Praise for *Jeff Herman's Guide to Book Publishers, Editors & Literary Agents*

"Nothing beats *Jeff Herman's Guide*."
— **Jack Canfield**, coauthor, *Chicken Soup for the Soul* series

"Jeff Herman has done a service to every writer who wants to make a living in this business. Every author should have a copy on their shelf."
— **Chip MacGregor**, literary agent

"Everything you need to get started."
— **Cheryl Richardson**, *New York Times*–bestselling author of *Stand Up for Your Life*

"*Jeff Herman's Guide* remains the Rosetta Stone of writerly success."
— **James Broderick, PhD**, BookPleasures.com

"I got my agent by using this guide!"
— **Meg Cabot**, *New York Times*–bestselling author of *The Princess Diaries*

"When you get to the 'finding the agent' stage, check out *Jeff Herman's Guide*. I found it very useful because it gives more background on agents. Keep in mind that publishing is very personality driven."
— **Emily Giffin**, *New York Times*–bestselling author of *First Comes Love*

"I sent my proposal and sample pages to ten agents selected from *Jeff Herman's Guide* and was shocked to receive interest from three of them. I celebrated when I signed with an agent and again when my first book was sold."
— **Jacqueline Winspear**, *New York Times*–bestselling author of *Maisie Dobbs*

"Here's my two cents: I used *Jeff Herman's Guide*. It includes a huge list of agents, interviews about what they are looking for, and useful info on big and small presses."
— **Kristy Woodson Harvey**, author of *Lies and Other Acts of Love*

"If you are only going to get one book on this subject, *Jeff Herman's Guide* is the one I recommend. When I was looking for an agent, this was the book that showed me how. The only thing is, you have to do what it says."
— **Marie Bostwick**, author of *Between Heaven and Texas*

Also by Jeff Herman

Write the Perfect Book Proposal: 10 That Sold and Why
(with Deborah Levine Herman)

Jeff Herman's GUIDE TO BOOK PUBLISHERS, EDITORS & LITERARY AGENTS

Who They Are, What They Want, How to Win Them Over

28th Edition

Jeff Herman

New World Library
Novato, California

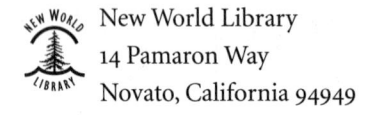

New World Library
14 Pamaron Way
Novato, California 94949

Copyright © 2018 by Jeff Herman

All rights reserved. This book may not be reproduced in whole or in part, stored in a retrieval system, or transmitted in any form or by any means — electronic, mechanical, or other — without written permission from the publisher, except by a reviewer, who may quote brief passages in a review.

Page 440, "An Editor of One's Own": Original article copyright © 2007; 2014 revision copyright © by Marlene Adelstein, Linda Carbone, Ruth Greenstein, Alice Peck, Alice Rosengard, Katharine Turok, and Michael Wilde

Text design by Tona Pearce Myers
Index by Carol Roberts

Library of Congress Cataloging-in-Publication data is available.

First printing, October 2018
ISBN 978-1-60868-584-4
Ebook ISBN 978-1-60868-585-1
Printed in the USA

New World Library is proud to be a Gold Certified Environmentally Responsible Publisher. Publisher certification awarded by Green Press Initiative.
www.greenpressinitiative.org

10 9 8 7 6 5 4 3 2 1

*This edition is dedicated to
those who are new to writing and publishing.
You are needed.*

CONTENTS

Introduction | Jeff Herman ... ix

Part 1. Advice for Writers

Introduction: Perfectly Imperfect Advice and Random Thoughts | Jeff Herman ... 3
Literary Agents: What They Are and What They Do | Jeff Herman ... 5
Write the Perfect Query Letter | Jeff Herman and Deborah Herman ... 20
You (Might) Belong in the Slush Pile (or Elsewhere) | Jeff Herman ... 26
The Knockout Nonfiction Book Proposal | Jeff Herman ... 32
Dumb-Ass Random Questions and Answers | Jeff Herman ... 38
When Nothing Happens to Good (or Bad) Writers:
   a.k.a. Ignored Writer Syndrome (IWS) | Jeff Herman ... 48
The Writer's Journey: The Path of the Spiritual Messenger | Deborah Herman ... 50
Tribulations of the Unknown Writer (and Possible Remedies) | Jeff Herman ... 55
Post-publication Depression Syndrome (PPDS) | Jeff Herman ... 59
The Business of Writing | Jeff Herman ... 61
Every Writer Needs to Meet Zero | Jeff Herman ... 72

Part 2. Publishing Conglomerates

Introduction to the Big 5 | Jeff Herman ... 77
Hachette Book Group ... 80
HarperCollins Publishers ... 87
Macmillan Publishers ... 95
Penguin Random House ... 102
Simon & Schuster ... 120

Part 3. Independent Presses

Introduction: Planet Independent | Jeff Herman	131
The Listings	134

Part 4. Literary Agents

Introduction: Planet Literary Agent | Jeff Herman	171
The Listings	173

Part 5. Independent Editors

Introduction: Editors vs. Scammers | Jeff Herman	437
An Editor of One's Own | Members of Words into Print	440
When to Call the (Book) Doctor | Sandi Gelles-Cole	446
Trust and Perfect Fit | Michael Wilde	449
The Listings	452
Acknowledgments	465
Glossary	467
Index	493
Advice for Writers	493
Publishers and Imprints	494
Agents and Agencies	496
Independent Editors	498
Publishers, Imprints, and Agents by Subject	499
About the Author	529

INTRODUCTION

In the beginning, some three decades ago, my primary mission for this book was to expose valuable information that was cloaked by tradition and a measure of volition. Relishing my self-appointed role as a 26-year-old outsider with nothing to lose and no loyalty to the status quo, I endeavored to smash the codes, reveal names and addresses, and give strategies for beating what I viewed as an arthritic system that deserved disrespect. My early impression was of an iron curtain designed to lock writers out and editors in. I perceived an inbred subculture of isolated intellectuals who published books they liked, written by people they were comfortable with. Their power was amplified by layers of inaccessibility and invisibility. It seemed to me that, regardless of talent, most writers were pathetically clueless about how to penetrate the system, and the publishers' uniform submission protocols seemed deliberately obstructive. Literary agents, then as now, provided pathways to publication, but they also preferred to be obscure and hard to find. Unlike today, agents were expected to keep low profiles outside the inner circle.

During the past 30 years, technological and economic disruption has brought significant changes, and the above impressions are a little less relevant. But this book still packs valuable, timely insights, innovative strategies, and data from an insider who prefers to self-identify as an outsider. Perhaps nothing is more nullifying than an unwanted result deemed unchangeable, but different efforts can manifest different results.

Jeff Herman

Part 1
ADVICE FOR WRITERS

What You (Might) Need to Know about Publishing, Even If It (Not You) Is Boring and Stupid

INTRODUCTION
PERFECTLY IMPERFECT ADVICE AND RANDOM THOUGHTS

Jeff Herman

Except for a few hiatuses, I have been in the book-publishing business since the early 1980s, when I was in my early twenties. I entered the business without any forethought. I wasn't an avid book lover or English major. My primary mission was to be respectfully employed in a Manhattan skyscraper where people wore jackets and ties and performed seemingly important tasks. That was my projection for post-college success, and I imagined it as glamorous and exotic. Reality was a hard, slow grind compared to the glorious images painted by youthful endorphins and innocence. Getting what we wish for can be easier than living with the consequences.

In the summer of '81, shortly after graduating from an Upstate New York college, I was clinging to a greasy pole in a sweltering subway car when I saw an ad that would direct my life going forward. "I Found My Job in the *New York Times*," said the ad's smiling generic white-man-in-a-suit, with his paper opened to the Help Wanted section. For me it was the right promise at the right time.

Over the next few weeks I answered countless blind ads for a variety of entry-level jobs. One day someone with a harried- and tired-sounding voice called to schedule an interview. I showered and showed up on time in a clean suit. I said little and tried to smile and nod on cue. The only question I recall was if I could start work the following Monday (it was a Friday) for $200 a week (1981) as a "publicity assistant." It was a small independent book-publishing company with a compelling list and history. I was second-in-command of the firm's two-person publicity department, which entitled me to do the filing, phone answering, and typing (on a huge IBM Selectric) — none of which I knew how to do before doing it. I knew nothing about publishing or what the job entailed. My most important attributes may have been a calm persona of sanity and an apparent willingness to follow orders. Or maybe it was just my sincere promise to show up. In a nutshell, that explains how I "chose" the business I am in.

I tell this vignette because people often ask how I got into the business. But there's also a larger reason why I share this. I didn't have much of a plan or fixed direction, but yet I arrived somewhere and along the way made decisions (good or otherwise), grew, and helped make constructive things happen for myself and others. Maybe it's okay to not know what we want or where we are going in order to accomplish what we should. When I was young, a wise man told me that "man plans, God laughs," and I have subsequently heard that phrase many times. Frankly, I had to *grow into* understanding what that meant, and I frequently question it all over again. Perhaps writers shouldn't overplan what they write or will write. For sure, they can't fully control what happens to their work after they write it, short of destroying it.

Because it can be useful to consider what others say about what you do and wish to achieve, I have generated this section of the book. Read what you will with absolute discernment. Not all of it is for you, and all of it is imperfect — same as you and me. The only perfection is that you and I are here now together.

LITERARY AGENTS: WHAT THEY ARE AND WHAT THEY DO

Jeff Herman

Think of a venture capitalist: those people who invest their resources in other people's talents and dreams in exchange for a piece of the glory and profits. The capitalist's skill is the ability to choose wisely and help manifest the endeavor. Literary agents are conceptually similar. For an industry-standard 15 percent commission ("ownership"), we invest considerable measures of time, expertise, and faith in the writers we choose to represent. Our professional credibility is on the line with each pitch we make. We don't directly provide the cash; part of our job is to get the publisher to put its money on the line. If you stick with the trajectory of information that follows, the reasons why most writers elect to have an agent will become clear.

Publishers Overtly Discourage Unagented/Unsolicited Submissions

A typical publisher's in-house functions include product acquisition and management, back-office administrative tasks, editing, production, distribution, sales and marketing, accounting, and numerous other indispensable aspects related to publishing a book and running a business. However, the creation of almost all editorial content is outsourced — unlike magazines and newspapers, books are rarely written by in-house staff; publishers are entirely dependent on "freelance" writers, including you.

If people stopped writing new books, publishers wouldn't have anything new to publish. So it might seem counterintuitive and ironic that traditional publishers make it difficult, if not impossible, for writers to submit their work for consideration. But from the publisher's perspective it's about being functional, not courteous. For every book that gets published at a given moment, there are at least 1,000 manuscripts vying for the same opportunity at the same time. Imagine George Clooney or your favorite heartthrob standing in Times Square, without any barriers or security, announcing that he's looking for a new wife. It would be a chaotic situation, and it's possible he and others would be trampled to death. This illustrates why publishers feel the need to barricade themselves against writers even though they can't exist without them. Not only do publishers lack in-house writers; they also lack an infrastructure for screening and filtering unagented/unsolicited works.

How Do Publishers Find Books to Publish?

Solicitation. Proactive editors sometimes have their own book ideas and will seek people to write them. They might read various literary publications in which virgin content is often debuted, and then contact the writers who impress them. Editors might also scan the news for interesting events and discoveries and then reach out to the people involved. Whenever the editor commences the conversation and offers someone the opportunity to be published, it is solicitation (not the illegal kind).

Agency representation. Editors rely on agents to do the hardcore screening and weeding, and to only represent writers and works that merit publication. Editors don't have time to screen hundreds of works in order to discover one they can publish; they don't have to, because the agents do it for them. When an editor receives a submission from a trusted agent, he or she immediately assumes the work is professionally qualified and deserves quality attention.

Having an agent equals having access to editors. Not having an agent usually means the opposite, no matter how good the work might be.

Who Do Agents Work For?

The majority of literary agents are self-employed small-business people. They work for neither the publisher nor the writer but are indispensable to both for different reasons. The agent's constant interest is to generate commissions against the client's advance and subsequent royalties. The healthier the agent can make the client, the healthier the agent can make herself. The agent's revenues are tied to the client's revenues, and this mutuality of interests drives the agent to make the client as successful as possible.

Agents have clear lines they won't/can't cross on behalf of a client. There are a finite number of publishers and an infinite number of potential clients. An agent can replace an unsatisfied client in a minute and perhaps can never replace an aggrieved publisher. Losing a publisher as a possible customer for future submissions is like permanently losing a large percentage of the business. In practice, it's rare for the agent to be forced into making such choices, and the agent will usually manage to preempt destructive conflicts by simply telling the client what is and isn't acceptable or possible.

The client needs to understand that a literary agent isn't the same as a litigator and won't relentlessly fight for issues that often can't be achieved anyway, such as a 20-city media tour. The agent's interests will stray from the client's interests if the agent-publisher relationship becomes threatened due to the client's actions or demands. However, any author who becomes more problematic than profitable will unilaterally burn all his bridges anyway. An author's profitability must always outpace her negatives, or she will be of diminishing value to both the agent and the publisher. However, agents usually confront publishers if they violate or ignore contracts and what's customary. If a publisher disrespects the client, the agent will feel as if he is being similarly abused and will push back. A key distinction is that for the agent you're a "client," whereas for the publisher you're an "author."

How Do Agents Make Money?

In the context of the agency-client relationship, agents make a 15 percent commission from all the advance and royalty revenues the agent's efforts enable the client to earn.

The above percentage pertains to the moneys received from the US publishers, which usually is the lion's share, if not the only source, of all revenue. The percentages assessed against subsidiary rights from deals made by the agent will vary by agency. For translation deals, most of the time US agents team with foreign agents in the respective countries, and the foreign agent wants at least 10 percent off the top, which generally is charged to the author in addition to the US agent's commission. That's the way it's done. If the US publisher controls the foreign rights, which they often do, the same subagent deal is also usually involved, except now the US publisher is also taking a cut. This sounds like a lot of dealings absent the author, but few authors can make these arcane deals unilaterally and they are the primary beneficiaries. Think of it as free money.

How Do False Agents Make Money?

Bogus agents make money in countless ways other than by doing what real agents do. Bogus agents tend not to ever sell works to traditional publishers and don't operate on the basis of earning commissions. Instead, they may offer amazing promises and an itemized menu of nonagent services, like simply reading your work for a fee. Sometimes they will offer a range of editorial services that are not necessarily useful or needed. If someone says she will be your agent if you pay her money, then she isn't a bona fide agent.

Legitimate agencies receive hundreds of unsolicited pitches each month. If a modest fraction of these were converted into a $100 "reading (consideration) fee," it would be a substantial monthly windfall without accountability. Eventually, the internet often exposes such scams, but by that time the bogus agent may have changed the company's name and be busy exploiting fresh pods of unjaded writers. It's like changing a parking spot if your time limit expires. Sometimes law enforcement will step in, but even then individual monetary losses probably won't ever be recouped, though valuable lessons hopefully will have been learned.

What's the Association of Authors' Representatives (AAR)?

The AAR is nothing like the Bar Association, American Medical Association, or any other mandatory-membership professional organization. Agents don't have to belong to or be licensed by any outside entity to be legal. The AAR can loosely be compared to a nonprofit country club minus a physical address, paid staff, and the usual accoutrements. A large fraction of agents choose to join the AAR because it offers a collegial way to network with other agents and find relief from their cloistered offices. To varying degrees, agents are compelled to be competitive with each other for clients, and AAR meetings serve as a refreshing "no-kill" zone where they can presumably be friends with others who understand what they do for a living.

AAR membership is restricted to agents who have made a specific number of actual book deals within a specific time frame and promise to adhere to the AAR's strict codes of conduct. The majority of codes are generic common sense, and a lot of space could be saved if they simply stated "Don't break the law"; but overeducated people prefer to deliberate over everything, and we have all been conditioned to make work for America's bloated legal establishment. However, some of the codes are archaic and prevent many qualified agencies from wanting to join. For instance, members are proscribed from establishing separate divisions dedicated to nonagent fee-based services, like editing, collaborating, and helping writers self-publish. The fast-changing nature of publishing has made it impossible for an ever-increasing number of boutique agencies to rely only on commission-based services, and agents are exceptionally qualified to provide these kinds of ancillary services in-house.

What Services and Assets Do Agents Provide in Exchange for Their Commissions?

1. They deliver access to the appropriate editors at traditional publishing companies. Few writers can achieve the same level of access without an agent because editors don't want to do mass screening; they rely on the agents to do that on their behalf.
2. The agents know who the appropriate editors and publishers are for the works they represent.
3. Agents can accelerate the sales process by going to many publishers simultaneously with the same project, which sometimes creates a competitive bidding war, called "auction."
4. Agents know how to tweak and improve the work in order to maximize its sale to a publisher.

5. Agents understand publisher contracts and how to modify the language to the writer's advantage.
6. Agents know how to assess a work's potential monetary value and are positioned to negotiate the best terms possible.
7. Agents help clients understand how to interact with editors and publishers after the publisher's contract is signed.
8. Agents can provide valuable consultations about what is marketable.
9. Agents help writers understand what to expect from the publisher post-contract and post-publication, and continue to consult and advocate indefinitely.

What Won't Agents Do as Part of Their Commission?

I can't speak for all agents, or even for myself in all situations, but generally speaking, agents shouldn't be counted on as editors, as they probably don't have time for perfecting or fixing afflicted manuscripts in detail, assuming they even have that skill set. Nor do they ordinarily act as publicists or sales reps. Agents may be able to provide excellent referrals for these and other needs, or may even have excellent in-house divisions for generally fee-based services. Though there's nothing inherently wrong about an agent providing fee-based services, the agent should make it clear that these services are absolutely separate from commission-based services and that representation isn't contingent on retaining the fee-based services.

How Do You Get an Agent?

Getting an agent might not be as difficult as you think. But if you're not thinking about it, don't expect it to be easy. If it were easy, you'd have no reason to buy this book. Some writers make it look easy, but what are you actually seeing? Observing a person's accomplishments absent their likely struggles is rarely worthwhile. Here are some things to consider when trying to land an agent.

- **Expect rejections.** The prima facie percentages are disconcerting. On average, agents reject about 98 percent of what's pitched. There's no rational reason for them to represent something without believing they can sell it to a publisher. Doing so would simply be a waste of everyone's time and not a good way for the agents to leverage their editor relationships. So the odds are that you will receive rejections.
- **Pitch the right agents.** Most agents have areas of editorial specialization and categories they rarely, if ever, deal with. You might have an excellent romance novel, but if you pitch only to agents who never handle romances, your rejection rate

will be 100 percent. Conversely, only pitching to appropriate agents might give you a 100 percent "yes" rate. You need to find out who the right agents are for your work, and there are many proven ways to do that. Start by using the agency section in this book, where more than 150 agents disclose what they want. Agencies' websites often include a clear statement about what to pitch and what not to bother them with. Visit physical bookstores that have a large shelf of books in your category and read the acknowledgments sections; most of the time the author's agent will be acknowledged. Join local and national organizations that either specialize in your category or seem to have many like-minded members, and make friends. Friends will often share valuable information and experiences with each other and may even make valuable introductions on your behalf. If you enter the community with a sense of generosity, you will receive much generosity in turn.

- **Prepare to become a pitcher.** It won't matter how good your content is if you fail to properly pitch it. Writers can greatly compensate for editorial mediocrity by embellishing their pitch skills. Fear of rejection prevents many talented people from reaching their full potential. Replacing fear with hunger and determination removes all limitations. It's often not the most talented people who rise to the top of their fields but those who want it the most.

- **Good pitching is power.** The publishing business is about editorial content, so your pitch will need to be expressed in the form of a pitch letter, often referred to in "pub-speak" as a query letter. *Query* means you are asking a question or making a request, which in this context means asking the agent to consider representing your work. Agents receive thousands of queries every year, and reading them can be a mind-numbing process. In order to be competitive it's best to avoid asking for anything while offering everything. A pitch should be designed as offering something of value that will directly benefit the agent — an enticement, a seduction. For advice on writing the best pitch possible, please refer to the essay dedicated to this subject (see page 20).

- **Pitch by email and snail mail.** Use both simultaneously. I'm serious. Agency digital submission boxes are overflowing, and not just with legitimate pitches. The internet is a blessing and a curse for all the obvious reasons. In the early years of the current century, emails were still relatively exotic and appreciated, and not everyone had fully "switched" yet. There was the "You've got mail" announcement each time we booted up and maybe a mere dozen emails every 24 hours, mostly spamless. Dealing with inboxes today is like flossing teeth after a corn-eating orgy. Ironically, hardcopy mail has now become exotic and thus might be seen and read much more quickly than the digital version of the same material. So why not hedge your bet by using both conveyance methods? Yes, some agents say they prefer that you use their digital mailboxes. But what they really prefer is what works out best in the long run. Shoot for best-case results, and everyone will be happy in the end. However, you might want to mention at the end of your letter that you've sent it via both hardcopy and email.

An unimportant side note: Many of my veteran publishing colleagues still refer to receiving submissions "over the transom," which is a dated metaphor for anything that's unrequested. Until about 50 years ago, most New York offices had open windows above hallway entrances, which were called "transoms." Most mail and other deliveries were simply tossed into the offices through the transoms.

- *Pitch in batches.* If you're not in a big hurry to get published, meaning you're willing to wait many years, you should only pitch one agent at a time. Frankly, some agents will never respond, period. Others may take a very, very long time. These are understaffed mom-and-pop businesses, and dealing with recent submissions is often a low priority compared to servicing current clients. Do yourself a favor and pitch about 10 agents at a time. Pitching more than that at a time isn't wise, because you may see ways to constantly upgrade your pitch with each cycle. Every four weeks, if you're still in limbo, go out there with a fresh batch of 10 pitches. Most successful authors have a bloody past of rejections and humiliations; amass your bloody past as efficiently as possible so that you can reach your future while still breathing.

  There are obvious exceptions. If you make a connection with a particular agent you like and he invites your submission, then play it out on an exclusive basis, but not forever. If he disappears from your radar for more than four to eight weeks, it may be time to play the field.

- *Sell yourself to the agent.* The agent is already 98 percent sure he doesn't need you. Even if he skips reading your work and goes straight to "reject," there's a less than 2 percent chance that he made a mistake. It's incumbent upon you to make the agent think you could be one of the magic 2 percent and avoid giving the impression you are one of the 98 percent.

- *Put yourself in the shoes of an agent.* What does an agent want? Commission-eligible clients, moron. What doesn't an agent want? If you can't answer this question by yourself, then you really are a moron. To date, no one has ever chastised me for using the word *moron*. I think it's because the term has no clinical meaning or history, unlike, for example, the "R" word. My wife and I sometimes call each other "idiot" or "moron"; we take turns being one or the other. It's especially fun when we do it in public. I think I'm telling you this so that you don't take me, or yourself, too seriously.

What Else Should You Know about Agents?

Literary agents aren't that smart. Nor are they especially stupid. In other words, they're pretty much like everyone else, and that probably includes you. A combination of geography, subculture, native interests, and accessible opportunities brings people to agenting. I might not have become an agent if I were not a New Yorker, and had not been conditioned to be a "mind worker" by family, community, and subculture. Joining the military, for instance, would have marked me as an extreme outlier in my world, as opposed to a conformist if I were from Tennessee. Many agents are former in-house book editors; it's a way for them to move on while still using the skills and connections they possess. Some agents were nurtured from when they were career virgins, meaning they landed an entry-level job in an agency, instead of in a publishing house, perhaps fresh out of college.

My assumption is that agents are self-structured and self-motivated, and are okay with being alone much of the day. Otherwise, I can't imagine them liking the job. They also need to be able to say no a lot, which is actually much nicer than not giving clear answers out of misplaced politeness or an exaggerated need to never be disliked. It helps if they have an appetite for risk taking. An ability to delay gratification and be patient comes in handy. A deep capacity for tolerating disappointment and setbacks will need to be acquired along the way if it's not a native characteristic. A keen awareness of basic human emotional needs and aspirations is a bonus, though not a necessity. Many agents are introverts to the point of being downright antisocial but hopefully learn how to be accepting and tolerant of others without judgment. Some agents are exceptionally gregarious and hypersocial, which can be an immense advantage in a universe mostly populated by reticent souls.

Do Agents and Editors Have Similar Traits?

The primary difference is that editors get paychecks, whereas most agents are self-employed and get paid only if they generate commissions. Agents can become millionaires if they strike the right deals, whereas in-house editors can become rich only through marriage, through an inheritance, or by becoming an owner/partner instead of an employee where they work. Agents run businesses and are risk takers, whereas editors serve the needs of the companies they work for.

Do Agents and Editors Make "Sweetheart" Deals?

Yes, all the time, but we prefer not to think about it that way. There are fewer than 1,000 full-time acquisitions editors and agents in total, and an even smaller core of those who are the most active. We have to keep working within this tight circle to get our mutual needs met. The system succeeds for writers because agents must push author revenues in order to push their own revenues. Writers are the conduits through which agents eat, and they're the people who generate the raw material that editors can't live without.

Who Can Be an Agent?

Anyone can self-declare him- or herself a literary agent. Of course, succeeding as an agent is a different story. Finding raw product is actually easy, because so much is generated all the time. But knowing how to discern the tiny fraction of the unfiltered mass content that publishers will pay for is mostly an acquired skill. Forming direct relationships with editors is an unrestricted process, but they won't buy what they don't want, no matter how strong the agent-editor relationship is. Knowing what publishers will pay for is tantamount to knowing what the public will pay for. I'm not aware of any academic tracks or books about how to become an agent. As said elsewhere, no licensing or accreditation is needed. You don't need to be hired by an agency to be an agent. The only measure is the ability to be self-sustaining as an agent. Once someone crosses that perimeter, they are a true agent.

What If an Agent Offers You Representation?

Bull's-eye. Mazel tov. Before you commit, settle any unfinished business with other agents who are still considering your work. Tell them you have an offer and need to make an immediate decision. Before accepting an agent's offer, you're entitled to ask reasonable questions and do some due diligence:

- Ask for a list of books the agent has sold to publishers, including the publishers' and authors' names. Some or all of this information might already be posted on the agent's website.
- Check the internet for any "bad news." But be discerning about what you read. Disgruntled people often publicly rant in ways that are unfair, if not entirely untrue.
- Have a conversation about why he likes your book, how he plans to sell it, how much he thinks he can get for it, the time frame, and if he believes in sexual monogamy (just checking if you're awake).

ADVICE FOR WRITERS

How Do You Know If Your Agent Is Doing a Good Job?

If your agent gets you a book deal with a traditional publisher, then she most likely did a good job for you. However, typically agents can sell only about half the works they represent in any given 12-month period. Having representation should mean your work is actively receiving quality access to eligible editors, but that doesn't guarantee that any of them will make an offer. In fact, most agented works probably never get published, especially in the literary fiction zone. Editorial quality is just one factor determining what does and doesn't get traditionally published. If a particular category or concept is overpublished, for instance, many excellent prospects become surplus product. Timing is important but impossible to foresee or control, though many people wish they could or think they can. You can't get a deal without correct access, but access won't guarantee you a deal.

What If the Agent Is Unable to Sell Your Work?

If your work is unsold after a long time (six months to a year), you should determine what the problem is and what the next steps might be. Upon request, the agent should let you know where the work was submitted, each submission's status, and any available details about rejections received. In consultation with your agent, it might be a good idea to consider some revisions or ways to tweak what editors are seeing.

Try to nail down whether the agent is still confident about selling the work. Sometimes an agent might no longer be confident but is reluctant to release a work he has already invested himself in. The bottom line is, does the agent plan to keep actively pitching the work? In the absence of that crucial intent, there's no good reason for the agent to hold you and your work in limbo, and you should arrange a friendly release. Getting a new agent requires following the same process you used when getting your first agent, but you'll need to disclose your history at the outset, which could be an obvious turnoff.

It might not be anyone's fault that your work remains unsold, least of all your agent's. Often it wouldn't have mattered who was representing it. Putting an unsold manuscript on the back burner for a year or so and working on something else might be the best move, instead of permanently burning your agent relationship. Many successful fiction writers were unable to sell the first manuscript(s) they wrote until after they finally became successful with a later manuscript. There's no law that says your works have to be published in the order in which you wrote them.

Agent-jumping is tricky. It's not easy to get an agent in the first place, and agents may not see any reason to be enthusiastic about representing a work that your previous agent failed to sell. But if the work wasn't widely circulated or shown to the right editors, a new agent might see fresh opportunities or ways to fix what's broken. You should be clear with yourself about why you want to switch agents, or you are likely to encounter the same grievances all over again.

What Will Happen to Agents as a Category over the Next Several Years?

This question makes most agents uncomfortable, because trends are not favorable. As I see it, literary agents will continue to be as important as ever in the context of traditional publishing. Actually, their standing and purpose have never been at risk. The problem is that traditional publishing will continue to become a less friendly environment for editors, writers, and, by extension, their agents. Writers and agents are in the same beleaguered boat. Each year, more agencies will either close or merge to form larger agencies, and a diminishing number of new agents will enter the business. Those at greatest risk will be the boutique agencies that are most reliant on maintaining a fresh flow of new deals, as opposed to having the luxury of resting on their laurels. Publishers are acquiring fewer books and paying less for most of the books they still acquire. In order to survive, many boutique agencies will be compelled to offer related fee-based services, such as editing, collaborating, consulting, and helping writers self-publish.

Do Agents Sell Everything They Represent?

Only if they represent very few projects. Agents usually know at the outset which projects are likely slam dunks and which are comparatively marginal. But this business is loaded with surprises; agents plan, and the process laughs at them. They hedge their bets by signing up more projects than they expect to actually get offers for. In fact, the ratio is probably less than 50/50 for the toughest categories, such as literary fiction. However, no bona fide agent will intentionally represent a project that he doesn't feel is viable, unless there are other compelling reasons to do so.

What's the Typical Agent's Sales Process, and How Long Does It Take?

Velocity is an agent's and writer's friend. You would presumably prefer not to observe your own book launch from heaven, which probably happens more than you realize. (I'm assuming all writers go to heaven, of course.) Usually, the agent will make a multiple submission, which means selecting approximately a dozen appropriate editors from distinct houses or divisions within the same house. Agents know which houses/divisions and which editors might be inclined to like the project in hand. The agent might make calls to prescreen or sell the project or might just go ahead and email it over and then follow up to see what the early response is.

Email has greatly altered the pitch process for agents. Until 1999 or so, almost all submissions were made in hardcopy. Agents had to run up large photocopying and delivery balances and had to allocate a lot of physical space for storing everything. Now everything tends to go by email, which makes it easier and cheaper to deal with. However, the relative ease of the submission process has served to increase quantity, not quality.

Agents typically follow up for some kind of response from each of the editors in cycles of one to four weeks, depending on the project and other circumstances. However, editors can't make instant unilateral decisions without going through in-house protocols. An editor may like a project but be prevented from acquiring it by his colleagues for a variety of reasons, such as list redundancies or because the sales department vetoes it.

The agent keeps the process from stagnating by making subsequent submissions as needed. Sometimes the agent will use the rejections as a learning opportunity and encourage the client to revise the work accordingly. Sometimes it may be as simple as altering the title to something more compelling or clear. If/when a genuine offer is close at hand, the agent might attempt to provoke a competitive bidding process. If at least two publishers are eager to acquire the same work, the agent might hold a formal auction in which the competing houses are forced to blindly bid against one another until only one house remains standing. But don't get too excited; auctions are the exception, not the rule.

Sometimes an agent will have good reasons to give a specific editor an exclusive or preemptive opportunity to consider and make an offer on a particular project before anyone else. The agent will generally set a deadline by which a verbal deal needs to be made.

How long might all of this take before a verbal deal is in hand? For certain kinds of nonfiction, such as basic how-to books, within eight weeks the agent may have a deal or know there probably won't be a deal. Arcane nonfiction or fiction by unpublished writers might require a much longer time. A slow process doesn't necessarily mean the agent isn't doing the job; some projects compile many rejections over time before finding the right editor at the right publisher at the right time.

How Do Agents Find Their Clients?

Agents need clients in order to function. An agent without clients is like a playboy without girlfriends. Yet some agents seem to be elusive to the point of invisibility, at least from the potential client's point of view. Not all agents want or need new/more clients, so those agents will make themselves unavailable. Most agents, to varying degrees, are always looking for new product, which means they are looking for new clients. But follow the sequence of the last sentence: the word *product* precedes *client*, because it's the viability of the product that counts. Writers who write salable products will get agents and publishers. Don't forget that the industry and the reader are interested in the product first and the author second, if at all. Over time successful authors become interesting to their readers as people and effectively become the product, but it doesn't start out that way. Of course, the author's ability to help promote her books forms a large part of how agents and publishers assess the value of the product.

Agents discover clients by responding to submissions and referrals; by attending conferences; by writing books or appearing in books; by proactively reaching out to experts, victims, celebrities, or whoever might have a sellable story or program to write about. Most agents are willing to scan and reject thousands of submissions a year to find a few dozen projects they feel confident about selling to publishers.

If You Get 20+ Agent Rejections, Is It Unlikely You'll Get an Agent?

Don't answer the above question affirmatively or it will be your truth, and it shouldn't be. Of course, there is the little matter of talent or the lack thereof, and that can't be dismissed as unimportant. But let's get real: a lot of highly talented people live below the poverty line, and a lot of mediocre people are self-made millionaires. On average, unsuccessful people are no smarter or dumber than successful people. Being gifted doesn't mean you'll manifest your natural gifts.

If you want to get published, be prepared to scratch your way to the surface and struggle. Countless others have and are, and can prove it. Success is the great equalizer because actual performance counts much more than latent potential. Of course corruption and nepotism are perpetual factors in all endeavors, but so what? I assure you that some of the best-written manuscripts are, and will remain, unpublished only because the authors did a poor job trying to get them published. Conversely, some of the most mediocre (or worse) manuscripts are successfully published simply because the authors did such a stellar job at getting published that they overcompensated for editorial deficits. Hunger and determination frequently outmatch raw talent.

Agents aren't in lockstep with each other and often make dumb decisions, just like everyone else. Receiving 20+ agent rejections could mean many things; that your work "sucks" may not be the correct assessment. Many masterpieces were rejected countless times along the way. Maybe you've been submitting your romance novel to sci-fi agents. Maybe those first 20 are over capacity and not taking new clients. Maybe you need to rewrite your pitch letter. Maybe you just need to keep trying. Babe Ruth had many more strikeouts than homers, and two-thirds of the time Ted Williams didn't get past the batter's box. Some flowers bloom early, some bloom later. You can only fail if you quit.

How Do Agents Like to Work with Their Clients?

How do you like to work with your significant other, neighbors, children, bosses, and subordinates? Exactly — it depends on the people in question. There is no one way agents interact with their clients. Some agents are loquacious, and some might be on the autism spectrum (seriously). However, there are certain universal professional protocols that should be expected and followed. You're entitled to know what your agent's plan and schedule for selling your work are, and it's appropriate to know where your work has been submitted and the results. If many weeks go by without any word, you should check in for news. If nothing is happening, you should determine if your agent has lost confidence and hasn't gotten around to telling you yet.

Good clients ask good questions and can discern good answers. Like "What if I tweak the overview — will that change the way editors are seeing the project?" Or "How about I generate a list of 10 prestigious people who are likely to endorse and recommend the book?" These aren't really questions; they are proactive solutions. If a particular work isn't selling, the agent will eventually shift her focus to other prospects. She might refocus on selling your work in time, or she might not. As a writer, you can't afford to interminably sleep in your agent's limbo zone. You have the most to gain and the most to lose. However, you don't want to motivate your agent to fire you; he may simply need some encouragement and fresh ideas from you. There's nothing unusual about having to resell yourself to your agent all over again, and a dose of humility never kills us. Before accepting or requesting termination of the relationship, maybe you should think about re-energizing your agent's confidence in you.

Is It Okay to Switch Agents?

Agent-hopping happens a lot, especially for writers who have already been published. Published writers are at an advantage because agents see them as proven commodities. Unpublished writers seeking to switch are often perceived as having been "fired" by their last agent; at any rate, they still haven't earned their first stripe.

When I hear from a published author who wants to change agents, the first thing I ask is, "Why?" Certain answers are reasonable, and others are alarm bells. I think it's okay if the writer expresses that it's simply not a mutually satisfying relationship. Of course, it's probably a bogus and evasive answer, but that's exactly why it's okay. I respect that the author just wants to move on without any annoying whining or backstabbing (we can always save that for later). An alarm bell rings when the author complains about low advances, low book sales, or lack of publisher support. The first thing that enters my mind is: could I have done better? This question is especially meaningful if I happen to respect the agent in question. Even if the author is a decent commodity, agents are wary of authors who are serial jilters or bigmouths.

What Kind of Client Do Agents Dislike?

That's a loaded question because it meshes business with personal. The real question is: what are the agent's priorities as a businessperson? It's theoretically possible that an agent might tend to release the clients she likes the most. Why would that happen? Because all the likability in the world can't compensate for a book that doesn't sell. If a likable client is deadweight, he's an endangered client. If an obnoxious client is sufficiently and reliably profitable, she's safe. If you are a superstar who generates the rent money, you can get away with behaving like Godzilla. No one will like you, but everyone will want a piece of you.

How Come Rejection Letters Are Generic, and Why Are There No Useful Comments?

Reading and evaluating manuscripts is very time-consuming and requires special expertise. It's impossible for an agent to dedicate any measure of his time to providing that level of service pro bono to the people he is rejecting. Any expectation to the contrary is naive, misguided, and unreasonable.

WRITE THE PERFECT QUERY LETTER

Jeff Herman and Deborah Herman

The query is a short letter of introduction to publishers or agents, encouraging them to request to see your fiction manuscript or nonfiction book proposal. It is a vital tool, often neglected by writers. If done correctly, it can help you avoid endless frustration and wasted effort. The query is the first hurdle of your individual marketing strategy. If you can leap over it successfully, you're well on your way to a sale.

The query letter is your calling card. For every book that makes it to the shelves, thousands of worthy manuscripts, proposals, and ideas are knocked out of the running by poor presentation or inadequate marketing strategies. Don't forget that the book you want to sell is a product that must be packaged correctly to stand above the competition.

A query letter asks the prospective publisher or agent if she would like to see more about the proposed idea. If your book is fiction, you should indicate that a manuscript or sample chapters are available on request. If nonfiction, you should offer to send a proposal and, if you have them, sample chapters.

The query is your first contact with the prospective buyer of your book. To ensure that it's not your last, avoid common mistakes. The letter should be concise and well written. You shouldn't try to impress the reader with your mastery of all words over three syllables. Instead, concentrate on a clear and to-the-point presentation with no fluff.

Think of the letter as an advertisement. You want to make a sale of a product, and you have very limited space and time in which to reach this goal.

The letter should be only one page long, if possible. It will form the basis of a query package that will include supporting materials. Don't waste words in the letter describing material that can be included separately. Your goal is to pique the interest of an agent or editor who has very little time and probably very little patience. You want to entice her to keep reading and ask you for more.

The query package can include a short résumé, media clippings, or other favorable documents. Do not get carried away, or your package will quickly come to resemble junk mail. If you're sending a hardcopy package, include a self-addressed stamped envelope (SASE) with enough postage to return your entire package. This will be particularly appreciated by smaller publishing houses and independent agents.

For fiction writers, a short (one- to five-page), double-spaced synopsis of the manuscript will be helpful and appropriate.

Do not waste money and defeat the purpose of the query by sending an unsolicited manuscript. Agents and editors may be turned off by receiving manuscripts of 1,000+ pages that were uninvited and that are not even remotely relevant to what they do. Though digital submissions obviously don't consume physical space, nobody enjoys a cluttered, overburdened inbox.

The query follows a simple four-part format (which can be reworked according to your individual preferences):

- Lead
- Supporting material/persuasion
- Biography
- Conclusion/pitch

Your Lead Is Your Hook

The lead can either catch the agent's or editor's attention or turn him off completely. Some writers think getting someone's attention in a short space means having to do something dramatic. Agents and editors appreciate cleverness, but too much contrived writing can work against you. Opt instead for clear conveyance of thoroughly developed ideas, and get right to the point.

Of course, you don't want to be boring and stuffy in the interest of factual presentation. You'll need to determine what is most important about the book you're trying to sell, and write your letter accordingly.

You can begin with a lead similar to what you'd use to grab the reader in an article or a book chapter. You can use an anecdote, a statement of facts, a question, a comparison, or whatever you believe will be most powerful.

You may want to rely on the journalistic technique of the inverted pyramid. This means that you begin with the strongest material and save the details for later in the letter. Don't start slowly and expect to pick up momentum as you proceed. It will be too late.

Do not begin a query letter like this: "I have sent this idea to 20 agents/publishers, none of whom think it will work. I just know you'll be different, enlightened, and insightful and will give it full consideration." There is no room for negatives in a sales pitch. Focus only on positives — unless you can turn negatives to your advantage.

Some writers make the mistake of writing about the book's potential in the first paragraph without ever stating its actual idea or theme. Remember, your letter may never be read beyond the lead, so make that first paragraph your hook.

Avoid bad jokes, clichés, unsubstantiated claims, and dictionary definitions. Don't be condescending; agents and editors have egos, too, and have power over your destiny as a writer.

Supporting Material: Be Persuasive

If you are selling a nonfiction book, you may want to include a brief summary of hard evidence, gleaned from research that will support the merit of your idea. This is where you convince the agent or editor that your book should exist. This is more important for nonfiction than it is for fiction, where style and storytelling ability are paramount. Nonfiction writers must focus on selling their topic and their credentials.

You should include a few lines showing the agent or editor what the publishing house will gain from the project. Publishers are not charitable institutions; they want to know how they can get the greatest return on their investment. If you have brilliant marketing ideas or know of a well-defined market for your book where sales will be guaranteed, include this rather than other descriptive material.

In rereading your letter, make sure you have shown that you understand your own idea thoroughly. If it appears half-baked, the agents and editors won't want to invest time fleshing out your thoughts. Exude confidence so that the agent or editor will have faith in your ability to carry out the job.

In nonfiction queries, you can include a separate table of contents and brief chapter abstracts. Otherwise, that material can wait for the book proposal.

Your Biography: No Place for Modesty

In the biographical portion of your letter, toot your own horn, but in a carefully calculated, persuasive fashion. Your story of winning the third-grade writing competition (it was then that you knew you wanted to be a world-famous writer!) should be saved for the documentary done on your life after you reach your goal.

In the query, all you want to include are the most important and relevant credentials that will support the sale of your book. You can include, as a separate part of the package, a résumé or biography that will elaborate further.

The separate résumé should list all relevant and recent experiences that support your ability to write the book. Unless you're fairly young, your listing of academic accomplishments should start after high school. Don't overlook hobbies or non-job-related activities if they correspond to your book story or topic. Those experiences are often more valuable than academic achievements.

Other information to include: any impressive print clippings about you; a list of your broadcast interviews and speaking appearances; and copies of articles and reviews about any books you may have written. This information can never hurt your chances and could make the difference in your favor.

There is no room for humility or modesty in the query letter and résumé. When corporations sell toothpaste, they list the product's best attributes and create excitement about the product. If you can't find some way to make yourself exciting as an author, you'd better rethink your career.

Here's the Pitch

At the close of your letter, ask for the sale. This requires a positive and confident conclusion with a phrase such as "I look forward to your speedy response." Such phrases as "I hope" and "I think you will like my book" sound too insecure. This is the part of the letter where you go for the kill.

Be sure to thank the reader for his or her attention in your final sentence.

Finishing Touches

When you're finished, reread and edit your query letter. Cut out any extraneous information that dilutes the strength of your arguments. Make the letter as polished as possible so that the agent or editor will be impressed with you, as well as with your idea. Don't ruin your chances by appearing careless; make certain your letter is not peppered with typos and misspellings. If you don't show pride in your work, you'll create a self-fulfilling prophecy: the agent or editor will take you no more seriously than you take yourself.

Aesthetics are important. If you were pitching a business deal to a corporation, you would want to present yourself in conservative dress, with an air of professionalism. In the writing business, you may never have face-to-face contact with the people who will determine your future. Therefore, your query package is your representative.

For hardcopy submissions, you should invest in state-of-the-art letterhead — with a logo! — to create an impression of pride, confidence, and professionalism. White, cream, and ivory paper are all acceptable, but you should use only black ink for printing the letter. Anything else looks amateurish. If agents or editors receive a query letter on yellowed paper that looks as if it's been lying around for 20 years, they will wonder if the person sending the letter is a has-been or a never-was.

For electronic submissions, keep your email formatting simple and readable, and be sure to include all your contact information. Also, most agents' websites include detailed guidelines for electronic submissions. Be sure to adhere to them, or your work might be rejected solely because you have not followed the rules.

Don't sabotage yourself by letting your need for instant approval get the best of you. Don't call agents or editors. You have invited them to respond, so be patient. Then prepare yourself for possible rejection. It often takes many nos to get a yes.

One more note: This is a tough business for anyone — and it's especially so for greenhorns. Hang in there.

Query Letter Tips

If you have spent any time at all in this business, the term *query letter* is probably as familiar to you as the back of your hand. Yet no matter how many courses you've attended and books you've read about this important part of the process, you may still feel inadequate when you try to write one that sizzles. If it's any consolation, you're far from being alone in your uncertainties. The purpose of the query letter is to formally introduce your work and yourself to potential agents and editors. The immediate goal is to motivate them to promptly request a look at your work, or at least a portion of it.

In effect, the letter serves as the writer's first hurdle. It's a relatively painless way for agents and editors to screen out unwanted submissions without the added burden of having to manhandle a deluge of unwanted manuscripts. They are more relaxed if their inboxes are filled with 50 unanswered queries as opposed to 50 uninvited 1,000-page manuscripts. The query is a very effective way to control the quality and quantity of the manuscripts that get into the office. And that's why you have to write a good one.

The term *query letter* is part of the lexicon and jargon of the publishing business. This term isn't used in any other industry. I assume it has ancient origins. I can conjure up the image of an English gentleman with a fluffy quill pen composing a most civilized letter to a prospective publisher for the purpose of asking for his work to be read and, perchance, published. Our environments may change, but the nature of our ambitions remains the same.

Let's get contemporary. Whenever you hear the term *query letter*, you should say to yourself "pitch" or "sales" letter. Because that's what it is. You need the letter to sell.

Here are a few more tips to make your query letter the best it can be.

- ***Don't be long-winded.*** Agents/editors receive lots of these things, and they want to mow through them as swiftly as possible. Ideally, the letter should be a single page with short paragraphs. (I must admit I've seen good ones that are longer than a page.) If you lose your reader, you've lost your opportunity.

- *Get to the point; don't pontificate.* Too many letters go off on irrelevant detours, which makes it difficult for the agent/editor to determine what's actually for sale — other than the writer's soapbox.
- *If sending your letter on hardcopy, make it attractive.* When making a first impression, the subliminal impact of aesthetics cannot be overestimated. Use high-quality stationery and typeface. The essence of your words is paramount, but cheap paper and poor print quality will only diminish your impact.
- *Don't say anything negative about yourself or your attempts to get published.* Everyone appreciates victims when it's time to make charitable donations, but not when it's time to make a profit. It's better if you can make editors/agents think that you have to fight them off.

Why Not Simply Submit Your Manuscript?

You might be wondering why you can't bypass the query hurdle and simply submit your manuscript. You may do that — and no one can litigate against you. But if you submit an unsolicited manuscript to a publisher, it's more likely to end up in the so-called slush pile and may never get a fair reading. If it's sent to an agent, nothing negative may come of it. However, most agents prefer to receive a query first.

Sending unsolicited nonfiction book proposals is in the gray zone. Proposals are much more manageable than entire manuscripts, so editors/agents may not particularly mind.

But you may want to avoid wasting time — and, in the case of hardcopy submissions, money — sending unwanted proposals. After all, the query is also an opportunity for you to screen out those who clearly have no interest in your subject.

Also, you shouldn't be overly loose with your ideas and concepts. After all, you can't protect ideas in the context of writing and publishing. You don't want to become overly cautious, but neither do you want to be a runaway train. Focus on pitching your ideas to those who are genuinely qualified to help you manifest them.

These pointers, in combination with the other good information in this book and all the other available resources, should at least give you a solid background for creating a query letter that makes a lasting impression.

For Deborah Herman's biography, see page 54.

YOU (MIGHT) BELONG IN THE SLUSH PILE (OR ELSEWHERE)

Jeff Herman

It's not you per se who might belong in the slush pile; it's your written product. Slush piles used to be almost entirely physical, whereas now they probably exist about 80 percent "in the cloud." Perhaps the term should be changed to *slush cloud*, which sounds much tastier than a *slush pile*. My question is: What are publishers doing with all the extra physical space that was formerly used for slush piles? But let me back up.

Most traditional publishers have a written policy that they won't accept or consider unagented/unsolicited submissions. If not submitted by a literary agent, the work is unagented. If no one at the company invited you to submit your work, it is unsolicited. If your work falls into either category, you're an "Un." In the context of publishing, a Un is a noncitizen or an untouchable. That sounds harsh, but it's the most accurate way to paint it, and it's virtually every writer's starting point. No one is born with or inherits a book deal. The good news is that it's entirely within every writer's power to self-mutate from being a Un to becoming an agented or solicited writer. You most likely already believe that, or you wouldn't be reading this book.

So what happens to Uns' submissions? They get returned, thrown out, or placed in the slush pile with countless other Uns' submissions.

Why does this policy exist? Because for every book traditionally published there are more than 1,000 manuscripts trying to be published at the same point in time. Publishers don't have the in-house staff to screen what's submitted to find the fraction of a percentage they can publish. Instead, they make direct solicitations for writers and experts they might want, or they rely on the several-hundred-strong literary agency community to do the screening and essentially nominate what's publishable.

What happens to the slush pile? That's an interesting question for which I have no scientifically proven answers, but I do have true anecdotes. Every once in a while, a low-level person in the editorial hierarchy will volunteer without prodding to wander through the slush pile and randomly select something to read, and occasionally they find a gem. Excellent books have been discovered in the slush pile and successfully published, and it will keep on happening. But trying to get published through the slush is like trying to pay for college with lottery scratch-offs.

A Random Prediction

Thousands of years from now, a new species or civilization will discover ancient manuscripts and digital archives within the ruins of a once-great metropolis that had been abruptly destroyed by a surging sea. They will have no context for any of it and will ponder and debate its significance at the highest levels. Unknown to them, they will have unsealed a massive slush pile, the unpublished manuscripts written with love and passion by thousands of ordinary people from a lost and little-understood society.

A museum will be constructed for the purpose of housing and displaying the wit, wisdom, and dysfunctions of this period from Earth's beleaguered past. In one fell swoop, an entire slush pile will finally be published.

A True Story

Approximately 20 years ago, there lived a man in Florida who was unable to get an agent or a publisher for his fiction manuscript. Then he had an idea. He was an admirer of a Pulitzer Prize–winning novel named *The Yearling*. The work had been published more than 50 years earlier, sold millions of copies, and was made into a feature film starring a young Gregory Peck. Though no longer a popular book, it still sold tens of thousands of copies each year as a classic reprint.

Our hero repurposed the book into a raw manuscript and changed its title and the author's name. Only someone familiar with the classic book would have recognized the manuscript as blatant plagiarism. He then proceeded to make unagented and unsolicited submissions of "his" work to all the usual publishing prospects. What happened next was easily predictable. In some cases, he never received any response, ever. Some publishers at least returned the manuscript, clearly unread, with an unsigned letter stating that unagented/unsolicited submissions would not be considered, ever.

Refreshingly, he actually received some genuine rejection letters seemingly written by entry-level editors and interns. The letters were brief and dismissive and expressed no appreciation for the work's merits or encouragement for its prospects. One of these rejection letters was from the same publisher that was still profitably publishing *The Yearling*.

What Does the Above Story Tell Us?

Even though the above story is 20 years old, it's no less telling today. At first blush, we see that a bestselling, Pulitzer Prize–winning novel that was made into a major motion picture couldn't even get itself arrested. What's unseen is what's most crucial, which is that the work's merits were worthless in the absence of genuine *access*. Without access, you don't really exist and the game can't begin. The dude didn't have an agent, was unsolicited, and didn't do anything to get quality access. The negative outcome is unsurprising for those who have been to the rodeo.

Publishers have surrounded themselves with firewalls to avoid being trampled by the relentless surge of eager writers. Having an agent is tantamount to a VIP bypass. For editors it's a safe assumption that a book that's agented merits *access*.

What If You Can't Get an Agent? Join the Battle of the Uns!

If you bang your head against a publisher's firewall, the wall won't move but your head will. Though it makes no sense to throw yourself against the wall, it's wise to remember that all walls have inherent limitations that can be exploited.

What if you can't get an agent? You are far from alone and are in excellent company; many superb writers don't connect with agents when first starting out. Fortunately, there are ways to get access to editors and get published even if you don't have an agent. Here's a big secret: publishers actually will consider unagented/unsolicited submissions, but they don't want you to know that. In fact, they may not even know it themselves. Remember this: the rule exists for their convenience, not yours. If you rigidly follow their rules, you're only serving them, not yourself. It's reasonable for you to consider ways to bypass the rule. Ironically, your success will also be the publisher's success; it's a win-win.

Guess what? Being published isn't only for the best writers, though it's invariably for those who are the best at getting published. Writing and getting your writing published are distinct endeavors. No one can keep you from writing, but you can be prevented from traditionally publishing your work. Guess what? Mediocre writers are frequently published while countless überwriters are left stranded at the gate. How does that happen? Keep reading.

1. No agent? No problem. Appoint yourself as your agent, and be your only client. You can even sign a contract with yourself and assign a 15 percent commission to your doppelgänger agent. What does this mean? Learn what an agent needs to know by finding out who publishes books like yours and who the appropriate editors are at each of those houses. You can do that by using this book, researching on Amazon and bookstore shelves, and reading the acknowledgments sections of similar books for editor names.

2. Cold-call. Another trick is to cold-call publishers asking to be routed to the editorial departments of the divisions/programs in question. Once a live voice says something like "Editorial," you'll have reached your destination. The next step is to cajole this person into giving you the name of an editor for romance titles or for whatever category your manuscript falls into. Accumulating relevant editor names will enable you to bypass the slush pile. Actually submitting your work to a real person who helps make crucial decisions is a tremendous upgrade from sending it to "Editorial Department" or "Submissions." Your work needs to be directed to an actual person with the genuine clout to acquire books. If the editor is interested in your work, you will enter the exalted "solicited" zone, which means you have avoided the knee-jerk deportation to the slush graveyard. You will have achieved access…

3. Know what editors do. You can't deeply understand what someone else does if you have never done it yourself. But gaining superficial knowledge about their basic functions and needs is immensely better than complete ignorance or misinformation. Obviously, editors edit, but not as much as you might think or as much as they might prefer. An accurate job description for today's editor could easily be Product Acquisition and Management. Notice that the word *editor* doesn't even appear? That's because they are not being paid or rewarded for their editing skills. In fact, those secondary tasks are often outsourced (to the chagrin of fussy authors). Book publishers no longer provide the intense fact-checking and word-smashing that urbane publications like the *New Yorker* are still famous for. In fact, some unsatisfied authors use their own funds to hire editors to go beyond what their publishers will do.

An editor's career track is tied to the success of the books that he acquires, not that he edits. Critically acclaimed books that are economic failures are not good for an editor's career unless they also attract commercially successful books to the editor. An editor's career success will match the commercial success of the books he or she acquires, regardless of the books' literary or cultural standing.

What's a successful career for an editor? Frankly, I can't imagine how most of them manage to support a full household in the Northeast unless both spouses are gainfully employed or there's a trust fund. Many years of toil are required before decent six-figure incomes are attained. In 1981 my entry-level publishing job paid $5 per hour, which was okay for a 22-year-old at that time. That same job today probably pays about $15 per hour, but I don't think the 300 percent increase has kept pace with New York's inflation rate. For instance, back then TV was still free and landlines were the only option, at less than $20 per month.

Let's keep our eyes on the ball. Editors need to acquire good product (books) in order to justify their employment. Your job as a writer is to give it to them. If you succeed at giving them what they need, you will get what you want (a deal). It's really that simple, yet too many writers don't seem to get it. They approach editors on their knees asking for mercy and attention, which is also how they confront agents. That's not pitching; that's begging, and it's unappealing. Don't be a beggar; be a giver and a maker. Initiate the process by communicating your intent and power to make everyone else very happy. You don't have to actually believe it any more than you believed you were really Juliet when you portrayed her in the school play. When you pitch your work, what you feel about yourself doesn't have to match how you want other people to feel about you. In fact, how other people see you might be more accurate than how you see yourself. No one wants losers for clients or authors. Don't ever apologize for being a writer who wants to get published; your apology might be accepted, but your manuscript won't be. When pitching your work, please believe you are offering others a generous opportunity to share your inevitable success. I have been pitched thousands of times by phone, in person, and through written expression. Arrogance, delusions of grandeur, and an unwarranted sense of entitlement are powerful turnoffs. But presenting a negative persona about one's own abilities and prospects can be even worse. Between these extremes there's plenty of space for a compelling blend of humility and confidence.

Editors can't make unilateral decisions about what to acquire or how big an advance to offer. When they discover something they want, they are required to sell and defend it at so-called editorial meetings. Other editors may act like the devil's advocate, testing the editor's resolve and whether she has fully considered the risks. Strong editors can usually get what they want, whereas marginal editors often don't. An editor who mostly fails to get green-lighted should be calling the headhunters, because he's already been marked for failure by his peers.

Also at these meetings is the in-house sales staff. If they say, "We can't sell it," it's game-over for that book. If they call their contacts at Barnes & Noble and Amazon and they say, "We won't order it," it's game-over for that book. If someone calls one of the company's boss-people, and she says, "I don't care what anyone else says, I want that book," it's game-on. So what can you do? Hedge your bet by learning how to impersonate the boss's phone voice and make sure she's heard loud and clear. If you can pull off a con like that, there's no reason you can't also generate a bestseller. Seriously, make sure you give editors (and your agent, if you have one) all the ammunition they might need to get the job done on your behalf.

4. Know what publishers do. If you have ever seen a book, then you know what publishers do. More specifically, they curate editorial products that the marketplace will presumably support; they produce them into consumable formats; they make them appealing; they get them into the hands of reviewers, media contacts, and key bloggers; they produce print and digital catalogs for distribution to retail accounts and employ salespeople to generate orders; they maintain inventory, fulfill orders, issue invoices, and manage the accounting; they pay authors varying percentages of revenues received; they sell subsidiary rights; they do what few authors can do by themselves. If I left anything out, *I'm sorry*. You go ahead and spend your spring weekends writing all of this not knowing if anyone will even bother to read it. IS ANYONE ACTUALLY READING THIS? Prove it: jeff@jeffherman.com.

Perhaps the most significant value that traditional publishers provide is credibility. Everyone in the business and throughout the supply chain knows that each traditionally published book is like a lucky sperm, or maybe we should say a "sperm with merit." Forget about sperms. For every book that publishers choose, at least 1,000 have been rejected. And publishing a book isn't cheap. Separate from the advance, the typical book costs at least $25,000 of a publisher's overall resources; much more if large inventories are called for.

By the way, having an agent shouldn't excuse you from learning everything you can about how the business works. The more you know, the better you will be at helping your agent and yourself get the best results possible.

I am confident that this runaway essay has given everything that was promised and more. The journey continues.

THE KNOCKOUT NONFICTION BOOK PROPOSAL

Jeff Herman

The quality of your nonfiction book proposal will invariably make the difference between success and failure. Before agents and publishers will accept a work of fiction (especially from a newer writer), they require a complete manuscript. But nonfiction projects are different: a proposal alone can do the trick. This is what makes nonfiction writing a much less speculative and often more lucrative endeavor (relatively speaking) than fiction writing.

You may devote five years of long evenings to writing a 1,000-page fiction manuscript, only to receive a thick pile of computer-generated rejections. Clearly, writing nonfiction doesn't entail the same risks, for the simple reason that you don't have to write an entire manuscript before you can begin pitching it. On the other hand, writing fiction is often an emotionally driven endeavor in which rewards are gained through the act of writing and are not necessarily based on rational, practical considerations. Interestingly, many successful nonfiction writers fantasize about being fiction writers.

As you'll learn, the proposal's structure, contents, and size can vary substantially, and it's up to you to decide the best format for your purposes. Still, the guidelines given here serve as excellent general parameters.

Appearance Counts

Much of what follows becomes less relevant, or perhaps not possible, if all your material is conveyed solely through digital transmission. However, even digital items should look as good as possible, and many people greatly prefer to print a hardcopy to read from. In my opinion, physicality is still king (or queen) when it comes to making best impressions.

- Your proposal should be printed in black ink on clean, letter-sized (8½" x 11"), white paper.
- Letter-quality printing is by far the best. Make sure the toner or ink cartridge is fresh and that all photocopies are dark and clear enough to be read easily. Publishing is an image-driven business, and you will be judged, perhaps unconsciously, on the physical and aesthetic merits of your submission.

- Always double-space, or you can virtually guarantee reader antagonism — eyestrain makes people cranky.
- Make sure your proposal appears fresh and new and hasn't been dog-eared, marked up, or abused by previous readers. No editor will be favorably disposed if she thinks that everyone else on the block has already sent you packing. You want editors to think you have lots of other places to go, not nowhere else.
- Contrary to common practice in other industries, editors prefer not to receive bound proposals. If an editor likes your proposal, she will want to photocopy it for her colleagues, and your binding will only be in the way. If you want to keep the material together and neat, use a binder clip; if it's a lengthy proposal, clip each section together separately. Of course, email submissions negate the above issues.

Proposal Contents

A nonfiction proposal should include the following elements, each of which is explained below:

- Title page
- Overview
- Biographical section
- Marketing section
- Author platform
- Competition section
- Promotion section
- Chapter outline
- Sample chapters

Title page. The title page should be the easiest part, but it can also be the most important, since, like your face when you meet someone, it's what is seen first.

Try to think of a title that's attractive and effectively communicates your book's concept. A descriptive subtitle, following a catchy title, can help you achieve both goals.

It's very important that your title and subtitle relate to the book's subject, or an editor might make an inaccurate judgment about your book's focus and automatically dismiss it. For instance, if you're proposing a book about gardening, don't title it *The Greening of America*.

Examples of titles that have worked very well are:

How to Win Friends and Influence People by Dale Carnegie
Think and Grow Rich by Napoleon Hill

Baby and Child Care by Dr. Benjamin Spock

How to Swim with the Sharks without Being Eaten Alive by Harvey Mackay

And, yes, there are notable exceptions: an improbable title that went on to become a perennial success is *What Color Is Your Parachute?* by Richard Bolles. Sure, you may gain confidence and a sense of freedom from such exceptional instances. By all means let your imagination graze during the brainstorming stage.

However, don't bet on the success of an arbitrarily conceived title that has nothing at all to do with the book's essential concept or reader appeal.

A title should be stimulating and, when appropriate, upbeat and optimistic. If your subject is an important historic or current event, the title should be dramatic. If a biography, the title should capture something personal (or even controversial) about the subject. Many good books have been handicapped by poorly conceived titles, and many poor books have been catapulted to success by good titles. A good title is good advertising. Procter & Gamble, for instance, spends thousands of worker hours creating seductive names for its endless array of soap-based products.

The title you choose is referred to as the "working title." Most likely, the book will have a different title when published. There are two reasons for this:

1. A more appropriate and/or arresting title may evolve with time.
2. The publisher has final contractual discretion over the title (as well as over a lot of other things).

The title page should contain only the title, plus your name, address, telephone number, and email address — and the name, address, and phone number of your agent, if you have one. The title page should be neatly and attractively spaced. Eye-catching and tasteful computer graphics and display-type fonts can contribute to the overall aesthetic appeal.

Overview. The overview portion of the proposal is a terse statement (one to three pages) of your overall concept and mission. It sets the stage for what's to follow. Short, concise paragraphs are usually best.

Biographical section. This is where you sell yourself. This section tells who you are and why you're the ideal person to write this book. You should highlight all your relevant experience, including media and public-speaking appearances, and list previous books, articles, or both, published by or about you. Self-flattery is appropriate — so long as you're telling the truth. Many writers prefer to slip into the third person here, to avoid the appearance of egomania.

Marketing section. This is where you justify the book's existence from a commercial perspective. Who will buy it? For instance, if you're proposing a book on sales, state the number of people who earn their living through sales; point out that thousands of large and small companies are sales dependent and spend large sums on sales training, and that all sales professionals are perpetually hungry for fresh, innovative sales books.

Don't just say something like "My book is for adult women, and there are more than 50 million adult women in America." You have to be much more demographically sophisticated than that.

Author platform. The platform has become a crucial piece of the proposal in recent years. It's expected that as a minimum the author is sufficiently savvy about social media to have a large digital network of like-minded "friends" who can be tapped to purchase the book. It's all about the number of relevant people ("communities") you can access, and the expectation that they will either buy your book or at least tell others about it ("viral marketing"). Mention the number of contacts you have through social media, as well as subscribers to your newsletter or professional services, and be as specific as possible about the numbers who visit your website.

Competition section. To the uninitiated, this section may appear to be a setup to self-destruction. However, if handled strategically, and assuming you have a fresh concept, this section wins you points rather than undermining your case.

The competition section is where you describe major published titles with concepts comparable to yours. If you're familiar with your subject, you'll probably know those titles by heart; you may have even read most or all of them. If you're not certain, just check Amazon or AbeBooks, where pretty much anything ever published is listed. If the titles in question are only available through "resellers," and not the original publishers, they are most likely out of print. Don't list everything published on your subject — that could require a book in itself. Just describe the leading half dozen titles or so (backlist classics, as well as recent books) and *explain why yours will be different.*

Getting back to the sales-book example, there is no shortage of good sales books. There's a reason for that — a big market exists for sales books. You can turn that to your advantage by emphasizing the public's substantial, insatiable demand for sales books. Your book will feed that demand with its unique and innovative sales-success program. Salespeople and companies dependent on sales are always looking for new ways to enhance sales skills (it's okay to reiterate key points).

Promotion section. Here you suggest possible ways to promote and market the book. Sometimes this section is unnecessary. It depends on your subject and on what, if any, realistic promotional prospects exist.

If you're proposing a specialized academic book such as *The Mating Habits of Octopi*, the market is a relatively limited one, and elaborate promotions would be wasteful. But if you're proposing a popularly oriented relationship book along the lines of *The Endless Orgasm in One Easy Lesson*, the promotional possibilities are also endless. They would include most major electronic broadcast and print media outlets, advertising, maybe even some weird contests.

You want to guide the publisher toward seeing realistic ways to publicize the book.

Chapter outline. This is the meat of the proposal. Here's where you finally tell what's going to be in the book. Each chapter should be tentatively titled and clearly abstracted.

Some successful proposals have fewer than 100 words per abstracted chapter; others have several hundred words per chapter. Sometimes the length varies from chapter to chapter. There are no hard-and-fast rules here; it's the dealer's choice. Sometimes less is more; at other times a too-brief outline inadequately represents the project.

At their best, the chapter abstracts read like mini-chapters — as opposed to stating "I will do...and I will show..." Visualize the trailer for a forthcoming movie; that's the tantalizing effect you want to create.

Also, it's a good idea to preface the outline with a table of contents. This way, the editor can see your entire road map at the outset.

Sample chapters. Sample chapters are optional. A strong, well-developed proposal will often be enough. However, especially if you're a first-time writer, one or more sample chapters will give you an opportunity to show your stuff and will help dissolve an editor's concerns about your ability to actually write the book, thereby increasing the odds that you'll receive an offer — and you'll probably increase the size of the advance, too.

Nonfiction writers are often wary of investing time to write sample chapters since they view the proposal as a way of avoiding speculative writing. But this can be a short-sighted view; a single sample chapter can make the difference between selling and not selling a marginal proposal. Occasionally, a publisher will request that one or two sample chapters be written before they make a decision about a particular project. If the publisher seems to have a real interest, writing the sample material is definitely worth the author's time, and the full package can then be shown to additional prospects, too.

Many editors say that they look for reasons to reject books and that being on the fence is a valid reason for rejecting a project. To be sure, there are cases where sample chapters have tilted a proposal on the verge of rejection right back onto the playing field!

Keep in mind that the publisher is speculating that you can and will write the book upon contract. A sample chapter will go far to reduce the publisher's concerns about your ability to deliver a quality work beyond the proposal stage.

What Else?

There are a variety of materials you may wish to attach to the proposal to further bolster your cause. These include:

- Laudatory letters and comments about you
- Laudatory publicity about you
- A headshot (but not if you look like the Fly, unless you're proposing a humor book or a nature book)
- Copies of published articles you've written
- Videos of TV or speaking appearances
- Any and all information that builds you up in a relevant way, but be organized about it — don't create a disheveled, unruly package

Length

The average proposal is probably between 15 and 30 double-spaced pages, and the typical sample chapter is an additional 10 to 20 double-spaced pages. But sometimes proposals reach 100 pages, and other times they're 5 pages in total. Extensive proposals are not a handicap.

Whatever it takes!

DUMB-ASS RANDOM QUESTIONS AND ANSWERS

Jeff Herman

By being snarky, I bet I got your attention. And now that I have it, hold on to your hat, because there's more to know. By the way, did your grade-school teachers ever say, "There's no such thing as a stupid question," before asking if there were any questions? Well, they were wrong. I've attended a lot of writers' conferences and have entertained many stupid questions. However, I tended to hear the same stupid questions over and over again. It finally dawned on me that a large percentage of writers had the same stupid questions. Besides, where do we draw the line between a stupid and a smart question, and who gets to decide? I came to the decision that stupid isn't bad, but choosing to remain stupid might be. And I concede it's kind of stupid for me to think about stuff like this with such intensity.

What Is an Advance?

The advance is the money that a traditional publisher gives you in exchange for granting them the exclusive right to publish your book. Unless you breach the terms of the publisher's contract, you never have to return the advance, even if your book sells only three copies. However, all royalty income will be charged against the advance, so you won't see any more money until your royalties (see below) surpass the advance.

How Are Advances Determined?

The amount of the advance is roughly determined by the publisher's best estimation of how many copies and subsidiary rights they can sell within the first year of publication. Presidential aspirant Hillary Clinton can easily command many millions of dollars as a single advance, because the publisher can count on making a lot of money by publishing her book. At the other extreme, your obscure neighbor Jim James will probably be ecstatic to receive a more typical $5,000 advance for his recipe book about ways to boil water.

What Are Royalties?

Traditional publishers pay their authors a percentage of the book's revenues. Many variables determine the royalty percentage, and publishers don't all offer the same structure. However, the following structure is accurate more than half the time: Hardcovers start at 10 percent of the listed retail price and escalate to 15 percent after 15,000 copies are sold. Paperbacks are usually fixed at 7.5 percent of the list price. However, many retailers are able to force publishers into granting them better than 50 percent discounts. These are known as "high-discount" sales, and every book contract contains fine print allowing the publisher to pay a significantly reduced royalty against copies sold at high discount. Refusing to grant the high discount often means losing the sale and the royalty altogether. The lower royalty is "justified" because the publisher's profit margin is supposedly also reduced. You or your agent can negotiate these kinds of contingencies to a point but won't be able to entirely negate them.

Most independent presses pay royalties on the basis of "net" receipts, which means what the publisher receives from the bookstore. Most of the time, wholesalers, bookstores, and other retailers pay publishers around 50 percent of the list price for print books. However, the independent presses usually manage to equalize the royalty situation for their authors by simply doubling the royalty percentages. For instance, whereas a list royalty might be 7.5 percent, a net royalty might be 15 percent.

Paperback originals are much more common now than they were in the past. Publishers will only issue a hardcover edition if confident about selling a requisite number of units. Library sales were much more robust in the past, and libraries greatly preferred hardcovers because they were more durable. Hardcover profit margins are much higher than those for paperbacks, but only some books can command a $30+ list price, and no one wants to end up losing more revenues than were generated. For obvious reasons, paperbacks sell many more copies, and most hardcovers are converted to paperback after the first year anyway, unless they do not have good sales, in which case they may simply disappear from print without ever migrating to paperback.

Digital sales have surged over the past few years and represent a large percentage of overall sales. However, the rapid growth seems to be leveling off lately, though I'm not sure anyone knows why. It may simply be that most readers who prefer digital jumped on the bandwagon all at once. In any case, authors tend to receive 25 percent of the publisher's net earnings from each digital sale.

What Happens after You Deliver Your Finished Manuscript to Your Publisher?

First, congratulations for having a traditional publishing deal and for meeting your deadline. Your publisher will take 30 to 60 days to have someone read the manuscript and make all kinds of suggestions and demands about what to revise or add. You get to decide if you want to make the suggested changes or if you want to protest them. It's okay to disagree, but unless you convince your publisher to see it your way, by contract it's their way or the highway and you may have to return the advance. The work isn't considered to be accepted until the publisher says so, at which point you'll get another advance payment. In my long experience, serious editorial grievances between authors and publishers are rare.

Next, the manuscript goes into production (including line editing/copyediting, typesetting, and proofreading), which takes several months and is like what happens to a cow that's repurposed into a sirloin steak, except nothing gets killed and rendered. Your publisher will consult with you about cover and title ideas. They get final say, though a consensus is greatly preferred. Then the book is posted in the frontlist of the publisher's catalog (print or digital), which goes to all booksellers.

Will the Publisher Promote Your Book?

If you mean will they pay to send you on a multicity or even a uni-city media tour, the answer is usually no. Every traditional publisher has in-house publicity and marketing departments that will, to varying degrees, try to get you interviewed by relevant media outlets and send the book to prospective reviewers and bloggers. But here's a sobering fact: Fortune 500 companies like Procter & Gamble pay their in-house sales and marketing professionals healthy six-figure incomes, and many of them have MBAs from the top programs. This isn't a model that publishers can even remotely afford to follow. Though talented people work for the publishers, the in-house staffs are small and most titles are neglected. The small number of books that received the biggest advances will consume the most attention, because the publisher needs to recover its relatively huge investments in those titles. In fact, the publisher might even pay to outsource some of the marketing to help maximize sales.

It's wise for most authors to learn how to be a self-marketing machine. One of the attributes that probably made you attractive to your publisher in the first place was the fact that you wouldn't be dependent on them to drive sales.

There are significant differences between the ways corporate houses and smaller houses market their books. Large publishers can afford to lose money a lot of the time, thanks to their huge backlist catalogs. Smaller presses lack that kind of cash cushion and must be doubly certain that every dollar spent is likely to generate more than $1 in return. They need to make every book as successful as possible, but they can't afford placing big bets.

What's an "Author Platform"?

Platform is one of the more recent terms to enter the publishing world's collective conversation, and, for better or worse, it has become something of an obsession. If misunderstood, a platform can become more like a gallows.

A platform is everything you already possess or can quickly manifest to almost guarantee that your book will be commercially successful. This is where your editorial ability could become secondary to other qualities. Specifically, publishers want to be convinced that you have mature and vibrant social media and professional networks, which need to exist largely in cyberspace for optimal speed, volume, and value. You're expected to receive high-volume, quality traffic to your website, and to appear often and early whenever you or your subject is searched for. Basically, they want you to be able to enter a few clicks and sell 10,000 copies minimum. There are authors who can do that and much more. The good news is that you don't have to spend a lot of money or be a techno-geek to learn how to become an internet player. Furthermore, there are few rules and truly no limitations to what can be done. New marketing paradigms emerge all the time from humble home-based jockeys. When people say, "That won't work," you should assume they might be 100 percent wrong.

When it comes to internet marketing, nothing succeeds until it does. It's simply a matrix of infinite problems and challenges waiting to be manipulated. Human psychology is the ultimate arbiter for what does and doesn't work. For instance, Facebook succeeds because it gives people the feeling of instant connection to friends and family, which is a primal instinct. What people have always wanted the most is what they will always want the most, and technology has not changed that fact.

If you don't have much of a platform, some agents and editors will automatically dismiss you for that reason alone. But please don't throw in the towel, because there are countless ways to compensate for whatever is lacking in your overall package. For obvious reasons, I want my clients to have vibrant platforms. But guess what? I have signed up and sold projects by authors who totally lacked conventional platforms, and their books did well. I'm sure the same is true for most of my colleagues. Caveat: There are many expensive services and products promising to make you a platform avatar. There are also many good books devoted to the subject for less than $25 each.

Fiction writers don't get a break in this regard, though they need to have a different kind of platform than authors who write self-help books. Fiction writers greatly benefit from popular fan pages, for instance.

Why Have Ebooks Changed the Business?

Obviously, it's expensive to print, store, and ship physical books. Because most retail sales are based on consignment, which means that the stores can return unsold books instead of paying the publisher for them, all books are printed at significant risk. Ebooks bypass all of the above, which means publishers potentially save tens of thousands of dollars in speculative overhead. If everyone simply decided to buy only ebooks, it's hard to say how many jobs and functions would disappear. But once the dust settled, stability would eventually return, and many of the same players would still be standing. Digital publishing has made self-publishing much more viable and is a great opportunity for entrepreneurial independent publishers. The real wild card is that no one knows what the eventual balance will be between physical books and ebooks, but recently ebook sales have leveled off in most areas. Fiction and self-published ebooks remain strong, and that's not likely to change.

Physical bookstores have had to readjust what they do and how they attract readers in their community, because if enough sales shift to digital, there simply won't be enough reason for them to continue existing, especially if Amazon continues to gobble up market share of all print sales. Recently, Amazon has opened physical bookstores, and it will be interesting to see what happens with those outlets. Barnes & Noble has had to adjust and close stores, and seemed on the brink of disappearing because of its huge inventory of stores, warehouses, staff, and other capital-draining infrastructure. So far, they have found ways to remain viable, but time will tell if that sort of retail bookstore is sustainable. In contrast, mom-and-pop stores require little capital investment and tend to be embedded in their communities as preferred destinations for recreational book shopping, even if their prices are a bit higher. For many people, selecting and reading books isn't a function; it's a passion. For them, boutique venues and the "book experience" are inviolable. If their love is passed on to future generations, then technology's dictates will be slightly thwarted.

What's Happening with Ebooks?

Tracked ebook sales have leveled off over the past couple of years and currently make up about 25 percent of all book sales. However, *tracked* is the key word here, because most ebooks are self-published, and that makes it difficult to measure aggregate sales. I'm going to go against common wisdom here by predicting that by 2020, overall ebook sales will taper off to about 10 percent of the book market, in favor of enhanced physical books. By *enhanced* I mean that physical books will be exceptionally alluring for reasons beyond mere editorial content. Currently, most paperback editions are only marginally more attractive than a newspaper; they are meant to be discarded. But we are a visual and tactile species. In the near future, digital reading will be equal to digital sex — accessible, better than nothing, and comparatively uncomplicated. But newly upgraded physical editions will be more desirable for the same reasons that people tend not to like blank walls.

Barnes & Noble and thousands of mom-and-pop booksellers must agree that print books are here to stay. The number of independent stores is growing, not shrinking, and

B&N is showing a tenacious spirit. This wouldn't be happening in an atmosphere of doom. Needless to say, every ebook sale and every online sale is at the expense of physical bookstores. But readers love shopping in bookstores, and there's nothing that online sellers can do to match that experience.

Why Do Publishers Fight with Amazon?

During the first decade of this century, publishers were frequently in public contention with Barnes & Noble, and no one had any issues with Amazon. But over the past several years Amazon has become the strongest single force in publishing, while B&N has been struggling to redefine itself.

Publishers squabble with Amazon for reasons similar to those for which European countries squabble with Russia. It's about who will dominate the present and the future. The irony is that Amazon decisively won the fight when they introduced the Kindle ereader several years ago, but some publishers still don't realize that they have already lost the war and that it's time to sue for peace.

Amazon is the only player with an innovative spirit, and that's the essence of the conflict. Oh, Amazon also happens to be rather selfish, greedy, and imperialistic, but that's the nature of corporate competition and combat. Any of the Big 5 publishing houses could have accessed their parent company's deep pockets to internally capitalize the creation of digital readers in advance of the Kindle, or could have partnered with Sony or one of the other early ereader producers. This would have given them unilateral control over the editorial product and a competitive digital delivery system. It's no accident that the early radio and TV set manufacturers were also the first content producers. In fact, self-retailing their own digital products through their own readers might have been a brilliant strategy for the major publishers. But instead they all sat on their hands and conducted business as usual while Amazon created the future, and therefore Amazon now owns it.

Over the past couple of years, the publisher-Amazon wars have mostly dropped from the headlines, and a palatable détente seems to be prevailing by mutual choice. The drama wasn't good for Amazon's image, and unmasked that the publishers can bark but can't actually bite. However, tensions remain high and new contention is potentially around the corner.

When a publisher refuses to comply with Amazon's dictates, Amazon can (and often does) simply stop selling that company's products as part of the free two-day shipping Prime program, or explicitly states that delivery will require excessive delays, which hurts the publisher much more than it hurts Amazon. True, consumers can easily buy the embargoed products elsewhere, and many do. However, several million consumers pay $119 (might be more by the time you read this) a year to be Amazon Prime members, which entitles them to free, fast shipping and easy ordering. Most of these consumers won't shop elsewhere unless they *really* want the embargoed product.

Publishers can't exist without Amazon, nor can they defend themselves against Amazon, which is why they also hate Amazon. The largest houses attempted to take a unified stand against Amazon's domination in 2012 by forming an alliance with Apple, and were subsequently sued by the federal government for their troubles. Ultimately, they were collectively fined many millions of dollars as part of a settlement for allegedly acting in concert with one another in violation of antitrust codes. Amazon emerged unscathed and more confident than ever.

When publishers lose sales, their authors lose money. So it's no surprise that the largest author organizations have anti-Amazon tantrums in unison with agents and publishers. But as I said elsewhere, Amazon won the war before it was actually fought. The publishers' best leverage is that Amazon can't afford to kill them; it needs the publishers to generate the books that it sells the most of. A scorched-Earth approach has never been contemplated by either side because they both live from the same soil.

By the way, Amazon has been a godsend for self-publishers because it provides the only comprehensive, full-service retail platform with massive traffic.

What about Self-Publishing?

I've heard self-publishing causes blindness and hair to grow on your palms. This book is about traditional publishing, which will remain the preferred method for the vast majority of writers into the foreseeable future. That said, self-publishing is a viable alternative, but you'd better understand what it is and isn't before choosing it.

I read somewhere that more than 1,000,000 "books" will be self-published in 2019. Most of them are digital or print-on-demand (POD). But what this staggering figure doesn't reveal is that at least 95 percent of self-published books sell fewer than 10 copies a year. As a self-publisher, are you prepared to invest enough resources to not be one of the 95 percent? Do you even know what that investment means? Sadly, many self-publishers retain an array of expensive services that promise them the moon but end up delivering credit-card debt. Yes, a fraction of self-publishers are exceedingly successful or at least self-satisfied with the results. But most of them have probably leveraged their preexisting business skills and connections to make it work. They probably had a realistic business plan and budget in place before pulling the trigger, the same as they would with any other self-financed venture.

Today, anyone can self-publish anything at any time. That's the easy part, but self-selling/marketing and self-distributing are where most self-publishers fall down the stairs. Brick-and-mortar retailers aren't interested in stocking self-published books. Amazon will give you a webpage, but that will mean nothing if you don't drive sales to the page.

If you know who your customers are likely to be, how many there are, and how to reach them, then self-publishing might make more sense than traditional publishing. And it's better to self-publish than no-publish if you can't get a traditional deal. But don't get bamboozled by expensive self-publishing packages. You can make it happen for less than $1,000 — or even less than $100 if you don't need a professional copyedit and cover design — and take it one frugal step at a time from there. Many excellent books (mostly self-published) are devoted to the subject.

Here's the flip side: Self-publishers are filling important editorial niches that traditional publishers neglect. For instance, some of the bestselling craft, hobby, and specialized how-to books are self-published. So are many of the bestselling "fan fiction" titles in such categories as vampires and zombies. Most of these successful self-publishers have figured out online selling and don't want to do business through traditional retailers because they would make much less money going the traditional route. It's likely that the importance of self-publishers as niche micropublishers will explode over the next few years. Maybe you can get a piece of the action.

What about Distribution for Self-Publishers?

Lack of distribution has always been the biggest obstacle for self-publishing, and that's not destined to change. However, most traditionally published books also struggle for meaningful distribution, for the simple reason that store space is extremely limited in comparison to the number of books that are traditionally published. Most published authors are frustrated about the fact that they rarely find their own books in bookstores, even if they have a Big 5 publisher. Publishers can't dictate what gets shelved; stores will stock what they are most likely to sell the most of based on consumer demand. The exception is that retail placement is for sale, meaning that the author and/or publisher can pay for retail visibility. However, publishers will only do this if they think the product will move. Visibility doesn't guarantee that sales will recover the cost.

What's Really Going on in Book Publishing?

A relatively quiet under-the-radar storm is continuing to disrupt the foundations of book publishing. On the surface it seems as if we are in a stable period in which the Big 5 are consolidating their dominance, Amazon continues to dictate how everyone must behave, and independent publishers struggle for market share against the billion-dollar constellations. But most observers are failing to see what's really happening in plain sight. The term *self-publishing* no longer does justice to what many people are accomplishing outside the traditional system. You can become a successful publisher of your own and other people's books without any budget to speak of. In fact, there's little evidence that big spending equals big sales.

Viable content is crucial, but that doesn't mean you have to comply with what the professionals say. Industry insiders were relentlessly critical of the editorial quality of *Fifty Shades of Grey* and even boasted that they would have immediately rejected it. But as we all know, it bypassed the system and became a multimillion-dollar property, because millions of people liked it. Don't make the mistake of assuming that the publishing establishment knows best about what the public wants to read. Your opinion as an experienced reader is no less valid than that of someone who reads and edits for a living.

Obviously, strong content is only the beginning, not the destination. The key is to get people who "talk a lot" to read and like your book. What's most incredible about the internet is that anyone can seemingly become "a person of influence" to millions of like-minded people. A single shout-out about a new sponge by a housewife from Kansas with thousands of kindred followers can generate tremendous ecommerce revenues. And if the conversations continue and customers stay loyal, the success will be self-sustaining.

This is what's happening in publishing as you read this: online reviewers, bloggers, and social media users with big followings are dictating which books succeed. But you probably don't know it yet because no one knows how to measure the numbers. The sole money counter is Nielsen BookScan, but it only measures what flows through established retailers, and much of the book market has migrated elsewhere. However, that "elsewhere" is mostly Amazon. Amazon is an easy sales platform for self-publishers, even though Amazon takes at least 30 percent of the gross revenue. Many readers use Amazon as their first book search engine and preferred sales venue when looking for a title or author they have heard about. Unless your site is easily findable through a Google search, Amazon is probably the only reliable way for people to find and buy your book.

The irony here is that Amazon was initially seen as a godsend for traditional publishers that were desperately trying to break up Barnes & Noble's de facto cartel of the retail book market. Ultimately, publishers unknowingly jumped from the frying pan into the fire. Amazon has become an even tougher taskmaster than B&N and also offers an ideal way for writers to reject conventional publishers.

Is Self-Publishing Good for Democracy?

The ascent of the internet was supposed to bring down totalitarian governments, which is exactly what happened in the 1980s and 1990s. And self-publishing goes hand in hand with the internet, since anything can be uploaded and subsequently downloaded. But throughout the current decade democracies are struggling. Even in the US, basic freedoms are being eroded.

The ability to freely transmit information has proved to have a boomerang impact. Ugly belief systems have poisoned millions of people through the internet. The problem isn't the availability of information, but what people do with the information. The internet is loaded with information telling people not to kill others in the name of their gods, but it doesn't help. Governments can block egregious information from being spread through the internet in territories they control, but there are countless ways for sophisticated users to override those obstructions. The internet is simply an inert channel that has nothing to do with human nature. At the end of the day, individuals have the power to decide who they are and what they will do. Unfortunately, bad information can be more compelling and influential than good information.

Now here's the good news, which you already know: You are your own universe. The world might be insane, but you don't have to be. Writing and publishing is your potential game changer regardless of what's happening all around you. You can create yourself any way you want to. You are free to write, and read, what you will. And you never need to be alone. The fight for decency is far from over. In fact, decency is by far the will of the majority; it just doesn't make for good headlines. The internet is indestructible even if access is vulnerable. Keep yourself free, and follow only yourself. If enough people do only that, the world will be fine.

Will Traditional Publishing Become Extinct Anytime Soon?

That's very unlikely. However, midsize independent publishers are endangered because many of them lack the cash flow to survive a fast-changing environment and can't jettison fixed costs fast enough. Many indies disappeared in the first half of this decade, but the survivors are hanging in and seem to be figuring things out. Unless there's an unforeseen disruption on the horizon, the situation should remain stable. Small presses will manage to survive simply because they are small and can more easily manage their overhead and shift to digital publishing and POD as needed. The Big 5 can't fail because of their billion-dollar backlist catalogs. In a worst-case scenario, all they have to do is stop acquiring expensive frontlist titles and just rely on midlist acquisitions and backlist sales. Their revenues would plummet, but ironically their profit margins would soar.

WHEN NOTHING HAPPENS TO GOOD (OR BAD) WRITERS
a.k.a. Ignored Writer Syndrome (IWS)

Jeff Herman

"I will not be ignored!" screams Alex Forrest, the book editor played by Glenn Close, to her philandering lover, played by Michael Douglas, in the classic film *Fatal Attraction*.

What perfect karma: a book editor being ignored, even though her job was not relevant to the conflict. Too bad about the rabbit, though.

It's an inalienable truth that any writer who aggressively pitches his or her work will encounter abundant rejections along the way. You know that. But what you may not have been prepared for was the big-loud-deafening nothing at all. You followed the given protocols; have been gracious, humble, and appreciative; and have done nothing egregious. And you would never boil a rabbit. So what's your reward? Absolutely nothing; you have been ignored.

A document stating that your work has been rejected, even if clearly generic, may be a much more welcome outcome than the silence of an empty universe. At least that formal rejection letter reflects that you are part of a genuine process. True, you have been turned away at the gate, but it still seems that you belong to a fraternity of sorts. It's like you're an understudy, or simply wait-listed. Your existence is acknowledged, even if unwelcome, whereas to be ignored is proof of nothing. Nature abhors a vacuum, and any writer with nerve endings will understand why soon enough, if not already.

I write this essay because of the frequent feedback I receive from readers complaining about the unresponsiveness of editors and agents. I have carefully considered this phenomenon and how it must negatively affect the morale and stamina of those who are endeavoring in good faith to be published. I have decided that to be ignored deserves its own category in the travails of writing, and that it inflicts even more pain and frustration than the proverbial rejection. I shall designate it with a logical term: *ignored*.

Why are so many writers ignored by editors and agents? I will respond to that with questions of my own. Why are so many children ignored? Why are so many of the poor and needy ignored? Why are so many social problems ignored? I could ask this question in countless ways, and the primary universal answer would essentially remain the same: it's far easier to do nothing.

Let's get back to our specific context. As I mention elsewhere, agents and editors have demanding, often tedious, workloads that overwhelm the typical 40-hour workweek (they tend to put in way more hours than that, even though they can rarely bill by the hour or receive extra pay). They are rewarded for generating tangible results, which is most often measured in the form of monetary revenues. Taking the time to respond to writers, even in a purely perfunctory manner, might be the courteous thing to do, but neither their businesses nor their bosses will reward their kindness. You may feel that such inaction is a misguided and shortsighted "policy," and you might be right, but it doesn't change the facts as they are.

Does being ignored mean that you have actually been read and rejected? This question can't be answered, because you're being ignored. It's possible that someone did read your work and rejected it, and then simply neglected to reply to your email or threw out your proposal even if an SASE was attached. Why would someone do that? Because it's much easier to, and they can't justify the time it would take to answer as many as 150 submissions per week. It's also possible that your submission has not been read and may never be read, because nobody is available to screen the "incoming" in any organized fashion. It's not out of the question that submissions will accumulate in numerous piles, boxes, and email inboxes for several years before they are simply discarded, never to be opened. Does this strike you as harsh or ridiculous? Whatever; it is the way it is.

What is certain is that if your work is read and accepted, you will hear about it. In closing, my message to you is that you not allow being ignored to diminish your dreams and goals. It's simply a part of the process and part of the emotional overhead you might encounter on your road to success. It's also a crucial reason why you should not put all your manuscripts in "one basket." To do so may be tantamount to placing your entire career in a bottomless pit. Making multiple submissions is reasonable and wise if you consider the possible consequences of granting an exclusive without any deadline or two-way communications. Please refer to the other essays and words of advice in this book to keep yourself from becoming a victim of Ignored Writer Syndrome (IWS).

THE WRITER'S JOURNEY
The Path of the Spiritual Messenger

Deborah Herman

If you have decided to pursue writing as a career instead of as a longing or a dream, you might find yourself focusing on the goal instead of the process. When you have a great book idea, you may envision yourself on a book-signing tour or as a guest on a talk show before you've written a single word.

It's human nature to look into your own future, but too much projection can get in the way of what the writing experience is all about. The process of writing is like a wondrous journey that can help you cross a bridge to the treasures hidden within your own soul. It is a way for you to link with God and the collective storehouse of all wisdom and truth, as it has existed since the beginning of time.

Many methods of writing bring their own rewards. Some people can produce exceptional prose by using their intellect and their mastery of the writing craft. They use research and analytical skills to help them produce works of great importance and merit.

Then there are those who have learned to tap into the wellspring from which all genius flows. They are the inspired ones who write with the intensity of an impassioned lover. I refer to them as "spiritual writers," and they write because they have to. They may not want to, they may not know how to, but something inside them is begging to be let out. It gnaws away at them until they find a way to set it free. Although they may not realize it, spiritual writers are engaged in a larger spiritual journey toward ultimate self-mastery and unification with God.

Spiritual writers often feel as if they're taking dictation. Spiritual writing — in any genre: nonfiction, sci-fi, women's fiction, whatever — has an otherworldly feeling and can teach writers things they would otherwise not have known. It is not uncommon for a spiritual writer to read something after a session in "the zone" and question if indeed she wrote it.

Writing opens you up to new perspectives, much like self-induced psychotherapy. Although journals are the most direct route for self-evaluation, fiction and nonfiction also serve as vehicles for a writer's growth. Writing helps the mind expand to the limits of the imagination.

Anyone can become a spiritual writer, and there are many benefits to doing so, not the least of which is the development of the soul. On a more practical level, it is much less difficult to write with flow and fervor than it is to be bound by the limitations of logic and analysis. If you tap into the universal source, there is no end to your potential creativity.

The greatest barrier to becoming a spiritual writer is the human ego. We treat our words as if they were our children — only we tend to be neurotic parents. Children are not owned by parents, but rather must be loved, guided, and nurtured until they can carry on, on their own.

The same is true for our words. If we try to own and control them like property, they will be limited by our vision for them. We will overprotect them and will not be able to see when we may be taking them in the wrong direction for their ultimate well-being. Another ego problem that creates a barrier to creativity is our need for constant approval and our tendency toward perfectionism. We may feel the tug toward free expression but will erect blockades to ensure appropriate style and structure. We write with a "schoolmarm" hanging over our shoulders, waiting to tell us what we are doing wrong.

Style and structure are important to ultimate presentation, but that is what editing is for. Ideas and concepts need to flow like water in a running stream. The best way to become a spiritual writer is to relax and have fun. If you are relaxed and pray for guidance, you'll be open to intuition and higher truth. However, writers tend to take themselves too seriously, which causes anxiety, which exacerbates fear, which causes insecurity, which diminishes their self-confidence and leads ultimately to mounds of crumpled papers and lost inspiration. You are worthy. Do not let insecurity prevent you from getting started and following through.

If you have faith in a Supreme Being, the best way to begin a spiritual writing session is with the following writer's prayer:

Almighty God [Jesus, Allah, Great Spirit, etc.], Creator of the Universe, help me to become a vehicle for your wisdom so that what I write is of the highest purpose and will serve the greatest good. I humbly place my [pen/keyboard/recording device] in your hands so that you may guide me.

Prayer helps to connect you to the universal source. It empties the mind of trash, noise, and potential writer's blocks. If you are not comfortable with formal prayer, a few minutes of meditation will serve the same purpose.

Spiritual writing as a process does not necessarily lead to a sale. The fact is that some people and concepts have more commercial potential than others. Knowledge of the business of writing will help you make a career of it. If you combine this with the spiritual process, it can also bring you gratification and inner peace. If you trust the process of writing and make room for the journey, you will grow and achieve far beyond your expectations.

Keep in mind that you are not merely a conduit. You are to be commended and should take pride in the fact that you allow yourself to be used as a vessel for the Divine. You are the one who is taking the difficult steps in a world full of obstacles and challenges. You are the one who is sometimes so pushed to the edge that you have no idea how you go on. But you do. You maintain your faith and you know that there is a reason for everything. You may not have a clue what it is…but you have an innate sense that all your experiences are part of some bigger plan. At minimum they create good material for your book.

In order to be a messenger of the Divine you have to be a vessel willing to get out of the way. You need to be courageous and steadfast in your beliefs because God's truth is your truth. When you find that your inner truth does not match that of other people, you need to be strong enough to stay true to yourself. Your soul, that inner spark that connects you to all creation, is your only reliable guide. You will receive pressure from everywhere. But your relationship with your creator is as personal as your DNA. You will be a house divided if you try to please other people by accepting things they tell you that do not resonate with your spirit.

When you do find your inner truth, your next challenge is to make sure that you do not become the person who tries to tell everyone else what to believe. When a spiritual writer touches that moment of epiphany, it is easy to become god-intoxicated. There is no greater bliss than to be transformed by a connection to the source of all creation. It is not something that can be described. It is individual. This is why it is important for a spiritual writer to protect this experience for another seeker. The role of a spiritual messenger who manifests his or her mission through the written word is to guide the readers to the threshold of awakening. Bring them to the gate, but allow God to take them the rest of the way. Your job is to make the introduction. From there the relationship is no longer your responsibility. Your task is to shine the light brightly for some other seeker to find it.

It is difficult to believe so strongly in something while feeling unable to find anyone to listen to you. If you try too hard, you might find that there are others who will drain your energy and life force while giving nothing in return. They may ridicule you and cause you to step away from your path. You do not have to change the world by yourself. You need to do your part. Whether it is visible or as simple as letting someone know you care, you are participating in elevating the world for the better. Some people like it exactly as it is. There are those who thrive on chaos and the diseases of the soul. Your job as a spiritual writer is to protect your spirit as you would your own child. Do not give away your energy; make it available for those who truly want it and will appreciate it. When you write, expect nothing in return. While following the protocols of the business world, do not set your goal too high, such as transforming people's souls. If you do, you will elevate your responsibility beyond the capability of simple humans. If you do the groundwork, God will do the rest.

The world of the spiritual writer can be a very lonely place. It is easier to love God, creation, and humanity than it is to feel worthy of receiving love in return. Those of us who devote our energy to trying to make a difference through our writing forget that God has given us this gift as a reward for our goodness, faith, and love. It is a two-way street. What we give we can also receive. It maintains the balance. It replenishes our energy so we can continue to grow and fulfill our individual destiny. We are all loved unconditionally. God knows everything we have ever thought, done, or even thought about doing. We judge ourselves far more harshly than God ever would. We come into this world to learn and to fix our "miss"-takes. We only learn through object lessons. We have free will. Sometimes we have to burn our hands on the stove several times before we learn that it is too hot to touch. I personally have lived my life with the two-by-four-to-the-head method. While not recommended, it is the only way I have been able to learn some of my more difficult lessons. I have often considered wearing a helmet.

When we connect with our inner truth, we can become intoxicated with our own greatness. Writing is a very heady thing, especially if we are able to see our name in print. If we have people listening to what we have to say, we can believe that we are the message and forget that we are merely the messenger. Spiritual writers need to start every day by praying for humility. If we don't, and there is danger that we are going to put ourselves before the purity of Divine truth, we will not be able to be the pure vessel that we had hoped to become. The universe has methods of protecting itself. We will experience humiliation to knock us down a few pegs, to give us the opportunity to get over ourselves. I have experienced many instances of humorous humiliation, such as feeling amazed with myself only to literally fall splat on my face by tripping over air. No injury except to my inflated pride. God has a sense of humor.

On a more serious note, spiritual messengers who are taken in by their own egos are vulnerable to negativity. The information they convey becomes deceiving and can help take people off their paths. This is why spiritual writers should always begin each session with a prayer to be a vessel for the highest of the high and for the greater good. While readers have the choice to discern the wheat from the chaff, in this time of rapid spiritual growth, it is important to help seekers stay as close to their paths as possible. There is no time for major detours. We all have a lot of work to do.

We are all here to improve the lives of one another. We are blessed to live in an information age, in which we can communicate quickly and clearly with one another. However, technology also serves to make us separate. We all cling to our ideas without respecting the paths of others. We are all headed to the same place, the center of the maze, where there is nothing and everything all at once. We are all headed for the place of pure love that binds all of us to one another. We don't want to get caught up with trivial arguments about who is right and who is wrong. Our goal right now needs to be to foster everyone's path to his or her own higher truth. We share what we have so others can find it, without wasting time arguing the point to win them to our side. Too many battles have been fought over who is the most right. We all come from the same source.

When it comes down to it, spiritual writers are the prophets of today. You are here to express the voice of God in our world in ways that we as human beings can understand. We need to listen to the essence of the message rather than focusing on who is the greater prophet. In the business of writing, there is no sin in profit. But in the mission of writing, we must not forget that we all answer to the same boss and serve the same master.

You are also a messenger. When you agree to be a spiritual writer, you are also agreeing to bring light into the world. This is no small commitment. Remember to keep your ego out of it. While it is important to learn to promote and support your work, you must not forget that you are the messenger and not the message. If you keep this at the center of your heart and remember that you serve the greater good, you are a true spiritual writer who is honoring the call. May God bless you and guide you always.

Deborah Herman, wife and business partner of Jeff Herman, considers herself a mystic literary agent. She is the author of *Spiritual Writing from Inspiration to Publication* (Atria, 2001), which is currently being updated to reflect the digital age. Herman is a micro-publisher, editor, and marketing consultant. She does high-level author branding and digital marketing strategies based on the three certifications she received from the Rutgers Mini-MBA program: Digital Marketing Strategy, Social Media Strategy, and Entrepreneurship. She has recently launched a niche and kitsch online indie bookstore called Bookstock Bookshop. It can be found at www.micropublishingmedia.com, where she also features the books she publishes under her many imprints. Herman is the coauthor of the recent title *Member of the Family: My Story of Charles Manson, Life Inside His Cult, and the Darkness That Ended the Sixties.* Her Twitter handles are @spiritualagent and @digitaldeborah.

TRIBULATIONS OF THE UNKNOWN WRITER (AND POSSIBLE REMEDIES)

Jeff Herman

Many nations have memorials that pay homage to the remains of their soldiers who died in battle and cannot be identified. In a way, it seems that the legions of unpublished writers are the Unknown Writers. As has been expressed elsewhere in this book, it cannot be assumed that the works of the unknown writer are of any lesser quality than those works that achieve public exposure and consumption, any more than those soldiers who died were less adept than those who got to go home. To the contrary, perhaps they were *more* adept, or at least more daring, and therefore paid the ultimate price.

No warrior aspires to become an unknown soldier, let alone a dead soldier. Every soldier prefers to believe that her remains will be known, that they will perhaps even explain what happened toward the end and will be presented to her loved ones for final and proper farewells. It is much the same for the writer. No writer worth her ink wants to believe that her legacy of expression will be forever unknown. Even if her other accomplishments in life are magnificent, it is still those words on the pages that she wants revealed, preferably while she's still around to experience and enjoy it.

Obviously, in life and beyond, there are many unknown writers. That's just the way it is.

It may just be that the fear of living and dying as an unknown writer is the extra push you need to bring your work to the first step on the road to publication — getting your work noticed by a publishing professional, be it agent or editor. If you are still reading this essay, then it is absolutely true that you are willing to try harder to reach that goal. In recognition and respect for your aspirations and determination, I will provide additional insights and strategies to help you help yourself avoid the fate of the unknown writer.

But let's make sure that your goals, at least in the early stages of your publishing life, are reasonably measured. It is suitable to imagine yourself one day at the top of the publishing food chain. Why not? Genuine humans have to be there at any given moment, so why not you? However, it is improbable that you will arrive there in one step. Your odds will be enhanced through your dedication to learning, calculating, and paying the necessary dues. For the purposes of the lesson at hand, I will encourage you to focus on the more humble goal of simply transitioning to the realm of being a published writer. For sure, there is more to do after that, but we will leave those lessons for other places in this book, and for other books.

Ways to Be Seen in a Crowd

Established literary agencies, including yours truly's, are inundated with unsolicited query letters (both hardcopy and digital), proposals, pieces of manuscripts, and entire manuscripts. This stream of relentless *intake* easily runs from 50 to 150 uninvited submissions per week, depending on how visible the agency in question is to the world of writers at large. These numbers do not account for the many works that the agency has requested or was expecting from existing clients. Frankly, many successful agents are simply not hungry for more than what they already have and make efforts to be as invisible and unavailable as possible.

The above scenario only tells of the agencies. It's likely that the publishers, both big and small, are receiving the same in even greater volumes, which is of dubious value since many publishers prefer not to consider anything that is unsolicited or unrepresented, period.

How can your work go from being an unseen face in the crowd to a jack-in-the-box whose presence cannot be denied? Here are some suggested steps.

1. ***Don't merely do what everyone else is already doing.*** That doesn't mean that you should entirely refrain from doing what's conventional or recommended. After all, the beaten track is beaten for a reason: it has worked before and it will work again. But be open to the possibility of pursuing specific detours along the way. Look upon these excursions as a form of calculated wildcatting. If nothing happens, or if you end up puncturing the equivalent of someone's septic tank, then just take it as a lesson learned.

2. ***Make yourself be seen.*** A pile of no. 10 envelopes is simply that, and none of the component envelopes that form the pile are seen. Someone once sent me a letter shaped like a circle. It could not be grouped with that day's quota of query letters; it demanded to be seen and touched and dealt with, immediately. Another time I received a box designed as a treasure chest, which contained an unsolicited proposal. I did not appreciate receiving a bag of white powder with a certain proposal. The powder was flushed down the toilet and the manuscript returned without being read. Digital queries are even more prone to disappear into a sea of sameness. But maybe that's why the email gods created the subject line: so that you can say something that can't be ignored.

3. *Be generous.* Most submissions are actually a demand for time, attention, and energy. During a long day in the middle of a stressful week in the throes of a month in hell, an agent will see none of those submissions as good-faith opportunities from honorable people. To the contrary, they will feel like innumerable nuisances springing forth from the armpits of manic brain-eating zombies, with drool and odor. I can recall opening a package to find a handwritten card from a stranger telling me how much he appreciated my contributions to the business and how much I have helped him and others, etc., etc. I always remember those kinds of things; wouldn't you?

4. *Don't be a nag, be a gift.* Everyone likes gifts, and nobody likes nags. So why do so many aspiring writers (and others) act like nags? It's counterintuitive. Of course, nature teaches us from the moment we are born that the noisy baby gets the tit. Passivity invites neglect. Noise attracts attention. What an interesting conundrum. Nagging is bad. Passivity leads to death. Noise can't be ignored. Well, all of that is equally valid, and none of it disqualifies the original point that you are a gift, so act like one.

5. *Keep knocking, even after the door is opened.* That does not make sense, and it might not be appreciated. But if someone were to keep knocking on my door even after I opened it, I would simply have to ask that person why he or she is doing that, and therein is the beginning of a conversation. Of course, it may all go downhill from there, but then it may not. What happens next depends on the nature of the conversation that has just been launched, regardless of its weird genesis.

6. *Don't ask for anything, but offer whatever you can.* If that is the energy projected throughout your communications, you will attract due wealth. However, the word *due* is rather crucial in this context. A well-intentioned worm may end up on the end of a fishhook, and a nasty frog may be well fed all summer. Too often people stop at just being nice, and then they become prey. Is it fair that they are eaten for doing nothing at all? Actually, that's exactly what they asked for, to end up nourishing the needs of others. We must all serve a purpose, and we must all consume to survive. If you don't wish to be consumed, then don't present yourself for that. The universe is a layered place of lessons and challenges, and being a writer is just one of many ways to play the game. Don't just give yourself away, any more than you would throw yourself away. If you value the gems you wish to share, you will discern to whom to grant them, and simply refuse to participate with others.

7. ***Know your gifts and appreciate them.*** I can tell right away when I am reading a query letter from a writer who believes in herself and the quality of her product, and I can see those who are not so sure that they should even be trying. Sometimes the writer is apologetic, or even goes as far as asking me if he should be trying. Ironically, the writer's quality as a writer cannot be predicted by his native sense of self-worth. In fact, great literature has emerged from the hearts of those who are seemingly committed to a life of losing. But there is a logical explanation for that: To each writer is assigned a muse. Some writers may hate themselves while loving their muse, and it shows.

POST-PUBLICATION DEPRESSION SYNDROME (PPDS)

Jeff Herman

If you're struggling to get published, then this essay isn't for you, yet. If you're currently under contract, now is a good time to read this. If you have already been published and experienced what the above title indicates, then hopefully this essay will help you heal and realize you are far from alone.

You don't need to be reminded how much passion, fortitude, and raw energy goes into crafting your work, followed by the grueling process of getting it published. What you're probably not prepared for is the possibility of post-publication blues.

No one directly discusses or recognizes this genuine condition because newly published authors are expected to be overjoyed and grateful for the achievement of being published. After all, each published author is among the fortunate "one out of a thousand" struggling writers who make it to the Big Show. In reality, people who reach the pinnacle of success in any field of endeavor will often feel an emotional letdown in the wake of their accomplishment. The feeling can be comparable to a state of mourning, as the thrill of chasing the goal instantly evaporates and is replaced by nothing. Writers are especially prone to wallowing alone, as theirs is a solitary process by design, and only other writers who have been through the same cavern can be truly empathetic.

Emotional letdowns happen when results don't fulfill expectations. Everything preceding the point of publication involves drama, excitement, and anticipation. Butterflies flutter in the belly, and endorphins soar through the brain. One day the writer's goal will be manifested in the body of a published book, and the self-constructed dreams will be displaced by a reality that seems to lack sizzle. What follows might feel sad and unnourishing. No matter how much is achieved, it might feel as if something crucial were left behind.

Achieving awesome goals is a reward unto itself, but it may not be enough to satisfy what's needed. The writer's imagination may have drawn fantastic pictures of glamorous celebrity parties, profound talk-show appearances, instantaneous fame, and goblets of money. But just as the explosive passions and idealized assumptions of first love might be followed by an anticlimactic consummation, finally receiving the bound book in hand might prove to be surprisingly uneventful.

Sometimes the publication is everything the writer hoped for, which of course is a wonderful outcome. But for many it feels like nothing much happened at all. The media aren't calling; few people show up for signings/readings; and, perhaps most upsetting of all, friends and relatives report that the book can't be found. Meanwhile, no one from the publisher is calling anymore, and they act like their job is done. In truth, most of the publishing team is probably absorbed with publishing the endless flow of new books, whereas what's already been published is quickly relegated to "yesterday's list." A chirpy in-house publicist may be available, but she may not appear to be doing or accomplishing much while adeptly saying imprecise things in a glib, patronizing manner.

There's abundant information available about how to be a proactive author and successfully compensate for the universal marketing deficits endemic to the book-publishing business. But that's not the purpose of this essay. For sure, it's constructive to take practical steps for mitigating disappointments and solving existential problems, but such activities may also distract the troubled writer from the tender places crying somewhere inside. These feelings must be recognized and soothed. Even bestselling writers get the blues.

Seeking or initiating communities of "published writers in pain" should be what the doctor ordered. If done right, such personal connections will help level the loneliness and despair that define post-publication depression. However, the community must consciously dedicate itself to a positive process. Nothing useful will be accomplished by reinforcing anger, resentment, or a sense of victimhood. Even worse is unsupportive competitiveness or negativity that pushes people down. And — as can happen in any inbred community — distortions, misinformation, and poor advice might circulate with a bogus badge of credibility.

Life is rarely a clear trail. If it looks to be, then unexpected destinations are likely to prevail. Writers will eat dirt and wear thorns in exchange for self-compassion and self-discovery. Pain isn't punishment but a consequence that expands the writer's integrity, authenticity, and relevance. Post-publication depression is an item on a menu in a script written by the writer for the writer. Never fear the pain; just be prepared to live through it and learn from it, and to help others do the same.

THE BUSINESS OF WRITING

Jeff Herman

I decided to provide this section for you folks who want to skip ahead, or perhaps already arrived, and are prepared to dive into the business details of being a paid writer, as opposed to a hobbyist.

$$$$ (+/−)

Let's begin with some sobering information: Genuine research shows that the vast majority of Americans who write for money cannot possibly support themselves, not to mention their families, from writing. The study doesn't include people whose day jobs entail writing, such as journalists. Furthermore, the research only includes people who have actually managed to have their book(s) traditionally published for advances and/or royalties; those yet to be published, or self-publishing, aren't skewing the numbers downward.

The lack of financial rewards suggests that most writers are primarily driven by passions that have little to do with money. There's simply no other way to explain why millions of people dedicate thousands of precious hours, often for decades, to the arduous craft of writing. If money were the focus, few people would write. Humans don't want to work for free, but many choose to write for free, or at least with the knowledge that money and recognition are unlikely outcomes.

If you're reading this book, you don't need to be told why people write without the benefit of knowing the destination. When one labors in harmony with one's heart, time explodes and joy is touched. Perhaps we are most fulfilled when pursuing our dreams. Liberation from practical mandates, combined with uncensored creative expression, is more precious than rubies. When we transform dense burdens into realms of truth and acceptance, we tread a healing path that purifies the soul.

Collectively, we are mere statistics, and the courses of our lives are predicted at birth. Individually, we are legions of free souls with the innate capacity for unstoppable self-expression and creation. Even the harshest forms of external conformity and oppression cannot distort what's real or dictate what matters to you. If you stay free, you cannot fail.

The Author-Agency Relationship and Contract

What happens next if an agent offers to represent you? Because I have never had an agent, I can only convey how I tend to work with my clients as an agent. Though I suspect that my methods and protocols are generally similar to how my esteemed colleagues function, I cannot overemphasize how individualized agents are. Only a small fraction of us work for large organizations that require a measure of in-house conformity and consistency. The vast majority of independent agents can only be defined within the context of each agent's distinct personality, and you probably won't discern that by studying their externally produced, generic websites. Added to this mysterious cocktail is the fact that zero writers are AI. The nature of the author-agent relationship can be as varied and unpredictable as mating season at the Bronx Zoo.

The above condition is likely to affect only the personal dealings between agents and authors. The publishing process as a whole embraces institutionalized ways of conducting business that regulate how far writers and agents can wander from the reservation. In that light, here's what will probably happen once an agent wants to represent you.

He or she will want to meet you by phone to make a human connection, answer questions, ask questions, and explain the process. If you are within reasonable driving range, go ahead and invite yourself to visit the agent and consummate the relationship in person. But more than 80 percent of the time, face-to-face meetings are impractical and don't matter anyway. It's primarily a content-driven business; you're not trying to be a model, actor, or TV newscaster. All of those skill sets are valued, but your work is what will ultimately carry you. With obvious exceptions, you outside of your writing may not need to exist, and sometimes it would actually be better if you didn't.

She or he will want you to sign a contract. When I started agenting in the 1980s (no, I'm not yet 60. Are you?), I was surprised to learn that more than a few agents didn't bother having written agreements with their clients. They were "old-school" folks descended from a time when human beings were required to be more visible to each other and therefore more transparent and accountable. It's hard for me to imagine what that must have been like. If you ever saw the movie *Wall Street*, you'll quickly gauge New York's ethical temperature during the fast-paced '80s. I don't think I'm overly cynical by defining that time as "in praise of greed." Things have calmed down since then, maybe because people have learned to be more self-protective. Nowadays, I suspect that all agents will want to memorialize their client relationships in writing, which is actually to everyone's advantage.

Here are the primary items the contract will likely cover:

- ***Representation and compensation:*** This will probably specify a per-project assignment applying only to the work you pitched the agent. It will be on an exclusive basis, meaning that neither you nor anyone else can simultaneously pitch the work. It will state the agent's commission, which is almost always 15 percent of the advance and royalties for as long as the book is in print. (Bear in mind that legitimate agents don't make a commission if they fail to sell the work. If the agent is providing nonagent fee-based services, those items should be covered in a separate document that has nothing to do with the agenting services.) The contract will assign representation to various ancillary rights, such as translations, ebooks (which nowadays is really a primary right), audio, and film.

- *Termination:* There should always be peaceful ways for people to go away and leave each other alone, and that's the purpose of this section. There might be a specified time limit within which the agent must either "put up or get out"; though there is usually an easy way for both parties to extend the period if mutually desired. My contract states that either party can terminate the contract anytime, no excuses needed. Of course, termination applies only to the future and can't have retroactive effect, meaning that the author can't delete the agent's commission or other entitlements embedded in deals already made on the author's behalf by the agent.

- *Duration:* As stated above, the agent's commissions relevant to deals made on the author's behalf are generally irrevocable. Going forward, most agents will want to represent the publisher's option book, meaning the author's next book, which the author is required to exclusively show the publisher. A fraction of the time there is no option mandate, and much of the time the publisher rejects the next work anyway or might not match what another publisher is willing to pay. Even in the absence of a formal option, the agent will probably expect to represent future deals with the same publisher for books that are conceptually similar to the first work. In the absence of any of the above or similar contingencies, both parties will typically be free to decide whether to keep working together regarding future projects.

Are agency contracts enforceable? Yes, assuming the agent isn't in breach and the contract is clearly written, doesn't include anything illegal, doesn't entail provable deception, and isn't absurdly outside the bounds of practices customary to publishing.

Are agency contracts negotiable? Anything is negotiable on the basis of leverage. Most authors don't have much leverage and probably won't manage to change anything that's of primary importance to the agent, such as the commission percentage. But there are several items the agent might not care much about and will agree to modify upon request. For instance, the agent might figure that there are zero film prospects for your sales-coaching book and will agree in a nanosecond to delete that from the contract. You should be able to ask the agent to explain anything that's unclear or bothersome. A frequent strategic error is for the author to retain a lawyer with zero publishing knowledge to vet the agent's contract. It usually wastes the author's money and can cast a destructive monkey wrench into the author-agent relationship at a crucial juncture — the beginning. If you don't like the contract and feel that it's inconsistent with customary best practices, you're best off not signing it.

What follows is my standard agency-author contract. It has never been touched by an attorney, has gone through many revisions over time, and will probably be changed again and again depending on the nature of the business, and my mood. I believe that a good contract almost always generates harmony, even if no one makes any money. The point is to lay out clear boundaries, understandable and practical responsibilities, all knowable contingencies, and how to one day maybe say goodbye in the absence of drama.

AGENCY-AUTHOR AGREEMENT

This Agreement, issued on APRIL 1, 3018, between The Jeff Herman Agency LLC (Agency) and FRANZ KAFKA (Author), will put the following terms and conditions into effect when signed by the parties.

Representation

Author exclusively authorizes Agency to represent and seek a publisher for his work ("Project") stated/described below.

Agency Commissions

If Agency sells Project to a Publisher, Agency will be Agent-of-Record for Project's duration with Publisher, including its licensees, assignees and successors; and Agency will be assigned as a third-party beneficiary a commission equal to 15% of moneys Publisher pays to Author's account.

Said commission will apply to Project's foreign/translated editions; reprinted/reformatted editions; revisions; illustrated or graphic editions; audio and digitized editions. Said commissions will carry over to a subsequent project Author chooses to publish with same Publisher resulting from Publisher-Author contract option language. Commissions shall also apply to subsequent Author project(s) with same Publisher that is conceptually derivative of the initial Project, or a series of titles for which the initial Project is the de facto "Flagship" title.

If Agency uses foreign subagents to help generate foreign deals, Agency's commission will be 10% and subagent's commission will be 10%.

Agency will endeavor to include language in Author-Publisher contract requiring Publisher to pay 85% of moneys directly to Author and 15% directly to Agency. If Publisher pays Author's moneys to Agency, Agency will forward funds to Author within 10 business days of receipt.

This Agreement will be binding upon Author's estate, successors, or assignees.

Amendment(s), Release
This Agreement can be amended through written expression if signed by the parties.

Either party may unilaterally release him/herself from this Agreement through written expression. However, Agency's standing and entitlements regarding prevailing Author-Publisher contract(s) cannot be retroactively revoked by Author. Additionally, Agency's standing and entitlements per this Agreement will apply in full pertaining to any deals accepted by Author that were generated by Agency prior to being released.

Unless amended or superseded by subsequent agreements, this Agreement will automatically apply in full to concurrent or future projects the Author explicitly authorizes the Agency to represent through written expression.

Agreed:

THE JEFF HERMAN AGENCY LLC, JEFFREY H. HERMAN
Signature: _____

Author: FRANZ KAFKA
Signature: _____

Project(s) description/working title represented:
SECRETS OF SELF-EXTERMINATION FOR MULTI-LIMBED BEINGS

Why Some Agents Charge Fees

Although this potentially loaded issue is addressed more than once elsewhere in these pages, I find it to be a recurring question that needs to be addressed from various angles.

As recently as the beginning of the current decade, it was generally verboten for agents to charge fees for anything, or to muddle and conflate their services. But economic disruption changed the rules as the traditional agent model became unsustainable for many boutique firms. Forming new agencies from scratch is more prohibitive than at any time in memory. Commission-based cash flow is erratic even for established firms. It's become more difficult to sell fresh projects, especially for large advances, and overall book sales have been stagnant for years. Furthermore, a growing and uncharted chunk of book consumption is clearly being claimed by self-publishers, which is good for them but not for agents. As a consequence, it has become more common and acceptable for agencies to offer fee-based editorial and marketing services. For obvious reasons they are uniquely qualified to deliver such services.

Conflicts of interest emerge if the agency fails to keep clear borders between its agent and nonagent functions. For instance, a writer shouldn't be made to feel that representation is contingent upon buying a package of services from the agent. A definite red flag is when a so-called agent's website is mostly focused on selling fee-based services or if a rapid response to a submission is largely dedicated to selling its services. It's easy for an editorial services firm to masquerade as a traditional agency in order to seduce dollars from unsuspecting writers.

I'm not trying to flood you with paranoia; I simply want you to be an educated writer. The overall process works best when everyone is transparent and cognizant. Buying editorial services from an agent should be an excellent investment, assuming you know what it does and doesn't entail.

What about Reading Fees?

Nearly 200 legitimate agents are willing to consider your submission, free of charge. It follows that there's no practical reason to pay someone to review your submission. With few exceptions, reading-fee firms are running a lucrative scam. Why bother struggling for elusive commissions if dozens of writers are granting you $100 or more every month? The scammers often compound the hoax by issuing long and flattering responses that are actually designed to lure larger expenditures for dubious services. No genuine agent would make absurd predictions about your prospects in the context of asking you to open your wallet.

Is It Important to Like Your Agent?

Frankly, how important is it to like anyone you do business with? Actually, the answer probably depends on how you define what it means to like someone and to what extent "likability" matters to you in general. And it never hurts to be open-minded about your own likability. Once you've been around the block a couple of times in life, you might decide that respecting those you work with is more valuable than liking them. Someone who will get the job done and not rip you off should be your starting point; mere positive chemistry is a nonessential fringe benefit. Of course, you never know where things might go. One of my first clients nearly 30 years ago eventually became my wife.

Rejection

Why is rejection in this section of the book? Well, I have to put it somewhere, and it's inevitably a large part of the business of publishing. I suppose we could just as accurately use the word *No*. It would save space to simply click and send a single-worded email with the word *No*, but that's not the accepted protocol.

Years ago when I was more snarky, I would dryly tell people that I include a fast-food job application with each rejection letter, and that I see it as a service not an insult. Eventually I finally realized that few were laughing, and some were perhaps even taking me literally. That wasn't the effect I wanted. I was simply trying to lighten up a subject that writers viscerally fear and hate.

Writers perceive rejection as they would a horrible contagion. Reaching a level of emotional comfort with the concept of rejection seems to be an undiscovered country for most writers, regardless of how successful they might be. In fact, it's often the most successful writers who are the most fragile. Perhaps they fear that their stellar plateaus rest upon foundations of Play-Doh and can collapse before they see it crumbling.

Let's be scientific about it. You're better off receiving formal closure, even if it's an impersonal kiss-off, than eternal dead air. Rejection at least confirms that you entered the ring. The absence of any response might cause you to question your own existence. Rejection is a shout-out and affirmation that you are "here" and did make contact at some level. Writers should never permit themselves to wallow in shame, embarrassment, or defeat in the face of rejection. Such sentiments are both understandable and absolutely irrelevant, and will unnecessarily poison the ground beneath your feet.

Like most agents, I use a form rejection letter most of the time. It isn't possible to do more than that. However, I've designed my letter to be as buffered and affirming as possible. No human is empowered to truly reject what others create, but we are entitled to choose what we want to work with. No one can negate your writing any more than you can command them to like it. Rejection shouldn't be conflated with destruction.

Writers are actually the most powerful party in the equation, because they are the sole creators of the golden eggs. The rest of us just build infrastructures. Agents and publishers curate, tweak, and manipulate; and readers consume. All of that matters, but the power to create is the supreme element. Without writers, there's no edifice or sustenance for anyone else in the publishing world. Always honor your precious individuality without cleaving yourself from the esteemed collective to which you belong by choice. No one can remove you from your given destiny unless you let go.

Agents and editors have a special responsibility to avoid damaging a person's aspirations and potential. Naturally, the rejection process inflicts pain, but that should never be the intention. Pain doesn't have to be attached to offensive motives, and in its purest form can be constructively transformative.

Below is the rejection template I've used for years. I've received many nice comments about it and only a handful of unfounded and sometimes weird complaints.

THE JEFF HERMAN AGENCY, LLC

Dear Author,

There's no easy way to compose a form rejection letter and no easy way to receive one.

Your submission was reviewed, and we decided not to represent it. This doesn't mean it won't be right for another agent or a publishing house. Many successful books have been rejected many times for many reasons before becoming successful. Sometimes poor decisions are made, and my agency is no exception. Like all established agencies, we are only able to represent a small fraction of the many prospects we see.

Due to the large volume of submissions we receive, we cannot write a personal letter to you. Please understand we have not charged you anything. Our compensation is derived from the discovery and successful sale of written works. Therefore, our review and rejection process must be managed as efficiently as possible.

Please don't give up or become discouraged. There are many opportunities out there. We want you to succeed even if it causes us to kick ourselves for letting you get away. Thank you for giving us a chance.

Sincerely, Jeffrey H. Herman

PS: I realize this might be a very late response. If so, I apologize for the unintended discourtesy. Perhaps you have landed a deal by now. Please succeed!

PO Box 1522 • 29 Park Street, Stockbridge, MA 01262
413-298-0077 • jeff@jeffherman.com • www.jeffherman.com

What's a Copyright, and How Does Someone Own One?

If you write it, you own it. That truly sums up the law. Of course, don't forget to put your name on it. If you're simply pitching the work, you don't need to file any paperwork supporting your ownership. If you decide to self-publish, there's an easy online copyright form. If your work is traditionally published, your publisher will handle the paperwork on your behalf.

Copyright ownership is rarely contested, probably because most written products aren't worth stealing, and ownership is usually a well-established fact once a property becomes worth pilfering.

There are important limitations to what can be copyrighted. For instance, you probably can't copyright an abstract idea or concept. Book titles are very difficult to copyright unless already covered by an existing copyright or patent.

What Are Libel and Slander?

Jim Johnson gets drunk and urinates in the middle of Main Street most evenings. Maybe you shouldn't publish that kind of information about an actual person named Jim Johnson without a confirming police report, a photo, or a preponderance of eyewitness testimony. Use common sense. Don't publicly write untrue or unverified information about other people, especially with malice, or they might sue you and win money if they can show monetary, emotional, or reputational damages. You need to also refrain from saying nasty and unfounded things about others with your mouth in public. Even mean-spirited social gossip can be expensive if someone can prove harmful intentions and meaningful damages, such as losing customers or a contract.

Every publishing contract includes dense language requiring the author to indemnify the publisher against any damages incurred from the writer's screwups, even if inadvertent or unforeseeable. This is rarely an issue, because the vast majority of writers manage to avoid stealing and telling lies, whatever the temptations. But when they do, it sometimes becomes big news.

What's Cease and Desist?

I like this term because it has rhythm and is self-duplicating. I think it means stop doing something specific, and don't stop stopping. I think you need to prove to a judge that someone is or will unfairly cause you meaningful damages in real time. President Trump unsuccessfully filed a C&D against the publisher of *Fire and Fury*, but he probably helped sell thousands of extra copies for his troubles. Sometimes writers and publishers publish presumably original content that's actually owned by a third party. As a consequence, they could get served with a C&D, which might be quite costly and inconvenient depending on how many copies are in inventory, in stores, or in the distribution pipeline. Large companies have insurance for these contingencies.

The Downside of Self-Publishing

Over the past few years it's become amazingly easy and inexpensive to self-publish. Of course, just like with traditional publishing, the singular fact that a book is for sale doesn't mean people will know about it, let alone buy it.

What I've been seeing as an agent is that some writers assume that self-publishing is a way to transition into traditional publishing. It no longer surprises me how many authors pitch their self-published works to me for representation. This strategy is unlikely to succeed unless you manage to sell a large volume and can show that the sales pace is sustainable. Obviously, any publisher will acquire a proven cash cow if they feel it will keep giving milk without consuming much grass (see *Fifty Shades of Grey*). However, many big-selling self-published books don't lend themselves to the kinds of retail consumer venues that traditional publishers are modeled to work with, and might be better off as self-published.

The most common kiss of death for self-published books is the absence of meaningful sales, which generally includes an Amazon sales ranking somewhere near Pluto or beyond. Agents and publishers are likely to dismiss your work sight unseen if it's been made abundantly evident that you have no ability to sell the book on the basis of your own resources — meaning you don't have the proverbial platform.

If you're considering self-publishing, you should at least generate a written plan for how and where you intend to sell copies. You don't want to just throw your baby into the wind without a realistic map and destination in mind. If you're thinking, "What does that mean?" you may not be ready to self-publish. Traditional publishers are allowed to acquire and release books without a proper plan, assuming they have a capital reserve to absorb the losses. Self-publishers have much more at stake.

The Author Platform

This, too, is discussed elsewhere in these pages, but it's one of those publishing concepts that can't be overly examined. In fact, there are more than a few books (mostly self-published, by the way) dedicated to this fraught and often misunderstood subject.

It's easy to think you know a healthy platform when you see one. The author tends to be all over the media, and a lot of people appear to be interested in consuming information from or about her or him. Often, these kinds of people are referred to as celebrities. And then a lot of the time no one buys their book for reasons that perhaps should have been seen before the fact. But it's worth jumping in without much due diligence because these books can be gold mines.

A more reliable platform is that of the noncelebrity who brings self-sustaining and self-expanding popularity and credibility in specific communities known to buy books. Examples are self-help/how-to experts and fiction writers with broad online fan enthusiasm.

Authors without conventional platforms can be, and frequently are, successfully published anyway because they have off-the-radar platforms that don't fit the usual paradigm. The majority of writers should endeavor to be seen in this light, probably because it's the only light available for them. What does this mean? Well, the possibilities are infinite and might be staring you in the face without your knowing it. I've seen unknown people write hugely successful books about such arcane subjects as bizarre ways to organize homes or how to be successful at something called "pony conventions." We live in a big world with an untracked array of passionate interests and avocations, and their respective gurus might be known only within the vibrant villages where they exist as resident superheroes. Many of these villages are quietly populated or visited by millions of book-buying fans.

In closing, always see obstructions as a means of discovering gaps, open windows, and the weakest points between the mud and Sheetrock that appear as walls.

EVERY WRITER NEEDS TO MEET ZERO

Jeff Herman

Hold a simple calculator in your hand and enter 0 + 0. Obviously, the result will be 0. Now enter 0 - 0. Again, the result will be 0. Next, multiply any value by 0, and you end up with 0. And any number subtracted from 0 results in the same number less than 0 (0 − 7 = −7).

On one hand we are taught that zero is nothing ("You're a zero"). But the same rules infuse zero with apocalyptic powers. How can "nothing" also be the most decisive and possibly destructive digit in the numerical tool kit? Any first grader with the insight to ask that question could get sent down to special education. Basic arithmetic forces us to accept a distorted and conflicted reality, which causes a lot of observable phenomena to seem incomprehensible, if not impossible. It's much easier to dismiss the existence of what can't be explained, even if it's right in front of us.

If there's a conspiracy against human potential, it begins with a self-burdened intellectual cult commonly referred to as math, and Ground Zero is its war against the true value and meaning of zero. We are forced to shred our imaginations through a false arbiter that won't tolerate variance. When our children lament how much they despise math, we should listen, because, as taught and used, it holds them back.

Don't blame the calculators. Don't blame anyone. Accepted paradigms are imprinted into us from the moment of birth and can stubbornly prevail for countless generations. An abrupt challenge of what's commonly considered to be real could provoke a spiral of social chaos and cause its promoters to be destroyed. Change is best when done gently in measured doses. Collectively and individually, there's a thin, fragile line between revelation and insanity. Seeing the truth and losing the lie is a painful, unregulated test that flirts with madness.

Albert Einstein and his peers managed to take us far in a relatively short span because enough of us were ready to go for the ride. No one managed to kill the messengers that time. But in his midlife, Einstein hit a theoretical wall that permanently sidelined his progression. Basically, his manipulation of numbers refused to explain observable outcomes, and he refused to accept that his numbers might be the problem. More than six decades later, scientists are struggling mostly against one another to codify what they are seeing. Nonscientific terms like *randomness*, *spooky*, and *wormhole* are frequently used as a way to categorize the massive list of observable phenomena that defy science's sanctioned laws and methods, not to mention simple logic.

What's especially unfair is that scientists frequently concoct their own mythologies to explain the unexplainable. For instance, we are taught that all energy and matter were compressed into a tiny ball that somehow exploded and became everything that we can see and measure. Maybe that's exactly what happened. But what created the super-ball, and why did it blow up? And why is that any less or more credible than a nameless entity creating everything on a whim? If you subscribe to the ball creation theory, you are called rational. If you subscribe to the entity creation theory, you might be considered ignorant or uneducated.

We are taught that life was somehow formed in some kind of pool of water, and that the same thing might have happened on other planets. But why did that never happen again on Earth? And why are other new "lives" not emerging in the same way as the original one did? I'm not defending religion or debasing science, but I am saying that we don't have to choose between the two, especially since they are birds of the same feather: possible explanations for what we don't know. It follows that you are free to create your own theories, even if you throw them out five minutes later. There are no fixed answers to pretty much any question you ask. What is certain is that your native creativity is part of your design, and you should never let anyone interfere with it, especially your thinking and writing.

Visually, o (zero) reflects its mysteries. Its oval shape doesn't have a beginning or an end. We can't accurately measure its circumference without destroying it because we are unable to determine the true value of pi (not even the most powerful computers have figured out that one). Because zero has no value, having zero money means you're flat broke, and adding zero to your wealth won't make you any richer. But if Donald Trump multiplied his wealth by zero, he would be instantaneously broke. How can nothing have the power to destroy everything, and why do we accept this conundrum?

Obviously, something cannot be both nothing and everything. But what if the existence of "nothing" is impossible? What if "something" is invariably everywhere and can be whatever we say it is? When we dream, the impossible often prevails. But it's deemed to be impossible only while we're awake, not while we're experiencing it when asleep. Why is one state more real than the other? Can you prove that it is? The better question is: why bother to prove it? What if you accept that everything is a luscious mystery and that you can morph it however you want to? Just be your own "Alice." This is the kind of liberation that will unbind your mind to create marvelous possibilities in your writing, and in your reality.

Part 2
PUBLISHING CONGLOMERATES

INTRODUCTION TO
THE BIG 5

Jeff Herman

The term *Big 5* has become the insider vernacular for referring to the largest book publishers in the US. It was the Big 6 until two of them, Penguin and Random House, got married in 2013. It isn't just size that qualifies for membership in this dubious collective. In fact, a handful of independent publishers are large enough (10-figure revenues) to be included, but several unique characteristics, in addition to size, separate the Big 5 from the largest of the independents.

1. Foreign Ownership

More than half of America's book-publishing infrastructure is foreign owned. Foreign acquisitions commenced in the 1980s and peaked in recent years without much noise or pushback. Global forces have been consolidating all forms of mass media for decades, and book publishing is no exception. However, the Big 5's domestic operations have remained largely staffed and managed by Americans, and the books are still mostly written by Americans for Americans.

Is massive foreign ownership something to be concerned about? I suggest we should be watchful without succumbing to prejudice or paranoia. Any country's culture is greatly influenced by the books its people read and write, so it should be disconcerting that foreigners have so much control over important aspects of our society and culture. What we really need to pay attention to is corporate control of cultural assets in general, regardless of address.

If it's of any relief, pretty much all the attractive American fish have already been gobbled up. For sure, there will still be meaningful acquisitions and mergers over the next few years, but they will occur at a more modest pace and magnitude.

2. Books Are a Small Fraction of the Parent Company's Matrix

Massive and burgeoning commercial enterprises such as cable/broadcast TV, digital games, websites, pop-culture magazines, sports teams, and entertainment are the primary focus for most corporate parents. Book revenues can't come close to these other income streams, and the imbalance will only become more pronounced in the future.

Most of the corporations are publicly owned and traded. Important decisions must ultimately satisfy each firm's board of directors and shareholders. Losing money, or failing to make enough money, is unsustainable. "Art" is valued on the basis of dollars and power.

A natural question is: Why do these multinational corporations want to own retro book companies? The answer: money follows power. Correct, few books make big money; but money isn't the only way to measure power. The top 20 percent of a country's population in terms of education and income are culturally and politically dominant, and are also the most reliable market for books. Even the most authoritarian governments and conformist societies must appease, manipulate, deceive, or intimidate the top social echelons. Certain books will deliver levels of influence, prestige, credibility, and power way beyond what the relatively paltry revenues suggest.

3. Frequent Reorganization and (Too) Many Imprints/Divisions

It's the nature of multinational conglomerates to keep on eating, which is frequently followed by indigestion. As a result, each of the Big 5 is an obese amalgamation of programs with distinct traditions. Integrating the diversity of formerly rogue asteroids into cooperative orbits is never a simple task. To the contrary, it's messy and contentious. Competitive overlapping programs often end up in the same corporate "family," and because corporations abhor redundancies, perfectly viable programs are often suffocated. Many legacy brands within the Big 5 exist in name only and have ceased reflecting their storied histories apart perhaps from their inherited backlists, or some people's sentimental memories.

What Does the Conglomeration of Publishing Mean?

1. ***Less risk taking.*** Editors are not encouraged to stray from the corporate mission, which is to make money or face the consequences. Renegade thinking doesn't fit in because it threatens the status quo, and entrenched stakeholders will defend their prerogatives at all costs.

2. ***More "sameness."*** What worked before becomes the model to follow, which discourages any methods that don't align with what's comfortable. Failure often breeds steady decay, not rebirth.

3. ***Steady irrelevance concealed by apparent success.*** The lack of forward motion negates innovation, and banality is rewarded. Lack of competition enables domination of the bestseller lists and therefore compounds in-house complacency.

Suddenly, something fresh and better is born and must be killed, acquired, or copied, or else the game changes and power is shifted.

4. ***You belong or you don't.*** In China, it helps a lot to be a member of the Communist Party. In America, it helps to be published by the Big 5. However, this being America, opportunities aren't monopolized. The independents, and self-publishers, will always raise their flags high, sometimes higher.

THE LISTINGS

HACHETTE BOOK GROUP ❖ www.hachettebookgroup.com

1290 Avenue of the Americas, New York, NY 10104, 212-364-1200

Hachette belongs to Lagardère, a huge French media conglomerate. Frenchly, I mean frankly, I mispronounced this name for many years. I don't speak French, at least not on purpose, but I thought the *t*'s were silent, so I used to say something like "Hachay." Silly me; it turns out it's pronounced more like the tool, so that you hear the *t*'s. Anyway, it's only fair that the French have a place at the table with the British and the Germans in America's media universe, and Time Warner was eager to divest its low-margin book-publishing portfolio.

The transaction was made in 2006, except that the new entity was prevented from using the high-profile brand, Warner, and the relevant imprints had to be retitled. It took the industry a little while to get used to the fact that the name Warner Books was permanently retired, but life went on. Little, Brown was included in the package.

In 2016, Hachette acquired the Perseus Book Group, which was a relatively large privately owned collection of previously independent niche houses. At the time of this writing, Perseus has been bloodlessly integrated into the Hachette matrix, and most of its preexisting divisions and separate addresses have been allowed to carry on as if nothing much happened. This suggests that Hachette wasn't merely looking to acquire an instant backlist catalog and actually wants the kind of multibrand editorial diversity enjoyed by its more deeply entrenched competitors.

Unless otherwise specified, Hachette editors' email addresses follow this format: firstname.lastname@hbgusa.com.

GRAND CENTRAL ❖ www.grandcentralpublishing.com

This is the brand name Hachette generated to replace Warner, which they are forever banned from using even though they acquired all of Warner's book-publishing assets. I assume it relates to the nearby Grand Central Station, which is a place of daily prayer for millions of commuters (they pray that the trains are on time). I never liked the name they chose, and I doubt they have any concern about my opinions, but I get to say what I want to in this tiny pocket of self-expression. And it's still a free country.

Gretchen Young, Executive Editor. General commercial nonfiction, business, pop culture, self-help.
Millicent Bennett, Executive Editor. Commercial fiction; general nonfiction, including memoir and narrative.
Lindsey Rose, Senior Editor. Commercial fiction.
Maddie Caldwell, Editor. Nonfiction, including memoir and narrative.
Suzanne O'Neill, Editor. Pop culture and humor.
Karen Kosztolnyik, Editor in Chief. Commercial fiction, including women's themes and romance.
Wes Miller, Senior Editor. Commercial fiction, including thriller and mystery.
Beth de Guzman, Publisher, Paperbacks and Digital. Commercial fiction and nonfiction as paperback and digital originals (as opposed to reprinted editions).
Katherine Stopa, Assistant Editor. Commercial nonfiction, including cooking, lifestyle, advice.
Ben Sevier, Publisher. Commercial fiction and nonfiction.

HACHETTE BOOKS

In 2014 the name Hachette Books displaced the name Grand Central Publishing as the conglomerate's de facto flagship name, and I don't think many people cared one way or the other. The imprint publishes the usual gamut of commercial frontlist fiction and nonfiction works.

(Ms.) Krishan Trotman, Senior Editor. Nonfiction, including current events, popular science, narrative.
Mauro DiPreta, Publisher. Commercial nonfiction, including business, sports, historical memoir, narrative.
David Lamb, Assistant Editor. General nonfiction, including history, current events, media.
Paul Whitlatch, Senior Editor. Commercial nonfiction, including current events, narrative, sports, pop culture, humor.
Michelle Howry, Executive Editor. Commercial nonfiction, including self-help, diet, parenting, business, health, lifestyle.
Amanda Murray, Executive Editor. Nonfiction.

TWELVE ❖ www.twelvebooks.com

Twelve was established in August 2005 with the intention of publishing only 12 books a year, though that's no longer the annual cutoff point. The mostly nonfiction imprint wants to create the intention that each title is extra-super-special, not just another book about whatever.

Sean Desmond, Publisher. Politics, current events, business, narrative, memoir.

GRAND CENTRAL LIFE & STYLE ❖ www.grandcentrallifeandstyle.com

As might be surmised by its name, this imprint focuses on wellness, beauty, fashion, the home, cooking, diet, fitness, relationships, inspiration, and related subjects.

Karen Murgolo, Editorial Director. Diet, health, cooking, personal finance.
(Ms.) Morgan Hedden, Assistant Editor. Cooking, diet.
Leah Miller, Senior Editor. Health, diet, parenting.

FOREVER YOURS ❖ www.forever-romance.com

This is the imprint dedicated to all areas of romance and love.

Leah Hultenschmidt, Editorial Director.
(Ms.) Alex Logan, Senior Editor.
Lexi Smail, Assistant Editor.

ORBIT ❖ www.orbitbooks.net

This is the science fiction and fantasy imprint.

Brit Hvide, Senior Editor.
Sarah Guan, Editor.

HACHETTE NASHVILLE ❖ www.faithwords.com ❖ www.centerstreet.com

7128 Holt Run Drive, Nashville, TN 37211

A common strategy for the big NY houses is to locate their religion- and faith-oriented programs somewhere in the heartland. In some cases, the programs in question actually originated in middle America as independent programs before being swallowed by the bigger fish. Frankly, New York isn't the ideal cultural environment for valuing and nurturing books of this nature. It's smart to allow these programs to prevail in like-minded communities.

The Nashville satellite houses two imprints: FaithWords tends to focus on nondenominational Christian-themed books on faith and lifestyle advice, including some fiction. Several celebrity televangelists and similar public personalities are published here. Center Street's titles tend to avoid direct theological connections while clearly being in sync with a Christian point of view, or at least perfectly compatible. Here you will find a wide range of nonfiction self-help/how-to/motivational/inspirational titles.

Kate Hartson, Executive Editor.
Virginia Bhashkar, Editor.
Keren Baltzer, Editor.

LITTLE, BROWN AND COMPANY ❖ www.littlebrown.com

LB began life in 1837 and has been one of America's premier book brands ever since. A few decades ago it was consumed by Time Warner, and then it was inherited by Hachette. Its mission and independence seem to have prevailed. Its backlist catalogs (adult and children's) are massive and probably generate nine-figure revenues per year without any marketing needed.

(Ms.) Tracy Behar, Executive Editor. Health, psychology, self-help, parenting, science, lifestyle.
Judy Clain, Editor in Chief. Commercial fiction, including mystery.
Ben George, Senior Editor. Commercial fiction; narrative nonfiction.
Vanessa Mobley, Executive Editor. Narrative, current events, history, politics.
(Ms.) Asya Muchnick, Executive Editor. Crime fiction; narrative nonfiction, history, biography, cultural history, popular science.
Michael Szczerban, Executive Editor. Food, cooking, lifestyle, science, humor, illustrated works.
(Ms.) Jean Garnett, Editor. Nonfiction, including women's interest, social issues, gender issues.
(Ms.) Reagan Arthur, Publisher. Commercial fiction; memoir, true crime.
Carina Guiterman, Associate Editor. Commercial fiction, graphic novels; illustrated nonfiction.
Philip Marino, Senior Editor. Culture, current events, sports, politics.

MULHOLLAND BOOKS ❖ www.mulhollandbooks.com

This program is dedicated to generating top-notch hardcover crime novels, thrillers, and spy stories.

Josh Kendall, Editorial Director. Commercial fiction, including mystery, thriller.
Emily Giglierano, Editor. Commercial fiction.

LITTLE, BROWN CHILDREN'S

LB began publishing children's books in 1926 and currently issues about 135 new titles a year. It publishes picture books, fiction and nonfiction in both paperback and hardcover for middle grade and young adult. LB Kids produces novelty media-tie-in books. Poppy publishes for teen girls.

Deirdre Jones, Editor. Middle grade.
Alvina Ling, Editor in Chief. Middle grade, young adult.
Pam Gruber, Senior Editor. Young adult.
Megan Tingley, Publisher. Picture books, middle grade.
Andrea Spooner, Executive Editor. Picture books, fantasy, young adult.
Lisa Yoskowitz, Executive Editor. Middle grade, young adult.
Kheryn Callender, Editor. Picture/illustrated middle grade and young adult.
Nikki Garcia, Editor. Picture books, young adult.
Rex Ogle, Editor. Middle grade.

Jimmy Patterson

Celebrity author James Patterson has his very own branded children's program. Leveraging his nickname was a smart move, and he's the author of many of the titles. The fiction and nonfiction list appears to be especially fun and lighthearted, without being frivolous.

Jenny Bak, Editorial Director. Middle grade, young adult.
(Ms.) Aubrey Poole, Editor. Middle grade, young adult.

THE PERSEUS BOOKS GROUP ❖ www.perseusbooks.com

Perseus is a large constellation of once-independent presses, now known as imprints. In a much-anticipated acquisition, Hachette bought Perseus in early 2016. Please see the Hachette description above for additional comments.

Basic Books ❖ www.basicbooks.com

Since 1952, Basic has helped explain many conversations and conflicts in the areas of history, science, sociology, psychology, politics, business, and current affairs.

Lara Heimert, Publisher. General history, culinary history.
(Mr.) TJ Kelleher, Associate Publisher. Science, natural history, computer science, economics.
Dan Gerstle, Senior Editor. History, politics, current events.

Brian Distelberg, Editor. Politics, law, sociology, technology, media.
Leah Stecher, Editor. History, politics, current events.

Da Capo Press ❖ www.dacapopress.com

Da Capo continues its long history of publishing books about general history, pop culture, music, sports, and popular business. Da Capo Lifelong Books — essentially an imprint within an imprint — specializes in pregnancy, parenting, health, fitness, and relationships.

Renee Sedliar, Editorial Director, Lifelong Books. Health, fitness, cooking, spiritual wellness, advice.
Bob Pigeon, Executive Editor. History, military history, politics, current affairs.
Ben Schafer, Executive Editor. Culture, entertainment, music, media, science, American counterculture.
Dan Ambrosio, Senior Editor. Popular business, health, wellness, personal improvement, parenting, advice.
Claire Schulz, Editor. Healthy eating cookbooks, health, parenting.

Nation Books ❖ www.hachettebookgroup.com/imprint/perseus/nation-books

116 East 16th Street, New York, NY 10003

Nation Books continues to be editorially related to *The Nation* magazine, which focuses on current events, politics, and deep-dive social exposés and narratives.

Alessandra Bastagli, Editorial Director; abastagli@nationbooks.org. Domestic and international affairs, politics, current events, social issues, economics.
Katy O'Donnell, Editor; katy@nationbooks.org. Social issues and current events.

Public Affairs ❖ www.publicaffairsbooks.com

As implied by its distinctive name, Public Affairs publishes books about current events, government, economics, business, politics, foreign affairs, and investigative journalism/narrative. Obviously, it appears to overlap with Nation Books. However, they maintain separate offices and have slightly different mandates and constituencies. Redundancy isn't detrimental in the book business, assuming the titles don't directly compete for space and revenue.

Colleen Lawrie, Senior Editor. Business, current events.
Benjamin Adams, Executive Editor. Science, current affairs, economics, psychology.

Clive Priddle, Publisher. Economics, political history, sociology, current events.
John Mahaney, Contributing Editor. Business, economics, personal finance.
Peter Osnos, Editor at Large. Current events, politics.

Running Press ❖ www.runningpress.com

2300 Chestnut Street, Suite 200, Philadelphia, PA 19103, 215-567-5080

Since 1972, Running Press has been an innovative book packager and merchandiser, meaning that many of their books are unconventionally designed and often show up where other books don't. "Impulse" or "gift" describes their distinctive formula, though conventional is also welcome. They generate a varied list of adult and children's titles in such areas as pop culture, humor, food and cooking, crafts, and lifestyle.

Kristen Green Wiewora, Editor. Cooking, crafts.
Jennifer Kasius, Editorial Director. Relationships, humor, lifestyle, advice.
Cindy De La Hoz, Editor. Relationships, parenting, health, women's self-help.
Jess Fromm, Editor. Humor, reference, illustrated, lifestyle, health.
Shannon Connors, Editor. Lifestyle, cooking, self-help/how-to.
Jordana Tusman, Senior Editor. Relationships, lifestyle, humor.
Julie Matysik, Editorial Director, Running Press Kids.

Seal Press ❖ www.sealpress.com

According to Seal's website, "A book can change a woman's life." They publish self-help and narrative books for, by, and about women. My understanding is that male writers should not apply, regardless of content, which strikes me as an archaic, if not illegal, restriction. But they do work with male agents, and I've never held back from pitching them appropriate projects or shaking hands with their editors at conferences; nor should you.

Laura Mazer, Executive Editor. Women's/gender issues, popular psychology.
Stephanie Knapp, Senior Editor. Gender issues, fitness, health, advice, parenting.

Weinstein Books ❖ weinsteinbooks.com

Gone…and I assume you know why.

HARPERCOLLINS PUBLISHERS ❖ www.harpercollins.com

195 Broadway, New York, NY 10007, 212-207-7000

HarperCollins is owned by News Corp and is technically Australian. However, its founder and dominant shareholder, Australian Rupert Murdoch, became a naturalized US citizen in 1985. News Corp is a huge international media conglomerate, of which book publishing reflects a tiny fraction of revenues and an even smaller fraction of profits. News Corp's monetary heartland and mass-market reach are tied to its 10-figure Fox TV and film operations.

Rupert Murdoch purchased Harper in 1989 and has done a good job making it into a commercially self-sufficient enterprise, while leaving room for important books that don't necessarily make any money. The firm is an amalgam of many legacy brands from the good old days of mom-and-pop publishing. As is the case throughout Big-Corp-Pub, the brands and their culturally invaluable catalogs bring immense credibility and gravitas to the parent firm, even if their frontlists have little in common with the brand's historic identity.

Unless otherwise specified, Harper editors' email addresses follow this format: firstname.lastname@harpercollins.com.

AMISTAD ❖ amistad.hc.com

Amistad publishes nonfiction and fiction books about African American history and culture.

(Ms.) Tracy Sherrod, Editorial Director.

AVON ❖ www.avonromance.com

Since 1941, Avon has been one of the strongest brand names in mass-market romance and women's fiction. It also maintains a powerful position in erotica, paranormal, and urban fantasy themes.

Erika Tsang, Editorial Director. Romantic suspense, "dark, angsty" historical romance.
May Chen, Executive Editor. Contemporary and historical romance, paranormal fiction.
Nicole Fisher, Editor. Erotic and contemporary romance.
Carrie Feron, Executive Editor. Romance, women's fiction.
Elle Keck, Editor. Romance, women's fiction.

BROADSIDE BOOKS ❖ www.broadsidebooks.com

Specializes in conservative political and public-policy books.

Eric Nelson, Editorial Director.

ECCO BOOKS

Formerly a small independent press, Ecco was acquired by Harper in 1999 and is currently a "boutique-ish" publisher of wide-ranging quality fiction and nonfiction, including memoir, "new voices," contemporary cookbooks, science, politics, current affairs, and history.

Dan Halpern, Editor in Chief. Fiction; cultural history.
Megan Lynch, Editorial Director. Fiction.
Zachary Wagman, Executive Editor. Thriller, mystery.
Denise Oswald, Executive Editor. Science, politics, current affairs.

HARPER

The Harper imprint is the heartland of HarperCollins and has existed since the early part of the 19th century. Whether independent or corporate owned, it has always maintained a full range of quality fiction and nonfiction books and carries a deep backlist.

(Ms.) Terry Karten, Executive Editor. General fiction, science fiction, fantasy.
Jonathan Jao, Executive Editor. Current events, politics.
Jennifer Barth, Executive Editor. Fiction, mystery/crime; memoir.
(Ms.) Gail Winston, Editor. General fiction; general nonfiction, parenting, relationships, culture.
Emily Griffin, Executive Editor. New fiction.
Jonathan Burnham, Publisher. General fiction; current events, politics, political history.
Sara Nelson, Executive Editor. General fiction.
Sofia Groopman, Editor. New fiction; current events, social history.
Erin Wicks, Associate Editor. Fiction; current events, memoir.

HARPER BUSINESS ❖ www.harperbusiness.com

This boutique imprint specializes in hardcover business biography, memoir, narrative, trends, history, and cutting-edge ideas.

(Ms.) Hollis Heimbouch, Editor.
Stephanie Hitchcock, Editor.

HARPERCOLLINS LEADERSHIP

This is a very new program dedicated to publishing books about (surprise!) leadership, especially in the context of business and large organizations. The program is absorbing the entire catalog of the previously independent entity AMACOM Books, which was the publishing division of American Management Association.

Tim Burgard, Senior Editor.
Jeff James, Publisher.

HARPER DESIGN

Exceptionally well-produced illustrated books in a wide range of subjects, including fashion, media, art, pop culture, music, crafts, lifestyle, interior design, cooking.

Cristina Garces, Editor.
Marta Schooler, Editor.

HARPERONE ❖ www.harperone.com

201 California Street, San Francisco, CA 94111, 415-477-4400

Formerly named HarperSanFrancisco, this cherished imprint has deliberately been maintained on the "other coast" for more than 30 years. It publishes a deep list of serious books about religion, science, alternative health, and new ideas in business and life.

Michael Maudlin, Editorial Director. Spiritual practices/philosophy, politics.
Gideon Weil, Editorial Director. Health, diet, science.
Julia Pastore, Executive Editor. Health, wellness, diet, lifestyle.
Kathryn Renz Hamilton, Editor. Lifestyle, self-help, science, spirituality.
Hilary Lawson, Editor. Humor, alternative health and lifestyle, feminism, alternative culture.
(Ms.) Sydney Rogers, Editor. Spiritual self-help, health, women's interest.
Anna Paustenbach, Assistant Editor. Self-help, relationships.

HARPER PERENNIAL

This imprint exists mostly for the purpose of reprinting Harper's successful hardcover books into evergreen backlist paperbacks. But it also publishes many quality fiction and nonfiction paperback originals in a wide range of "boundary-pushing" topics.

Laura Brown, Editor. Fiction, thriller, mystery; humor.
Amy Baker, Editor. Fiction.

HARPER VOYAGER ❖ www.harpervoyagerbooks.com

Voyager specializes in science fiction, fantasy, supernatural, and horror.

David Pomelico, Editorial Director.
Kelly O'Connor, Assistant Editor.
Rebecca Lucash, Editorial Assistant.
(Ms.) Priyanka Krishnan, Editor.
Chloe Moffett, Editor.

HARPER WAVE ❖ www.harperwave.com

Wave is a relatively new imprint specializing in innovative perspectives in mind-body-spirit, wellness, and lifestyle.

Karen Rinaldi, Publisher.
Julie Will, Editorial Director.
Sarah Murphy, Editor.

WILLIAM MORROW

Founded in 1926, Morrow is one of the major legacy names in American publishing. It was merged into the HarperCollins conglomerate a number of years ago. Its frontlist and exceptionally robust backlist address a full range of fiction and nonfiction categories and subjects.

Cassie Jones, Executive Editor. Cookbooks, health.
Rachel Kahan, Executive Editor. Fiction.
Kate Nintzel, Executive Editor. Fiction.
Tessa Woodward, Senior Editor. Fiction.
David Highfill, Executive Editor. Fiction: mysteries, thrillers, crime.
Emily Krump, Senior Editor. Fiction.
Emma Brodie, Editor. Health, humor, graphic/illustrated works, advice, lifestyle.
Peter Hubbard, Executive Editor. Military and political history and stories.
Jessica Williams, Senior Editor. Fiction.
(Ms.) Liate Shelik, Publisher. Fiction, including women's.
Jennifer Brehl, Director of Editorial Development. Fiction; celebrity memoir.
Nick Amphlett, Associate Editor. Quirky reference and history.
Matt Harper, Executive Editor. Sports, true crime.

CUSTOM HOUSE ❖ info.harpercollins.com/customhouse

This is a small imprint for "specially handled" provocative nonfiction and fiction.

Geoff Shandler, Editorial Director.

DEY STREET BOOKS ❖ deystreet.harpercollins.com

Dey Street Books is a relatively new imprint. Harper's headquarters is adjacent to Dey Street in lower Manhattan, hence the moniker for this division. Dey Street tends to publish pop-culture narratives and celebrity/high-profile titles likely to attract large fan-driven media attention.

(Ms.) Carrie Thornton, Editorial Director. Memoir, lifestyle, pop culture.
Julia Cheiffetz, Executive Editor. Memoir, narrative, biography, politics.
Matthew Daddona, Editor. Sports, popular media, pop culture.
Jessica Sindler, Senior Editor. Lifestyle, current affairs, pop culture.

HARLEQUIN ❖ www.harlequin.com

Harlequin is one of the world's leading publishers of romance titles. Their catalog covers every imaginable romance theme in both adult and teen categories, divided into multiple imprints with clearly assigned names. It might be useful to review the website's catalog of recent acquisitions for a snapshot of current orientations for each of the many imprints. In the romance sector, tastes and culture are a rapidly moving ball, and today's flavor of the month can quickly become retro. The firm was acquired by HarperCollins in 2014, though its editorial and marketing functions have remained largely autonomous. In fact, few dedicated readers would ever notice or care where the proverbial corporate buck stops as long as the products meet expectations.

Editors' email addresses follow this format: firstname.lastname@harlequin.com.

Julia Williams, Editor. Desire, Historical Romance, and Medical Romance imprints.
(Ms.) Stacy Boyd, Senior Editor. Desire and Romantic Suspense imprints.
Patience Bloom, Senior Editor. Intimate Moments, Romantic Suspense, Intrigue, and Love Inspired imprints.
Carly Silver, Assistant Editor. Romantic Suspense and Nocturne imprints.
Susan Litman, Assistant Editor. Special Edition imprint.
Elizabeth Mazer, Editor. Suspense, Historical, and Inspired imprints.

Gail Chasan, Senior Editor, Special Edition Imprint.
Shana Asaro, Editor, Inspired and Suspense imprints.

Harlequin TEEN ❖ www.harlequinteen.com

Paranormal, dystopian, horror, and romance appropriate for the young adult market, presumably girls.

Lauren Smulski, Associate Editor.
Michelle Meade, Editor.

Mira Books ❖ www.mirabooks.com

Contemporary and historical psychological and suspense thrillers.

Kathy Sagan, Senior Editor.

Graydon House ❖ www.graydonhousebooks.com

Graydon positions itself as a boutique imprint for "highly commercial" frontlist women's fiction. In other words, they're modeled to avoid the general Harlequin formula of producing dozens of mass-market paperbacks per list, and strive for bestseller lists and high Amazon rankings.

Susan Swinwood, Editorial Director. Historical themes.
Melanie Fried, Editor. Historical and contemporary themes.
Allison Carroll, Editor. Dating/relationship and edgy romance themes.
Brittany Lavery, Assistant Editor. Fringe, unconventional love stories.

Park Row Books ❖ www.parkrowbooks.com

Park Row was launched in 2016 for the purpose of acquiring an open range of commercial fiction eligible for bestsellerdom.

Erika Imranyi, Editorial Director.
Liz Stein, Senior Editor.
Matalie Hallak, Editorial Assistant.

Hanover Square Press ❖ www.hanoversqpress.com

Hanover was launched in 2017 with the stated mission of publishing strong frontlist fiction and nonfiction categories, including thriller, history, true crime, and high-profile narratives.

Peter Joseph, Editorial Director.
John Glynn, Editor.

HARPERCOLLINS CHRISTIAN PUBLISHING ❖
www.harpercollinschristian.com

A while back, Harper saw "the light," but not in the same way you might. They saw where the money was. The American Christian community is huge and loves books about faith. Harper knew better than to try building a religion program from scratch. Instead, they purchased two of the most successful and long-standing firms in the Christian community: Thomas Nelson and Zondervan.

Thomas Nelson ❖ www.thomasnelson.com

501 Nelson Place, Nashville, TN 37220, 615-889-9000

With roots going back to Scotland more than 200 years ago, Nelson may be the oldest Christian publisher in the world and probably has the biggest catalog. Originally known for its Protestant Bibles and church/Sunday school–related products, it publishes a large range of faith-based books for adults and children.

Editors' email addresses follow this format: firstinitiallastname@thomasnelson.com.

Brian Hampton, Publisher. Nonfiction.
Amanda Bostic, Publisher. Inspirational Christian fiction.
Webster Younce, Executive Editor. Nonfiction.
Jenny Baumgartner, Editor. Faith, self-help, relationships, women's interest.

Zondervan ❖ www.zondervan.com

5300 Patterson Avenue SE, Grand Rapids, MI 49530, 616-698-6900

For more than 80 years Zondervan has been a powerhouse publisher of Bibles as well as Christian-themed books for adults and children.

Carolyn McCready, Executive Editor; carolyn.mccready@zondervan.com. Nonfiction.

Zondervan Children's ❖ www.zondervan.com/children.html

Fiction and nonfiction faith-based books for children through young adult.

Jillian Manning, Editor.
Barbara Herndon, Editor.

HARPERCOLLINS CHILDREN'S BOOKS ❖ www.harpercollins.com/childrens

As would be expected, Harper has a deep children's program consisting of many legacy and relatively recent imprints.

Balzer + Bray

Balzer is best known for beautifully illustrated and packaged children's and middle grade books, and young adult novels.

Alessandra Balzer, Co-Publisher.
Donna Bray, Co-Publisher.
Kristin Daly Rens, Executive Editor.

Greenwillow Books

A well-respected boutique imprint since 1974, Greenwillow publishes quality books for children of all ages that aim to go into a little more emotional and social depth than usual.

Martha Mihalick, Associate Editor.
Virginia Duncan, Publisher.

HarperCollins Children's Books

Harper is the flagship within the flagship and the heartbeat of the entire children's program in terms of volume and depth.

Nancy Inteli, Editorial Director.
Sara Sarget, Executive Editor.
(Ms.) Tamar Mays, Editor.
(Mr.) Chris Hernandez, Editor.

HarperTeen ❖ www.harperteen.com

This imprint was recently created to publish exactly what its name implies.

Rosemary Brosnan, Editorial Director.

Katherine Tegen Books

This is a boutique home for books that tell "meaningful stories with memorable characters" for children through teens.

Katherine Tegen, Publisher.
Ben Rosenthal, Editor. Young adult.
(Ms.) Alex Arnold, Editor.

MACMILLAN PUBLISHERS ❖ us.macmillan.com

175 Fifth Avenue, New York, NY 10010, 212-674-5151

Macmillan is owned by the large German conglomerate Verlagsgruppe Georg von Holtzbrinck, whose name can't be memorized or said fast, if at all, by Americans unless seriously intoxicated or when moving pianos. The firm doesn't have any evident history in the chemical, plumbing fixtures, propagation, or armaments industries. Macmillan is a very familiar publishing brand and serves as the designated flagship umbrella encompassing many other legacy publishing brands that have been sequentially acquired, passed around, and ultimately amalgamated into relative stasis. The events are emblematic of the corporate creative destruction and reformation of America's media assets into obscure foreign-owned galaxies. Though Macmillan is a celebrity brand for book people, its current incarnation is several generations removed from its origins as a powerful UK book publisher. Like a ball tossed in the absence of gravity, rights to the Macmillan name have been bought and sold several times in recent years, and the name even disappeared for a time. In fact, Macmillan has been permanently severed from its original catalogs, which have been acquired and prevail elsewhere under other names.

FARRAR, STRAUS AND GIROUX ❖ www.fsgoriginals.com

175 Varick Street, New York, NY 10014, 212-741-6900

This one is a jackpot brand universally recognized for discovering and nurturing excellent works by new writers. In 1946 the firm was partly founded by refugee Euro-Semites who dedicated themselves to publishing edgy new voices whose works were unwelcome elsewhere for unsavory reasons. Its current program hasn't strayed, but it's no longer a particularly unique venue. The firm was acquired by Holtzbrinck in 1994.

Editors' email addresses follow this format: firstname.lastname@fsgbooks.com.

(Ms.) Alex Star, Executive Editor. History, politics, current events.
Amanda Moon, Editor. Popular science, *Scientific American* imprint.
Eric Chinski, Editor in Chief. Fiction; current events, history.
Emily Bell, Senior Editor. Fiction; general nonfiction.
Jonathan Galassi, Publisher. Fiction; serious nonfiction.
Jenna Johnson, Executive Editor. Fiction and nonfiction.
Jeremy Davies, Editor. Fiction and nonfiction.
Colin Dickerman, Executive Editor. American cultural history, politics.

FLATIRON BOOKS ❖ us.macmillan.com/flatiron-books

175 Fifth Avenue, New York, NY 10010, 212-674-5151

Flatiron is a relatively new and editorially autonomous boutique imprint that will endeavor to justify its ongoing existence by publishing a full range of frontlist fiction and nonfiction books that enough people will buy. The interesting name is derived from the iconic office building they are in. Furthermore, most of the program's description about itself is dedicated to warning ambitious writers NOT to submit unsolicited work to any of their editors, and they promise to auto-delete or destroy any such submissions. In other words, they truly don't want to know you. However, don't believe everything you read, especially if said by the publishers.

Editors' email addresses follow this format: firstname.lastname@flatironbooks.com.

Bob Miller, Publisher. Health, politics, pop culture.
James Melia, Editor. Fiction; current events.
Jasmine Faustino, Associate Editor. Pop culture.
Kara Rota, Editor. Humorous commentary, pop culture, cooking.
Caroline Bleeke, Editor. Fiction.

HENRY HOLT AND COMPANY ❖ us.macmillan.com/henryholt

175 Fifth Avenue, New York, NY 10010, 212-674-5151

Holt has been a premier publishing brand since 1866. It still carries a strong reputation as a general fiction and nonfiction publisher with genres including mystery, thriller, social sciences, and current events.

Editors' email addresses follow this format: firstname.lastname@hholt.com.

Serena Jones, Executive Editor. Popular science, political history.
Michael Signorelli, Senior Editor. Fiction; popular science.
Libby Burton, Senior Editor. Fiction; cultural history, self-help, politics, interesting narrative/memoir.
Gillian Blake, Editor in Chief. Cultural history, popular science.
Stephen Rubin, Publisher. Current events, cultural history.
Paul Golob, Executive Editor. Sports, current events, politics, history.

Metropolitan Books

This Holt imprint was established in 1995 for the purpose of publishing fiction and nonfiction books with a slightly fringe or quirky orientation — just a little outside the mainstream but often perfectly conventional nonetheless.

Riva Hocherman, Executive Editor; riva.hocherman@hholt.com. Graphic novels; social issues, politics.

ST. MARTIN'S PRESS ❖ us.macmillan.com/smp

175 Fifth Avenue, New York, NY 10010, 212-674-5151

Here's another well-respected publishing giant that was conglomerated early this century. SMP has managed to maintain itself as it was before the plague and tends to have much less editorial turnover/attrition than other legacy programs. In other words, it has been a reliably stable planet in an unpredictable solar system.

Editors' email addresses follow this format: firstname.lastname@stmartins.com.

George Witte, Editor in Chief. Literary fiction; current affairs, investigative journalism.
Tim Bartlett, Executive Editor. Current issues, business stories, narrative.
Elizabeth Beier, Executive Editor. Commercial fiction; problem-solving nonfiction, pop culture, cookbooks.
Laurie Chittenden, Executive Editor. Women's fiction; inspiring memoir.
Elisabeth Dyssegaard, Executive Editor. Social history, current issues.
Jennifer Enderlin, Executive Vice President. Commercial fiction, including paperback originals.
Michael Flamini, Executive Editor. History, politics, nature, performing arts, food.
Michael Homler, Senior Editor. Crime fiction, thriller; biography, quirky narrative, popular science, sports.
Holly Ingraham, Editor. Women's contemporary fiction, mystery, thriller, romance.
Keith Kahla, Executive Editor. Commercial fiction.
Elizabeth Lacks, Associate Editor. Crime, suspense, historical fiction, Southern-themed fiction; personal narrative about compelling experiences.
Vicki Lame, Associate Editor. Women's, literary, and historical fiction; inspiring memoir and narrative.
Marcia Markland, Executive Editor. Crime and supernatural fiction; animal and nature topics, social issues.

April Osborn, Associate Editor. Mystery, thriller, women's fiction.

Monique Patterson, Editorial Director of Romance. Romance, paranormal, multicultural-themed fiction.

Daniela Rapp, Senior Editor. Narrative nonfiction, pets, quirky, popular science, travel stories, pop culture, animals.

Marc Resnick, Executive Editor. Military narrative, sports, adventure, pop culture, music.

Catherine Richards, Senior Editor. Thriller, mystery, suspense.

Eileen Rothschild, Editor. Romance, women's fiction.

Charles Spicer, Executive Editor. Men's and women's commercial fiction, crime fiction; true crime, history, pop culture.

Jennifer Weis, Executive Editor. General and young adult fiction; health/medicine, women's interest.

Karen Wolny, Executive Editor. Current events, interesting trendy concepts, social issues, American culture, politics, history.

Peter Wolverton, Executive Editor. Commercial fiction, thriller, fantasy, mystery; sports stories.

Sally Richardson, Publisher. History, politics, current affairs.

Joel Fotinos, Editorial Director of newly formed program dedicated to mind-body-spirit titles.

Thomas Dunne Books ❖ us.macmillan.com/thomasdunne

Dunne is a close sibling to St. Martin's, and they seem to frequently share each other's editors. Perhaps the single distinguishing aspect is that Mr. Dunne still exists and has been laboring as a hands-on editor since before he was given his own imprint in 1986.

Editors' email addresses follow this format: firstname.lastname@stmartins.com.

Thomas Dunne, Publisher. British fiction. Politics, history, science, current events, popular culture.

Stephen Power, Executive Editor. Politics, current affairs, sports, popular culture.

Minotaur ❖ us.macmillan.com/minotaurbooks

Established in 1999, Minotaur specializes in a boutique list of quality crime fiction. Many Dunne and SMP editors also acquire under this imprint.

Editors' email addresses follow this format: firstname.lastname@stmartins.com.

Keith Kahla, Editor.
Kelley Ragland, Editorial Director.
Charles Spicer, Editor.
Andrew Martin, Publisher.

All Points Books

This small imprint was recently established as a home for politically and socially conservative points of view.

Adam Bellow, Editorial Director.

CELADON BOOKS ❖ us.macmillan.com/publishers/celadon-books

This boutique imprint is so new that its first list won't appear until 2019. Frankly, nothing truly unique can be said about the program's mission: it will publish an open range of fiction and nonfiction hardcovers intended to be "bestseller eligible" (a term I made up just now, I think). What is notable is that the program is being built by very successful veterans — people actually over the age of 40. Their combined experiences and connections might create a powerful alchemy, or an expensive sizzle. Always the optimist, I predict that this program will catch on and emerge as a preferred home by many.

Editors' email addresses follow this format: firstname.lastname@celadonpublishers.com.

(Ms.) Jamie Raab, Publisher.
Deb Futter, Co-Publisher.
Randi Kramer, Editorial Assistant.
Ryan Doherty, Executive Editor.

PICADOR ❖ us.macmillan.com/picador

Picador was established in 1995 as an imprint for literary fiction and nonfiction. That doesn't sound innovative, but hatching imprints is how large houses try to refresh themselves and reward veteran editors who will never earn the salaries they would be worth in other businesses. Picador is also where all the Macmillan divisions repurpose many of their successful titles as paperback cash cows.

Editors' email addresses follow this format: firstname.lastname@picadorusa.com.

Elizabeth Bruce, Editor. Thriller, general fiction.
Anna deVries, Executive Editor. Political and cultural affairs.

(Mr.) Pronoy Sarkar, Editor. Politics, current affairs, culture.
Stephen Morrison, Publisher. Fiction, mystery, crime fiction; true crime.

TOR/FORGE ❖ www.tor.com

175 Fifth Avenue, New York, NY 10010, 212-674-5151

Tor publishes a premier line of mostly science fiction and fantasy. Forge publishes a wider range of commercial fiction, including historical, thriller, mystery, women's, modern Westerns, military, and young adult novels, as well as some nonfiction relevant to the fiction themes. Many if not most of their books are paperback originals.

Unless otherwise specified, editors' email addresses follow this format: firstname.lastname@tor.com.

Patrick Nielsen Hayden, Associate Publisher; pnh@tor.com. Science fiction, fantasy.
Liz Gorinsky, Senior Editor. Science fiction, fantasy.
Miriam Weinberg, Senior Editor. Science fiction, fantasy.
Kristin Sevick, Senior Editor. Mystery, thriller.
Jennifer Gunnels, Editor. Science fiction, fantasy.
Devi Pillai, Associate Publisher. Science fiction, fantasy.
Diana Pho, Editor. Science fiction, fantasy.
Bob Gleason, Editor. Thriller.
Claire Eddy, Editor. Science fiction, fantasy.
Linda Quinton, Publisher. Science fiction, fantasy.

MACMILLAN CHILDREN'S ❖ us.macmillan.com/mackids

Encompasses many vibrant and deeply rooted imprints.

Farrar, Straus and Giroux Books for Younger Readers

This program boasts a huge catalog of children's classics going back to the 1950s. Its frontlist program includes everything from preschool to young adult.

Editors' email addresses follow this format: firstname.lastname@fsgbooks.com.

Janine O'Malley, Executive Editor.
Wesley Adams, Executive Editor.
Joy Peskin, Editorial Director.
Grace Kendall, Editor.

Feiwel and Friends ❖ us.macmillan.com/publishers/feiwel-and-friends

Publishes across the board from prereaders to age 16. "Our books are friends for life" is the program's inspiring motto.

Editors' email addresses follow this format: firstname.lastname@macmillan.com.

Liz Szabla, Associate Publisher.
Jean Feiwel, Publisher.
Anna Roberto, Editor.
Holly West, Editor.

Henry Holt Books for Young Readers

Holt's program is noted for its high-quality picture books, chapter books for young readers, and novels for young adults.

Editors' email addresses follow this format: firstname.lastname@hholt.com.

Tiffany Liao, Editor.
Christian Trimmer, Editorial Director.

Roaring Brook Press ❖ us.macmillan.com/publishers/roaring-brook-press

This imprint was founded in 2002 and publishes for young readers of all ages. (Like me, you may be wondering how all these imprints manage to live with one another. The answer is, they just do, and the editors are glad to have their jobs.)

Editors' email addresses follow this format: firstname.lastname@roaringbrookpress.com.

Katherine Jacobs, Senior Editor.
Emily Feinberg, Editor.
Connie Hsu, Senior Editor.
Claire Dorsett, Editor.

First Second Books ❖ firstsecondbooks.com

This is a recent imprint dedicated to graphic novels and cartoon collections that can cross over from children's to young adult and adult.

Editors' email addresses follow this format: firstname.lastname@firstsecondbooks.com.

Calista Brill, Executive Editor.
Mark Siegel, Editorial Director.

PENGUIN RANDOM HOUSE ❖ www.penguinrandomhouse.com

December 13, 2013, was perhaps both the most anticlimactic and the most meaningful day in the modern history of American and international publishing. On this day, amid the noise of Christmas consumption, Random House and Penguin legally finalized their friendly merger. It was a gentle event that the Justice Department seemingly ignored. The metaphorical equivalent of an old-growth forest abruptly collapsed in the woods. Everyone knew but no one listened.

In fairness, the handwriting had been on the wall for more than a decade. And there's still plenty of handwriting to be parsed about what might follow. There's still room for more compression both within and between the entities. Though both Penguin and Random House maintain a clear American footprint, don't be fooled. Ownership is primarily German and secondarily British, although a plurality, perhaps even a majority, of revenues are American. More importantly, book sales are a comparatively small fraction of overall revenues and profits for the corporate parent.

What follows is a breakdown of an especially large and fluid matrix of 250+ amalgamated divisions and imprints with ancient legacies and new mandates. However, the merger-digestion process is still sorting itself out, and it's possible that by the time you read this some programs will have been reverted to the dust from which everything derives.

RANDOM HOUSE

1745 Broadway, New York, NY 10019, 212-782-9000

CROWN PUBLISHING GROUP ❖ www.crownpublishing.com

Until 1988, Crown was a thriving independent, family-owned house, and there was a noticeable measure of protest and concern when Random House announced its consumption of Crown. People understood that it represented an early stage of the corporate consolidation of independent mom-and-pop publishing. Today, Crown stands as a large, autonomous division encompassing many distinct imprints.

Editors' email addresses follow this format: firstinitiallastname@randomhouse.com.

Julian Pavia, Executive Editor. Science fiction, fantasy, thriller, general fiction.
Rachel Klayman, Executive Editor. Science, politics, current events.
Amanda Cook, Executive Editor. Science, current affairs, business, social history.
Hilary Ruben Teeman, Senior Editor. Fiction.
Kevin Doughten, Executive Editor. Politics, contemporary biography, arts/culture.

Emma Berry, Editor. Political and social issues.
Nathan Roberson, Editor. Fiction; sports.

Crown Archetype

This is a recent hardcover boutique program focused on books by or about celebrities and high-profile events.

Tricia Boczkowski, Editorial Director.
Jennifer Schuster, Executive Editor.
Mary Reynics, Executive Editor.

Convergent Books

This is a relatively new boutique program focused on inspiration, motivation, and self-improvement.

David Kopp, Executive Editor.

Currency

This program is dedicated to books by high-profile business leaders and about trend-setting business practices.

Roger Scholl, Executive Editor.

Crown Forum

Political and social commentary books with a conservative orientation.

Derek Reed, Editor.

Clarkson Potter

This imprint has an impressive pre–Random House history. For many years it was where you'd find a huge array of frontlist and backlist books dedicated to food, cooking, lifestyle, crafts/hobbies, decorating, and entertaining, and that tradition remains solid.

Amanda Englander, Senior Editor. Cooking, food, lifestyle, organizing.
Sara Neville, Editor. Lifestyle.
Jennie Zellner, Associate Editor. Pop culture.

Harmony Books

This imprint is a long-lived brand whose standing within RH has ebbed and flowed for years. At one time it was the designated New Age, spirituality, mind-body-spirit program. In recent years it has tended to avoid fringe topics while focusing on trendsetting books about diet, health, relationships, culture, self-help, popular psychology, and self-improvement.

Diana Baroni, Editorial Director.
Donna Loffredo, Editor.

Hogarth

I didn't understand the meaning of this name until I discovered that it was the name of Virginia Woolf's publishing house. This is a relatively new boutique imprint dedicated to discovering and publishing fiction that is a little more "adventurous" (lifted from their website).

Alexis Washam, Executive Editor.

Ten Speed Press

6001 Shellmound Street, Emeryville, CA 94608, 510-285-3000

Many publishing professionals were sorry to see this formerly independent publisher fall into the corporate abyss. But that tends to happen when a firm's founder/owner retires, dies, or simply wants to cash out while he or she can. Kudos to Penguin Random House for keeping Ten Speed on the other coast. The press is famous for its quirky, high-production-quality, innovative list of books about food, careers, test prep, humor, health, and perhaps anything else you might think of.

Editors' email addresses follow this format: firstname.lastname@tenspeed.com.

Julie Bennett, Editorial Director. Cookbooks, popular reference, lifestyle.
Lisa Westmoreland, Executive Editor. Popular reference, test-taking/education guides, creativity, writing, how-to, cooking, crafts.
Kaitlin Ketchum, Editor. Illustrated and lifestyle how-to books.
Emily Timberlake, Senior Editor. Food, cooking.
Jenny Wapner, Executive Editor. Food, cooking, crafts, art.
Lorena Jones, Editor in Chief. Health and wellness, food, careers, entrepreneurship.
Patrick Barb, Editor. Arts and crafts.
Kelly Snowden, Editor. Cooking.

Anne Goldberg, Associate Editor. Cooking, lifestyle, pop culture.
Ashley Pierce, Editorial Assistant. Cooking, diet, practical self-help.

Rodale Books ❖ www.rodalebooks.com
733 Third Avenue, New York, NY 10017

Rodale Books has been the book division of Rodale Media for more than twenty years. Rodale is best known as a publisher of magazines devoted to healthy lifestyles and diet. The book program has published many excellent books reflecting the health-wellness philosophy but has probably been a drag on overall corporate profits and resources. In 2017 the catalog and use of the name were offered for sale. Frankly, it didn't appear as if publishers were lining up to compete for the entity, which is a sign that the formerly vibrant pace of "inside" acquisitions is on pause and that outside equity isn't marching in. Eventually, a deal was closed with PRH. As of this writing, no major changes to the program have been made or announced, and it's business as usual.

Editors' email addresses follow this format: firstname.lastname@rodale.com.

Jennifer Levesque, Editorial Director. Diet, fitness, cooking, sports, parenting, lifestyle.
Mark Weinstein, Executive Editor. Sports, fitness, health.
Dervla Kelly, Senior Editor. Illustrated cooking and lifestyle books.
Marisa Vigilante, Senior Editor. Health, diet, wellness, lifestyle.
Anna Cooperberg, Editorial Assistant. Mind-body-spirit.
Danielle Curtis, Editorial Assistant. Narrative, motivation, inspiration, science.
Eric Wight, Editor. Health, nature, and lifestyle themes (adult); children's fiction and nonfiction.

Three Rivers Press

This is the trade paperback division for the Crown program. Most of its catalog is devoted to evergreen backlist nonfiction titles originally published by Crown. But it also publishes a wide range of trade paperback nonfiction originals.

Matt Inman, Senior Editor; minman@penguinrandomhouse.com. Celebrity narrative, celebrity humor.

WATERBROOK MULTNOMAH PUBLISHING GROUP ❖
www.waterbrookmultnomah.com

10807 New Allegiance Drive, #500, Colorado Springs, CO 80921, 719-590-4999

Launched by Random House in 1996, the division exclusively publishes books for Protestant Christians of all ages about how to live a Christian lifestyle. As per routine with corporately owned religious book divisions, the program is based thousands of miles away from the New York parent company's headquarters.

Susan Tjaden, Editor; stjaden@randomhouse.com.
Andrew Stoddard, Editor; astoddard@randomhouse.com.

KNOPF DOUBLEDAY PUBLISHING GROUP ❖ knopfdoubleday.com

Knopf ❖ www.knopfdoubleday.com/imprint/knopf

The firm was founded by Alfred Knopf in 1915 and is still one of the few "Rolls Royce / Cartier"–level brand names in American publishing. "Smart people" have always been enthusiastic bookbuyers. In fact, they used to be the only bookbuyers. It's fitting that programs exist essentially for them. Within publishing's circle of circles, getting published by Knopf puts you at the head of the line, though you will probably be more reliant on your trust fund than your royalties.

Editors' email addresses follow this format: firstinitiallastname@randomhouse.com.

Tim O'Connell, Editor. Fiction; interesting narrative.
Andrew Miller, Senior Editor. Journalistic narrative, current events, politics.
Sonny Mehta, Editor in Chief.
(Ms.) Jordan Pavlin, Executive Editor. Fiction; narrative.
Diana Tejerina Miller, Editor. Fiction.
Robin Desser, Editorial Director. Fiction and nonfiction.

Doubleday ❖ knopfdoubleday.com/imprint/doubleday

Founded in 1897, Doubleday is one of the great publishing brands, though now it's one of many brands decapitated from their foundational souls. The brand has had a rocky tenure as part of the RH "family." But what is a publisher worth if it can't maintain brand value? The ironic answer is that few readers care who the publisher is when they buy a book; but it still means a lot to the people who work in the book business, especially authors and booksellers. Doubleday continues a wonderful tradition of publishing excellent fiction and nonfiction frontlist books.

Editors' email addresses follow this format: firstinitiallastname@randomhouse.com.

(Mr.) Yaniv Soha, Senior Editor. Popular science, medicine/health, contemporary narrative.
Margo Shickmanter, Associate Editor. Fiction
(Mr.) Gerry Howard, Executive Editor. Fiction; cultural biography, narrative, memoir.
(Ms.) Kris Puopolo, Executive Editor. Political history and narrative.
(Ms.) Lee Boudreaux, Executive Editor. Fiction.
Bill Thomas, Editor in Chief. Current events, politics, fiction.
Robert Bloom, Editor. Horror, thriller, mystery.

Schocken Books ❖ knopfdoubleday.com/imprint/schocken

Though lately an obscure and little-heard-from imprint, Schocken has a dramatic and brilliant history. In fact, the entire program is literally a refugee from Nazi Germany. The Schocken family took advantage of the opportunity to gather up their valuable copyrights and make a run for it while still possible. An unintended benefit of the Nazi race laws was that all Jewish writers needed to be consolidated into Jewish-owned publishing houses, so just before they "left the room," the Schockens ended up with the rights to such literary giants as Kafka. Today the firm publishes an annual handful of titles relevant to Jewish cultural history and themes.

(Ms.) Altie Karper, Editor; akarper@randomhouse.com.

RANDOM HOUSE ❖ www.randomhousebooks.com

If you're a little confused, just be glad not to be part of the management team that has to keep figuring out how to align, or keep alive, its wealth of Brahmin brands that have been amalgamated many times over. The RH imprint carries the glory and burden of the Random House history, which has been one of America's premier publishing brands since 1925. RH was a large independent firm until about a generation ago, when it was acquired by the Newhouse family. A few years later it was acquired by the German-owned media goliath Bertelsmann, which made a lot of blood money during the middle of the 20th century as the Nazi Party's exclusive designated publisher. The assignment was especially lucrative because millions of people were required to buy the books (sounds a little like the contemporary textbook market). On our side of the lake, not even Donald Trump can force people to buy his books (yet). Today's Random House has one of the biggest and most lucrative backlist catalogs in the world, and its frontlist always consists of a highly respected and diverse assortment of good books.

Editors' email addresses follow this format: firstinitiallastname@randomhouse.com.

Andy Ward, Editor in Chief. Nonfiction, science, sports, business, current events.
Will Murphy, Executive Editor. Fiction and nonfiction.
Andrea Walker, Executive Editor. Fiction.
Ben Greenberg, Executive Editor. American culture and entertainment, current affairs.
Kate Medina, Executive Editor. Fiction; memoir, narrative, social issues.
Hilary Redmon, Executive Editor. Narrative, memoir, social issues.
Caitlin McKenna, Senior Editor. Fiction, thriller; American history, culture.
Molly Turpin, Editor. Politics, social issues, history.
Mark Warren, Editor. Memoir, narrative.

BALLANTINE BOOKS

BB was conceived as an innovative unattached firm in 1952 with what at the time was an unusual vision: specializing in mass-market paperback originals, which the old guard disrespected. There was a time not that long ago when paperbacks were the exception. Following WWII, publisher-entrepreneurs broke the cultural glass ceiling by placing paperbacks in unthinkable venues like grocery stores. Somewhere along the line, Random House gobbled up BB, and their destinies have been entwined ever since. BB continues to perform its primary purpose as a publisher of a wide assortment of popular fiction categories and some nonfiction, mostly in paperback. Several recognizable brand names prevail within BB, each with its own rich history.

Pamela Cannon, Executive Editor. Cooking, food.
Sara Weiss, Senior Editor. Personal finance, self-help.
Marnie Cochran, Executive Editor. High-concept self-help, health, parenting, diet, cooking.
Brendan Vaughan, Executive Editor. Narrative, sports, military, current affairs.

DEL REY

According to the RH website: "Del Rey Books began as an imprint of Ballantine Books in 1977. Founded by editors Judy-Lynn and Lester del Rey, Del Rey is now one of the world's foremost publishers of science fiction, fantasy, and speculative fiction, as well as media and pop culture titles."

Tricia Narwani, Editor.

LOVESWEPT ❖ www.randomhousebooks.com/loveswept-flirt

You won't find how-to books about death or taxes here, unless they include cleavage and abs. It's a women's fiction/romance list, most of which seems to be published in digital only.

Sue Grimshaw, Editor at Large.
Junessa Viloria, Editor.
Shauna Summers, Editor.

ONE WORLD ❖ www.oneworldlit.com

This relatively new boutique imprint focuses on multicultural perspectives about the past, the present, and the future, in both fiction and nonfiction.

Nicole Counts, Editor.
(Mr.) Chris Jackson, Editor in Chief.
Victory Matsui, Editor.

SPIEGEL & GRAU

Some years ago two smart veteran editors were given the space and budget to create and manage their own dedicated list. Large houses often do that as way to maybe shake up internal motivation and creativity, and it's possible something special will bloom. If it doesn't work they just shut it down and move any successful titles into an existing backlist program. Fortunately, this boutique imprint has been self-sustaining for more than 10 years.

Julie Grau, Co-Publisher. Literary fiction; celebrity books, narrative nonfiction, prescriptive nonfiction.
Cindy Spiegel, Co-Publisher. Fiction; groundbreaking nonfiction.
Annie Chagnot, Editor. Self-help, memoir, narrative.

RANDOM HOUSE CHILDREN'S BOOKS ❖ www.rhcbooks.com

RHCB is arguably the largest and busiest children's publisher in the known universe. Its list includes Dr. Seuss books (game-over), and there are several imprints.

Alfred A. Knopf Books for Young Readers

Full spectrum of children's books. The list and the brand were part of the original Knopf–Random House merger.

Melanie Cecka, Publisher.
Nancy Siscoe, Senior Executive Editor.
Erin Clarke, Senior Executive Editor.
Katherine Harrison, Editor.
Michelle Frey, Executive Editor.
Jennifer Brown, Editor.
Kelly Delaney, Editor.
Julia Maguire, Editor.
Karen Greenberg, Editor.

Crown Children's

Although this imprint retains the Crown name, it was placed within the RH program following the merger. It publishes a dynamic and commercial list of titles for all young age groups, ranging from nonreaders (picture books) to young adult.

Emily Easton, Publisher.
Phoebe Yeh, Publisher.

Delacorte

Publishes a wide range of middle grade and young adult novels and nonfiction.

Wendy Loggia, Senior Executive Editor.
Beverly Horowitz, Publisher.
Krista Marino, Senior Executive Editor.
Kate Sullivan, Senior Editor. Young adult.
Rebecca Weston, Editor. Middle grade.
Kelsey Horton, Associate Editor.

Random House Books for Young Readers

The flagship imprint within the flagship program, this is where Dr. Seuss and Babar live. The program covers every category and age group.

Maria Modugno, Editorial Director.
Caroline Abbey, Editor. All areas.
Anna Membrino, Editor.
Shana Corey, Editor.
Alice Jonaitis, Executive Editor.
Jenna Lettice, Editor.
Heidi Kilgras, Editor.

Schwartz and Wade

Established in 2005 as a boutique imprint specializing in highly designed illustrated books. Middle grade through young adult fiction and nonfiction.

Anne Schwartz, Editorial Director.
(Mr.) Lee Wade, Co-Director.
Ann Kelley, Associate Editor.

PENGUIN ❖ www.penguin.com
375 Hudson Street, New York, NY 10014, 212-266-2000

Penguin is the other half of the huge conglomeration of a plurality percentage of America's traditional publishing assets. Ironically, it's not American owned, even though most revenues are generated in America. Needless to say, every kind of book you can imagine is probably published by one or more of the numerous brands, imprints, and divisions found herein.

Unless otherwise specified, editors' email addresses for all Penguin imprints follow this format: firstinitiallastname@penguinrandomhouse.com.

AVERY ❖ www.penguin.com/publishers/avery

Avery was acquired by Penguin in 1999. It had been a successful independent publisher specializing in cutting-edge health lifestyle, science, and psychological self-help books, and that orientation has been maintained.

Caroline Sutton, Editor in Chief.
Lucia Watson, Executive Editor.
Megan Newman, Publisher.

Pam Krauss Books

This is a micro-imprint managed by the veteran über-foodie editor Pam Krauss. She acquires top-notch cookbooks for her own imprint and some for the Avery imprint.

Pam Krauss, Publisher.

BERKLEY ❖ www.penguin.com/publishers/berkley

Berkley, which includes the NAL brand, is one of the most prestigious mass-market book brands in publishing. More than 50 years ago, the company was created around the revolutionary concept of publishing books that ordinary people would like to read, printing them as affordable paperbacks, and distributing them where real people shopped for nonbook products. Hence, the term *mass-market publishing* was born. Today, Berkley continues to publish a diverse list of commercial fiction and nonfiction titles as paperback originals, and some frontlist hardcovers. Its Prime Crime imprint is devoted to cozy mysteries.

Cindy Hwang, Editorial Director. Romance.
Claire Zion, Editor in Chief. Romance.
Kate Seaver, Executive Editor. Women's fiction, romance.
Danielle Perez, Executive Editor. Mystery, thriller.
Kerry Donovan, Executive Editor. Romance.
Tom Colgan, Editorial Director.
Michelle Vega, Senior Editor. Prime Crime.
Amanda Bergeron, Executive Editor. Suspense, thriller.
Kristine Swartz, Editor. Women's fiction, romance.

Ace/Roc Books

Ace was founded in 1953 as a science fiction/paranormal/fantasy publisher. Many of the classics that you have and haven't heard of still prevail on its backlist. The program has been eaten several times by corporations but continues to survive with minimal alterations to its mission.

Anne Sowers, Executive Editor.
Rebecca Brewer, Editor.

BLUE RIDER PRESS ❖ www.penguin.com/publishers/blueriderpress

Blue Rider was created in 2011 for the purpose of generating a special, "high-rent" space for some of the veteran editors and their highly esteemed authors, fiction and nonfiction. The term *Blue Rider* has obscure origins from more than 100 years ago as a culturally renegade arts movement based in pre-WWI Munich — but you already knew that.

David Rosenthal, Publisher. Fiction and nonfiction.

DAW ❖ www.penguin.com/publishers/daw

DAW was founded as an independent press in 1971 and was the first program to be exclusively dedicated to science fiction and fantasy. That mandate continues to thrive. Disclosure: other than their divergent origins, I don't know how to differentiate this program from the Ace program, though that's not meant to imply that there are not significant differences.

Betsy Wollheim, Editor.
Katie Hoffman, Editor.

DUTTON ❖ www.penguin.com/publishers/dutton

Dutton's history as a major American publisher can be traced to 1852, when Edward Payson Dutton heard the calling to publish Christian books. Over the generations the firm has been resurrected and reincarnated many times. Today it is a premium imprint specializing in top-selling (that's always the plan) fiction and nonfiction hardcover books.

John Parsley, Editor in Chief. Fiction; current issues/events, popular science, contemporary culture and history.
Stephen Morrow, Executive Editor. Science, economics, psychology, investigative journalism.
Jill Schwartzman, Executive Editor. Pop culture, music, narrative, biography, high-profile self-help, politics.
Jessica Renheim, Senior Editor. Mystery, thriller, crime fiction.
Maya Ziv, Executive Editor. Fiction; memoir, social issues.
Stephanie Kelly, Editor. Fiction.
Brent Howard, Executive Editor. Military history and memoir, political events and history.

THE PENGUIN PRESS ❖ www.penguin.com/publishers/penguinpress

This is the one that gets to use the flagship brand name, which has a distinguished history originating in London. Today's Penguin Press (US) was rebooted in 2003 as a home for distinguished nonfiction and fiction titles. Disclosure: Even though I've been in the business for three decades, I don't have solid language for describing how some of these imprints actually differ from one another. But I have learned that in-house overlapping is common in publishing, probably because it's easier to manage everything in clustered pockets of humanized endeavors, as opposed to massive piles of redundancies.

Ann Godoff, Publisher. Current affairs, cultural history, arts, politics.
Scott Moyers, Publisher. Current affairs, politics, sports, humorous commentary.
Virginia Smith, Executive Editor. Current affairs, cultural history, popular science.
Emily Cunningham, Editor. Fiction; current events.
Christopher Richards, Editor. Political memoir.
William Heyward, Editor. Fiction; cultural history.

PORTFOLIO ❖ www.penguin.com/publishers/portfolio

Portfolio was established in 2001 as a boutique destination for commercial books about business, technology, and investing, including narrative business stories, history, and philosophy.

(Mr.) Adrian Zackhein, Publisher.
Stephanie Frerich, Executive Editor.
Natalie Horbachevsky, Editor.
Niki Papadopoulas, Editorial Director.
Bria Sandford, Senior Editor.
Leah Trouborst, Associate Editor.
(Mr.) Kaushik Viswanath, Associate Editor.

G. P. PUTNAM'S SONS ❖ www.penguin.com/publishers/gpputnamssons

Now here's a big brand from 1838 that was its own domain for more than a century and even had its own skyscraper. Now it's a brand with a marvelous backlist and frontlist that successfully competes for commercial primacy.

Sally Kim, Editorial Director. Commercial fiction.
Mark Tavani, Executive Editor. Thriller; sports, current affairs, history, science.
Kerri Kolen, Executive Editor. Wide range of popular nonfiction and narrative, including pop culture, current affairs, humor, investigative journalism.

Sara Minnich, Senior Editor. Contemporary and historical fiction, upmarket mystery and thriller; narrative history, popular science, travel narrative, current affairs.

Tara Singh Carlson, Executive Editor. Women's fiction, suspense, historical, magical realism.

RIVERHEAD BOOKS ❖ www.penguin.com/publishers/riverhead

Riverhead was created in 1994 as an editorially autonomous imprint for cutting-edge commercial fiction and high-end nonfiction hardcover originals. It has generated a healthy backlist and is a reliable producer of successful and award-winning frontlist titles.

Rebecca Saletan, Editorial Director. Literary fiction; current events, environmental issues, multicultural subjects, food, travel.

Sarah McGrath, Editor in Chief. Literary fiction and narrative nonfiction.

Laura Perciasepe, Editor. Wide range of literary fiction and narrative nonfiction.

Courtney Young, Executive Editor. Social, business, and technological trends, popular science.

Cal Morgan, Executive Editor. Fiction. Cultural history, social issues.

SENTINEL ❖ www.penguin.com/publishers/sentinel

This small imprint specializes in right-wing political and social opinions.

Bria Sandford, Senior Editor.

TARCHER PERIGEE ❖ www.penguin.com/publishers/tarcherperigee

The Tarcher and Perigee programs were merged in late 2015. This was a smart consolidation because there was substantial editorial overlap between the kinds of practical and alternative lifestyle, health, spiritual, and self-help categories that both programs already excelled at. Fortunately, the Tarcher name has been maintained, since it has a strong tradition of publishing innovative works, going back to the days when it was an independent West Coast press.

Marian Lizzi, Editor in Chief. Wide-ranging self-help categories, including popular business, lifestyle, popular psychology, narrative.

Joanna Ng, Editor; jong@penguinrandomhouse.com. Personal growth, popular psychology, parenting.

Sara Carder, Editorial Director. Parenting, advice, self-help.

Lauren Appleton, Editor. Creativity, mindfulness, self-help.

Nina Shield, Editor. Prescriptive self-help, personal finance, popular business, inspiration, health.

Amanda Shih, Assistant Editor. Popular business, humor.

PENGUIN BOOKS ❖ www.penguin.com/publishers/penguinbooks

Okay, this confuses me, too. Correct, there's an imprint named Penguin Press, and a completely distinct imprint named Penguin Books. Not my idea, but it seems to work out anyway. There are crucial differences between the two programs. This Penguin services relatively more "high-brow," "intellectual, "scholarly" type readers. These books are suitable for college adaptations and for people with frontal lobes oozing out of their skulls. This isn't how the publisher would describe itself; it's simply my interpretation for myself, and I guess you're stuck with it if you're actually reading this.

Patrick Nolan, Editor in Chief. Popular philosophy and social issues.

John Siciliano, Senior Editor. Classic reprints and commentaries about the Classics, cultural history, food.

Meg Leder, Executive Editor. Relationships, psychology, popular science.

(Mr.) Sam Raim, Associate Editor. Political and social history, popular reference.

VIKING BOOKS ❖ www.penguin.com/publishers/vikingbooks

Viking is an important legacy publishing brand founded in 1925 that has published many impressive and long-lived books ever since.

Andrea Schulz, Editor in Chief. Mystery, literary fiction; narrative nonfiction.

Wendy Wolf, Associate Publisher. History, science, psychology, politics, culture, current affairs.

Paul Slovak, Executive Editor. High-end commercial fiction; cultural history, natural history.

Carole Desanti, Executive Editor. Literary fiction, commercial fiction; health, psychology.

Rick Kot, Executive Editor. Current affairs, science, business stories, history, arts/culture.

Joy de Menil, Executive Editor. History, international issues, economics, science.

Laura Tisdel, Executive Editor. Literary fiction; women's interest, parenting, memoir, narrative.

Allison Lorentzen, Executive Editor. Literary/upmarket fiction; pop culture, narratives.

Brian Tart, Publisher.

Lindsey Schwoeri, Senior Editor. Fiction; social issues, gender issues.
Kathryn Court, President. Fiction; memoir.

PENGUIN YOUNG READERS GROUP ❖ www.penguin.com/children
345 Hudson Street, New York, NY 10014

There are many vibrant historic imprints meshed here from both Penguin and Random House, and each of their antecedents.

Dial Books for Young Readers ❖ www.penguin.com/publishers/dialbooksforyoungreaders

Established in 1961, Dial is a busy hardcover program of books for preschool through young adult. They were an industry pioneer in the introduction of multicultural and specifically African American themes.

Lauri Hornik, Publisher.
Jessica Garrison, Senior Editor.
Kate Harrison, Executive Editor.
(Ms.) Namrata Tripathi, Editorial Director.
Lucia Monfried, Senior Editor.
(Ms.) Stacey Friedberg, Associate Editor.
Dana Chidiac, Associate Editor.
Ellen Cormier, Assistant Editor.

Dutton Children's Books ❖ www.penguin.com/publishers/duttonchildrensbooks

Dutton is the oldest continuously operating children's publisher in America. That may explain why Winnie the Pooh and his friends live here. Today, Dutton is a boutique middle grade/young adult imprint and publishes a relatively small list of new fiction titles.

Andrew Karre, Editor.

Grosset & Dunlap

GD tends to publish nonfiction paperback series for ages 0 to 12.

Renee Hooker, Editor.

Philomel Books ❖ www.penguin.com/publishers/philomel

Established in 1980, Philomel focuses on picture books for preschoolers, and fiction for middle grade through young adult. One of its specialties is attracting books written from or about other cultures.

Michael Green, Publisher.
Jill Santopolo, Executive Editor.
Liza Kaplan, Editor.
Talia Benamy, Assistant Editor.
Cheryl Eissing, Assistant Editor.

G. P. Putnam's Sons Books for Young Readers ❖ www.penguin.com/publishers/gpputnamssonsbooksforyoungread

This is one of the imprints blessed and/or burdened with a flagship moniker, in this case dating back to 1838. Today Putnam publishes about 50 new titles a year, all of which are hardcover fiction, from picture books to young adult.

Jennifer Besser, Publisher.
(Ms.) Stacey Barney, Executive Editor.
Arianne Lewin, Executive Editor.
Susan Kochan, Associate Editorial Director.
Stephanie Pitts, Editor.
Kate Meltzer, Associate Editor.
Amelia Frick, Editorial Assistant.

Razorbill ❖ www.penguin.com/publishers/razorbill

Publishes about 50 middle grade to young adult titles a year, both fiction and nonfiction. How many kids (or adults) know what a razorbill is? Part of the program's identity is to be a little more fringe or edgy.

Ben Schrank, Publisher.
(Ms.) Casey McIntyre, Associate Publisher.
Julie Rosenberg, Editor.
Marissa Grossman, Associate Editor.
Jessica Harriton, Assistant Editor.

Viking Children's Books ❖
www.penguin.com/publishers/vikingchildrensbooks

Established in 1933, Viking has a proud and rich history. Today, they publish about 60 fiction and nonfiction books a year for pre-readers to teenagers.

Kenneth Wright, Publisher.
Kendra Levin, Executive Editor.
Leila Sales, Editor.
(Ms.) Tracy Gates, Editor.
(Mr.) Alex Ulyett, Associate Editor.

SIMON & SCHUSTER ❖ www.simonandschuster.com

1230 Avenue of the Americas, New York, NY 10020, 212-698-7000

Simon & Schuster was founded in 1924 by Richard L. Simon and Lincoln Schuster. The firm was sold to Marshall Field (the man, not the store, though he also owned the store) in 1944 and was repurchased by its founders following Field's death in 1957. It was sold to Gulf+Western in 1975, which morphed into Paramount Communications in 1989. In 1994 Paramount was acquired by Viacom. In 2006, Simon & Schuster was split off from Viacom and made into a separate company, though still part and parcel of Viacom (it confuses me too). The corporate situation has been uneventful since then. As revealed below, S&S is both an imprint and an umbrella for several distinct programs with varying levels of independence, and there are semiautonomous imprints within the divisions.

Editors' email addresses for all Simon & Schuster imprints follow this format: firstname.lastname@simonandschuster.com.

ATRIA PUBLISHING GROUP ❖ www.atria-books.com

Atria (the plural of *atrium*) are centralized spaces open to Earth's natural elements. Considering I had to look that up even though I know everything about everything, chances are good that most people are as clueless as I was about what that name is supposed to make us feel. In fact, I thought S&S made up that name to sound fancy. Maybe if plebeian venues such as malls didn't have atria, the program would have been named Atrium; though clearly I digress. Atria was formed in 2002 by repackaging several of S&S's trade programs into a coherent universe of wide-ranging fiction and nonfiction subjects. Over time, several divisions have been germinated within Atria's garden(s).

Peter Borland, Editor in Chief. Commercial fiction; narrative nonfiction, memoir, biography, pop culture.

Johanna Castillo, Executive Editor. Fiction, including women's, thriller, historical; nonfiction, including inspirational, self-help, Spanish translation.

Sarah Cantin, Senior Editor. Fiction, including historical, suspense; nonfiction, including travel stories, pop culture, narrative.

(Ms.) Jhanteigh Kupihea, Senior Editor. Upmarket women's romance and psychological suspense; pop culture.

(Mr.) Rakesh Satyal, Senior Editor. Celebrity, pop culture, digital influencers, emerging trends.

Todd Hunter, Editor. Fiction, including political, suspense, mystery, thriller; African American topics.

Daniella Wexler, Editor. Literary and upmarket fiction; pop culture, psychology, humor.

Sarah Pelz, Executive Editor. Health, diet, wellness, self-help, relationships, parenting, spirituality, style, inspiration, memoir, cooking.

Haley Weaver, Assistant Editor. Literary fiction, suspense, women's fiction, LGBTQ fiction; pop culture.

(Ms.) Loan Le, Assistant Editor. Psychological thriller, historical fiction, women's fiction.

Melanie Perez, Assistant Editor. Pop culture, Latin interest, translations.

Sean Delone, Editorial Assistant. Mystery, suspense; current events.

Emily Bestler Books ❖ www.simonandschusterpublishing.com/emily-bestler

One way for an editor to reach the top, without starting their own company, is to get their own division named for them within the corporate matrix. Frankly, many veteran editors probably earn this honor, but only a few achieve it. It would simply be impractical to make it a routine event, and what is deserved often has little relation to what is given in any competitive enterprise. When an editor shows her- or himself to be a consistent earner and an above-average magnet for hot projects, and has formed powerful alliances within the firm, that person is eligible for their own imprint. And Ms. Bestler has certainly earned the honor in all respects.

Emily Bestler, Senior Vice President, Editor in Chief. Upmarket fiction and nonfiction.

Lara Jones, Assistant Editor. Mystery, thriller, suspense, women's fiction.

37 Ink

Fiction and nonfiction titles with African American themes.

Dawn Davis, Publisher.

Chelcee Johns, Editorial Assistant.

Enliven Books ❖ simonandschusterpublishing.com/enliven

Best described as a micro-boutique, this program focuses on nonfiction in the areas of inspiration, motivation, spirituality, health and wellness, and environmental issues.

(Ms.) Zhena Muzyka, Publisher at Large.

Howard Books ❖ simonandschusterpublishing.com/howard-books

216 Centerview Drive, Suite 303, Brentwood, TN 37027

S&S acquired this independent press in 2006 to gain a footprint in the vibrant Christian/faith-based publishing world and achieve membership in the Evangelical Christian Publishers Association. It's not by accident that the firm has been maintained in Tennessee, as opposed to being relocated to S&S's Manhattan headquarters. The program publishes a large list of theological, inspirational, and pop-culture titles in both fiction and nonfiction. Chelsea Handler's books wouldn't be found here. But *Duck Dynasty* titles thrive due to the Robertson family's frequent Christian-friendly references.

Philis Boultinghouse, Senior Editor. Celebrity-driven nonfiction inspirational books.
Beth Adams, Executive Editor. Inspirational fiction and nonfiction.
Becky Nesbitt, Editor at Large. Inspirational fiction and nonfiction.
Kristen O'Neal, Editorial Assistant. Faith-based fiction and nonfiction.

GALLERY BOOKS ❖ simonandschusterpublishing.com/gallery-books

This division was established from scratch in 2009. Its purpose is to be a distinct platform for publishing "fresh voices" (picture a gallery with pictures) in both fiction and nonfiction, with a clear focus on pop culture, entertainment, celebrities, and multimedia tie-ins, which makes sense considering that Viacom is a sister company.

Louise Burke, President and Publisher. Major projects.
Lauren McKenna, Executive Editor. Women's fiction, historical and contemporary romance; pop culture.
Alison Callahan, Executive Editor. "Ambitious" fiction; narrative nonfiction, memoir.
Jeremie Ruby-Strauss, Senior Editor. "Blockbuster nonfiction," celebrity, pop culture, diet/fitness, multimedia tie-ins.
Abby Zidle, Senior Editor. Romance, suspense, thriller, women's fiction, historical fiction; pop culture.
Ed Schlesinger, Senior Editor. "Dark" fiction, horror, science fiction, fantasy, crime fiction; media tie-ins.
Adam Wilson, Senior Editor. Supernatural, thriller, romance, urban fiction, fantasy; pop culture and inspirational narratives.
Marla Daniels, Editorial Assistant. Romance, women's fiction.
Natasha Simons, Editor. Upmarket horror and "women in jeopardy"; pop culture, online personalities, current events, lifestyle.
Kate Dresser, Editor. Women's fiction; self-help, pop culture.

Molly Gregory, Editorial Assistant. Women's fiction; pop culture, unique narrative.

Jackie Cantor, Senior Editor. Historical and contemporary women's fiction; personal memoir.

THRESHOLD EDITIONS ❖ thresholdeditions.com

This boutique imprint was created to publish books about conservative political concepts or by notable conservative pundits.

Mitchell Ivers, Editorial Director.

Natasha Simons, Editor.

Hannah Brown, Editorial Assistant.

NORTH STAR WAY ❖

North Star, formed in 2015, can be viewed as an innovative work in progress, or perhaps as an experiment with room to fail until it succeeds. The concept is that people who have an energetic social media footprint are competitively well positioned to support their own books. North Star endeavors to provide these highly qualified authors with a wide range of ancillary benefits that traditional publishers often neglect. The program is geared for a wide range of mass-market motivation/self-help/how-to topics.

Michele Martin, Publisher.

Diana Ventimiglia, Editor.

SCRIBNER ❖ www.simonandschusterpublishing.com/scribner

Scribner is one of the extra-holy names in American publishing. When it was founded in 1846 by Charles Scribner and Isaac Baker, the company had a religious orientation. Scribner's sons saw greener, secular pastures, and within a few decades the firm was arguably the number one publisher of nonreligious American literature — which explains why the name became Charles Scribner's Sons as opposed to "& Sons," I assume. The house also launched and managed its own bookstore chain, as New Yorkers over the age of 50 will fondly recall. The forensics for how Scribner became an S&S satellite is a little like tracing the mammalian food chain. In 1984 Macmillan ate Scribner. Several years later Paramount ate Macmillan. Gulf+Western ate Paramount, which then became Viacom, which ate CBS. The sons are long dead, so now it's simply Scribner. Without much notice, the corporate overlords might decide one day that Scribner is an unprofitable redundancy, and it will disappear. That's what happened to the Free Press several years ago. However, the Scribner name will most likely always be repurposed somewhere in the realm of publishing, because it's essentially immortal.

Colin Harrison, Editor in Chief. Current events, culture, politics, history, sports, science, true crime.

Rick Horgan, Executive Editor. Current events, thought-leader books, social issues, business, popular psychology, true crime.

Kathryn Belden, Executive Editor. Social/cultural history.

Daniel Loedel, Editor. Fiction; popular science.

Valerie Steiker, Executive Editor. Fiction; cooking, memoir.

Sarah Goldberg, Assistant Editor. Fiction; social/cultural history, popular science.

Sally Howe, Assistant Editor. Fiction; contemporary culture, mental health, race and gender issues.

SIMON & SCHUSTER ❖ simonandschusterpublishing.com/simonandschuster

In addition to being the iconic name of the entire house (mansion), Simon & Schuster is also the name of one of its distinct divisions. Due to the rash of mergers, contractions, and nervous breakdowns endemic to the book business, there are numerous editorial overlaps and shared facilities, and even some healthy competition, between the divisions within each of the corporate entities. The S&S imprint's specialness is marked by the fact that it is the carrier of the nearly century-old (1924) name and possesses an immense backlist with many of the best books ever published in the United States. In fairness, the same can be said for most of the legacy brands that have been permitted to remain attached to their historic catalogs. S&S's vibrant frontlist program can best be summed up as a wide spectrum of commercial fiction and nonfiction.

Alice Mayhew, Editorial Director. History, politics, biography, philosophy, entertainment, pop culture.

Marysue Rucci, Editor in Chief. Commercial fiction; narrative nonfiction.

Priscilla Painton, Executive Editor. Political biography, memoir, narrative, history, politics, science, religion, economics, US current events.

Trish Todd, Vice President and Executive Editor. Popular and literary fiction; practical nonfiction, lifestyle, psychology, humor.

Robert Bender, Executive Editor. History, current events, popular science, film, music, business narrative, investing, baseball.

(Mr.) Jofie Ferrari-Adler, Executive Editor. Fiction; politics, current affairs, history, military history, sports, narrative/investigative journalism, music.

Ben Loehnen, Executive Editor. Fiction; business, economics, psychology, science, nature, religion.
Karyn Marcus, Senior Editor. Upmarket suspense; popular science, social trends, animals, celebrity tie-ins.
Ira Silverberg, Senior Editor. Literary fiction; serious nonfiction.
Johanna Li, Associate Editor. Literary fiction; cultural history.
Emily Graff, Editor. Commercial and literary fiction; US history, current affairs, food.
Jonathan Cox, Editor. Literary fiction; philosophical narrative, science, nature, technology, politics.
Stuart Roberts, Associate Editor. History, current affairs, business, science, politics.
Julianna Haubner, Associate Editor. Literary fiction; investigative journalism.
Zack Knoll, Assistant Editor. Culinary/food, illustrated works.
Megan Hogan, Associate Editor. "Strange history," popular science, narrative.
Sean Manning, Senior Editor. Fiction; business, "cultural explorations."
Christine Pride, Senior Editor. Literary fiction; race, gender, and cultural issues.
Amar Deol, Associate Editor. True crime, current events, sports, music, politics.
(Ms.) Andurina Panezo, Editorial Assistant. Multicultural themes and voices.

TOUCHSTONE BOOKS ❖ www.simonandschusterpublishing.com/touchstone

Touchstone can best be described as a fusion catchall program combining frontlist original (fiction and nonfiction) titles and evergreen backlist cash cows. It's common for huge publishers to keep legacy brands alive, even if there's no unique purpose and substantial overlap with other imprints. You can never predict if new divisions will live or die, so bets are hedged through a process of cluttering clusters. Sometimes the new brands fail, and then the old brands become a welcome refuge for the surviving titles and editors, and vice versa.

Tara Parsons, Editor in Chief. Commercial fiction.
Lauren Spiegel, Senior Editor. Pop culture, humor, narrative.
Matthew Benjamin, Executive Editor. Narrative and prescriptive nonfiction, investigative journalism, self-help, diet/fitness, men's interest.
Kaitlin Olson, Assistant Editor. Suspense, women's fiction.
Trish Todd, Executive Editor. Fiction; psychology, self-help/how-to, lifestyle, humor.
Cara Bedick, Senior Editor. Health, wellness, diet, cooking, lifestyle, parenting, science.

SIMON & SCHUSTER CHILDREN'S PUBLISHING

S&S is especially noted for its large and wide-ranging children's program, which includes several distinct divisions/imprints.

Aladdin ❖ simonandschusterpublishing.com/aladdin

This dynamic imprint specializes in fiction and nonfiction picture books and chapter books for pre-readers to middle grade.

Liesa Abrams, Editorial Director. Fantasy and action-adventure stories.
Alyson Heller, Editor. "Tweens" themes and characters, multicultural themes.
Karen Nagel, Executive Editor. Picture and chapter books, "funny and inventive formats."
Amy Cloud, Editor. "Boy-centric" stories, humorous and "grounded fantasy."
Mara Anastas, Publisher.
Tricia Lin, Editorial Assistant. "Social exploration" and fantasy themes.

Atheneum Books for Young Readers ❖ simonandschusterpublishing.com/atheneum

Founded in 1961, AB publishes a full range of picture books, middle grade books, and teen titles. It has been a trendsetter in publishing books with multicultural and social themes.

Caitlyn Dlouhy, Editorial Director.
Richard Jackson, Editorial Director.
(Ms.) Reka Simonsen, Executive Editor. Middle grade novels that will "hook" kids into becoming avid readers.
Emma Ledbetter, Senior Editor. Picture books, chapter books, middle grade novels, humor.
(Ms.) Alex Borbolla, Assistant Editor. Quirky, irreverent picture books, serious young adult, humor.

Beach Lane Books ❖ simonandschusterpublishing.com/beach-lane

Founded in 2008, the program covers all ages and formats with a primary focus on "lyrical, emotionally engaging" picture books.

Allyn Johnston, Publisher.
Sarah Jane Abbott, Assistant Editor.
Andrea Welch, Executive Editor.

Little Simon ❖ simonandschusterpublishing.com/little-simon

Noted for innovative and attractive books for young children.

Jeffrey Salane, Editorial Director.
Hannah Lambert, Editor.
Valerie Garfield, Publisher.
Cindy Kim, Editorial Assistant.

Margaret K. McElderry Books ❖ simonandschusterpublishing.com/margaret-k-mcelderry-books

A boutique imprint formed in 1972 by its legendary namesake. Well respected for a full range of author- and character-driven works for all ages in all formats.

Karen Wojtyla, Editorial Director. "Attracted to works with strong dialogue, vivid settings and characters."
Annie Nybo, Assistant Editor.
(Ms.) Ruta Rimas, Senior Editor. "Books that challenge preconceived notions."

Paula Wiseman Books ❖ simonandschusterpublishing.com/paula-wiseman-books

This boutique program, founded in 2003, has published dozens of award-winning picture books, novelty books, and even novels. They prefer works that are "timeless and centered in emotion."

Paula Wiseman, Publisher.
Sylvie Frank, Editor.
Sarah Jane Abbott, Editorial Assistant.

Saga Press ❖ www.sagapress.com

Young adult science fiction, fantasy, urban and supernatural titles.

Joe Monti, Executive Editor.
(Ms.) Navah Wolfe, Editor.

Salaam Reads ❖ www.salaamreads.com

Founded in 2016, the program specifically publishes stories about Muslim children, families, and communities for readers of all faiths and backgrounds.

(Ms.) Zareen Jaffery, Executive Editor.

Simon Pulse ❖ www.simonandschusterpublishing.com/simonpulse

Boundary-pushing fiction for teenagers. Strives to be "daring and edgy."

Jennifer Ung, Editor.
Nicole Ellul, Editor.

Simon & Schuster Books for Young Readers ❖ www.simonandschusterpublishing.com/bfyr

Simon & Schuster is the name of one of its own children's divisions. It's a large program covering all ages and formats. As mentioned elsewhere, it's common for large houses to maintain multiple overlapping divisions. In most cases, the various imprints predated the corporate mergers by many decades, which is why the corporate name is also frequently one of the premier imprint names: it already existed for a long time.

David Gale, Editorial Director. Contemporary middle grade and teen fiction.
(Ms.) Zareen Jaffery, Executive Editor. Commercial and literary fiction for teens and middle grade; teen nonfiction.
Liz Kossnar, Editor. Contemporary young adult fiction.
Catherine Laudone, Assistant Editor. Contemporary young adult fiction. Middle grade fiction. Chapter books with series potential.
Krista Vitola, Senior Editor. Literary and commercial middle grade fiction.
Alexa Pastor, Associate Editor. Literary and commercial picture books.
Amanda Ramirez, Editorial Assistant. Diverse young adult and middle grade literature.
Alyza Liu, Editorial Assistant. Translated genre fiction with "postcolonial" themes.

Part 3
INDEPENDENT PRESSES

INTRODUCTION
PLANET INDEPENDENT

Jeff Herman

Here's the other half of publishing. Any publisher, no matter how large, that's not owned by one of the Big 5 corporate houses is by default an independent publisher. Some of them are micropublishers with revenues in the 4 figures, and some are huge with revenues into the 10 figures. See my introduction to the Big 5 section (page 77) for a fuller discussion about what separates the two categories.

In recent decades the world has become commercially globalized and homogenized. Most resources have been consolidated into efficient multinationals that overwhelm localized preferences and habits. Corporate conquest has disrupted all nations and people, and technology has been used as a soulless ally.

It only took a few years for dozens of once-vibrant mom-and-pop firms to either join the Big 5 or go out of business. The carnage has stopped, mostly because there isn't much left to grab. The few who managed to "hang in" have adjusted by becoming stronger and smarter. "Micro-mergers and acquisitions" and service-sharing arrangements are the strategies that have enabled many to survive. Creating better products, combined with intelligent financing, can also make a difference. However, the birth rate of new independent publishers is a far cry from days gone by.

Which Publishers Are and Aren't Listed Here?

I am solely responsible for selecting the houses in this section. I chose them on the basis of their recent history, proven sustainability, and confirmation they are legitimate traditional publishers, as opposed to fancy self-publishers or deceptive predators. I avoided the multitude of kitchen-table micropublishers because there's no way to discern their competence. I skipped academic and professional association publishers because relatively few people have the highly specialized skill sets and professional résumés those programs require. Finally, I left out Canadian publishers for the simple reason that they're not allowed to publish original books written by non-Canadians. The Canadians are less restricted when licensing the rights to books initially published elsewhere, which is of no help to anyone who hasn't yet been published in the US.

What Advantages Do Independent Houses Offer Compared to the Big 5?

Let's begin by saying that most independent houses are able to do everything the corporate houses do in terms of marketing, quality production, editing, sales, and distribution. It's unusual for the bestseller lists not to include a decent number of independently published books.

The primary advantage is that the vast majority of independent publishers are actually owned and operated by a select group of human beings, not 20,000 shareholders. Decisions are made on the basis of people's hearts and guts, not technical modalities. There are far fewer obstacles to risk taking, and authors are less likely to get lost in the bureaucracy. For these and other reasons, independent publishers tend to be more creative, innovative, and risk-tolerant — and a lot more fun to work with.

Importantly, independent houses are much more likely to objectively consider submissions that are unagented/unsolicited simply because they don't receive nearly as many agented submissions as the Big 5.

What Are the Disadvantages?

Frankly, I feel they are minimal. The primary disadvantage is that the Big 5 can and do pay large advances. The irony is that in practice this rarely happens. In fact, most Big 5 advances are on par with what the independents pay for comparable titles. More importantly, I'm not aware of any evidence showing a difference in total earnings (advance plus royalties) over a book's lifetime between corporate and independent houses for comparable titles. Nor am I aware of any evidence that the Big 5 sell more copies on average over a book's lifetime than the independents do for comparable titles.

Agents definitely prefer selling books to the Big 5 because the potential for a larger advance is always there, and each of the Big 5 acquires many, many more books than most of the independents can afford to.

Keep in mind that typical John Grisham, Stephen King, Danielle Steel, etc., fans neither know nor care who the publishers are. Readers are only focused on the author, not his or her publisher. They also care about price, and perhaps what vendors they spend money with. Only industry insiders pay attention to who someone's publisher is. No writer should ever feel second-class because they are with a relatively obscure publisher. It's not a step down and might even be a step up considering the extra attention indie books often receive. As I said above, it's common for the bestseller lists to be populated by more than a few independently published titles. You probably don't know that because, like most people, you don't care, which further proves the point.

Independent publishing is one of the crucial safety nets against the industry's possible intellectual and creative suffocation. Current economic realities mandate the existence of multinational corporate empires. Naturally, these huge entities are no more or less enlightened than governments. The individuals who work for them surely have the best of intentions, but they're handcuffed by corporate mandates.

It's plausible that 10 years from now 90 percent of the book business will be controlled by three entities. In that case, the remaining 10 percent, and those whom they publish, will be on the front lines in a war against corporate conformity and control. Approach this section with the wisdom that independent publishing is both a practical option and a philosophical mission.

THE LISTINGS

ABC-CLIO ❖ www.abc-clio.com
130 Cremona Drive, Santa Barbara, CA 93117, 805-968-1911

This company is over 50 years old, and I don't know what all the letters actually stand for, which probably doesn't matter. However, they publish an impressive list of reference and academic books for educators and students in all age ranges, covering many subjects. Their products are organized within several imprints and subsidiaries, some of which were formerly independent presses before being acquired by ABC.

Praeger ❖ www.abc-clio.com/praeger.aspx

Praeger appears to be the most "submission-friendly" of the ABC-CLIO imprints. It focuses on academic books about psychology, education, health, politics, current events, history, military issues, business, and religion.

Hilary Claggett, Senior Editor; hclaggett@abc-clio.com.

ABINGDON PRESS ❖ www.abingdonpress.com
201 Eighth Avenue South, Nashville, TN 37202, 800-251-3320

Founded in 1789, Abingdon is the official publisher of the United Methodist Church. As would be expected, it publishes a wide range of faith-, inspiration-, and curriculum-based books, including fiction. Its fiction program includes contemporary and historical romances, suspense, mystery, and Amish themes. The program prides itself on publishing a diversity of religious opinions.

Constance Stella, Senior Acquisitions Editor; cstella@abingdonpress.com.
David Teel, Editor; dteel@abingdonpress.com.

ABRAMS ❖ www.abramsbooks.com
195 Broadway, New York, NY 10007, 212-206-7715

Beginning in 1949, Abrams was the first US-based publisher to specialize in art and illustrated books, commonly referred to as *coffee-table books*. The firm continues that tradition in many areas, including cooking, crafts, comics, gardening, and interior design. But that's not all. It has a vigorous children's program and publishes nonillustrated books about culture, science, current events, and history. And some fiction.

Editors' email addresses follow this format: firstinitiallastname@abramsbooks.com.

Holly Dolce, Editorial Director. Cooking/food, decorating.
David Cashion, Executive Editor. Fiction; current events, film, pop culture.
Garrett McGrath, Associate Editor. Travel, cooking/food, photography.
Michael Sand, Publisher. Illustrated books about art, cooking.
Karrie Witkin, Director, Gift and Paper Products.
Shawna Mullen, Associate Publisher. Crafts, how-to, design.
Rebecca Kaplan, Senior Editor. Lifestyle.
Jamison Stoltz, Executive Editor. Film, art history, culture, food, popular science.

Abrams Books for Young Readers

Picture books, illustrated nonfiction for preschool through young adult, and graphic novels.

(Ms.) Tamar Brazis, Editorial Director.
Erica Finkel, Editor.
Howard Reeves, Editor at Large.
Anne Heltzel, Editor.
Maggie Lehrman, Executive Editor.

AKASHIC BOOKS ❖ www.akashicbooks.com
232 Third Street, Suite A115, Brooklyn, NY 11215, 718-643-9193

Dedicated to publishing urban-themed literary fiction and political nonfiction by writers whom the establishment has "ignored" or refused to publish.

Ibrahim Ahmad, Editorial Director; info@akashicbooks.com.

AMACOM BOOKS ❖ www.amacombooks.org

In early 2018, this publisher announced the sale of its assets, which basically means its catalog, to HarperCollins, where it will become part of a new division still in formation, Harper Leadership. It doesn't appear that the brand, AMACOM, will remain in use.

AMERICAN ACADEMY OF PEDIATRICS ❖ www.aap.org

Division of Consumer Publishing, 345 Park Boulevard, Itasca, IL 60143, 800-433-9016

This program was created to provide quality educational information for parents and caregivers on a wide variety of health issues.

Submissions should be directed to newpubs@aap.org.

ANDREWS MCMEEL PUBLISHING ❖ www.andrewsmcmeel.com

1130 Walnut Street, Kansas City, MO 64106, 816-581-7500

AM was founded in 1970 and originally named Universal Press Syndicate. The firm became extremely successful at syndicating a huge roster of illustrators, cartoonists, and columnists to an archaic physical-content delivery vehicle referred to as "newspapers." The book program was founded as an organic way to repurpose its talented clients. The firm is also famous for its calendar and gift book programs. In recent years, the frontlist program has been downsized to a tight list of mostly cookbooks, gift books, calendars, and cards, with some lifestyle, pop culture, humor, and middle grade fiction titles.

Editors' email addresses follow this format: firstinitiallastname@amuniversal.com.

Patty Rice, Editor. Humor, gift, health, illustrated gift books.
(Ms.) Jean Lucas, Editor. Illustrated cookbooks, lifestyle.
Michael Nonbello, Creative Director of Calendars and Greeting Cards.
Kristy Melville, President of Book Division.
Allison Adler, Editor. Pop culture, illustrated books, humor.

ARTE PÚBLICO PRESS ❖ www.artepublicopress.com

4902 Gulf Freeway, Building 19, Room 100, Houston, TX 77204, 713-743-2843

This is the most established publisher of books by US-based Hispanic writers in fiction, nonfiction, and children's categories.

Writers are requested to submit projects electronically using the Submission Form available on their website (artepublicopress.com/manuscript-submissions-form), and to send any questions to submapp@uh.edu.

BAEN BOOKS ❖ www.baen.com

PO Box 1188, Wake Forest, NC 27588

Baen is a veteran independent publisher of quality science fiction and fantasy books. The good news is that they actually welcome unsolicited manuscripts for acquisition consideration. However, they don't want it to be a particularly personal process where authors get to interact with real people — not a unique preference. The best method is to visit their website and follow the stated submission protocol.

BAKER PUBLISHING GROUP ❖ www.bakerpublishinggroup.com

6030 East Fulton Road, Ada, MI 49301, 616-676-9185

Baker claims to publish books that represent historic Christianity and the diverse interests of evangelical readers. The firm was founded in 1924 by a recent Dutch immigrant, Herman Baker, and became a thriving enterprise. Today's Baker comprises several imprints, most of which have their own storied histories.

Editors' email addresses follow this format: firstinitiallastname@bakerbooks.com.

Baker Books ❖ www.bakerpublishinggroup.com/bakerbooks

Baker publishes a large list of Christ-centered nonfiction self-help and reference books for laity and clergy.

The publisher requests that writers follow the submission protocol provided on their website.

Bethany House ❖ www.bakerpublishinggroup.com/bethanyhouse

Bethany began more than 50 years ago and is a leader in inspirational fiction, including romance and suspense. Its nonfiction program includes Christian living, theology, and "eternity."

Kim Bangs, Editor.

Revell ❖ www.bakerpublishinggroup.com/revell

Revell has been publishing Christian books for more than 125 years. Subjects include inspirational and educational fiction, self-help, marriage/family issues, and youth books.

Andrea Doering, Editor.
Kelsey Bowen, Editor.
Vicky Crumpton, Editor.

BEACON PRESS ❖ www.beacon.org
24 Farnsworth Street, Boston, MA 02210, 617-742-2110

Beacon has been a breath of independent air since 1854. It currently publishes books that seem to be about causes, social conditions, theories, and events that have affected, or are affecting, our lives. Women's and environmental subjects are welcome. Health-care issues receive a lot of attention. Although it would be unfair to say that the firm has any political or social agendas, it's clear that many of their books wouldn't be welcome by the Far Right or fundamental-religious communities.

Editors' email addresses follow this format: firstinitiallastname@beacon.org.

Helen Atwan, Director. Public health and legal issues.
Amy Caldwell, Executive Editor. Religion from a cultural and historical perspective, science and society, women's studies.
(Ms.) Gayatri Patnaik, Editorial Director. African American issues and history, LGBT issues, alternative views of American history.
Joanna Green, Senior Editor. Social justice, environmental, economic, and judicial issues.
(Ms.) Rakia Clark, Senior Editor. Social issues, media, criminal justice.
Rachael Marks, Editor. Educational issues.
Will Myers, Editor. Environmental sustainability issues.

BENBELLA BOOKS ❖ www.benbellabooks.com
10300 North Central Expressway, Suite 530, Dallas, TX 75231, 214-750-3600

BenBella is a successful, independent, entrepreneurial, outside-the-NYC-box boutique publisher. They tend to publish commercial self-help nonfiction books on timely subjects or by writers with self-marketing skill sets. They also publish narratives and true crime.

Glenn Yeffeth, Publisher; glenn@benbellabooks.com.

BERRETT-KOEHLER PUBLISHERS ❖ www.bkconnection.com

1333 Broadway, Suite 1000, Oakland, CA 94612, 510-817-2272

This successful West Coast independent press publishes an eclectic and interesting list of business-oriented books that large publishers might pass over for the wrong reasons. Their books are practical and traditional, and author "platforms" are of course critical. If the late Abbie Hoffman had written a real self-help business book, this is one of the venues he might have seriously considered.

Neal Maillet, Editorial Director; nmaillet@bkpub.com.

BEYOND WORDS PUBLISHING ❖ www.beyondword.com

20827 NW Cornell Road, Suite 55, Hillsboro, OR 97124, 503-531-8700

Beyond Words has actually been a division of Simon & Schuster for many years. However, their origins are independent, and their current editorial process appears to be separate from that of their corporate overlord, so I've made an executive decision to list them as independent. If you've heard of *The Secret*, you'll understand what this boutique player is capable of accomplishing; it's plausible that the New York publishing matrix would have reflexively rejected that book with comments like "trite" or "too downmarket." BW tends to publish books that are generally designated as mind-body-spirit.

Richard Cohn, Publisher; richard@beyondword.com.

BLOOMSBURY PUBLISHING ❖ www.bloomsbury.com/us

1385 Broadway, New York, NY 10018, 212-419-5300

Founded in 1986, Bloomsbury qualifies as a multinational independent press with active English-language programs in England, Australia, and India. They publish a varied list of mostly narrative nonfiction books that most sentient beings would be impressed by, even if not inclined to read. They also publish cookbooks, children's books, and literary fiction. It's possible that many Bloomsbury books would be rejected by corporate houses as "noncommercial" or too academic. Fortunately, the big players are often wrong about what books readers will indeed buy when given the chance.

Editors' email addresses follow this format: firstname.lastname@bloomsbury.com.

Anton Mueller, Executive Editor. Current affairs, politics, film/media.
Nancy Miller, Editorial Director. Social and cultural issues.

Lea Beresford, Senior Editor. Fiction and nonfiction.
Sarah Shumway, Senior Editor. Children's publishing program.
Liese Mayer, Editorial Director. Fiction.
Callie Garnett, Editor. Fiction; memoir.
Ben Hyman, Senior Editor. True crime, political history, social issues.

CENTRAL RECOVERY PRESS ❖ www.centralrecoverypress.com

321 North Buffalo Drive, Suite 275, Las Vegas, NV 89129, 702-868-5830

This publisher specializes in books about addiction recovery, behavioral therapies, and general wellness. I'm surprised the casinos don't run them out of town. But then again, it makes sense to have a place to refer "clients" to after they lose their shirts.

Nancy Schenck, Executive Editor; nschenck@centralrecoverypress.com.
Vallery Killeen, Editor; vkilleen@centralrecoverypress.com.

CHELSEA GREEN PUBLISHING ❖ www.chelseagreen.com

85 North Main Street, Suite 120, White River Junction, VT 05001, 802-295-6300

Founded in 1984 (which, prior to 1984, seemed like it would be an important year), Chelsea is a top-notch publisher of books about sustainable/green living, which can be summarized as "consumption minus destruction." What makes CG especially unique is that it's entirely employee owned.

Editors' email addresses follow this format: firstinitiallastname@chelseagreen.com.

Joni Praded, Senior Editor. Environmental issues.
Ben Watson, Senior Editor. Organic gardening and agriculture, natural science.
Michael Metivier, Associate Editor. Landscaping.
Fern Bradley, Senior Editor. Farming, gardening, community action.
Brianne Goodspeed, Senior Editor.
(Ms.) Makenna Goodman, Senior Editor. Food, integrative medicine.

CHICAGO REVIEW PRESS ❖ www.chicagoreviewpress.com

814 North Franklin Street, Chicago, IL 60610, 312-337-0747

The press was founded in 1973, has nearly 1,000 titles in print, and owns five distinct imprints. Subjects include crafts, film, food, history, music, parenting, pop culture, popular science, sports, travel, women's interest, and children's books.

Editors' email addresses follow this format: firstinitiallastname@chicagoreviewpress.com.

Cynthia Sherry, Publisher. Nonfiction children's books, travel, popular science, progressive politics, gardening.
Jerome Pohlen, Senior Editor. History, gardening, education, popular science, young adult nonfiction, landscaping.
(Mr.) Yuval Taylor, Senior Editor. Music, film, history, civil rights history.
Lisa Reardon, Senior Editor. Children's and young adult nonfiction, parenting, feminism.

CHRONICLE BOOKS ❖ www.chroniclebooks.com

680 Second Street, San Francisco, CA 94107, 415-537-4200

Chronicle claims to have been born on the day that paper was invented in the year 105 CE, even though there's no record of the firm's existence prior to 1967 CE. The nature of their claim accurately reflects Chronicle's irreverent publishing personality. Here you will find a delightful array of cleverly packaged and designed theme-oriented books/products for children, adults, and anyone who likes things that are silly and/or useful. Many of their books are quite useful in such arcane areas as how to survive an apocalypse.

I was recently reprimanded (gently) by a pileup (not that many) of their editors for publishing their names and direct email addresses. They greatly prefer for writers to follow the protocols dictated (suggested) on their website (www.chroniclebooks.com/submissions).

CLEIS PRESS / VIVA EDITIONS ❖ www.cleispress.com / www.vivaeditions.com

101 Hudson Street, Suite 3705, Jersey City, NJ 07302, 646-257-4343

This publisher could also be named Over-the-Top Press. Cleis outs itself as "the largest sexuality and queer publisher in America." But their catalog seems to have something for everyone and even offers a lot of books that aren't about orgasms. Viva appears to be a home for nonsexual books about lifestyles and relationships.

Hanna Bennett, Editor; acquisitions@vivaeditions.com.

COFFEE HOUSE PRESS ❖ www.coffeehousepress.org

79 Thirteenth Avenue NE, #110, Minneapolis, MN 55413, 612-338-0125

I'm very happy that there's a publisher with this perky name. Coffee House is a nonprofit company, something many publishers would never admit to. They publish books, poetry included, that their editors deem to be genuine works of art. Guess what? There's a market for that. More specifically, they publish short story collections, essay collections, and memoir.

(Mr.) Chris Fischbach, Publisher; fish@coffeehousepress.org.

THE COUNTRYMAN PRESS ❖ www.countrymanpress.com

500 Fifth Avenue, New York, NY 10110, 212-354-5500

Countryman has a long and distinguished history as an independent publisher of books devoted to healthy lifestyles, nature, travel, self-sufficiency, pets, and animals. The firm is now owned by W. W. Norton and shares their offices. But their mission and independence still thrive, so I made an executive decision to list them separately.

Ann Triestman, Editorial Director; atriestman@wwnorton.com.

DeVORSS & COMPANY ❖ www.devorss.com

PO Box 1389, Camarillo, CA 93011

Since 1929, DeVorss has been publishing books about metaphysics, spirituality, and New Thought concepts, which can also be captioned as mind-body-spirit. The company also distributes and markets titles published by others that are in harmony with its own catalog. The house appears to be affiliated with the Unity Church, which provides an organized blending of Eastern and Western spiritual concepts and belief systems.

Editorial@devorss.com

WM. B. EERDMANS PUBLISHING CO. ❖ www.eerdmans.com
2140 Oak Industrial Drive NE, Grand Rapids, MI 49505, 616-459-4591

Founded in 1911, Eerdmans is an independent publisher of Christian books ranging from academics to theology, Bible studies, and religious history and reference. The founder's motto still holds true: *The finest in religious literature.* The firm prides itself on publishing objective viewpoints throughout the "Christian spectrum" without favoring any single Christian perspective. They also have a Young Readers program.

I recommend that writers follow the submission guidelines provided on the website (www.eerdmans.com/pages/about/submission-guidelines.aspx).

ENTREPRENEUR PRESS ❖ entrepreneurmedia.com/books
18061 Fitch, Irvine, CA 92614, 949-622-7106

Entrepreneur Press is a division of the popular magazine named *Entrepreneur*. As would be expected, they publish books about zoology and proctology. That was a test to see if anyone actually reads what I break my finger bones writing. Per their website, their books "aim to provide actionable solutions to help entrepreneurs excel in all ventures they take on." In fact, they generate a rich assortment of cutting-edge how-to/self-help and reference books for anyone in business, even if not self-employed.

Jennifer Dorsey, Editor; jdorsey@entrepreneur.com.

EUROPA EDITIONS ❖ www.europaeditions.com
214 West 29th Street, Suite 1003, New York, NY 10001, 212-868-6844

Europa is an independent publisher of literary fiction, nonfiction, and "high-end crime" fiction. Founded in 2005, the firm specializes in bringing some of Europe's best books to American readers, and vice versa. Authors from several dozen nations, including the US, are published by Europa. It's safe to assume that the firm favors books by Americans that will have international appeal and relevance.

Editors' email addresses follow this format: firstnamelastname@europaeditions.com.

Michael Reynolds, Editor in Chief.
Kent Carroll, Publisher at Large.
Eva Ferri, Acquiring Editor of Foreign Fiction.

THE EXPERIMENT PUBLISHING COMPANY ❖
www.theexperimentpublishing.com

220 East 23rd Street, #301, New York, NY 10010, 212-889-1659

This is a relatively young boutique, specializing in health, lifestyle, and wellness. I sense that it's currently a moving target in terms of ownership, but I'm confident that the catalog and the firm's special flavor will settle somewhere prior to press time.

Editors' email addresses follow this format: firstnamefirstletteroflastname@theexperimentpublishing.com.

Jennifer Kurdyla, Editor.
Matthew Lore, Publisher.
Anna Bliss, Editor in Chief.
(Ms.) Batya Rosenblum, Editor.

FANTAGRAPHICS BOOKS ❖ www.fantagraphics.com

7563 Lake City Way NE, Seattle, WA 98115, 206-524-1967

Since 1976, Fantagraphics has published cartoon/comic artists — likely several of your favorites — and that tradition prevails to the present day.

Gary Groth, Editor; fbicomix@fantagraphics.com.

GRAYWOLF PRESS ❖ www.graywolfpress.org

250 Third Avenue North, Suite 600, Minneapolis, MN 55401, 651-641-0077

Graywolf is committed to "discovering and energetically publishing" contemporary American and international literature (fiction and nonfiction). They "champion writers in all stages of their careers" and look for "diverse voices." In other words, this is a not-for-profit publisher that won't let potential lack of sales dissuade them from publishing what they deem to be great books. However, in practice, because their catalog is known to be carefully curated by exceptionally astute people, anything they publish is immediately considered to be wonderful by a core community of devoted readers; which is a little like running for mayor of New York City once you get the Democratic nomination. Of course, it's a subjective process, but like-minded communities are by definition homogeneously subjective.

Ethan Nosowsky, Editorial Director; nosowsky@graywolfpress.org.

GROVE ATLANTIC ❖ www.groveatlantic.com
154 West 14th Street, New York, NY 10011, 212-614-7850

"An independent literary publisher since 1917." Several formerly independent programs coexist under this revered umbrella, though they appear to share the same editorial team. Grove is respected for their "curated" quality catalog. They publish a wide range of fiction and nonfiction categories. Corporate houses would quickly dismiss many books published here due to a commercially risk-averse culture.

Editors' email addresses follow this format: firstinitiallastname@groveatlantic.com.

Amy Hundley, Senior Editor. Fiction and nonfiction.
Peter Blackstock, Senior Editor. Fiction.
Joan Bingham, Executive Editor. Fiction and nonfiction.
Elisabeth Schmitz, Editorial Director. Fiction and nonfiction.
Zachary Pace, Assistant Editor. Nonfiction.
George Gibson, Executive Editor. American history, current affairs/events, culture, science.
Corinna Barsan, Senior Editor. Fiction and nonfiction.
Allison Malecha, Associate Editor. Fiction.

Grove Press

Grove was founded in 1947 in America's bohemian heartland (at that time), Greenwich Village, and quickly made a name for itself by publishing numerous bad boys who used foul language, practiced unorthodox sexual methodologies, liked to induce hallucinations, and even tended to compulsively "typewrite" (meant as a cutting criticism at the time). Much ground has been covered along the road since then. In 1993 Grove and Atlantic Monthly Press merged their DNA to become a perfectly respectful and self-supporting publisher of wide-ranging fiction and nonfiction works that tend to have intriguing titles by authors with exotic or sensuous names, which you'll definitely want to read in the absence of noise or other enticements for nimble brains and bodies.

Atlantic Monthly Press

The only obvious distinction (in these times) between the Atlantic and Grove imprints is that Atlantic publishes only hardcover books, whereas Grove also publishes paperback originals and reprints. Atlantic was formerly owned by the literary-culture magazine *Atlantic Monthly*.

The Mysterious Press ❖ www.mysteriouspress.com

Here you will find hardcore noir and adrenaline stimulation, both the old-time classics and new titles by those who dare to attempt following in their footsteps.

HARVEST HOUSE ❖ www.harvesthousepublishers.com

PO Box 41210, Eugene, OR 97404, 800-547-8979

From the publisher's mission statement: "To glorify God by providing high-quality books and products that affirm biblical values…and proclaim Jesus Christ as the answer to every human need." Since 1974, this nondenominational Christian press has published a large list of practical and accessible self-help books for adults and children about how to confront life's challenges in Christian ways. They also publish inspirational fiction.

Kyle Hatfield, Editor; kyle.hatfield@harvesthousepublishers.com.
Terry Glaspey, Editor; terry.glaspey@harvesthousepublishers.com

HAY HOUSE ❖ www.hayhouse.com

PO Box 5100, Carlsbad, CA 92018, 760-431-7695

Hay House is a pacesetter in the mind-body-spirit book categories. Many of the most financially successful self-help gurus are published by Hay House (not to be confused with their subsidy/vanity division, Balboa Press). They publish a diversity of nonfiction titles relevant to self-improvement with spiritual or metaphysical slants. They also publish kindred nonbook merchandise.

Editors' email addresses follow this format: firstinitiallastname@hayhouse.com.

Patty Gift, Director of Acquisitions.
Anne Bartel, Editor.
Sally Mason-Swaab, Editor.

HAZELDEN PUBLISHING ❖
www.hazelden.org/web/public/publishing.page

PO Box 176, Editorial Department, RW-15, Center City, MN 55012, 651-213-4213

Hazelden's stated mission is to help people recognize, understand, and overcome addiction and related problems and challenges. This is the in-house publishing arm of one of the most respected and pioneering recovery facilities in the world. Their books are consistent with the proverbial 12-step approach.

Vanessa Torrado, Editor for Consumer Books; vtorrado@hazelden.org.

HEALTH COMMUNICATIONS, INC. ❖ www.hcibooks.com

3201 SW 15th Street, Deerfield Beach, FL 33442, 945-360-0909

"Changing lives one book at a time" (from publisher's website), HCI claims to select books that help readers achieve abundance, consolation, and healing through a huge range of self-help subjects for adults and teens. HCI enjoyed many years in the sun publishing the *Chicken Soup for the Soul* series.

Allison Janse, Editor; ajanse@hcibooks.com.

HOUGHTON MIFFLIN HARCOURT ❖ www.hmhco.com/hmh-books

125 High Street, Boston, MA 02110, 617-351-5000
3 Park Avenue, New York, NY 10016, 212-420-5800

HMH is an amalgamation of several revered houses with deep American roots (200+ years, according to its website). It qualifies as one of the largest independent firms, as opposed to a corporate firm, because its owners only publish books — a wide commercial list of fiction and nonfiction for adults and children.

Editors' email addresses follow this format: firstname.lastname@hmhco.com.

(Mr.) Alex Littlefield, Senior Editor (NY). Current affairs, social history.
Justin Schwartz, Executive Editor (NY). Cookbooks, food, lifestyle.
Susan Canavan, Senior Executive Editor (MA). Sports history, contemporary history.
Bruce Nichols, Publisher (NY). Political history, current events, health issues, popular psychology and science.
Lauren Wein, Executive Editor (NY). Fiction, thriller.
Deanne Urmy, Senior Executive Editor (MA). Politics, current affairs, health, women's interest.
Rick Wolff, Senior Executive Editor (NY). Business, sports.
Naomi Gibbs, Editor (NY). Mystery, general fiction; popular science, memoir/narrative.
Helen Atsma, Editorial Director (NY). Fiction.

Stephanie Fletcher, Editor (MA). Cooking.
Deb Brody, Editor in Chief (NY). Lifestyle, healthful living, advice.
Pila Garcia-Brown, Editor (NY). Fiction, thriller.
Jenny Xu, Editor (NY). Fiction.
Eamon Dolan, Editorial Director, Eamon Dolan Books (NY). American history, military history, social issues, current affairs/events.
(Ms.) Rux Martin, Editorial Director, Rux Martin Books (MA). Cooking.

HOUGHTON MIFFLIN HARCOURT CHILDREN'S

Picture books, middle grade through young adult.

Margaret Raymo, Senior Executive Editor (MA).
Ann Rider, Executive Editor (MA). All areas plus fantasy.
Kate O'Sullivan, Senior Editor (MA). Picture books.

Clarion

Dinah Stevenson, Editor at Large (NY).
Lynne Polvino, Editor (NY). Picture books.
Anne Hoppe, Associate Publisher (NY). All areas plus fantasy.
Jennifer Greene, Editor (NY). Picture Books.

HUMAN KINETICS PUBLISHERS, INC. ❖ www.humankinetics.com

PO Box 5076, Champaign, IL 61825, 800-747-4457

HK is a well-established publisher of books, journals, and educational content relevant to health, physical education, sport sciences, recreation, and dance. Founded in 1973, "Human Kinetics leads the world in providing information relevant to physical activity" (from their website).

acquisitions@hkusa.com

INNER TRADITIONS / BEAR & COMPANY ❖ www.innertraditions.com

PO Box 388, Rochester, VT 05767, 802-767-3174

For more than 30 years, these two firms, recently merged, have published a rich list of books about ancient mysteries, Celtic studies, Eastern religions, healing arts, martial arts, Tantra, tarot, and many related subjects.

Jon Graham, Editor; jon@innertraditions.com.

KENSINGTON PUBLISHING ❖ www.kensingtonbooks.com

119 West 40th Street, New York, NY 10018, 800-221-2647

Founded in 1974, Kensington is one of the largest independent publishing houses in the US today, best known for its dense lists of category/genre mass-market fiction and some nonfiction, all divided into several imprints.

Editors' email addresses follow this format: firstinitiallastname@kensingtonbooks.com.

Dafina

African American–themed romance titles.

Selena James, Executive Editor.

Kensington

Kensington covers the whole waterfront of category commercial fiction; some self-help and popular-psychology nonfiction; and true crime.

John Scognamiglio, Editor in Chief. Mystery, crime, historical romance, gay fiction.
Alicia Condon, Editorial Director. Sexy romance, Amish/inspirational romance.
(Ms.) Esi Sogah, Editor. Romance, American historical.
Michaela Hamilton, Executive Editor. Mystery, thriller, science fiction; true crime, pets, pop culture, military history.
Martin Biro, Editor. Romance, mystery, science fiction.
Wendy McCurdy, Editorial Director. Women's categories, suspense, intrigue, paranormal, erotica.
Tara Gavin, Executive Editor. Romance, historical, multicultural.

Denise Silvestro, Executive Editor. Nonfiction, including health/wellness, relationships, parenting, lifestyle, pop culture.

Elizabeth May, Assistant Editor. Romance, women's, mystery.

LIVERIGHT ❖ books.wwnorton.com/books/affiliatecontent.aspx?id=24633

500 Fifth Avenue, New York, NY 10110, 212-354-5500

Liveright is presently owned by Norton and shares its facilities, including a dedicated parking spot in Norton's website. But I chose to give it a distinct listing to keep it from being passed over. Founded in 1917 as Boni & Liveright, this was the home of Faulkner, Freud, Hemingway, and many other literary icons (at least some of the time). Its current purpose seems to be publishing original fiction and nonfiction in the areas of history, politics, current events, memoir, and narrative.

Robert Weil, Executive Editor; rweil@wwnorton.com.

Katie Adams, Senior Editor; kadams@wwnorton.com.

LLEWELLYN WORLDWIDE ❖ www.llewellyn.com

2143 Wooddale Drive, Woodbury, MN 55125, 651-291-1970

Founded in 1901, Llewellyn is one of the largest independent mind-body-spirit publishers. Per their website, their mission is "to be the world's leading provider of works for personal growth and the transformation of Body, Mind and Spirit." Specific topics include Wiccan, New Age, metaphysics, wellness, and kindred nonbook products.

Angela Wix, Editor; angelaw@llewellyn.com.

MANIC D PRESS ❖ www.manicdpress.com

Box 410804, San Francisco, CA 94141, 415-648-8288

I'm sorry, but I'm at a loss for how to reflect what this publisher is about, but I'll give it my best shot. If you wrote a heavily illustrated book, fiction or nonfiction, that June Cleaver, Donna Reed, or Ted Cruz would consider unacceptably perverse, then you have found a possible home.

mss@manicdpress.com

MCGRAW-HILL PROFESSIONAL ❖ www.mhprofessional.com

2 Penn Plaza, 9th Floor, New York, NY 10121, 212-904-2000

McGraw-Hill is a large international media corporation. Because their trade book program is relatively small and focused, similar to a boutique, it makes sense to include them as an "indie." The McGraw-Hill brand has a long and deep history as a top publisher of all varieties of books. But for many years the firm has focused strictly on publishing high-quality business books in areas such as finance, personal investing, management, entrepreneurship, and technology.

Editors' email addresses follow this format: firstname_lastname@mcgraw-hill.com.

Donya Dickerson, Editorial Director. All business categories.
Noah Schwartzberg, Editor. Investing, management, human resources, real estate.
(Ms.) Casey Ebro, Senior Editor. Self-improvement/career skills, leadership, marketing.
Cheryl Ringer, Editor. Business self-help, leadership, marketing, careers.

MILKWEED EDITIONS ❖ www.milkweed.org

1011 Washington Avenue South, Suite 300, Minneapolis, MN 55415, 612-332-3192

Founded in 1980, Milkweed calls itself an independent publisher of literature and proclaims that its purpose is to "identify, nurture, and publish transformative literature [poetry, fiction and nonfiction, and young adult], and build an engaged community around it." The company depends on donations in addition to revenues for its survival. Having that safety net obviously enables its editors to be extra-risky and not entirely beholden to traditional profit-and-loss protocols.

Daniel Slager, Publisher; daniel_slager@milkweed.org.

NATIONAL GEOGRAPHIC BOOKS ❖
www.nationalgeographic.com/books

1145 17th Street NW, Washington, DC 20036, 202-857-7359

This is the book-publishing arm of the prestigious organization with the same name. Any subject you might see in the magazine is eligible for the book program.

Lisa Thomas, Editorial Director; lithomas@ngs.org.

NAVAL INSTITUTE PRESS ❖ www.usni.org/store/books

291 Wood Road, Annapolis, MD 21402, 410-268-6110

Per its website: "An independent forum for those who dare to read, think, speak, and write to advance the professional, literary, and scientific understanding of sea power and other issues critical to global security." In spite of its name and location, this nonprofit organization receives no public funding; nor is it affiliated with the Naval Academy or Department of Defense. The firm is most famous for discovering and publishing works of mass-market military fiction by a new writer named Tom Clancy.

Richard Latture, Editor in Chief; rlatture@usni.org.

NEW DIRECTIONS ❖ www.ndbooks.com

80 Eighth Avenue, New York, NY 10010

An independent publisher dedicated to experimental literature, influential translations, and avant-garde poetry. I took all that from the website. So what does it mean? Well, you could view their catalog, but here's my spin: quality stuff written for people with the focus to do deep-dive reading, thanks to their cherished days as English PhD candidates somewhere in the Great Lakes region. Disclosure: I'm prone to stereotyping. For instance, I envision beards (only on the men).

Barbara Epler, Editor in Chief; bepler@ndbooks.com.

NEW HARBINGER PUBLICATIONS ❖ www.newharbinger.com

5674 Shattuck Avenue, Oakland, CA 94609, 800-748-6273

New Harbinger prides itself on generating a primo catalog of scientifically sound yet cutting-edge self-help books in many areas of physical, mental, and spiritual health and personal growth. The press is proud of publishing books that many mental-health and other health professionals use and refer patients to.

Editors' email addresses follow this format: firstname@newharbinger.com.

Elizabeth Hollis Hansen, Editor. Mental health and treatment programs.
Jess O'Brien, Editor. Psychology, parenting.
Wendy Millstine, Editor. Parenting, yoga, health and wellness, spiritual themes.

NEW HORIZON PRESS ❖ www.newhorizonpressbooks.com

PO Box 669, Far Hills, NJ 07931, 908-604-6311

NHP focuses on true crime, "battles for justice," medical drama, incredible true stories, women's and men's interest, and parenting. Many of its books are optioned for TV and film.

JoAnne C. Thomas, Editor; jct@newhorizonpressbooks.com.

THE NEW PRESS ❖ www.thenewpress.com

120 Wall Street, 31st Floor, New York, NY 10005, 212-629-8802

Founded in 1992, The New Press publishes serious "activist" books that promote a better understanding of vital domestic and international issues that mainstream commercial houses aren't modeled to deal with. They can afford to do this because they are a nonprofit subsidized by private-sector donors (I don't know who). I feel it's safe to say that most of their books would be considered left of center both politically and socially, though they don't appear to be aligned with any specific parties or organizations.

Marc Favreau, Executive Editor; mfavreau@thenewpress.com.

NEW WORLD LIBRARY ❖ www.newworldlibrary.com

14 Pamaron Way, Novato, CA 94949, 415-884-2100

In 1977, at a kitchen table, Whatever Publishing was born. The firm quickly prospered, and within a few years its name was changed to something a little more serious sounding, per the above. Today it's an eight-figure enterprise. The firm publishes about three dozen new titles each year in the areas of personal consciousness, personal growth, self-help, creativity, prosperity, philosophy, spirituality, wellness, animals, nature/environment, and many related subjects — even book publishing.

Georgia Hughes, Editorial Director; georgia@newworldlibrary.com.
Jason Gardner, Executive Editor; jason@newworldlibrary.com.

W. W. NORTON & COMPANY, INC. ❖ www.wwnorton.com

500 Fifth Avenue, New York, NY 10110, 212-354-5500

What began in someone's living room more than 90 years ago has become the largest publishing company owned entirely by its employees. That sounds like a kibbutz, though I'm sure there's an economic/political hierarchy. The firm strives to publish books about influential issues and events that cross into all conceivable areas of human endeavor and discovery. If the Public Broadcasting System had a book division, Norton might be it. They also publish a respected fiction list.

Editors' email addresses follow this format: firstinitiallastname@wwnorton.com.

Matt Weiland, Senior Editor. Popular science, political issues, cultural history.
John Glusman, Editor in Chief. Popular science, contemporary social issues, cultural and military history.
Brendan Curry, Senior Editor. Current events, social issues, popular science.
Jill Bialosky, Senior Editor. Fiction; health, social issues, women's interest, memoir.
Tom Mayer, Senior Editor. Politics, current events, business narrative.
Alane Mason, Executive Editor. Cultural, social, and political history.
Amy Cherry, Senior Editor. Social history, African American history and culture, gender issues, personal narrative.
(Ms.) Quynh Do, Editor. Popular science, Asian philosophy.

NO STARCH PRESS ❖ www.nostarch.com

245 8th Street, San Francisco, CA 94103, 415-863-9900

No Starch claims to be "the finest in geek entertainment." Maybe you know what that means better than I. They have an excellent list of books about all areas of computing that appear to be both entertaining and educational. They also have a lot of books about games, LEGO, science, and math.

Editors' email addresses follow this format: firstname@nostarch.com

Tyler Ortman, Senior Editor.
Liz Chadwick, Editor.
Jan Cash, Associate Editor.
Annie Choi, Associate Editor.

THE OVERLOOK PRESS ❖ www.overlookpress.com

141 Wooster Street, New York, NY 10012, 212-673-2526

Founded in 1971, Overlook successfully publishes a large, eclectic list of fiction and non fiction titles in such areas as history and culture.

Peter Mayer, Publisher; pmayer@overlookny.com.

PAULIST PRESS ❖ www.paulistpress.com

997 Macarthur Boulevard, Mahwah, NJ 07430, 800-218-1903

According to its website, Paulist "publishes the best in Catholic thought since 1972." The company is part of the Paulist Fathers and strives to bring Catholic-based education, wisdom, healing, growth, and inspiration to all peoples.

Rev. Mark-David Janus, CSP, Editorial Director; submissions@paulistpress.com.

PEACHTREE PUBLISHERS ❖ www.peachtree-online.com

1700 Chattahoochee Avenue, Atlanta, GA 30318, 404-876-8761

Since 1977 Peachtree has published quality children's books, from picture books to young adult fiction and nonfiction. In adult categories they publish titles about parenting, health, and anything about the American South.

Kathy Landwehr, Associate Publisher; klandwehr@peachtree-online.com.

PEGASUS BOOKS ❖ www.pegasusbooks.com

148 West 37th Street, 13th Floor, New York, NY 10018, 646-343-9501

Pegasus publishes a wide-ranging list including history, philosophy, culture, and fiction.

Editors' email addresses follow this format: firstname@pegasusbooks.us.

Jessica Case, Associate Publisher. Upmarket crime and suspense fiction; history, popular science, culture.
Katie McGuire, Assistant Editor. Historical fiction and mystery.
(Mr.) Bowen Dunnan, Editorial Assistant. Historical fiction and mystery.
(Mr.) Claiborne Hancock, Editor in Chief.

INDEPENDENT PRESSES

PELICAN PUBLISHING COMPANY ❖ www.pelicanpub.com

1000 Burmaster Street, Gretna, LA 70053, 504-368-1175

Pelican is best known for travel guides, architectural reviews, holiday-themed books, specialized cookbooks, some fiction, and children's books. As might be expected, many of its titles are relevant to the Gulf Coast. In fact, surviving natural disasters, not to mention the economy, has often been the company's greatest challenge. Founded in 1926, the firm has a backlist catalog of more than 2,500 titles and is one of the largest independently owned houses in the South.

Nina Kooij, Editor in Chief; editorial@pelicanpub.com.

THE PERMANENT PRESS ❖ www.thepermanentpress.com

4170 Noyac Road, Sag Harbor, NY 11963, 631-725-1101

Since 1978, this micropublisher has sustained itself by publishing literary fiction, and some nonfiction, that serious readers can't ignore. Near zero capitalization has never been a worthy excuse for failure in the book business, for the simple reason that quality will outlast all the hype that money can buy. The key has always been patience and the ability to resist making risky expenditures. During times of easy credit it's only too easy to overspend and overborrow, which is why so many worthy independent presses ultimately disappear. We should all pay attention to why some small presses, like this one, prevail.

Editors' email addresses follow this format: firstname@thepermanentpress.com.

Martin Shepard, Co-Publisher.
Judith Shepard, Co-Publisher.
Chris Knopf, Co-Publisher.

PROMETHEUS BOOKS ❖ www.prometheusbooks.com

59 John Glenn Drive, Amherst, NY 14228, 716-691-0133

Prometheus defines itself as a leading publisher of popular science, philosophy, humanism, psychology, and perhaps any other topic you can think of. In actuality, this is a somewhat controversial publisher that tends to publish deliberately confrontational and provocative content. For instance, if you want to challenge organized religion, New Age concepts, or unproven alternative-health protocols, this might be your home. The house can't be nailed down as politically left-wing or right-wing. They simply seem to like material that's supported by logic and hard science, as opposed to emotions, sentimentality, or wishful thinking.

Steven Mitchell, Editor; smitchell@prometheusbooks.com.

QUARTO PUBLISHING GROUP ❖ www.quartoknows.com
100 Cummings Center, Beverly, MA 01915, 800-328-0590

This was a tough house for me to get my head around because it seems to exist in tiny pieces spread wide and far. But many of its pieces have long and deep histories in specific areas. Quarto is showing one of the ways that an independent publisher can establish deep roots and broad lists without becoming overextended. Though there are many imprints, each with a focused mission, Fair Winds and Harvard Common Press are the only programs I was able to track recent acquisition activity for on the basis of my research. But that doesn't mean the other programs are inert. Indeed, they might be very robust.

Fair Winds Press ❖ www.quartoknows.com/Fair-Winds-Press

Since 2001, this confident firm has handsomely packaged books about fitness, special diets, parenting, sex, and a wide range of other self-help/how-to categories.

Editors' email addresses follow this format: firstname.lastname@quarto.com.

Jess Haberman, Acquisitions Editor.
Jill Alexander, Executive Editor.
Amanda Waddell, Editor.

Harvard Common Press ❖ www.quartoknows.com/Harvard-Common-Press
535 Albany Street, Boston, MA 02118, 617-423-5803

This well-established independent press was acquired by the Quarto Group in early 2016. The company has never had anything to do with Harvard but is named for Harvard Common, which is an actual place that anyone can name their company after without permission. Since 1976, the company has been a successful producer of high-quality and uniquely positioned food books and cookbooks. They are also noted for their excellent taste in parenting and childbirth titles.

editorial@harvardcommonpress.com

QUIRK BOOKS ❖ www.quirkbooks.com

215 Church Street, Philadelphia, PA 19106, 215-627-3581

In view of their name, it would be appalling for any of their books to be ordinary, not to mention dull. Quirk's website welcomes "off-the-wall" novels; "playful" cooking, lifestyle, and craft books; and "cool photography or crazy illustrations." Most of their books have high production value, meaning they are meant to be seen and touched, not just read. They have a strong children's program and also publish nonbook merchandise.

Editors' email addresses follow this format: firstname@quirkbooks.com.

Jason Rekulak, Publisher.
Rick Chillot, Editor.
(Ms.) Blair Thornburgh, Editor.

RED WHEEL ❖ www.redwheelweiser.com

65 Parker Street, Newburyport, MA 01950, 978-465-0504

What we have here is a synergistic consolidation of several legacy brands. The respective imprints publish in a wide range of mind-body-spirit categories, including metaphysics, alternative health, yoga, relationships, and practical business/entrepreneurship. The Weiser imprint seems to have a tighter focus on the occult, esoteric philosophies, and the "old" religions. Conari Press has a strong footprint in women's interest. Hampton Roads seems to have a solid handle on New Age and fringe concepts and unorthodox spirituality. The recently acquired Career Press brings a strong history of practical books for small businesses and entrepreneurs. The various programs seem to be geographically spread out, with the above address serving as the administrative home base.

Editors' email addresses follow this format: firstinitiallastname@rwwbooks.com.

Peter Turner, Associate Publisher.
Michael Pye, Associate Publisher, Career Press division.
Christine LeBlond, Senior Acquisitions Editor.
Greg Brandenburgh, Associate Publisher.

REGNERY PUBLISHING, INC. ❖ www.regnery.com

300 New Jersey Avenue NW, Washington, DC 20001, 202-216-0600

Fidel Castro will never be a Regnery author (doesn't help that he's dead). Neither will Hillary Clinton. But their names are frequently referenced in unflattering ways in many of Regnery's books. Without going to the blatant extremes of fascism, this is where right-wingers are at home, and more than a few of them have landed on the *New York Times* bestseller list. Regnery publishes political narratives/memoirs, and toothy exposés about public figures and issues that tend to be controversial.

Editors' email addresses follow this format: firstinitiallastname@eaglepub.com.

(Mr.) Alex Novak, Associate Publisher.
Marji Ross, Publisher.
Harry Crocker, Executive Editor.
Tom Spence, Editor.
Gary Terashita, Editor. Regnery Faith division.

ROWMAN & LITTLEFIELD ❖ www.rowman.com

4501 Forbes Boulevard, Lanham, MD 20706, 301-459-3366
5360 Manhattan Circle, Boulder, CO 80303, 303-543-7835
200 Park Avenue South, Suite 1109, New York, NY 10003, 212-529-3888

In recent years, Rowman has accumulated an impressive portfolio of independent presses with strong positions in their respective professional and academic communities (including Globe Pequot and Lyons Press). Under its own name, Rowman publishes a huge list of nonfiction titles for scholars and consumers in the humanities and social sciences.

Editors' email addresses follow this format: firstinitiallastname@rowman.com.

Susan McEachern, Editorial Director (CO). International studies, geography, history, regional studies.
Suzanne Staszak-Silva, Executive Editor (NY). Health, psychology, sexuality, food studies, military life studies, criminal justice, crime studies, careers, small business, technology.
Marie-Claire Antoine, Senior Acquisitions Editor (NY). Security, terrorism, intelligence, diplomacy, Middle Eastern and African politics.
Sarah Stanton, Senior Acquisitions Editor (CO). Sociology, religion, criminology.

Leanne Silverman, Acquisitions Editor (CO). Anthropology, archaeology, communications.

Tom Koerner, Publisher (MD). Educational market.

Charles Harmon, Executive Editor (CO). Library/information sciences, museum studies.

Jonathan Sisk, Senior Executive Editor (MD). American government, US history.

Stephen Ryan, Senior Acquisitions Editor (MD). Arts, entertainment, pop culture for adult and young adult markets.

Christen Karniski, Editor (CO). Sports.

Kathryn Knigge, Editor (MD). Military life, green living, criminal justice, true crime.

Globe Pequot ❖ www.globepequot.com
246 Goose Lane, Guilford, CT 06437, 203-458-4500

Specializes in regional travel guides throughout the US, books of regional interest and regional history, and popular reference. Books about animals and parenting also seem to have some traction here.

Rick Rinehart, Editor (MD). Travel, pop culture, history, film.

Holly Rubino, Senior Editor (CT). Pets, animals, lifestyle.

Gene Brissie, Editor (CT). American history, current events, military stories.

SASQUATCH BOOKS ❖ www.sasquatchbooks.com
1904 Third Avenue, Suite 710, Seattle, WA 98101, 206-467-4300

Sasquatch is known for its innovative and eclectic list of nonfiction books about food and wine, travel, lifestyle, gardening, and nature. Many of its books are relevant to the Pacific Northwest region.

Hannah Elnan, Senior Editor; helnan@sasquatchbooks.com.

SCHOLASTIC INC. ❖ www.scholastic.com
557 Broadway, New York, NY 10012, 212-343-6100

Scholastic is the largest publisher of children's and young adult books and educational products in the world. They publish for both consumer distribution and classroom adoption.

Editors' email addresses follow this format: firstinitiallastname@scholastic.com.

Aimee Friedman, Editorial Director.
Jody Corbett, Senior Editor.
David Levithan, Publisher.
Orli Zuravicky, Senior Editor.
Mallory Kaas, Editor.
Lisa Sandell, Executive Editor.
Amanda Maciel, Executive Editor.

Arthur A. Levine Books ❖ www.arthuralevinebooks.com

This boutique imprint was created by Mr. Levine in 1996. They are highly respected for the production and editorial quality of the books they publish.

Arthur Levine, Editorial Director; alevine@scholastic.com.

SEVEN STORIES PRESS ❖ www.sevenstories.com

140 Watts Street, New York, NY 10013, 212-226-8760

Founded in 1995, Seven Stories was named for the seven original authors who took a leap of faith to be published by this untested start-up. In the nonfiction zone, SS is proud of its large list of political and social-advocacy books. In fiction, the house has been a champion for new voices.

Dan Simon, Publisher; dansimon@sevenstories.com.

SHAMBHALA PUBLICATIONS ❖ www.shambhala.com

4720 Walnut Street, Boulder, CO 80301, 888-424-2329

This house was conceived during the hippie sixties in San Francisco by a group of devout Mormons who ingested LSD that had been inserted into a batch of Big Macs as part of a CIA experiment. Well, the San Francisco part is true, anyway. To sum it up, this is a successful publisher of books that are compatible with Eastern philosophies, esoteric philosophy, yoga, martial arts, natural health, crafts, creativity, and green living.

Beth Frankl, Editor; bfrankl@shambhala.com.

SKYHORSE PUBLISHING ❖ www.skyhorsepublishing.com

307 West 36th Street, 11th Floor, New York, NY 10018, 212-643-6816

Skyhorse is a gutsy horse, in that they entered independent publishing when many others were leaving (that is, in 2006). Their founder had the requisite experience and connections to survive, expand, and thrive as an independent publisher. Their eclectic list includes history, politics, rural living, sports, health, humor, hobbies, self-help, conspiracy theories, and even some fiction.

Editors' email addresses follow this format: firstinitiallastname@skyhorsepublishing.com.

Nicole Frail, Editor. Romance, young adult fiction; relationships, lifestyle, popular reference, pets, parenting.
Joseph Craig, Editor. Social issues, history, true crime.
Leah Zarra, Editor. Cooking, yoga, health, diet, lifestyle.
Kim Lim, Editor. Women's interest, advice, parenting.
Alexandra Hess, Editor. Mystery/crime fiction; current issues, culture, film.
Michael Campbell, Editor. True crime, self-help, how-to.
Veronica Alvarado, Editor. Animals, sports, nature.

SMITHSONIAN BOOKS ❖ www.smithsonianbooks.com

600 Maryland Avenue SW, Suite 6001, Washington, DC 20024, 202-633-6012

SB publishes a variety of nonfiction titles, many of which are illustrated, about the kinds of subjects relevant to the museum's amazing exhibits, such as American history, technology, culture, science, and space/aviation.

Carolyn Gleason, Director; cgleason@si.edu.

SOHO PRESS ❖ www.sohopress.com

853 Broadway, New York, NY 10003, 212-260-1900

Soho endeavors to publish bold new literary voices, international crime fiction, and young adult fiction. Most of their books are fiction, with the occasional memoir or narrative.

Editors' email addresses follow this format: firstinitiallastname@sohopress.com.

Mark Doten, Executive Editor.
Juliet Grames, Associate Publisher.
(Ms.) Amara Hoshijo, Editor.

SOUNDS TRUE, INC. ❖ www.soundstrue.com

413 South Arthur Avenue, Louisville, CO 80027, 800-333-9185

ST was founded in 1985. "To disseminate spiritual wisdom" is their stated mission. Audio was its only format for many years, which explains the firm's name. The company grew and thrived, and successfully entered the traditional print fray in 2005. Its most popular categories include health, inspiration, meditation, music, self-empowerment, spirituality, and yoga.

Editors' email addresses follow this format: firstnamefirstletteroflastname@soundstrue.com.

Caroline Pincus, Editor at Large.
Jennifer Y. Brown, Acquisitions Editor.
(Ms.) Jaime Schwalb, Editor.

SOURCEBOOKS ❖ www.sourcebooks.com

1935 Brookdale Road, Naperville, IL 60563, 630-961-3900
232 Madison Avenue, Suite 1100, New York, NY 10018, 212-414-1701
18 Cherry Street, Milford, CT 06460, 203-876-9790

Launched in 1987, Sourcebooks has managed to become one of the most dynamic and fastest-growing independent presses in the country. They have been a little ahead of the curve by acquiring even smaller presses with proven niches and by discovering authors with preexisting marketing and sales connections and corporate tie-ins. Sourcebooks has not been coy about helping to discover the digital future. They are especially strong in children's and romance categories and have a large footprint in all areas of nonfiction, including gift books and calendars. Basically, this is a risk-tolerant publisher that knows how to see and follow the money.

Editors' email addresses follow this format: firstname.lastname@sourcebooks.com.

Deb Werksman, Editorial Director (CT). Romance (all categories), women's fiction.
Mary Altman, Editor (NY). Romance (all categories).
Cat Clyne, Editor (NY). Romance, women's fiction, erotica.
Shana Drehs, Editorial Director (IL). Women's and historical fiction; women's interest, parenting, relationships, self-help, pop culture, gift items, inspiration.
Steve Geck, Editorial Director (NY). Children's book programs.
Todd Stocke, Editorial Director (IL). Books that include impressive multimedia applications and author platforms.

Anna Michels, Senior Editor. Literary fiction, mystery, thriller; practical and prescriptive nonfiction, gift books, inspiration, humor, quirky history.

Grace Menary-Winefield, Associate Editor (NY). Adult fiction; quirky self-help, weird history.

Annette Pollert-Morgan, Editorial Manager (NY). Books for teens and young adults.

Meg Gibbons, Editor (IL). Popular business, motivation, self-help, inspiration.

SQUARE ONE PUBLISHERS, INC. ❖ www.squareonepublishers.com

115 Herricks Road, Garden City Park, NY 11040, 516-535-2010

SQ1 was founded in 2000 by veteran publishing innovator Rudy Shur. Most of his titles are self-help- or how-to-oriented by experts in their respective fields, with a strong emphasis on alternative health and lifestyle titles. But there's also an assortment of general fiction and nonfiction titles, as well as cookbooks. As with most independent publishers, acquisitions often depend on the editor's heart and intuition, as opposed to mere statistics. Actually, statistics would suggest that most small presses shouldn't even exist.

Rudy Shur, Founder and Publisher; sq1info@aol.com.

THAMES & HUDSON ❖ www.thamesandhudson.com

500 Fifth Avenue, 6th Floor, New York, NY 10110

Though now owned by Norton, the house continues to maintain its 70-year tradition as a publisher of illustrated books on art, architecture, design, photography, fashion, and travel.

Roger Thorp, Editor; rthorp@thames.wwnorton.com.

TIN HOUSE BOOKS ❖ www.tinhouse.com

2617 NW Thurman Street, Portland, OR 97210, 503-473-8663

Tin House Books follows the same tradition as the company's much-loved magazine of the same name, which is to carefully curate an eclectic list of fiction and nonfiction, as well as some poetry. The firm isn't averse to introducing new voices. It seems that their primary criterion is the depth and uniqueness of the writing. This isn't where you'll find a how-to book about salesmanship, but you might discover the next Kerouac.

Editors' email addresses follow this format: firstname@tinhouse.com.

Thomas Ross, Assistant Editor.
Michelle Wildgen, Executive Editor.
Masie Cochran, Editor.
Emma Komlos-Hrobsky, Associate Editor.

TURNER PUBLISHING COMPANY ❖ www.turnerpublishing.com

424 Church Street, Suite 2240, Nashville, TN 37219, 615-255-2665

It may sound like a cliché, but Turner (no relation to Ted) is one to watch. While many large and small presses are standing still or withering away, Turner is quickly expanding. Though fast growth is often the kiss of death in any business, digital technology has become publishing's great equalizer, because content doesn't have to be solely printed and physically managed, and the content generators (authors) provide outsourced, low-cost labor. Turner recently grabbed a lot of attention by purchasing the rights to several thousand general nonfiction titles that Wiley no longer wanted to carry. With a single signature, Turner became a midsize publisher that few insiders were familiar with, yet. They appear to be on the prowl for all kinds of nonfiction and fiction titles, though specific subject preferences may become clearer in the near future.

Stephanie Beard, Editor; sbeard@turnerpublishing.com.

TYNDALE HOUSE PUBLISHERS, INC. ❖ www.tyndale.com

351 Executive Drive, Carol Stream, IL 60188, 800-323-9400

Stated purpose: "Minister to the needs of people through literature consistent with biblical principles." They publish a wide list of Christian-based fiction, nonfiction, and children's books. Many of the top names in Christian publishing are Tyndale authors. Their most famous (some might say infamous) and successful program was the *Left Behind* fiction series.

Jon Farrar, Acquisitions Director; jonfarrar@tyndale.com.

ULYSSES PRESS ❖ www.ulyssespress.com

PO Box 3440, Berkeley, CA 94703, 510-601-8301

The firm seems to be publishing something for every nonfiction category you can think of, so it's difficult, if not impossible, to clearly define what they won't consider. One overriding attribute is made evident by viewing their catalog: every book seems to have a clear title and is for a well-focused market.

(Ms.) Casie Vogel, Editor; casievogel@ulyssespress.com.

VERSO BOOKS ❖ www.versobooks.com
20 Jay Street, Suite 1010, Brooklyn, NY 11201, 718-246-8160

Long story short, Verso publishes the kinds of books that Bernie Sanders reads and that Paul Ryan does not.

Andrew Hsiao, Editor; submissions@versobooks.com.

WILEY ❖ www.wiley.com
111 River Street, Hoboken, NJ 07030, 201-748-6000

Though Wiley isn't listed as one of the corporate houses, it is an international billion-dollar content generator. In recent years, the firm seems to have been selling off its consumer trade book assets and focusing more on the high-ticket professional and academic markets. Many of its $100+ books have such arcane titles and content that I could never accurately paraphrase what they are about. However, Wiley is still publishing a large list of trade books in the areas of finance, banking, marketing, investing, and general business. A compelling side note: Wiley family members have been actively engaged in the operation since the company's foundation more than 200 years ago.

Unless otherwise specified, editors' email addresses follow this format: firstinitiallastname@wiley.com.

Richard Narramore, Senior Editor; richard.narramore@wiley.com. General business subjects with strong author platforms.
(Ms.) Shannon Vargo, Editor. General practical business subjects.
Bill Falloon, Executive Editor. Investing and personal finance.
(Mr.) Sheck Cho, Executive Editor. Technology.
Matt Holt, Editorial Director. General business.

WORKMAN PUBLISHING COMPANY ❖ www.workman.com

225 Varick Street, New York, NY 10014, 212-254-5900

Workman has been a bold independent innovator since 1968. Its clever calendars, humor titles, and gift/illustrated products have always profitably complemented its traditional books. The company has frequently excelled at capturing an inordinate measure of market share in cluttered categories. This is especially true for its *What to Expect* pregnancy and parenting series. Workman's books run the full gamut of nonfiction categories and children's books; for them the key seems to be how to differentiate what they publish in the eyes of the consumer. Ordinary isn't their model. Workman has acquired several excellent programs, listed below, which have been allowed to maintain their distinctive cultures and locations.

Editors' email addresses follow this format: firstname@workman.com.

Megan Nicolay, Editor. Cooking, crafts, hobbies, humor, illustrated.
Suzie Bolotin, Editor in Chief. Interesting nonfiction titles.
Maisie Tivnan, Editor. Yoga, health, parenting, how-to.
Margot Herrera, Senior Editor. Health, women's interest, parenting.
Kylie Foxx McDonald, Editor. Food, cookbooks.
Samantha O'Brien, Associate Editor. Nonfiction.
Mary Ellen O'Neill, Senior Editor. Parenting, humor, self-help.

Artisan ❖ www.workman.com/imprints/artisan

Artisan specializes in publishing nicely packaged and illustrated books about fashion, decorating, food, dining, and cooking.

Judy Pray, Executive Editor.
Lia Ronnen, Publisher.

Algonquin Books ❖ www.algonquin.com

PO Box 2225, Chapel Hill, NC 27515

This formerly independent publisher has been allowed to maintain its special fingerprints since being acquired by Workman many years ago. And they still hold to their stated mission to "publish quality fiction and nonfiction by undiscovered writers." Many of their books have a distinct Southern feel and flavor. They also publish children's books.

Unless otherwise specified, Algonquin editors' email addresses follow this format: firstname@algonquin.com.

Amy Gash, Executive Editor; amyg@algonquin.com. Memoir, narrative, popular psychology, sports, social issues.

Chuck Adams, Executive Editor. Fiction.

Betsy Gleick, Editor. Fiction.

Kathy Pories, Executive Editor. Fiction.

Elise Howard, Publisher, Algonquin Young Readers.

Krestyna Lypen, Editor, Algonquin Young Readers.

Storey Publishing ❖ www.storey.com

210 Mass MoCA Way, North Adams, MA 01247, 413-346-2100

Storey's stated mission is to publish "practical information that encourages personal independence in harmony with the environment." This publisher may have been ahead of its time and is now clearly on time, since many of its books are dedicated to all aspects of sustainable/green living. They also publish an excellent assortment of books about small farming, pet care, crafts, gardening, and nature.

Deborah Balmuth, Publisher; deborah.balmuth@storey.com.

Part 4
LITERARY AGENTS

INTRODUCTION
PLANET LITERARY AGENT

Jeff Herman

Here are the listings for 104 literary agencies and 176 individual agents, most of whom provide the information you need to make intelligent choices about whom to pitch and how to do it.

Who Is and Isn't Listed in This Edition?

To the best of my knowledge, only qualified agents are included. Please let me know if you disagree (jeff@jeffherman.com). I invited more agents than are here and would have gladly included most of them, but to be included, agents must respond to my survey, even if they only list name and website, and many did not. Some agents are at full capacity and don't want to receive unsolicited submissions, and I didn't make adequate contact with everyone I tried to. As you know or soon will, spam filters and unfriendly agency mailboxes can be impenetrable. By the way, I received more than a few boilerplate rejection letters from agents in response to my invitation to include them in this book.

Bottom line: I can confidently say that at least 98 percent of the agents in this section are legitimate. But just because someone isn't here doesn't mean they aren't a real agent.

What's a "Fee-Charging" Agent?

I hope there are no reading-fee agents in this listing. If there are, it's because they conned me, and you need to let me know (jeff@jeffherman.com). A legitimate agent shouldn't charge for the simple purpose of considering your work for representation. Anyone who does is probably not really an agent, which means they never actually sell anything to legitimate publishers.

Think about this: I receive several hundred unsolicited queries each month, as do many of my peers. If I converted a fraction of them into check-stuffed envelopes and PayPal credits, I'd have a nice revenue stream and wouldn't have to rely on commissions. Real agents don't make money from reading your work; they make it from successfully selling your work to a traditional publisher for a 15 percent commission. However, there are a few acceptable exceptions to this rule. A small number of legitimate agents request a modest fee (less than $100) in order to defray the cost of employing people to do first reads. I have included one or two of them because their policies are transparent, they have genuine track records, and you can easily bypass them.

THE LISTINGS

ANDREA BROWN LITERARY AGENCY, INC. ❖ www.andreabrownlit.com

Agents: President: Andrea Brown; Executive Agent: Laura Rennert; Senior Agents: Caryn Wiseman, Jennifer Laughran, Jennifer Rofé, Kelly Sonnack; Jamie Weiss Chilton; Agents: Jennifer Mattson, Kathleen Rushall; Associate Agents: Laura Perkins, Jennifer March Soloway

What would you be doing right now if not responding to this survey? Reading a client manuscript.

What would you be if not an agent (other than a dog, cat, or other mammal)? We truly love what we do, but if we had to choose something else, it would be something related to children's books: editing, publishing, bookselling, etc.

Do you think independent (noncorporate) publishing will be stronger, weaker, or the same over the next few years? We've been very impressed with many of the smaller presses, who have found ways to shine in the market. We hope to see them grow even stronger in the next few years.

Please describe your professional history. The Andrea Brown Literary Agency was founded in August 1981 and has offices in the San Francisco Bay Area, San Diego, Los Angeles, New York, and Chicago. Our agency specializes in children's literature. We work to bring light to the voices and perspectives of new writers as well as nurture and develop the careers of experienced authors. Our goal, whether seeking to secure a publishing contract for a first book or a fiftieth book, is to make sure our clients are not only published but published well.

Our agents have backgrounds in New York publishing, editing, academia, business, teaching, marketing, public relations, writing, and film, and one of our strengths as an agency is that we work collaboratively. Our clients have the benefit not only of their individual agent's expertise but of the combined experience and vision of the group.

How would you define the "client from hell"? Thankfully, we don't have any clients from hell.

Do you think Earth was created a few thousand years ago or several billion years ago? Several billion.

Please list five books you recently agented. We have 11 agents and have many fantastic books we love, including award winners and debuts, and it would be too difficult to choose only five. Please refer to our website for a list of our recent deal highlights.

Please describe the kinds of books you want to agent. All categories of children's books, both fiction and nonfiction, in a wide range of genres and subjects. We are actively seeking well-written stories, and we'd love to hear from fresh new voices and perspectives under-represented in literature. To learn more about our individual tastes and wish lists, please refer to the agents page of our website, www.andreabrownlit.com.

What should writers submit for consideration, and how should they send it? Per our submission guidelines, a query should include a query letter and the first 10 pages of the manuscript or the complete text of a picture book project copied into the body of the email. Please, no attachments, except for illustrations (in JPEG format) or picture-book dummies (in PDF format).

Do you think there are too many, too few, or just enough agents? There seem to be many agents right now — perhaps more than the market can bear — but the market has a way of self-adjusting.

Do you think Amazon will become the country's largest employer within 10 years? It's a possibility. Or maybe we'll all end up working for Elon Musk someday.

Why do you think some books become super-successful (beyond the obvious reasons)? Sometimes it's simply the right book at the right time, offering a story that fulfills a common need in readers.

Do you think agents are likely to become millionaires? Anything's possible, but it's definitely not the norm.

Do you think agents tend toward certain personality types? Thankfully, there are many different agent types to match the many different writer and illustrator types.

Do you think writers tend to be more or less narcissistic than the population at large? No more than the rest of us. Plus, they usually have a valuable inner critic that tends to keep their ego in check.

Knowing what you know now, would you become an agent again? In a heartbeat!

Why did you choose to become an agent? All of us love literature, and we love writers. We understand that writing is a passion, an intensely personal calling, and a longtime dream for many, and we hope to help make the dream of publication possible. We have great respect for authors, and we share the writer's passion — that is why we are literary agents.

Do you think many talented writers fail to get published for avoidable reasons? If so, what are some of those reasons? Often, talented writers submit their work too soon. Their project has potential, but they have yet to revise and elevate the work enough for publication.

ANDREA HURST & ASSOCIATES, LLC ❖ andreahurst.com

Agent's name and contact info: Andrea Hurst, info@andreahurst.com

What would you be doing right now if not responding to this survey? Walking my miniature poodle.

What would you be if not an agent (other than a dog, cat, or other mammal)? A bestselling novelist.

Do you think independent (noncorporate) publishing will be stronger, weaker, or the same over the next few years? Stronger.

Please describe your professional history. I bring over 25 years' experience in the industry. I am a developmental book editor for publishers and authors, a bestselling Amazon author, an instructor for the MFA creative writing program at the Northwest Institute of Literary Arts, and a webinar presenter for *Writer's Digest*. As a literary agent, I selectively represent high-profile adult nonfiction and well-crafted fiction. My clients and their books have appeared on *The Oprah Show*, *The Ellen DeGeneres Show*, *Good Morning America*, and the National Geographic network and in the *New York Times*.

How would you define the "client from hell"? Unreasonable expectations and unprofessional.

Please list five books you recently agented. *Magnolia Nights*, *Sweet Tea Tuesdays*, *The Buried Book*, *Rejected Writers' Bookclub*, *Pancakes in Paris*.

Please describe the kinds of books you want to agent. Women's fiction and suspense.

What should writers submit for consideration, and how should they send it? If they are experienced writers with strong sales, self-published or traditional, email me a query at info@andreahurst.com.

How do you feel about self-publishing, and what do you see happening with it in the near future? I am very open to it; I have self-published my own novels and do agent-assisted self-publishing.

Why do you think some books become super-successful (beyond the obvious reasons)? They hit an archetypal vein.

Do you think agents are likely to become millionaires? Occasionally.

Knowing what you know now, would you become an agent again? Yes.

ANNIE BOMKE LITERARY AGENCY ❖ www.abliterary.com

PO Box 3759, San Diego, CA 92163, 619-634-3415

Agent's name and contact info: Annie Bomke, submissions@abliterary.com

What would you be doing right now if not responding to this survey? Having a solo dance party to "Mi Gente" or compulsively looking at my Facebook page but not posting anything.

What would you be if not an agent (other than a dog, cat, or other mammal)? Psychology fascinates me, so probably something in that field. Or I'd be on *Dancing with the Stars*. If I could find a way to combine those two, I'd give up agenting.

Do you think independent (noncorporate) publishing will be stronger, weaker, or the same over the next few years? As the major publishers become more and more narrow in their acquisitions, indie publishing will become increasingly stronger. They'll offer a wider scope of books that will serve underserved audiences and just bring more variety to the market in terms of genres and topics.

Please describe your professional history. During college, I interned at *Zoetrope: All-Story*, a literary magazine founded by Francis Ford Coppola. Then I worked at Margret McBride Literary Agency for seven and a half years, first as an intern, then as the royalties and foreign-rights agent, until I opened my own agency in 2011.

How would you define the "client from hell"? An author who refuses to take feedback and doesn't listen. Also authors who send angry emails to their editors at 3 AM. It's important for an agent to be clear about what (if any) major changes he or she expects before signing an author. Agents and authors have to make sure they're on the same page, or else they're going to be fighting the whole way. So a warning sign is if authors hem and haw about what changes they're willing to make and won't give an agent a straight answer or if they make half-assed attempts to address the agent's concerns that don't actually do anything. I once worked with an author who, instead of making changes to address my feedback or telling me why she didn't agree with it, would argue why it was unnecessary to address such concerns in the actual manuscript. For example, if I asked her to expand on an idea, she would write in the manuscript itself something like, "If some want a more thorough explanation of X, they can refer to my earlier chapter where I addressed it." Talk about passive-aggressive!

Do you think Earth was created a few thousand years ago or several billion years ago? It was a really long time ago. That's all I know. I wasn't there.

Please list five books you recently agented. *The Introvert Entrepreneur* by Beth Buelow (Perigee), *Class Reunions Are Murder* by Libby Klein (Kensington), *Dodging and Burning* by John Copenhaver (Pegasus Crime), *Midnight Snacks Are Murder* by Libby Klein (Kensington), *Restaurant Weeks Are Murder* by Libby Klein (Kensington).

Please describe the kinds of books you want to agent. On the fiction side, I love character-driven stories; mystery (cozies, gritty police procedurals, and everything in between); psychological thrillers, literary/psychological horror, and magical realism; historical, women's, literary and upmarket, and contemporary young adult fiction; and books with diverse characters. So if you have a literary/psychological thriller set in Nazi Germany with a gay protagonist, I'd love to see it. I'm a sucker for books set in the Victorian era, retellings of *Hamlet* and other classics, and books about famous historical figures.

For nonfiction, I'm looking for fresh prescriptive business, self-help, and health/diet books with a great platform. I also love memoir with a fresh voice (funny or serious), narrative nonfiction on an unusual topic, and big-concept popular psychology books. I'm fascinated by topics, like behavioral economics (for example, *Predictably Irrational* by Dan Ariely), that explore some aspect of why people do the things they do from either a psychological or biological perspective.

What should writers submit for consideration, and how should they send it? For fiction, writers should submit a query letter, synopsis, and the first two chapters. For nonfiction, writers should submit a proposal and at least two sample chapters. I accept email submissions and snail mail submissions. For email submissions, I prefer the above-mentioned things pasted in the body of the email, though attachments are okay as long as they're either in Word doc or PDF format. For snail mail submissions, please include a SASE (self-addressed stamped envelope).

How do you feel about self-publishing, and what do you see happening with it in the near future? Self-publishing is a great option for authors who have had trouble getting published by a traditional publisher and want to get their work out there. I just always tell authors to promote the hell out of their self-published books, because if they want a traditional publisher for their future books, it can be difficult if the sales figures for their self-published books aren't amazing.

In the near future, the number of self-published books will expand exponentially, but I don't foresee any improvements in the way self-published books are perceived in the market or how lucrative self-publishing is. If anything, the larger number of self-published books will further dilute the market and make it that much harder for any self-published author to become a runaway success.

Do you think there are too many, too few, or just enough agents? There are far too many, which is why I'm participating in the Agent Hunger Games this year. May the best agent prevail! Just kidding. I think there are a fine number of agents.

Do you think Amazon will become the country's largest employer within 10 years? Probably. Either them or the supercomputers that will enslave us all someday.

Why do you think some books become super-successful (beyond the obvious reasons)? Luck and timing (which is basically just luck).

Do you think agents are likely to become millionaires? (Hysterical laughter.)

Do you think agents tend toward certain personality types? No, I don't think agents fit into a certain personality type. There are the super-extroverted phone talkers who make up the agent stereotype, the more introverted types who are in agenting because they like to read, and everything in between.

Do you think writers tend to be more or less narcissistic than the population at large? I don't think there's any direct correlation between writing and narcissism, so I don't think authors are any more or less narcissistic than anyone else.

Knowing what you know now, would you become an agent again? (Hysterical laughter resumes.)

Why did you choose to become an agent? I fell into agenting because I wanted to work in publishing while living at my mom's house. Literary agencies were the only form of publishing in San Diego, so I got an internship at one, and the rest is history.

Do you think many talented writers fail to get published for avoidable reasons? If so, what are some of those reasons? Yes, there are definitely avoidable reasons why authors don't get published. One is not properly researching the agents you're querying, which can lead to querying agents who don't represent your genre, and then getting so discouraged by the rejections that you stop querying.

Another is not properly researching the expectations of the market for your book and querying a book that doesn't fit within market norms. One such norm is word count. It's difficult, for example, to sell an adult novel that is shorter than 60,000 words or longer than 120,000 words. Yes, it happens every once in a while, but you can't rely on being the exception to the rule, especially when you're a debut author. You tip the odds in your favor by following market norms.

I also often receive queries for "young adult" books that don't fit into the young adult genre because the protagonist is the wrong age. A young adult book should have a protagonist who is high-school age (14–18), and yet I receive queries for young adult books with a 12-year-old or a 30-year-old protagonist. These authors aren't aware of the expectations of the genre, so they are querying books that don't meet market norms.

So the best way to tip the odds in your favor is to educate yourself on the publishing industry. You can do this by joining organizations (like Mystery Writers of America), attending conferences, subscribing to publishing magazines or blogs, reading books, listening to podcasts, etc.

I also urge writers to be knowledgeable about the genre they're writing in and the expectations of that genre. Perhaps the easiest way to accomplish this is to be a fervent reader of the genre you're writing in, analyze the books you read to determine what makes them special, and apply those lessons to your own writing.

THE AUGUST AGENCY LLC ❖ www.augustagency.com

Agent's name: Cricket Freeman, Founder and Principal Agent

What would you be doing right now if not responding to this survey? Sometimes I can squeeze out time to read, watch movies, travel, hike, canoe, walk the beach, or visit with other writers, my favorite people. This past year I returned to a passion from my youth — construction — working in my spare time with my architectural designer husband to design and renovate several houses. Among them is August Words House, a tropical writer's retreat. (Now a shameless plug: please visit www.augustwordshouse.com.)

What would you be if not an agent (other than a dog, cat, or other mammal)? A writer. It is how I entered this industry, as a working freelancer. For several years I've been neck-deep in researching and writing a whale of a creative nonfiction book on early aviation history amid the effervescent, intoxicating 1920s. But I cannot ignore that being an agent has brought me considerable rare gifts: friendships with delightful, generous, and spellbinding people from all over the globe, many my clients. My life is infinitely richer for it. And the best gift of all: while in Oregon as a speaker at a writers' conference a decade ago, at dinner at a volunteer's home, I first met Mr. Freeman on a hilltop under a meteoric sky. Destiny? Methinks so.

Do you think independent (noncorporate) publishing will be stronger, weaker, or the same over the next few years? With distance comes perspective, so I can see trends in my literary crystal ball. These are heady times, ripe with possibility. The major publishers, often referred to as legacy publishers, will always be the gold standard for authors, the definition of having arrived, of being a success at writing — no matter what this freewheeling publishing environment brings to surprise us, and no matter how many readers authors have, how many books they sell, or how much money lands in their pockets. Legacy publishers will still dominate, pulling huge numbers per book, and self-publishers will continue to roam in huge numbers, pulling small numbers per book. What my crystal ball does show me is an ever-widening middle space for the independent publishers to gain ground, once again giving readers a broad range of choices.

Please describe your professional history. Encouraged by bestselling author friends, I directed my creativity and entrepreneurial spirit to the writing business in the 1980s, freelancing for magazines (more adventure than money) and business clients (more money than adventure). Then I slaved as the editor in chief of a national full-color, glossy trade magazine for too long a time, overseeing design, ad sales, editorial, and staff and still managing to write 1,100 damn fine words a day, day after day, for print. As a result, after decades of writing, I tend to measure my writing credits by the pound. Reaching out to other writers, in 2001 I founded the August Agency, a literary agency, and in 2014 came augustwords.org, a network of writers' resources supporting literary and literacy charities. Later I expanded again with August Words Publishing, specializing in unique books by exceptional authors for select readers. Along the way, for nearly 30 years I've served as a writing instructor, in venues from writers' conferences and workshops to community-college classes.

I'm a proud fifth-generation Floridian, what locals call a "skeeter beater" (someone whose intrepid family was brave enough, wild enough, or criminal enough to be here before the advent of mosquito control, when a palm broom hung by each front door, so you could beat the skeeters off your body before entering). When it comes to my writing and business creativity, I don't grow where bananas don't grow, so my agency is based in South Florida. At the time I founded the August Agency, locating an agency anywhere outside New York City was considered foolhardy, so we maintained a NYC branch for many years. By the time the recession rolled around and the internet ruled business, we all opted for sunshine and more fiscal efficiency.

How would you define the "client from hell"? Have you heard about the writer whose career got snuffed?

> There's this writer. An insecure, desperate writer. But also a skilled, impassioned writer. A writer who's as deft with her pen as a musketeer with his sword, and with as much heart. Fueled by her hopes, this writer pushes forward in her quest till she discovers an agent who believes in her pen. The writer thinks she's finally arrived as a writer. Nothing can stop her now. She dreams of buzzing up the

New York Times bestseller list, touring the world amid exploding flashbulbs, and laughing it up with Ellen and Kimmel.

But then one day, before the writer finds her place in the sun, she overreacts and goes off on her agent. She jumps to a crooked conclusion, blames her agent for anything and everything, has a bad hair day, gets cursed by an evil witch — take your pick. Whatever triggers it, she acts like a screaming, kicking two-year-old. She shrieks at her agent, she sends flaming emails, she resorts to name-calling, ad nauseam. Even when the agent tries to reach out to her, the writer refuses to see it, much less apologize. Somehow, in her convoluted thinking, her bizarre actions and blistering words are justified.

Once the storm is over, all the writer hears is a deafening silence. The agent casts her adrift. The writer's career is over before it truly begins, she doesn't understand why, and her heart is broken. Moreover, the agent cries at such a loss on the rocks of shortsightedness.

The moral of this tragic tale? Throw a temper tantrum and you commit career suicide. Remember, publishing at this level is a relatively small community. It doesn't take too many tantrums, large or small, before word gets around branding you "difficult," "unpredictable," "psychotic." Why does this singlehandedly kill off an otherwise promising career? It destroys trust, from which everything else flows. When a writer throws a conniption fit, the agent immediately asks herself: "Would she throw a tantrum with an editor? Or — oh, my! — with a reader at a book signing?" Such embarrassment is something an agent or editor will not accept, no matter the writer's talent. Remember, agents are looking not only for good writers, but also for professional ones.

Do you think Earth was created a few thousand years ago or several billion years ago? I just don't see the relevance of this question to the publishing business.

Please list five books you recently agented. Not all our clients' projects are books, although that is how most of them first come to us. We have sold their works for hardcover, trade paper, and mass-market paperback editions, but also as digital, film, audio, serial, reprint, gaming, and foreign rights. Outlets have included academic presses, genre presses, regional houses, content providers, and educational testing services as well as traditional advance-paying publishers, such as Career Press, John Wiley & Sons, Praeger, Gale, and AMACOM Books. (A representative title is *The Office Politics Handbook* by Jack Godwin, PhD.) I have always believed in the gift of small presses to discover, develop, appreciate, and publish those fabulous, entertaining, and invaluable books we all adore but the Big Guys can't be bothered with and thus ignore. Our literary services have expanded to include one such small commercial press: August Words Publishing. (Another shameless plug: please visit www.augustwordspublishing.com.)

Please describe the kinds of books you want to agent. We are a discreet agency that has worked quietly since 2001, in the US and internationally, offering highly personalized service to an exclusive group of exceptional writers. Primarily we handle mainstream nonfiction, creative nonfiction, narrative nonfiction, memoir, and crime fiction. We favor persuasive and prescriptive nonfiction works, each with a full-bodied narrative command and an undeniable contemporary relevance. We enjoy untangling literary Gordian knots — an intricate story operating on multiple levels — whether historical crime thrillers, narrative memoir, contemporary creative nonfiction, or anything in between. We do *not* handle children's books, screenplays, poetry, short stories, romance, Westerns, horror, fantasy, or sci-fi. We do not charge fees for our literary representation services. We earn standard commissions on payments, advances, and royalties.

What should writers submit for consideration, and how should they send it? More than three-quarters of our clients have come to us through writers' conferences, so it's obvious that's the best way for us to connect. In fact, invite me to your conference to teach a workshop and hear pitches, and in a scheduled one-on-one or even during the ride from the airport you can pitch your book and pick my brain mercilessly, and we'll plot your career objectives. *Note*: We only accept submissions at a conference or by referral. However, periodically we are open to over-the-transom submissions through the submission form on our website. Unfortunately, we cannot consider queries that come to us any other way. Tip: The best queries are easier said than done. They're simple, but also slippery. They only have two paragraphs, one about the book and one about you — but those paragraphs must be flawless and golden.

How do you feel about self-publishing, and what do you see happening with it in the near future? Decades ago, before digital publishing and long before the August Agency, I had Possibilities Press, which provided prepublication preparation for small publishers and self-publishers: ghostwriting, editing, book design, cover design, printing, binding, and market analysis. Even with a professionally produced book, many self-published authors discovered a steep uphill climb. We've come so far since then, from glue pots and typesetting to the click of a mouse, from social shunning in literary circles to encouragement and acceptance. At last, from the reader's viewpoint, every book is on equal ground, no matter if it is published by one of the major houses, an academic press, a small regional publisher, a few-books-a-year micropress, or directly by the author. It's an amazing new playground with lots that's new and exciting. (Heads up: Always be cautious of bullies lurking in the shadows ready to pocket your lunch money.) One thing I have seen is that large publishers today are now viewing self-published books as test-marketed; low sales numbers brand a book as not testing well, but books with high sales numbers are deemed to have test-marketed well and are therefore worthy of a look. The number-one thing still true for self-published books today is: If truth be told, is it ready for prime time? Is it a quality book in every aspect, writing, editing, and production? Remember, you only get one shot at your reader with this book, whether an agent, editor, or buyer.

Do you think there are too many, too few, or just enough agents? I see that opportunities for writers are growing with each year, that having an agent is becoming more necessary in some areas yet less so in others, and that boutique agencies who foster authors' careers, like the August Agency, are becoming scarcer each year.

Do you think Amazon will become the country's largest employer within 10 years? Amazon is at once a blessing and a curse. It is an amazing research tool, a bargain-hunter's paradise, a self-pubbed author's champion, a midlist author's savior, and an industry revolutionizer. But it can also be a competition smasher, an industry monopolizer, a literary bully, and a hometown-bookstore assassin. When Amazon coughs, the industry holds its breath. And yet it has also allowed little upstart August Words Publishing to distribute books on equal footing with other publishers and in 14 countries. Consequently, one day I adore it, the next I loathe it — much like spinach.

Why do you think some books become super-successful (beyond the obvious reasons)? You just can't ignore the obvious reasons: that a new book has a fresh perspective or a unique author's voice or is just, well, a damn fine book. Many would then argue for the business acumen of the author who placed the work into fitting hands to push it forward — whether agent, editor, or publisher (including themselves). Beyond all that, I chalk up the success of many über-successful books to the "lining up of the planets." In other words, timing. And that's something no one has much control over. So concentrate on the things you can control, in particular the first three.

Do you think agents are likely to become millionaires? I don't see being an agent as a job or career fueled by a strong drive for money. It's a lifestyle, like being a professional writer, artist, or musician. A lifestyle is your passion. The work comes first, and if your work is authentic and your instincts are sound, funds will follow.

Do you think agents tend toward certain personality types? Like all occupations, every personality will turn up sooner or later. However, one common trait I've seen over the years is that agents who've been at it a long time are attentive to detail and passionate about their clients and their works.

Do you think writers tend to be more or less narcissistic than the population at large? Many narcissistic people wander into writing, naively thinking it's perfect for them because it will happily sustain their belief that the world revolves around them. But not many survive the rigors to become professional, working authors. (See "the client from hell" above.)

Why did you choose to become an agent? I didn't go to university to be a literary agent. After all, who does? You wander through the back door from somewhere close at hand: a publishing house, a law office, a media company — and usually because someone opened the door and invited you in. In my case, I was an experienced freelance writer and former national magazine editor in chief who knew my way around the publishing world, plus I'd been a real estate broker who boogied through contracts. When I pitched a book at a conference, an agent recognized my value and recruited me. A year later when I was up to my eyeballs in intriguing work, he wandered out the door. I stayed. Being an entrepreneur, I then founded my own agency.

Knowing what you know now, would you become an agent again? Tough, tough question. After all, hindsight is always 20/20. In the years I've been an agent, publishing has experienced an era of extreme change, from all hardcopy to digital and beyond. This sea change pushed and pulled every aspect of the industry like saltwater taffy. What was once true is no longer, and what was unimaginable is now commonplace. One thing it never was is static — or boring. When you get right down to it, that's probably why I've stayed, when so many of my colleagues have gone on to other careers. It's kept me on my toes to try to keep up, expanding our literary services in new marketplaces. I do love new challenges.

Do you think many talented writers fail to get published for avoidable reasons? If so, what are some of those reasons? When literary agents accept writers as clients, they expect to be working with confident professionals who can produce the top-shelf, professional-level materials necessary for agents to do their job effectively. We look for that professionalism in every interaction with prospective clients — queries, emails, phone calls, personal interactions with us and with others — and do not have time to teach it. Yeah, writers are thrown into the deep end of the publishing ocean and expected to swim on their own. Listen to your grandma here: be prepared, do your homework, be kind, bring joy. And heed Miss Aretha, too: R-E-S-P-E-C-T. Any less than 100 percent professionalism simply will not cut it. Ever.

BETSY AMSTER LITERARY ENTERPRISES ❖

amsterlit.com, cummingskidlit.com

Agent's name and contact info: Mary Cummings, Agent, Books for Kids and Teens, b.amster.kidsbooks@gmail.com

What would you be doing right now if not responding to this survey? Reading submissions from prospective clients or pitching work to editors.

What would you be if not an agent (other than a dog, cat, or other mammal)? An opera singer. If I was good at it. But I'm not, so I will stick to listening to opera. However, I *am* good at being an agent for kids' books!

Do you think independent (noncorporate) publishing will be stronger, weaker, or the same over the next few years? On balance, probably the same.

Please describe your professional history. For 14 years I was education director at the Loft Literary Center in Minneapolis, where I curated an annual festival of children's literature. I also hired judges from among top editors in the field for the $25,000 McKnight Award in Children's Literature. Those editors formed the base of my contacts, though I've built many more. In addition to overseeing classes in children's lit at the Loft, I directed the entire program for writers of screenplays, novels, poetry, etc. In that capacity, I hired Betsy Amster on many occasions to teach workshops. When I left the Loft in 2008, I joined the agency to bring expertise in kid and teen lit.

Among my sales are picture books, chapter books, and novels to such houses as Viking; Little, Brown; Henry Holt; Imprint; Paula Wiseman Books, Simon & Schuster; Abrams; Farrar, Straus and Giroux; Holiday House; Walker; Knopf; and others.

How would you define the "client from hell"? I'm happy to say I don't have any of them.

Do you think Earth was created a few thousand years ago or several billion years ago? Umm. I will go with the overwhelming evidence of science on this.

Please list five books you recently agented. *Where Is My Balloon?* by Ariel Bernstein (Paula Wiseman Books, Simon & Schuster), *Merry Christmas, Sleep Tight* by J. Theron Elkins (Zondervan Children's), *Bike and Trike* by Elizabeth Verdick (Paula Wiseman Books, Simon & Schuster), *When Numbers Met Letters* by Lois Barr (Holiday House), *Warren and Dragon: 100 Friends* and *Warren and Dragon: Weekend with Chewy* by Ariel Bernstein (two-book deal, Viking).

Please describe the kinds of books you want to agent. I represent fiction, poetry, and lyrical nonfiction for preschoolers through teens. I'm especially seeking middle grade novels and picture books. I like stories about times, places, and people underrepresented in children's and teen lit. Friendship stories, great read-aloud picture books, nonrhyming picture books, and stories about important relationships, coming-of-age milestones, and holidays (including ones for minority communities) are always welcome. For novels, I especially like magic realism or fantasy mixed with real world and also historical fiction. Work tied to school standards and lyrically written nonfiction (arts, sciences, mindfulness, social awareness) are also welcome. I'm also seeking picture books and chapter books for young middle grade by author-illustrators. I do *not* want material for adults.

What should writers submit for consideration, and how should they send it? See guidelines at either amsterlit.com or cummingskidlit.com. No attachments! For picture books, embed the full manuscript. For longer works, embed the first three pages and include some bio info and a one-sentence summary of the manuscript, plus any information on competing titles, potential audience, marketing, etc.

How do you feel about self-publishing, and what do you see happening with it in the near future? I shy away from projects that have been self-published, but I think it will continue to be an important and attractive option for many people.

Do you think there are too many, too few, or just enough agents? If we're staying in business and getting great material into the hands of editors, there are probably just enough.

Do you think Amazon will become the country's largest employer within 10 years? Maybe. But they'll probably have more and more robots, so who knows.

Why do you think some books become super-successful (beyond the obvious reasons)? There are tipping points around topics. Something that would not have caught fire at one point will be sensationally attractive and important less than a year later because of various happenings in society. When a book comes out at exactly the right moment, it can exceed all reasonable expectations of success.

Do you think agents are likely to become millionaires? A very few.

Do you think agents tend toward certain personality types? There are probably some personality types that are more likely than others to become successful agents. I would not say there is any one type.

Do you think writers tend to be more or less narcissistic than the population at large? Probably less. With exceptions, of course. Most writers are people with curiosity, talent, and idiosyncratic insight who turn these gifts into stories that benefit us all.

Knowing what you know now, would you become an agent again? Absolutely.

Why did you choose to become an agent? I love children's books and have always loved nurturing artists and writers. Helping them bring their dreams to reality in the form of books that kids will learn from, laugh or cry over, and read under the covers at bedtime because they can't stop reading is just the most fun and rewarding thing to do.

Do you think many talented writers fail to get published for avoidable reasons? If so, what are some of those reasons? Talent is essential, but not sufficient. Submitting a manuscript with language errors or in less than the very best shape possible is the mark of someone who is unprofessional or impatient, or both. Language errors tend to show up early; I stop reading when I see them. I don't know how many times I've read a novel manuscript that was good for the first 20 pages or so, then began to sag or show erratic pacing, and concluded with the final chapters showing uninspired word choices or clichéd plot elements and other signs of rushing and carelessness. Ignoring submission guidelines or pitching wildly and blindly are other common mistakes that will likely result in the writer not being taken seriously and the submission immediately tossed.

BJ ROBBINS LITERARY AGENCY ❖ www.bjrobbinsliterary.com

Agent's name and contact info: BJ Robbins, robbinsliterary@gmail.com

What would you be doing right now if not responding to this survey? Reading.

What would you be if not an agent (other than a dog, cat, or other mammal)? Not that I would have ever pursued this, but I would have made a great FBI agent or detective.

Do you think independent (noncorporate) publishing will be stronger, weaker, or the same over the next few years? The same.

Please describe your professional history. I started in publicity at Simon & Schuster, then moved to Harcourt, where I was director of marketing and then senior editor. I moved to LA and started my agency in 1992.

How would you define the "client from hell"? I feel fortunate to have clients who are professional and don't exhibit hellish behaviors.

Please list five books you recently agented. *Mongrels* by Stephen Graham Jones, *Blood Brothers* by Deanne Stillman, *Shoot for the Moon* by James Donovan, *Reliance, Illinois* by Mary Volmer, *Mapping the Interior* by Stephen Graham Jones.

Please describe the kinds of books you want to agent. I love a great story beautifully told. Doesn't matter what subject or whether it's fiction or nonfiction.

What should writers submit for consideration, and how should they send it? Writers should check out my website, bjrobbinsliterary.com, see if their project will be a good fit, and follow my submission guidelines.

How do you feel about self-publishing, and what do you see happening with it in the near future? It's fine for certain kinds of books that have a specific niche audience. I believe it will continue as it is now, with a handful of books breaking out each year.

Knowing what you know now, would you become an agent again? Yes.

Why did you choose to become an agent? I had moved to LA and wanted to continue to work with writers, and it felt like the logical choice.

BLUE RIDGE LITERARY AGENCY, LLC ❖ www.blueridgeagency.com

Agent's name and contact info: Dawn Dowdle, query@blueridgeagency.com

What would you be doing right now if not responding to this survey? Editing manuscripts.

What would you be if not an agent (other than a dog, cat, or other mammal)? No idea. I love being an agent.

Do you think independent (noncorporate) publishing will be stronger, weaker, or the same over the next few years? Independent publishers will be stronger over the next few years. They are filling the gaps left by larger publishers.

Please describe your professional history. I started out reviewing cozy mysteries. Then I opened Sleuth Editing. I enjoyed editing manuscripts and working with authors. I also ran Mystery Lovers Corner (which was later bought but is not in service at this time). A writer I knew made the comment, "I wish we could do this ourselves," when she was looking for an agent. I did some research on the industry and what the role of an agent was and opened my agency 10 years ago. My agency now has contracts with 4 of the Big 5 publishers and many independent publishers.

How would you define the "client from hell"? A client who doesn't communicate well, is not open to editing, and does not meet deadlines on a regular basis.

Do you think Earth was created a few thousand years ago or several billion years ago? I believe Earth was created by God.

Please list five books you recently agented. A Literal Mess, Southern Sass & Killer Cravings, Knot My Sister's Keeper, Expiration Date, and Back Home at Firefly Lake.

Please describe the kinds of books you want to agent. I enjoy representing cozy mysteries with female protagonists, Amish romances, and other romances, especially historical and suspense. I do not represent paranormal romances or erotica.

What should writers submit for consideration, and how should they send it? They should follow the instructions at www.blueridgeagency.com, as I use Query Manager and there is a button on my website to lead them right to the submissions information.

How do you feel about self-publishing, and what do you see happening with it in the near future? It is the way to go for many books. I expect to see more authors going hybrid.

Do you think there are too many, too few, or just enough agents? There is always room for more agents.

Do you think Amazon will become the country's largest employer within 10 years? I don't know about the largest employer, but I do see them as a large employer who is growing all the time.

Why do you think some books become super-successful (beyond the obvious reasons)? If anyone can figure out the exact formula, they can make millions. It takes a great book, with good promotion. It seems that the books that become super-successful usually have a large word-of-mouth buzz. They need to go viral.

Do you think agents are likely to become millionaires? Not most of the agents.

Do you think agents tend toward certain personality types? I don't know. I think most want to help authors and enjoy seeing an author's book come to fruition.

Do you think writers tend to be more or less narcissistic than the population at large? No.

Knowing what you know now, would you become an agent again? Yes. I wish I had done it when I was younger. I really enjoy this. But I also know that my previous careers all helped prepare me for the work I'm doing now.

Why did you choose to become an agent? To help authors become published, especially newer authors.

Do you think many talented writers fail to get published for avoidable reasons? If so, what are some of those reasons? Yes, I do. Many don't take the time to learn their craft. They don't study what editors and agents are looking for. Many submit their work to the wrong agents or editors or before their book is ready. They also don't learn the parameters of their genre.

BRADFORD LITERARY AGENCY ❖ www.bradfordlit.com

5694 Mission Center Road #347, San Diego, CA 92108

Agent's name and contact info: Laura Bradford, laura@bradfordlit.com (do not send queries to this address), queries@bradfordlit.com

What would you be if not an agent (other than a dog, cat, or other mammal)? Some kind of entrepreneur or other kind of small-business owner. Maybe I'd invent some widget that everyone decided was essential to their lives and make a fortune selling them on TV.

Do you think independent (noncorporate) publishing will be stronger, weaker, or the same over the next few years? The thing about independent publishing is that because of the size, it can be agile and respond really well to the market. But the market can be volatile, and publishing is always a gamble, so it is very easy for independent publishers (any publishers, really) to make a few bad calls on books and fail to make the revenue they need to survive and thrive. In theory, an independent publisher could be the best place for an outside-the-box book, but certainly a smaller press is somewhat less insulated against risk. I think these things have always been true, so I see independent publishing staying the same over the next few years. Unless you meant independent publishing as a synonym for self-publishing, in which case my answer is different.

Please describe your professional history. I have a BA English literature from the University of California at San Diego. I came to agenting pretty much straight out of college. I started with my first agency as an intern less than six months after I graduated. I started my own agency in 2001.

How would you define the "client from hell"? Writers come in infinite variety, and I am pleased to work with a lot of different "types." As for some characteristics I don't particularly love, it is hard to work with someone who has unrealistic expectations, isn't a team player (and publishing *is* a team sport), and does not respect deadlines. My least favorite of all? Someone who doesn't comport themselves professionally in public. That includes online dealings.

Do you think Earth was created a few thousand years ago or several billion years ago? Is this a real question?

Please list five books you recently agented. *Our Year of Maybe* by Rachel Lynn Solomon (Simon Pulse), *The Spitfire Girls* by Soraya M. Lane (Lake Union), *Vox* by Christina Dalcher (Berkley), *Serious Moonlight* by Jenn Bennett (Simon & Schuster), *Whiskey Sharp: Torn* by Lauren Dane (HQN).

Please describe the kinds of books you want to agent. I handle commercial fiction, specifically genre fiction. I love romance (all subgenres), mystery, thrillers, women's fiction, urban fantasy/speculative fiction, upper middle grade, and young adult. I do some select nonfiction as well.

What should writers submit for consideration, and how should they send it? A simple, professional query letter is very important, one that is specific, articulate, and concise. I don't need an author to be zany to grab my attention; just cut right to the heart of what your manuscript is about and give me a strong hook. Don't be vague. As far as submissions go, please email a query letter along with the first chapter of your manuscript and a synopsis (all pasted into the body of the email) to queries@bradfordlit.com. Please be sure to include the genre and word count in your cover letter. To keep it from falling into spam, the subject line should begin with the word *Query* and be followed by the title of the manuscript and any *short* message you would like us to see.

How do you feel about self-publishing, and what do you see happening with it in the near future? It is a growing part of the publishing landscape, and it can be a wonderful thing. I like that authors have more options, access, and control than they ever have before. Some authors are self-publishing in a smart way and finding a lot of success with it. Other authors are not being smart about it but still finding success. Still others are not finding that they enjoy being entrepreneurial or that they are not happy with the amount of return they are getting for the work that they put in. It is ideal for some authors and not for others, but it's nice that it is a viable option for all. I have many authors who are publishing traditionally as well as self-publishing. I don't think that it has to be an either/or thing. And I do think that agents have a place in that landscape.

Do you think there are too many, too few, or just enough agents? There are a ton of agents in business, but I don't have any opinion about whether there are too many. If they can generate enough business to survive, I guess it's fine. The number of agents in the business doesn't really have an effect on me and my bottom line, really. There are a gazillion other agents with tastes totally different from mine, and our paths will never cross. Sometimes agents do compete for authors, but if there was only one other agent in the world and that agent and I wanted the same author, it would create more competition than if there were a thousand other agents in the world who had zero interest in that author. I'm not sure the number of agents in business overall matters much to me.

Do you think Amazon will become the country's largest employer within 10 years? No.

Do you think agents are likely to become millionaires? Some agents who rep books that become cultural phenomena already are, but I'd say most agents will never get close to being millionaires.

Do you think agents tend toward certain personality types? Agents tend to be organized (because we have to be) and flexible (because we have to be), maybe a little bossy, but generally very patient.

Knowing what you know now, would you become an agent again? I would do it all over again in a heartbeat. I totally adore my job.

Why did you choose to become an agent? Once upon a time, I thought I might like to be a novelist, and I joined Romance Writers of America, so I could learn what was what. At my first meeting, the speaker was a literary agent, which was something I had never heard of before. I was instantly fascinated. I researched what the job was and how to go about getting started. It was the perfect job for someone who loved books and business and allowed me to be around my favorite people: authors.

Agent's name and contact info: Jennifer Chen Tran, jen@bradfordlit.com

What would you be doing right now if not responding to this survey? Reading and editing a book proposal.

What would you be if not an agent (other than a dog, cat, or other mammal)? A teacher or lawyer.

Do you think independent (noncorporate) publishing will be stronger, weaker, or the same over the next few years? Hopefully stronger.

Please describe your professional history. Originally from New York, I am a lifelong reader and experienced member of the publishing industry. Prior to joining Bradford Literary in September 2017, I was an associate agent at Fuse Literary and served as counsel at The New Press. I obtained a BA in English literature from Washington University in St. Louis and my JD from Northeastern School of Law in Boston.

How would you define the "client from hell"? A client who has unreasonable expectations regarding the publishing journey; someone who demands more of my time and attention than necessary and doesn't trust me to execute the best deal for his or her investment; someone who calls a little too often.

Do you think Earth was created a few thousand years ago or several billion years ago? I don't know. Only God and the dinosaurs know the real answer.

Please list five books you recently agented. *Spark!* by Ted Anderson (middle grade graphic novel trilogy, Lion Forge, fall 2019); *Get Peached: Recipes and Stories from the Peached Tortilla* by Eric Silverstein (cookbook, Sterling Epicure, spring 2019); *I Will Love You Forever* by Cori Salchert (Barbour Books / Shiloh Run Press, March 2018); *Breaking Up and Bouncing Back* by Samantha Burns (Ixia Press, May 2018); *The Art of Escaping* by Erin Callahan (young adult debut, Amberjack, June 2018).

Please describe the kinds of books you want to agent. My ultimate goal is to work in concert with authors to shape books, both fiction and nonfiction, that will have a positive social impact on the world — books that also inform and entertain. I am very interested in diverse writers and #ownvoices from underrepresented or marginalized communities, strong and conflicted characters who are not afraid to take emotional risks, stories about multigenerational conflict, war and postwar fiction, and writing with a developed sense of place. In nonfiction, I love books that broaden my worldview or shed new light on "big ideas."

In fiction, I am looking for women's fiction (contemporary, upmarket, literary), select young adult (must have distinct voice), select middle grade, and graphic novels and visually driven projects. In nonfiction, I am looking for narrative nonfiction (biography, current affairs, medical, investigative journalism, history, how-to, music, pop culture, travel), cookbooks and culinary projects, lifestyle (home, design, beauty, fashion), business books (social entrepreneurship, female- and/or minority-led businesses, and innovation), select memoir with an established platform, parenting, relationships and psychology, and mind-body-spirit titles.

What should writers submit for consideration, and how should they send it? For fiction, please email a query letter along with the first chapter of your manuscript and a synopsis pasted into the body of your email; be sure to include the genre and word count in your cover letter. For nonfiction, please email your full nonfiction proposal, including a query letter and a sample chapter.

How do you feel about self-publishing, and what do you see happening with it in the near future? It is a good option for those who do not want to obtain a traditional publishing deal. I see more authors considering it as a viable option and more agents partnering with writers who have previously self-published.

Do you think there are too many, too few, or just enough agents? There are too few agents of color and those who want to champion underrepresented writers in particular. The publishing industry, agents included, is too homogeneous. Therefore, there are too few agents who are representative of our diverse country.

Do you think Amazon will become the country's largest employer within 10 years? Probably.

Why do you think some books become super-successful (beyond the obvious reasons)? Because they are different. Whether it's the topic, the writing, or the buzz, some sort of edge drives book sales. I think that positive PR, media exposure, and good old word of mouth are still what drive book sales, but you cannot deny the power of social media or endorsements from those with a large following (e.g., Oprah).

Do you think agents are likely to become millionaires? No. Only a few. Most of us do it because we love it, not necessarily for financial reward. One can hope, though.

Do you think agents tend toward certain personality types? Yes. We are driven. We like to help others. We are service-oriented. There can be some big egos here and there, but overall we are helpful, friendly types who love books!

Do you think writers tend to be more or less narcissistic than the population at large? Probably slightly more narcissistic, but that narcissism, or I should say focus and reflection on oneself (to characterize it more accurately), probably makes for better writers and, hence, better writing.

Knowing what you know now, would you become an agent again? Yes, but I probably would have saved up more before diving in.

Why did you choose to become an agent? Many reasons. I love books. I love the written word. I have a penchant for the artistic. I like to help others. Most of all, I wanted to help diversify the publishing world. I felt, when I began, that the world of books wasn't diverse enough with regard to both those working in the industry and the types of books being published. That's true to this day, and I want to do something about it, being a person of color and a child of immigrants myself.

Do you think many talented writers fail to get published for avoidable reasons? If so, what are some of those reasons? Yes. Hubris is the number-one avoidable reason — not believing or being open-minded enough to consider revisions or another way of seeing things. You have to be flexible if you want to get published. It really is a team effort, and it behooves a writer to pay attention to what his or her agent or editor says, to what beta readers say, to feedback from your writers' circle, etc.

CARNICELLI LITERARY MANAGEMENT ❖ www.carnicellilit.com

7 Kipp Road, Rhinebeck, NY 12572

Agent's name and contact info: Matthew Carnicelli, President, queries@carnicellilit.com

Please describe your professional history. I began my publishing career at Dutton, where as an editor I worked with many great writers of fiction, history, and current events, including Christopher Bram, Sandra Mackey, Martin Duberman, Vice President Al Gore, William J. Mann, Judith Warner, Cornel West, and Cathleen Schine. At Contemporary Books and McGraw-Hill, I became enthralled with strong health writing and business and sports books, working with such authors as John Wooden, Victoria Moran, Dr. Robert Brooks, Gail Ferguson, Roland Lazenby, and Robert Kurson. I became an agent in 2004 in order to have more control over the depth of my work with clients and to focus only in areas that interested me intellectually and creatively, and over the past decade I've represented such notable authors as *Sports Illustrated* reporter Jim Gorant, brain and movement expert Anat Baniel, political pundit Dave "Mudcat" Saunders, historian Brian McGinty, *Meet the Press* moderator Chuck Todd, economist Joseph P. Quinlan, and graphic novelist Derf Backderf.

  I graduated from Washington University in St. Louis and received a master's degree in English literature from the University of Toronto. I have taught college-level nonfiction writing and enjoy leading writing workshops. I've been on panels at numerous writers' conferences and have lectured on publishing at places like Georgetown University; the *Wall Street Journal* and *Bloomberg* regularly call upon me to comment on publishing and other topics.

Please list five books you recently agented. Derf Backderf, *Kent State: A Graphic Novel* (Abrams ComicArts); Justin Gifford, PhD, *Cleaver: A Life of Insurrection* (Chicago Review Press); Megan Koreman, PhD, *The Escape Line: How the Ordinary Heroes of Dutch-Paris Resisted the Nazi Occupation of Western Europe* (Oxford University Press); Roland Lazenby, *Showboat: The Life of Kobe Bryant* (Little, Brown); Brian McGinty, *The Rest I Will Kill: William Tillman and the Unforgettable Story of How a Free Black Man Refused to Become a Slave* (Norton); Natalie Neelan, *Rebel at Work: How to Innovate and Drive Results When You're Not the Boss* (Diversion); Nicholas J.C. Pistor, *Shooting Lincoln: Matthew Brady, Alexander Gardner, and the Race to Photograph the Story of the Century* (Da Capo).

Please describe the kinds of books you want to agent. My goal as a literary agent is to help provocative thinkers and great writers express themselves more clearly and navigate the tricky terrain to get their books out into the world. I've always been a big believer in the power of breakthrough ideas and stories to change the world in a big way. Over the past two decades, first as an editor and then as a literary agent, I've had the good fortune to work with a vast array of prominent journalists, business leaders, health experts, media figures, and policy makers: former vice president Al Gore analyzing environmental change, brain and movement expert Anat Baniel writing about vitality, fashion icon Marc Ecko defining authenticity, sports biographer Roland Lazenby exploring Michael Jordan's greatness, civil rights leader Mel White examining the religious right, and TV commentator Chuck Todd explaining presidential leadership. But I've always been on the lookout for breakthrough new talent, too, and I am equally as proud to have represented such groundbreaking books as health writer Laurie Edward's history of chronic illness, cultural historian Justin Gifford's biography of Iceberg Slim, graphic novelist Derf Backderf's take on Jeffrey Dahmer, business strategist Gino Wickman's primer on how to get traction in your business, public-health advocate Michele Simon's takedown of the food industry, Felicia C. Sullivan's memoir of growing up in Brooklyn, historian Emerson "Tad" Baker's history of the Salem witch trials, science journalist Dan Drollette's report on the hunt for rare animals in Vietnam, sex therapist Michael Aaron's examination of the biggest sexual myths, and business reporter Loren Steffy's account of the BP disaster.

I'm always looking for new nonfiction submissions from authors with the appropriate credentials in the areas of current events, biography, memoir, history, business, health, science, self-help, psychology, sports, and pop culture. For fiction, I'm mainly interested in accessible literary fiction and, from time to time, good political and medical thrillers.

What should writers submit for consideration, and how should they send it? I hope that writers will spend some time reviewing my website to familiarize themselves with the types of books I represent. Then please write a clear, straightforward query letter that will make me beg to see your proposal or manuscript. Please limit your query to one page in the body of the email and know that I won't open any email queries with attachments. Tell me why your project is so important, timely, and salable and why you are the only author with the right credentials to write it. Convince me to ask you to send me more.

CORVISIERO LITERARY AGENCY ❖ www.corvisieroagency.com

275 Madison Avenue, 14th Floor, New York, NY 10016, 646-992-1647

Agent's name: Marisa Corvisiero

What would you be doing right now if not responding to this survey? Playing Xtronaut with my twins or reading.

What would you be if not an agent (other than a dog, cat, or other mammal)? An attorney.

Do you think independent (noncorporate) publishing will be stronger, weaker, or the same over the next few years? They will be weaker. Many don't offer the resources needed to add value above self-publishing.

Please describe your professional history. I am a practicing attorney who started agenting eight years ago and never looked back.

How would you define the "client from hell"? Someone who doesn't follow instructions and expects you to do the work for them.

Do you think Earth was created a few thousand years ago or several billion years ago? Four billion years ago. I'm an astrophysics nerd and love your questions!

Please list five books you recently agented. Kiss My Boots by Harper Sloan, Forever My Girl by Heidi McLaughlin, Jed and the Junkyard War by Steven Bohls, and many more.

Please describe the kinds of books you want to agent. Amazing love stories, thrillers, science fiction, and adventure stories for all ages.

What should writers submit for consideration, and how should they send it? Send a query, a two-page double-spaced synopsis, and the first five pages of the finished manuscript by uploading to querymanager.com/query/marisacorvisiero.

How do you feel about self-publishing, and what do you see happening with it in the near future? I love when authors hybrid-publish. When they self-publish correctly, it can help grow a career.

Do you think there are too many, too few, or just enough agents? Just enough.

Do you think Amazon will become the country's largest employer within 10 years? Undoubtedly, especially if Walmart's numbers go down. Amazon may surpass its number-one standing sooner than 10 years and is well on its way with its recent acquisition of Whole Foods.

Why do you think some books become super-successful (beyond the obvious reasons)? Some books hit the market at just the right time and resonate with the audience that craved the story.

Do you think agents are likely to become millionaires? Depends on so many things.

Do you think agents tend toward certain personality types? More often than not the work speaks for itself. Other times agents and authors connect on a personal level and join forces to make projects work, depending on the personality types of agent and author. There are partners for everyone.

Do you think writers tend to be more or less narcissistic than the population at large? This is a very broad generalization. Yes, some are, but the introverts in the bunch balance the scale.

Knowing what you know now, would you become an agent again? Absolutely!

Why did you choose to become an agent? I love books, knowledge, and stories. Agenting allows me to work on the things I love while using my problem-solving, writing, negotiating, and legal skills. It's a job tailor-made for me.

Do you think many talented writers fail to get published for avoidable reasons? If so, what are some of those reasons? Yes, mostly writing to make money, publishing to become famous, partnering with the wrong agent, failing to behave professionally, and not learning from peers and about the industry.

Agent's name and contact info: Jennifer Haskin, Junior Agent, jenn@corvisieroagency.com, 913-832-6199

What would you be doing right now if not responding to this survey? Reading requested manuscripts or writing.

What would you be if not an agent (other than a dog, cat, or other mammal)? An author and portrait artist.

Do you think independent (noncorporate) publishing will be stronger, weaker, or the same over the next few years? It will be in great demand, just as it is now. It is considered a good "middle ground" for some authors between self-publishing and "Big 5" publishing. In fact, as more and more authors choose to publish themselves as well as a few others, I believe many more independent companies will appear, making it easier for the flooding of lower- and varied-quality books into the market.

Please describe your professional history. After I began helping another agent with her slush pile and looking for appropriate publishers, she asked me if I was interested in joining the ranks of independent literary agents. I was delighted and began to learn the ins and outs of the publishing world. As a writer, I had joined several writing guilds and was invited to many conferences. Those are my favorite events to date. I love learning new aspects of the literary journey, going new places, and meeting new people, authors, agents, and editors. After more than a year of being an independent agent, signing clients, and helping them get published, I joined with a New York–based agency as an apprentice to learn its procedures and was promoted to junior agent.

How would you define the "client from hell"? I love all my clients. I don't choose authors I don't connect with. That said, sometimes people change or end up not being what one expects. A "client from hell" would be someone who wants my services, but doesn't believe they need me or feels that their manuscript is above change, not trusting me to have their best interest at heart and thinking that my goals are not the same as theirs.

Do you think Earth was created a few thousand years ago or several billion years ago? Interesting question for this type of questionnaire. I may be controversial, but here goes. The Earth was made several billion years ago by a creator who formed our universe with a great deal of pressure and a bang. A famous book says that it was created in a day; however, that same book says that a day is as a thousand years to the creator. I think that number was one that the people of that time could understand. I believe that a day to the creator is a billion years or so. One day for the Earth, one day for the water, the animals, etc. I believe in religion *and* science. The creator would have had to be a scientist to create the complexity of cell system design.

Please list five books you recently agented. *Accidental Lawyer* by Kim Hamilton, *Death in Disguise* by Karen Neary, *Light a Candle for Me* by Jenni DeWitt, *Blue Pearl* by Sammi Goldberg, *The Last Outpost* by Jay Sandlin, *The Elementalist* by V. V. Mont.

Please describe the kinds of books you want to agent. I have a passion for all types of young adult. I love fantasy, sci-fi, and dystopian. I will accept those genres in the adult market as well.

What should writers submit for consideration, and how should they send it? Writers should submit polished manuscripts, except for nonfiction, erotica, horror, or picture books. Do not send your first draft "just to see how it goes." Find beta readers to help you with your self-editing, and go through as many drafts as you can. Then expect to be given more edits, by both the agency and your publisher. Agents will not take a manuscript that needs more than a little work. If you feel that you are one edit away from being published, go to my page on our agency website and click the button that says "Submit Here": www.corvisieroagency.com/jennifer-haskin.html.

How do you feel about self-publishing, and what do you see happening with it in the near future? It has been a long-standing belief of many that self-publishers are people who couldn't make it with the "real" publishers. Of course, this does happen, but it is not always the case. There are some hidden gems in the flood of self-published books pouring into the market. I think the number of unedited or poorly edited books being self-published unfortunately affects the expected quality of all the other books that may be worth Big 5 publication. There are many reasons why one would choose to publish oneself, but most of the authors I know have an ultimate goal of Big 5 publication.

Do you think there are too many, too few, or just enough agents? There are millions and millions of books, and they all have an author. Think about all the traditionally published books in your local library. Of course, there are copies and multibook authors, but all those books needed an agent. How long would it take you to count them all? As long as there are publishers, there will be a need for more agents, especially as many of them go on to other positions in publishing.

Do you think Amazon will become the country's largest employer within 10 years? I haven't heard that before, but I can certainly see it. With Prime, it's easier to shop on Amazon and receive the item at your door two days later than to run to Walmart or Target. This depends on your need for the item, of course, and whether you can wait; the nation gets lazier with each generation.

Why do you think some books become super-successful (beyond the obvious reasons)? I'm not sure that the reasons are obvious. There are the luck of the draw and trends in readership that shape the market. You have to be in the right place at the right time. As far as publishing goes, it's all subjective. You have to find the agent who is passionate about your work, and they have to find the publisher who sees the vision. It's like finding the one black fish in the koi pond. Things move and trends change, and you can't be the second werewolf love story they like; you have to be the first.

Do you think agents are likely to become millionaires? This one made me chuckle. You would have to be the agent of a multimillionaire author. Everyone wants to find the next J.K. Rowling, but even then, many agents passed on her. As I said before, you have to be passionate about the book. No one knows which books are going to "hit it big."

Do you think agents tend toward certain personality types? Not on purpose, but all people tend to gravitate toward charismatic, genuine artists who are humble and nonconfrontational. I know I do. I need creative writers who have confidence, but can still recognize good advice and will fix problem spots in their manuscript. And I like nice, helpful people like myself. I want to help authors realize and access their dream.

Do you think writers tend to be more or less narcissistic than the population at large? No. Narcissism is simply overconfidence, and I don't know any super-confident writers who feel more capable than everyday engineers, business owners, child-care workers, self-help gurus, etc. To me, narcissism is a character trait of individual people rather than businesses.

Knowing what you know now, would you become an agent again? Absolutely. I love my job. There is nothing as satisfying as helping people and giving them their dream-come-true.

Why did you choose to become an agent? As an author, I enjoy learning more about the literary world; and as an agent, I get to make lots of new friends in the publishing business, help clients achieve their goals, and watch them become successful authors. It's a gratifying position.

Do you think many talented writers fail to get published for avoidable reasons? If so, what are some of those reasons? There are so many things that can sabotage good writers. Not being willing to edit, not researching their agent, not being educated about the publishing process enough to recognize a bad deal or an unsavory contract. Authors want and need to trust their agent, but don't know what their agent can and can't do; they don't know their comp titles or what publishers they fit the best with. Or some good writers know so much about the process that they second-guess their knowledgeable agent at every turn and self-sabotage. There is a fine line between knowing enough to make good choices and trusting in the industry insiders they've chosen to do what's best and have their interests at heart.

Agent's name and contact info: Kaitlyn Johnson, queries: querymanager.com/query/KaitlynJohnson; nonquery emails: kaitlyn@corvisieroagency.com

What would you be doing right now if not responding to this survey? Editing *Writer's Digest* workshop partials.

What would you be if not an agent (other than a dog, cat, or other mammal)? A copyeditor or developmental book editor.

Do you think independent (noncorporate) publishing will be stronger, weaker, or the same over the next few years? For a while, it'll stay the same, as even newer small presses are cropping up. But my hunch is it'll grow stronger as writers begin turning to this avenue for publishing aid.

Please describe your professional history. After graduating from Emerson College in 2016, I was the copyeditor/proofreader for the academic press codeMantra and a literary intern for Corvisiero. I also began my own freelance editing business, K. Johnson Editorial, in 2016. In 2017, I worked in development and as a conference assistant for GrubStreet, Boston, and briefly acted as young adult editor for Accent Press. I am now a junior agent with Corvisiero Literary Agency, currently seeking to build my list.

How would you define the "client from hell"? Clients from hell refuse to implement edits or even to talk them through and brainstorm; also clients who need constant attention and hand-holding.

Do you think Earth was created a few thousand years ago or several billion years ago? I believe our planet was formed billions of years ago.

Please list five books you recently agented. Still currently building my list.

Please describe the kinds of books you want to agent. I want to agent vivid world building and characters I could reach out and touch, they're so clearly crafted. I also want all the feels and sarcasm. I'm a big dork, so I love things that can get a bit campy or fandom-like; stories should also be diverse, as it is in the real world. In contemporary, though, I love deep stories from unique perspectives.

What should writers submit for consideration, and how should they send it? I want upper middle grade — adult, fantasy, urban fantasy, historical fiction, and contemporary (and a dash of romance). Writers can submit their query, synopsis, and first five pages to querymanager.com/query/kaitlynjohnson.

How do you feel about self-publishing, and what do you see happening with it in the near future? Self-publishing is a valid avenue for some writers. It gets books out there that perhaps aren't grabbing the publishing world yet. The one thing I'd like — and we've been seeing an uptick in this already — is better editing possibilities for writers seeking self-publishing. These titles need just as much editing as a traditionally published book, and I hope writers are able to find it.

Do you think there are too many, too few, or just enough agents? There are *a lot* of agents. I don't know that I'd say too many, but the competition has clearly grown for agents over the years. But it's great. Writers have more opportunities to find someone they connect with and can form a great working relationship with.

Do you think Amazon will become the country's largest employer within 10 years? I am completely unsure on this. At the rate they're going, it looks like it. I hope physical bookstores, though, outlast it. It'd be a shame to see the corporation take over in the physical book-buying world.

Why do you think some books become super-successful (beyond the obvious reasons)? Many books become successful because they have their finger on the pulse of what's affecting people in the real world. This can be any genre. Even fantasy has themes and elements woven into it that mirror current news. Books that don't shy away or create numb views of life grab the audience and hold on.

Do you think agents are likely to become millionaires? No! This actually made me laugh. Maybe some agents will, who knows. But most aren't here for the money. We're here to take great books and find a place for them in the public. We're here to help writers tell stories. If an agent is there for the money, they're probably in the wrong business.

Do you think agents tend toward certain personality types? Not necessarily. I've met so many different personalities in this industry: introverts, extroverts, sharks, killer whales, heavy-editing or light-editing, funny, serious. It's a job that attracts people through a common interest, but the people themselves often seem so different from one another.

Do you think writers tend to be more or less narcissistic than the population at large? That's too broad a question. Writers are just like the population at large. Some are narcissistic; some aren't. Just like your coworkers or family members. I don't think being a writer makes you more likely to lean either way.

Knowing what you know now, would you become an agent again? I would've tried to do it sooner! My eyes were fastened on editing, which I still do and still love. But agenting is a world I didn't understand and wasn't sure was the fit for me. Now, though, I love everything it entails, and I just wish it could've been in my life earlier.

Why did you choose to become an agent? I became an agent because there are so many stories out there that need to be told, but often don't get the chance. My goal is to find these stories, to do everything possible so the world can see them. Writing is more than pages and ink. It's a part of the person's core, and it's one of the most emotional and vulnerable jobs out there. So I realized being an agent meant I could help writers on the way, take a little bit of the worry and burden out of it, and let them focus on creating.

Do you think many talented writers fail to get published for avoidable reasons? If so, what are some of those reasons? Many well-written stories might be passed over due to bad behavior on the writer's part. It's sad to see that, but if I realize a writer isn't a great person — has harmful ideals, picks fights, thinks they are above agent or editor guidelines — it immediately makes me not want to work with them.

Agent's name and contact info: Cate Hart, cate@corvisieroagency.com

What would you be doing right now if not responding to this survey? Reading.

What would you be if not an agent (other than a dog, cat, or other mammal)? An author, maybe an editor.

Do you think independent (noncorporate) publishing will be stronger, weaker, or the same over the next few years? It will continue to get stronger. We may lose some, while others will grow.

Please describe your professional history. I interned for almost a year before being promoted to an apprentice agent at Corvisiero Literary Agency. After about six months I was promoted again. I have been an agent for almost four years.

How would you define the "client from hell"? An author who doesn't fully understand all that goes into the business of publishing, is unable to disassociate unrealistic expectations from reality, and feels their publisher should do everything for them including revisions and marketing.

Do you think Earth was created a few thousand years ago or several billion years ago? Billions of years ago.

Please list five books you recently agented. Stroke of Midnight, Dusk Until Dawn, Break of Day, plus three more in the same series from Kensington's Lyrical Press; *Beautiful Crazy* and *Beautiful Mess* from Sourcebooks Casablanca.

Please describe the kinds of books you want to agent. I represent commercial fiction, primarily middle grade, young adult, romance, historical, some science fiction and fantasy, and select nonfiction.

What should writers submit for consideration, and how should they send it? Query, one- to two-page synopsis, and the first five pages of the work.

How do you feel about self-publishing, and what do you see happening with it in the near future? It is a viable path for some authors, but shouldn't be done without careful planning and understanding.

Do you think there are too many, too few, or just enough agents? Just enough.

Do you think Amazon will become the country's largest employer within 10 years? Maybe.

Why do you think some books become super-successful (beyond the obvious reasons)? Because of the right networking done by authors, word of mouth, and that the book's subject or theme created a resonance the public wanted at that moment.

Do you think agents are likely to become millionaires? I wish.

Do you think agents tend toward certain personality types? Yes.

Do you think writers tend to be more or less narcissistic than the population at large? I don't think so.

Knowing what you know now, would you become an agent again? Absolutely.

Why did you choose to become an agent? Because I love books and the writing process, encouraging authors, and selling their books.

Do you think many talented writers fail to get published for avoidable reasons? If so, what are some of those reasons? Sure. One is they don't persevere. Publishing is subjective, but rejections can be taken personally. It can be hard to separate that.

Agent's name and contact info: Kortney Price, Junior Agent, emails: kortney@corvisieroagency.com

What would you be doing right now if not responding to this survey? Answering emails, reading submissions, editing clients' manuscripts, and all the little things that come with the day-to-day life of an agent.

What would you be if not an agent (other than a dog, cat, or other mammal)? There's no other job I'd rather have, but if I absolutely couldn't be an agent, I'd probably want to own my own bookstore. It'd be your stereotypical small-town bookstore, on Main Street or in the square, a small, homey place, the kind with ladders on the bookshelves, lots of sunlight, a cat, comfy chairs, and tea.

Do you think independent (noncorporate) publishing will be stronger, weaker, or the same over the next few years? I find it difficult to predict anything with the current political climate, but I'm optimistic that so long as publishers focus on producing quality works, they'll be successful in the coming years.

Please describe your professional history. I started out in publishing in 2014 as an intern with Andrea Hurst & Associates. After that I moved on to intern with both Inklings Literary Agency and Amphorae Publishing Group. I was an associate agent with Holloway Literary before I found my home with Corvisiero in October 2017.

How would you define the "client from hell"? The biggest things I value in potential clients are patience and professionalism, so I guess the most difficult partnership for me to work in would be one where a client lashes out at me for the slow-moving processes of publishing. If my authors need to yell and scream about how frustrated they are, I'm here to listen. However, if someone was continually aiming their anger at me or especially if they were taking it to social media, I'd have a hard time working in that environment.

Do you think Earth was created a few thousand years ago or several billion years ago? Not sure. I wasn't there.

Please list five books you recently agented. As a new agent, I haven't sold to any publishers quite yet, but I have a wonderful team at Corvisiero and spectacular clients who are helping me to change that.

Please describe the kinds of books you want to agent. I'm a big fan of the books that allow you to escape into fantastic worlds and visit faraway places. Humor, art, artists, antiques and old buildings, and strong, quirky family dynamics are always welcome. I've also worked in the special-needs community for most of my life, so I'm especially drawn to stories featuring characters with special needs.

For middle grade I'm looking for adventure and survival stories, mystery, science fiction, and fantasy. For young adult I'm looking for psychological thrillers, "geeky" or "artsy" romance, magical realism, fantasy of any flavor, science fiction, and steampunk. As far as adult literature goes, I'm selectively looking for fantasy or paranormal featuring ghosts, time travel, ancient curses, and did I mention time travel? For more, check out my page at www.corvisieroagency.com.

What should writers submit for consideration, and how should they send it? If you think your story is a good fit for what I'm looking for, you can send in your query using my form at querymanager.com/query/kortneyprice. Please include your query, a synopsis, and the first five pages of your manuscript.

How do you feel about self-publishing, and what do you see happening with it in the near future? I am not against self-publishing if authors choose that route because they would like to be in control of their story's cover, sale price, and branding. I'm totally on board if authors are ready and willing to work harder than they've ever worked before. The upfront costs can be high when you need to hire a professional to edit your manuscript and someone to design the cover, and it's a lot of work in marketing afterwards. Also know that if you self-publish your manuscript, there's a very big chance that you're not going to be able to publish that story or the next books in the series traditionally without astronomical sales. I don't see self-publishing changing a whole lot in the future, although with the times we're living in nothing is certain.

Do you think there are too many, too few, or just enough agents? Every time I get word that there's another offer on a manuscript I love or have offered on, I grumble that there are too many agents. Ha-ha. In all seriousness, I think there are just enough. If everyone were looking for the same genres, then it would be a bit crowded, but interests are still varied enough. So we have a wonderful community of passionate people here to help authors.

Do you think Amazon will become the country's largest employer within 10 years? There's no denying that retail takes up a large percentage of America's workforce; if I remember right, it was the third largest employer overall. I'm no expert by any means, but with online shopping pushing some brick-and-mortar stores out of business and assuming that the number of people being hired by Amazon is equal to or less than the number of those losing their jobs in retail, it would make sense to me to see that industries such as health care would remain on top despite Amazon's growth. Again, I majored in English. Predicting what/who will be the largest employer in the country in 10 years should probably be left to people much smarter than me. Ha-ha.

Why do you think some books become super-successful (beyond the obvious reasons)? The books that become wildly successful are authentic stories being told to an audience that is hungry to hear what they have to say. The social and political climates have a huge impact on what the masses are reading, but these change so rapidly, it's incredibly difficult to chase trends. If you want your story to be hugely successful, write from your heart about issues that matter to you. The rest is a matter of luck and timing.

Do you think agents are likely to become millionaires? Ha! No, not unless the lottery or an amazing inheritance is involved. We don't do what we do for the money. We're here because we're passionate about what we do.

Do you think agents tend toward certain personality types? I don't think there's a specific type of personality that all agents love. We're all different, and so the kinds of people we're drawn toward will be just as varied. The trick is finding the agent you can work well with. That's the agent you will want working with you long-term.

Do you think writers tend to be more or less narcissistic than the population at large? I wouldn't say writers are more narcissistic than the population at large. I mean, think of how many rejections even the most successful of authors have to suffer through. The writers I've met and know are wonderful, humble people with hearts of gold.

Knowing what you know now, would you become an agent again? Yes. Hands down. I love my job, and even when it gets chaotic or the hours have me stretched thin, I can't imagine my life without it. It's a core part of who I am.

Why did you choose to become an agent? I love books. I enjoy helping people. Getting excited about books and helping authors for a living seemed to make perfect sense for me as a person.

Do you think many talented writers fail to get published for avoidable reasons? If so, what are some of those reasons? I believe some do. Little things like ignoring word count guidelines, not proofreading your query before sending, and not researching the agent before sending material are super-avoidable, but I continually receive queries with these issues. If I'm absolutely in love with a story, however, the small things can be overlooked or fixed. The biggest reason I'll reject a work even if I think it has potential is in attitude and professionalism. It's important to keep a level head and a professional image. We all get upset, but take a second, minute, or hour to breathe before responding or posting anything.

CREATIVE MEDIA AGENCY ❖ www.cmalit.com
212-812-1494

Agent's name and contact info: Paige Wheeler, paige@cmalit.com

What would you be doing right now if not responding to this survey? At this time of year (December), I am preparing for an active start to the new year. This involves preparing pitches and submissions to editors, reviewing the status of current projects, chasing subsidiary rights submissions (film, audio, etc.), brainstorming new income streams for backlist titles, etc.

What would you be if not an agent (other than a dog, cat, or other mammal)? I was an editor prior to becoming an agent, so I suppose I would still be working on that side of the desk!

Do you think independent (noncorporate) publishing will be stronger, weaker, or the same over the next few years? Independent publishing has been growing stronger over the past few years, but I feel that it is at a bit of a tipping point. Authors will continue to explore and utilize self-publishing, but I don't think in the next year or so it will continue to make the major inroads it has previously. That stated, major mergers and acquisitions occurring in corporate publishing will certainly cause current authors to be orphaned, so it's interesting times, for sure.

Please describe your professional history. I began my career in London with Euromoney Publications before moving back to the States to work as an editor for Harlequin/Silhouette and then as an agent for the Artists' Agency. I founded Creative Media Agency in the 1990s as a boutique independent agency; then I partnered with two others to start up Folio Literary Management in New York City. I left Folio in the summer of 2014 to relaunch CMA with an emphasis on providing a more personalized and highly detailed focus on my clients and their work rather than running and managing a growing firm.

How would you define the "client from hell"? I'm lucky enough to work with a stable of wonderful writers, but I think most agents try to avoid a client who is uncooperative and highly impatient and doesn't seem to understand the nature of the publishing industry.

Do you think Earth was created a few thousand years ago or several billion years ago? Several billion!

Please list five books you recently agented. *Three Christmas Wishes* by bestselling author Sheila Roberts (in the *Life in Icicle Falls* series); *Twilight Wife* by A. J. Banner, author of the breakout hit *The Good Neighbor*; *Dead and Breakfast* by Kate Kingsbury (first in the *Merry Ghost Inn* series); *Edinburgh Twilight* by Carole Lawrence (the debut title of a new detective series, *Ian Hamilton Mysteries*); and *The Future She Left Behind* by Marin Thomas (a standalone women's fiction title). We generally have anywhere between 15 and 50 titles published every year, so it's hard to pick just a few.

Please describe the kinds of books you want to agent. Fiction: commercial fiction, women's fiction, romance, mystery, thrillers. Nonfiction: narrative nonfiction, self-help, pop culture, women's interest, business.

What should writers submit for consideration, and how should they send it? Queries should be emailed to paige@cmalit.com. The subject heading should include the word *Query*. Fiction queries should include the first five pages of the manuscript. Nonfiction queries should include an extended author bio and the marketing section of your book proposal.

How do you feel about self-publishing, and what do you see happening with it in the near future? Self-publishing is a tough business, even for the most experienced writers. Like a few other agencies, we recently launched a self-publishing division — CMA Digital — to help clients with backlist titles and new work self-publish. Through this branch, I (and my office manager, Ana-Maria Bonner) offer to partner with current clients in getting their work up quickly and maximizing profit, so that they can invest more of their own time in doing what they love — writing.

Do you think there are too many, too few, or just enough agents? I love the quote, "Publishing is a tiny industry atop a huge hobby," and I'd imagine that as its gatekeepers the number of successful agents reflects that.

Do you think Amazon will become the country's largest employer within 10 years? Even though Amazon is certainly expanding and making major acquisitions, I doubt it will become the country's largest employer — but it certainly feels that way, doesn't it?

Why do you think some books become super-successful (beyond the obvious reasons)? It starts with a fabulous premise and good writing. Outside of having a phenomenal editor and a significant marketing budget, word of mouth can sometimes be the best tool for generating success. I want all of my authors to promote themselves — with the aim of encouraging readers to amplify that noise!

Do you think agents are likely to become millionaires? Anyone getting into agenting to get rich quick has incredibly unrealistic expectations.

Do you think agents tend toward certain personality types? Yes and no. Agents are people, just like everyone else, which means they each have preferences in the personalities they work with best. In a business partnership, though, agents need to be able to put those likes and dislikes aside to champion the work. If the differences are too extreme, though, then it is likely best to dissolve the partnership.

Do you think writers tend to be more or less narcissistic than the population at large? Writers I've worked with are eager to hone their craft through editorial suggestions and are completely open to revisions. Even my experienced clients accept these notes and work with the editor to polish the work.

Knowing what you know now, would you become an agent again? My first love was always reading. After learning I was also pretty business-savvy and enjoyed sales, what else could I ever do but be an agent?

Why did you choose to become an agent? I enjoy learning new things and discovering new talent. Also, the ability to wear multiple hats appeals to me. Over the course of my career, I have honed many skills and learned to wear many hats, including those of reader, editor, salesperson, and dealmaker. I discovered that I loved combining these skills and talents and that I could use them to forge a career I loved.

Do you think many talented writers fail to get published for avoidable reasons? If so, what are some of those reasons? Of course, it all starts with the query letter. Even if the actual manuscript is beautifully written, I won't get to look at it if the query letter fails to pique my interest. There is also the communication factor. Are the authors able to follow the directions given to them, and do they communicate in a professional and respectful manner? Finally, how much work are the authors willing to put into marketing themselves? If the expectation is that the publisher will do all the work, that writer may not be ready for the life of a published author.

CSG LITERARY PARTNERS / MDM MANAGEMENT ❖

www.csgliterary.com

127 Hillside Avenue, Cresskill, NJ 07626, 201-569-9213

Agent's name and contact info: Steven Harris, steven@csgliterary.com

Do you think independent (noncorporate) publishing will be stronger, weaker, or the same over the next few years? Same.

Please describe your professional history. Began in book publishing in 1971 with Warner Books, and then NAL/Penguin from 1976 to 1998. Founded online fund-raising company with backing from Microsoft and Compaq from 1998 to 2005, at which time I founded this agency.

Do you think Earth was created a few thousand years ago or several billion years ago? Several billion.

Please list five books you recently agented. Spiritual Fertility (Hay House); *My Dear Boy* (Potomac Books); *Owning Bipolar* (Kensington); *Step into Your Moxie* (New World Library); *This Is How I Save My Life* (Simon & Schuster).

What should writers submit for consideration, and how should they send it? We are interested in: current events, career, reference, biography, business/investing/finance, cookbooks, history, humor, mind-body-spirit/inspiration, health, lifestyle, pop culture, self-help, sports, science; also memoir and children's nonfiction, but only if heavily platformed! Email a query letter with a proposal attached.

How do you feel about self-publishing, and what do you see happening with it in the near future? Self-publishing is a viable enterprise for authors with a very large platform, but publishing with a traditional publisher is generally the way to go.

Knowing what you know now, would you become an agent again? Yes.

Why did you choose to become an agent? Love to see deserving books and authors get published.

DANA NEWMAN LITERARY, LLC ❖ dananewman.com

1800 Avenue of the Stars, 12th Floor, Los Angeles, CA 90067

Agent's name and contact info: Dana Newman, dananewmanliterary@gmail.com

What would you be doing right now if not responding to this survey? Following up on emails.

What would you be if not an agent (other than a dog, cat, or other mammal)? Practicing law full-time instead of part-time as I do now.

Do you think independent (noncorporate) publishing will be stronger, weaker, or the same over the next few years? Stronger. Independent and small presses serve an important role in the publishing ecosystem and can be a great fit for certain projects. They don't have the budgets or marketing and publicity muscle that the larger publishers have, but they're usually staffed by hardworking, dedicated people who are passionate about publishing good books and can take risks larger publishers can't. They have more flexibility and can adapt to changing market conditions faster.

Please describe your professional history. I have a BA in comparative literature from University of California at Berkeley and a JD from University of San Francisco School of Law. I founded my literary agency in 2010. Prior to becoming a literary agent, I worked for 14 years as in-house counsel for the Moviola companies in Hollywood, CA, providers of entertainment and communications technologies. In addition to representing authors as a literary agent, I'm also a transactional and intellectual property attorney, advising content creators and entrepreneurs on contracts, copyrights, trademarks, and licensing.

How would you define the "client from hell"? A writer who has unreasonable expectations about the realities of the book business, won't accept any feedback on their work, has no interest in marketing and promoting their work, is unprofessional, is disrespectful of the author-agent and author-editor relationships, and has no sense of humor. I can usually tell if a writer is going to be challenging to work with based on the way they communicate — both what they say and how they say it.

Do you think Earth was created a few thousand years ago or several billion years ago? No idea — science is not my strong suit.

Please list five books you recently agented. *Crawl of Fame* by Julie Moss and Robert Yehling (Pegasus), *Diagnosis Female* by Emily Dwass (Rowman & Littlefield), *Climbing the Hill* by Jaime Harrison and Amos Snead (Ten Speed), *Nora Murphy's Country House Style* by Nora Murphy (Vendome), *A Court of Refuge* by Ginger Lerner-Wren (Beacon).

Please describe the kinds of books you want to agent. I'm interested in representing practical nonfiction (business, health and wellness, self-help, psychology, parenting, technology) by authors with smart, unique perspectives and established platforms. I love compelling, inspiring narrative nonfiction in the areas of memoir, biography, history, pop culture, current affairs, women's interest, social trends, science, and sports. My favorite genre is literary nonfiction: true stories, well told, that read like a novel you can't put down. On the fiction side I'm looking for a very select amount of literary fiction and upmarket women's fiction (contemporary and historical).

What should writers submit for consideration, and how should they send it? Email a query letter to dananewmanliterary@gmail.com that identifies the category, title, and word count and provides a brief overview of your project, credentials, platform, and previous publishing history, if any. For fiction submissions, please send a query letter and the first 5 pages of your book in the body of the email (no attachments). If I'm interested in your material, I'll email you a request for a full proposal (for nonfiction) or a synopsis and the first 20 pages (for fiction). Unfortunately, I can't respond to every query I receive. Be sure to include your contact details (email address and phone number), relevant writing experience (articles, books), or writing awards.

How do you feel about self-publishing, and what do you see happening with it in the near future? Self-publishing can be a great option for those writers who have the means and ability to handle all aspects of the publishing process or put together a team of experts to help them. It's easier than ever to upload an ebook and have it distributed to major online retailers, but it's another thing to have that book be well-edited with a striking professional cover, receive impactful reviews and media attention, and sell a lot of copies. The success stories are wonderful, but they represent a very small percentage of all the self-published books out there, most of which don't find an audience and fail to sell.

Do you think there are too many, too few, or just enough agents? To me, as an agent trying to sell projects, it feels like there are too many, but I'm sure to the writers seeking publication it feels like there aren't enough. So perhaps there are just enough.

Do you think Amazon will become the country's largest employer within 10 years? It's starting to look that way.

Why do you think some books become super-successful (beyond the obvious reasons)? That magical coalescence of good timing, the right marketing and promotion, and word of mouth.

Do you think agents are likely to become millionaires? From selling books, no.

Do you think agents tend toward certain personality types? Most of them are bookworms, but other than that I've encountered a wide range of types of people who are agents.

Do you think writers tend to be more or less narcissistic than the population at large? Certainly the act of writing a memoir is inherently self-focused, but I think most writers are motivated by a desire to help, share, or engage with others.

Knowing what you know now, would you become an agent again? I would absolutely do it again — I wish I'd started sooner.

Why did you choose to become an agent? I'm a lifelong book lover, and after working as an in-house attorney in the entertainment industry for many years, I knew I wanted to bring those skills and my passion for reading to a position in publishing. Having worked in entertainment during the transition from analog to digital platforms in film editing and audio recording, I was excited about the new technologies and business models for the creation and distribution of books that were emerging.

Do you think many talented writers fail to get published for avoidable reasons? If so, what are some of those reasons? Yes. Failing to learn about the business of publishing; sending work out too soon before it's ready; not accepting when a project suffers from a fatal flaw and refusing to listen to feedback and rework it.

Optional shout-outs/comments: Thank you, Jeff Herman, for creating this guide, which is a wonderful resource for writers!

DEFIORE AND COMPANY LITERARY MANAGEMENT, INC. ❖

www.defliterary.com

47 East 19th Street, 3rd Floor, New York, NY 10003

Agent's name and contact info: Miriam Altshuler, querymiriam@defliterary.com

Please describe your professional history. I began my career at Russell & Volkening, where I worked for 12 years with such writers as Anne Tyler, Eudora Welty, Joseph Campbell, Nadine Gordimer, and Bernard Malamud. In 1994 I established my own agency, which I ran for 21 years until I joined DeFiore and Company in early 2016.

Please list five books you recently agented. *The Light We Lost* by Jill Santopolo, *Survivor Café* by Elizabeth Rosner, *The Truth as Told by Mason Buttle* by Leslie Connor, *Everything Must Go* by Jenny Fran Davis, *The Shadow Daughter: A Memoir of Estrangement* by Harriet Brown.

Please describe the kinds of books you want to agent. I specialize in adult literary and commercial fiction, narrative nonfiction, and books for children. First and foremost, I respond to voices and stories that are character-driven. I search for books that draw me in and give me a new perspective on a world I don't know or make me think more deeply about a world I do know. I seek books with a heart and writers with wonderful storytelling abilities.

In fiction, I am most interested in family sagas, historical novels, and stories that offer a new twist or retelling of some kind. I do not work with adult romance, sci-fi, or fantasy. In nonfiction, I love memoir, narrative nonfiction, and self-help (as long as it is not too prescriptive). I particularly respond to books that have an important cultural, social, or psychological focus. For children's books, I focus primarily on young adult and middle grade, and my tastes vary broadly in those areas. It always comes back to the voice and the heart of a story for me.

What should writers submit for consideration, and how should they send it? I only accept email queries. For all manuscript queries, please send an email to querymiriam@defliterary.com that includes (1) a brief description of your book — I really want to know what you feel the heart of your book is, in one or two sentences; (2) a brief relevant bio; and (3) the first chapter pasted in the body of the email; attachments will not be opened.

Agent's name and contact info: Caryn Karmatz Rudy, caryn@defliterary.com

What would you be doing right now if not responding to this survey? Reading a manuscript!

What would you be if not an agent (other than a dog, cat, or other mammal)? I would be a book reviewer. Imagine just reading piles of books and picking the ones you like best and bestowing praise upon them! And if they weren't worthy of praise, I'd just skip those reviews!

Do you think independent (noncorporate) publishing will be stronger, weaker, or the same over the next few years? The same.

Please describe your professional history. I was an editor at Warner/Grand Central for 17 years before joining DeFiore in 2010.

How would you define the "client from hell"? A client who doesn't trust my opinion/perspective.

Do you think Earth was created a few thousand years ago or several billion years ago? The real question is: Will the Earth be here for another billion years or just another few decades?

Please list five books you recently agented. Never Have I Ever by Joshilyn Jackson (Morrow, 2019), Ashes of Fiery Weather by Kathleen Donohoe (Houghton Mifflin Harcourt, 2016), The Way She Wears It by Dallas Shaw (Morrow, 2017), Beyond Birds and Bees by Bonnie J. Rough (Seal, 2018), Heartstrong by Amy Bloch and Colleen Kapklein (St. Martin's, 2019).

Please describe the kinds of books you want to agent. I love voice-driven fiction, ideally in the sweet spot between literary and commercial (but who doesn't?) and have a soft spot for witty, unreliable narrators. I also gravitate toward women's interest nonfiction, with a focus on parenting, relationships, lifestyle, and fitness, and narrative nonfiction.

What should writers submit for consideration, and how should they send it? A query letter with five pages pasted in the body of the email.

How do you feel about self-publishing, and what do you see happening with it in the near future? For some projects it is a very viable option, but I tend to stick with more traditional publishers, both large and independent.

Do you think there are too many, too few, or just enough agents? There are so many amazing writers out there for agents to discover — we've got a great array to choose from, so I'd say just enough. We need more editors, though!

Do you think Amazon will become the country's largest employer within 10 years? Yes.

Why do you think some books become super-successful (beyond the obvious reasons)? The stars have to align just right. There are so many superb books that don't find their readership every year, but with a passionate author, agent, editor, and publicist, there's always a shot — and if I didn't believe that, I couldn't be in this business!

Do you think agents are likely to become millionaires? Sadly, not often.

Do you think agents tend toward certain personality types? Agents are as different as the writers we represent.

Do you think writers tend to be more or less narcissistic than the population at large? I plead the fifth.

Knowing what you know now, would you become an agent again? Yes!

Why did you choose to become an agent? I loved being an editor, but wanted more freedom to develop all the projects I loved and not be limited to the tastes of one house.

DENISE SHANNON LITERARY AGENCY, INC. ❖
deniseshannonagency.com

121 West 27th Street, Suite 303, New York, NY 10001, 212-414-2911

Agent's name and contact info: Denise Shannon, submissions@deniseshannonagency.com

Please describe your professional history: After 16 years representing authors at Georges Borchardt, Inc., and International Creative Management (ICM), I formed my own agency in 2002. My clients have received numerous awards and honors, including the Pulitzer Prize, the National Book Award finalist medal, the PEN/Hemingway Award, the MacArthur Fellowship, and the Whiting Writer's Award.

Please list five books you recently agented: *Toscanini* by Harvey Sachs (Norton), *Night at the Fiestas: Stories* by Kirsten Valdez Quade (Norton), *The North Water* by Ian McGuire (Henry Holt), *The Man Who Shot Out My Eye Is Dead* by Chanelle Benz (Ecco), *A Simple Favor* by Darcey Bell (Harper).

Please describe the kinds of books you want to agent: Particular areas of interest include literary fiction, narrative nonfiction, biography, journalism, politics, social history, health, and business.

What should writers submit for consideration, and how should they send it? Email a description of the available book project and a brief bio including details of any prior publications. We will reply and request more material if we are interested. Queries may also be sent by post, accompanied by a self-addressed stamped envelope, to Denise Shannon Literary Agency, Inc., 121 West 27th Street, Suite 303, New York, NY 10001. Please do not send queries regarding fiction projects until a complete manuscript is available for review. We request that you inform us if you are submitting material simultaneously to other agencies.

DIANA FINCH LITERARY AGENCY ❖

dianafinchliteraryagency.blogspot.com

116 West 23rd Street, Suite 500, New York, NY 10011, 917-544-4470
(no queries by phone, please)

Agent's name and contact info: Diana Finch, diana.finch@verizon.net

What would you be doing right now if not responding to this survey? Reading clients' work, editing same, and submitting it!

What would you be if not an agent (other than a dog, cat, or other mammal)? Good question. People always ask me if I'm a teacher — I think I give off teacher vibes. So does that mean I'd be a teacher? I do find that I'm more and more interested in politics, mostly on the local level, in response to what's going on in the world.

Do you think independent (noncorporate) publishing will be stronger, weaker, or the same over the next few years? About the same. The independent publishers that have survived so far are the strong ones, the ones that have adapted. Although a number of those depend on grants, and apparently grants are now harder to come by, so we shall see.

Please describe your professional history. I'm a faculty brat — my father chaired the English and drama departments at Dartmouth College — and have a BA in English cum laude from Harvard, where as cocaptain I worked with my field hockey teammates to see the benefits of Title IX come to women's collegiate sports. I earned an MA in American literature from Leeds University, England, because after Harvard, where the reading lists in American lit courses featured authors who were alumni of Harvard, I wanted to study the field from a bit more of a distance.

I started out in publishing as an editorial assistant at the very collegial St. Martin's Press, where I acquired my first books and learned about all the operations of a publishing house from the inside — invaluable experience for an agent. I trained as an agent at Sanford Greenburger Associates and then the Ellen Levine Literary Agency, where I handled foreign and serial rights in addition to my own clients, before opening my own agency in 2003.

How would you define the "client from hell"? None of my clients, I am glad to say. Someone with unrealistic expectations and an underestimation of the work involved in getting published. A writer who can't revise.

Do you think Earth was created a few thousand years ago or several billion years ago? Billions. Apparently the big bang was 13.8 billion years ago, so can we say the Earth was created in that event? To me, 13.8 is more than "several." And what's fascinating to me is how we get to that estimate.

Please list five books you recently agented. *The Journeys of the Trees* by Zach St. George (Norton); *Owls of the Eastern Ice* by Jonathan Slaght (Farrar, Straus and Giroux); *Cutting School: Privatization, Segregation and the End of Public Education* by Cornell professor Noliwe Rooks (The New Press); *Beyond $15: Immigrant Workers, Faith Activists, and the Revival of the Labor Movement* by Jonathan Rosenblum (Beacon); and an English-language translation of *Bundahishn*, the Zoroastrian creation myth (Oxford University Press).

Please describe the kinds of books you want to agent. I love to represent wonderfully imaginative, gripping stories written in a distinctive, engaging voice. For nonfiction, I am excited about popular science and social justice, and I love math, history, progressive politics, narrative nonfiction, sports, journalism, environmentalism from all angles including business and lifestyle, smart business advice, and health. Because I've always been successful at selling foreign rights, I love to handle both novels and nonfiction that will appeal to translation publishers as well as to the global English-speaking market.

What should writers submit for consideration, and how should they send it? First choice: A query letter through my site at dianafinchliteraryagency.blogspot.com. The submission form also asks for the first 10 pages (for fiction) or a proposal and sample chapters (for nonfiction). Submitting this way allows writers to easily check on the status of their query. And the software platform, Submittable, was written by my client Michael FitzGerald, and I helped test the beta version!

Second choice: By email, with the text of the query in the body of the email, not as an attachment, and with a subject heading that includes the word *Query*. The first 10 pages for fiction and a proposal and sample chapters for nonfiction may be included with the query as an attachment. Word files are hugely preferred to PDFs.

How do you feel about self-publishing, and what do you see happening with it in the near future? Whether it's successful depends a great deal on the author's personality and on the genre. The bloom is off the rose, people are realizing how difficult it is to do well, and the novelty factor is gone. Strategies that can make self-published books successful — such as fast, frequent publication — often don't work as well for books published traditionally. It's pretty clear to me that it's no longer a satisfying alternative for writers who just haven't been able to interest a traditional publisher in their work — there has to be a valid, positive reason for self-publishing, where pricing is such a factor.

Do you think there are too many, too few, or just enough agents? If you believe in market forces, you'd say there are just enough. I do think it is harder to become an agent and remain one, and many young agents, and some older ones, have separate side gigs or are trying different business models, perhaps charging for extensive editing, for example.

Do you think Amazon will become the country's largest employer within 10 years? Considering that Walmart, the largest, has nearly 2 million more employees than Amazon, I'm not sure. Amazon would have to have offices and warehouses in many more locations to catch up with Walmart. And there are products that are resistant to being bought by mail, delivery, or download — the human urge to physically go out and gather items is an instinctive one, hard to eliminate.

Why do you think some books become super-successful (beyond the obvious reasons)? Timing, and they reach a certain word-of-mouth tipping point.

Do you think agents are likely to become millionaires? Some agents, who concentrate on representing bestsellers — yes.

Do you think agents tend toward certain personality types? I did, before my first job at an agency (Sanford Greenburger Associates), where there were six or seven full agents, each one a very different personality!

Do you think writers tend to be more or less narcissistic than the population at large? I'm not sure "narcissistic," with its negative connotations, is the right term here. "Self-centered," "self-focused," or "inwardly focused" perhaps. And "sensitive." And are there temperamental differences between fiction and nonfiction authors? Yes, there are.

Knowing what you know now, would you become an agent again? If it meant becoming an agent in the same era — the 1980s — yes, I would.

Why did you choose to become an agent? I became an agent when it was time to move up from the assistant-editor ranks, and the older editors I knew all advised me that if they were my age, they'd become agents, because agents flourish when their authors do, and opportunities are unlimited. In my first job as an agent I saw that although the editor is often caught in the middle — as the author's champion at the publishing house, but always an employee of the publisher — the agent is wholly on the side of the author, and that is where I want to be.

Do you think many talented writers fail to get published for avoidable reasons? If so, what are some of those reasons? How avoidable these things are often depends on circumstances, but I think the answer is yes. Talented writers may not have the time and conditions necessary to finish a full-length work. Or they may not be interested in or inclined to write within genre boundaries, and these days publishers are very insistent that books conform neatly to specific genres, often for marketing reasons that have to do with sales, distribution, and promotional concerns, not editorial ones.

DOUG GRAD LITERARY AGENCY ❖ www.dgliterary.com
156 Prospect Park West, #3L, Brooklyn, NY 11215

Agent's name and contact info: Doug Grad, doug.grad@dgliterary.com

What would you be doing right now if not responding to this survey? Taking a nap.

What would you be if not an agent (other than a dog, cat, or other mammal)? A professional saxophone player. Or center fielder for the Mets.

Do you think independent (noncorporate) publishing will be stronger, weaker, or the same over the next few years? Boy, that's a tough one. On the one hand, it seems like the rich keep getting richer, so perhaps the small publishers will be weaker. On the other hand, the big publishers are vacating so much of the market, there are gaps for the smaller publishers, so perhaps they will be stronger. Which probably means both will cancel each other out, and it'll be about the same.

Please describe your professional history. Editor of both fiction and nonfiction for 22 years at imprints at Simon & Schuster, Random House, Penguin, and HarperCollins. Numerous bestsellers on the *New York Times* list as well as *Publishers Weekly*, Barnes & Noble, *USA Today*, and local lists. An editor in corporate publishing when it was a fun, moneymaking business. Became an agent in 2008, about six months before the economy fell apart, and have managed to hang in by tooth and nail. (Yes, it's a cliché. I know.) I now rep authors on both the fiction and nonfiction sides of the adult market. As I tell my friends, I may not ever get rich doing this, but I'm never bored!

How would you define the "client from hell"? The client from hell is one who puts you through the ringer out of ignorance, stubbornness, orneriness, and stupidity. Then they don't take your advice. Then they blame you when things go wrong because they didn't take your advice. The beauty part of having my own agency is if a client acts like a total and complete asshole, I can fire them. Life is too short to deal with jerks. And there are many jerks in this industry.

Do you think Earth was created a few thousand years ago or several billion years ago? Earth was created on November 13, the day Felix Unger was asked to remove himself from his place of residence. That request came from his wife.

Please list five books you recently agented. *The Next Great Generation: Vietnam Veterans and How They Changed America* by Joseph L. Galloway and Marvin J. Wolf, *Game Face: A Lifetime of Hard-Earned Lessons On and Off the Basketball Court* by Bernard King with Jerome Preisler, *Please Don't Feed the Mayor* and *Alaskan Catch* by Sue Pethick, *A Hole in the Ground: The Second Avenue Subway, a Century in the Making* by Michael Hunt and San Fischler, *A Serial Killer's Daughter* by Kerri Rawson.

Please describe the kinds of books you want to agent. Books that sell. Books that have a wide interest to the general reading public. Books that interest me personally. Books that are well written and intelligently thought out. Books that are fun and escapist. Books with lots of explosions in them! ☺

What should writers submit for consideration, and how should they send it? Query letter first as an attached Word doc. Or just a short email. Send to: query@dgliterary.com. If I like the pitch, I'll ask for more material.

How do you feel about self-publishing, and what do you see happening with it in the near future? Self-publishing is not the panacea that it's thought to be. Some writers who can't get published see it as a legitimate choice. And for those writers whose work is well done and who are willing to put significantly more time, effort, and money into it than they'd ever thought they'd have to, self-publishing is a good choice. To do it well is not easy. To do it badly is really easy, however. It's going to remain the minor leagues for most authors — perhaps as a place to get noticed and picked up by a real publisher. For the extreme few, it will become a success story unto its own, and they'll never need a real publisher. Good luck to anyone who chooses to go down that road. You're gonna need it.

Do you think there are too many, too few, or just enough agents? Far too many. They should all send their best clients to me. All kidding aside, probably too many, but I don't know how many of us are actually making a living doing this.

Do you think Amazon will become the country's largest employer within 10 years? It's a race to the bottom with Walmart. May not even take 10 years. Woe to all of us.

Why do you think some books become super-successful (beyond the obvious reasons)? Great market presence — authors who promote like crazy, publishers who support that promotion, market saturation in terms of distribution, and somehow just getting lucky and striking a chord with the reading audience.

Do you think agents are likely to become millionaires? Not anymore. Twenty-plus years ago, yes. Now, no.

Do you think agents tend toward certain personality types? For some it's a shared inability to put up with corporate BS any longer. There aren't too many around from the Swifty Lazar school of dealmaking these days.

Do you think writers tend to be more or less narcissistic than the population at large? Oh. My. God. More. Like so much more.

Knowing what you know now, would you become an agent again? Yes, but I would have done it in the 1990s.

Why did you choose to become an agent? I became tired of the corporate BS. The job of being an editor changed, and not for the better. With the coming of ebooks and social media, the editor's job doubled or tripled overnight. When a boss of mine told me I was "spending too much time editing," I knew that it was time to get out of the corporate publishing world. Besides, after 22 years, I didn't feel there were any new challenges. When you're an editor, you always need a backup plan, and for a number of years I'd been thinking about joining the "dark side." There was something very attractive to me about being my own boss, making my own hours, working with who I wanted, and not having to answer to anyone. Except my wife, of course.

Do you think many talented writers fail to get published for avoidable reasons? If so, what are some of those reasons? So many reasons. Where to start?

1. Not being open to criticism — real criticism. Having your friends and relatives tell you, "It's really good!" is not taking criticism.
2. Not learning genre conventions. Don't set out to break the conventions — the rules are in place because they work, because readers want and expect them. Never disrespect the readers.
3. Combining genres. Sounds like fun. May be fun. Marketing nightmare.
4. Can't self-edit. This is a big one. Keep it short. Keep it simple. Keep it moving.
5. Lack of either a great story or great characters. Writers can write great prose, but they need to tell a story that readers care about, and they need to create characters readers want to spend time with.
6. Being a Jerk, Part I. Your agent may work for you, but that doesn't mean he or she will lick your boots. You can get people to work harder for you if you're nice to them. Duh!

7. Being a Jerk, Part II. Don't stalk at writers' conferences. Or genre conferences. Or show up at an agent's doorstep unannounced. Unless you like seeing jail cells from the inside.

I think that's enough for now!

DUNHAM LITERARY, INC. ❖ www.dunhamlit.com

Agent's name and contact info: Jennie Dunham, queries: query@dunhamlit.com

What would you be doing right now if not responding to this survey? Reading, reviewing, and responding. Or writing a pitch and submitting!

What would you be if not an agent (other than a dog, cat, or other mammal)? I'm not sure. Some possibilities: a special-collections librarian, an avant-garde filmmaker, a professor of literature.

Do you think independent (noncorporate) publishing will be stronger, weaker, or the same over the next few years? We hope that the non–Big 5 will grow stronger, larger, and more able to pay substantial advances. The consolidation of the major publishers and the diminishing of the midlist has made this business really tough. Few writers start out with substantial sales right from the start, and the midlist allows them to grow.

Please describe your professional history. I worked at three literary agencies, John Brockman Associates, Mildred Marmur Associates, and Russell & Volkening, respectively, before starting my own.

How would you define the "client from hell"? A writer who wants more control over the book and process than is industry standard, who makes unreasonable demands, and who acts unprofessionally.

Do you think Earth was created a few thousand years ago or several billion years ago? Billions.

Please list five books you recently agented. Ten Horse Farm by Robert Sabuda, *Bad Kitty Camp Days* by Nick Bruel, *The Five Forms* by Barbara McClintock, *Every Father's Daughter* by Margaret McMullan, *Gangster Nation* by Tod Goldberg.

Please describe the kinds of books you want to agent. I represent all ages of children's books, from novelty through young adult, and literary fiction and nonfiction for adults. I'm looking for character-driven books with a commercial hook and writers with strong platforms.

What should writers submit for consideration, and how should they send it? We ask for a one-page query letter and the first five pages of the manuscript, all included in the body of an email sent to query@dunhamlit.com.

How do you feel about self-publishing, and what do you see happening with it in the near future? Traditional publishing acts as a quality-control filter. The trend I see is many writers wanting to see themselves in print before their writing is ready to be successful through a traditional publisher. Self-publishing allows writers to have complete control of their books in all aspects from creation to selling. Traditional publishing offers credibility, visibility, and distribution channels that are not always available to self-published writers. It's a choice each writer must make, and no single answer is right for all writers.

Do you think there are too many, too few, or just enough agents? The issue is not so much the number of agents, but the training and experience that new agents get in order to represent authors well. Writing, editing, and agenting are all apprentice businesses. I should add that it's healthy to have competition.

Do you think Amazon will become the country's largest employer within 10 years? I don't have a crystal ball, but it certainly seems on track to be so.

Why do you think some books become super-successful (beyond the obvious reasons)? If I could answer that, I would be representing only those books! But it's not predictable. That is both the challenge and the fun of the business. It is always a thrill when a book achieves great success.

Do you think agents are likely to become millionaires? All parts of publishing are tough and too infrequently have large financial recompense.

Do you think agents tend toward certain personality types? I don't like to generalize that way. Just as there are many types of editors and writers, there are many types of agents. We are all similar in loving books and wanting to be involved in their creation.

Do you think writers tend to be more or less narcissistic than the population at large? Again, I don't like to generalize that way. And I'd rather not define people as narcissistic. All writers have narcissistic moments, and these times have both positive and negative repercussions for writers.

Knowing what you know now, would you become an agent again? I love books and advocating for writers. So, yes!

Why did you choose to become an agent? By accident. Perhaps the best one that happened to me. In college I thought I might want to be an editor, and after an editorial internship the job I got was at an agency. I liked being involved with different types of books, which is easier to do, I think, as an agent than as an editor. And I also loved giving support to authors.

Do you think many talented writers fail to get published for avoidable reasons? If so, what are some of those reasons? Writing takes a lot of work, and it's not an easy process. One of the easiest ways to get waylaid is not being open to guidance. Agents and editors are trying to help writers get the best book possible that will sell well. It's a balance to keep the artistic integrity of a book and its marketability.

Agent's name and contact info: Bridget Smith, queries: query@dunhamlit.com

What would you be doing right now if not responding to this survey? Writing up notes on a new manuscript for a client — I may have chosen the easier task first!

What would you be if not an agent (other than a dog, cat, or other mammal)? I nearly went to grad school for archaeology, so possibly an academic or whatever kind of practical job you can get as an archaeologist — I confess I was watching a lot of *Bones* when I entertained this idea!

Do you think independent (noncorporate) publishing will be stronger, weaker, or the same over the next few years? We hope that the non–Big 5 will grow stronger, larger, and more able to pay substantial advances. The consolidation of the major publishers and the diminishing of the midlist has made this business really tough. Few writers start out with substantial sales right from the start, and the midlist allows them to grow.

Please describe your professional history. After college, I did an internship at Don Congdon Associates, followed by a freelance position as slush reader for Tor.com and a part-time job at a used bookstore in my hometown. I started at Dunham Literary as Jennie's assistant in June 2011, and I slowly started taking on clients around the end of 2012.

How would you define the "client from hell"? Someone who doesn't want to take editorial feedback, doesn't trust my expertise, and can't accept and roll with the disappointments that are inevitable in an industry that relies so heavily on taste and luck.

Do you think Earth was created a few thousand years ago or several billion years ago? Well, what I "think" doesn't really matter here — the science is clear. I studied human evolution under one of the global experts, and I have seen the fossils from tens of thousands of years ago.

Please list five books you recently agented. *The Nine* by Tracy Townsend, *Foolish Hearts* by Emma Mills, *The Window* by Amelia Brunskill, *Camp Griftwood* by Lee Gjertsen Malone, and *The Dream Peddler* by Martine Fournier Watson.

Please describe the kinds of books you want to agent. I represent middle grade, young adult, and adult fiction, and in general I want well-written, complex, moving stories with a lot of heart and a little bit of humor. I want characters who bind me to them and make me feel everything they feel. I want perspectives that I haven't read before and fresh, hooky premises. As for genre, I love upmarket/book club fiction (also known in young adult and middle grade as contemporary realistic fiction), historical fiction, and speculative fiction (including genre sci-fi/fantasy).

What should writers submit for consideration, and how should they send it? We ask for a one-page query letter and the first five pages of the manuscript, all included in the body of an email sent to query@dunhamlit.com.

How do you feel about self-publishing, and what do you see happening with it in the near future? It's a great option for the kind of person who wants complete control over the entire publishing process, but if you're not willing to be — or hire and oversee — the editor, cover designer, publicist, and more, it might not be your best course.

Do you think there are too many, too few, or just enough agents? There are certainly a lot! I've been in situations where I've been one of a dozen or more agents offering on a project, which is nerve-wracking for us and overwhelming for the writer (albeit the good kind!). But the issue here is not so much the competition over one manuscript as it is the bigger picture: if that many agents have similar enough taste to fight each other on one project, that many agents will also have other projects that they'll be submitting to the same group of editors, who can only buy a finite amount. The problem, I suppose, is not ultimately that there are too many agents, but that there are too few publishers.

Why do you think some books become super-successful (beyond the obvious reasons)? There's a massive element of luck in this business. Does the book hit at exactly the moment the audience wants it? Does it have an element that will make readers press it into the hands of everyone they know? Does the president violate the First Amendment by trying to prevent its publication? Any of these things can make a book blow up, but at the two-year mark, where many books are acquired, it's hard to predict whether they'll happen.

Do you think agents are likely to become millionaires? Hah! If only.

Do you think agents tend toward certain personality types? There's a wide range of personality types who are drawn to agenting, but they do tend to be a little more outgoing, a little more independent, and a little more opinionated on practical matters.

Do you think writers tend to be more or less narcissistic than the population at large? I do think it takes a certain amount of narcissism (or at least confidence) to decide your work is worth sharing with the world, but then the very act of fiction writing requires erasure of self and immersion into another. So I guess my answer is: both.

Knowing what you know now, would you become an agent again? I feel like I am continually choosing to be an agent with every new client I sign and every new submission I send out. It's an active process!

Why did you choose to become an agent? In part because it was the first job I was offered after college — but I kept up with it because I liked the intimacy of working directly with writers, the satisfaction of holding something I helped make in my hands, and the complete freedom to choose what projects interested me. I've always been a book lover, and I'm thrilled to be involved on this side.

Do you think many talented writers fail to get published for avoidable reasons? If so, what are some of those reasons? Not finishing a novel is probably the biggest pitfall! Once you've cleared that hurdle — and it's a big one — some of the others are not finding people who will give you honest and thoughtful feedback on the manuscript, not learning how to write a captivating query letter, and making demands before you even know if the agent is interested in the book. There's no shortage of good writers out there; given the choice, I'll always prefer a client who sees me as a valued partner.

EBELING & ASSOCIATES ❖ www.ebelingagency.com

Agent's name and contact info: Michael Ebeling, michael@ebelingagency.com

What would you be doing right now if not responding to this survey? Surfing, mountain biking, yoga, hiking.

What would you be if not an agent (other than a dog, cat, or other mammal)? I would probably be an amateur athlete of some type.

Do you think independent (noncorporate) publishing will be stronger, weaker, or the same over the next few years? They will be stronger over the next five years, especially if they get ahead of the curve on how to market books.

Please describe your professional history. I have been a professional marketing and sales person my entire career. I have marketed and managed everything from health-food stores to insurance and cars, and a long period of my career has been spent managing high-profile authors.

How would you define the "client from hell"? The client who thinks their book and their message is the best in the world. They have entitlement issues and expect us to be available whenever they reach out.

Do you think Earth was created a few thousand years ago or several billion years ago? Several billion years.

Please list five books you recently agented. *Running on Empty No More, The Complete Book of Juicing, Get It!, The Bra Book 2, The Recipe Hacker Confidential.*

Please describe the kinds of books you want to agent. Prescriptive nonfiction. Self-help, business, psychology, spirituality.

What should writers submit for consideration, and how should they send it? Query letter and book proposal via email.

How do you feel about self-publishing, and what do you see happening with it in the near future? It depends on an author's purpose for writing their book. Self-publishing is a great idea if they have programs and products they are using the book to upsell.

Do you think there are too many, too few, or just enough agents? Just enough. The market will dictate that based on who stays in business and who does not.

Do you think Amazon will become the country's largest employer within 10 years? Yes.

Why do you think some books become super-successful (beyond the obvious reasons)? Because the books connect with readers, and the best way to sustain long-term sales is by word of mouth. The other reason a book is successful is that authors figure out how to include their book in their sales funnels that produce sales passively through a tailored email sequence.

Do you think agents are likely to become millionaires? Yes, the top ones!

Do you think agents tend toward certain personality types? Yes, and lean away from others.

Do you think writers tend to be more or less narcissistic than the population at large? More.

Knowing what you know now, would you become an agent again? Yes, but I do think the role of an agent will change over the next 5 or 10 years.

Why did you choose to become an agent? I felt like I could help a lot of people get their messages out to the world.

Do you think many talented writers fail to get published for avoidable reasons? If so, what are some of those reasons? No, I think they fail to get published because the publishing world has placed so much emphasis on having a large platform. Most authors have no clue about this huge requirement until they start sending out query letters to agents.

THE EVAN MARSHALL AGENCY ❖ www.evanmarshallagency.com

1 Pacio Court, Roseland, NJ 07068-1121, 973-287-6216

Agent's name and contact info: Evan Marshall, evan@evanmarshallagency.com

Please describe your professional history. I received my bachelor's degree from Boston College and then attended the Radcliffe Publishing Procedures Course. I began my publishing career as a book editor, working at Houghton Mifflin, Ariel Books, New American Library, Everest House, and Dodd, Mead. I then became a literary agent, working at the Sterling Lord Agency for three years before founding my own agency in 1987. I am the author of several nonfiction books, including *The Marshall Plan for Novel Writing*, now available as software, and 10 mystery novels.

Please list five books you recently agented. *The Taster* by V.S. Alexander, *The Bloody Black Flag* by Steve Goble, *The Maverick's Snowbound Christmas* by Karen Rose Smith, *Never Speak* by John Manchester, *Nemesis* by Joe Yogerst.

Please describe the kinds of books you want to agent. Full-length adult and young adult fiction in all genres.

What should writers submit for consideration, and how should they send it? Send a query letter, the first three chapters of the novel, and a synopsis of the entire novel — all in the body of the email — to evan@evanmarshallagency.com. If we are interested, we will ask to see more.

How do you feel about self-publishing, and what do you see happening with it in the near future? Self-publishing has made it possible for millions of authors who couldn't get through the New York gates to make their work available to the world; many authors are not even bothering to try the traditional publishers. In self-publishing, strict categories in fiction are not as important, and a lot of fresh new work is being done. Authors have far more control over how their work is marketed and sold. In the near future more authors who are unable to sell in any numbers will drop out, reducing the number of self-published titles per year.

Knowing what you know now, would you become an agent again? Yes.

Why did you choose to become an agent? I started on the editorial side, wanted to work on a broader range of books, and switched to the agenting side.

FINEPRINT LITERARY MANAGEMENT ❖ fineprintlit.com

207 West 106th Street, Suite 1D, New York, NY 10025, 212-279-6214

Please list five books the agency recently represented. *Thirty Days a Black Man* by Bill Steigerwald, *Dreamland* by Sam Quinones, *A Secret History of Witches* by Louisa Morgan, *Fizzopolis* by Patrick Carman and Brian Sheesley, *The Last Volcano* by John Dvorak, *The Divided City* by Luke McCallin, *Starfish* by Akemi Dawn Bowman, *Red Sky* by Chris Goff, *August Snow* by Stephen Mack Jones, *The Improv: An Oral History* by Budd Friedman and Tripp Whetsell.

Agent's name and contact info: Laura Wood, laura@fineprintlit.com

With over 20 years in the publishing industry, Laura has a broad perspective on the book-publishing industry, having worked in-house at publishers large and small and also as a buyer. Laura was previously merchandising manager for barnesandnoble.com. As the science and nature editor, she bought books in the categories of science and nature, reference, home and garden, and science fiction/fantasy.

Laura has experience at a range of publishing houses, from the Harmony Books imprint of Crown to Duke University Press and Columbia University Press, and was the associate publisher of Council Oak Books, an independent book publisher. Laura holds a master's degree in publishing studies from New York University. Her master's thesis explored the market for serious trade nonfiction. Early in her publishing career she was an assistant at the Condé Nast publications *Vogue* and *Glamour*. Before that Laura studied at the Laban Centre for Movement and Dance in London. One of her life goals is to be known as the dancing science editor.

Laura specializes in serious nonfiction, especially in the areas of science and nature, along with substantial titles in business, history, and other areas by academics, experienced professionals, and journalists. Laura enjoys hanging out with scientists and academics in general and believes in bringing their findings to a wide audience. Her client list includes NASA scientists, animal behavior experts, paleontologists, physicists, and award-winning science journalists, among others. Laura is also developing a select list in genre fiction only (no poetry, literary fiction, or memoir) in the categories of science fiction, fantasy, and mystery. Preference given to SFWA and MWA members.

Agent's name and contact info: Lauren Bieker, lauren@fineprintlit.com

After a brief career in the fashion industry, Lauren made her move to publishing as an intern for agent Paige Wheeler. She moved to FinePrint to assist with day-to-day administrative tasks but is now developing her client list and is open to queries.

Lauren is looking for commercial and upmarket women's fiction and some well-crafted and differentiated young adult novels. She is also open to select dystopian science fiction as well as high-concept and literary fiction works. She appreciates great storytelling and is a sucker for outstanding writing and convincing characters. While primarily interested in fiction, she will consider nonfiction proposals related to the world of fashion. Please note: Lauren is *not* looking for religious fiction, horror, fantasy, or political/military fiction.

Lauren writes during her free time and has been published on various online platforms. She has attended many writing workshops and intensives, including the National Academy of Writing's intensive at Cambridge University in the UK.

Agent's name and contact info: June Clark, june@fineprintlit.com

June received her MA in writing and publishing from Emerson College, with a focus on playwriting. Her play *Separation Anxiety* was produced at the Brimmer Street Theater in Boston. A monologue from the play is featured in *One on One: The Best Women's Monologues of the 21st Century*. A published author, June cowrote *Signature for Success: How to Analyze Handwriting and Improve Your Career, Your Relationships, and Your Life* (with Arlyn Imberman) and *The Complete Book of Astrology* (with Ada Aubin). She is also the author of *The Everything Baby Name Book* (2nd and 3rd editions).

Before moving into publishing, June worked in the cable-TV industry handling affiliate relations, marketing, and promotion for Showtime, Group W Cable, and the New England Cable Co-op, and then worked for several promotion agencies as a consultant and copywriter on campaigns for cable networks including Food Network, HBO, A&E, and Nickelodeon. She is the recipient of a Cable ACE / Emmy award.

As an agent-at-large and the agency's online administrator, June built a strong client list with a focus on nonfiction projects in the areas of entertainment, self-help, parenting, reference, how-to, food and wine, style/beauty, and prescriptive business titles. Though June is *not* currently seeking new clients, she is focusing on platform building, promotion, and editorial consulting for emerging authors through her company, Get There Media.

Agent's name and contact info: Peter Rubie, peter@fineprintlit.com

What would you be doing right now if not responding to this survey? Answering email or reading queries and manuscripts.

What would you be if not an agent (other than a dog, cat, or other mammal)? A professional writer and a jazz musician. (Wait! I do that already.)

Do you think independent (noncorporate) publishing will be stronger, weaker, or the same over the next few years? The indie market has stabilized and will stay somewhat at the level it's at now. Some companies will grow stronger (BenBella is a great example of this). As the demands of corporate publishing dictate what the Big 5 can afford to publish, the smaller companies will be drawn in to fill the vacuum the Big 5 create.

Please describe your professional history. I began as a journalist in England, working in Fleet Street and for BBC Radio news before mobbing to New York, where I was the editor of a local newspaper in Manhattan. After a stint as a freelance editor and writer, I was hired to be a senior editor at Walker and Co.; after six years I left to become a literary agent. I formed my own company in 2000, which merged with another agency in 2007 to form FinePrint. In the meantime, I have written and published fiction and nonfiction and started an independent editorial company (Lincoln Square Books) that consults and advises authors how to publish themselves properly using myself and a network of experienced professionals. The two companies are *not* connected, but they are siblings, given the changing nature of the publishing industry and the technological opportunities available to entrepreneurial authors.

How would you define the "client from hell"? This is a client who has unrealistic and uninformed views and expectations of what the publishing industry is these days and what it (and their agent) can do for them. Someone who argues with you when you try and help them learn how to navigate the shoals of authordom. An author who believes their own press, and worse, expects us all to validate their belief that they should be treated like a million-book-selling author, when in fact they are either unpublished or have sold only a few thousand copies.

Do you think Earth was created a few thousand years ago or several billion years ago? Really? You mean it wasn't created by a certain Republican president at the moment of his birth?

Please describe the kinds of books you want to agent. I specialize in a broad range of high-quality fiction and nonfiction. In nonfiction I specialize in narrative nonfiction, popular science, spirituality, history, biography, pop culture, business and technology, parenting, health, self-help, music, and food. I am a sucker for outstanding writing. In fiction I represent literate thrillers, crime fiction, science fiction and fantasy, military fiction, literary fiction, middle grade, and some boy-oriented young adult fiction.

What should writers submit for consideration, and how should they send it? Go to the website and see the instructions for submissions. Generally we much prefer electronic submission with attachments to hardcopy these days.

How do you feel about self-publishing, and what do you see happening with it in the near future? For some these days self-publishing is a valid route to take. Where the "Hey, kids, let's put on a show" approach falls down is that the authors taking this route don't spend enough time and attention on professional standards of editing and book design and think they are naturally gifted at marketing and sales rather than understanding these are skills that take time to learn.

Do you think there are too many, too few, or just enough agents? Each agent has a niche they develop and so they attract authors who live in the shadow of those niches. The more successful in general that agents are in understanding their niche (or niches), the more successful they will eventually be.

Do you think Amazon will become the country's largest employer within 10 years? No. I remember when the Berlin Wall would never fall and women were doomed to be sexual victims of powerful predators in order to get on in their chosen career. Nothing is immutable or inevitable, as our lifetime has ably demonstrated.

Why do you think some books become super-successful (beyond the obvious reasons)? If I knew the answer to this, I'd have a *lot* more money than I do currently.

Do you think agents are likely to become millionaires? Not unless their clients do.

Do you think agents tend toward certain personality types? If you mean good writers who like to collaborate in the exercise of their craft, then yes.

Do you think writers tend to be more or less narcissistic than the population at large? It's true that writers — though, in truth all artists — often become self-involved in their obsession with writing/creating something, particularly at a professional level, but that is more a sign of commitment and perfectionism than it is of narcissism. It's also true that when you're really up close and personal with someone involved in a genuinely creatively process, it's relatively easy to mistake one thing for the other. In the sense it's not about you, but often about them and their sometimes constipated creative struggles.

Knowing what you know now, would you become an agent again? Only if I couldn't make a living as a full-time writer writing what I want to write.

Why did you choose to become an agent? Like many things in my life, I kind of fell into it, having been a writer who was also an editor who became an agent, yada yada yada, as I mention above. If you can't always do what you love to do most exclusively, then you can sometimes manipulate things so that you are doing the next best thing. And for me that was editing, and then being an editorially focused agent who works with writers who *are* making a success out of their writing. It does also take one away from a myopic view of the world and forces a more objective perspective.

Do you think many talented writers fail to get published for avoidable reasons? If so, what are some of those reasons? Often it's because they don't want to compromise with the demands of commercial publishing. After all this talk of art and creativity, it's important to remember that publishing is a *business* first and foremost, and the demands of sustaining profitable enterprises perforce narrow one's options sometimes. But it really depends on what you mean by "get published" these days. The indie publishing world and the mainstream world overlap more than ever now, and one feeds the other more commonly than before.

FOLIO LITERARY MANAGEMENT / FOLIO JR. ❖

www.foliolit.com, www.foliojr.com

630 Ninth Avenue, Suite 1101, New York, NY 10036, 212-400-1494

Agent's name and contact info: John Cusick, john@foliolit.com, Twitter: @johnmcusick

What would you be doing right now if not responding to this survey? I would be responding to client emails before diving into the day's manuscript edits.

What would you be if not an agent (other than a dog, cat, or other mammal)? In high school I wanted to join the CIA, but my foreign-language skills are abysmal. Today, if I weren't a literary agent, I'd probably run a food blog or YouTube channel.

Do you think independent (noncorporate) publishing will be stronger, weaker, or the same over the next few years? I imagine it could be a struggle to stay afloat as an independent publisher with book sales down across the industry; however, indies seem well poised to discover and break out new talent.

Please describe your professional history. I started as a personal assistant and dog walker and worked my way up to agent's assistant before eventually building my own client list with Scott Treimel NY. In 2013 I moved to Greenhouse Literary, where I expanded my list to include *New York Times* bestsellers and award winners. In 2015 I joined Folio Literary Management / Folio Jr., where my list has continued to grow. My focus has always been on young adult and middle grade novels, with occasional forays into nonfiction and graphic novels.

How would you define the "client from hell"? An author who expects fabulous success in exchange for doing as little work as possible.

Do you think Earth was created a few thousand years ago or several billion years ago? The Earth is 4.5 billion years old but looks great for its age.

Please list five books you recently agented. *Puddin* by Julie Murphy, sequel to her *New York Times* bestseller *Dumplin*; *We Hunt the Flame* by Hafsah Faizal; *Seven Deadly Shadows* by

Courtney Alameda and Valynne Maetani; *Saints & Misfits* by S. K. Ali; *The Seven Torments of Amy and Craig* by Don Zolidis.

Please describe the kinds of books you want to agent. Generally I'm after middle grade and young adult novels in a variety of genres, but with a particular focus on high-concept contemporary realistic stories, fantasy, and all manner of stories by a diverse range of voices. I want the books that kids will sneak, steal, or borrow in secret, those personal, dangerous, lifesaving stories.

What should writers submit for consideration, and how should they send it? Please email your query along with the first 2,500 words of your manuscript, with the word *Query* in the subject line, to john@foliolit.com. I try to respond to all queries; however, if you do not hear from me within 30 days, please consider it a pass.

How do you feel about self-publishing, and what do you see happening with it in the near future? It's a market that will continue to grow, particularly in the field of prescriptive nonfiction (which I don't typically represent). I'm always happy to see new work from previously self-published authors.

Do you think there are too many, too few, or just enough agents? For authors, choice is good, and today there are more agents than ever. However, if it were up to me, the list would include myself and maybe three other agents with vastly different tastes.

Do you think Amazon will become the country's largest employer within 10 years? I have no idea. I'm hoping in 10 years we'll all be living in Elon Musk's colonies on Mars.

Why do you think some books become super-successful (beyond the obvious reasons)? What are the obvious reasons? I'd like to know what those are so I can try to replicate them. But basically, books that become super-successful are the ones that make us feel something we need to feel (joy, sorrow, hope, inspiration). These are the books we share and talk about and gift to friends. These titles are the most successful because people care about them. It's only after people care that a book becomes a "sensation."

Do you think agents are likely to become millionaires? Oh, my goodness, I hope so.

Do you think agents tend toward certain personality types? Yes. There's a certain self-directed ambition, chutzpah, and imagination in the agent mentality. You've got to be driven, quick on your feet, and savvy. And there's another quality that doesn't often fall into the fast-talking agent cliché, and that's a kind of compassion. Some agents are caretakers by nature, I think, and want to look after, help, protect, and nurture their clients.

Do you think writers tend to be more or less narcissistic than the population at large? Less. It's all that outward focused energy, the quality of being an observer who chronicles the world.

Knowing what you know now, would you become an agent again? Absolutely.

Why did you choose to become an agent? It's an engaging, difficult, and rewarding job that's also creative. You help people realize their dreams, while also shepherding (one hopes) great new books into the world. Nothing is more challenging or gratifying than that.

Do you think many talented writers fail to get published for avoidable reasons? If so, what are some of those reasons? Talent is only a small piece of the pie. Failing to do your research when seeking an agent, expecting the world to shower you with praise and riches, or writing *only* for your own satisfaction are factors that prevent good writers from getting published, or published well. Writing is a creative and personal enterprise — publishing is about making money with your writing. Forgetting that being a published author is really a business can sometimes hamper a writer's success.

Agent's name and contact info: Erin Harris, eharris@foliolitmanagement.com

What would you be doing right now if not responding to this survey? When I'm not working, I love to travel, visit art museums, go to the theater, binge-watch engrossing television (usually something crime-based or with a speculative twist), enjoy a glass of wine, and read. I read a lot.

What would you be if not an agent (other than a dog, cat, or other mammal)? I can't imagine being anything other than a literary agent; it's my passion. However, if I had to do something else, I'd go back to school, get my PhD in literature, and become a professor.

Do you think independent (noncorporate) publishing will be stronger, weaker, or the same over the next few years? Independent publishers play a vital role in the publishing ecosystem, often publishing bold, risk-taking debut voices in literary fiction and narrative nonfiction. I believe and hope they will continue their good work for years to come. Some of my favorite recent books have been published by the indies.

Please describe your professional history. I joined the publishing industry in late 2007 and worked at the Irene Skolnick Literary Agency for about five years, first as an assistant and then as a junior agent. During that time, I pursued my MFA in Creative Writing at The New School, where I honed my editorial skills and got to experience what it's like to sit on the other side of the desk. This experience has served me well in the work I do with my authors. In 2012, I joined Folio Literary Management, where I continue to build my list in literary fiction, narrative nonfiction, and select young adult titles.

Outside of the office, I'm an active participant in New York's literary community. I'm a member of *Epiphany Magazine*'s board and a founder and curator of H.I.P. Lit, a literary event series.

How would you define the "client from hell"? Fortunately, I haven't encountered the "client from hell," but I think the agent-author relationship works best when there is clear communication, transparency, mutual respect, and realistic expectations. We work tirelessly on behalf of our authors — agenting is a labor of love, more of a lifestyle than a job — and it's always nice when authors communicate gratitude.

Do you think Earth was created a few thousand years ago or several billion years ago? Billions.

Please list five books you recently agented. Pulitzer Prize and National Book Award Finalist Carla Power's *Prodigal Children*, following her debut memoir *If the Oceans Were Ink*, an account of the cutting-edge field of deradicalization and its pioneers — including soldiers, "formers," Islamic scholars, and families — as they seek new ways to solve the global problem of violent extremism, told through the interconnected stories of four remarkable mothers from the United States, Pakistan, Germany, and the UK (Spiegel & Grau, Penguin Random House); Indie Next Pick Author Erica Ferencik's *The River at Night*, a "raw, relentless, and heart-poundingly real" (Ruth Ware, *New York Times* bestselling author) thriller set against the harsh beauty of the Maine wilderness that charts the journey of four friends as they fight to survive the aftermath of a white-water rafting accident (Scout Press, Simon & Schuster); Katrin Schumann's *The Forgotten Hours*, a debut novel ripped from the #metoo headlines exploring the fallout on a well-to-do family after a teenager accuses her best friend's father of a shocking transgression; and a second novel, *The House of a Thousand Eyes*, set in the art world of late 1960s America and on a Baltic island as the Iron Curtain descends, about one woman's quest to reconcile her troubled past and discover the fate of the daughter she was forced to leave behind (Lake Union, Amazon Publishing); MacDowell Colony Fellow and published poet Kit Frick's *See All the Stars*, pitched as in the tradition of E. Lockhart, Lauren Oliver, and Kara Thomas, a young adult debut about the thrills of first love, the pain of betrayal, and the complexities of female friendship, in which an 18-year-old must navigate her last year of high school in the wake of a mysterious accident for which she's been blamed (Margaret K. McElderry Books, Simon & Schuster Books for Young Readers); Oxford University professor emeritus and founder of the Power Shift Forum for Women in the World Economy Linda Scott's *The Double X Economy*, based on her blog of the same title, an account of global sexism, putting forth the cutting-edge theory that women, due to systemic exclusion, have emerged as a distinct economic group, the "Double X Economy," and that, if allowed to reach their full potential, could spur prosperity while solving humankind's most debilitating problems, pitched as the feminist answer to Thomas Piketty's *Capital* (Faber & Faber, UK).

Please describe the kinds of books you want to agent. I want to agent books that transport the readers to a world they've never seen or books that make them see our world differently.

I want to agent books that celebrate language and tell incredible stories, whether real or imagined. I want to agent books that are socially engaged and feature underrepresented voices. I want to agent books that interrogate, challenge, delight, and reinvent.

I represent books in three main categories: literary (and upmarket) fiction, narrative nonfiction, and select young adult titles. In *literary (and upmarket) fiction*, I'm mainly seeking novels, but I'm also open to thematically unified or linked short story collections. I enjoy family sagas, atmospheric novels with a strong sense of place, literary novels rooted in a speculative tradition that reaches beyond genre, books that engage with history, elevated suspense and literary mysteries, and narratives that play with form and structure. Strong female characters, diverse perspectives, and an enticing premise are also things I look for. In *nonfiction*, I'm interested in subject-driven narratives, "big idea" books, essay collections, feminism, books that promote social justice, and memoirs that transcend the author's personal experience to shed light on larger themes or societal concerns. I especially enjoy working with journalists. In *young adult titles*, I'm looking for dazzling writing, original premises, and masterful storytelling in the following categories: speculative, fantasy, contemporary realistic, contemporary with elements of magic, and psychological suspense.

What should writers submit for consideration, and how should they send it? Please query me at eharris@foliolitmanagement.com. You should include your query letter (description of your project and your writing bio) and the first 10 pages of your manuscript or nonfiction proposal pasted into the body of the email.

How do you feel about self-publishing, and what do you see happening with it in the near future? If authors have the marketing muscle it takes to promote their own books, then self-publishing can be a good alternative for writers who haven't found a home with a traditional publisher.

Do you think there are too many, too few, or just enough agents? We work in a competitive but collegial industry, and I value my professional relationships with my peers, both at Folio and at other agencies. There are many kinds of books and many kinds of agents. It's all about finding the right fit, and so it's great that emerging writers have choices.

Do you think Amazon will become the country's largest employer within 10 years? It's possible.

Why do you think some books become super-successful (beyond the obvious reasons)? Some books are set up to be successful, while others are underdogs — they strike the right chord in the zeitgeist and take off. It's always tremendously exciting when this happens. My best advice to writers is to always write the very best book you can, the book of your heart that feels wholly authentic and true to you — and to read voraciously and omnivorously.

Do you think agents are likely to become millionaires? This question made me chuckle. You don't go into agenting because it's a surefire thing or even a steady-paying job (most agents work on commission). You do this because you absolutely love it and can't stomach the thought of doing anything else.

Do you think agents tend toward certain personality types? I don't think there's one definitive "agent" personality, but I will say that you need to be extroverted, aggressive, fearless, tenacious, resilient, organized, and compassionate to be a successful agent.

Do you think writers tend to be more or less narcissistic than the population at large? Tough question. Like most creative people, writers tack between self-effacement and self-aggrandizement. (Here's a secret: agents do, too.) When you lay yourself bare on the page and create something public for others to judge and consume, of course you're going to be more caught up in assessing your own image than, say, someone who's not in the public eye. Agents make themselves vulnerable in a similar way. I think "narcissism," if we can call it that, is a very human response to living in a constant state of self-imposed vulnerability.

Knowing what you know now, would you become an agent again? In a heartbeat.

Why did you choose to become an agent? It was an accident. I didn't know what I wanted to do with my life. I had an English degree and a background in theater. I answered an ad on Craigslist for an internship at a literary agency, and I wound up falling in love with the work on my first day. I haven't looked back since.

Do you think many talented writers fail to get published for avoidable reasons? If so, what are some of those reasons? The mistake I see talented writers make most frequently is that they get caught up in the outcome rather than the process. You can't write well from a place of desperately wanting success; you have to write from a place of truth and passion that honors the work itself.

Agent's name and contact info: Jeff Kleinman, jeff@foliolit.com

What would you be doing right now if not responding to this survey? Reading one of nine novels or editing one of six proposals in my inbox. Or out having cocktails with my colleagues. Or both. (Kidding.)

What would you be if not an agent (other than a dog, cat, or other mammal)? Practicing intellectual property law or training horses, or both.

Do you think independent (noncorporate) publishing will be stronger, weaker, or the same over the next few years? It's going to continue to get stronger — focusing on areas that have been less of a focus for big commercial presses.

Please describe your professional history. After graduating from the University of Virginia, I studied Renaissance history in Italy for several years, went to law school, and then joined an art and literary law firm. A few years later, I joined the Graybill and English Literary Agency before becoming one of the founders of Folio in 2006.

How would you define the "client from hell"? Someone who doesn't listen, doesn't incorporate suggestions, and believes that the world "owes" him or her a bestseller.

Do you think Earth was created a few thousand years ago or several billion years ago? It saddens me to even think that this is a question that needs an answer.

Please list five books you recently agented. *The Marsh King's Daughter* by Karen Dionne, *The Luster of Lost Things* by Sophie Chen, *Ginny Moon* by Benjamin Ludwig, *Jackie's Girl: My Life with the Kennedy Family* by Kathy McKeon, *The Reminders* by Val Emmich.

Please describe the kinds of books you want to agent. Very well written character-driven novels; some suspense, thrillers, historicals; otherwise mainstream commercial and literary fiction; prescriptive nonfiction (health, parenting, aging, nature, pets, how-to, etc.); and narrative nonfiction (especially books with a historical bent, but also art, nature, ecology, politics, military, espionage, cooking, equestrian, pets, memoir, biography).

What should writers submit for consideration, and how should they send it? For fiction, write a fabulous book with a fresh voice and compelling, unique perspective and be able to sum up that book in a single, smart, intriguing sentence or two. For nonfiction, *enhance your credentials*. Get published, or have some kind of platform or fresh perspective that really stands out above the crowd. Show me (so I can show a publisher) that you're a good risk for publication. Email only (no attachments, please). Include a cover letter and perhaps a few pages of a sample chapter and/or an overview/summary.

How do you feel about self-publishing, and what do you see happening with it in the near future? It absolutely has its place — especially for projects that are more workmanlike, less voice-driven.

Do you think there are too many, too few, or just enough agents? I don't have a clue. I see the same agents again and again, and they're always great fun people to hang out with.

Do you think Amazon will become the country's largest employer within 10 years? Ten? Why not five? Or two?

Why do you think some books become super-successful (beyond the obvious reasons)? They tap a vein in the country's zeitgeist — something that's been lurking below the surface, waiting for someone to bring it into the sunlight and examine it with care and deliberation.

Do you think agents are likely to become millionaires? Golly, I sure hope so. As soon as it happens, I'm gonna buy me a boat.

Do you think agents tend toward certain personality types? Agents tend to be outgoing and very self-motivated. This can be a grueling grind of a business, and you need a certain amount of optimism, stick-to-itiveness, and drive to make the job work.

Do you think writers tend to be more or less narcissistic than the population at large? Vastly more self-involved — that's what makes a good writer. But "self-involved" doesn't necessarily mean "narcissistic."

Knowing what you know now, would you become an agent again? I feel like I don't know anything now. But if I could do it all over again, I'd go into computer science. No question about it.

Why did you choose to become an agent? My law firm shared offices with an agency, and I did several book contracts. Gradually, I started reading manuscripts, talking to writers, and before long, there I was — a literary agent.

Do you think many talented writers fail to get published for avoidable reasons? If so, what are some of those reasons? The biggest reason is that talented, wonderful writers pick familiar or disagreeable premises for their books — so agents and editors steer clear.

Agent's name and contact info: Marcy Posner, marcy@foliolit.com, 212-400-1494

What would you be doing right now if not responding to this survey? Reading, streaming TV, spending time with my grandchildren.

What would you be if not an agent (other than a dog, cat, or other mammal)? Go back to being a librarian, especially now with all of this cool technology.

Please describe your professional history. Please visit the agency website.

How would you define the "client from hell"? I only had one client from hell who called me nine times a day to read me paragraphs from his new work.

Please describe the kinds of books you want to agent. Fiction: mostly commercial women's fiction, historical, psychological thrillers, young adult, some middle grade, suspense especially. Nonfiction: narrative nonfiction, history, psychology.

What should writers submit for consideration, and how should they send it? Please query me at marcy@foliolit.com. Please include a query letter and the first 50 pages of your finished manuscript or proposal as an email attachment.

Why did you choose to become an agent? After a decade on the other side as an editor, everyone I knew told me I should become an agent. I listened to them and haven't turned back since.

FRASER-BUB LITERARY, LLC ❖ www.fraserbubliterary.com

401 Park Avenue South, 10th Floor, New York, NY 10016

Agent's name and contact info: MacKenzie Fraser-Bub, mackenzie@fraserbubliterary.com, 917-524-6982

What would you be doing right now if not responding to this survey? Reading, running, or baking.

Do you think independent (noncorporate) publishing will be stronger, weaker, or the same over the next few years? Stronger.

Please describe your professional history. I began my career in publishing as a teenager reading manuscripts and writing readers' reports at the Crown Publishing Group, a division of Penguin Random House. I am a veteran of the Columbia Publishing Course, having taught and worked there. I also spent several years at Simon & Schuster (Touchstone Books), in one of the industry's finest marketing departments, before becoming an agent at the venerable Trident Media Group. There, I quickly built a diverse list that included multiple *New York Times* and *USA Today* bestselling titles, including romance, new adult, women's fiction, cookbooks, and science fiction. In 2016 I established my own agency, Fraser-Bub Literary.

How would you define the "client from hell"? Unreasonable professional expectations coupled with poor communication skills.

Please list five books you recently agented. *Clean Snacks* (cookbook) by Arman Liew (Countryman), *Our Prince of Scribes: Writers Remember Pat Conroy* (anthology) by Nicole Seitz and Jonathan Haupt, eds. (University of Georgia Press), *Dolls* (fiction) by Anna Snoekstra (MIRA), *The Summer House* (fiction) by Hannah McKinnon (Emily Bestler Books), *Slippery Rock* series (fiction) by Kristina Knight (Harlequin).

Please describe the kinds of books you want to agent. Fiction: women's fiction, romance, new adult, young adult with crossover appeal, historical fiction, female-driven mystery, thrillers, and crime. Nonfiction: fashion, food, exercise, diet, and design; cookbooks (especially healthy eating and baking and specialty diet/nutrition); popular psychology, self-help, and relationships; and true crime.

What should writers submit for consideration, and how should they send it? Send a query plus the first chapter in the body of an email to submissions@fraserbubliterary.com.

How do you feel about self-publishing, and what do you see happening with it in the near future? In the right circumstances self-publishing is a great choice. I predict the continued success of hybrid authors.

FULL CIRCLE LITERARY ❖ www.fullcircleliterary.com

Submissions: For each of our agents, please use the Submissions Form on our website. No email or phone queries, please! You can also view our agent bios, updated "wish lists," and latest submission status on our website.

Agents:

Stefanie Sanchez Von Borstel is a literary agent and cofounder of Full Circle Literary, an entrepreneur, and a mom with more than 20 years of experience in trade book publishing. Prior to agenting, she worked in editorial, publicity, and trade marketing with Penguin and Harcourt Children's Books. She enjoys tapping her publicity and marketing background to champion writers and artists. Stefanie represents fiction and nonfiction children's books and select adult nonfiction. Recent books include: Celia C. Pérez's middle grade debut, *The First Rule of Punk* (Viking), which was selected as a Kids' Indie Next Book and named to many Best Book of the Year lists including *Kirkus, School Library Journal, Horn Book,* and NPR lists; Susie Ghahremani's author-illustrator debut, *Stack the Cats* (Abrams), a *Kirkus* Best Book of the Year and Amazon Best Book of the Year; and Juana Martinez-Neal's *Alma* (Candlewick). On the adult nonfiction side: *A Glorious Freedom: Older Women Leading Extraordinary Lives* by Lisa Congdon (Chronicle), and *Balanced & Barefoot: How Unrestricted Outdoor Play Makes for Strong, Confident and Capable Children* by Angela Hanscom (New Harbinger).

Adriana Domínguez has 20 years of experience in publishing. Prior to becoming an agent, she was executive editor at HarperCollins Children's Books, where she managed the children's division of the Rayo imprint. Before that, she was children's reviews editor at *Críticas* magazine, published by *Library Journal.* Adriana has performed editorial work for both children's and adult book publishers. She is also a professional translator, a member of the Brooklyn Literary Council, which organizes the Brooklyn Book Festival, and one of the founders of the Comadres and Compadres Writers Conference in New York City. Adriana is based on the East Coast. Recent books include: illustrator Ana Aranda's debut, *The Chupacabra Ate the Candelabra,* written by Marc Tyler Nobleman (Nancy Paulsen, Penguin); Emma Otheguy's biography of poet and Cuban national hero José Martí,

Martí's Song for Freedom (Lee & Low), which received five starred reviews; and *Bravo!*, by the award-winning team of Margarita Engle and Rafael López (Macmillan); as well as many award-winning and bestselling biographies and memoirs, such as *Little Melba and Her Big Trombone* by Katheryn Russell-Brown and *Taking Flight: From War Orphan to Star Ballerina* by Michaela and Elaine DePrince.

Taylor Martindale Kean is a graduate of the College of William and Mary, where she studied English and Hispanic studies. Taylor is looking for young adult fiction, literary middle grade fiction, and young adult and middle grade nonfiction. She is interested in finding unique and unforgettable voices in contemporary, fantasy, historical, and magical realism novels. She is looking for books that demand to be read. More than anything, Taylor is looking for diverse, character-driven stories that bring their worlds vividly to life and voices that are honest, original, and interesting. Recent deals include: *The Names They Gave Us*, the newest contemporary young adult novel from Schneider Family Book Award winner Emery Lord (Bloomsbury); *Wild Beauty* by Anna-Marie McLemore (Feiwel & Friends, Macmillan), *School Library Journal* Best Book of 2017, *Kirkus Reviews* Best Book of 2017, Chicago Public Library Best of the Best Book 2017, 2017 Booklist Editors' Choice; *The Someday Birds*, by Sally J. Pla (HarperCollins), 2017 Dolly Gray Children's Literature Award Winner, New York Public Library Best Book of 2017.

Lilly Ghahremani cofounded Full Circle Literary with Stefanie. But here's how it really began for her. After graduating from law school, she joined a small law firm that represented authors. Although she loved finessing the perfect deal for authors, she realized that what she loved even more was working closely with them. She wanted to be part of the entire creative process, helping to grow and manage their careers. So she decided to apply her powers of persuasion to advocating for writers at all stages of their careers. Recent deals include: *The Sh!t No One Tells You*, Dawn Dais's tell-all parenting series; *The Latin Kitchen*, popular West Coast chef Isabel Cruz's new Latin cookbook; *Hello Color* by the founder of the lifestyle blog *The Crafted Life*, Rachel Mae Smith; *The Complete Guide to Paying for College* by family finance guru Leah Ingram (Career Press); and *Bean Sprouts Kitchen* by the cofounders of the popular kids' restaurant, Shannon Seip and Kelly Parthen.

FUSE LITERARY ❖ www.fuseliterary.com

PO Box 258, La Honda, CA 94020

Agent's name and contact info: Laurie McLean, laurie@fuseliterary.com (do not use for queries)

What would you be doing right now if not responding to this survey? Doing book deals.
What would you be if not an agent (other than a dog, cat, or other mammal)? A geologist

or archaeologist. I'd have to study hard because my master's degree was in journalism, but it would be worth it.

Do you think independent (noncorporate) publishing will be stronger, weaker, or the same over the next few years? Stronger.

Please describe your professional history. I was a journalist, then a marketing professional, then an author, then a literary agent. All great jobs.

How would you define the "client from hell"? Someone who is so convinced their writing is spectacular that they will not edit or even consider changes of any kind to their opus.

Do you think Earth was created a few thousand years ago or several billion years ago? C'mon. Billions. But I guess it depends on which parallel universe you hail from.

Please list five books you recently agented. Behind the Vale and two more by Brian D. Anderson ($230,000 audio deal from Audible); *Nessie's Quest* by Melissa D. Savage (Crown Books for Young Readers); *Shadow of the Fox* and three more by Julie Kagawa (Harlequin Teen); *Cinderella Boy* and two more by Kristina Meister (Riptide); *On Thin Ice* and one more by Susan Cliff (Carina, Harlequin).

Please describe the kinds of books you want to agent. Middle grade, young adult, and adult genre fiction (fantasy, science fiction, romance, mystery, thrillers, suspense, horror, weird Westerns).

What should writers submit for consideration, and how should they send it? I am closed to unsolicited submissions. I depend on referrals and conference requests.

How do you feel about self-publishing, and what do you see happening with it in the near future? I love self-publishing for many reasons too numerous to mention here. At Fuse I specialize in hybrid authors, because I feel that it is the most stable way for an author to make a sustained living, having one foot in self-publishing and one in traditional publishing. I also see hybrid authors as having the story as the core of their author brand and then expanding it into all kinds of areas such as video games, movies, streaming, television, epics, flash fiction, plays, etc.

Do you think there are too many, too few, or just enough agents? Too many. Hah!

Do you think Amazon will become the country's largest employer within 10 years? No, I think the government has that locked up.

Why do you think some books become super-successful (beyond the obvious reasons)? Buzz. Current events. Gestalt.

Do you think agents are likely to become millionaires? Do you know the best way to make a million dollars as an agent? Start with three million dollars.

Do you think agents tend toward certain personality types? Agents tend to be more outgoing and extroverted, on the whole. We have to be, because our business partners are mainly creative introverts. We're also good at sales and marketing.

Do you think writers tend to be more or less narcissistic than the population at large? Less.

Knowing what you know now, would you become an agent again? Absolutely. I love my job.

Why did you choose to become an agent? It's the perfect blend for me of my right and left brain hemispheres. Creative and analytical all in one package.

Do you think many talented writers fail to get published for avoidable reasons? If so, what are some of those reasons? Not researching their potential business partner (agent) with as much passion as they use for their writing, so they select the wrong agent and it sets them back. Another reason is chasing trends. That is a fool's errand. And the third reason is they allow critique groups or other people to water down their writing, so their strong, true voice no longer rings through.

Agent's name and contact info: Michelle Richter, querymichelle@fuseliterary.com

What would you be doing right now if not responding to this survey? Reading.

What would you be if not an agent (other than a dog, cat, or other mammal)? A professional organizer.

Do you think independent (noncorporate) publishing will be stronger, weaker, or the same over the next few years? Stronger.

Please describe your professional history. I graduated from the University of Massachusetts at Boston with a degree in economics and a minor in Russian. I spent a number of years working in banking and finance in Boston and Baltimore before moving to New York City to attend Pace University's publishing program, where I obtained a master's degree and am now an adjunct professor. I worked at St. Martin's Press for eight years, before joining Fuse Literary in 2014.

How would you define the "client from hell"? One who doesn't want to listen to solid advice and is high-maintenance.

Do you think Earth was created a few thousand years ago or several billion years ago? Several billion years ago.

Please list five books you recently agented. *The Unrepentant* by E.A. Aymar, *Hollywood Homicide* by Kellye Garrett, *The Ingredients of Us* by Jennifer Gold, *America's Next Reality Star* by Laura Heffernan, *Chasing the Wind* by C.C. Humphreys.

Please describe the kinds of books you want to agent. Women's or book-club fiction, contemporary romance, mystery, suspense, thrillers (more like Harlan Coben than Tom Clancy), and select historical fiction. I also seek the following nonfiction: pop culture, science, medicine, economics, and sociology from recognized experts in their fields. See www.fuseliterary.com for more information. I'm open to young adult contemporary or young adult crime fiction as well.

What should writers submit for consideration, and how should they send it? A query and their first 20 pages pasted in the body of an email.

How do you feel about self-publishing, and what do you see happening with it in the near future? It can be a good fit for an author, whether for all their work or just one project. But writers must realize that they need to do (or hire people to do) all the jobs a publisher would do for them to succeed. These include an editor, a cover designer, perhaps a publicist and/or marketing manager if they lack those skills (and they likely do). And they need to figure out distribution if it's a print book and not just an ebook.

Do you think there are too many, too few, or just enough agents? Just enough.

Do you think Amazon will become the country's largest employer within 10 years? It's possible.

Why do you think some books become super-successful (beyond the obvious reasons)? Sometimes it's a great story hook, taps into something in the zeitgeist, or fills a need that wasn't being met.

Do you think agents are likely to become millionaires? No.

Do you think agents tend toward certain personality types? No, there's a range of personalities.

Do you think writers tend to be more or less narcissistic than the population at large? This feels like a trick question.

Knowing what you know now, would you become an agent again? Yes.

Why did you choose to become an agent? I love being able to work with writers, to develop their work and their careers with them, but I have greater autonomy as an agent.

Do you think many talented writers fail to get published for avoidable reasons? If so, what are some of those reasons? Yes. Sometimes, they have a great idea, but at the wrong time. Some are too shy or self-deprecating to effectively promote their work. We all suffer from the impostor syndrome sometimes. Fake it till you make it.

Agent's name and contact info: Tricia Skinner, queries: queryme.online/querytricia

What would you be doing right now if not responding to this survey? Finishing up a promising manuscript. This one is exciting!

What would you be if not an agent (other than a dog, cat, or other mammal)? An editor.

Do you think independent (noncorporate) publishing will be stronger, weaker, or the same over the next few years? Indie publishing will be stronger. I also think we'll see some indie mergers that will change the landscape in a good way.

Please describe your professional history. I started as a newspaper reporter, ended up in corporate communications, jumped over to game-industry relations, and ended up an author and an agent.

How would you define the "client from hell"? Unprofessional and unrealistic.

Do you think Earth was created a few thousand years ago or several billion years ago? Are you asking about Earth 1, Earth 2, or one of the other Earths from different dimensions?

Please list five books you recently agented. Level Up by Cathy Yardley, Not of This World by Tracy St. John, Forget You by Nina Crespo, The Breakup Bash by Nina Crespo, and an upcoming book by Synithia Williams.

Please describe the kinds of books you want to agent. Romance, science fiction, fantasy, historical. I enjoy blended genres (such as historical fantasy or fantasy romance). I mainly seek adult and young adult, but I would enjoy a great middle grade. It almost goes without saying that I have a fondness for diverse settings and people in all genres.

What should writers submit for consideration, and how should they send it? I use a submission portal to better manage queries. I ask for the query letter (no more than 3 or 4 paragraphs) and the first 20 pages of the first chapter (no prologues).

How do you feel about self-publishing, and what do you see happening with it in the near future? I love self-publishing. I buy a lot of indie books, and my client list includes successful indie authors. I think it's evolving fine without my predications. Just keep going, authors!

Do you think there are too many, too few, or just enough agents? I don't know. I think Fuse Literary has the right mix of agents, and our team is a great size.

Do you think Amazon will become the country's largest employer within 10 years? I wouldn't be surprised.

Why do you think some books become super-successful (beyond the obvious reasons)? Most books hit at the "right" time. It could be tied to a specific event that triggers people to want to see the story told from a fictional bent. It's always interesting to see something through a different lens.

Do you think agents are likely to become millionaires? Are we talking about different dimensions again?

Agent's name and contact info: Gordon Warnock, Partner, querygordon@fuseliterary.com, Twitter: @gordonwarnock

What would you be doing right now if not responding to this survey? Reading submissions. Folks, feel free to blame Jeff Herman for the wait.

What would you be if not an agent (other than a dog, cat, or other mammal)? Likely an editor or author coach. I love career building, and I love fixing manuscripts up to get them ready for market.

Do you think independent (noncorporate) publishing will be stronger, weaker, or the same over the next few years? I plan to vote for those who fund the arts and support small businesses.

Please describe your professional history. I started interning at an agency for my own personal use as a writer, and I fell in love with it. I found success fairly early; they offered me a job before I'd graduated college, and they fast-tracked me to becoming a senior agent. After way too long with that company, Laurie and I started Fuse, and we've since grown to a thriving team of eight sharp and diverse agents covering most of the trade market.

How would you define the "client from hell"? Hunched, moaning, pungent, with an incessant hunger for brains.

Do you think Earth was created a few thousand years ago or several billion years ago? Jeff, seriously.

Please list five books you recently agented. *The Night Child* by Anna Quinn; *Perceptual Intelligence* by Brian Boxer Wachler, MD; *This Is What a Librarian Looks Like* by Kyle Cassidy; *The Everything Series* by Kerry Lonsdale; *Losing the Girl* by Mari Naomi.

Please describe the kinds of books you want to agent. My nonfiction list is comprised of recognized experts with a significant platform (see www.fuseliterary.com for more info). I have a soft spot for quirky nonfiction steeped in pop culture, nerd culture, or punk culture; bonus points if the book is part of a larger project backed by celebrities and an enthusiastic fan base. My fiction list runs the gamut of women's fiction from literary to commercial, charming to thrilling. I also represent verse novels and graphic novels for young adult and middle grade.

What should writers submit for consideration, and how should they send it? Email is best, but also feel free to pitch me if you meet me at a conference or an online pitch fest. Follow my submission guidelines. I love it when folks follow directions. The most current info can always be found at www.fuseliterary.com.

How do you feel about self-publishing, and what do you see happening with it in the near future? I'm all for it if it makes sense for the author. I like using it as a tool for career development, but the beauty of it is that anyone can publish at any time for any reason. That's an essential part of today's healthy publishing ecosystem.

Do you think there are too many, too few, or just enough agents? More agents, more diverse agents, and more voices being represented, please.

Do you think Amazon will become the country's largest employer within 10 years? It's possible but not what I spend my day thinking about.

Why do you think some books become super-successful (beyond the obvious reasons)? I see it as a matter of the right kind of material connecting with what a particular audience is feeling at the moment. Nobody can predict it exactly, which is one reason why it's so magical when it happens. It's an industry of probabilities, educated judgment calls, and setting folks up for fulfilling potential.

Do you think agents are likely to become millionaires? Possible, yes; likely, no. Turnover in this industry as a whole is high, and many talented new agents move on to other careers before they've given themselves enough of a chance to succeed.

Do you think agents tend toward certain personality types? I love meeting other agents (and writers, too!), because, as different as we might be, on some level we're all tremendous book nerds.

Do you think writers tend to be more or less narcissistic than the population at large? More inquisitive, likely more introspective, but not necessarily narcissistic.

Knowing what you know now, would you become an agent again? One hundred percent.

Why did you choose to become an agent? Given the choice, I couldn't turn it down. It really is the best job.

Do you think many talented writers fail to get published for avoidable reasons? If so, what are some of those reasons? Of course. I'm sure I've passed on brilliant folks who didn't follow guidelines, didn't submit in a genre I represent, or didn't take enough time to edit their work before sending it.

Agent's name and contact info: Carlisle K. Webber, carlisle@fuseliterary.com, queries: querycarlisle@fuseliterary.com

What would you be doing right now if not responding to this survey? Training for a half marathon.

What would you be if not an agent (other than a dog, cat, or other mammal)? An opera singer.

Do you think independent (noncorporate) publishing will be stronger, weaker, or the same over the next few years? About the same.

Please describe your professional history. After years of working as a librarian, I attended the Columbia Publishing Course. I then interned at a large NYC agency, worked a few years at a boutique NYC agency, and joined Fuse Literary after moving to San Francisco.

How would you define the "client from hell"? The client from hell is a micromanager, doesn't know where their book fits in the marketplace, and can't behave on social media.

Do you think Earth was created a few thousand years ago or several billion years ago? Several billion. I'm a big fan of Neil deGrasse Tyson's podcast.

Please list five books you recently agented. This Side of Night, High White Sun, The Far Empty, The Stolen Sky, The Breaking Light.

Please describe the kinds of books you want to agent. For young adult and middle grade, I am seeking all genres; for adults, I'm interested in mystery, thriller, suspense, horror, women's fiction, and popular fiction. I have a special place in my heart for books that are very dark (or even a little dark) or that are filled with characters who aren't necessarily good, but who are always interesting.

What should writers submit for consideration, and how should they send it? Writers should submit a query letter and 10 pages of their work through my Query Manager form: querymanager.com/query/querycarlisle. They can learn more about what kinds of books I represent at my agency page: www.fuseliterary.com/carlisle-webber.

How do you feel about self-publishing, and what do you see happening with it in the near future? Self-publishing can be great for the right authors. In the future, we may see fewer self-published books overall, but more that are edited, marketed, and published well because authors understand the responsibilities that come with self-publishing.

Do you think there are too many, too few, or just enough agents? For what I represent, I think there are just enough. If I represented nonfiction, I might have a different outlook.

Do you think Amazon will become the country's largest employer within 10 years? Maybe, if they buy Walmart, McDonald's, and some pro sports teams, car companies, and the like.

Why do you think some books become super-successful (beyond the obvious reasons)? They speak to a wide range of feelings and experiences. Successful books are always greater than the sum of their parts and give readers something to think about beyond what the characters do on the page.

Do you think agents are likely to become millionaires? Anything is possible, though some things are less likely than others.

Do you think agents tend toward certain personality types? Every agent I know is tenacious and an avid reader. They also keep their expectations high not just for their clients, but for themselves.

Do you think writers tend to be more or less narcissistic than the population at large? They are neither more nor less narcissistic than any other artistic population.

Knowing what you know now, would you become an agent again? Yes. If I didn't want to be an agent, I wouldn't be one.

Why did you choose to become an agent? Agenting combines two things I both love to do and am good at doing: advocating for clients and matching books to readers. I also love working with authors on building their brand and planning their long-term careers.

Do you think many talented writers fail to get published for avoidable reasons? If so, what are some of those reasons? I do think most talented writers find a home eventually, but not every talented writer finds a home for their first book or even the book their agent signs for. As far as avoidable reasons, I'd have to say that the biggest reason an otherwise talented writer might fail to get published is that they send out the book before it's really finished. When a writer writes "The End," that's just the beginning. Agents have so little time to read unsolicited queries that if your book isn't as perfect as you can get it, we're going to pass on it.

GLOBAL LION INTELLECTUAL PROPERTY MANAGEMENT, INC. ❖
globallionmanagement.com

PO Box 669238, Pompano Beach, FL 33066, 754-222-6948

Agent's name and contact info: Peter Miller, President and CEO, peter@globallionmgt.com

What would you be doing right now if not responding to this survey? Representing an author, selling their book, or optioning their movie rights.

What would you be if not an agent (other than a dog, cat, or other mammal)? A movie producer or an artist.

Do you think independent (noncorporate) publishing will be stronger, weaker, or the same over the next few years? Stronger. Yes, the entertainment industry has changed. It might be considered the wild West, and all people involved in publishing need to embrace the change and learn how to deal with it in the 21st century.

Please describe your professional history. I've been a literary and film producer, manager, and publisher for decades. I began my career in New York as a literary agent and was the cofounder of Writers House. I went off on my own to form the Peter Miller Agency, which then became PMA Literary & Film Management. That spawned a film production company that became Millennium Lion. From there I formed Global Lion Intellectual Property Management. Additionally, I cofounded the independent publishing company The Story Planet with my client and friend Lou Aronica and still remain a stockholder. I've been involved in the production/representation of 25 films and still have many motion picture and television/cable series in development.

How would you define the "client from hell"? I can offer many descriptions, but I'll suggest a few. A client who doesn't use the internet or a computer. One who insists on calling or emailing you a dozen times a day. A client who constantly complains about paying a commission or thinks they own you because you represent them.

Do you think Earth was created a few thousand years ago or several billion years ago? It's definitely more than a few thousand years.

Please list five books you recently agented. *You, Your Child, and School* by Ken Robinson and Lou Aronica; *Red Wine* by Jeff Jenson, Mike D. Simone, and Kevin Israeli; *In the Footsteps of Jesus* by Jean-Pierre Isbouts; *Inside the Atheist Mind* by Anthony DeStefano; *Young Leonardo* by Jean-Pierre Isbouts and Christopher Heath Brown.

Please describe the kinds of books you want to agent. Cutting-edge narrative nonfiction, transformational/spiritual, futuristic healing remedies, anything that would help make the world a better place. I am also interested in cutting-edge fiction that has global potential as well as film potential.

What should writers submit for consideration, and how should they send it? See the submission guidelines on our website, and email us your query.

How do you feel about self-publishing, and what do you see happening with it in the near future? Social media has become an ever-present ingredient necessary for any author to be published in the modern world. Consequently, we spend a lot of time coaching our clients to learn how to build their brand, fan base, and community in order to drive the sales of their books.

Do you think there are too many, too few, or just enough agents? Just enough.

Do you think Amazon will become the country's largest employer within 10 years? Yes.

Why do you think some books become super-successful (beyond the obvious reasons)? Fads still have a presence in the marketplace. For example, what made *Titanic* so successful is that young teenage girls were going to see the movie as many as 10 times. Consequently, that broadcast a global recognition of all things Titanic-related. In the modern world, video games can drive sales. But traditionally, I'm enamored with book franchises like *Harry Potter*, *The Hunger Games*, *Jason Bourne*, the new *Star Wars* canon novels or any way the book industry flourishes as a by-product of other media.

Do you think agents are likely to become millionaires? Yes.

Do you think agents tend toward certain personality types? Yes.

Do you think writers tend to be more or less narcissistic than the population at large? More.

Knowing what you know now, would you become an agent again? No.

Why did you choose to become an agent? It just happened. I'm a born salesman, and I always fantasized about being a movie producer, which I have become.

Do you think many talented writers fail to get published for avoidable reasons? If so, what are some of those reasons? Unfortunately, the modern world of technology and the power of marketing in media versus the enormous number of books that are published each year (1.5 million) as a result of Amazon's CreateSpace has created a situation wherein the marketing of a book can become as important as the quality of the book itself.

Additional agents at Global Lion: Matthew Gill, Assistant; Charlie Serabian, Assistant

HARTLINE LITERARY AGENCY ❖ www.hartlineliterary.com

123 Queenston Drive, Pittsburgh, PA 15235, 412-829-2483

Agent's name and contact info: Jim Hart, jim@hartlineliterary.com

What would you be doing right now if not responding to this survey? Reading a manuscript!

What would you be if not an agent (other than a dog, cat, or other mammal)? A full-time musician.

Do you think independent (noncorporate) publishing will be stronger, weaker, or the same over the next few years? The number of independently published books will continue to rise, but if the quality of those books is not there, then that makes indie publishing weaker. There will continue to be a small percentage of authors who will continue to do well with their indie-published books.

Please describe your professional history. I've been a full-time literary agent for five years. I've been a prepress manager for a large direct-mail publication, and I've managed a soup kitchen/food bank/meals on wheels.

How would you define the "client from hell"? A writer who will not take direction or suggestion.

Do you think Earth was created a few thousand years ago or several billion years ago? My position on that is fluid. Lately I don't find the answer as that critical to me. I find it more important to acknowledge that there is a Creator who spoke everything into existence.

Please list five books you recently agented. *Spiritual Wisdom for a Happier Life* by Dr. Mark W. Baker (Revell), *Unblemished Trilogy* by Sara Ella (Thomas Nelson), *Journey into Silence* by Chaim Bentorah (Whitaker House), *Renewed* by Leigh Powers (FaithWords), *Confessions of an Adoptive Parent* by Mike Berry (Harvest House).

Please describe the kinds of books you want to agent. I represent nonfiction and fiction for both the Christian/inspirational market and the general market. Nonfiction: leadership, social issues, biography, Christian living, church growth, parenting, music/entertainment, and self-help. Fiction: literary, suspense/thrillers, speculative, sci-fi, fantasy, romance (contemporary, historical, suspense, Amish), women's fiction, young adult. I am *not* looking for devotionals, children's, or middle grade.

What should writers submit for consideration, and how should they send it? A full proposal, as a Word document, attached to an email.

How do you feel about self-publishing, and what do you see happening with it in the near future? Self-publishing can be a good option for a writer, but they must be willing to pay a good freelance editor and a talented graphic artist for the cover. Self-publishing will continue to grow.

Do you think there are too many, too few, or just enough agents? It's becoming a crowded field.

Do you think Amazon will become the country's largest employer within 10 years? It's possible.

Why do you think some books become super-successful (beyond the obvious reasons)? Those books have a message that resonates with readers in a strong way. It's often a case of the right book at the right time, which I don't think can be predicted.

Do you think agents are likely to become millionaires? No. (But I'm trying.)

Do you think agents tend toward certain personality types? Not really.

Do you think writers tend to be more or less narcissistic than the population at large? I find that my clients are quite humble. But we do come across a percentage who seem to be narcissistic.

Knowing what you know now, would you become an agent again? Probably, but perhaps with a different focus. I may have begun with a stronger emphasis on nonfiction.

Why did you choose to become an agent? Hartline is a family-owned business, and the time was right for me to jump in.

Do you think many talented writers fail to get published for avoidable reasons? If so, what are some of those reasons? One of the most avoidable reasons is failing to craft an excellent proposal for their book. They have to be able to succinctly identify their intended audience, and they need to be somewhat cognizant of how to reach that audience. The number of books published each year is staggering (traditional and self-published). There are definitely steps a good writer can take, along with a determined literary agent, but it's still a challenge to get noticed in the crowd.

HARVEY KLINGER, INC. ❖ www.harveyklinger.com

300 West 55th Street, Suite 11V, New York, NY 10019

Agent's name and contact info: David Dunton, david@harveyklinger.com

What would you be doing right now if not responding to this survey? Writing a submission letter. Or taking down a dead tree in my yard.

What would you be if not an agent (other than a dog, cat, or other mammal)? A park ranger.

Do you think independent (noncorporate) publishing will be stronger, weaker, or the same over the next few years? Roughly the same.

Please describe your professional history. I worked in editorial at Prentice Hall Press and then Fireside/Touchstone (Simon & Schuster) for seven years, then left to tour with a band for a year. After getting that out of my system, I signed on with Harvey Klinger and have never looked back.

How would you define the "client from hell"? Someone who calls to scream at me, then hangs up, then calls back, crying, to apologize. Someone who doubts I know what I'm doing. Also, someone who has their nonpublishing lawyer relative look at a publisher's contract and then send me many pages of alarmed questions.

Do you think Earth was created a few thousand years ago or several billion years ago? The latter.

Please list five books you recently agented. Tara Altebrando, *The Opposite of Here* (Bloomsbury Children's); Robert Gordon, *Memphis Rent Party* (Bloomsbury); Robert Elder, *The Mixtape of My Life* (Running Press); Tom Beaujour and Richard Bienstock, *Nothin' but a Good Time* (St. Martin's); Ed Ward, *The History of Rock & Roll*, vol. 2 (Flatiron).

Please describe the kinds of books you want to agent. Adult nonfiction (narrative, essay, memoir, biography, pop culture), young adult fiction (particularly contemporary), middle grade fiction (contemporary, sci-fi, fantasy).

What should writers submit for consideration, and how should they send it? A query letter and five sample pages.

How do you feel about self-publishing, and what do you see happening with it in the near future? I don't read much that was originally self-published, so I don't have an opinion about it. Writers frustrated by the process of finding an agent and publisher have taken and will continue to take this route. Some love it.

Do you think there are too many, too few, or just enough agents? Too many by a lot.

Do you think Amazon will become the country's largest employer within 10 years? Probably.

Why do you think some books become super-successful (beyond the obvious reasons)? I haven't a clue, to be honest. I've seen well-connected authors with vast social networks publish books that have done nothing, and vice versa. It's more likely, of course, that a highly visible author will do better.

Do you think agents are likely to become millionaires? No. But if they stick with it long enough, they should be able to make a perfectly decent living.

Do you think agents tend toward certain personality types? I know so few agents that it's hard for me to see whether this is the case.

Do you think writers tend to be more or less narcissistic than the population at large? How can I answer this without looking either ignorant or like a jerk?

Knowing what you know now, would you become an agent again? Absolutely.

Why did you choose to become an agent? It was a great way to be in publishing without all the corporate nonsense of working for a publisher.

Do you think many talented writers fail to get published for avoidable reasons? If so, what are some of those reasons? Many talented writers fail to get published, but not necessarily for avoidable reasons. I remain astonished by the crapshoot that is the book-publishing process.

Agent's name and contact info: Andrea Somberg, andrea@harveyklinger.com, 212-581-7068

What would you be doing right now if not responding to this survey? Reading manuscripts and searching for the next bestseller.

What would you be if not an agent (other than a dog, cat, or other mammal)? A freelance editor.

Do you think independent (noncorporate) publishing will be stronger, weaker, or the same over the next few years? There are so many smaller houses doing amazing work these days, and because of innovation in the distribution and marketing process, that will only continue.

Please describe your professional history. I've been an agent for over 15 years, working at the Donald Maass Agency and Vigliano Associates before joining Harvey Klinger in 2006.

How would you define the "client from hell"? I've never had a client from hell, but I guess that, if I had to imagine one, they would be very unpleasant. But if that was the case, I probably wouldn't be working with them to begin with.

Please list five books you recently agented. Ruth Emmie Lang's *Beasts of Extraordinary Circumstance* (St. Martins, finalist for BOMC's Book of the Year Award); Dana Mele's young adult *People Like Us* (Putnam Children's, Penguin Random House); Barbara Binns's middle grade *Courage* (HarperChildrens); Mithu Storoni's *Stress-Proof: The Scientific Solution to Building a Resilient Life and Brain* (Perigee, Penguin Random House); Hannah Howard's memoir *Feast* (Little A).

Please describe the kinds of books you want to agent. My list is quite diverse, and I'm looking for books in almost every genre, including young adult and middle grade. The only things I am not looking for are picture books and graphic novels.

What should writers submit for consideration, and how should they send it? A query letter and the opening five pages in the body of an email to andrea@harveyklinger.com.

How do you feel about self-publishing, and what do you see happening with it in the near future? The Big 5 publishers are taking on fewer projects these days, and so self-publishing can be a very viable option for a lot of people. The only thing I caution is that if you self-publish a book and then want to place another project with a traditional publisher, it can be hard to do unless the initial book has sold *very* well (i.e., tens of thousands if not hundreds of thousands of copies).

Do you think there are too many, too few, or just enough agents? Part of what is so great (and so tough) about this industry is that it's so subjective. There have been a lot of times that I've passed on a project, but another agent has loved it, and vice versa. It's great to have so many agents, because it means that there is more of a chance that a particular manuscript will find its perfect fit. That being said, it's important to make sure that the agent is reputable and has the connections and the experience to be a good advocate for your book.

Why do you think some books become super-successful (beyond the obvious reasons)? One of the most exciting things about reading a great book is the ability to talk about it with others. As a result, a lot of readers gravitate to the same titles, because they want to have that shared, communal experience.

Do you think agents are likely to become millionaires? No one gets into this business for the money. But, yes, I do think that it is very possible.

Do you think agents tend toward certain personality types? The best agents are those who are enthusiastic, optimistic, and driven. This is a business that is rife with setbacks, and it's important for an agent to have the persistence to keep on going.

Knowing what you know now, would you become an agent again? Yes, definitely! Absolutely no regrets.

Why did you choose to become an agent? I love to read, and I love to work with people who love to read.

Do you think many talented writers fail to get published for avoidable reasons? If so, what are some of those reasons? Some writers might give up too soon. There are a lot of wonderful agents out there, and sometimes it's just a matter of finding the right fit.

HEATHER JACKSON LITERARY AGENCY ❖ www.hjlit.com

Agent's name and contact info: Heather Jackson, heather@hjlit.com

What would you be doing right now if not responding to this survey? Reading, editing, or brainstorming with an author or editor.

What would you be if not an agent (other than a dog, cat, or other mammal)? Can't imagine a different profession that would be as interesting, exciting, or satisfying.

Do you think independent (noncorporate) publishing will be stronger, weaker, or the same over the next few years? Depends on the company; if led by a thoughtful, imaginative, and daring management team, then I'd say stronger.

Please describe your professional history. I've spent my life in books; first as an editor for 25 years and now as an agent. I feel blessed to meet and brain-meld with the talented people I've been privileged to work with over the years.

How would you define the "client from hell"? Someone who is dishonest, unkind/cruel, or disrespectful toward others. Life is too short.

Do you think Earth was created a few thousand years ago or several billion years ago? Is this a trick question?

Please list five books you recently agented. *We Need to Talk* by Celeste Headlee, *Breaking Free* by Rachel Jeffs, *The Last Wolf* by Maria Vale, *Motherland* by Elissa Altman, *OMD* by Suzy Amis Cameron.

Please describe the kinds of books you want to agent. As I say on my website, those works that make you want to press the pause button on all your duties and responsibilities and curl up in a corner for hours and read — and that can range in subject area from narrative to prescriptive nonfiction on through to commercial fiction.

What should writers submit for consideration, and how should they send it? I do not review unsolicited manuscripts, but I will accept query letters at query@hjlit.com. I make it a point to let authors know, though, that, as awful as it feels to wait with no response, I only reach out regarding works I am interested in reviewing.

How do you feel about self-publishing, and what do you see happening with it in the near future? I don't know that I "feel" anything about it per se; it's another available vehicle for some to share their work. For those with a major ability to move books in large numbers, it can make good, great sense to explore.

Do you think there are too many, too few, or just enough agents? I believe that the pool is big enough for everybody to swim in happily together. Every individual brings their own unique talents and tastes to bear in the works and authors with which they partner.

Do you think Amazon will become the country's largest employer within 10 years? For book publishing or in general? I don't begin to know the answer to either question.

Why do you think some books become super-successful (beyond the obvious reasons)? What are the obvious reasons? I believe that for a book to become super-successful folks need to be talking about it; there needs to be great word of mouth that continues to spur its sales on, and of course readers need to feel some deep connection to something within its pages.

Do you think agents are likely to become millionaires? Some do, some don't. I imagine it, like anything in life, depends on the agent and their authors.

Do you think agents tend toward certain personality types? I've absolutely no idea. If you were to ask me whether publishing folks were often of a certain personality type, I'd say yes, but I don't know that I'd be able to isolate it to agents in particular.

Do you think writers tend to be more or less narcissistic than the population at large? This question presupposes a belief that writers are narcissistic; I don't know that I believe one can make such a generalization. As to the population at large, I don't know the data about narcissism.

Knowing what you know now, would you become an agent again? Absolutely.

Why did you choose to become an agent? As an editor I felt hamstrung by the books I was allowed to work on and the narrowness of the genres I could work within; also, the author advocacy could get a little muddled, since I was working for the publisher, not the author. Not so on this side of the desk. I can work on any project that delights me and that I think I can find a supportive editorial home for within trade publishing.

Do you think many talented writers fail to get published for avoidable reasons? If so, what are some of those reasons? There are those who don't want to look at the marketplace as a whole — review what has and hasn't worked or is or isn't currently working — in the crafting of their work. I get all the reasons why someone might take this stance. But it neglects the fact that publishing is a business, and it is reviewing the current and past sales and basing their future lists on the genres they see are currently working. For instance, you might write a brilliant vampire story, but if publisher after publisher has seen a decline in that genre's sales, it will be a tough road to get an editor on board for your work. Or an insightful editor might see there's an opportunity, but that's harder to come by when going up against BookScan.

INKWELL MANAGEMENT ❖ inkwellmanagement.com

521 Fifth Avenue, Suite 2600, New York, NY 10175

Agent's name and contact info: Stephen Barbara, 646-517-2833, fax: 212-922-0535, stephen@inkwellmanagement.com

What would you be if not an agent (other than a dog, cat, or other mammal)? Completely unclear. I have no practical skills outside of the ability to identify, sell, support, and nurture writers.

Please describe your professional history. I got my start in 2006 as the contracts director of the Donald Maass Agency. Slowly but surely, I began signing my own clients and eventually ended up at InkWell Management as a full-time agent, representing a list of more than 50 authors. That's where I am today.

How would you define the "client from hell"? I can take all comers, and a challenging personality isn't a barrier to entry for me, if it's someone I really admire. I do think, though, that you should listen to someone's advice (at least with *some* frequency), if you've taken the trouble to hire and pay them to be your agent.

Please list five books you recently agented. *Bonfire* by Krysten Ritter, a nationally bestselling mystery novel from the star of Netflix's *Marvel* series *Jessica Jones*. *The Cabin at the End of the World*, the next horror masterpiece from Bram Stoker Award winner and World Fantasy Award nominee Paul Tremblay, this one a twist on the home-invasion novel. *Strange Practice* by Vivian Shaw, the first of a trilogy, launched in 2017, featuring Greta Helsing, London-based doctor to the city's supernatural community. *Replica* by Lauren Oliver, a *New York Times* bestselling young adult novel with a speculative twist that takes place in the Haven Institute, a facility where "replicas," or human models, are born, raised, and observed; optioned for film by Awesomeness. *The Hired Girl* by Newbery Medalist Laura Amy Schlitz, a *New York Times* bestselling historical novel for young people in which a girl who yearns for love, education, and a finer life after being raised in crushingly difficult circumstances on a farm in Pennsylvania runs away to Baltimore in 1911; winner of the Scott O'Dell Award.

Please describe the kinds of books you want to agent. I generally like a big story — big ideas and a big canvas — and writers with a real authoritative style or simply a unique voice. I sometimes think of my list as a sort of publishing version of "mixed martial arts" — there's children's and adult books, literary and commercial fiction, fiction and nonfiction, novels and screenplays even. I like to straddle those lines and have found there's a richness in being able to work in these different disciplines and develop an expertise for various categories. A few categories that I've done particularly well with are elevated genre fiction for adults, teen fiction, and quality middle grade.

What should writers submit for consideration, and how should they send it? A brief query letter by email is fine, with a concise pitch of the project along with the first five pages of the manuscript as a sample.

Do you think there are too many, too few, or just enough agents? Too many! To quote Lynn Nesbit in a recent *Poets and Writers* interview, "There are more writers than readers — and more agents than writers. I don't know how they all make a living."

Why do you think some books become super-successful (beyond the obvious reasons)? Publishing is funny, because everyone is an expert on why a book succeeded or failed after publication, but the longer I've been in the business, the more I feel that some books are simply never going to be popular just based on their subject matter; and we can learn a lot by looking at the books that readers actually like to read.

Do you think agents are likely to become millionaires? Sure. But to quote Michael Cader, in "*New York Post* dollars."

Do you think agents tend toward certain personality types? I would hope that most of us are aggressive on behalf of our clients, but at the same time honest and professional in our dealings. I can't speak for anyone else, but that is the type of colleague I've been lucky to have at InkWell.

Do you think writers tend to be more or less narcissistic than the population at large? More, of course. But in fairness, the publishing industry seems designed to bring out our worst neuroses.

Knowing what you know now, would you become an agent again? One hundred percent! It's given me such an interesting life, working with a group of really brilliant people on all different kinds of books. No day is the same, and there's always something new to learn. That's what gets me out of bed in the morning.

IRENE GOODMAN LITERARY AGENCY ❖ irenegoodman.com

Agent's name and contact info: Irene Goodman, irene.queries@irenegoodman.com

What would you be doing right now if not responding to this survey? Reading a proposal and watching the news at the same time.

What would you be if not an agent (other than a dog, cat, or other mammal)? A political campaign manager.

Do you think independent (noncorporate) publishing will be stronger, weaker, or the same over the next few years? Both stronger and weaker. Stronger because more authors will figure out how to do it, and weaker because many of them will crowd the market with yet more ecrap.

Please describe your professional history. It all started in the land of Goshen, where I toiled among the peons for coins thrown by passing noblemen. Then I started working for a publisher and got to see what agents did. I looked at that and thought I would be good at it. So I did it. I became a specialist in romance novels, which were booming at the time. Then I got sick of them, except for the very best, and reinvented myself doing everything else. After a long parade of bestsellers, I am not energized by same old, but will fight to the death for something that excites me. When those come along, I am like a tank.

How would you define the "client from hell"? I can't say. It's not printable. But oh, the stories these walls could tell.

Do you think Earth was created a few thousand years ago or several billion years ago? Both. I think science and poetry are easily reconciled, although there is a third alternative.

Please list five books you recently agented. *The Blue and the Gray* by Linda Lael Miller (title TBD), *Parisian Charm School* by Jamie Cat Callan, *Survivors Club* by Michael Bornstein and Debbie Bornstein Holinstat, *An Unquiet Grave* by Sharyn McCrumb, *Typhoon Fury* by Clive Cussler and Boyd Morrison.

Please describe the kinds of books you want to agent. Something brilliant. Something wonderful. Something different.

What should writers submit for consideration, and how should they send it? They should look at our website and do exactly what it says. Really.

How do you feel about self-publishing, and what do you see happening with it in the near future? It is here to stay, and it will increase as authors become more sophisticated, but it will also crowd the market with authors who are only so-so but make a lot of noise.

Do you think there are too many, too few, or just enough agents? Too many. Some of them don't seem to know what they are doing.

Do you think Amazon will become the country's largest employer within 10 years? Could be. They seem to be aiming for total world domination.

Why do you think some books become super-successful (beyond the obvious reasons)? Because they are good and they hit the right note. They are by savvy authors who understand they need to be more than authors. And because publishers anoint certain books and get behind them.

Do you think agents are likely to become millionaires? Of course.

Do you think agents tend toward certain personality types? No, but they all need to be bitten by the bug. The definition of a good salesperson is someone who sells. They can be quiet, loud, aggressive, courtly, or strange — as long as they sell books.

Do you think writers tend to be more or less narcissistic than the population at large? More narcissistic than Forrest Gump, but less narcissistic than Donald Trump. Anyone who becomes an author is automatically narcissistic. It can't be helped. I have been an author, and I was as nuts as anyone else.

Knowing what you know now, would you become an agent again? It's all I know how to do. Maybe it would be smarter to become a techie with one of those standing desks and high-end headphones, but I don't know how to do that.

Why did you choose to become an agent? Because I understood that I could get people to do what they needed to do even if they didn't know it. As a young assistant back in the day, I once walked a check through the company for an author who wasn't getting any attention from anyone else. I found it thrilling to make that happen.

Do you think many talented writers fail to get published for avoidable reasons? If so, what are some of those reasons? Sure. They write off-market. They fail to recognize that poor numbers are actually going to hurt them, no matter the reason. They don't learn to think like a publisher, who wants only to make money. They fail to utilize basic but crucial concepts, such as pacing, positioning, and voice.

Additional agents at Irene Goodman Agency: Miriam Kriss, Barbara Poelle, Rachel Ekstrom, Kim Perel, Victoria Marini, and Whitney Ross

JABBERWOCKY LITERARY AGENCY, INC. ❖ awfulagent.com

Agent's name and contact info: Joshua Bilmes, President, queryjoshua@awfulagent.com

What would you be doing right now if not responding to this survey? Reading through lots of emails, negotiating contracts, and always trying to do the best I can for my clients.

What would you be if not an agent (other than a dog, cat, or other mammal)? Santa Claus. Nothing is better than giving people gifts and helping make their dreams come true.

Do you think independent (noncorporate) publishing will be stronger, weaker, or the same over the next few years? Weaker. Amazon is going to squeeze independent publishers and authors even harder.

Please describe your professional history. I have been an agent for almost 30 years, having made my professional debut at the Scott Meredith Literary Agency in 1986. In 1994 I founded JABberwocky Literary Agency.

My path to owning my own literary agency started in high school, when I sent monthly letters to the editor of *Analog*, the leading science fiction magazine, critiquing each issue.

These letters so impressed Betsy Mitchell, the magazine's associate editor, that she offered me the chance to do freelance readers' reports and other work for her when she joined Baen Books shortly after its inception. The publishing industry and I took an immediate liking to one another, and I started at Scott Meredith soon after graduating from the University of Michigan with a BA in history.

Although my path to becoming an agent went through the science fiction genre, my interests were and are far broader. In the mystery genre, the Hardy Boys led to the Three Investigators, and from there to Agatha Christie, Perry Mason, the 87th Precinct, and John le Carré. I became a *Variety* junkie during high school and read it every week for as long as there was a weekly *Variety*. My college degree in history introduced me to the *New Republic*, and I now keep up on things with the *New Yorker*, *Rolling Stone*, and multiple newspapers. There's always time for a good movie, and tennis and Australian rules football are often my background music.

Do you think Earth was created a few thousand years ago or several billion years ago? Several billion. Go ask *all* of the world's peer-reviewed experts.

Please list five books you recently agented. A Deal with the Devil by Elaine Viets, *Sleep like a Baby* by Charlaine Harris, *Legends of the First Empire* by Michael Sullivan, *Finder* by Suzanne Palmer, *Quillifer* by Walter Jon Williams.

Please describe the kinds of books you want to agent. View my specific guidelines at this website: awfulagent.com/agents/joshua-bilmes.

What should writers submit for consideration, and how should they send it? View my specific guidelines at this website: awfulagent.com/agents/joshua-bilmes.

How do you feel about self-publishing, and what do you see happening with it in the near future? There is a space for it, but I am biased toward traditional publishing.

Do you think there are too many, too few, or just enough agents? Enough.

Do you think Amazon will become the country's largest employer within 10 years? No.

Why do you think some books become super-successful (beyond the obvious reasons)? The right combination of luck and hard work. Having a great agent doesn't hurt either!

Do you think agents are likely to become millionaires? Not particularly, but it is a fun job to have nonetheless.

Do you think agents tend toward certain personality types? Absolutely! They are all hardworking, literate people.

Do you think writers tend to be more or less narcissistic than the population at large? More narcissistic than accountants, but less narcissistic than our current president.

Knowing what you know now, would you become an agent again? Yes.

Why did you choose to become an agent? It's a lot more fun than digging ditches.

Do you think many talented writers fail to get published for avoidable reasons? If so, what are some of those reasons? You can be talented at writing but have no connections to editors at traditional publishers. Make sure you get an agent if you want to give yourself the best chance of being traditionally published.

Additional agents at JABberwocky Literary Agency: Eddie Schneider, Vice President, queryeddie@awfulagent.com; Lisa Rodgers, Agent, querylisa@awfulagent.com

JANKLOW & NESBIT ASSOCIATES ❖ www.janklowandnesbit.com

285 Madison Avenue, 21st Floor, New York, NY 10017, 212-421-1700

Agent's name: Emma Parry, submissions@janklow.com

What would you be doing right now if not responding to this survey? Editing a proposal.

What would you be if not an agent (other than a dog, cat, or other mammal)? Some other sort of advocate for good ideas.

Do you think independent (noncorporate) publishing will be stronger, weaker, or the same over the next few years? I hope stronger. I love seeing new players enter the territory.

Please describe your professional history. See my profile on our website.

How would you define the "client from hell"? Not someone I ever need to meet.

Do you think Earth was created a few thousand years ago or several billion years ago? I incline scientific.

Please list five books you recently agented. Americana, Mr. Dickens and His Carol, Bleaker Island, The Futilitarians, Utopia for Realists.

Please describe the kinds of books you want to agent. See my profile on our website.

What should writers submit for consideration, and how should they send it? A short overview of the book, note on the author, and opening chapter or 10 pages.

How do you feel about self-publishing, and what do you see happening with it in the near future? I'm glad writers have the option, and I've enjoyed working with one or two writers who've come via that route, but discoverability and accountable accounting are hard to come by in the self-publishing seas, and unless the self-published book does phenomenally well, critically or commercially, the odds of securing a conventional deal for that same book are vanishingly small.

Do you think there are too many, too few, or just enough agents? A few more than there were, but the waters don't feel too crowded.

Do you think Amazon will become the country's largest employer within 10 years? Very possibly.

Why do you think some books become super-successful (beyond the obvious reasons)? Timing and attention.

Do you think agents are likely to become millionaires? Very few.

Do you think agents tend toward certain personality types? Probably.

Do you think writers tend to be more or less narcissistic than the population at large? Pass.

Knowing what you know now, would you become an agent again? Yes.

Why did you choose to become an agent? I love helping writers make money.

Do you think many talented writers fail to get published for avoidable reasons? If so, what are some of those reasons? Running out of time and/or money when they might have paced themselves differently, maybe.

Optional shout-outs/comments: I'd like to think there's justice in who makes the cut, and to keep helping see that justice done.

JEANNE FREDERICKS LITERARY AGENCY, INC. ❖

www.jeannefredericks.com

221 Benedict Hill Road, New Canaan, CT 06840, 203-972-3011

Agent's name and contact info: Jeanne Fredericks, jeanne.fredericks@gmail.com

Describe the kinds of works you want to represent. I like to represent practical, popular reference by authorities, especially in health, science, fitness, gardening, and women's interest. I'm also interested in cooking, elite sports, parenting, environment, lifestyle, and antiques/decorative arts.

Describe what you definitely don't want to represent. I do not represent genre fiction (e.g., horror, occult fiction, true crime, romance, Westerns, and sci-fi), juvenile, textbooks, poetry, essays, plays, short stories, pop culture, guides to computers and software, politics, pornography, overly depressing or violent topics, memoirs that are more suitable for one's family or that are not compelling enough for the trade market, manuals for teachers, or workbooks. I rarely represent fiction, and only for existing clients whose novels are a normal outgrowth of their nonfiction writing.

How do you want writers to pitch you? Please query by email without attachments to jeanne.fredericks@gmail.com or by mail with a SASE. No phone calls, faxes, or deliveries that require signatures, please.

Describe your education and professional history. BA, Mount Holyoke College, 1972, major in English, Phi Beta Kappa; Radcliffe Publishing Procedures Course, 1972. MBA, New York University Graduate School of Business (now called Stern), major in marketing, 1979. I established my own agency in 1997 after being an agent and acting director for Susan P. Urstadt, Inc. (1990–96). Prior to that, I was an editorial director for Ziff-Davis Books (1980–81); acquiring editor, the first female managing editor, and assistant managing editor for Macmillan's Trade Division (1974–80); assistant to the editorial director and foreign/subsidiary rights director of Basic Books (1972–74). Member of AAR and Authors Guild.

How did you become an agent? I reentered publishing as an agent because the flexible hours and home-based office were compatible with raising young children. I enjoy working with creative authors who need my talents to find the right publishers for their proposed books and to negotiate fair contracts on their behalf. I am still thrilled when I open a box of newly published books by one of my authors, knowing that I had a small role in making it happen. I'm also ever hopeful that the books I represent will make a positive difference in the lives of many people.

Knowing what you do now, would you do it again? If not, what might you do instead? Yes, I would do it again. I enjoy the long-term relationships I have with my authors, the daily challenges of learning something new such as ebook publishing, reviewing promising proposals, pitching proposals that I love to publishers, and managing auctions.

Do you charge fees? (If yes, explain.) I do not charge any fees.

What do you like to do when you're not working? I enjoy travel and visiting our grown children and grandson, swimming, yoga, hiking, walking with friends and my Lab, reading, traveling, casual entertaining, gardening, photography, volunteering at church and other local organizations, good conversations with friends, and of course reading. I am hoping to return to crew, which was my key outside interest for 10 years.

List some of the titles you recently placed with publishers. *The Secret Language of Cells* by Jonathan Lieff, MD (BenBella); *Coming to Our Senses about Concussion* by Elizabeth

Sandel, MD (Harvard University Press); *The Autoimmune Disease Handbook* by Julius Birnbaum, MD (Johns Hopkins University Press); *How to Build Your Own Tiny House* by Roger Marshall (Taunton); *Chefs & Company: 75 Top Chefs Share More Than 180 Recipes to Wow Last-Minute Guests* by Maria Isabella (Page Street); *The Colorful Dry Garden: Over 100 Flowers and Vibrant Plants for Drought, Desert & Dry Times* by Maureen Gilmer (Sasquatch); *Storm of the Century* and *For Sale — American Paradise: How Our Nation Was Sold an Impossible Dream in Florida* by Willie Drye (Lyons); *The New England Catch* by Martha Murphy (Globe Pequot); *Yoga Therapy: The Ultimate Guide to Yoga for Health and Wellness* by Larry Payne, PhD, Eden Goldman, DC, and Terra Gold, DOM (Basic Health/Turner); *Yoga Nidra for Stress Relief* by Julie Lush (New Harbinger); *Treasure Ship: The Legend and the Legacy of the S.S. Brother Jonathan, The Raging Sea,* and *Sentinel of the Seas* by Dennis M. Powers (Sea Ventures Press); *The Creativity Cure: A Do-It-Yourself Prescription for Happiness* by Carrie Barron, MD, and Alton Barron, MD (Scribner); *The Scarlett Letters: The Making of the Film* Gone with the Wind by John Wiley, Jr. (Taylor); *The American Quilt* by Robert Shaw (Sterling); *Waking the Warrior Goddess: Dr. Christine Horner's Program to Protect against and Fight Breast Cancer* by Christine Horner, MD (Basic Health); *Lilias! Yoga: Your Guide to Enhancing Body, Mind, and Spirit in Midlife and Beyond* by Lilias Folan (Skyhorse); *Artful Watercolor* by Carolyn Janik and Lou Bonamarte (Sterling); *The Smart Guide to Single Malt Scotch Whisky* by Elizabeth Riley Bell and *Smart Guide to Understanding Your Cat* by Carolyn Janik (Smart Guides); *A Woman's Guide to Pelvic Health: Expert Advice for Women of All Ages* by Elizabeth E. Houser, MD, and Stephanie Riley Hahn, PT (Johns Hopkins University Press).

Describe your personality. I love to learn about many subjects, so I continue to be enthused about working with authors who want to share their expertise with others. I favor building and nurturing long-term relationships with authors, but remain open to new talent. I'm an optimist who likes to work with people who see problems as challenges to overcome and know that good results in publishing stem from insight, monitoring trends, hard work, and attention to detail as well as keeping up with new technologies and ways of doing things. My background makes me think on many levels when representing clients — as an MBA, editor, agent, and enthusiastic reader. Though I can be firm and persistent in negotiations, I believe in old-fashioned courtesy and respect among colleagues and love working as a team in creating and marketing a book that will have lasting value.

What do you like reading/watching/listening to on your own time? I am an eclectic reader who enjoys literary fiction, groundbreaking research-based nonfiction that makes me think in new ways, inspirational books, tempting cookbooks, gardening books, and ones with breathtaking photos. I enjoy classical music as a background to reading and editing (Beethoven, Mozart, Chopin, Brahms, Bach), but I love to dance to classic rock, ethnic music, jazz — anything with a good beat that makes me want to move to the music. I'm a big fan of *The Crown, Victoria, Downton Abbey, Foyle's War, Northern Exposure, Doc Martin, Call the Midwife, Poirot,* films of Jane Austen's classics, other PBS productions, and *So You Think You Can Dance.* I lived in England during my college vacations and my mother was raised there, so I am quite an Anglophile.

Do you think the business has changed a lot over the past few years? If yes, please explain. Yes, there has been quite a dramatic change in what publishers expect from an author. It used to be that if a nonfiction author had authority, could write well, chose a fresh angle on a subject of interest to enough people, and was "promotable," he or she had a good shot at getting a contract. Now publishers also require authors to bring ready-made markets with them, especially in terms of social media. Even smaller publishers expect this. The practical reality behind these new requirements is that the bookstores and chains focus on carrying books by authors who are already known. My concern is that this is leading to contracts being given to too many people who are simply popular online and to too few well-qualified authors who haven't managed to create a following online. Building an online presence requires time and a certain amount of extroversion, which doesn't necessarily jibe with the typical reserved writer or the busy professional who doesn't have time to spend on such pursuits. I am somewhat nostalgic for the days when books were acquired on the basis of an experienced editor's judgment that someone could write well about something worth reading and had the potential to learn from the publicity department how to promote the book.

What do the "Big 5" mean to you? A necessary concentration of power and economies of scale in back-office, selling, and inventory functions due to the competition of Amazon and other forms of entertainment. From the perspective of an agent, though, it means fewer publishers to pitch, fewer auctions, and less leverage for securing higher advances, better royalties, and improved contractual language.

How do you feel about independent/small presses? I believe that they can sometimes do a better job publishing a book long term than the Big 5 when they focus on niche markets and actively sell and promote their backlists. Some of my authors who have published with small publishers have sold more copies than authors published by the Big 5.

What are your feelings about self-publishing? Self-publishing opens up opportunities for many aspiring writers and levels the playing field to a certain extent, since self-published authors can sometimes publish successfully and earn more money than with publishers. They can also have more control over the key decisions in publishing. The problem is discoverability in a world where there are far too many books being published. Unless the self-published author has written a high-quality book and is willing to put in the time to build a marketing platform and fine-tune the metadata for discoverability, the book may sell so few copies that all the effort put into writing and publishing will seem worthless. Also if authors aspire to publish POD (print-on-demand) paperbacks, they may be surprised by what they need to know and do to prepare a book for publication.

Do you think Amazon is good or bad — or both — for the book business? I used to feel that Amazon was the hated behemoth that used its clout to drive out small publishers and independent booksellers who couldn't compete with their discounted pricing and speedy fulfillment of orders. I still think that there is some truth to that statement, but over time I realized that I had to admit that I liked the convenience and low prices of buying on their site and I also found the site an excellent tool for research. I admire how Amazon staff continually learn and improve their ways of doing business and take the time to meet with agents to educate them about their way of publishing. Now that I am involved with publishing some ebooks and POD books with them, I have respect for their quick sizing up of opportunities, taking the steps to make publishing seem understandable and doable, and their one-on-one support to agents who are publishing books in their "White Glove" program. To remain competitive, publishers and other book retailers are going to have to be proactive in keeping pace by finding ways to offer more or something better or different than Amazon; otherwise, they may find that they will go the way of so many independent bookstores.

What do you like and dislike about your job? I feel honored to work with smart, persevering authors to help them achieve their dream of being published and then to help them build their writing careers. I find auctions thrilling since they generally yield the highest advances for my authors. Negotiating contracts, though tedious, is satisfying at the end when I know I've used my experience to get the best terms and contractual language for my client. I feel energized by meeting with editors and learning what they like and want. I also enjoy the role of diplomat, since I know the publishing side of the business and can therefore more easily help the author and publisher resolve issues that inevitably arise during the publishing process. What I don't like is rejecting queries and proposals (especially ones that are good, but by authors with insufficient marketing platforms). I also dislike feeling that I can never be caught up since there is an endless flow of emails that keep tugging me away from the more substantive work such as reading proposals I've requested or helping an author fine-tune a submission package.

What are the ways prospective clients can impress you, what are the ways they can turn you off? I am impressed by authors who are true authorities on the subject of their books, have a fresh angle or new research, and can convincingly explain why the proposed book is different, better, and needed by large, defined audiences. I am drawn to authors who are not only sought after as speakers by their peers, but also by the public. Due to the current expectations by publishers, I also take notice of authors who have already established an SEO-optimized website and who regularly engage online with their anticipated trade audiences. I prefer working with authors who are polite, patient, and willing to work hard to make their proposal ready for submission. I also appreciate authors who are familiar with my website and therefore know what kinds of books I like and what I like to see in a proposal.

What turns me off is a cold call or query from someone who tells me about a book that is totally unsuited for my line of books. I am repelled by queries that seem grandiose, complaining, gross, depressing, uninformed about the competition, poorly written, or sloppily proofread.

How would you describe the "writer from hell"? An arrogant, pushy, self-centered, unreliable writer who does not understand publishing or respect my time and who vents anger in an unprofessional way. Fortunately, I've rarely encountered such a person in this business. When I sense an overly inflated ego in the initial correspondence and communication, I steer clear of the person.

Describe a book you would like to write. Hmm…no idea! My head is too full of the books that others have written or aspire to write. Maybe I will write my own sometime in the future when I have more time to reflect on the life I've lived and what I want to pass on to the next generation.

Do you believe in a higher and/or lower power? Yes, I believe in God, but I also believe that a person needs to work to make opportunities and achieve success in life. I have been active in my church for decades and as the trustee of a foundation that fosters small group ministries and Bible study for people from any denomination. I also believe strongly in science and evolution.

Is there anything you wish to express beyond the parameters of the preceding questions?

Just that I urge authors to be resilient in the face of the inevitable rejections, learn from constructive criticism, and embrace learning new technologies and marketing methods.

THE JEFF HERMAN AGENCY, LLC ❖ www.jeffherman.com

PO Box 1522, Stockbridge, MA 01262, 413-298-0077

Agent's name and contact info: Jeff Herman, jeff@jeffherman.com

What would you be doing right now if not responding to this survey? Napping is what I would want to do, but most likely it would be some work-related or domestic task, like I have to change the furnace filters but hate going into the basement.

What would you be if not an agent (other than a dog, cat, or other mammal)? I've been doing this for so long (30 years), I truly don't know where else I might have ended up.

Do you think independent (noncorporate) publishing will be stronger, weaker, or the same over the next few years? Good question (I wrote all the questions, by the way). I predict that we have a standoff. The "corps" and the "indies" will keep the current ratio as is, until the next great disruption.

Please describe your professional history. Not much. In my 20s I worked for a small publishing company in the publicity department and for a public-relations firm doing corporate marketing. Thinking I was getting "old," I opened my own business at age 26 in 1985 with some money I had saved, and here I am.

How would you define the "client from hell"? If someone became a client, it means they did a good job making themselves appear not to be from hell, and that level of deception is pretty hellish. No one enjoys working with crazy-makers, liars, thieves, or people who tend to yell and complain too much. Uh-oh, who am I channeling here?

Do you think Earth was created a few thousand years ago or several billion years ago? Both and otherwise. Our experience and perception of time isn't necessarily the only way time functions. For instance, antimatter doesn't seem to interact with time in a way we understand; neither do thoughts. I advise not bothering to answer such silly questions, even though I obviously wrote it and did answer it.

Please list five books you recently agented. *Member of the Family: My Story of Charles Manson, Inside His Cult, and the Darkness That Ended the Sixties* (Morrow), *The Dictator Pope: The Inside Story of the Most Tyrannical Papacy in Modern Times* (Regnery), *The Dawn Prayer (or How to Survive in a Secret Syrian Terrorist Prison)* (BenBella), *Becoming Facebook* (AMACOM), *No B.S. Guide to Business* book series (18 titles and growing, Entrepreneur Press).

Please describe the kinds of books you want to agent. Bring me your expressions of thought; telling of life; perceptions of deeds; experiences of sentiments; choices made and paths denied. Additionally, I tend toward various areas within the adult nonfiction categories.

What should writers submit for consideration, and how should they send it? I prefer email because paper takes space and organization attention. Query letters are fine. Attachments with proposals, manuscripts, etc., are also okay.

How do you feel about self-publishing, and what do you see happening with it in the near future? Only do it if you can push direct-to-consumer sales. Otherwise it will look as if your book failed in the eyes of the world.

Do you think there are too many, too few, or just enough agents? I should be the only agent, and my clients should be the only writers. Actually, more agents will generate more opportunities for writers to get traditionally published; so in that context there can never be too many agents, any more than there can be too many writers.

Do you think Amazon will become the country's largest employer within 10 years? Top five.

Why do you think some books become super-successful (beyond the obvious reasons)? Humans are herd animals. People will purchase books on the basis of what their cultural and community leaders tell them they should read. Go for and score at the top, and the mandate will trickle down to the people.

Do you think agents are likely to become millionaires? It was more likely 20 years ago. The pie gets sliced differently today.

Do you think agents tend toward certain personality types? Loners. Independent-minded. Self-structured. Need internal gratification. Opposite of manic. Low-key and intense at the same time.

Do you think writers tend to be more or less narcissistic than the population at large? Creative people in general tend to be a little narcissistic simply because they don't function as part of a team when working. However, I also think they can have a huge awareness of other people's needs and feelings, even if not especially empathetic.

Knowing what you know now, would you become an agent again? I don't think I'd want to start from scratch today, because the opportunities for reliable growth just aren't what they used to be. However, I do see new paths that combine agenting with other functions and don't only rely upon the commission model.

Why did you choose to become an agent? Freedom. Interesting work. Potentially lucrative. Intellectually rewarding. Independence. Self-expression.

Do you think many talented writers fail to get published for avoidable reasons? If so, what are some of those reasons? Failure to make/keep allies. Failure to motivate and reward others. Failure to be grateful, humble, generous, tolerant, self-adjusting, resilient, tenacious…

THE JENNIFER DE CHIARA LITERARY AGENCY ❖ www.jdlit.com

299 Park Avenue, 6th Floor, New York, NY 10171, 212-739-0803

Agent's name and contact info: Jennifer De Chiara, jenndec@aol.com

Please describe your professional history. I was a literary agent at two established New York City literary agencies before I started my own agency in 2001. Before that I was a freelance editor for Simon & Schuster and Random House. I've also been a writing consultant to major corporations, and I've been a writer since I could hold a pencil. I was also a dancer and an actress, but I had to stop when I got tired of eating ramen noodles.

How would you define the "client from hell"? Someone who listens to the advice of their friends over mine, doesn't respect my time, and has unrealistic expectations of the publishing industry.

Please list five books you recently agented. A Day So Gray (picture book) by Marie Lamba (Clarion Books), *Hazy Bloom* (middle grade) by Jennifer Hamburg (Scholastic), *Three Truths and a Lie* (young adult) by Brent Hartinger (Simon & Schuster), *Tippi: A Memoir* (adult nonfiction) by Tippi Hedren (HarperCollins), *The One-Way Bridge* (adult fiction) by Cathie Pelletier (Sourcebooks).

Please describe the kinds of books you want to agent. Nonfiction: celebrity memoirs and biographies, books about anything and everything Hollywood, pop culture, true crime, social issues, politics, health and wellness. I'm open to just about any topic, but the author has to have a platform. Adult fiction: literary, commercial, horror, mystery, historical — anything and everything, really. Children's fiction: picture books, middle grade, and young adult — I'm open to every genre, but no high fantasy or science fiction.

What should writers submit for consideration, and how should they send it? Email only; we don't accept manuscripts or queries by regular mail. For picture books, email the query along with the manuscript in the body of the email. Complete submission guidelines are on my agency website, www.jdlit.com.

Knowing what you know now, would you become an agent again? Yes.

Why did you choose to become an agent? To make writers' dreams come true, and to have a hand in great books that will, hopefully, inspire, inform, and in their own way change the world.

Do you think many talented writers fail to get published for avoidable reasons? If so, what are some of those reasons? Some writers are their own worst enemies, for too many reasons to list here. But a willingness to learn from publishing professionals, a positive attitude, hard work, and appreciation for the hard work of others go a long way.

Agent's name and contact info: Alexandra Weiss, Associate Agent, alexweiss.jdlit@gmail.com, 212-739-0803

What would you be doing right now if not responding to this survey? Reading queries.

What would you be if not an agent (other than a dog, cat, or other mammal)? If I had paid better attention in my math and physics classes (instead of reading books under my desk), I'd probably be an astrophysicist or aspiring astronaut, preferably one of the first headed to Mars.

Please describe your professional history. I hold a BFA in Creative Writing and Publishing from Columbia College Chicago. Previously, I worked for Bustle.com as a books and features writer and an acquisitions editor for an award-winning fiction and nonfiction anthology. In addition to interning with the Jennifer De Chiara Literary Agency for over two years before joining as an associate agent, I interned with boutique book publicist Kaye Publicity. I've also held a number of different PR and marketing positions. I'm an avid volunteer for numerous literary organizations, including Story Week, Young Chicago Authors, and Printers Row Lit Fest.

Do you think Earth was created a few thousand years ago or several billion years ago? Earth is approximately 4.54 billion years old.

Please describe the kinds of books you want to agent. I'm currently seeking children's literature (picture books, middle grade, and young adult) in every genre. For fiction, I am always looking for stories that intertwine magic and mythology or use space, science, and other STEM-related fields as a main source of inspiration. Diverse stories and #ownvoices are also incredibly important to me. I'm a big traveler and am always eager to learn about different cultures, countries, and ways of life. I'm eagerly looking for stories centered around strong and smart female leads as well as adventurous, risk-taking characters. If a story has a bright and whimsical voice, I'm instantly hooked. For nonfiction, I'm particularly interested in books that highlight the wonders and importance of nature and the universe, from galaxies to the Galápagos Islands. I'd love to find a story that teaches me something new or makes me look at the world differently.

What should writers submit for consideration, and how should they send it? Please email a query letter with the word *Query* in the subject line to alexweiss.jdlit@gmail.com. Please send the first 20 pages in the body of the email, along with a 1-paragraph bio and a 1-paragraph synopsis.

How do you feel about self-publishing, and what do you see happening with it in the near future? It works for some writers who are prepared to take on the work that self-publishing demands and isn't a great fit for others. It really just depends on the book and the author.

Knowing what you know now, would you become an agent again? Absolutely. To me, there's nothing more rewarding than working with passionate writers and helping them share their incredible work with the world.

Why did you choose to become an agent? Books and writing have always played an important role in my life. While I was in school, I found myself eager to read and edit my classmate's stories any chance I could. I took every publishing course that was offered and learned all about the role of a literary agent. From that point on, I was determined to become an agent. Shortly after, I interviewed a literary agent (Victoria Selvaggio), and she offered me an internship with Jennifer De Chiara. The rest is history (and a dream come true).

Do you think many talented writers fail to get published for avoidable reasons? If so, what are some of those reasons? There's an endless list of reasons why some writers get published and others don't. It's always important for writers to remain kind, patient, and open-minded. Sometimes those things can make all the difference when it comes to getting an agent, editor, or publishing deal.

Agent's name and contact info: Stephen Fraser, Senior Literary Agent, fraserstephena@gmail.com, 212-739-0803

What would you be doing right now if not responding to this survey? Reading.

What would you be if not an agent (other than a dog, cat, or other mammal)? A teacher.

Do you think independent (noncorporate) publishing will be stronger, weaker, or the same over the next few years? Small publishers are doing some very interesting things right now. This will continue and will blossom in years to come.

Please describe your professional history. After getting a degree in English literature and a master's degree in children's literature, I worked as an editor for 25 years at major New York houses including Simon & Schuster and HarperCollins. I began agenting 13 years ago.

How would you define the "client from hell"? Someone who embarrasses both themselves and the agency with bad behavior.

Please list five books you recently agented. *Catching a Storyfish* by Janice Harrington, *Reaper* by Kyra Leigh, *The Green Umbrella* by Jackie Azua Kramer, *Alice Paul and the Struggle for Women's Rights* by Deborah Kops, *The Messenger* by Carol Lynch Williams.

Please describe the kinds of books you want to agent. I'm looking for prestige books with high literary quality that will win major awards and receive multiple starred reviews.

What should writers submit for consideration, and how should they send it? Email submissions only, after a query.

How do you feel about self-publishing, and what do you see happening with it in the near future? Often self-publishing means an author is impatient with a traditional publishing route.

Do you think there are too many, too few, or just enough agents? There are a lot of agents, but I don't believe in competition. There is a rightness to it, and authors will find the right agent for them.

Why do you think some books become super-successful (beyond the obvious reasons)? Often there is something in the zeitgeist that a book hits. But you can't second-guess this. I do think that a good book will always find the proper home.

Do you think agents are likely to become millionaires? I'm still working on it.

Do you think agents tend toward certain personality types? There are as many different types of agents as there are types of editors and writers.

Do you think writers tend to be more or less narcissistic than the population at large? I love writers and all creative people. Some are needier than others; some are a bit unhinged; but they are all wonderful. Writers need to be carefully nurtured.

Knowing what you know now, would you become an agent again? Probably sooner.

Why did you choose to become an agent? There were no senior editorial spots at the time, and a friend asked me to join her agency.

Do you think many talented writers fail to get published for avoidable reasons? If so, what are some of those reasons? It takes not just talent but also fortitude, patience, and a sense of humor. I've seen talented writers give up too soon.

Agent's name and contact info: Cari Lamba, Associate Literary Agent, cari.jdlit@gmail.com, 212-739-0803

Please describe your professional history. Prior to officially joining the team of agents, I interned for the Jennifer De Chiara Agency for eight years. I knew I wanted to join the publishing world and help writers bring their books to life through this internship. I graduated from Franklin and Marshall College with a BA in English literature. I also studied literature at the Advanced Studies in England Program. I have experience as a bookseller and in publicity and content writing for online publications. I have been published in *Writer's Digest* and have taught webinars for *Writer's Digest* as well.

How would you define the "client from hell"? Instead, I would like to describe my ideal client. This is someone I'm able to communicate openly with, is responsive to changes, and is patient and understands that projects can take a lot of time.

Please describe the kinds of books you want to agent. I'm currently looking for middle grade, both fiction and nonfiction picture books, and adult commercial fiction. In children's books I'm interested in wacky plots and characters that drive the story. I like contemporary stories that are both humorous and heartfelt. Although I am not interested in stories with high fantasy, I would welcome elements of the fantastic and otherworldly. I want novels that will resonate with children without being didactic. In picture books I'm looking for unique ideas with fun and quirky elements as well as sweet, endearing stories. In nonfiction I'm especially looking for strong female role models. In adult commercial fiction I'm looking for original plot and clever characters. Although I'm not interested in romance novels, elements of romance are welcome. I also have particular interest in mystery/detective fiction and novels with culinary ties. I'm *not* interested in science fiction, horror, high fantasy, Christian fiction, political novels, or books with extremely violent elements.

What should writers submit for consideration, and how should they send it? To submit to me, please email a query letter with the word *Query* along with the title of your work in the subject line to cari.jdlit@gmail.com. Please send the first 20 pages in the body of your email, along with a 1-paragraph bio and a 1-paragraph synopsis. No attachments will be opened.

Why did you choose to become an agent? As mentioned in my bio, I interned for the agency for years prior to joining the team. I knew I wanted to do something in publishing, but being an agent would allow me to really help writers succeed. I wanted to be in a position where I could be involved in the business side of publishing while also holding close relationships with authors to help them throughout their entire career. Being an agent was a perfect fit for me.

Agent's name and contact info: David Laurell, 212-739-0803

What would you be doing right now if not responding to this survey? Scooping up Yorkie poop and cleaning the kitty litter box.

What would you be if not an agent (other than a dog, cat, or other mammal)? In a perfect world, either the host of *The Tonight Show Starring David Laurell* or a Tahitian basket weaver.

Do you think independent (noncorporate) publishing will be stronger, weaker, or the same over the next few years? It will grow stronger as production quality increases and digital media continues to evolve, giving authors more tools to self-promote and market their books beyond what an independent publisher may be able or willing to do.

Please describe your professional history. I was a television writer, producer, reporter, and anchor prior to working as a communications specialist, book ghostwriter, newspaper journalist/columnist, and managing editor and editor in chief for various national magazines. I also lost my mind for a time and served as an elected official, but am now a fully recovered politician.

How would you define the "client from hell"? A bloviating, narcissistic, prevaricating, yellow-haired, real-estate magnate turned politician who believes his dealmaking skills rise to the level of art.

Do you think Earth was created a few thousand years ago or several billion years ago? I'm thinking several billion plus eight.

Please describe the kinds of books you want to agent. I'm most interested in celebrity biographies and autobiographies and all genres of pop culture, entertainment, broadcasting, professional sports, and politics from any era. I am also open to fresh takes on unique collectors and collections and compelling stories of motivation, inspiration, faith, positive aging, and self-improvement.

On the fiction side, I am always on the lookout for unique and well-plotted stories about nontraditional, unconventional, or extraordinary families or individuals that are infused with passion, irony, sarcasm, intelligence, insight, kindness, hope, inspiration, and humor. I love richly presented quirky characters with unforgettable personalities. Think *Being There*, *The World According to Garp*, *Postcards from the Edge*, *Running with Scissors*, *Forrest Gump*, and the play/film *August: Osage County*.

What should writers submit for consideration, and how should they send it? Although fresh baked goods are always a nice bribe, er, I mean, touch, to start the process, they should just simply email a 1-page query letter that includes a brief synopsis of their book, their bio or résumé, contact information, and the first 2 chapters or 20 pages of their manuscript to dclaurell@gmail.com with the word *Query* and the submission's title in the subject line.

How do you feel about self-publishing, and what do you see happening with it in the near future? It is a viable option for some authors and books. As for the future, see my answer above with regard to independent publishing.

Do you think there are too many, too few, or just enough agents? Until some retire or die, there is only room for seven and a half more.

Do you think Amazon will become the country's largest employer within 10 years? You're asking me what will happen in the American corporate structure over the next 10 years? I don't even know what I'm going to have for dinner tonight.

Why do you think some books become super-successful (beyond the obvious reasons)? If anyone knew that answer, there would be no books published other than super-successful ones — and that would prove to be one of the world's greatest shames.

Do you think agents are likely to become millionaires? Yeah, sure! Maybe even billionaires or trillionaires! In fact, I'm even thinking bazillionaires! Yeah, bazillionaires! That's the ticket!

Do you think agents tend toward certain personality types? To be a really good one — a great one — an agent must embrace work and love providing service to others.

Do you think writers tend to be more or less narcissistic than the population at large? Narcissistic? No. Exaggerators? Yes. Millions of my friends who are writers exaggerate, nonstop, 24/7, 365 days a year. It makes me so mad that I kill them.

Knowing what you know now, would you become an agent again? Yes. Unless Charlize Theron begged me to give it all up and run away with her, preferably to Tahiti.

Why did you choose to become an agent? As with the person who is owned by a cat, I didn't choose it as much as it (or, more specifically, the amazingly talented woman who is my agent) chose me. I think she did so because I love to work (and I emphasize the word *work*) with creative and interesting people, and few things thrill me more than seeing their dreams become a reality.

Do you think many talented writers fail to get published for avoidable reasons? If so, what are some of those reasons? There are two main reasons. The first one is that they cling to unrealistic expectations and, no matter how their agent, editor, or publisher may advise them — creatively or from a business standpoint — they choose to only do things their way. The other is that they love to talk about their ideas, but don't actually plant their derrière in front of a computer and use their fingers to tap the keys to transform their thoughts and ideas into a string of 90,000 words that tell a story.

Agent's name and contact info: Damian McNicholl, damianmcnichollvarney@gmail.com, 212-739-0803

Do you think independent (noncorporate) publishing will be stronger, weaker, or the same over the next few years? It will be the same.

Please describe your professional history. I studied law at Cardiff University, am a member of the New York State Bar, and practiced as an attorney. I'm also the author of the critically acclaimed novels *A Son Called Gabriel,* which was an ABA Booksense Pick and Lambda Literary Award finalist, and *The Moment of Truth,* from Pegasus Books.

How would you define the "client from hell"? I have only great clients, but I think they'd be writers who are excessively needy and constantly seeking contact when there is nothing to discuss.

Please list five books you recently agented. I'm a new agent building my list.

Please describe the kinds of books you want to agent. In a nutshell, I represent literary fiction that hits the sweet spot between commercial and literary, exciting narrative nonfiction, and memoir. For specific details, see my agent listing at www.jdlit.com.

What should writers submit for consideration, and how should they send it? A succinct and exciting query letter and the first 15 pages by email.

How do you feel about self-publishing, and what do you see happening with it in the near future? It works for some writers, especially genre fiction.

Why do you think some books become super-successful (beyond the obvious reasons)? Luck and tapping into the cultural zeitgeist.

Knowing what you know now, would you become an agent again? Yes. It's exciting working at the Jennifer De Chiara Literary Agency.

Why did you choose to become an agent? I'm interested in representing exciting, interesting writers and their work.

Agent's name and contact info: Victoria Selvaggio, Associate Agent, vickiaselvaggio@gmail.com, 212-739-0803

What would you be doing right now if not responding to this survey? As an agent I'm constantly prioritizing, even as I complete this survey. I never know what will come across my desk and when, from both clients and aspiring writers. And being organized is a big part of staying on top of the volume of work that comes my way.

What would you be if not an agent (other than a dog, cat, or other mammal)? I love remodeling homes, refurbishing antique/old furniture, and designing. All allow me to tap into my creative side, like I do as an agent. My last project was turning an old ladder into a coffee table. It's beautiful, and I'm asked all the time where I purchased it. But, as much as I love doing these other things, working as an agent is a good fit for me. It satisfies my creative side in a more intellectual way.

How would you define the "client from hell"? As I tend to be positive, looking for the good qualities in a writer, I'm not a huge fan of someone who is arrogant, defensive, or unprofessional. Of course, though, I'm quite selective about how and to whom I offer representation, and I'm honored to say that all JDLA clients I represent are wonderful. Together, we are a team, working toward the same goal. Always.

Please list five books you recently agented. *Applesauce Day* by Lisa Amstutz (Albert Whitman), *Today We Go Birding* (tentative title) by Lisa Amstutz (Albert Whitman, fall 2018), *Maple Syrup from the Sugarhouse* by Laurie Lazzaro Knowlton (Albert Whitman), *Mother Ghost: Spooky Rhymes for Halloween* by Rachel Kolar (Sleeping Bear, fall 2018), *Amphibiology: 30 Activities and Observations for Exploring the World of Amphibians* by Lisa Amstutz (Chicago Review Press).

Please describe the kinds of books you want to agent. I'm seeking board books, picture books, chapter books, middle grade, young adult, new adult, and adult. I am interested in nonfiction and fiction in all genres. I especially love thrillers and all elements of weird, creepy stuff. If it's out of the box and it will make me think and think, long after I'm done reading, send it to me. On the flip side, I yearn for books that make me laugh, cry, and wonder about the world.

What should writers submit for consideration, and how should they send it? Please email a query to vickiaselvaggio@gmail.com and put the word *Query* in the subject line of your email. For queries regarding children's and adult fiction, please send the first 20 pages in the body of your email (no attachments or links), along with a 1-paragraph bio and a 1-paragraph synopsis. For queries regarding a nonfiction book, please attach the entire proposal as a Word document (the proposal should include a sample chapter), along with a 1-paragraph bio and a 1-paragraph synopsis of your book in the body of your email (no attachments or links). Please send only one project at a time.

How do you feel about self-publishing, and what do you see happening with it in the near future? Years before I knew I wanted to become an agent, I wrote and self-published two titles. I'm happy for the experiences they've brought, but I do find myself wishing I had learned more about the publishing industry and the writing process. Although neither title was ever submitted to an agency or editor, neither title was ever revised (revision is a huge part of the writing process).

If writers wish to follow this path, I usually encourage lots of research (there are scams out there) and lots of revision and editing before publication. It's also important to consider how this publication will affect writers' future projects and the writers themselves. As with traditionally published books, being represented in the best way possible is important.

Knowing what you know now, would you become an agent again? Absolutely! Books have always been such an important part of my life. I can't imagine where I would be without them. And now, knowing that I have a part in the process of stories evolving into books is one of the highlights of my job. Although rejection is a huge part of the process, there are no words to describe how I feel when I learn that a manuscript will become a book, one that will have a place on a shelf in a library, store, or child's room, and that readers will have the chance to fall in love, just like the author did, and I did, and those involved in the acquisitions process.

Why did you choose to become an agent? We are all destined for the "right" path. Becoming an agent was mine! After several years as regional advisor for the Society of Children's Book Writers and Illustrators, Northern Ohio, and becoming a published author myself, I found myself limited on what I could do to help writers and illustrators reach their goals. I was able to provide tools (education, motivation, inspiration), but building careers was out of reach, so I strived to make it reachable. For me, I love, love, *love*, working one-on-one with my clients! Although all jobs have their disadvantages, I can't seem to find many as an agent. I love going to work every day. It's as simple as that!

Do you think many talented writers fail to get published for avoidable reasons? If so, what are some of those reasons? Yes. This list could be quite long, so I'm listing just a few things to consider when looking for representation:

- Read, read, read in the genre or age category you're writing in. And then write, write, write.
- Research, research, research. Finding the best author-agent match is important.
- Follow submission guidelines. It is possible that you're receiving rejections simply because you're not following instructions. Guidelines are given for reasons — following them shows that you're able to do what is asked.
- Be pleasantly persistent. I have a "query status" in place for those who have submitted manuscripts to me, yet very few agents do this. Don't think that what is standard for the industry is standard for every agent. We're all different.
- Have your manuscript critiqued, and be open to what works and, more importantly, what doesn't. Many writers' organizations offer free critique events; consider joining. Conferences and events offer many opportunities.
- Accept rejection. It is something that happens in every career and in all aspects of life. Learning to embrace rejection will inadvertently make you a stronger writer.

Agent's name and contact info: Roseanne Wells, queryroseanne@gmail.com, Twitter: @RivetingRosie

What would you be doing right now if not responding to this survey? I'd be reading (for work). Or reading (for pleasure). I'm also likely to be cooking or baking, watching TV (big into *Steven Universe* and *Brooklyn Nine-Nine*, and rewatching *White Collar* at the moment), hanging out with friends, or trying to keep my plants alive.

Please describe your professional history. I joined the Jennifer De Chiara Literary Agency as an associate agent in 2012. Previously with the Marianne Strong Literary Agency, I also worked as a proofreader at a magazine group and several other places and as a special sales/editorial assistant at a small illustrated publisher. I discovered my passion for book publishing during my internship at W. W. Norton. Since becoming an agent, I've worked as an advocate and partner to my clients; traveled to numerous writing conferences as a faculty member and speaker to meet writers; taught craft and publishing classes for *Writer's Digest*, Gotham, and other outlets; and published in print and online to help writers.

Please describe the kinds of books you want to agent. In all categories, I'm eager to see diverse and underrepresented authors, marginalized stories, and crossover or blended genres. Adult nonfiction: I'm looking for authors who have a unique story to tell, have built a strong platform, and are dedicated to reaching their audience. I like narrative nonfiction, select memoir, science (popular or trade, not academic), history, religion (not inspirational or Christian), travel, humor, food/cooking, pop culture, illustrated/gift books with a strong angle and similar subjects. Adult fiction: I'm interested in science fiction and fantasy; con/heist stories, especially featuring art, jewelry, or tech; smart detective novels (more Sherlock Holmes than cozy mysteries); and select literary fiction.

Children's: I'm eager to see diverse voices and marginalized stories, unique narrative structures that support the story, and unreliable narrators. I'm looking for young adult and middle grade of all genres that connect me to a strong main character and a phenomenal voice. I'm also open to picture books, especially from author-illustrators. I love cranky, mischievous characters that grow throughout the narrative and stories that are fun and hilarious for children (and the adults who will read them 500 times). Nonfiction picture books in STEM, science, arts, and biographies are a big plus for me. I'm not interested in rhyming picture books or overly sweet and sentimental stories.

What should writers submit for consideration, and how should they send it? Please email a 1-page query letter to queryroseanne@gmail.com with the word *Query* and your title in the subject line. Please include your contact information and the first 20 pages pasted into the body of the email below the letter. Picture-book authors should send 1 manuscript; I may request more if I'm interested. Illustrators should copy and paste artwork into the body of the email and send an expanded link (no bit.ly or vren23 types of links) to an online portfolio. No attachments will be opened. You will receive an automatic message once you submit. I only accept email queries, and any queries sent by regular mail will not be considered.

How do you feel about self-publishing, and what do you see happening with it in the near future? Self-publishing can be a great option for people who are working on their platform or want to take on the responsibility of being their own publisher. My concern comes when people self-publish as a quick fix or put work out before it's ready because they are "testing the market," after which they approach agents with an already published book or book 2 in a self-published series. Unless you are selling thousands of copies per week, a publisher won't be interested in the reprint rights. If you are going to self-publish with the intention of building your readership, approach it thoughtfully and purposefully, with a marketing plan and realistic goals. And send an agent your next book.

JENNIFER LYONS LITERARY AGENCY ❖
www.jenniferlyonsliteraryagency.com

151 West 19th Street, 3rd Floor, New York, NY 10011

Agent's name and contact info: Jeff Ourvan, jeff@jenniferlyonsliteraryagency.com

What would you be doing right now if not responding to this survey? Reading some interesting new works.

What would you be if not an agent (other than a dog, cat, or other mammal)? Investing my lottery winnings.

Do you think independent (noncorporate) publishing will be stronger, weaker, or the same over the next few years? Independent publishing will continue to gain strength and influence.

Please describe your professional history. I've been a commercial fisherman, geologist, political consultant, attorney, and, for the past five years, a writer, editor, and literary agent.

How would you define the "client from hell"? I don't think I've ever had one.

Do you think Earth was created a few thousand years ago or several billion years ago? Earth, several billion years ago; life, not so sure.

Please list five books you recently agented. Christopher Knowlton's *A Bubble in the Sun* (Eamon Dolan Books), Christy Farley's *The Princess and the Page* (Scholastic), Cory Taylor's *How Hitler Was Made* (Prometheus), Tim Bakken's *The Denial* (Bloomsbury), Sara Alexander's *440 Steps to the Sea* (Kensington).

Please describe the kinds of books you want to agent. Especially looking for narrative nonfiction in the fields of history, science, politics, sports, and finance. Also commercial fiction, including young adult, romance, thriller, mystery, and sci-fi.

What should writers submit for consideration, and how should they send it? Kindly send a query by email with no more than five sample pages of writing (if you must).

Do you think agents are likely to become millionaires? I'll let you know when it happens to me.

Do you think writers tend to be more or less narcissistic than the population at large? No. Writers are our collective eyes on the world.

Knowing what you know now, would you become an agent again? Yes.

Why did you choose to become an agent? It combines my love of writing and editing with my legal and communications background. And the creative spirit is a force for peace. Much more satisfying than working in a corporate law firm.

JILL COHEN ASSOCIATES, LLC ❖ www.jillcohenassociates.com

Agent's name and contact info: Jill Cohen, jcohen.ny@gmail.com

What would you be doing right now if not responding to this survey? Having dinner or drinks with clients and authors.

What would you be if not an agent (other than a dog, cat, or other mammal)? A corporate CEO.

Do you think independent (noncorporate) publishing will be stronger, weaker, or the same over the next few years? Weaker.

Please describe your professional history. Founder and publisher of Condé Nast books, president of Random House Direct Marketing, publisher of Time Warner Bulfinch Press, Senior VP of QVC new business development.

How would you define the "client from hell"? The one who calls daily and doesn't pay the bills.

Do you think Earth was created a few thousand years ago or several billion years ago? Several billion.

Please list five books you recently agented. Carolyne Roehm, *A Constant Thread*; Mark Sikes, *Beautiful*; Gil Schafer, *A Place to Call Home*; Bunny Williams, *A House by the Sea*; and Chara Shreyer, *Art House*.

Please describe the kinds of books you want to agent. High-profile authors in fashion, beauty, or interior design — all with incredible taste and the willingness to invest in spectacular photography,

What should writers submit for consideration, and how should they send it? Send me a well-written outline — email and attach visual samples. Send me the platform and a sample of the work.

How do you feel about self-publishing, and what do you see happening with it in the near future? It's great for the right authors — specialty categories including architecture, etc.

Do you think there are too many, too few, or just enough agents? I don't pay attention to the agents.

Do you think Amazon will become the country's largest employer within 10 years? Yes.

Why do you think some books become super-successful (beyond the obvious reasons)? Clever marketing, connections, and hardworking authors.

Do you think agents are likely to become millionaires? Not in my category of publishing (lifestyle and design books).

Do you think agents tend toward certain personality types? I don't hang out with agents, so I wouldn't know.

Do you think writers tend to be more or less narcissistic than the population at large? More.

Knowing what you know now, would you become an agent again? Yes, but not in book publishing.

Why did you choose to become an agent? It chose me. I was a publisher for 30 years, transitioned out of corporate, and wanted to find a home for my talented authors. It just happened.

Do you think many talented writers fail to get published for avoidable reasons? If so, what are some of those reasons? They don't know how to properly approach or market themselves. They don't do the proper homework. I publish lifestyle, illustrated luxury books, and when an author sends me a submission for a science fiction novel, I know they haven't done their homework, so I delete the email.

JOHN HAWKINS & ASSOCIATES, INC. ❖ www.jhalit.com

80 Maiden Lane, Suite 1503, New York, NY 10038

Agent's name and contact info: Anne Hawkins, ahawkins@jhalit.com

What would you be doing right now if not responding to this survey? Reading.

What would you be if not an agent (other than a dog, cat, or other mammal)? A museum curator.

Do you think independent (noncorporate) publishing will be stronger, weaker, or the same over the next few years? Same.

Please describe your professional history. I joined John Hawkins & Associates in 1996 as an agent. Prior to that I had careers in business administration and English education.

How would you define the "client from hell"? Uninformed, unrealistic, and resistant to any kind of constructive feedback.

Do you think Earth was created a few thousand years ago or several billion years ago? Seriously?

Please list five books you recently agented. Tasha Alexander, *Death in St. Petersburg*; John Giltrap, *Final Target*; Miranda Beverly-Whittemore, *Bittersweet* and *June*; Reavis Wortham, *Hawke's Prey*; Taylor Stevens, *Liar's Paradox*.

Please describe the kinds of books you want to agent. Adult literary and commercial fiction, including all types of crime fiction. Serious nonfiction on public policy, nature and the outdoors, history, philosophy, and science.

What should writers submit for consideration, and how should they send it? For fiction, a query letter, brief synopsis, and the first three chapters. For nonfiction, a query letter and proposal. I prefer email queries.

How do you feel about self-publishing, and what do you see happening with it in the near future? Self-publishing is here to stay. For many, it is a way to see their words in print. For a very few, it is a preferable and more lucrative way to make a living as an author.

Do you think there are too many, too few, or just enough agents? There can never be too many competent agents. The key word here is *competent*.

Do you think Amazon will become the country's largest employer within 10 years? The government will always be our largest employer.

Why do you think some books become super-successful (beyond the obvious reasons)? Only Nostradamus knows.

Do you think agents are likely to become millionaires? No.

Do you think agents tend toward certain personality types? Not at all.

Do you think writers tend to be more or less narcissistic than the population at large? No.

Knowing what you know now, would you become an agent again? Yes.

Why did you choose to become an agent? I love books and working with people directly. I also enjoy using both my right-brain creative side and my left-brain analytical side, and this is a job that exercises both.

Do you think many talented writers fail to get published for avoidable reasons? If so, what are some of those reasons? I believe that many authors are unsuccessful in their attempt to get published simply because they don't do sufficient homework before starting the process. This can range from unfamiliarity with the conventions of the type of book they are writing, to selecting the wrong agent, to signing a contract with unfavorable provisions. Publishing is a business, and the more authors know about it in advance, the better their decisions will be.

Agent's name and contact info: Annie Kronenberg, annie@jhalit.com

What would you be doing right now if not responding to this survey? Reading through submissions! Lately our agency has had an influx of really strong, original queries, and we have to work hard to stay on top of them all.

What would you be if not an agent (other than a dog, cat, or other mammal)? A ballet dancer. It requires the same skills, essentially — passion, flexibility, balance, and a lot of snacks.

Do you think independent (noncorporate) publishing will be stronger, weaker, or the same over the next few years? Stronger. I believe there will always be a place for traditional publishing, readers who want literature that has been selected and polished by the big editors. But the trend toward independence in all industries can't be ignored, and there's definitely a place for that too.

Please describe your professional history. Prior to joining John Hawkins & Associates as an assistant in 2016, I worked as an intern at Writers House under Jodi Reamer and Alec Shane.

How would you define the "client from hell"? Anyone who wears those weird shoes that look like feet. Also, a writer who views agents as adversaries rather than advocates.

Do you think Earth was created a few thousand years ago or several billion years ago? Several billion, though I believe the bestselling book of all time says the contrary, and I would've loved to have represented it.

Please list five books you recently agented. None, yet! I've assisted with *Hiddensee* by Gregory Maguire, *The Bird King* by Willow Wilson, *At Briarwood School for Girls* by Michael Knight, *Death in St. Petersburg* by Tasha Alexander, and a forthcoming novel by Joyce Carol Oates.

Please describe the kinds of books you want to agent. I'm a huge fan of young adult fiction, older middle grade fiction, science fiction, and horror, particularly stories with fantastical elements rooted in reality and characters with quirky senses of humor. I love finding young adult authors with literary voices. Some of my favorite books include *Mischling* by Affinity Konar, *Slade House* by David Mitchell, *Coraline* by Neil Gaiman, *Never Let Me Go* by Kazuo Ishiguro, and *Let the Right One In* by John Ajvide Lindqvist.

What should writers submit for consideration, and how should they send it? Writers should submit a brief letter about their book (genre, word count, synopsis) and their writing background. Include the first 3 chapters or about 30 pages as a Word doc attachment. Queries can be sent to annie@jhalit.com, jha@jhalit.com, or via snail mail.

How do you feel about self-publishing, and what do you see happening with it in the near future? Not all books that deserve to be published actually end up that way. It's great that there's a way for writers to put their work out into the world all on their own. As technology advances, there will be even more routes for self-publishing. I'd like to see more curation in the self-publishing world; since the market is flooded, it'd be nice to have a way to highlight the gems.

Do you think there are too many, too few, or just enough agents? I'll say too many simply because almost anyone can call themselves an agent, even if they don't have the necessary experience, affiliations, or accreditations. An author has to do their research to find trustworthy, reputable agencies.

Do you think Amazon will become the country's largest employer within 10 years? I hope not! The value of independent bookstores can't be overstated. The browsing/discovery process simply doesn't exist in the same way on Amazon.

Why do you think some books become super-successful (beyond the obvious reasons)? Books that hit on something in the public consciousness, strike a nerve, or shock or comfort us in pertinent ways are bound to reach a certain level of success.

Do you think agents are likely to become millionaires? Depends on the size of their bitcoin investment.

Do you think agents tend toward certain personality types? Most agents tend to be driven, passionate, and curious. Maybe it's because I'm green, but I genuinely like, on a personal level, all of the agents I've met.

Do you think writers tend to be more or less narcissistic than the population at large? It varies, just as it does in the general population. Writers have to be self-critical in their craft, but writing can also be a very self-indulgent art.

Knowing what you know now, would you become an agent again? Of course!

Why did you choose to become an agent? I've always loved the process of discovery, finding that novel that you deeply connect with. To be the first one to make that discovery and then to get to connect with the author and launch their career is incredibly exciting to me.

Do you think many talented writers fail to get published for avoidable reasons? If so, what are some of those reasons? Failing to submit your work is the obvious one. There are so many talented writers out there who just sit on their work because they're intimidated by the process. Put your work out there — worst-case scenario, you'll learn a lot for your next attempt.

JULIA LORD LITERARY MANAGEMENT ❖ www.julialordliterarymgt.com

38 West Ninth Street, #4, New York, NY 10011, 212-995-2333

Agents' names and contact info: Julia Lord, Ginger Curwen, query@julialordliterarymgt.com

What would you be doing right now if not responding to this survey? *Julia:* Reading! Traveling, hiking, anything in the outdoors, playing the piano, going to the theater.

Ginger: Reading! Travel, tennis, cross-country skiing, drawing, walking my dog.

Do you think independent (noncorporate) publishing will be stronger, weaker, or the same over the next few years? We believe it will be stronger.

Please describe your professional history. *Julia* began her agenting career in 1985 working for actors. She opened the talent agency's literary department representing writers for film, television, and theater. She moved to books eventually, opening Julia Lord Literary Management in 1999. Her mission is very hands-on — to work with writers to develop their careers — from idea through publication and marketing. Her office is known for its steadfast commitment to each and every author and book project.

Ginger represents thrillers and mysteries. Ginger's previous publishing experience includes positions at Barnesandnoble.com, HarperCollins, American Booksellers Association, Bantam Books, and Random House.

Please list five books you recently agented. Thomas Cathcart and Daniel Klein's *I Think, Therefore I Draw* (Patrick Nolan, Penguin), Julie Fenster's *Cheaters Always Win* (Sean Desmond, Twelve), Ann Telnaes's *Trump's ABCs* (Gary Groth, Fantagraphics), Michael Kaufman's *Count Me In!* (Dan Smetanka, Counterpoint), Elizabeth Rush's *Rising: Essays from the Disappearing American Shore* (Joey McGarvey, Milkweed).

Please describe the kinds of books you want to agent. Nonfiction: narrative nonfiction, reference, biography, history, humor, science, adventure, philosophy, military. Fiction: general, literary, historical, suspense, mystery, and thrillers.

What should writers submit for consideration, and how should they send it? Please follow our guidelines on the website and query us at query@julialordliterarymgt.com.

JULIE A. HILL AND ASSOCIATES, LLC ❖

Agent's name and contact info: Julie Hill, hillagent@aol.com

What would you be doing right now if not responding to this survey? Reading!

What would you be if not an agent (other than a dog, cat, or other mammal)? I would work in commercial real estate.

Do you think independent (noncorporate) publishing will be stronger, weaker, or the same over the next few years? Stronger.

Please describe your professional history. Twenty years an agent. Former food and travel writer. Also spiritual writer (astrology).

How would you define the "client from hell"? Calls to chat or talk about his or her "process," does not take advice or direction. In the worst case, seems to hear advice but sends a proposal that is not ready. (Quick road to finding another agent.)

Do you think Earth was created a few thousand years ago or several billion years ago? God only knows.

Please list five books you recently agented. Biz/tech titles and travel titles.

Please describe the kinds of books you want to agent. More biz titles.

What should writers submit for consideration, and how should they send it? A perfect proposal, ready to be shown to pubs. Electronic or hardcopy.

How do you feel about self-publishing, and what do you see happening with it in the near future? More of it.

Do you think there are too many, too few, or just enough agents? Too many.

Do you think Amazon will become the country's largest employer within 10 years? Mmm…no.

Why do you think some books become super-successful (beyond the obvious reasons)? If I knew, I could retire in luxury.

Do you think agents are likely to become millionaires? No.

Do you think agents tend toward certain personality types? Yes.

Do you think writers tend to be more or less narcissistic than the population at large? More.

Knowing what you know now, would you become an agent again? Mmm…no.

Why did you choose to become an agent? Love writers. Love, love, love contracts.

Do you think many talented writers fail to get published for avoidable reasons? If so, what are some of those reasons? Failure to take advice from publishing professionals. It's tragic to watch.

KIMBERLEY CAMERON & ASSOCIATES ❖

www.kimberleycameron.com

1550 Tiburon Boulevard, #704, Tiburon, CA 94920, 415-789-9191

Agent's name and contact info: Amy Cloughley, amyc@kimberleycameron.com; submission form: kimberleycameron.com/amy-cloughley.php; Twitter: @amycloughley

Please describe your professional history. After studying creative writing and earning a BS in magazine journalism, I held positions that straddled the line between editorial and marketing — managing a magazine, advertising campaigns, and marketing projects. I first got into book publishing via an internship at my agency until I ultimately started taking on my own clients, coaching writers through classes and conferences, and participating in the myriad of opportunities that agenting has opened up. Certainly my journalism background laid the groundwork for my appreciation of tightly written prose and love of a unique story, whereas my marketing background provided a base for the business side of book publishing. Now I can leverage my background in both words and business to benefit my clients.

How would you define the "client from hell"? As long as clients understand that I have other clients (and a personal life!), we are usually fine. I also treat all my clients as business professionals and partners in this endeavor, and I really need the same courtesy returned.

Please list five books you recently agented. *The Shadows We Hide* by Allen Eskens (Mulholland, fall 2018), *Where Bad Things Abide* by Allen Eskens (Mulholland, 2019), *Every Single Secret* by Emily Carpenter (Lake Union, May 2018), *Till the Day I Die* by Emily Carpenter (Lake Union, March 2019), *Seven Mountains* by Kimi Cunningham Grant (Amberjack, May 2019).

Please describe the kinds of books you want to agent. I look for unique, clear voices with smart, tightly written prose. I have a soft spot for distinctive, strong, contemporary characters set in small towns and always look for an unexpected story arc, a suitable pace, and a compelling protagonist. I am actively building my client list with both debut and veteran writers.

Fiction: literary and upmarket fiction as well as commercial — including well-researched historical (prefer 1800s or later) and well-told women's fiction. Also love a page-turning mystery, suspense, or domestic thriller with unexpected twists and turns. Nonfiction: narrative nonfiction when the plot and characters are immersed in a culture, lifestyle, discipline, or industry. Travel or adventure memoir. *Not* currently focusing on: military/government thrillers, fantasy, sci-fi, or young adult projects.

What should writers submit for consideration, and how should they send it? Please complete my submission form found at kimberleycameron.com/amy-cloughley.php. The form requires the first 50 pages of author's completed, polished manuscript.

How do you feel about self-publishing, and what do you see happening with it in the near future? Self-publishing is a good option for the writers who want to control and manage every aspect of their projects — hiring private editors, cover and book design, distribution, promotion, etc. — but it isn't for everyone.

Why did you choose to become an agent? Working as a literary agent is a lovely balance of all of my favorite things: providing editorial feedback, pitching to the editors, negotiating deals, and the thrill of helping writers reach their goals. (There really is nothing better than that!) It is truly a business of relationships at every stage. I enjoy the business side of agenting as much as the creative, and I think that all of the positions I have held (and the many, many books I have read) have proved to be the perfect base for this career.

THE KNIGHT AGENCY ❖ knightagency.net

232 West Washington Street, Madison, GA 30650, 706-752-1157

Agent's name: Lucienne Diver

What would you be doing right now if not responding to this survey? Working like a fiend.

What would you be if not an agent (other than a dog, cat, or other mammal)? A fiction or travel writer.

Do you think independent (noncorporate) publishing will be stronger, weaker, or the same over the next few years? There will always be ebb and flow, but traditional publishing is particularly strong right now. With so many books and authors out there, it's become difficult to stand out without the distribution, promotional and marketing deals, experience, and relationships that publishing houses have built up over the years. That said, authors who have the time, talent, and temperament to work the system will continue to do well independently.

Please describe your professional history. Over the course of 25 years in the industry, I've built a strong list of bestselling and award-winning authors. I spent my first 15 years in New York at Spectrum Literary Agency, which was a fantastic experience. I've been with the Knight Agency for the past 10 years, where I continue to specialize in all manner of commercial fiction, young adult through adult, particularly science fiction and fantasy, mystery and suspense, romance and women's fiction.

How would you define the "client from hell"? Someone who sabotages his or her own career by blowing deadlines or refusing to be edited or arguing with reviewers or … There are many paths to self-sabotage.

Do you think Earth was created a few thousand years ago or several billion years ago? Is this a trick question?

Please list five books you recently agented. *Wolfkiller River* by Rachel Caine (third book in the series after *Stillhouse Lake* and *Killman Creek*), *The Other Sister* by Sarah Zettel, untitled by N. K. Jemisin, *Time's Children* by David B. Coe.

Please describe the kinds of books you want to agent. I want to agent brilliant books with either an original approach or a unique voice, preferably both. I don't want a book I feel already exists, but something new and exciting that will spark a passionate response in others.

What should writers submit for consideration, and how should they send it? The Knight Agency's submission guidelines are available at knightagency.net/submission-guidelines. In brief, submissions should include a one-page query letter and the first five pages of the manuscript pasted into the body of the email. Our address for submissions is: submissions@knightagency.net.

Additional agent at the Knight Agency: Pamela Harty, pamela.harty@knightagency.net

THE LA LITERARY AGENCY ❖ www.laliteraryagency.com

PO Box 46370, Los Angeles, CA 90046, 323-654-5288

Agent's name and contact info: Maureen Lasher, maureen@laliteraryagency.com

Describe the kinds of works you want to represent. I like to represent the same kind of books that I buy for myself from a bookstore. At the top of my nonfiction list is narrative nonfiction, which is storytelling. The subjects are eclectic, and I can't put them in one category, so here are brief log lines describing some of our narrative nonfiction books that illustrate what I like to represent.

Light My Fire by Ray Manzarek (Putnam): Ray re-creates how he founded The Doors with Jim Morrison and takes you on their trip; he wrote the first draft by pencil on yellow legal pads. *Beyond the Limits* by Stacy Allison (Little, Brown): Stacy tells how she became the first American woman to crest Mt. Everest; her sample chapter focused on the moment when she and two other climbers realized that they had enough oxygen for only one person to summit. *Where the Money Is* by William Rehder (Norton), FBI Special Agent, who is the world's foremost expert on bank robberies. *Uppity* by Bill White (Grand Central): professional baseball player, voice of the Yankees for 18 years, and president of the National League for 5 years, White is the first African American to reach that level in any sport. *Sweet Life* by Barry Manilow (McGraw Hill), an intelligent, funny, talented writer. *Never Too Late* by Bobby DeLaughter (Scribner): a criminal prosecutor, DeLaughter solved the mystery of Medgar Evers's murder 30 years after the crime when, by chance, he found the missing weapon in the closet of a judge — his father-in-law (the judge wasn't hiding the gun; he didn't know it was the missing piece of evidence in the case).

Fiction is both easier and harder to define. Like everyone in publishing, we long for compelling, beautifully written novels. It can be historical, contemporary, literary, commercial, mystery, suspense. Reality check: It's difficult to sell a first novel, but it happens every day.

We don't work with romance novels (although it's huge now), horror, Westerns, science fiction, juvenile or young adult (also huge), or books on how to solve world problems. Our website (www.laliteraryagency.com) will give you a broader overview of our books.

Describe your education and career history. After graduating from Brown University with a concentration in history, I entered publishing in the college division of Prentice Hall, later acquired by Simon & Schuster. After five years of commuting from Manhattan, over the George Washington Bridge to Fort Lee, I was happy to move to Random House, which was within walking distance of my apartment. At Random House, I was associate manager of advertising, responsible for marketing Random House titles to schools, colleges, and libraries. I then became director of advertising and publicity for Liveright, now an imprint of Norton.

After marriage and a baby, I moved to Los Angeles with my husband, Eric, who was CEO of Nash Publishing, which was eventually merged into extinction. Because we both had extensive publishing experience, we launched an independent publishing imprint with Houghton Mifflin. The imprint focused on commercial fiction (several were *New York Times* bestsellers) and a travel guide series that grew to over 20 titles. During that time, we were reading many excellent manuscripts that didn't fit the profile of our imprint. This led to the creation of our literary agency, which provided us with wider latitude in placing titles.

What do you like to do when you're not working? I've had some interesting side trips from agenting. When I moved to Los Angeles, I learned how to fabricate jewelry — mostly in silver. Invited to a party in New York, I wore as much of my new jewelry as I could put on — earrings, two silver cuffs, three rings, a necklace, and a belt buckle. A woman approached me to inquire where I had purchased the pieces. Her name was Vera Wang, then accessories editor at *Vogue*. For the next year, my jewelry was featured every month on the editorial pages of *Vogue* and was sold in major department stores such as Bloomingdale's. I enjoyed designing and making jewelry, but didn't see it as a career, so I returned to publishing.

I've been knitting since I was ten. A few years ago, I coauthored a knitting book, *Teen Knitting Club* (Artisan). I love knitting, yarn, and knitting books.

What do you want to tell new/unpublished writers? The internet has opened the floodgates and made it more complicated for writers and agents to find each other. When it's obvious to me that I'm one of scores of agents who have received the same email, I'm reluctant to spend any time on it. Nevertheless, I have connected with some writers on the internet.

Don't give up on the internet, but here's some advice on how to use it. Try to personalize your approach to an agent. Read the acknowledgments in books that are like yours and email a note to the agent referring to the book. Ask everyone you know if they know someone in the publishing world, and try to get, at least, an email introduction. Comb through books like this so you can write an email that stands out. Look at your college alumni listings and use that shared experience as an introduction. Don't open your letter with "Dear Sir."

How would you describe the "client from hell"? This is an extreme example, but it happened. Eric and I were scheduled to be on an agent panel in Los Angeles, sponsored by the New York–based Volunteer Lawyers for the Arts. The event was widely publicized. Then we and the Volunteer Lawyers group in New York received anonymous letters explaining why we weren't qualified to be on the panel. The letters were also filled with anti-Semitic rhetoric and physical threats. The police, thankfully, took it seriously. They had a plan. Two policemen went with us to the conference in plain clothes and when the moderator said that we couldn't be there, a man walked out, clearly angry. The police followed him and brought him in for questioning. He revealed that, months before, we had turned down his novel.

If the person is already a client and I want to take a Valium before each phone conversation, I try to end the professional relationship as quickly as possible. Today, it's easy for someone who feels ignored, insulted, or unhappy to use the internet to vent his or her anger at you. Hopefully, you can spot that kind of person early and not get involved.

Describe your job and what you like about it. Most of the time I work as an editor, and that's what I truly enjoy. For nonfiction, it's essential to have a stellar, best-on-the-editor's-desk proposal. I work editorially with our clients on the book proposal, which is harder to write than the book; but when you have it right, you will have a blueprint for your book. In 20 or 30 or 40 pages, the proposal has to do it all. What's the best way to define your book? What will you cover in each chapter? Is the overview effective? What is the best structure for the book? Are the sample chapters good enough? What qualifies you to write the book? And on and on.

Working with fiction is quite different. Publishers make their decisions based on reading the complete novel. Right now I'm working with several writers I met through the internet. We had no personal connection, but I was taken by their submission letter. With both writers I've done extensive editorial work to get their books ready to submit. We communicate in two ways: on the phone and on the computer (most of the time). I'm not copyediting (punctuation, spelling, etc.), but working on structure, characters, dialogue, and pacing.

Truthfully, I never know where I will find a wonderful book. When our daughter was in college, she went to a lecture given by Norma McCorvey (a.k.a. Jane Roe of *Roe v. Wade*). Surprised that nobody had ever asked Norma to tell her story, we paired her with a writer, and HarperCollins published *I Am Roe*. A small slice of history: Norma learned about the historic Supreme Court decision *Roe v. Wade* when she opened up the Dallas daily newspaper lying on her doorstep and read the front-page article about herself.

What are your feelings about self-publishing? If all you care about is to see your book in print, go for it. If you believe that when your book is in print, the world will find it, reevaluate your conclusion. If you have a huge success, you won. Winners are rare.

Do you think Amazon is good or bad — or both — for the book business? Answering as a customer: I like Amazon. I'm a member of Amazon Prime and joined audible.com years ago — before Amazon bought them.

I go to the Barnes & Noble at The Grove in LA about once a week. Their children's section is a playground with books. Their display tables highlight books by category like historical fiction or biography. You can sit in the café with a cappuccino and look through a pile of new titles. Every year I renew my membership card. If Barnes & Noble closes, I'll be devastated.

Answering as an agent: The publishing business is changing, but I don't have a clue how it will sort itself out. Amazon is a major force. It will be a huge loss to book lovers and the publishing industry if Barnes & Noble can't survive because of Amazon. Books aren't going away.

LEVINE | GREENBERG | ROSTAN LITERARY AGENCY ❖
www.lgrliterary.com

307 Seventh Avenue, Suite 2407, New York, NY 10001, 212-337-0934

Agent's name and contact info: Danielle Svetcov, Agent, dsvetcov@lgrliterary.com

Describe the kinds of works you want to represent. Novels, graphic novels, journalism, science, reported memoir, food/cooking, and humor. More specifically, I want to represent novels like *I Capture the Castle*, *The Truth According to Us*, *The Shipping News*, and, er, *Jane Eyre*; I want to represent graphic novels like *Roller Girl*; I want to rep journalism/history like *Devil in the White City* and journalism/science like *The Immortal Life of Henrietta Lacks*; I want to rep memoir like *Don't Let's Go to the Dogs Tonight*; food and recipe books like *Blood, Bones & Butter* and *Twelve Recipes*; and, as for humor, anything, so long as it's yours and no one else's and you've thought long and hard about how to deliver humor in book form.

Describe what you definitely don't want to represent. Self-help, erotica, and other extreme exhibitionism.

How do you want writers to pitch you? Write me a letter. Be yourself, and be economical. Try to convey your abilities as a writer. Tell me who you are and why you have written what you've written; create enough drama in the note to get me interested in hearing more. Include a proposal and/or small sample from the book.

Describe your education and professional history. California public schools, Northwestern University's J-school, Boston University culinary "camp" certificate program, Warren Wilson College MFA.

How did you become an agent? I answered an ad on Craigslist, which led to a 5-hour-a-week job assisting an agent who'd just moved from New York to San Francisco to start her agency's West Coast office. The 5 turned into 10, then 20, then however many hours it took to get the job done. I began selling my own books about 5 years into the gig. I still work for the agency I began assisting in 2002. I'm the only agent at LGR based in California.

Knowing what you do now, would you do it again, or what might you do instead? Yes.

Do you charge fees? If yes, please explain. Not fees, just commissions on sales, 15 percent, the standard commission charged by agents.

When and where were you born and where have you lived? Born in northern California, 1973. I've lived in Marin County, CA; Evanston, IL; Albuquerque; Chicago; Oxford (England); New York City; Boston; and Washington, DC. Not in that order.

What do you like to do when you're not working? Read, hike, cook, talk through it all with smart friends.

List some of the titles you recently placed with publishers. *Why We Swim* by Bonnie Tsui (Algonquin), *Semicolon* by Watson Mason (Ecco), *Suffragist City* by Bridget Quinn (Chronicle), *Amboy* by Alvin Cailan (Houghton Mifflin Harcourt).

Describe your personality. Conscientious, practical, encouraging, impatient, eye-roller.

What do you like reading/watching/listening to on your own time? I'm a big fan of Newbery-quality middle grade books and tend to shake down our local kids' librarian for the candidates each year; I spend a lot of free time reading those titles and feeling 12, my favorite age. I love a good British mystery (the *Matthew Shardlake* series, the *Flavia de Luce* series, and the Sherlock spin-offs by Laurie R. King have kept me busy over the years, though the last is actually an American doing a mean impression). Favorite comedic writers (book and/or TV): David Sedaris, Zach Galifianakis, Bill Murray. TV taste runs to *Game of Thrones* (though the violence tips my scales some days), *Catastrophe*, *The Wire*, *Man in the High Castle*, and pretty much anything made by the BBC (*Jewel in the Crown*, *The Forsythe Saga*, et al.). You can frequently find me parked in my driveway, listening to a chapter of *Ramona the Brave*, *The Secret Garden*, or an episode of the Longform, More Perfect, or Slow Burn podcasts.

Do you think the business has changed a lot over the past few years? It doesn't seem drastically different from when I began. Still have to find talent. Still have to edit and shape proposals and manuscripts. Still have to cultivate relationships with editors. There are certain kinds of projects — spin-offs from blogs, Vine, Instagram, etc. — that seem to sell faster than ever before; but those are the pop-culture projects. They've always been freaks of nature. I don't know the time before the internet. Maybe it was easier then…

What do the "Big 5" mean to you? The publishers who pay the most and have the greatest ability to distribute a book, here and abroad.

How do you feel about independent/small presses? They're wonderful and absolutely essential at this moment when so few "biggies" exist. They are the presses that often find the next generation of great writers, take the first risk on them, launch them.

What are your feelings about self-publishing? It's a lot harder than it looks, and you'd better love to glad-hand and market if you have a desire to succeed as a self-published author.

Do you think Amazon is good or bad — or both — for the book business? Both. Like marriage, it's complicated.

What do you like and dislike about your job? I like that it's an ongoing education, that I'm in contact with talented and creative people, and that I can help them navigate this world. I don't like the feeling I sometimes get that it's impossible to be heard anymore. I suppose that comes from a discomfort and generalized worry about the pace and habits of the modern world, specifically the modern media cycle, which publishing is part of or at least depends on. I'd like to find new ways to spread the gospel of books.

Describe a book you would like to write. So many, and one will be published in 2019, hopefully, *Park, Place* (Dial Books for Young Writers).

Do you believe in a higher and/or lower "power"? Sometimes.

Agent's name and contact info: Victoria Skurnick, vskurnick@lgrliterary.com

What would you be doing right now if not responding to this survey? Dealing with manuscripts.

What would you be if not an agent (other than a dog, cat, or other mammal)? A writer.

Do you think independent (noncorporate) publishing will be stronger, weaker, or the same over the next few years? With the rise of Amazon, independent publishers are in a special position to become stronger, to fight the corporate tide.

Please describe your professional history. Started as promotion/advertising director at Holt, went on to become an editor, a commercial fiction writer (half of pseudonymous "Cynthia Victor"), an editor at trade houses (Pocket and St. Martin's), and then editor in chief of the Book-of-the-Month Club before coming to LGR 10 years ago.

How would you define the "client from hell"? A person who does not live up to his or her commitments, is sloppy or late, or is unable to listen hard enough to the editor or agent to make a book the best it can be.

Do you think Earth was created a few thousand years ago or several billion years ago? The latter.

Please list five books you recently agented. *The Paris Spy* by Susan Elia MacNeal, *Half Moon Bay* by Alice LaPlante, *The Unexpected President* by Scott Greenberger, *Jumping at Shadows* by Sasha Abramsky, *The Man in the Crooked Hat* by Harry Dolan.

Please describe the kinds of books you want to agent. Literary fiction or suspense fiction with strong characters and voice; nonfiction, especially books on history or politics, quirky big-idea books.

What should writers submit for consideration, and how should they send it? Writers should email a query letter with a concise description of the book. If l find the query interesting, I will ask for a full manuscript (if fiction) or a full proposal (if nonfiction).

How do you feel about self-publishing, and what do you see happening with it in the near future? Self-publishing can be a rewarding alternative, especially if a writer has great connections with large groups of readers. If writers do not have some kind of built-in audience, it will be a full-time job to publish their books. It can work, but it is more of a challenge than is often indicated in the media.

Do you think there are too many, too few, or just enough agents? I have no opinion.

Do you think Amazon will become the country's largest employer within 10 years? Yes, indeed.

Why do you think some books become super-successful (beyond the obvious reasons)? Luck, timing, quality — and magic.

Do you think agents are likely to become millionaires? Nope.

Do you think agents tend toward certain personality types? Not really. I know agents who are shy, outgoing, meticulous, slobby, relentless, and lazy.

Do you think writers tend to be more or less narcissistic than the population at large? Absolutely not, though they are often lonelier and in need of support. It can be a most solitary endeavor.

Knowing what you know now, would you become an agent again? Absolutely.

Why did you choose to become an agent? It combined everything I did earlier, picking books, finding authors of quality, finding the words to interest an audience (or, in this case, an editor and publisher). And it's fun!

Do you think many talented writers fail to get published for avoidable reasons? If so, what are some of those reasons? They are long-winded or stubborn or untalented — that about covers it.

LINDA KONNER LITERARY AGENCY ❖

www.lindakonnerliteraryagency.com

10 West 15th Street, Suite 1918, New York, NY 10011

Agent's name and contact info: Linda Konner, ldkonner@cs.com

What would you be doing right now if not responding to this survey? Playing poker or going to the theater.

What would you be if not an agent (other than a dog, cat, or other mammal)? An author (I have written or cowritten eight books).

Do you think independent (noncorporate) publishing will be stronger, weaker, or the same over the next few years? Weaker.

Please describe your professional history. Author or coauthor of eight books, including *Why Can't a Man Be More like a Cat?* and *The Last 10 Pounds*. Former editor in chief of *Weight Watchers Magazine*; a features editor at *Redbook*, *Seventeen*, and *Woman's World*; founding editor of *Richard Simmons & Friends* newsletter. Launched my literary agency in 1996. Currently represent approximately 50 writers of nonfiction.

How would you define the "client from hell"? One who doesn't follow instructions (from me, or his or her editor or publicist), misses deadlines.

Do you think Earth was created a few thousand years ago or several billion years ago? ??

Please list five books you recently agented. *Get Money: How to Live the Life You Want, Not Just the Life You Can Afford*; *Overcoming Opioid Addiction*; *The Reducetarian Cookbook: 125+ Easy, Healthy & Delicious Plant-Based Recipes for Omnivores, Vegans and Everyone in Between*; *Silver Hair: Say Goodbye to the Dye and Let Your Natural Light Shine*; *Graceful Exit: How to Advocate Effectively, Take Care of Yourself and Be Present for the Death of a Loved One*.

Please describe the kinds of books you want to agent. Like those listed above, that is, written by top experts in their field with a solid author platform and with a talented writer if necessary.

What should writers submit for consideration, and how should they send it? Via email: one- or two-paragraph book summary and one- or two-paragraph author bio, including the size of their following via social media, traditional media, and websites they blog for; lectures, podcasts, or webinars done in the last one or two years; affiliations with companies that might brand or promote their book.

How do you feel about self-publishing, and what do you see happening with it in the near future? I still love the business and hope it continues. I'm happy to see print publishing continuing and audiobook publishing exploding.

Do you think there are too many, too few, or just enough agents? Not sure.

Do you think Amazon will become the country's largest employer within 10 years? Probably.

Why do you think some books become super-successful (beyond the obvious reasons)? ??

Do you think agents are likely to become millionaires? Likely? Probably not, but many are or can be.

Do you think agents tend toward certain personality types? Yes.

Do you think writers tend to be more or less narcissistic than the population at large? Not sure.

Knowing what you know now, would you become an agent again? Yes — in fact I would have started 10 years earlier.

Why did you choose to become an agent? I was tired of being an author and an editor and wanted to try something new within publishing.

Do you think many talented writers fail to get published for avoidable reasons? If so, what are some of those reasons? They give up too soon. And they take rejection personally. Editors and agents don't have all the answers!

THE LISA EKUS GROUP ❖ lisaekus.com

57 North Street, Hatfield, MA 01038

Agents' names and contact info: Lisa Ekus, lisaekus@lisaekus.com, 413-247-9325; Sally Ekus

What would you be doing right now if not responding to this survey? Lisa: Reading fiction.

What would you be if not an agent (other than a dog, cat, or other mammal)? I would love to be a gardener.

Do you think independent (noncorporate) publishing will be stronger, weaker, or the same over the next few years? They'll be stronger!

Please describe your professional history. I received a BA from Barnard College (1979). I worked at Random House and Crown Publishers. I have owned the Lisa Ekus Group for the past 35 years. Our boutique agency represents hundreds of culinary writers through our Literary Agency, Consulting, Media Training, Talent Agency, and A La Carte divisions.

Please list five books you recently agented. We proudly list our titles in a catalog each season on our website, lisaekus.com.

Please describe the kinds of books you want to agent. Culinary(ish) nonfiction including cookbooks, health, nutrition, and women's health.

What should writers submit for consideration, and how should they send it? Writers should submit a full proposal for us to review, and the best way to do so is to send it to info@lisaekus.com. You can review our proposal guidelines at lisaekus.com/submission-requirements.

How do you feel about self-publishing, and what do you see happening with it in the near future? Self-publishing is a wonderful option for many.

Do you think there are too many, too few, or just enough agents? "Collaboration is the new competition."

Why do you think some books become super-successful (beyond the obvious reasons)? A combination of talent and content reigns!

Do you think agents tend toward certain personality types? Yes! They are empathetic, passionate, and advocators.

Knowing what you know now, would you become an agent again? I would do it all over again in a heartbeat!

Why did you choose to become an agent? I love to make dreams come true and find the right match of publisher and author. My passion for books made me an English major at Barnard, and I worked for a literary agent while still in college. There was never any question I would embark on a publishing career.

LISA HAGAN LITERARY ❖ lisahaganbooks.com

Agent's name and contact info: Lisa Hagan, lisa@lisahaganbooks.com

What would you be doing right now if not responding to this survey? Under the covers getting warm reading a good book.

What would you be if not an agent (other than a dog, cat, or other mammal)? A social worker — which is what I studied to be.

Do you think independent (noncorporate) publishing will be stronger, weaker, or the same over the next few years? I am concerned about the state of independent publishers and their ability to stay in the game.

Please describe your professional history. Agent for 25 years, and I hope for another 25.

How would you define the "client from hell"? One who doesn't listen.

Do you think Earth was created a few thousand years ago or several billion years ago? Really?

Please list five books you recently agented. *Zen Camera: Creative Awakening with a Daily Practice in Photography* by David Ulrich; *Turbo Metabolism: 8 Weeks to a New You — Preventing and Reversing Diabetes, Obesity, Heart Disease, and Other Metabolic Diseases by Treating the Causes* by Pankaj Vij, MD; *The Heart of Wellness: Bridging Western and Eastern Medicine to Transform Your Relationship with Habits, Lifestyle, and Health* by Kavitha M. Chinnaiyan, MD; *The Five Gifts: Discovering Hope, Healing and Strength When Disaster Strikes* by Dr. Laurie Nadel; *Ask Dr. Nandi: 5 Steps to Becoming Your Own #HealthHero for Longevity, Well-Being, and a Joyful Life* by Partha Nandi, MD.

Please describe the kinds of books you want to agent. Meaningful books that help the reader grow as a person. I want to be moved by the story or dive right into the self-help process to see if it works.

What should writers submit for consideration, and how should they send it? Please send an email query letter first.

How do you feel about self-publishing, and what do you see happening with it in the near future? I have made peace with it, as it is certainly not going away. If you are going to self-publish, hire a good editor. With the demand for platforms from traditional publishers, often this is the only way.

Do you think there are too many, too few, or just enough agents? When a writer approaches me with a project that I think is viable but not in my area of expertise and I assist them in finding a good agent, I think we have too few.

Do you think Amazon will become the country's largest employer within 10 years? I hope not.

Why do you think some books become super-successful (beyond the obvious reasons)? It has to be magic, where all of the pieces of the puzzle come together at the right time.

Do you think agents are likely to become millionaires? That would be nice.

Do you think agents tend toward certain personality types? Yes, I do, but underneath all of the bluster is a nice person.

Do you think writers tend to be more or less narcissistic than the population at large? Odd question.

Knowing what you know now, would you become an agent again? Absolutely. It is thrilling being an agent, and I love working with authors and publishers.

Why did you choose to become an agent? My mother was a literary agent, and her passion for books inspired me from childhood. I can't imagine doing anything else.

Do you think many talented writers fail to get published for avoidable reasons? If so, what are some of those reasons? They don't listen.

LITERARY MANAGEMENT GROUP, LLC ❖
literarymanagementgroup.com

PO Box 41004, Nashville, TN 37204, 615-812-4445

Agent's name and contact info: Bruce R. Barbour, Founder, brucebarbour@literarymanagementgroup.com

What would you be doing right now if not responding to this survey? Reading proposals.

What would you be if not an agent (other than a dog, cat, or other mammal)? Preparing manuscripts for production or consulting.

Do you think independent (noncorporate) publishing will be stronger, weaker, or the same over the next few years? Stronger, because they have to be smarter than the big operations. They can be more nimble and less risk-averse.

Please describe your professional history. My family has been in publishing since 1870, when my two uncles, Dwight Moody and Fleming Revell, began printing *Moody's Sunday School Lessons*, which he gave to kids on the streets of Chicago. I joined the family business, Fleming Revell, in 1976 and held executive positions through 1984, when we sold the firm to Scott Foresman. I cofounded Barbour Books and went on to serve in executive positions at Thomas Nelson and Random House. In 1995 I started Literary Management Group and have been helping authors get their books to market ever since. It's my calling and my life work.

How would you define the "client from hell"? They don't listen because they already know everything.

Do you think Earth was created a few thousand years ago or several billion years ago? Don't know, just happy I'm blessed to be aboard for the journey!

Please list five books you recently agented. *Two Chairs* by Bob Beaudine, inspirational/self-help (Worthy); *#Gospel* by Daniel Rice, a contemporary retelling of the book of Romans (Barbour); *Live to Win* by Tom Ziglar, motivation (Thomas Nelson); *A Stroke of Faith* by Mark Moore, autobiography (Hachette); *A Prairie Girl's Faith* by Steve Hines, the personal faith of Laura Ingalls Wilder (WaterBrook, Random House).

Please describe the kinds of books you want to agent. Unique perspective or twist on age-old truths.

What should writers submit for consideration, and how should they send it? Check my website for editorial guidelines and, if the book is a fit, email a query letter and attach a proposal using the template on the website.

How do you feel about self-publishing, and what do you see happening with it in the near future? I encourage authors to consider self-publishing if I think their idea is too small for a traditional publisher. There is no limit to this category, though distribution will primarily be online.

Do you think there are too many, too few, or just enough agents? Always room for one more who knows what they're doing!

Do you think Amazon will become the country's largest employer within 10 years? No clue.

Why do you think some books become super-successful (beyond the obvious reasons)? They hit a chord, resonate with a gazillion readers who can't stop talking about it to anybody who will listen.

Do you think agents are likely to become millionaires? Some, yes, but not many.

Do you think agents tend toward certain personality types? No.

Do you think writers tend to be more or less narcissistic than the population at large? Probably a bit more than the general population only because writing is such a solitary process, so they have to like themselves!

Knowing what you know now, would you become an agent again? Absolutely!

Why did you choose to become an agent? I wanted to help the right authors and publishers connect with each other.

Do you think many talented writers fail to get published for avoidable reasons? If so, what are some of those reasons? Idea is too small. Not qualified to write the book. Haven't done their homework. Haven't invested the time in learning to be a great writer. Wrong publisher.

LITERARY SERVICES, INC. ❖ www.literaryservicesinc.com

PO Box 888, Barnegat, NJ 08005

Agent's name: John Willig

What would you be doing right now if not responding to this survey? Reading.

What would you be if not an agent (other than a dog, cat, or other mammal)? A history or political science teacher — maybe even a professor.

Do you think independent (noncorporate) publishing will be stronger, weaker, or the same over the next few years? Stronger.

Please describe your professional history. I graduated from Brown University in 1976 and have worked in publishing for 40 years. I started in academic publishing as a college "traveler" (sales rep), became an editor at Harper & Row, a senior editor at WGL, and then executive editor for business professional/trade books at Prentice-Hall before starting Literary Services, Inc., in 1992. That's pretty much the résumé. I sincerely believe, though, that my "professional history" began when I became an avid reader as a young teenager. I would see my mother (God bless her Irish soul) come home from the library smiling, happy that she was able to get her favorite writers' new books without having to go on the waiting list. Who were these people who could make her so happy? To find out, I became a reader and lover of "stories well told."

How would you define the "client from hell"? I take very seriously my responsibility not to represent these types of writers, who are disrespectful of experience, arrogant, and disorganized and do not exhibit humility or a sense of humor.

Do you think Earth was created a few thousand years ago or several billion years ago? I'll take the billions.

Please list five books you recently agented. Yvonne Tally, *Breaking Up with Busy*; Rod Pyle, *Space 2.0*; Ed Gordon, PhD, *Divided on D-Day*; Diana Jones, PhD, *Leadership Material*; Steven Pantilat, *Life after the Diagnosis*.

Please describe the kinds of books you want to agent. Fresh, provocative, counterintuitive, contrarian, well-researched, and well-written presentations that "shine a new light" on a topic, event, company, or person. I work primarily in nonfiction categories with a strong interest in history, science, psychology, business, politics, current events, health and wellness, food and cultures, reference, and personal growth. I've also started to represent historical fiction in the mystery/crime and literary categories.

What should writers submit for consideration, and how should they send it? Per the submission instructions on our website, I prefer to initially receive a one-page email describing your work and professional activities. If interested, I will request your proposal and sample chapters.

How do you feel about self-publishing, and what do you see happening with it in the near future? Walt Whitman self-published/printed the original version of *Leaves of Grass* and with each new printing added new poems based on the reactions of his readers, a lesson in quality oftentimes lacking in self-publishers or self-funders. It's a very crowded marketplace, and to stand out many writers will need to seek out professionals providing editorial, design, production, and marketing (which begins with your writing) expertise and experience. Recognizing this need through the many conferences I have attended, I established a Content Coaching & Strategy service for writers considering self-publishing. It has led many writers to rethink their approaches (e.g., broad vs. narrow focus), titles, subtitles, contents, planned expenses, etc.

Do you think there are too many, too few, or just enough agents? It depends on the areas of interest and categories, but there always seem to be enough choices for writers.

Do you think Amazon will become the country's largest employer within 10 years? Yes.

Why do you think some books become super-successful (beyond the obvious reasons)? They connect with the zeitgeist. Think *The Life-Changing Magic of Tidying Up*, *You Are a Badass*, etc.

Do you think agents are likely to become millionaires? If they connect with the zeitgeist.

Do you think agents tend toward certain personality types? It's a big tent with all types of characters.

Do you think writers tend to be more or less narcissistic than the population at large? Tough to be more narcissistic these days than the population at large.

Knowing what you know now, would you become an agent again? Yes.

Why did you choose to become an agent? To work closely with talented writers.

Do you think many talented writers fail to get published for avoidable reasons? If so, what are some of those reasons? You may be a talented writer, but if you have a reputation of being an a-hole (which can be avoidable), then agents and editors might choose others to work with. You can be talented but writing in overpublished categories. You may be listening to your loving partner more than to your agent.

LIZA ROYCE AGENCY, LLC ❖ www.lizaroyce.com

1049 Park Avenue, New York, NY 10028, 212-722-1950
Twitter and Instagram: @lizaroyceagency; Facebook: Liza Royce Agency

Agents' names: Liza Fleissig, Ginger Harris Dontzin

What would you be doing right now if not responding to this survey? Liza: Spending time with my family is the most important thing. Whether skiing in Vermont, summering on the Cape, just doing jigsaw puzzles or watching TV, we are a pretty tight crew, and I am grateful every day for them.

What would you be if not an agent (other than a dog, cat, or other mammal)? Despite being vegan, I cook a ton of meat for my family, who joke I should open a restaurant called Beethoven's (get it, he composed but couldn't hear and I cook meat without tasting it). I also fantasize about going to medical school. I had all my credits but went to law school instead. So who knows? But I really *love* what I do, so for the long haul, here I am!

Do you think independent (noncorporate) publishing will be stronger, weaker, or the same over the next few years? They are only going to get stronger. They can be wonderful opportunities for some authors, especially debuts, where authors can get a little more hand-holding and attention. They can also provide stronger marketing in some cases, since a smaller list means more focus per book. The first LRA book to receive *New York Times* praise and multiple starred reviews was published by a small press.

Please describe your professional history. I graduated from the Wharton School of Business at the University of Pennsylvania and later went to Cardozo School of Law, where I graduated magna cum laude. I have practiced law for 20 years and was a partner in a litigation firm before founding LRA with Ginger. Prior to that, I worked in construction development and the banking industry.

How would you define the "client from hell"? Legends in their own mind, they are way too entitled and can't appreciate the importance of constructive criticism.

Please list five books you recently agented. *Car Trouble* (Harper Perennial), *Wish* (Scholastic), *Someone Else's Summer* (Running Press Kids, Hachette), *Hedy Lamarr's Double Life* (Sterling Children's), *The Last Trial* (Thomas & Mercer).

Please describe the kinds of books you want to agent. From picture books through adult projects, fiction and nonfiction, LRA welcomes strong voices and plot-driven works.

What should writers submit for consideration, and how should they send it? We prefer to receive queries via email at submissions@lizaroyce.com. Please include a brief synopsis, a little information about yourself, including any social-media platform and marketing ideas you may have, but do not send any attachments, as they will not be opened at this stage in the process.

How do you feel about self-publishing, and what do you see happening with it in the near future? In this crowded marketplace, many books that would have been published 5 or 10 years ago are being passed over as not being "different enough to stand out," and for those authors self-publishing can be a great way to jump-start their career. Caution: the writing still needs to be super-strong, and you need to constantly work sales and marketing if you expect to later break out to a traditional publisher. With that said, we took on a self-published book that later went on to be published by Thomas Nelson/HarperCollins and is now being courted for film. So anything is possible.

Knowing what you know now, would you become an agent again? *Yes* — just maybe wish I had started sooner!

Why did you choose to become an agent? I have always been under a strong sphere of influence from friends in the publishing industry, and I had been searching for something creative to do for a long time after my children were born. Besides, I guess when you come from an entrepreneurial family, it's in your blood to take risks and try new things!

LOWENSTEIN ASSOCIATES ❖ www.lowensteinassociates.com

Agent's name and contact info: Barbara Lowenstein, 212-206-1630

What would you be doing right now if not responding to this survey? Reading queries, following up on books out on submission.

What would you be if not an agent (other than a dog, cat, or other mammal)? We honestly can't imagine doing anything else other than working in the publishing industry in some capacity.

Do you think independent (noncorporate) publishing will be stronger, weaker, or the same over the next few years? We are excited by the innovative and brilliant work that's being published by small presses. We hope those presses will continue to grow and thrive in the coming years.

Please describe your professional history. Barbara Lowenstein started her publishing career at the Sterling Lord Agency as an assistant to the dramatic agent. She then moved on to Lancer Books, one of the last independent paperback houses at the time, where she created the first line of trade paperbacks in the industry. There, she published self-help, psychology, how-to, crafts, and cooking titles. After a brief stint as director of subsidiary rights for Walker Books, she started Lowenstein Associates. For over four decades, Barbara has represented the international bestselling author M. C. Beaton, known as the "Queen of Cozy Mysteries." Barbara also represents Ishmael Reed, MacArthur Genius Award winner, novelist, essayist, and poet; Cordelia Fine, winner of the prestigious Royal Society Science Prize for *Testosterone Rex*; and Carla Harris, vice chairman and managing director at Morgan Stanley and author of the extremely successful career and business books *Strategize to Win* and *Expect to Win*.

How would you define the "client from hell"? Someone who refuses to listen to or take his or her agent's advice and then blames the agent for the lack of a sale.

Do you think Earth was created a few thousand years ago or several billion years ago? We believe in science.

Please list five books you recently agented. *Testosterone Rex* by Cordelia Fine, *The Witches' Tree* by M. C. Beaton, *Death of a Ghost* by M. C. Beaton, *Strategize to Win* by Carla Harris, *The Complete Muhammad Ali* by Ishmael Reed.

Please describe the kinds of books you want to agent. Lowenstein Associates is accepting submissions for cozy mysteries, outstanding literary and commercial fiction, young adult and middle grade novels, and narrative nonfiction as well as nonfiction authors who have a strong platform and are leading experts in their field, including business, women's interest, psychology, health, science, and social issues. We particularly welcome submissions from women and writers of color.

What should writers submit for consideration, and how should they send it? For fiction, please send us a 1-page query letter along with the first 10 pages pasted in the body of the email to assistant@bookhaven.com. For nonfiction, please send a 1-page overview, table of contents, and a chapter breakdown pasted into the body of the email to assistant@bookhaven.com. Please put the word *Query* and the title of your project in the subject line of your email, and address it to the agent of your choice.

How do you feel about self-publishing, and what do you see happening with it in the near future? There have been more and more opportunities for self-publishing in recent years, especially with Amazon's print-on-demand services available through KDP. Great books have first been self-published and gone on to be discovered and republished by major presses. However, considering the high volume of books that are self-published, distinguishing the good from the bad can be an arduous task for readers. In this respect, agents and editors still serve a vital task in not only helping authors to develop their books but also vetting writing.

Do you think there are too many, too few, or just enough agents? There are probably too many.

Do you think Amazon will become the country's largest employer within 10 years? Amazon is growing larger and more powerful by the day. But we hope that readers will continue to support their local independent bookstores, which play a vital role in the publishing ecosystem.

Why do you think some books become super-successful (beyond the obvious reasons)? Compelling stories and unique characters will always appeal to readers. What also makes a big difference is the author's willingness to promote and market his or her work both in person and on social media and not just relying upon reviews or advertising to sell their writing.

Do you think agents are likely to become millionaires? Some do, most don't.

Do you think agents tend toward certain personality types? To be an agent requires not only an overwhelming passion for books, but also the ability to hustle and promote. The best agents will have both an open and an assertive personality.

Do you think writers tend to be more or less narcissistic than the population at large? Writers, generally speaking, are highly motivated and gracious people.

Knowing what you know now, would you become an agent again? Yes.

Why did you choose to become an agent? Love of good writing and the desire to nurture authors' careers and help bring good writing into the world.

Do you think many talented writers fail to get published for avoidable reasons? If so, what are some of those reasons? Yes and no. Even the best writers face a lot of rejection before they find success — rejection of their stories submitted to literary journals, rejection upon querying agents, and rejection from editors at publishing houses after they've acquired representation. It's a very tough process, and not everyone wants to stick it out. However, we do believe that writers who are talented and who persevere despite rejection or setbacks will eventually find success, especially if they are willing to take a hand in promoting their own material.

LYNN SELIGMAN, LITERARY AGENT

Upper Montclair, NJ 07043, 973-783-3631

Agent's name and contact info: Lynn Seligman, seliglit@aol.com

What would you be doing right now if not responding to this survey? I would probably be doing work now.

What would you be if not an agent (other than a dog, cat, or other mammal)? I might have been an international or copyright attorney.

Do you think independent (noncorporate) publishing will be stronger, weaker, or the same over the next few years? There will be more consolidation of corporate publishing, but there will also be independents starting up as well.

Please describe your professional history. After getting my MA from Columbia in French literature, I taught ESL (I also speak German and Spanish) in the NYC public schools, but soon decided to enter publishing. I worked at two small houses, Hawthorn Books and T.Y. Crowell, in editorial and subsidiary rights. I continued doing sub rights, first at Doubleday in foreign rights and then as manager of serial rights, after which I moved to Simon & Schuster in the same capacity until I became associate director of rights. From that position, I went to Julian Bach Literary Agency as an agent before becoming independent.

How would you define the "client from hell"? I usually take on clients with whom I feel I have a good rapport to begin with, so there are not usually any major problems. I am only bothered when a client disappears and won't answer my (or the editor's) calls, emails, or letters. But isn't that what clients complain of as well?

Do you think Earth was created a few thousand years ago or several billion years ago? I don't know and, honestly, don't care.

Please list five books you recently agented. *The Witch's Hunger* and *The Witch's Thirst* by Deborah LeBlanc, *Road to Temptation* and untitled Carrington Twins sequel by Terra Little, *Waiting for an Earl like You* by Alexandra Hawkins.

Please describe the kinds of books you want to agent. I enjoy representing both commercial and literary fiction as well as young adult fiction. I particularly like women's fiction, romance, and historical fiction. I also enjoy nonfiction such as memoir, narrative nonfiction, biography, history, entertainment, health, medicine, psychology, and science.

What should writers submit for consideration, and how should they send it? I used to only ask for hardcopy with an SASE, which is still acceptable, but I now look at email submissions as long as there are no attachments. I do like seeing a short sample of the writing, which can be attached to the email, but the best thing is to send me a really complete description of the project or book in the email itself.

How do you feel about self-publishing, and what do you see happening with it in the near future? Self-publishing is not going away, so we have to learn to work with it. I have a couple of writers who work with me and also self-publish, and I am fine with that as long as I know what they are doing and I get a chance to review the material to see if I think there is a market with a commercial publisher. I do believe both can coexist.

Do you think there are too many, too few, or just enough agents? What I think is irrelevant, as I believe there will always be people wanting to set up shop. That is their prerogative.

Do you think Amazon will become the country's largest employer within 10 years? Amazon is already huge and continues to grow and change. Even though books were their entree into publishing, they are much more interested in film and other subsidiary media.

Why do you think some books become super-successful (beyond the obvious reasons)? Especially in this era of social media, some works get a tremendous amount of buzz. Most of the really successful ones deliver to the reader in some way as well, as entertainment, information, quality of writing, etc. I think that is really important to success.

Do you think agents are likely to become millionaires? Ha-ha.

Do you think agents tend toward certain personality types? Most agents I know want to help writers and bring their work to an audience as well as make money doing it. That need to help is an important part of being a successful and happy agent.

Do you think writers tend to be more or less narcissistic than the population at large? It really takes all kinds of people in this world, and writers are no exception. I think any artist has to be a bit more narcissistic, if you want to call it that. An artist has to believe in the quality of his or her work, and that requires a certain amount of self-involvement.

Knowing what you know now, would you become an agent again? Probably. It has been a good field for me, although I could have done other things. It has always seemed to combine my interests — a love of books and reading, the fun of negotiation and working with different people and projects all the time, so I don't get bored.

Why did you choose to become an agent? See above. That combination made me want to do this job in publishing.

Do you think many talented writers fail to get published for avoidable reasons? If so, what are some of those reasons? Many talented writers fail to get published or reach the success they should. The market is so crowded with books, it takes a very loud voice to be heard. I also think publishers often take on projects and don't support their authors well, even to guiding them on how to promote their own books. This is one of the reasons many authors have turned to self-publishing. Even though they might not sell as many copies, they will sell what they can and the money is all theirs.

MALAGA BALDI LITERARY AGENCY ❖ www.baldibooks.com

Agent's name and contact info: Malaga Baldi, queries: info@baldibooks.com

What would you be doing right now if not responding to this survey? Reading a manuscript and falling asleep in bed.

What would you be if not an agent (other than a dog, cat, or other mammal)? A UPS driver. Brown uniforms. Love UPS.

Do you think independent (noncorporate) publishing will be stronger, weaker, or the same over the next few years? The same.

Please describe your professional history. In the mid-1970s I took off a year during college and worked as a mother's helper for Lois Wallace. Wallace had left William Morris to start her own agency. I got the publishing bug by meeting Erica Jong, Erich Segal, and Joan Didion at the very start of their careers. My first job in publishing was as secretary to the head of Ballantine Books publicity a zillion years ago. I then went on to work for two outstanding and remarkably different agents, Candida Donadio and Elaine Markson, before I went on my own in 1986. Thirty years in the school of hard knocks.

How would you define the "client from hell"? Rude, won't listen, knows everything, makes you cry. All in one client? Not yet.

Do you think Earth was created a few thousand years ago or several billion years ago? Several billion years ago. The Beatles would have been a much better band if they had juggled.

Please list five books you recently agented. *Furry Nation: The True Story of America's Most Misunderstood Subculture*, Joe Strike (Cleis, October 2017); *Urban Tantra: Sacred Sex for the Twenty-First Century*, 2nd ed., Barbara Carrellas (Ten Speed, December 2017); *A Wilder Time: Notes from a Geologist at the Edge of the Greenland Ice*, William W. Glassley (Bellevue Literary, February 2018); *Tomb of the Unknown Racist*, Blanche McCrary Boyd (Counterpoint, May 2018); *Why* To Kill a Mockingbird *Still Matters: What Harper Lee's Book and the Iconic American Film Mean to Us Today*, Tom Santopietro (St. Martin's, June 2018).

Please describe the kinds of books you want to agent. Intelligent, far-reaching, voicey fiction and hybrid nonfiction — creative nonfiction — narrative nonfiction that takes me to places I have never been before.

What should writers submit for consideration, and how should they send it? A knock-your-socks-off query letter, asking questions — enticing me. Make me want to drop everything I am doing to find out what happens at the end of your novel. For nonfiction, please bring to light a subject, idea, or situation we have long overlooked in a new and brilliant fashion.

How do you feel about self-publishing, and what do you see happening with it in the near future? If a self-published book is successful, a publisher will offer to reprint, distribute, and expand on your numbers, brand, or platform, perhaps even publish subsequent books. Many self-published books fit into categories (sci-fi, Westerns, romances, young adult, fantasy, etc.). Category fiction is not my area of expertise. I offer little to a title that already has an ISBN and a poor-to-modest history. Self-published books are often regional. Local bookstores support them, often competing with writers on book tours. Whether you are self-published or have a standard, old-fashioned publisher, get a website, make friends, campaign months ahead of time!

Do you think there are too many, too few, or just enough agents? Never enough. Always room for more agents. And *more good writers.*

Do you think Amazon will become the country's largest employer within 10 years? Probably one of the largest. We will end up working for the government at the rate we are going.

Why do you think some books become super-successful (beyond the obvious reasons)? Readers like to be entertained.

Do you think agents are likely to become millionaires? I want to be a millionaire.

Do you think agents tend toward certain personality types? There are good Virgos and bad Virgos. I am a bad Virgo.

Do you think writers tend to be more or less narcissistic than the population at large? Writers do think a lot. Narcissists think a lot about themselves.

Knowing what you know now, would you become an agent again? *Yes*. But I was expecting more cake.

Why did you choose to become an agent? Because I like the way writers think. I want to find out what happened.

Do you think many talented writers fail to get published for avoidable reasons? If so, what are some of those reasons? Define success and failure. It is all in the eye of the beholder. I believe good books get published. Goodwill, great art, music, books, etc., will survive. Am I naive? Who decides what is great? The point is to read as much as you can and make up your own criteria. As a gatekeeper, my criteria are something like: (1) Gosh, I wish I had written it! (2) He or she makes it look so easy. I wish I could do that. Could I? (3) This book made me a better person. Thank you for writing it.

MARSAL LYON LITERARY AGENCY, LLC ❖

www.marsallyonliteraryagency.com

PMB 121, 665 San Rodolfo Drive, 124, Solana Beach, CA 92075

Agent's name and contact info: Jill Marsal, jill@marsallyonliteraryagency.com

What would you be doing right now if not responding to this survey? Reading author submissions or responding to emails.

Do you think independent (noncorporate) publishing will be stronger, weaker, or the same over the next few years? We have seen a strong growth in independent publishing over the past few years, and it has opened many new publishing opportunities for authors that will continue in the next few years.

Please describe your professional history. I am a founding partner of the Marsal Lyon Literary Agency and have been in the publishing industry for 20 years. Previously, I worked as a literary agent with the Sandra Dijkstra Literary Agency for 8 years. I also have a strong legal background, hold a JD from Harvard Law School, and practiced as an attorney with Wilson Sonsini Goodrich & Rosati for 5 years in the Bay Area.

How would you define the "client from hell"? It is really important to have good communication and be responsive, so you can build a relationship. Warning signs for me would be a client who doesn't respond to phone calls or emails and doesn't seem excited about their work and taking steps to move forward in the publishing process.

Please list five books you recently agented. *The Boy at the Door* by Alexandra Dahl (Penguin Random House), *Farm-to-Fork Mystery* series by Lynn Cahoon (Kensington), *The 30-Minute Money Plan for Moms* by Catey Hill (Center Street, Hachette), *The Promise of Us* by Jamie Beck (Montlake), *Transform* by Professor Jo Boaler (HarperOne).

Please describe the kinds of books you want to agent. I am looking for all types of mystery, suspense, and psychological suspense as well as cozies and thrillers that keep the pages turning and have an original hook. I am also looking for commercial fiction: Southern fiction; all types of women's fiction; stories of family, friendships, secrets, interesting relationships, or multigenerations; and romance, including romantic suspense, historical, contemporary, and category romance. I welcome a dramatic story line and compelling characters in interesting situations or relationships. If you have a novel that has a highly original concept or voice, I would love to see it.

On the nonfiction side, my areas of interest include current events, business, health, self-help, relationships, psychology, parenting, history, science, and narrative nonfiction. I am particularly drawn to projects that will move readers or leave them thinking, make provocative arguments, share interesting research, or offer useful, new advice.

What should writers submit for consideration, and how should they send it? Writers should submit a query letter to jill@marsallyonliteraryagency.com.

How do you feel about self-publishing, and what do you see happening with it in the near future? Self-publishing offers many writers another opportunity for getting their work out there. It is important for authors to identify their goals in publishing when they are evaluating whether to go with a traditional publisher or an epublisher or to self-publish. We have authors who have chosen each of those paths, and many do a combination; hybrid authors are very common these days. It really depends on what an author is looking for from the publishing experience.

Why do you think some books become super-successful (beyond the obvious reasons)? For fiction, it starts with a great story, good writing, strong characters, a compelling hook, interesting twists or emotionally compelling developments, and strong marketing. And for nonfiction, super-successful books make readers think or see an issue in a new way, share engaging ideas that can lead readers to change their beliefs, actions, or understanding of an issue, and engage readers in a thoughtful manner.

Knowing what you know now, would you become an agent again? Yes, I love being an agent and working with terrific writers.

Why did you choose to become an agent? I love reading and editing and working with authors to make their manuscripts as strong as possible. It is such an exciting process to be able to work on a manuscript and take it from idea/concept to completed book. And, of course, it is such a great thing to take a manuscript on submission, then get "the call" from an editor, and then be able to make "the call" to the author. I like being a part of the process that brings readers books that can impact their lives, offer intriguing stories, take them to places they would never otherwise experience, and entertain and inspire.

Do you think many talented writers fail to get published for avoidable reasons? If so, what are some of those reasons? Yes, it is important for writers not to give up and to learn from any feedback they get with rejections, whether it is from agents or editors. Writers also need to make sure they are targeting the right agents and editors who handle and are interested in their type of work.

MARTIN LITERARY & MEDIA MANAGEMENT ❖

www.martinliterarymanagement.com

914 164th Street SE, Suite B-12, #307, Mill Creek, WA 98012, 206-466-1773

Agent's name and contact info: Sharlene Martin, President, sharlene@martinliterarymanagement.com

Note: Our email address is still the same, but we've changed our name from Martin Literary Management to Martin Literary & Media Management to reflect our increasing involvement in book-to-screen adaptations of our authors' books for feature films, television movies, and reality TV.

What would you be doing right now if not responding to this survey? The weather is cold right now, so I would definitely be watching films, especially those that are adaptations from books. In warmer weather I would be swimming.

What would you be if not an agent (other than a dog, cat, or other mammal)? A film and TV producer, which I already am, but it would then be a full-time occupation.

Do you think independent (noncorporate) publishing will be stronger, weaker, or the same over the next few years? I wish I had a crystal ball. But, alas, I don't.

Please describe your professional history. I've always been eclectic and entrepreneurial. In 1992 I started a production company with a former network journalist/broadcaster and was an independent producer for a number of years in addition to doing freelance casting for independent and feature films. Because of that experience, I was invited to join a reality-television production company and spent time doing acquisitions and talent management. It was there that I realized my love of show business found its greatest strength in working with passionate and highly skilled writers. I left to start Martin Literary Management, which has since expanded to become Martin Literary & Media Management, and the lovely success that has followed seems a natural result of the fact that I've never been happier in any line of work.

How would you define the "client from hell"? Self-entitlement is like a bad flu virus moving through our society. It manifests in the writing world in the form of half-baked written work accompanied by explanations for the unfinished condition and a tale of woe about the author's struggles in the task of getting the work to this stage. These people fail to appreciate the truth that everybody struggles if they endeavor to write truly and well, and writers who believe themselves unique in that regard have already revealed a cautionary tale about their lack of insight toward others. Such people seldom deliver meaningful work.

Do you think Earth was created a few thousand years ago or several billion years ago? I think the Earth is flat, reality is an illusion, and you, my friend, are not really reading this.

Please list five books you recently agented. Impossible Odds by Anthony Flacco with Jessica Buchanan (Atria, Simon & Schuster); Taking My Life Back by Rebekah Gregory with Anthony Flacco (Revell); The Cousteau Expeditions (four-book series) with Fabien Cousteau, James Fraioli, and Joe St. Pierre; Hilde Cracks the Case (six-book series) by Hilde and Matthew Lysiak (Scholastic); Wild Escape by Chelsia Marcius (Diversion).

Please describe the kinds of books you want to agent. I love to read meaningful memoirs, pop-culture subjects, true crime books, and celebrity-related books. As always, we have our long-standing devotion to great narrative nonfiction writing done with such depth of style and visual clarity that it is naturally adaptable to film.

What should writers submit for consideration, and how should they send it? I require a well thought out and concise query letter from a writer first. If the topic is of interest to me, I will then ask for submission of a full book proposal.

How do you feel about self-publishing, and what do you see happening with it in the near future? It isn't going away, because hope springs eternal. Send enough gamblers to

Vegas, and *somebody* is going to come home a winner. If you catch a wave of public interest in a self-publishing situation, you will make far more money than in a traditional royalty deal; i.e., if you sell a hundred thousand copies of a self-published book, you can then go out and buy a great house, take a magnificent world tour, or begin planning a comfortable retirement.

However, the vast majority of self-published books will fail, because the general public will never be made aware that they exist. Some of them are written well enough to stand beside anything published by a major house, although many are not. A large portion are not very good because the writers become impatient to see the work in print and stop the polishing process in its early stages. These raw efforts not only clog the market; they serve to diminish the potential size of that market by repeatedly burning those intrepid readers who venture into the swamps of self-published books, hoping to find that gem.

So, assuming you have written great stuff and polished it until your readers need dark glasses, then the secret is in the publicity. The challenge for you as a self-published writer is much like that of the traditional author in today's world. They probably get more help than you do, but that doesn't have to stop you. So, since the self-published author will rise or fall on the unjust gaze of public awareness, just like the folks with contracts from the Big 5 houses or the gang down at the university press, find an appropriate way to get awareness of your book in the public eye (the operative word here is *appropriate*). That means it will not help your writing career to grab for attention by doing something bizarre, like running naked into a major-league ball game, unless you are writing about someone who runs naked into major-league ball games. In that case, it could be your springboard to the bestseller list.

Do you think there are too many, too few, or just enough agents? Too many agents who aren't doing this full time. This isn't a hobby; it requires a huge amount of time and commitment.

Do you think Amazon will become the country's largest employer within 10 years? Again, I don't have a crystal ball, but I see a lot of areas of commerce and service yet to be tapped by them.

Why do you think some books become super-successful (beyond the obvious reasons)? Answer that and grow rich beyond your dreams. Nobody knows why trends appear. Sometimes it's a catchy title. Other times it's great cover art. Occasionally it's a great PR campaign with lots of money thrown at it by publishers or wealthy authors. But quite often, it's just really fabulous storytelling that strikes a chord with readers, and word of mouth takes over.

Do you think agents are likely to become millionaires? I believe the only people "likely" to become millionaires are crooked politicians, drug dealers, and kids with rich parents who give them their first million. Literary agents? I suppose anything is possible...and I love that there's always that "chance," as opposed to punching a time card.

Do you think agents tend toward certain personality types? Absolutely! We tend toward writers who are obsessed with the quality of their work and who uphold a firm work ethic about achieving their finest possible result, those who make no excuses.

Do you think writers tend to be more or less narcissistic than the population at large? My experience with that is a mixed bag. But I can tell you narcissistic people as a rule do not write well, because their condition prevents them from feeling the empathy and compassion necessary to write important work. They tend to produce a lot of half-baked pages, which they describe as brilliant and which they try to pass off by defending them as if their lives depended on the outcome. Passion is good, but too much of it can be used to cover inferior work — as if passion excuses carelessness. Experience has taught me that if you disappoint a narcissist, it will *always* be your fault.

Knowing what you know now, would you become an agent again? Yes, and I would have started sooner.

Why did you choose to become an agent? Simple: I love the written word. Although I was editor of my high-school literary magazine, I never realized my passion for books until much later in my career. I want to make a difference in writers' lives by helping them realize their dreams. It's how I realize my own, and this is the path that gets me to that place.

Do you think many talented writers fail to get published for avoidable reasons? If so, what are some of those reasons? Substance abuse, neurosis, lifetime habits of laziness, or lifetime habits of self-entitlement will absolutely stop a writer's dream in the starting gate. Quality fanatics tend to be the winners around here.

Agent's name and contact info: Adria Goetz, adria@martinlit.com

What would you be doing right now if not responding to this survey? Snuggling with my two kittens, Maple and Mulberry. Oh wait...I am. I'm a great multitasker.

What would you be if not an agent (other than a dog, cat, or other mammal)? A librarian.

Do you think independent (noncorporate) publishing will be stronger, weaker, or the same over the next few years? Stronger.

Please describe your professional history. I started as an intern at Martin Literary & Media Management when I was a bright-eyed 19-year-old studying creative writing at the University of Washington in Seattle. I was convinced I wanted to be an editor, but I thought taking an internship with a literary agency would be a great experience, because I wanted to see every angle of the publishing-industry beast. The internship was only supposed to last for a few months, but ended up lasting two years. When I graduated from college, they kept me around as an assistant for one year. I then attended the Columbia Publishing Course, a six-week intensive course on all aspects of publishing, held at Columbia University. When I returned, I knocked on Martin Literary's door and asked them if they'd be willing to take me under their wing and train me as an agent. And they said yes! My résumé also boasts of a local library job as well as a stint as a gelato scooper.

How would you define the "client from hell"? A client who doesn't understand that they are not my sole client. I'll leave it at that.

Do you think Earth was created a few thousand years ago or several billion years ago? Several billion years ago.

Please list five books you recently agented. *The Compendium of Magical Beasts* by Melissa Brinks and Lily Jones (Running Press, 2018), *Rice from Heaven* by Tina Cho (Little Bee Books, 2018), *A Dreadful Fairy Book* by Jon Etter (Amberjack, 2019), *When Day Is Done* by Natalee Creech (Sparkhouse Family, 2019), *Green Burial Guidebook* by Elizabeth Fournier (New World Library, 2018).

Please describe the kinds of books you want to agent. Specifically picture books, middle grade, young adult, and quirky gift books as well as books for the Christian market. Thematically, I look for books that delight readers, that help inspire wonder and imagination, that foster deep empathy and compassion for our fellow human beings, that provide rich character representation of marginalized groups, that take readers on an adventure, that uncover fascinating stories from history's footnotes, that explore issues of faith and how to apply Christ's teachings to our own life, that celebrate women and the female experience, that ask nitty-gritty questions and don't settle for easy answers, that make people disappointed when they have to close the book and go to bed, and that add a touch of magic to readers' lives.

What should writers submit for consideration, and how should they send it? I prefer a query letter and the first 10 pages of the manuscript pasted into the body of the email. I also really appreciate it when writers share their Twitter handles and whether or not they have a detailed synopsis/overview of their project.

How do you feel about self-publishing, and what do you see happening with it in the near future? Self-publishing has come a long way, and it's going to improve in the future, because people are starting to hold them more accountable.

Do you think there are too many, too few, or just enough agents? Just enough.

Do you think Amazon will become the country's largest employer within 10 years? I live in Seattle, and it certainly feels like most people I know are employed by them, so I'll say yes.

Why do you think some books become super-successful (beyond the obvious reasons)? Never underestimate the power of a clear, concise concept as well as a beautiful cover design.

Do you think agents are likely to become millionaires? Unfortunately, no. Nobody in publishing is in it for the money. We're in it because we want to keep in touch with the under-the-sheets-with-a-flashlight child in us.

Do you think agents tend toward certain personality types? Not in my experience. I've met shy wallflower agents as well as boisterous life-of-the-party agents. Most of us are quite friendly, though.

Do you think writers tend to be more or less narcissistic than the population at large? Ha! Some can swing that way, but I've found most writers swing the opposite way, where they are riddled with insecurities. Even after landing an agent. Even after landing a book deal. We're all still self-conscious teenagers cringing at our acne in the mirror. Metaphorically, of course.

Knowing what you know now, would you become an agent again? In a heartbeat.

Why did you choose to become an agent? Because I get to edit and develop creative work, work with writers, and play matchmaker — all from the comfort of my home.

Do you think many talented writers fail to get published for avoidable reasons? If so, what are some of those reasons? No.

Agent's name and contact info: Natalie Grazian, Associate Literary Manager, Adult Fiction, natalie@martinlit.com

What would you be doing right now if not responding to this survey? Looking up flash fiction prompts online. Or watching my dinner on the stove.

What would you be if not an agent (other than a dog, cat, or other mammal)? A tenth-grade high-school English teacher. I had an amazing one who confirmed my love of literature (here's to you, Ms. Falkner!).

Do you think independent (noncorporate) publishing will be stronger, weaker, or the same over the next few years? Stronger. Some are being acquired and distributed by bigger publishers, giving them wider reach.

Please describe your professional history. Sales representative for W. W. Norton; fiction editor of *The Santa Clara Review* literary magazine; writing tutor; remote intern for Amy

Cloughley at Kimberley Cameron & Associates; intern for Sharlene Martin at MLM, which led to my current job as an associate manager for adult fiction.

How would you define the "client from hell"? Anyone who assumes the worst of me when I suggest an edit.

Do you think Earth was created a few thousand years ago or several billion years ago? Those dinosaur fossils look real to me!

Please list five books you recently agented. Come back to me in a year. I'm newly minted.

Please describe the kinds of books you want to agent. I'm especially interested in contemporary fantasy, stories inspired by myths and fairy tales, dystopian sci-fi, historical fiction, allegory, satire, dark comedy, coming-of-age stories, and quest narratives. More than anything, I look for complex characters who make the unrelatable relatable and for a smart, distinctive narrative voice.

What should writers submit for consideration, and how should they send it? I accept queries for commercial, upmarket, and literary adult fiction. Please submit via email to natalie@martinlit.com. Include a query letter in the body of the email and attach the first 10 pages of your manuscript, preferably as a Word doc.

How do you feel about self-publishing, and what do you see happening with it in the near future? The avenues for self-publishing will become more accessible and varied, and it can be a great option for many books. It really depends on the author's goals.

Do you think there are too many, too few, or just enough agents? I want to say just enough.

Do you think Amazon will become the country's largest employer within 10 years? I see no end in sight, considering their rise so far. I asked my friend's Alexa, and she dodged the question.

Why do you think some books become super-successful (beyond the obvious reasons)? On a subliminal level, successful books tap into something that readers are nervous about or wishful for.

Do you think agents are likely to become millionaires? Did you team up with my parents to write this survey?

Do you think agents tend toward certain personality types? I tend toward people who are gracious, polite, and communicative. Of course, I'm looking for great storytellers, but I want trustworthy business partners as well.

Do you think writers tend to be more or less narcissistic than the population at large? Truly, I think writers tend more toward insecurity. Even the most brilliant ones.

Knowing what you know now, would you become an agent again? I'm too new to say.

Why did you choose to become an agent? For the love of books! Books have always been the constant in my life. I'm proud and thrilled to be part of the instrument that brings them into being.

Do you think many talented writers fail to get published for avoidable reasons? If so, what are some of those reasons? Talented writers will find a way to get published. It may take trial and error and just the right timing, but great writing has a luster to it — trust that someone will fall in love with it.

Agent's name and contact info: Clelia Gore, clelia@martinlit.com, 206-395-6565, www.cleliagore.com, Twitter: @MadmoiselleClel

What would you be doing right now if not responding to this survey? Probably evaluating queries, editing client manuscripts, or reading the latest buzz-y book in kid lit!

What would you be if not an agent (other than a dog, cat, or other mammal)? This is already a second career for me — I used to be an attorney. But if I could do something else entirely, I would simultaneously be a linguistics expert, a successful middle grade author, a mildly successful character actress, and a first lady of something with some medical expertise. That job exists, right?

Do you think independent (noncorporate) publishing will be stronger, weaker, or the same over the next few years? Stronger. Modern consumers have come to value localism and independent vendors and will choose special parts of their lives that they want to devote to indies that are uniquely capable of addressing their interests and needs. There are so many great indies out there — so many flavors of book publishers to choose from. For example, when I'm looking for a picture book with a quirky Euro-feel (as I often do), I know I can turn to the independent publisher Enchanted Lion and easily find a charmer.

Please describe your professional history. I graduated with an English and Communications degree from Boston College. I then earned my law degree from American University and practiced at a big and then at a small firm in Manhattan, primarily working in corporate and criminal litigation. Although I valued my experience as a lawyer, I decided to do a big pivot in my career toward something I felt more passionate about. I ended up getting my master's in publishing and writing from Emerson College, where I also taught undergraduate composition courses and interned for two major publishers. My husband's career brought us to Seattle in 2013, where I have been working as a literary agent specializing in books for children and young adults at Martin Literary & Media Management ever since.

How would you define the "client from hell"? A client from hell is a writer who doesn't sufficiently trust their agent or the process, who has a pattern of rejecting their agent's editorial or career advice, who is dishonest or not upfront with their agent — a client who chooses ego over art. In general, I don't positively respond to people who are not kind and respectful.

Do you think Earth was created a few thousand years ago or several billion years ago? Billion. Science!

Please list five books you recently agented. *Yoga Bunny* by Brian Russo, a picture book featuring a yoga-loving bunny (HarperCollins, 2016). *Philanthroparties: A Party-Planning Guide for Kids Who Want to Give Back* by Lulu Cerone, a monthly party-planning guide inspiring kids to incorporate social activism into their social lives (Aladdin / Beyond Words, 2017). *Superfail* by Max Brunner, illustrated by Dustin Mackay, a graphic middle grade novel about a team of "defective" superhero kids (Running Press Kids, 2017). *A Couch for Llama* by Leah Gilbert, a picture book featuring a family and a spunky couch-loving llama (Sterling, 2018). *Cousteau Expeditions* series by Fabien Cousteau and James Fraioli, illustrated by Joe St. Pierre, a graphic series inspired by the famous expeditioner and environmental activist (Margaret K. McElderry Books, Simon & Schuster, starting in 2018).

Please describe the kinds of books you want to agent. In general, I represent all books under the children's book umbrella — board books, picture books, chapter books, middle grade, and young adult fiction and nonfiction. I am especially looking for books that readers will feel a special connection to, books that they will want to reread. I am especially looking for books that allow kids who have been historically underrepresented in publishing to see themselves as heroes and heroines.

What should writers submit for consideration, and how should they send it? Send me a query via email that includes a short pitch (not a synopsis) of your book, the market for your book (comparable books), and a short bio. Please include the text of your manuscript within the body of the email (no attachments). For novel-length works, include the first 10 pages. For picture books, you can include the whole manuscript. For author-illustrators, include the manuscript text and provide a link to your online portfolio of sample work.

How do you feel about self-publishing, and what do you see happening with it in the near future? Self-publishing is a good resource for authors who have met a dead end trying to find a traditional publisher, those who want to bypass traditional publishing in general, or those who want to see their book come out fast or offer it to a very targeted audience. Self-publishing also offers readers a wider selection of books, often at low cost. The royalties paid to authors are certainly favorable, but it does put a big onus on the author to market the book. There are problems with quality control in self-publishing, but ultimately it can be a great way to create a satisfying experience for writers. I see self-publishing continuing to expand, and the quality-control issues ameliorating, but, all this being said, I do think traditional publishers will always exist as a trusted source for literature of all kinds.

Do you think there are too many, too few, or just enough agents? Agenting is a really, really tough business and, as a result, is a self-filtering industry — there's a lot of in-and-out. I don't have an opinion on whether the number of agents is right, but I do think the book-publishing industry as a whole, including at the agent level, could use more points of view, particularly those of people of color or voices not traditionally heard from. All of us can benefit from a more diverse population of gatekeepers like agents.

Do you think Amazon will become the country's largest employer within 10 years? Ubiquitous corporations like McDonald's and Walmart have been around for a long time and will continue to have Amazon beat in this way, but I do see Amazon continuing to expand its various arms and with that employing a large number of people in this country and beyond. Especially with the development of its HQ2.

Why do you think some books become super-successful (beyond the obvious reasons)? Don't we all wish we knew the definitive answer to this question!? If I had to come up with a magic equation, I think a super-successful book is well-timed — it touches upon an issue, experience, or trend that is resonating with a large population at that exact moment. It will also have that special sauce that connects with readers in a personal way — they, in some degree, see themselves in the book or the book reveals something about themselves or the world around them. Also, a successful and wide-reaching marketing and publicity program. And luck!

Do you think agents are likely to become millionaires? Most will not. Some do! That's part of what makes this job so exciting — there is no ceiling to your success, and it *could* be you. A mix of hard work, expertise, sharp instincts, smart strategizing, good timing, and that oft-elusive luck may get you there!

Do you think agents tend toward certain personality types? Not definitively, but a typical agent has to play several roles in the job, three most critically: (1) editor, so they have to have a creative side; (2) networker with industry folk and writers, so being a people person is important; and (3) advocate/negotiator, so business savvy is needed. Most successful agents have a mix of at least these three attributes. Oh, and they all love books!

Do you think writers tend to be more or less narcissistic than the population at large? Whew, loaded question! Writing often requires interior examination and pulling from your own experience, so I suppose there is an inherent narcissism in the action of writing. But I wouldn't label writers as more narcissistic than the general population.

Knowing what you know now, would you become an agent again? Absolutely. I probably would have been a bit more fearful at the start if I knew the realities of the long hard road ahead, but I would also know that the reward of helping bring a wonderful book into the world makes it all worth it.

Why did you choose to become an agent? First off, I love books and I love being in a creative industry. I also love that this job is a great marriage of all my skills and interests — it appeals to my creative side, uses my lawyer skills, and allows me to collaborate and connect with a lot of different kinds of people, something I both enjoy and believe I am good at.

Do you think many talented writers fail to get published for avoidable reasons? If so, what are some of those reasons? Some talented writers don't realize that the business side of this creative endeavor is really important to understand and master. It's important for them to equip themselves with as much knowledge about the publishing industry as they can — this will help position a writer for success. Also, sometimes it's just about timing.

MASSIE & MCQUILKIN LITERARY AGENTS ❖ www.mmqlit.com

27 West 20th Street, Suite 305, New York, NY 10011, 212-352-2055

Agent's name and contact info: Laney Katz Becker, laney@mmqlit.com

What would you be doing right now if not responding to this survey? This exact minute (it's during the week) I'd probably be responding to email from editors, authors, and colleagues and reading queries. The weekend is when I edit my clients' manuscripts and proposals, since that's when I'm guaranteed to have blocks of uninterrupted time.

What would you be if not an agent (other than a dog, cat, or other mammal)? I'd likely return to my roots — as an author. Maybe combine that with doing something to support the women's movement or feminist agenda.

Please describe your professional history. I graduated from Northwestern University and moved to New York City. My background is as a writer. I started as a copywriter at the ad agency J. Walter Thompson. Over the next two decades I continued my career as a copywriter (both on-staff at some of New York's best-known agencies and also as a freelancer). I also worked as a freelance journalist; my articles appeared in more than 50 magazines, including *Self*, *Health*, *Seventeen*, and *First for Women*. I am also an award-winning author of both fiction and nonfiction. Somewhere along the way, I decided that spending seven hours a day in my basement writing books was too solitary for me. I wanted to use my marketing, writing, and reading skills in a new and different way. The agenting world allows me to do just that — and it's never, ever solitary! Prior to joining MMQ, I was an agent at Markson Thoma Literary Agency and Folio Literary Management. My debut authors have made the *New York Times* national and international bestsellers' lists. They have also been selected as *Target Book Club* picks and the *B & N Discover Great New Writers* program.

How would you define the "client from hell"? Defensive writers who don't want to revise and who view agents simply as gatekeepers to editors. I'm also not a fan of writers who fail to say thank you. Writers who immediately send back revisions, rather than taking time to let things sit, reread what they've written, and then — only then — once they're certain their work can't be any better, send it back to me for my review.

Please list five books you recently agented. David Bell's most recent novel, *Somebody's Daughter* (his eighth suspense novel with me); *The Nazi Titanic* by Robert P. Watson (narrative nonfiction/history); *Killer Choice* by Tom Hunt, a debut thriller; Jennifer S. Brown's *Modern Girls*, historical women's fiction; *Fraver by Design* by Frank "Fraver" Verlizzo, a coffee-table book of Broadway theater posters.

Please describe the kinds of books you want to agent. I represent exactly the kinds of books I want to agent. If I don't love it, I don't take it on. Fiction: I gravitate toward anything well suited to book-club discussion, and I am a sucker for a fresh voice and well-defined characters. I also enjoy smart, psychological thrillers and suspense novels. Historical fiction is also a particular favorite. Nonfiction: I'm always on the prowl for narrative nonfiction, especially from journalists or experts. I am always looking for memoir and stories about fascinating subjects that teach me something new or expose me to different ideas, cultures, or people who make a difference in the world — *but only if the author has a strong national platform.* I do have a feminist bent, so that's also a subject I'm happy to read about. I do *not* represent romance, cozy mysteries, sci-fi, fantasy, paranormal, or dystopian fiction, nor do I handle young adult, children's, middle grade, or poetry.

What should writers submit for consideration, and how should they send it? I expect a well-written query that briefly tells me about you and your project. If it's fiction, embed the first chapter (or so) in the body of the email. If it's nonfiction, send the entire proposal. I only accept queries by email (laney@mmqlit.com).

Do you think agents are likely to become millionaires? Hahahahahaha.

Why did you choose to become an agent? The best part of my job is helping people attain their dreams. For some writers, the dream might be to be published for the first time "by a real publisher." For other writers, the dream might be to grow their careers or their readership. Whatever it is, I enjoy being part of it. But what I really love is finding that jewel in the slush pile and working with the author to polish it up and get it ready for submission.

MAX GARTENBERG LITERARY AGENCY ❖ www.maxgartenberg.com

912 North Pennsylvania Avenue, Yardley, PA 19067, 215-295-9230

Agents' names and contact info: Anne G. Devlin, agdevlin@aol.com; Dirk Devlin, dirk_devlin1@yahoo.com

Please describe your professional history. Anne: Max Gartenberg Literary Agency has long been recognized as a source for fine fiction and nonfiction. One of the oldest and most prestigious agencies in the US, it was established in 1954 in New York City and has since migrated to the Philadelphia area.

How would you define the "client from hell"? A client who demands unceasing attention and is never satisfied with the deal the agent brings (this client always has friends who got twice as much) and then delivers the manuscript late and in such disrepair that it is unacceptable. This is not an imaginary character.

Please list five books you recently agented. Beyond Your Baby's Checkup by Luke Voytas, MD (Sasquatch Books); *Penguins! Step into Reading* by David Salomon (Random House); *Everything a New Elementary Teacher Really Needs to Know and Didn't Learn in College* by Otis Kreigel (Free Spirit); *Jack and Lem: The Untold Story of an Extraordinary Friendship* by David Pitts (Da Capo); *Bold Venture* by Steven K. Bailey (Potomac Books).

Please describe the kinds of books you want to agent. Nonfiction, current affairs, education, parenting, health, fitness, food, how-to, self-help, business, women's interest, celebrity, true crime, sports, politics, history, music, biography, environment, pets, narrative nonfiction, and historical fiction.

What should writers submit for consideration, and how should they send it? Writers desirous of having their work handled by this agency should first send a one- or two-page query letter. Simply put, the letter should describe the material being offered as well as relevant background information about the writer. If the material is of interest, we will request a book proposal and sample chapters. Queries are accepted by both email and post. Please include a SASE for a reply via post.

How do you feel about self-publishing, and what do you see happening with it in the near future? Self-publishing is a last resort, as it lacks the support an author receives from a traditional publishing house's production department, marketing department, sales staff, and distributors. Authors who self-publish should understand that they will need to promote and publicize themselves in every possible venue and medium.

Why did you choose to become an agent? I chose to become an agent because it allows me to continuously learn and discover. As a former newspaper writer and editor as well as a marketing entrepreneur, I enjoy being part of the creation of a great book. I enjoy discovering authors, pitching book ideas, negotiating deals, and being part of an exciting and dynamic industry. I work with authors to help them shape proposals and manuscripts to interest editors.

Do you think many talented writers fail to get published for avoidable reasons? If so, what are some of those reasons? To be considered, write a brilliant query letter and, when asked, follow it up with a proposal as well and sample chapters or a manuscript that is even better. Be sure to include your qualifications and experience along with a synopsis of the work.

MENDEL MEDIA GROUP, LLC ❖ www.mendelmedia.com

115 West 30th Street, Suite 209, New York, NY 10001, 646-239-9896

Agent's name and contact info: Scott Mendel, submission queries: query@mendelmedia.com; business emails about licensing rights: scott@mendelmedia.com

What would you be doing right now if not responding to this survey? Reading. Or negotiating.

What would you be if not an agent (other than a dog, cat, or other mammal)? An academic scholar of literature and history.

Do you think independent (noncorporate) publishing will be stronger, weaker, or the same over the next few years? There will be more independent publishers than ever before.

Please describe your professional history. I was an academic at the University of Chicago and at the University of Illinois at Chicago, where I taught literature, until about 1999. I decided to leave academia and pursue a career in publishing, as I had written a book and been the managing editor of a magazine previously. At around this time, I met an agent in Chicago who had been for decades the only established literary agent there. She taught me the profession, and we became business partners for a while. Eventually we separated, she passed away, and I returned to New York, where I was born, to open my own agency in 2002.

How would you define the "client from hell"? I would avoid using that language, even to myself, to describe someone I have committed to representing. Some authors and agents are not a good fit for each other. I generally tell prospective clients from our first conversation that I tend to be very goal-oriented, which many writers love. But some authors do like their agents to be extremely process-oriented, which isn't my inclination. That is not to say that I don't actively develop projects with my clients. I do. But I need my authors to see themselves as professionals who are pursuing concrete goals and usually trying to take the most direct possible path to those goals.

Do you think Earth was created a few thousand years ago or several billion years ago? In the words of many successful improvisational comedians, "Why not both?" More seriously, I'm a believer in science. But I also understand that faith is the substance of things hoped for, the evidence of things not seen. The best science writers understand that.

Please list five books you recently agented. That's too few. Here is a longer list of recent and forthcoming books of mine that together give a good idea of the range of my clientele: *The Daughter of Sherlock Holmes* by Leonard Goldberg (St. Martin's, 2017), *How to Change a Life* by Stacey Ballis (Berkley, Penguin Random House, 2017), *The Tomb* by Stephanie Stuve-Bodeen (Feiwel & Friends, Macmillan, 2018), *The Dangerous Case of Donald Trump* by Bandy Lee (Thomas Dunne, 2017), *The Death of Democracy* by Benjamin Carter Hett (Henry Holt, 2018), *Sleeping with Napoleon* by Stephen Harding (Da Capo, Hachette, 2018), *All the Answers* by Michael Kupperman (Gallery 13, Simon & Schuster, 2018), *The Crisis* by Larry Diamond (Penguin Random House, 2018), *The Book Smugglers* by David Fishman (ForeEdge, 2017), *Saving Sin City* by Mary Cummings (Pegasus, 2018), *Mrs. Sherlock Holmes* by Brad Ricca (St. Martin's, 2017), *Edge of Order* by Daniel Libeskind (Crown, Penguin Random House, 2018), *Odd Birds* by Ian Harding (St. Martin's, 2017), *Hi, Anxiety* by Kat Kinsman (Dey Street, HarperCollins, 2016), *The Military Science of Star Wars* by George Beahm (Tor/Forge, 2018), *I Could Pee on This, Too: And More Poems by More Cats* by Francesco Marciuliano (Chronicle, 2017), *The True Tails of Baker and Taylor* by Jan Louch and Lisa Rogak (Thomas Dunne, 2016).

Please describe the kinds of books you want to agent. The list above is fairly representative. We represent nonfiction writers in most subject areas, from narrative to biography and serious analytic history to health and relationships. Our nonfiction clientele includes individual authors and institutions whose works, collections, archives, researchers, and/or policy experts contribute to important public discussions and debates. We also represent more lighthearted nonfiction projects when they suit the market particularly well. The agency's fiction writers principally write historical and contemporary multicultural fiction, contemporary thrillers, and mainstream women's fiction.

What should writers submit for consideration, and how should they send it? Email only, to query@mendelmedia.com. We no longer accept or read submissions sent by regular mail. For fiction queries, please paste a synopsis and the first 20 pages into the body of your email; for nonfiction queries, paste a completed proposal and sample chapters into the body of the email. For both fiction and nonfiction, also include a detailed letter about your publication history and the history of the project, if it has been submitted previously to publishers or other agents. Please do not send attachments, as we will not open them.

If we want to read more or discuss your work, we will call or email you directly. If you do not receive a personal response within a few weeks, we are not going to offer representation. In any case, however, please do not call or email to inquire about your query.

How do you feel about self-publishing, and what do you see happening with it in the near future? I don't have very strong feelings about self-publishing. My impression is that, for each very rare breakout success, hundreds of thousands of authors sell copies pretty much exclusively to their family and friends. It looks to me a bit like playing the lottery, but I suppose some people might say that very same thing about traditional trade publishing. I understand why authors go the self-publishing route, and I'm very happy to see when people succeed at it. But I don't believe it spells the end of trade publishing in our lifetime.

Do you think there are too many, too few, or just enough agents? I don't often quote Mao, especially when he was probably being murderously insincere, but here goes nothing: "Let a hundred flowers bloom; let a hundred schools of thought contend."

Do you think Amazon will become the country's largest employer within 10 years? Ten years is a lifetime in our current economy, but it certainly seems possible.

Why do you think some books become super-successful (beyond the obvious reasons)? The reasons vary so much that this would require a book-length answer. And a deck of tarot cards.

Do you think agents are likely to become millionaires? Lord willing, and the creek don't rise. And if they do become millionaires, I think it's a good thing, because it means at least some of their clients have become considerably wealthier and presumably reached a large readership with their books, while working with those agents.

Do you think agents tend toward certain personality types? We are mostly introverted book nerds at heart, just like most of the people reading these words.

Do you think writers tend to be more or less narcissistic than the population at large? There's plenty of narcissism to go around. Why pick on one profession?

Knowing what you know now, would you become an agent again? Yes.

Why did you choose to become an agent? Lack of a trust fund. Inability to cultivate practical skills in the boat-building trades. Oh, and a burning passion for great stories, well told.

Do you think many talented writers fail to get published for avoidable reasons? If so, what are some of those reasons? Sure. Book publishing is a long game, probably the part of the media with the longest lead time from the creation of original creative work to the dissemination of that work in public. It requires people to play well with others, for long periods. That isn't for everyone.

METAMORPHOSIS LITERARY AGENCY ❖

www.metamorphosisliteraryagency.com

Agent's name and contact info: Stephanie Hansen, info@metamorphosisliteraryagency.com

What would you be doing right now if not responding to this survey? Reviewing queries, reading manuscripts, chatting with acquisitions editors, emailing clients, and more.

What would you be if not an agent (other than a dog, cat, or other mammal)? A pilot.

Do you think independent (noncorporate) publishing will be stronger, weaker, or the same over the next few years? It would be best if all forms of publishing worked together more instead of competing against one another. If that happens, they'll all be stronger.

Please describe your professional history. I represent authors ranging from first-timers to those with multiple *New York Times* bestsellers. I've signed authors from small presses to major publishing house distribution. I received a master's in 2008 and creative writing specialization in 2017. Predominately I represent young adult sci-fi/fantasy, but have a secret addiction to romance. Although these are my favorites, I handle everything fiction, from children's books to adult thrillers. Previously an editor for *Mind's Eye Literary Magazine*, I became a part of Metamorphosis in July 2016. Originally looking to help Midwest authors garner the attention of major publishing houses despite residing in "flyover states," I found camaraderie with multiple agents and editors.

How would you define the "client from hell"? Someone with high if not impossible demands without hard work in return.

Do you think Earth was created a few thousand years ago or several billion years ago? Which Earth? JK. LOL. Several billion years ago.

Please list five books you recently agented. *The Ghost and the Wolf* by Shelly X. Leonn (currently negotiating contract), *Cookie & Milk* by Michele McAvoy (currently negotiating contract), *Immortal Sleepers: Blood Awakening* by Miranda Nichols, *Texting Prince Charming* by Patty Carothers and Amy Brewer, *The Affliction* by Wendy Marsh.

Please describe the kinds of books you want to agent. Young adult series, adult sci-fi/fantasy, thrillers, and romance. I'm intrigued by prose that flows as smoothly as poetry, unforgettable plot twists, and well-rounded characters.

What should writers submit for consideration, and how should they send it? Please send a query letter with a synopsis and the first three chapters pasted into the email to info@metamorphosisliteraryagency.com.

How do you feel about self-publishing, and what do you see happening with it in the near future? If an author has an established audience, it's a completely viable option for them. I personally love the team approach behind traditional publishing, but self-publishing will continue to grow.

Do you think there are too many, too few, or just enough agents? There are too few agents, editors, and shelf space, which is why self-publishing ebooks will continue to grow.

Do you think Amazon will become the country's largest employer within ten years? Yes, but they'll be superseded too.

Why do you think some books become super-successful (beyond the obvious reasons)? Luck, timing, and the market.

Do you think agents are likely to become millionaires? No, and that's not the reason I went into the business. Seeing an author reach their dream goal of being traditionally published is.

Do you think agents tend toward certain personality types? Literary agents may differ from agents in other industries. We're all avid readers, and some of us are writers too. These qualities do not usually lend themselves to the stereotype of the agent as an outgoing personality, though I do know many awesome literary agents with explosive personalities.

Do you think writers tend to be more or less narcissistic than the population at large? Since a good majority of the population are also writers, I'm unsure how to answer that question.

Knowing what you know now, would you become an agent again? Yes, but I'd do things differently.

Why did you choose to become an agent? In the pursuit to become published, I found myself connecting writers with editors and decided to capitalize on the discovered ability.

Do you think many talented writers fail to get published for avoidable reasons? If so, what are some of those reasons? Well, yes and no. Having a polished manuscript without plot holes is very important, and query letters can garner attention. But even with all of your ducks in a row, the odds in this industry are not in the writer's favor.

Agent's name and contact info: Amy Brewer, abrewer@metamorphosisliteraryagency.com

What would you be doing right now if not responding to this survey? I would be reading manuscripts.

What would you be if not an agent (other than a dog, cat, or other mammal)? I would continue to be a yoga teacher and a therapist.

Do you think independent (noncorporate) publishing will be stronger, weaker, or the same over the next few years? I think it will get stronger as long as the market demands it.

Please describe your professional history. I'm a published coauthor, so I know what it takes to go through the submission process. I've studied social media marketing for the last year so I can help my clients promote their books. I was an intern at Metamorphosis for about six months so I could fully understand the process of being an agent.

How would you define the "client from hell"? That isn't really who I am. I like everyone. Maybe a client who tried to stalk and kill me would be a client from hell?

Do you think Earth was created a few thousand years ago or several billion years ago? Several billion — we are all stardust.

Please list five books you recently agented. Coagenting, Wendy Million's *Movie Star Memories*, Mark S. Waxman's *The Virgin Gary*, Karla Kratovil's *Captain of My Heart*, Michelle Thorne's *Switching Addictions*, Katie Salvo's *The Old Mata Hari Trick*.

Please describe the kinds of books you want to agent. I want to agent books that I love to read. Any and all romance, young adult, fantasy, and LGBTQ+.

What should writers submit for consideration, and how should they send it? Please send a query, synopsis, and first three chapters of your completed manuscript to abrewer@metamorphosisliteraryagency.com.

How do you feel about self-publishing, and what do you see happening with it in the near future? I think self-publishing can be very liberating for people who feel they need to get their voices heard. I just hope people understand that once they make the choice to self-publish, it is very hard to traditionally publish the same story. I think we will see more hybrid authors in the future.

Do you think there are too many, too few, or just enough agents? There seem to be too few, because of the overwhelming number of writers. But I suspect that there are just enough.

Do you think Amazon will become the country's largest employer within ten years? Nope. The world is always changing and moving, and so are America's industry titans.

Why do you think some books become super-successful (beyond the obvious reasons)? The crass answer is that making a movie out of it makes it become a super-successful book. But the romantic in me wants to believe that it is the relatability of the characters and the passion of the author that work to create the magic that sells books.

Do you think agents are likely to become millionaires? Yes, if they win the lottery.

Do you think agents tend toward certain personality types? Hardworking is a shared trait; other than that, all the agents I know are very different from one another. I think it is important for writers to find the personality type of agent (whatever it might be) to complement them and their personality.

Do you think writers tend to be more or less narcissistic than the population at large? Good writers think more of their stories than they do of themselves. They want what is best for their stories, and I understand that. That isn't narcissism; it is passion and dedication.

Knowing what you know now, would you become an agent again? In a heartbeat. I love my job. I get to help people's dreams come true.

Why did you choose to become an agent? This is what I was meant to do — create relationships, communicate, and read, read, read. I'm just lucky enough to have been pointed to Metamorphosis at the right time in my life to be able to make it a career.

Do you think many talented writers fail to get published for avoidable reasons? If so, what are some of those reasons? Yes, I'm afraid they do. I find that writers assume that I know what they know. Some don't want to query or write a synopsis or look up what they need to include in a query letter. I know that all those things are really hard to do, but I appreciate the effort that writers give in dotting all their *i*'s and crossing all their *t*'s. It doesn't mean they are a bad writer or that their manuscript is bad; it just means they didn't take the time to research the agent or care enough to copyedit. I'd much rather have an author ask for help than to make assumptions or send off something that is unedited.

Agent's name and contact info: Patty Carothers, pcarothers@metamorphosisliteraryagency.com

What would you be doing right now if not responding to this survey? Reading comic books.

What would you be if not an agent (other than a dog, cat, or other mammal)? A writer and a cat-café owner extraordinaire or just a make-believe superhero.

Do you think independent (noncorporate) publishing will be stronger, weaker, or the same over the next few years? Stronger, I hope.

Please describe your professional history. A certified copyeditor, Oxford comma fan girl, and writer of the *Texting Prince Charming* series.

How would you define the "client from hell"? A client who believes in Maximum Vision Integrity — a.k.a. #MVI — one who does not want to accept constructive criticism to make their work better. I like working with my clients to make their stories tight, the best they can possibly be.

Do you think Earth was created a few thousand years ago or several billion years ago? Can I answer katrillions? Dinosaurs disprove the thousands-of-years theory.

Please list five books you recently agented. Movie Star Memories, Never Mine, Warrior Zero, HTBBFILWMBUF (acronym crazy, I know).

Please describe the kinds of books you want to agent. Ones that I would want to be BFFs with the protagonists of — or maybe even the antagonists, if it's really a good story.

What should writers submit for consideration, and how should they send it? Please send the query, first three chapters, and a synopsis to my email.

How do you feel about self-publishing, and what do you see happening with it in the near future? I think self-publishing is a good thing for the industry. It gives those undiscovered authors a chance to have their story loved by the masses. On the flip side, though, a lot of self-published works go unedited and can give other indie stories a bad rap as well.

Do you think there are too many, too few, or just enough agents? Good question. I think it all depends on supply and demand. As long as the writers keep writing wonderful stories, then there will remain a need to have quality agents to help see their dreams come to fruition.

Do you think Amazon will become the country's largest employer within ten years? I believe that Amazon will keep growing and growing and growing…

Why do you think some books become super-successful (beyond the obvious reasons)? Great marketing, of course. Authors who bond and interact with their fan base on social media tend to have the best chance of succeeding.

Do you think agents are likely to become millionaires? Ummm…no.

Do you think agents tend toward certain personality types? Yes. Those type A people (me) with cheery, go-get-them dispositions who don't ever give up without one heck of a good fight. And even then.

Do you think writers tend to be more or less narcissistic than the population at large? More narcissistic. Definitely. But in a fabulous, "I have to get these thoughts out of my head and down on paper so the voices will cease" way.

Knowing what you know now, would you become an agent again? Yes. Of course.

Why did you choose to become an agent? To help writers achieve their dreams.

Do you think many talented writers fail to get published for avoidable reasons? If so, what are some of those reasons? Writing genres that are not marketable. Having poor attitudes about the industry and how things work at large. General narcissistic tendencies.

MYERS LITERARY MANAGEMENT ❖ myersliterary.com

23 Waverly Place, #2-Y, New York, NY 10003

Agent's name and contact info: Eric Myers, eric@myersliterary.com

What would you be doing right now if not responding to this survey? Seeing a Sunday matinee of a foreign or independent film or going to an exhibit at a museum.

What would you be if not an agent (other than a dog, cat, or other mammal)? Possibly a New York tour guide. I love showing off my city.

Do you think independent (noncorporate) publishing will be stronger, weaker, or the same over the next few years? It will always be a haven for the books and authors that the majors are unwilling to take a chance on. But that still does not mean anyone stands to make much money in independent publishing. It's primarily a labor of love.

Please describe your professional history. I became a literary agent in 2002. Prior to that, I was a publicist on over 60 movies, including *Wall Street, Fatal Attraction, Scent of a Woman, Julie & Julia,* and many others. During that time I was also an author and had three nonfiction books published by St. Martin's Press: *Uncle Mame: The Life of Patrick Dennis* (2000), *Screen Deco: A Celebration of High Style in Hollywood* (1985), and *Forties Screen Style: A Celebration of High Pastiche in Hollywood* (1989). (The latter two were co-written with Howard Mandelbaum.) In addition, I've spent many years as a performing-arts journalist and critic. My articles and reviews have appeared in the *New York Times, Time Out New York, Opera News,* and many other publications and websites. In 2002 I joined the Spieler Agency as an agent and spent 13 terrific years there, then moved to Dystel, Goderich, and Bourret, where I spent 2 years before deciding to start my own agency, Myers Literary Management.

How would you define the "client from hell"? I'm lucky not to have had one of those yet! I guess the client from hell would not understand that there is a point of diminishing returns, where one must realize that a manuscript just is not working, cannot be improved, and will never find a home with a major publisher.

Do you think Earth was created a few thousand years ago or several billion years ago? Several billion. Sorry, I'm not a creationist.

Please list five books you recently agented. *The Girls' Auto Clinic Glove Box Guide* by Patrice Banks (Touchstone, Simon & Schuster, 2017), *Quackery* by Lydia Kang and Nate Pedersen (Workman, 2017), *Mr. Lemoncello's Great Library Race* by Chris Grabenstein (Random House Children's Books, 2017), *Full Disclosure* by Canada's Chief Justice Beverley McLachlin (Simon & Schuster Canada, 2018), *Welcome to Wonderland 3: Banana Shack Shake-Up!* by Chris Grabenstein (Random House Children's Books, 2018).

Please describe the kinds of books you want to agent. Young adult and middle grade novels, adult historical novels, adult thrillers, adult nonfiction of all varieties, including memoir, but only if the author comes with a strong preexisting platform. Publishers insist on that now. I'm not looking for mystery, literary fiction, picture books, short stories, or poetry.

What should writers submit for consideration, and how should they send it? For genres, please see above. If you have nonfiction, please send a proposal (including at least one sample chapter) along with your query letter. If you have fiction, please attach the first two chapters.

How do you feel about self-publishing, and what do you see happening with it in the near future? There are many worthy manuscripts that, for various reasons ranging from lack of author platform to a perceived limited readership, will never be acquired by a major publisher. For manuscripts such as these, the rise of self-publishing is the best thing that could have happened.

Do you think there are too many, too few, or just enough agents? I'd say the number of working agents out there is probably just about right.

Do you think Amazon will become the country's largest employer within 10 years? It's beginning to look that way.

Why do you think some books become super-successful (beyond the obvious reasons)? Publisher support counts for a great deal, and so does social media. In addition, sometimes the right book hits at just the right time, keying into a major current event or trend that might not have even been foreseen at the time of writing.

Do you think agents are likely to become millionaires? I already know a couple who are. Not me; not yet, anyway!

Do you think agents tend toward certain personality types? I like to think that they tend to be nurturing, but also know the right time for a little tough love.

Do you think writers tend to be more or less narcissistic than the population at large? One may say that many artists of all stripes tend to be somewhat narcissistic. However, the best of them are also observers: they are constantly observing those around them in order to draw from that and enhance their art. And that is sort of the opposite of narcissism, isn't it?

Knowing what you know now, would you become an agent again? Oh, yes! It was the best career decision I could have made. Working with authors is a wonderful gift.

Why did you choose to become an agent? I had written three books that were published and enjoyed working with agents. I realized that not only was it something I might be able to do; I knew it was the sort of profession I could continue to work in as long as I'd like, perhaps choosing to whittle my client list down to a precious few when I'm finally entering my dotage.

Do you think many talented writers fail to get published for avoidable reasons? If so, what are some of those reasons? A writer needs to be able to accept constructive criticism and to recognize what aspects of that criticism should be taken into consideration and implemented. That's the purpose of workshopping and critique groups; it's very rare that a first draft is anywhere near publishable.

Optional shout-outs/comments: I'm a real schoolmarm when it comes to punctuation, grammar, and spelling. Even the best authors can have trouble in this area — you should see some of F. Scott Fitzgerald's first drafts! It's worth having your query letters, sample chapters, and full manuscripts vetted by a copyeditor before you submit them to any literary professional. This costs money, but it can make a difference in whether an agent or acquiring editor will take you on.

NEW LEAF LITERARY & MEDIA, INC. ❖ www.newleafliterary.com

110 West 40th Street, Suite 2201, New York, NY 10018, 646-248-7989; email (not submissions): assist@newleafliterary.com

Describe the kinds of works you want to represent. Picture books, middle grade, young adult, adult, genre fiction, women's fiction, thrillers, romance, nonfiction of all kinds — basically everything.

How do you want writers to pitch you? Send us a query and your first five pages to query@newleafliterary.com. Submission guidelines are on our website.

List some of the titles you have recently placed with publishers. *Six of Crows* by Leigh Bardugo, *Red Queen* by Victoria Aveyard, *The Little World of Liz Climo* by Liz Climo, *Daughters unto Devils* by Amy Lukavics, *A Key to Extraordinary* by Natalie Lloyd.

Agents:

Joanna Volpe represents all brands of fiction, from picture books to adult novels. Her picture-book taste is the most eclectic, ranging from sweet to fun to smart to quirky. For other fiction (both adult and children's) she has an affinity for stories that have a darker element to them, whether they are horror, drama, or comedy. She's not the kind of reader who needs a romance in her novels, though she does appreciate a good one. On the nonfiction side her tastes are much more specific. For children she looks for topics that captivate kids: biographies, animal-related stories, all sciences, history, etc. Joanna also has an affinity for morbid, weird, or offbeat topics. In her adult nonfiction tastes, she tends toward all things geek-related, foodie books, travel books, and general pop culture and popular science. Overall, she's looking for anything that highlights underrepresented characters. More diversity, please!

Kathleen Ortiz is the director of subsidiary rights, overseeing audio, translation, and digital rights for the agency's titles. She regularly attends book trade shows around the world to sell titles to translation publishers and looks for new medium opportunities for our clients' books. Kathleen is also a literary agent and is actively seeking to sign more authors and illustrators, specifically fresh, new voices in young adult and animator-illustrator talent. In young adult she gravitates more toward beautiful and exceptional world building as well as contemporary stories whose main characters stay with the reader far beyond the pages. She would love to see a beautifully written young adult set within other cultures and experiences. On the illustration side, she loves animator-illustrators and their unique way of storytelling. Kathleen is *not* currently seeking middle grade, screenplays, or adult projects not listed above.

Suzie Townsend represents all brands of children's and adult fiction. She is actively looking to build her list. In adult, she's specifically looking for new adult, romance (all subgenres), fantasy (urban fantasy, science fiction, steampunk, epic fantasy), and crime fiction (mystery, thrillers). In children's she loves young adult (all subgenres) and is dying to find great middle grade projects. Suzie loves strong characters and voice-driven stories that break out of the typical tropes of their genres.

Mackenzie Brady got her start in publishing as an intern at Farrar, Straus and Giroux and FinePrint Literary Management. She then cut her teeth as an agent at Charlotte Sheedy Literary Agency before moving to New Leaf in 2014. She was a microbiologist in her prepublishing life, so she's always on the hunt for projects that bring new or wild facets of science to light. She is endlessly fascinated by the human body, especially the heart. Her taste in nonfiction extends beyond science books to memoir, lost histories, investigative journalism, epic sports narratives, and gift/lifestyle books. She is particularly interested in projects that move the cultural conversation forward and have a lasting impact on readers.

If you've written the next *Brain on Fire*, *The Power of Habit*, *Random Family*, *The Boys in the Boat*, *The Immortal Life of Henrietta Lacks*, *Autobiography of an Execution*, or *Young House Love*, she wants to see it. On the fiction side, Mackenzie represents a very select list of upmarket commercial/literary adult and young adult novels (think: *Everything I Never Told You*, *Station Eleven*, and *The Spectacular Now*). She also represents illustrators with or without book projects of their own.

Peter Knapp joined New Leaf as an agent in July 2015. Previously, he worked at the Park Literary Group, where he represented authors of middle grade and young adult fiction, and prior to that he was a story editor at Floren Shieh Productions, consulting on book-to-film adaptations for Los Angeles–based movie and TV entities. He graduated from NYU summa cum laude and lives in Brooklyn. At New Leaf, Peter will continue to represent authors of middle grade and young adult fiction across all genres, and he's also seeking out smart, high-concept adult fiction. He is genre-agnostic, as long as the writing is great — meaning a standout voice, complex characters (not just the protagonist), and plotting that keeps readers hooked from the first page through to the very end. In middle grade, he likes literary-award contenders, epic adventures (fantastical or not), and everything in between. He has a special place in his heart for middle grade that is spooky, funny, irreverent — or all three. In young adult, he wants character-driven contemporary, magical realism, epic fantasy (but it must feel fresh), and realistic stories with some type of twist (speculative, fantastical, or otherwise — such as *The Raven Boys*, *Bone Gap*, *We Were Liars*, etc.). For adult fiction, he wants high concept, voice-driven stories ranging from the highly commercial (such as *The Martian* or Blake Crouch's books) to the more literary (*The Age of Miracles*, *The Language of Flowers*). For all ages, Peter is always on the lookout for character-driven horror and suspense.

Jaida Temperly is very excited to be building her client list. Her clients include Kody Keplinger, Kirsten Hubbard, Eric Telchin, Amber McRee Turner, and Maggie Heinze. She also represents illustrators Betsy Bauer, James Lipnickas, and Genevieve Santos. After a brief stint in medical school at the University of Wisconsin–Madison, Jaida moved to New York City for an internship at Writers House. After five months, Jaida joined New Leaf Literary & Media, assisting Joanna Volpe for the past three years before starting to build her own list of clients. For children's, middle grade, and young adult titles, she's drawn to quirky, dark stories (*The Mysterious Benedict Society*, *Coraline*, *Escape from Mr. Lemoncello's Library*, *I Don't Like Koala*, etc.). For adult fiction, she loves those with strong mystery, high fantasy, or religious undertones (*The Westing Game*, *A Discovery of Witches*, and *The Da Vinci Code*).

THE PETER BEREN AGENCY ❖ peterberen.com

1201 Brickyard Way, Suite 315, Point Richmond, CA 94801, 510-821-5539, Skype: peterberenagency

Agent's name and contact info: Peter Beren, peterberen@aol.com

What would you be doing right now if not responding to this survey? Reading.

What would you be if not an agent (other than a dog, cat, or other mammal)? A publisher.

Do you think independent (noncorporate) publishing will be stronger, weaker, or the same over the next few years? Independent publishing grows stronger every year.

Please describe your professional history. I started my career in publishing at the age of 22 as a founding staff member and contributing editor of the alternative newsweekly the *Boston Phoenix* in 1969. After a brief stint with Intermedia, a multimedia company, I went west to pursue graduate studies in journalism at the University of California at Berkeley while freelancing for a variety of alternative publications, including *Clear Creek*, *Rags*, *Mother Jones*, and the *San Francisco Fault.* Joining the Berkeley-based alternative book publisher And/Or Press, Inc., I found my niche in book publishing in 1976 and have been working in the industry ever since.

From And/Or I went to Sierra Club Books as a marketing director in 1981, becoming publisher and licensing director in 1994. Since then I served as publisher for VIA Books for the California State Automobile Association and vice-president for publishing for Insight Editions, ending up as a literary agent and publishing consultant. Along the way, I was an acquisition field editor for Jeremy Tarcher (later the Tarcher imprint of Penguin) and author or coauthor of seven books including *The Writers Legal Companion*, *California the Beautiful*, and *The Golden Gate.*

My publishing career has spanned some 50 years, and I have been an editor, marketing director, licensing director, publisher, author, and agent. I approach being an agent from the perspective of being a publisher, and I am very involved with the shaping and positioning of book concepts in the marketplace of ideas.

How would you define the "client from hell"? I once had a client who claimed that he didn't need editing because God had dictated his manuscript.

Do you think Earth was created a few thousand years ago or several billion years ago? Several billion.

Please list five books you recently agented. *Our InstaMusic Memories: My Generation* by Baron Wolman, *Habits of a Happy Brain* by Loretta Breuning, *The Last Herd: Elephant Conservation in an Age of Extinction* by Art Wolfe and Sam Wasser, *A Headache in the Pelvis* by David Wise.

Please describe the kinds of books you want to agent. Original and creative nonfiction. I have a subspecialty in illustrated books of art and photography. The best example of that might be *Material World*, which I published at Sierra Club. My favorite genre is self-help, and I think the best example of a spectacular self-help book is *The Road Less Traveled*. I absolutely love working on pop-culture books, especially illustrated ones. Right now I'm moving into young adult and popular science.

What should writers submit for consideration, and how should they send it? A query by email.

How do you feel about self-publishing, and what do you see happening with it in the near future? Self-publishing is empowering for the writer and beneficial for the publishing industry as a sort of "farm league" for talent. It actually harkens back to our revolutionary times, like Tom Paine's self-published influential pamphlet *Common Sense*. Self-publishing is evolving and becoming more professional every day. I have worked directly with self-publishers as a consultant and also represented some self-published books for traditional publishing deals as an agent.

Do you think there are too many, too few, or just enough agents? It depends on who you ask. Authors probably think there are too few, agents will say there are too many, and publishers will say just enough.

Do you think Amazon will become the country's largest employer within 10 years? I have no idea.

Why do you think some books become super-successful (beyond the obvious reasons)? All books are sold by word of mouth. What spurs the word of mouth? Something that ignites readers and makes them missionary. Often in nonfiction, it's the ability of the author to speak in the voice of his or her audience like a friend talking to you in your kitchen.

Do you think agents are likely to become millionaires? I'm pretty sure the answer to this question is no.

Do you think agents tend toward certain personality types? All types with some things in common: curiosity and a love of books and ideas.

Do you think writers tend to be more or less narcissistic than the population at large? All artists are prey to narcissism to some extent.

Knowing what you know now, would you become an agent again? Yes. I would be an agent even if I won the lottery.

Why did you choose to become an agent? Because it's a form of lifelong learning. I love books and enjoy working with ideas and creative types.

Do you think many talented writers fail to get published for avoidable reasons? If so, what are some of those reasons? A lack of in-depth knowledge of the publishing business and how books are sold to publishers.

PETER LAMPACK AGENCY, INC. ❖ www.peterlampackagency.com

Agents' names and contact info: General queries: Andrew Lampack, andrew@peterlampackagency.com; foreign rights: Rema Dilanyan, rema@peterlampackagency.com

Please list five books you recently agented. The Gray Ghost by Clive Cussler and Robin Burcell, *Celtic Empire* by Clive Cussler and Dirk Cussler, *Shadow Tyrants* by Clive Cussler and Boyd Morrison, *The Rising Sea* by Clive Cussler and Graham Brown, *Feast of Lies* by Gerry Spence, *Late Essays* by J.M. Coetzee.

What should writers submit for consideration, and how should they send it? The Peter Lampack Agency no longer accepts material through conventional mail. When submitting, include a cover letter, author biography, and a one- or two-page synopsis. Please do not send more than one sample chapter of your manuscript at a time. Due to the extremely high volume of submissions, we ask that you allow four to six weeks for a response. We do not charge a reading fee or any fee for office services.

P.S. LITERARY AGENCY ❖ www.psliterary.com

2010 Winston Park Drive, 2nd Floor, Oakville, Ontario L6H 5R7, Canada, 416-907-8325, 212-655-9276, info@psliterary.com

What should writers submit for consideration, and how should they send it? Email only. Please send *just a query letter* to query@psliterary.com that consists of three paragraphs: (1) an introduction, including the title and category of your work (i.e., fiction or nonfiction and topic), an estimated word count, and a brief, general description; (2) a brief overview, which should read similar to back-cover copy; and (3) your bio, in which you tell us a little bit about yourself and your background (awards, affiliations, etc.).

Agent's name and contact info: Curtis Russell, President and Principal Agent, Twitter: @CurtisPSLA

Please describe the kinds of books you want to agent. I am currently acquiring both fiction and nonfiction. In fiction, I am seeking literary, commercial, mystery, thriller, suspense, romance, young adult, middle grade, and picture books. In nonfiction, I am looking for business, history, politics, current affairs, memoir, health, wellness, sports, humor, pop culture, popular science, and popular psychology.

Agent's name and contact info: Carly Watters, Vice President, Senior Literary Agent, and Director of Literary Branding; Twitter: @carlywatters; Instagram: @carlywatters

Please describe your professional history. I have a BA in English literature from Queen's University and an MA in publishing studies from City University London. After working at Bloomsbury and Kids Can Press in the rights departments and the Darley Anderson TV, Film, and Literary Agency as an agency assistant, I joined PSLA in 2010. In 2014 I was named VP and in 2017 added the role of director of literary branding; however, my primary focus continues to be as a literary agent.

Please list five books you recently agented. Seven Husbands of Evelyn Hugo by Taylor Jenkins Reid, *She Regrets Nothing* by Andrea Dunlop, *The Subway Girls* by Susie Orman Schnall, *Nobody Cares* by Anne T. Donahue, *Whole Bowls* by Allison Day.

Please describe the kinds of books you want to agent. Books that people want to talk about.

Why did you choose to become an agent? I love being a project manager through the entire process. Discovering talent, finding great author-publisher connections, negotiating contracts, selling sub rights, publicizing books, and helping writers navigate careers are all deeply satisfying parts of this job that I never tire of.

THE PURCELL AGENCY, LLC ❖ thepurcellagency.com

Agent's name and contact info: Tina P. Schwartz, querytinap@gmail.com, 847-702-6945

What would you be doing right now if not responding to this survey? Probably reading.

What would you be if not an agent (other than a dog, cat, or other mammal)? Hmm… maybe working with children in some capacity.

Do you think independent (noncorporate) publishing will be stronger, weaker, or the same over the next few years? Stronger.

Please describe your professional history. I started in advertising and media sales, then changed to writing and eventually agenting.

How would you define the "client from hell"? One who is a bully.

Please list five books you recently agented. Alone on the Shield; It's Not What You're Eating, It's What's Eating You; In My Shoes; Deep Novel Revision; Seven Suspects.

Please describe the kinds of books you want to agent. Engrossing young adult fiction, nonfiction for teens and adults.

What should writers submit for consideration, and how should they send it? For fiction, a query and three sample chapters; for nonfiction, a proposal (outline, sample chapter, competing titles, why *you* are the person to write this book). Send to tpaqueries@gmail.com.

How do you feel about self-publishing, and what do you see happening with it in the near future? Self-publishing can be a great avenue for some people, but it takes a *lot* of work to do it successfully! Authors need to research all that goes into it before jumping in blindly.

Do you think there are too many, too few, or just enough agents? Probably too few. With some bigger houses wanting agented authors only, it's difficult for the large number of authors to get representation. It's very competitive!

Do you think Amazon will become the country's largest employer within 10 years? Interesting question. Not sure.

Why do you think some books become super-successful (beyond the obvious reasons)? When a book touches a nerve with a large audience and is about something so relatable, it can't help but succeed.

Do you think agents are likely to become millionaires? Not the majority, but it would be nice!

Do you think agents tend toward certain personality types? Yes!

Do you think writers tend to be more or less narcissistic than the population at large? Less narcissistic, on average. Many writers are introverts.

Knowing what you know now, would you become an agent again? Absolutely.

Why did you choose to become an agent? I was helping a lot of my writer friends get published and was a writer myself gaining some success in publishing. I figured I don't usually write more than one book per year and needed more of an income with three kids who all want to go to college. So I learned what I could, tried to find an agency job in Chicago (small market for agents), and ultimately opened my own agency. I loved negotiating contracts when I was in advertising and media, so this married my two careers — writing and negotiating. It was the right choice for me, and I haven't regretted a single moment of this career.

Do you think many talented writers fail to get published for avoidable reasons? If so, what are some of those reasons? Perseverance. Usually, people are just a few noes away from a yes. It's a numbers game, so *keep submitting*! Also, if someone is talented but not willing to take edits, that will kill a career quickly! You have to be open enough to suggestions; I'm not saying take every single edit, but consider each point carefully.

Additional agents at the Purcell Agency: Kim McCollum, Catherine Hedrick; submissions: tpaqueries@gmail.com

RED SOFA LITERARY ❖ www.redsofaliterary.com

PO Box 40482, St. Paul, MN 55104, 651-224-6670 (no queries by phone, please)

Describe the kinds of works the agency represents. Our categories are described in detail at redsofaliterary.com/representative-categories.

Please list books the agency has recently placed with publishers: *Jack Cooper & the Ghost Girl*, by Chan Poling and Lucy Michell (University of Minnesota Press, 2019); *Bodies of Evidence: Evolution through Biology's Most Baffling Beasts*, Maggie Ryan Sandford (Blackdog & Leventhal, 2019); *Other Than Honorable*, by Claire O'Dell (Harper Voyager, 2018); *Robert E. Lee: An American Story*, Brandon Marie Miller (Calkins Creek, 2018); *Cocaine + Surfing: A Love Story!*, Chas Smith (Rare Bird Books, Hachette Australia, 2018); *Girl in the Grove*, Eric Smith (Flux Books, 2017); *Semiosis*, Sue Burke (Tor, 2018); *An Unkindness of Ghosts*, Rivers Solomon (Askashic, 2017); *Under the Pendulum Sun*, Jeannette Ng (Angry Robot, 2017); *The Haunted Serpent*, by Dora Mitchell (Sterling, 2018).

Agent's name and contact info: Dawn Frederick, Owner, Literary Agent, dawn@redsofaliterary.com

Please describe your professional history. Before publishing, I was a bookseller in the independent, chain, and specialty stores. I ended up in Minnesota due to my first publishing job, eventually becoming a literary agent at Sebastian Literary Agency. I have a BS in human ecology and an MS in information sciences from an ALA accredited institution. I'm also the cofounder of the Minnesota Publishing Tweet Up, the news chair for the Twin Cities Advisory Council for MPR, and a teaching artist at Loft Literary. I can be found on Twitter at @redsofaliterary.

How would you describe the "writer from hell"? Diva. If someone is bringing too much ego or showing signs of being a difficult client to work with, I will run (not walk) away from this person.

Describe the kinds of works you want to represent. I am always in search of a good work of nonfiction that falls within my categories (see my specific list at our website). I especially love pop culture, interesting histories, social sciences/advocacy, humor, and books that are great conversation starters. As for fiction, I am always in search of good young adult and middle grade titles. For young adult, I will go a little darker on the tone, as I enjoy a good gothic, contemporary, or historical young adult novel. For middle grade, I will always want something fun and lighthearted, but would love more contemporary themes too.

Describe what you definitely don't want to represent. Memoir, although it seems everyone ignores this request. I also prefer to represent books that aren't overly sappy, overly romantic, or didactic/moralistic. Also business how-to and self-help books aren't my cup of tea. It's best to not query me with ideas in these categories.

What should writers submit for consideration, and how should they send it? Outside of the correct way to query me (see our website), I want a pitch that is engaging, reflective of what I'm looking for, and provides the *who/what/why* perspective to why the author believes it's a good fit for the agency.

How do you feel about self-publishing, and what do you see happening with it in the near future? If you put the same amount of work and time that traditional publishers put into their books and the quality is just as good, I'm all in favor. But also it's important to not rush into the process without a plan or a team to support you along the way. And once the book is indie published, that means your new ideas will need to be taken to publishers, as opposed to just shopping the already published book.

Why did you become an agent? While working at a publishing house, I realized how much I missed selling the finished books, let alone the chance to meet so many authors beyond the completed book. The bookstore life had left this impression, and I realized that when a friend in grad school suggested I become an agent, it was in fact the best idea. I mentioned this to a friend, who it turns out knew Laurie Harper. And I haven't looked back since. It was meant to be. ☺

Knowing what you know now, would you become an agent again? My only change? I would have cut to the chase and become an agent straight out of grad school rather than waiting longer.

What are ways prospective clients can impress you, and what are ways they can turn you off? Showing a knowledge of my categories and helping me know they *are* the ones to write the book ideas being shared. This will always stand out. Additionally, always keeping our interactions personal and professional. Lacking any of the things I find important will generally not leave the best impression.

Agent's name and contact info: Laura Zats, Associate Literary Agent, laura@redsofaliterary.com

What would you be doing right now if not responding to this survey? Tweeting about one of my books that came out today. The world needs to know how good it is and that they can buy it!

What would you be if not an agent (other than a dog, cat, or other mammal?) I'm not sure what kind, but I'd be an entrepreneur or an integral part of a start-up that focuses on improving individual lives and communities.

Do you think independent (noncorporate) publishing will be stronger, weaker, or the same over the next few years? Stronger, for sure. There's a lot of innovation coming in this business, and it'll start with two people in a basement, I bet.

Please describe your professional history. I had the great luck of getting started in publishing before I graduated college, so I've never done anything else full-time. In this industry, however, I have spent some time freelancing, working with indie authors, and teaching. For the past three years, I've been on the board of the nonprofit Minnesota Book Publishers' Roundtable and am currently its president. I am also the founder and host of Print Run, a weekly publishing podcast, with agent Erik Hane. We write a monthly column for *Apex Magazine*. Find me online @LZats and look out for my #500queries series at the beginning of every year.

How would you describe the "writer from hell"? Hardheaded. Aggressive. Suspicious of me and wanting to dictate how I do my job. A troll on social media and a general loose cannon where their public image is concerned.

Describe the kinds of works you want to represent. I am looking for romance, science fiction, fantasy, and young adult books. I have a specific interest in feminist narratives and working with marginalized authors. Tonally, I am drawn to wit, banter, and gorgeous, lush, "literary" phrasing. I also love fresh storytelling techniques that might be more commonly seen in short stories. Thematically, I love seeing characters in new and nontraditional spaces; stories about identity formation, interpersonal relationships, and transgenerational trauma; and all different types of geekery.

Describe what you definitely don't want to represent. Nonfiction, including memoir. Adult mystery, thrillers, literary fiction. Fiction without quirky or distinctive hooks. Books that follow or fit in trends.

What should writers submit for consideration, and how should they send it? A simple query sent to my email address.

How do you feel about self-publishing, and what do you see happening with it in the near future? I am energized and excited about self-publishing. It's a great way to expand the market's definition of a "sellable" book. Many of my authors are hybrid authors, meaning they are self-publishing some books and going traditional with others.

Why did you become an agent? As much as I would love to think that I would make a good writer, I find myself at home in spaces where I can work with others (but still have agency over what I'm working on) and combine creative work with what can only be termed "management." Add that to my love of reading and enthusiasm for the book community, and you can see why I did it (even though I had no idea what an agent actually did at my first interview at Red Sofa).

Knowing what you know now, would you become an agent again? 10/10 would do again! I can't imagine my life being any different. I love being an author's biggest fan for a living.

What are ways prospective clients can impress you, and what are ways they can turn you off? They can impress me by knowing about my list and what my goals are as an agent before they query me. Essentially, doing research puts you ahead of 95 percent of everyone who queries me. I am turned off when authors don't follow submission guidelines or don't want to hear my advice.

Agent's name and contact info: Amanda Rutter, Associate Literary Agent, amanda@redsofaliterary.com

Please describe your professional history. I have no formal qualifications in literary arts — in fact, my degree subject was accounting. But my professional history includes being an acquisitions editor for Strange Chemistry, a freelance editor for Bubblecow and Wise Ink Publishing, and a book blogger.

Describe the kinds of works you want to represent. Science fiction/fantasy, the non–young adult ideas; young adult and middle grade science fiction/fantasy.

Describe what you definitely don't want to represent. I am definitely not a nonfiction person. I rarely read it myself, so I wouldn't know where to start to represent! Also, although I enjoy middle grade fiction and would be happy to represent, I won't take on picture books.

What should writers submit for consideration, and how should they send it? With an email (to amanda@redsofaliterary.com) stating the genre, the word count, and a brief pitch of the novel. I don't like being approached via social media unless I am taking part in a specific contest.

How do you feel about self-publishing, and what do you see happening with it in the near future? Positive in general. The increasing trend of authors treating it as a business and producing quality products is excellent and has introduced some really talented individuals to a wider readership.

Why did you become an agent? I was approached when I left Strange Chemistry and asked if I had ever considered a role as a literary agent. I hadn't before then, but gave the matter a great deal of thought and was pleased to accept a position with Red Sofa when offered.

Knowing what you know now, would you become an agent again? Ha, well, I suppose I could go back to accounting! I wouldn't change a thing. I love working with authors and publishers and discovering new stories and voices.

What are ways prospective clients can impress you, and what are ways they can turn you off? They can impress me with a sharp and concise pitch for their novel that conveys enough to entice me to read the novel without going on for paragraphs and paragraphs. I dislike authors who feel as though they don't need to follow the rules — don't finish a novel before submitting, don't include the information I ask for, etc.

Agent's name and contact info: Stacey Graham, Associate Literary Agent, stacey@redsofaliterary.com

Please describe your professional history. I have BS degrees in history and archaeology/anthropology from Oregon State University. I am the author of four books and multiple short stories, a screenwriter, ghostwriter, and editor.

How would you describe the "writer from hell"? A writer who rejects solid edits in favor of their own vision without consideration.

Describe the kinds of works you want to represent. Funny and/or spooky middle grade with a great voice, romance, quirky nonfiction for adults or middle grade.

Describe what you definitely don't want to represent. I am not looking to represent young adult, fantasy, sci-fi, or memoir.

What should writers submit for consideration, and how should they send it? A short query to stacey@redsofaliterary.com. If I feel that we're a good fit, I'll request the first three chapters or a finished book proposal.

How do you feel about self-publishing, and what do you see happening with it in the near future? Self-publishers are workhorses. They learn the best part of publishing — and the ugliest. It can be an excellent education for authors if they stick it out.

Why did you become an agent? After years of working in the field as a writer, I wanted to be a part of the business side of publishing. After speaking with my agent about working as an agent, she invited me to join her agency.

What are ways prospective clients can impress you, and what are ways they can turn you off? To impress me, show that you've researched how the business of publishing works. Be proactive in the publishing community either online or locally, and be open to constructive criticism to make the project stronger.

Agent's name and contact info: Erik Hane, Associate Literary Agent, erik@redsofaliterary.com

Please describe your professional history. I graduated from Knox College with a major in writing and went from school to the Denver Publishing Institute. My first publishing job came soon after, as an editorial assistant and then assistant editor at Oxford University Press. I then moved to the Overlook Press as an acquiring editor, working on primarily upmarket nonfiction (history, biography, popular science), but I was lucky enough to work on some novels as well. Overlook's broad trade-publishing range, combined with my experience at OUP, has me comfortable with a wide variety of projects, and I look forward to seeing and representing this variety at Red Sofa.

How would you describe the "writer from hell"? The writer from hell tries to be overly ornate rather than focusing on telling a good story and letting strong prose naturally develop. This person also doesn't like edits and doesn't trust me. If you and I are working together, I trust you as the author; I like your book and can picture it doing well. Trust me to do what I can to help you make it a success!

Describe the kinds of works you want to represent. Nonfiction: I love great stories and sharp commentary on just about anything, but off the top of my head I really like great writing on politics, race, social trends, leftism/socialism, video games, Weird Twitter, the intersection of sports and culture, and anything else you can convince me the world should care about. I also do more traditionally "academic" subjects for general readerships, like history and science (especially evolutionary studies).

Fiction: I typically like novels that are "realistic," though I do love light speculative elements if the book is closer to just "surreal" than overtly sci-fi/fantasy. I like novels that probably get called "literary" even as they fit into other categories. I love family stories, memorable settings (often historical or political) that matter to the book, characters with harebrained schemes, legends, folklore, religion, mythology, and games. I like when the impossible is grappled with in a realist setting; think *The Prestige*. I want "ambitious" novels that reach for something memorable — I'm not scared of a giant manuscript if it's got reason to be that long. Apropos of nothing, I'm a sucker for Scandinavian things.

Describe what you definitely don't want to represent. No memoir, children's, young adult, or middle grade for me.

What should writers submit for consideration, and how should they send it? For fiction, I'd love to see a pitch letter (perhaps one that includes some comp titles) and a first chapter; I will request more if interested. For nonfiction, a proposal that includes an overview of the project, a table of contents, a clear sense of who the author is and why he or she is the one to write the book, comparable titles, and some sample writing.

How do you feel about self-publishing, and what do you see happening with it in the near future? I like self-publishing as long as it's situational. I don't think it's a substitute for traditional publishing; traditional houses have too many resources and sales channels that are simply unavailable to most self-published authors. I do think self-publishing can work if the author has a clear platform for promoting the book. I also think it's important that if someone is willing to pay to have a book produced, he or she should be able to do so. But in most cases that should not be treated as an equivalent to being published by a house as far as expectations go.

Why did you become an agent? I love the "frontier" of it — finding writers doing fascinating things and helping them take a concept from idea stage to book. I love working deeply on something before a publisher even knows it exists, which is a freedom unique to agenting.

Knowing what you know now, would you become an agent again? Knowing what I do now, I would certainly go through the work and publishing experiences I've been lucky enough to have. Working in editorial departments at two vastly different houses has provided a frame of reference for the industry and has helped me learn what sorts of books I'd love to work on moving forward.

Do you think many talented writers fail to get published for avoidable reasons? If so, what are some reasons? Though I worked at first an academic house (albeit a large one) and then a tiny independent press, I really like the Big 5. Someone in our industry has to command enough size and power to balance out Amazon's sometimes difficult influence, at least in part. And obviously, some of the best books and some of the best editors I know are at Big 5 houses.

What are ways prospective clients can impress you, and what are ways they can turn you off? Clear vision impresses me. What is your book, and why should someone pay to read it? And I think something that turns off anyone in the publishing industry is oversized bluster or expectations. It's not that I don't think your book could do really, really well; but if from the outset all you want to talk about is how many copies printed, how many sold, etc., that's the wrong foot to start on and doesn't do justice to the process. Telling me you expect your book to be a bestseller is a bit empty; obviously I want that too! I'd rather focus on the book until it's truly time to talk commercial performance.

Agent's name and contact info: Liz Rahn, Subrights Agent, liz@redsofaliterary.com

Please describe your professional history. I graduated from Concordia College with a degree in English literature and attended the Denver Publishing Institute in 2015. I interned with Red Sofa for a year before officially joining the team as a subrights agent last July. During college and since then, I've done quite a bit of freelance editing, copy writing, and submissions reading for literary magazines.

How would you describe the "writer from hell"? The writer from hell comes into a conversation with an agent or editor thinking they have all the answers and are unreceptive to constructive edits. A good writer should trust that a good agent or editor will only make suggestions to make their book better.

How do you feel about self-publishing, and what do you see happening with it in the near future? Self-publishing can be a great way for authors to get their writing into the hands of readers, especially if they have a personal platform built on which to advertise their writing. It is certainly a different route of creating a book than going through a publishing house with a dedicated team for marketing and promoting your book. The two methods are not mutually exclusive for authors; you can publish both ways. But most houses will not publish a work that has already been self-published.

Why did you become an agent? My initial draw to publishing was a desire to work with authors. I started with Red Sofa as an intern simply looking to get publishing experience, but I ended up doing a lot with author relations at the agency and loved it. I get more opportunity to work closely with writers than I would at a publishing house.

Knowing what you know now, would you become an agent again? My original plan was to work in-house for a publisher and I ended up agenting instead, and it was the best thing that could have happened.

Do you think many talented writers fail to get published for avoidable reasons? If so, what are some reasons? There are a lot of reasons a talented writer may not get published. Above all, publishing is a fickle business. An author may have a really great book that just isn't right for the market at a certain time. My best advice is to be open to edit suggestions from agents and editors, and don't get disheartened if your first book doesn't get picked up. Keep writing and keep trying.

What are ways prospective clients can impress you, and what are ways they can turn you off? The best way to impress an agent is follow the guidelines and show that you picked that agent as a thoughtful choice, not just as a shot in the dark. Make sure you research the types of books an agent represents and how they take submissions. Not following their guidelines is an easily avoidable mistake.

REGAL HOFFMANN & ASSOCIATES, LLC ❖ rhaliterary.com

Agent's name and contact info: Claire Anderson-Wheeler, claire@rhaliterary.com

What would you be doing right now if not responding to this survey? Donning an extra pair of socks and sitting down to some (likely work-related) reading.

What would you be if not an agent (other than a dog, cat, or other mammal)? A tree.

Do you think independent (noncorporate) publishing will be stronger, weaker, or the same over the next few years? I would like to say stronger.

Please describe your professional history. Transatlantic.

How would you define the "client from hell"? A belligerent narcissist with a rapidly deteriorating prose style. (Luckily, all my clients are wonderful.)

Do you think Earth was created a few thousand years ago or several billion years ago? The latter.

Please list five books you recently agented. When You Read This by Mary Adkins; an illustrated graphic biography of David Bowie by Allred and Steve Horton; *Soon the Light Will Be Perfect* by Dave Patterson; on the children's / young adult side, All the Wind in the World by Samantha Mabry and *Time Castaways* by Liesl Shurtliff.

Please describe the kinds of books you want to agent. Books that tackle something. Books that spin a good yarn.

What should writers submit for consideration, and how should they send it? A cover letter, detailed synopsis, and first three chapters — by email is my preference.

How do you feel about self-publishing, and what do you see happening with it in the near future? It has its place, but what a sink-or-swim environment. It's not my area of expertise, so I wouldn't want to speculate too much on its future.

Do you think there are too many, too few, or just enough agents? Since it's commission based, the supply-and-demand effect is pretty strong.

Do you think Amazon will become the country's largest employer within 10 years? As long as it's not the arms industry.

Why do you think some books become super-successful (beyond the obvious reasons)? Everyone loves a "phenomenon" — it ties into our need for community, I think.

Do you think agents are likely to become millionaires? The 1 percent.

Do you think agents tend toward certain personality types? Somewhat. There are creative introvert types, and Jerry Maguire types, and a lot in between. And hipsters. We have some of them, too.

Do you think writers tend to be more or less narcissistic than the population at large? Are we including tweeters in your definition of writers?

Knowing what you know now, would you become an agent again? I hope so.

Why did you choose to become an agent? I wanted to make good things happen to good people.

Do you think many talented writers fail to get published for avoidable reasons? If so, what are some of those reasons? It depends what we mean by *avoidable.* Most great books eventually get published, even if they have to wait a while to catch the right wave. Many talented writers may fail to get a certain book published, but if they're truly talented, they will be published, even if not for that initial book.

Agent's name and contact info: Grace Ross, grace@rhaliterary.com

What would you be if not an agent (other than a dog, cat, or other mammal)? A scuba-diving instructor.

Do you think independent (noncorporate) publishing will be stronger, weaker, or the same over the next few years? Stronger.

Please describe your professional history. I started in editorial at Oxford University Press before jumping over to the agenting side of the industry, where I first worked as the digital marketing manager at Lowenstein Associates. I then worked under Denise Shannon at her agency before landing at Regal Hoffmann & Associates in 2016.

How would you define the "client from hell"? Someone who calls me in the middle of the night.

Do you think Earth was created a few thousand years ago or several billion years ago? The latter, of course — it pains me that this is even a debate nowadays.

Please list five books you recently agented. How about some authors I represent? Katie Knoll, Michael Jeffrey Lee, Molly Pascal, Ryan J. Burden, and Eugene Tracy, to name a few.

Please describe the kinds of books you want to agent. Books that engage with larger social issues, both fiction and nonfiction, all genres and languages.

How do you feel about self-publishing, and what do you see happening with it in the near future? It's great for some projects, but the vast majority are lost in the noise.

Do you think there are too many, too few, or just enough agents? Not enough outside of New York.

Do you think Amazon will become the country's largest employer within 10 years? Nope.

Do you think agents are likely to become millionaires? That's not why I became an agent.

Do you think agents tend toward certain personality types? Not really — we have to wear so many different hats that it combats that kind of homogeneity.

Do you think writers tend to be more or less narcissistic than the population at large? Uh.

Knowing what you know now, would you become an agent again? Absolutely.

Why did you choose to become an agent? Because I love working with creative people and advocating on their behalf, behind the scenes.

Agent's name and contact info: Markus Hoffmann, info@rhaliterary.com

What would you be doing right now if not responding to this survey? Surfing, reading, or hanging out in a jazz bar.

What would you be if not an agent (other than a dog, cat, or other mammal)? An opera director.

Do you think independent (noncorporate) publishing will be stronger, weaker, or the same over the next few years? Stronger.

Please describe your professional history. I started as a literary scout in London, then sold foreign rights for two major agencies in the same city before moving to the US in 2004, where once again I worked as a literary scout first. I joined Regal Literary in 2006 and was made a partner in what then became Regal Hoffmann & Associates in 2015.

How would you define the "client from hell"? On fire in all the wrong ways.

Do you think Earth was created a few thousand years ago or several billion years ago? The more important question for me is how we can make sure it'll last for another several billion years. (But the latter, obvi.)

Please list five books you recently agented. Wolfram Eilenberger, *Time of the Magicians* (Penguin Press US and Penguin Press UK); Elliot Reed, *A Key to Treehouse Living* (Tin House Books); Leland de la Durantaye, *Hannah versus the Tree* (McSweeney's); John Kaag, *Hiking with Nietzsche* (Farrar, Straus and Giroux); Philipp Blom, *Nature's Mutiny* (Liveright).

Please describe the kinds of books you want to agent. Books that know how to tell a story, whether fiction or nonfiction, in whatever genre, in any language.

What should writers submit for consideration, and how should they send it? A cover letter and 30 pages, following the guidelines on our website, please.

How do you feel about self-publishing, and what do you see happening with it in the near future? It'll continue to be 99.5 percent dross, and 0.5 percent amazing.

Do you think there are too many, too few, or just enough agents? Not enough good ones.

Do you think Amazon will become the country's largest employer within 10 years? No. Ever heard of automation?

Why do you think some books become super-successful (beyond the obvious reasons)? Because life isn't fair.

Do you think agents are likely to become millionaires? Not many of them, and even fewer good ones.

Do you think agents tend toward certain personality types? Looking at my fantastic colleagues, each of whom is different from the others, I'd have to say no.

Do you think writers tend to be more or less narcissistic than the population at large? The American or the global population?

Knowing what you know now, would you become an agent again? In a heartbeat.

Why did you choose to become an agent? Because I'm good at and love helping creative people make what they've created better.

Do you think many talented writers fail to get published for avoidable reasons? If so, what are some of those reasons? Truly talented writers will get published. Eventually.

RICHARD CURTIS ASSOCIATES, INC. ❖ www.curtisagency.com

Agent's name and contact info: Richard Curtis, President, rcurtis@curtisagency.com

What would you be doing right now if not responding to this survey? Listening to a Dickens audiobook.

What would you be if not an agent (other than a dog, cat, or other mammal)? A playwright.

Do you think independent (noncorporate) publishing will be stronger, weaker, or the same over the next few years? Same.

Please describe your professional history. Literary agent for four decades. Pioneered in digital publishing with the founding in 1999 of the first independent ebook publisher. Author of over 50 published books and of dozens of plays.

How would you define the "client from hell"? I actually wrote a story called "The Client from Hell," in which the narrator becomes the literary agent for an alien starfarer. The alien begins to suspect he is being cheated by movie studios and book publishers, so he destroys Earth. I'll bet nobody can claim a worse client than that!

Do you think Earth was created a few thousand years ago or several billion years ago? Come on, Jeff!

Please list five books you recently agented. Death of an Heir by Philip Jett (true crime); *Fata Morgana* by Steven Boyett and Ken Mitchroney (science fiction adventure); *A Single Spy* by William Christie (spy thriller); three novels in the *Savannah Reid* series by G.A. McKevett (romantic detective); *False Flag* by John Altman (thriller).

Please describe the kinds of books you want to agent. Spy thrillers, popular-science nonfiction, exciting contemporary romance.

What should writers submit for consideration, and how should they send it? Use the application form on the website, www.curtisagency.com.

How do you feel about self-publishing, and what do you see happening with it in the near future? You have to devote 100 percent of your time to being an author and 100 percent of your time to being a publisher.

Do you think there are too many, too few, or just enough agents? Always just enough.

Do you think Amazon will become the country's largest employer within 10 years? Don't know.

Why do you think some books become super-successful (beyond the obvious reasons)? Word of mouth.

Do you think agents are likely to become millionaires? Yes, if they inherit millions.

Do you think agents tend toward certain personality types? No.

Do you think writers tend to be more or less narcissistic than the population at large? Good writers are less narcissistic than the population at large. They must be empathetic to create believable characters.

Knowing what you know now, would you become an agent again? No.

Why did you choose to become an agent? I loved reconciling opposites and making all parties believe they have won something.

Do you think many talented writers fail to get published for avoidable reasons? If so, what are some of those reasons? Authors must start by loving to write, whether it gets published or not.

RITA ROSENKRANZ LITERARY AGENCY ❖

www.ritarosenkranzliteraryagency.com

440 West End Avenue, #15D, New York, NY 10024, 212-873-6333

Agent's name and contact info: Rita Rosenkranz, rrosenkranz@mindspring.com

Please describe your professional history. Former editor at major New York publishing houses.

Please list five books you recently agented. *A Mind for Numbers: How to Excel at Math and Science (Even if You Flunked Algebra)* by Barbara Oakley (Tarcher); *Get Lit Rising: Words Ignite. Claim Your Poem. Claim Your Life* by Diane Luby Lane and the Get Lit Players (Beyond Words, Atria Books); *We Regret to Inform You: A Survival Guide for Gold Star Parents and Those Who Support Them* by Joanne Steen (Central Recovery Press); *The Law of Small Things: Why Some People Really Act with Integrity and Why the Rest of Us Just Think We Do* by Stuart H. Brody (Berrett-Koehler); *Hitler and the Habsburgs* by James Longo (Diversion Books).

Please describe the kinds of books you want to agent. Projects that present familiar topics freshly and lesser-known subjects commercially and to which the author is tied for verifiable personal or professional reasons.

What should writers submit for consideration, and how should they send it? Best to start with a query, preferably sent electronically. Follow the guidelines on the website, www.ritarosenkranzliteraryagency.com.

Why did you choose to become an agent? I have an avid interest in the creative process that leads to a well-published book.

ROBIN STRAUS AGENCY, INC. ❖ www.robinstrausagency.com

229 East 79th Street, Suite 5A, New York, NY 10075, 212-472-3282, fax: 212-472-3833

Agents' names and contact info: Robin Straus, Agent, info@robinstrausagency.com; Katelyn Hales, Junior Agent, info@robinstrausagency.com

What would you be if not an agent (other than a dog, cat, or other mammal)? Robin: I love my work being an advocate for writers, working with them on many books, over many years. I would also probably have been happy being a doctor or raising horses and dogs.

Katelyn: I was a modern dancer in New York City before making the jump to publishing, so I've already done one of the things I'd do if I was not an agent! If I were not hopelessly unqualified, I'd happily be an astronaut and spend my career on the ISS.

Please describe your professional history. *Robin*: BA, Wellesley College; MBA, NYU School of Business. I started at Little, Brown, thinking I'd become an editor, but I became very interested in the business end, so I moved to subsidiary rights at Doubleday and then Random House. But I missed working with authors, and agenting seemed like the best way to combine everything. I joined Wallace & Sheil Agency for four years and started my own agency in 1983.

Katelyn: BA and BFA, Western Washington University. I joined the agency in 2015 after internships at Writers House and W. W. Norton.

Please describe the kinds of books you want to agent. *Robin*: High-quality literary fiction and nonfiction. The subject is of less importance than fine writing and research. I'm an eclectic reader, watcher, and listener! A good writer can make his or her work captivate me even when I'm not initially drawn to the subject. I don't like violence, however. Please don't send me "genre" fiction, screenplays, or juveniles.

Katelyn: Adult fiction and nonfiction. I love character-driven science fiction, fantasy, and speculative fiction, and I'm always excited by a surprising new take on the familiar. I'm drawn to the relationship between humans and technology, complex world building, and women in space and have a shameless soft spot for talking animals (e.g., Temeraire, Pantalaimon). I'm also looking for upmarket and literary fiction, books on pop culture and current affairs, and narrative nonfiction or memoirs with unusual and fresh perspectives. Recent books I loved (but did not agent) are *The Bear and the Nightingale* by Katherine Arden and *All the Birds in the Sky* by Charlie Jane Anders. Please don't send me romance or children's literature.

What should writers submit for consideration, and how should they send it? Please see our website for full submission information. We love to see a great query letter and sample material that speaks for itself. Caution: we are a very small agency and take on very few new clients. We also no longer accept submissions by regular mail. Email only, please!

Please do blow us away with your prose and ideas. Watch your grammar, avoid clichés, and don't overstate claims that a book is revolutionary. Be receptive to suggestions on how to improve your work, and understand that publishing works best as a collaborative effort. Be imaginative about how to market yourself and your books.

How do you feel about self-publishing, and what do you see happening with it in the near future? We think authors benefit most from working with skilled editors and publishers. There is a ton of junk being self-published.

How would you define the "client from hell"? We'd have to say someone who calls to complain every morning at 9 AM.

RODEEN LITERARY MANAGEMENT ❖ www.rodeenliterary.com

www.facebook.com/rodeenliterary, www.instagram.com/rodeenliterary

Agent's name and contact info: Lori Kilkelly, submissionslori@rodeenliterary.com

What would you be doing right now if not responding to this survey? Putting on real clothes to go to dinner.

What would you be if not an agent (other than a dog, cat, or other mammal)? I changed careers to become an agent — I'm not going back!

Please describe your professional history. I began working with Paul Rodeen in 2010 after attending the Denver Publishing Institute. Paul came up in the industry working at the right hand of publishing legend George Nicholson. I was Paul's intern, then assistant, then RLM's social-media director, and at last I felt well prepared to take on my own clients in 2013. My first two clients and I have sold 34 books together in those 5 years.

How would you define the "client from hell"? I don't, wouldn't, and haven't worked with anyone who could possibly be described that way. My clients are responsive, receptive to feedback, and always working to become their own personal best. I look for clients who take their work seriously, but don't take themselves too seriously.

Do you think Earth was created a few thousand years ago or several billion years ago? See my client Stacy McAnulty's recent nonfiction picture book *Earth! My First 4.54 Billion Years*. I sold that. ☺

Please list six books you recently agented. *What the Night Sings* by Vesper Stamper (Knopf); *The Miscalculations of Lightning Girl* by Stacy McAnulty (Random House); *Warren and Dragon* by Ariel Bernstein and Mike Malbrough (Penguin, Viking); *Eliza's Story* (the story of Elizabeth Schuyler Hamilton) by Camille Andros, illustrated by Tessa Blackham (Christy Ottaviano Books at Henry Holt, Macmillan); *Jasper & Ollie Go to the Pool* by Alex Willan (two-book deal with Doubleday); *Windows* by Julia Denos and E. B. Goodale (Candlewick).

Please describe the kinds of books you want to agent. I represent the full range of children's work from picture books to young adult, but I currently only rep picture-book writers who also write middle grade and/or young adult. The illustrators I rep are also writers. As for the kinds of books I want to agent, I love books that make me feel something — laughter, tears — that move me in some way.

What should writers submit for consideration, and how should they send it? We only accept submissions via email. If you're an author-illustrator, please send a dummy in PDF format, not larger than 5 MB. Please don't send a link to download. For middle grade and young adult, paste the first 50 pages into your email. If you're concerned about the formatting, you can also attach as a docx.

How do you feel about self-publishing, and what do you see happening with it in the near future? This is a way for so many people who are passionate about writing to put their work into the hands of readers.

Do you think there are too many, too few, or just enough agents? I haven't given it any thought, frankly. I'm inclined to believe there is plenty of fantastic talent to go around, so "just enough."

Do you think Amazon will become the country's largest employer within 10 years? Sadly, yes. I say sadly because I think local business is the crux of a community. Independent bookstore owners and booksellers are crucial to the success of new talent.

Do you think agents are likely to become millionaires? Hahahahaha.

Knowing what you know now, would you become an agent again? Without question.

Why did you choose to become an agent? It magically combines my love of reading with my love for working with creative people and ultimately puts mind-opening work into the hands of children and young adults.

THE ROHM LITERARY AGENCY ❖ therohmliteraryagency.com

Agent's name and contact info: Wendy Goldman Rohm, wendy@rohmliterary.com, 646-845-9185

What would you be doing right now if not responding to this survey? Writing, editing, reading, walking, cooking for friends, dancing wildly.

What would you be if not an agent (other than a dog, cat, or other mammal)? A sheet-metal worker. Ha ha. Not really.

Do you think independent (noncorporate) publishing will be stronger, weaker, or the same over the next few years? Stronger.

Please describe your professional history. Author, managing editor, author, features editor, agent, author, developmental editor, author-agent. Separately and simultaneously. ☺

How would you define the "client from hell"? I haven't had any. They're all angels. ☺

Do you think Earth was created a few thousand years ago or several billion years ago? It's a virtual planet; it has yet to be created correctly. ☺

Please list five books you recently agented. They're being bid on right now, so I'll tell you when the deals are done.

Please describe the kinds of books you want to agent. Literary fiction, narrative nonfiction, memoir, journalism, young adult, women's fiction, business.

What should writers submit for consideration, and how should they send it? By email, double-spaced, in Word or PDF format, with your name and contact information on the first page. Do not send unless you have sent a query letter first and we have asked for the full manuscript.

Knowing what you know now, would you become an agent again? Inevitably.

Why did you choose to become an agent? As an author, I was teaching in my spare time and began to get my students book contracts. I know the creative side and the business side of book publishing from having been involved in both sides for decades now. Unlike many agents, I'm an author and highly skilled editor myself.

Do you think many talented writers fail to get published for avoidable reasons? If so, what are some of those reasons? They don't know how to recognize what's wrong with the manuscript and need skills to hone a stronger story line, understand how point of view works, develop an authentic voice, restructure, or cut out the fat.

THE RUDY AGENCY ❖ rudyagency.com

Please list five books the agency recently represented. The Millennial Money Makeover by Conor Richardson (Red Wheel, Weiser); *Ghosted and Breadcrumbed* by Dr. Marni Feuerman (New World Library); *Isadora Duncan's Neck* by Tim Rayborn and Abigail Keyes (Skyhorse); *Murder in the News* by Robert Jordan, Jr. (Prometheus); *The Art of Creating Value* by Jeffrey Ansell (Praeger).

What should writers submit for consideration, and how should they send it? For nonfiction, send a relatively short query email that clearly states what the book is about, the genre, and why you are an appropriate person — or the best person — to write the book. If the query piques our interest, we will invite a proposal. The proposal should be emailed as a Word or PDF file and must contain both marketing-related information and a solid presentation of the editorial merits of the book. Include at least one sample chapter of the book and be clear about the status of the manuscript. For fiction, put a short synopsis and brief author bio in the body of an email. Please do not send the entire manuscript unless and until we ask you to send it.

Agent's name and contact info: Maryann Karinch, mak@rudyagency.com, 970-577-8500

What would you be doing right now if not responding to this survey? Catching up on my reading while sitting in front of a fire drinking spiked hot chocolate. (It's three days before Christmas.)

What would you be if not an agent (other than a dog, cat, or other mammal)? A writer. Oh, wait, I am a writer, too.

Do you think independent (noncorporate) publishing will be stronger, weaker, or the same over the next few years? Stronger.

Please describe your professional history. I have been a published author since 1994 and founded the Rudy Agency in 2004 when my agent had a baby. Before that, I did marketing communications for high-tech companies and trade groups. I am the author of 28 books, most of which focus on human health and behavior. I am a member of the Authors Guild and the Explorers Club and hold a BA and MA in speech and drama from the Catholic University of America, in Washington, DC. A former competitive athlete in gymnastics, bodybuilding, and adventure racing, I have also been a certified personal trainer through the American Council on Exercise since 1998.

How would you define the "client from hell"? Someone who thinks Copernicus was wrong, the Earth really is the center of the universe, and his or her house is the most important spot on Earth.

Do you think Earth was created a few thousand years ago or several billion years ago? I don't work for the CDC, so I'm allowed to say that I'm science-based.

Please describe the kinds of books you want to agent. Books that wake people up, get them exchanging ideas, and help make the world a better place.

How do you feel about self-publishing, and what do you see happening with it in the near future? It's perfect for authors who have identified a narrow market and know exactly how to reach that market. For example, someone queried me recently about a book aimed at families affected by a particular disease that very few people even know about. There is at least one organization that tries to inform and assist those families, so the channel to reach the audience is specific and in place.

Do you think there are too many, too few, or just enough agents? Just enough.

Do you think Amazon will become the country's largest employer within 10 years? Possibly. They are doing a lot of things right from the perspective of consumers.

Why do you think some books become super-successful (beyond the obvious reasons)? With nonfiction, it's because people whom readers respect tell them the book has information they must have or entertainment value that exceeds expectations. With fiction, I don't have any original thoughts, so all I would probably do is quote from *The Bestseller Code*.

Do you think agents are likely to become millionaires? Are pigs likely to get wings?

Do you think agents tend toward certain personality types? No, I don't. We exemplify diversity; I hear a version of that from authors fairly often.

Do you think writers tend to be more or less narcissistic than the population at large? No more and no less. I would describe most of the professional writers (as opposed to experts who happen to write) whom I've worked with as fearless and scared, ambitious and lazy, hopeful and depressed, overconfident and modest — just depends on how things are going at the moment.

Knowing what you know now, would you become an agent again? Yes.

Why did you choose to become an agent? I love nurturing talented people with an important message, and closing deals is fun.

Do you think many talented writers fail to get published for avoidable reasons? If so, what are some of those reasons? Yes. With nonfiction, many do not do their homework about the competitive landscape. They feel passionate about communicating what they know and perhaps do it very well, but don't take the competition seriously enough. And whether the work is fiction or nonfiction, they have to have a keen sense of whose critique has value. Refusing to rewrite something after a high-value critique is a self-sabotaging action.

Agent's name and contact info: Hilary Claggett, claggett@rudyagency.com

What would you be doing right now if not responding to this survey? Running, if not for the huge snowfall this morning.

What would you be if not an agent (other than a dog, cat, or other mammal)? A diplomat (per education), a lawyer, a journalist, a stand-up comedian, a bartender, or a musician.

Do you think independent (noncorporate) publishing will be stronger, weaker, or the same over the next few years? Stronger.

Please describe your professional history. I have worked in an editorial capacity in publishing for nearly 30 years, specializing in politics, international affairs, current events, history, military studies, journalism, environmentalism, business, economics, and finance. I have a master's degree in international affairs from Columbia University, where I specialized in Russian studies and national security, and a bachelor's degree in politics and Russian studies from the University of California. My hobbies have included motorcycle riding (2002–3), yoga (2004–7), and now running (2007–present). I have completed 173 races to date, including 3 50Ks, 14 marathons, 38 half marathons, and 38 5Ks.

How would you define the "client from hell"? Someone who refuses to write a book proposal and expects me to make a decision based solely on the manuscript. But then that person would not be a client. Also writers whose credentials are not related in the slightest to their manuscripts, the chief culprits being lawyers and engineers who want to fix the world's political or spiritual problems.

Do you think Earth was created a few thousand years ago or several billion years ago? Having been a reference editor for many years, I'm definitely pro-science. I also have a fondness for facts (and thorough documentation).

Please describe the kinds of books you want to agent. Books that make me think about something in a new way, inspire others, and contribute to the greater good.

How do you feel about self-publishing, and what do you see happening with it in the near future? Self-publishing is growing, and as it grows, so too does the variety in quality of self-publishing and hybrid "revenue-sharing" companies. Authors must be diligent in selecting a quality self-publisher — some are quite good, others have poor reputations. The most important thing an author should know about self-publishing is that we do not represent previously self-published authors. However, there are always exceptions — be upfront in disclosing whether your manuscript was self-published in any format, because we will discover it anyway.

Do you think there are too many, too few, or just enough agents? Certainly not too few.

Do you think Amazon will become the country's largest employer within 10 years? It depends on whether we count AI machines as employees, because in 10 years who knows what the mix will be. They might have the largest number of autonomous entities working without the largest number of humans employed, because AI may affect retail and supply chains more heavily (or earlier) than some other industries.

Why do you think some books become super-successful (beyond the obvious reasons)? I still have to read that book — it's on my shelf! For nonfiction, there is a strong correlation between sales and the author's existing marketing platform, specific marketing plan for the book, commitment, and energy. I once had a great book with a novel idea, flawless execution, and perfectly plausible marketing plan, but the author decided to turn his attention to producing a musical shortly after the book's publication. Needless to say, it died on the vine.

Do you think agents are likely to become millionaires? ☺

Do you think agents tend toward certain personality types? It helps to like meeting new people and learning new things, but any personality is capable of that.

Do you think writers tend to be more or less narcissistic than the population at large? I'll just say I've met more narcissists in other professions.

Knowing what you know now, would you become an agent again? Yes.

Why did you choose to become an agent? I love the unexpected nature of the work — you never know whom you'll meet or what you'll read, and sometimes it's very exciting. It's fun to look forward to checking email. It reminds me of the days when the postal mail actually contained pleasant surprises like letters or gifts, rather than bills and junk mail. Now email, too, is overwhelmed with promotions, petitions, and the like. So my agency email is free of all that electronic detritus.

Do you think many talented writers fail to get published for avoidable reasons? If so, what are some of those reasons? One of the biggest obstacles I've faced is authors who refuse to write their manuscript until they receive an advance. It is hard for publishers to make a decision sight unseen, especially if the manuscript is groundbreaking or interdisciplinary. Uncertainty does not lead to contract offers. This is not to say that one can't get a contract based on a proposal and a chapter or two. But if the book is unusual in any way, it's important to give publishers as much information about it as possible. Unrelated to that is an author's online presence. It's important that an author's profiles, comments, and activities are consistent with the book's message. This alignment makes social-media marketing possible, or at least much easier than it would be if you had some digital doppelgänger you were trying to hide.

SAVVY LITERARY SERVICES ❖ www.savvyliterary.com

3 Griffin Hill Court, The Woodlands, TX 77382, 281-465-0119; cell: 281-682-7518

Agent's name and contact info: Leticia Gomez, Founder and CEO, savvyliterary@yahoo.com

What would you be doing right now if not responding to this survey? Preparing manuscripts and book proposals for the submission process. Scouting for exciting, new projects to represent while drinking a glass of wine or sipping on a Lady Godiva chocolate martini.

What would you be if not an agent (other than a dog, cat, or other mammal)? A psychologist or life coach. I absolutely love talking to people and helping them get through the rough patches in their lives.

Do you think independent (noncorporate) publishing will be stronger, weaker, or the same over the next few years? Independent publishing is going to become more prevalent in the future. Mainstream corporate publishers are no longer giving away any "Get Published Free" cards as they did in the good ole days, leaving aspiring and emerging authors with no choice but to take matters into their own hands and publish independently (also see the question about self-publishing below).

Please describe your professional history. I've been working in the publishing industry since 1993. During this span of time, I have published my own newspaper, authored and published three books, and edited numerous fiction and nonfiction manuscripts written in both English and Spanish that have gone on to publication. Thus far in my career as a literary agent, I've placed more than 100 books and counting with independent and mainstream publishers. I have also brokered foreign translation rights and audio book rights. Several of my clients' published books and screenplays have been optioned for film and television.

As CEO and founder of Savvy Literary Services, one of the few minority-oriented publishing firms, I have worked hard to distinguish myself as a literary agent who can communicate effectively with the authors I represent. Four years ago, I began partnering with Ascendant Group, a branding and marketing firm, to offer an even greater level of support to aspiring authors. As director of Ascendant Publishing, I serve as the company's in-house publishing consultant and literary agent. Blending my experience as an author, literary agent, publishing consultant, and acquisitions editor, I am now truly excited to spearhead my own Hispanic book division, Café con Leche Books, which is an imprint of Atlanta-based Cosby Media Productions.

How would you define the "client from hell"? A client who is lazy and does not want to work with me toward publication has no business contacting me in the first place. Another definition of a "client from hell" is a writer who does not have a sense of humor.

Do you think Earth was created a few thousand years ago or several billion years ago? I am a firm believer in the seven creative days as described in the book of Genesis. I also believe that the way God views and measures time is completely different from the way humans do it.

Please list five books you recently agented. Enjeela Ahmadi-Miller's *The Walk*, a story of escape, adventure, endurance, determination, and self-will, as four children escape the war in Afghanistan and journey across Pakistan, Bangladesh, Nepal, and finally India to reunite with their family (to Erin Calligan-Mooney at Little A). New Orleans pastor Debra Morton's *Beyond the Storm: Coping Strategies to Thrive in the Aftermath of Any Challenge*, which will help people recover from the aftermath of tragedy, trauma, challenge, and crisis; find purpose in spite of it all; and push toward their destiny (to Jenny Baumgartner at Thomas Nelson, 2018). CEO of content-marketing firm T3 Custom Kevin Lund's *Conversation Marketing: How to Be Relevant, Involve Your Customer, and Communicate by Speaking Human*, which will help readers bridge the gap between traditional and New Age digital marketing (to Adam Schwartz at Career Press, 2018). Interventional cardiologist and chef Michael Fenster's *Food Shaman: The Art of Quantum Food*, which utilizes the tools of the ancient shamanic practitioners to provide the path to unleash our creative, healing energies in an easy-to-read, entertaining mix of well-researched scientific studies, new theories, entertaining stories and anecdotes, and thought-provoking perceptions across the spectrums of the human food experience (to Anthony Ziccardi at Post Hill Press, 2018). CEO of Alpha Shark Trading Andrew Keene's *Airbnb: A 21st-Century Goldmine*, in which the author offers his expertise and fresh perspective of the Airbnb model in a way that helps travelers and potential investors gain clarity on the whole new world of opportunities that it has opened up (to Anthony Ziccardi at Post Hill Press, 2018).

Please describe the kinds of books you want to agent. I am seeking book proposals and manuscripts written in English or Spanish in the following genres. Fiction: suspense thrillers, mystery, women's commercial fiction, fantasy, historical, humor, multicultural, paranormal, romance, erotica, young adult, and middle grade. Nonfiction: advice/relationship, biography, business, cooking, diet, health, history, politics, current affairs, how-to, humor, lifestyle, memoir, pop culture, parenting, religion/spirituality, sports, and true crime.

What should writers submit for consideration, and how should they send it? Please send me your best query via email and include synopsis and the first three chapters for fiction works or a completed book proposal for nonfiction projects.

How do you feel about self-publishing, and what do you see happening with it in the near future? I used to strongly advocate that authors should only self-publish their works as a last resort, when all hope had been lost of landing a traditional publishing deal. In my opinion, the two greatest challenges of self-publishing are that it requires authors to promote and market their books to the point of physical exhaustion and practically going broke and the lack of national print and ebook distribution. The chances of self-publishing success were extremely slim. However, the publishing landscape has changed dramatically.

In recent years a new model of publication known as independent/entrepreneurial publishing has been gaining more and more traction. The beauty of this new model is that it allows authors to keep all creative control of their content. In other words, they call all the shots while keeping the majority of the royalties. The best part of all is that national print and ebook distribution services that were once an elusive dream for self-published authors are now so easy to obtain. Of course, the best-case scenario for any author is to get published by Penguin Random House, HarperCollins, Simon & Schuster, the Hachette Book Group, or others like them. But for any author who has been forsaken by the Big 5, independent/entrepreneurial publishing makes a great consolation prize.

Do you think there are too many, too few, or just enough agents? I happen to think there is an extremely large quantity of literary agents these days, but they are not necessarily high-quality. Agents have become notorious for being unresponsive, difficult to reach, close-minded, arrogant, and on the lookout for an easy sale that doesn't require much leg work. More agents who have a strong work ethic and do not give up easily are needed.

Of course, I can't speak for other literary agents out there, but I operate on the basis of an open-door policy. When my clients wish to speak with me, all they have to do is pick up the phone and chances are I will answer it live. They don't have to hire a private detective to find me when I'm needed the most. If I don't happen to be available when they call, I will normally return their call within 24 to 48 hours. I sometimes joke with them by saying that if more than a week goes by without my returning their call, it means something has gone terribly wrong in my life or I am lying unconscious in a ditch somewhere. The point is I give each and every one of my clients easy access to me anytime they want it. And like my own children, they are always in the back of my mind. In a nutshell, I have a sunny disposition and wicked sense of humor (imagine finding that quality in a literary agent) and have been told that I have a heart the size of the Grand Canyon. My son once described me as an "Explosion of Sunshine" in a poem he was required to write in the sixth grade.

Do you think Amazon will become the country's largest employer within 10 years? As future generations become more and more isolated and dependent on technology, which grants instant gratification, I definitely foresee Amazon becoming one of the country's largest employers. Millennials and Generation Z would rather shop online than take a trip to the local mall.

Why do you think some books become super-successful (beyond the obvious reasons)? Every once in a blue moon, a book will come along that is highly unique in its content or fills a void that has been missing in the marketplace. The book's author is a lean, mean marketing machine who goes the extra mile to promote and market it every single day, at every given opportunity. Although the aforementioned are factors that definitely come into play whether a book is successful or not, ultimately it is up to the "publishing gods" to decide which books will become super-successful and which ones will tank miserably. In other words, sometimes it all just boils down to blind and dumb luck.

Do you think agents are likely to become millionaires? Realistically speaking, the majority of working literary agents today will never become millionaires unless all the stars in the universe become aligned just write (pun intended) and the publishing gods see fit to smile upon them. Granted, there are some agents who have become millionaires, but they are an exception to the rule. The truth is that for most of us, it's either feast or famine. I would love to become a millionaire — I mean what self-respecting agent in their right mind wouldn't want to reach super-rich status? I decided a long time ago to measure my success by the number of books I've placed and dreams I have made come true rather than by how much money I've made. I also make it a point to remind myself repeatedly that I became an agent because this is my passion, my true calling in life, and I believe in the power of the written word. End of story.

Do you think agents tend toward certain personality types? One of the things I tell my clients when I first begin working with them is that this is a highly subjective business. Many times, it all just boils down to a matter of personal taste. Each and every agent is a unique individual, and of course they will gravitate toward certain personality types. As for me, I like working with people who have a strong work ethic and a good sense of humor, because, believe me, in the brutal book-publishing world, there will always be a need for comic relief. I look for clients who are open-minded, take constructive criticism well, and are willing to put their full trust in me. If a client doesn't trust me, our relationship just isn't going to work out.

Do you think writers tend to be more or less narcissistic than the population at large? I don't necessarily think creative types are more or less narcissistic than noncreative individuals. It's really an individual trait on a case-by-case basis.

Knowing what you know now, would you become an agent again? I honestly don't think I would have done anything different, because it has been a truly incredible journey.

Why did you choose to become an agent? I chose to become an agent to help as many Latino and other ethnic minority writers as possible get their literary works published. Because, let's face it, these are the writers who are oftentimes underrepresented, misrepresented, or, worse yet, not represented at all. However, the landscape of publishing has changed so much since I first opened my doors. It seems as though, these days, any writer who has a pulse falls into the category of being an "underdog writer." I also became a literary agent because I needed a profession that was going to give me the flexibility to raise my children and always be there for them while they were growing up.

Do you think many talented writers fail to get published for avoidable reasons? If so, what are some of those reasons? The world is filled with talented writers. But what separates the successful ones from the ones who fail is the amount of grit they possess. A writer who does not procrastinate and has the ability to crank out one high-quality book manuscript after another will become published more often than those who are not proactive.

THE SCHISGAL AGENCY, LLC ❖ www.theschisgalagency.com

Agent's name and contact info: Zachary Schisgal, zach@theschisgalagency.com

What would you be doing right now if not responding to this survey? I would be sending an email, working on a proposal, or scrolling Instagram, alas.

What would you be if not an agent (other than a dog, cat, or other mammal)? I would be an editor, as I was for many years. There's a satisfaction in helping writers and creative people bring a vision to life, whatever the format or category.

Do you think independent (noncorporate) publishing will be stronger, weaker, or the same over the next few years? It will be weaker because of Amazon. But the resurgence of independent booksellers is a great thing for everyone — especially the communities they serve. Certainly, the continued merger of large publishers creates opportunities for smaller publishers, of which there are many really, really good ones.

Please describe your professional history. I was an editor for 20 years at William Morrow, Random House, and Simon & Schuster. I worked on a broad range of projects with a focus on commercial nonfiction.

How would you define the "client from hell"? The client from hell is rude and unprofessional to the people with whom he or she works. I'm pretty thick-skinned, but it's not acceptable for a client to be abusive toward a publicist or editor even when there are some difficult issues.

Do you think Earth was created a few thousand years ago or several billion years ago? I'll go with science on this one: several billion. But we are stardust ultimately.

Please list five books you recently agented. *Jimmy Buffett: A Good Life All the Way* by Ryan White; *Raw. Vegan. Not Gross* by Laura Miller; *The Selfie Vote* by Kristen Soltis Anderson; *Muskets & Applejack* by Mark Will-Weber; *Navy Seal Art of War* by Rob Roy.

Please describe the kinds of books you want to agent. Commercial fiction and nonfiction. In fiction, genre fiction like mystery or thriller that is meant to launch a series or presents a protagonist who can inhabit future works. In nonfiction, works written by authors for a known, intended audience that the author has a vehicle to reach (social media, TV, newspapers, etc.). But no memoir or fiction written by a first-person narrator.

What should writers submit for consideration, and how should they send it? I am happy to consider works sent by email with a Word doc or PDF. A cover letter, outline, and sample chapter are sufficient.

How do you feel about self-publishing, and what do you see happening with it in the near future? Self-publishing has always been a vibrant and important part of publishing. It will evolve as mobile companies get into the game and as works like fan fiction continue to be crowd-sourced.

Do you think there are too many, too few, or just enough agents? It's free market. The number changes to suit the marketplace.

Do you think Amazon will become the country's largest employer within 10 years? Probably not.

Why do you think some books become super-successful (beyond the obvious reasons)? With the focus on media and social media, we tend to overlook the immense effect of good old-fashioned word of mouth.

Do you think agents are likely to become millionaires? Not many. But a great editor I knew once remarked that when editors die, the obituary reads, "Lived in New York" (for example), but when agents die, it reads, "Lived in New York and Southampton."

Do you think agents tend toward certain personality types? Yes.

Do you think writers tend to be more or less narcissistic than the population at large? Let's just say that it's a function of spending a lot of time alone looking inward.

Knowing what you know now, would you become an agent again? I love agenting. Books are a hugely important part of our culture and history, but other forms of media have had a remarkable impact in recent years.

Why did you choose to become an agent? It shares many qualities with editing, from which I derive satisfaction. But it also comes with a financial stake in projects that editors don't share. That said, it's much more speculative.

Do you think many talented writers fail to get published for avoidable reasons? If so, what are some of those reasons? I am generally optimistic about a good book's chances of being published. But "being published" means many different things in this day and age. It might ultimately not be the publisher or format that an author had hoped for. Or it might not find its audience after publication for countless reasons. Publishers want good books on their list. I think part of that talent also has to be authors' ability to listen to the marketplace and make reasonable changes if they are not getting the response they hoped for.

SECOND CITY PUBLISHING SERVICES, LLC ❖
www.secondcitypublishing.com

Agent's name and contact info: Cynthia Zigmund, cynthia@secondcitypublishing.com

What would you be doing right now if not responding to this survey? Reviewing queries and proposals and pitching books to editors.

What would you be if not an agent (other than a dog, cat, or other mammal)? I love what I do; I don't waste my time thinking about what else I could be doing.

Do you think independent (noncorporate) publishing will be stronger, weaker, or the same over the next few years? Stronger; I'm already seeing an impact. Independents are willing to take risks corporations can't (or don't want to). Independents can afford to lead instead of follow when it comes to new ideas. Some of the best new books are coming out of independent presses — and people are beginning to notice.

Please describe your professional history. I've been in publishing my entire career, first as a publisher and now as an agent. Before founding Second City Publishing Services, I spent more than 20 years in New York and Chicago publishing, including positions at John Wiley & Sons and Irwin Professional Publishing (now McGraw-Hill). Six months after joining Dearborn Trade Publishing (now Kaplan Publishing) as executive editor, I was promoted to editorial director, and six months after that, I was named vice president and publisher. During my 10 years with Kaplan, the company released several business bestsellers and became a leading business-book publisher. After leaving Kaplan in 2006, I started Second City Publishing Services, an agency I run with my husband and business partner, Richard.

How would you define the "client from hell"? One who does not listen (and always second-guesses their agent and editor), is unwilling to accept feedback, and doesn't treat their book as a priority. If you don't take your career as a writer seriously, we aren't interested.

Do you think Earth was created a few thousand years ago or several billion years ago? You're kidding, right?

Please list five books you recently agented. *The Introvert's Edge* by Matthew Pollard, *Death at the Emerald* by Richard Koreto, *The Fifth Reflection* by Ellen Kirschman, *Think like an Entrepreneur* by Beverly Jones, *Decision Time* by Greg Bustin.

Please describe the kinds of books you want to agent. We are primarily interested in nonfiction books that are written by experts in their respective fields with a platform to support their books. Topics include business, current affairs, and science and nature. We are also interested in mystery as well as commercial and literary fiction.

What should writers submit for consideration, and how should they send it? Our guidelines are available at our website. For nonfiction we need a complete proposal (including a full marketing plan and sample chapter). For fiction, a finished manuscript — but please don't send us your novel until and unless you feel it is perfect and you've gotten feedback from your writing group.

How do you feel about self-publishing, and what do you see happening with it in the near future? We work with authors who do both; every project is different, and sometimes it's the better choice for a project. Self-publishing options continue to expand, and we're seeing more choices, but with that comes more pressure on authors to invest in marketing, promoting, and selling. But please don't come to us after you've self-published a book and sold 50 copies, now expecting us to find a commercial publisher for it.

Do you think there are too many, too few, or just enough agents? You can never have enough good agents.

Do you think Amazon will become the country's largest employer within 10 years? Don't know, and not sure I care.

Why do you think some books become super-successful (beyond the obvious reasons)? There are lots of reasons, but success is primarily due to luck and/or a strong platform.

Do you think agents are likely to become millionaires? I sure hope so.

Do you think agents tend toward certain personality types? Every agent, just like every author and every editor, cannot be lumped into a one-size-fits-all description.

Do you think writers tend to be more or less narcissistic than the population at large? See my answer to the above question.

Knowing what you know now, would you become an agent again? You bet.

Why did you choose to become an agent? I loved publishing (still do), but I was spending too much time in meetings and not enough time working with authors — plus, I wanted to take control of my life.

Do you think many talented writers fail to get published for avoidable reasons? If so, what are some of those reasons? Too many talented writers (fiction and nonfiction) don't understand that, at its core, publishing is a business. Publishers are in business to sell books. Too many talented writers aren't willing to put in the effort to make their book successful. For a fiction author that may mean having your manuscript professionally copyedited before sending it to an agent (or publisher). For a nonfiction author, that means having a strong and complete proposal and samples chapter(s). Too many talented writers assume that if they write it, people will buy it. Writing is only part of the formula for success. Your ability to market and sell yourself is a tipping point when it comes to success.

SEVENTH AVENUE LITERARY AGENCY ❖ www.seventhavenuelit.com

2052 124th Street, South Surrey, BC V4A 9K3, Canada

Agent's name and contact info: Robert Mackwood, Owner and Principal Agent, info@seventhavenuelit.com

What would you be doing right now if not responding to this survey? Reading manuscripts.

What would you be if not an agent (other than a dog, cat, or other mammal)? A high-school teacher.

Do you think independent (noncorporate) publishing will be stronger, weaker, or the same over the next few years? Stronger.

Please describe your professional history. This year will be my 35th year in book publishing: 8 years in Vancouver as senior publicist at Raincoast Books; 8 years at Bantam/Doubleday Canada in Toronto as VP, director of publicity and promotion; and 19 years back in Vancouver as a literary agent.

How would you define the "client from hell"? Someone who is extremely impatient — publishing is a marathon, not a sprint.

Do you think Earth was created a few thousand years ago or several billion years ago? Really?

Please list five books you recently agented. *Your Heart Is the Size of Your Fist*, a memoir (Brindle & Glass, a BC-based publisher); *The Idea of Canada: Letters from Our Governor-General* (Penguin Random House Canada); *Like Water over Stone*, a memoir (HarperCollins Canada); *The Mirror Method* (Brilliant Idea Books); *Headhunting for Ghosts* (Skyhorse, NYC).

Please describe the kinds of books you want to agent. Nonfiction only, *please*.

What should writers submit for consideration, and how should they send it? Send a query first, no attachments *ever* until asked. Do not send a query to multiple agents in one email — this will be deleted instantly, with no consideration — just so wrong.

How do you feel about self-publishing, and what do you see happening with it in the near future? It will ultimately be the only future.

Do you think there are too many, too few, or just enough agents? Too many — including me — and there will be a culling sometime soon.

Do you think Amazon will become the country's largest employer within 10 years? No.

Why do you think some books become super-successful (beyond the obvious reasons)? I am only speaking of nonfiction here: this will be an increasingly rare occurrence. A book has to be part of the everyday lexicon in our language — the "tipping point" as an example — and these used to happen much more frequently. That is what I consider to be super-successful.

Do you think agents are likely to become millionaires? Really?

Do you think agents tend toward certain personality types? To some degree — yes.

Do you think writers tend to be more or less narcissistic than the population at large? To some degree — yes.

Knowing what you know now, would you become an agent again? For the satisfaction of helping someone see their book well published and received — yes. For financial gain, no.

Why did you choose to become an agent? I liked the challenge of trying to find something publishers would publish.

Do you think many talented writers fail to get published for avoidable reasons? If so, what are some of those reasons? If someone is talented, they must reach out, understand something about publishing, share their work, listen, and be ready for rejection until someone sees that talent. That is usually a long road.

SHEREE BYKOFSKY ASSOCIATES, INC. ❖ shereebee.com

PO Box 706, Brigantine, NJ 08203

Agents' names and contact info: Sheree Bykofsky, President, shereebee@aol.com; Janet Rosen, janetellenrosen@gmail.com

What would you be doing right now if not responding to this survey? *Sheree*: Watching a cooking show like *Top Chef*, playing with a bulldog, or playing poker.

What would you be if not an agent (other than a dog, cat, or other mammal)? An attorney.

Do you think independent (noncorporate) publishing will be stronger, weaker, or the same over the next few years? Stronger.

Please describe your professional history. I have worked in almost every aspect of publishing. I have a master's in English and comparative literature from Columbia University. I was production manager at Bard Hall Press, executive editor at the Chiron Press, executive editor at the Stonesong Press, freelance accounting book editor at Macmillan (simultaneously), book author (simultaneously) of over 30 books, including five editions of *The Complete Idiot's Guide to Getting Published* (Alpha) by Sheree Bykofsky and Jennifer Basye Sanders (not for idiots) and my newest book, *The Kaizen of Poker* (ECW Press). I founded Sheree Bykofsky Associates, Inc., in 1991 in New York City and have been progressively building it. I moved my agency to New Jersey in 2007, but we are still a New York company. In recent years, I have absorbed the Doris S. Michaels Literary Agency and have exponentially increased my international deals.

How would you define the "client from hell"? It's very rare, thankfully. A client from hell would be a nonappreciative author who thinks agents are their hired assistants who should work according to the author's guidelines and not the agency's.

Do you think Earth was created a few thousand years ago or several billion years ago? I believe in the big-bang theory and am also a spiritual person.

Please list five books you recently agented. *Cells Are the New Cure* by Robin L. Smith and Max Gomez (BenBella); *Radical Repair* (working title) by Donald Laub, MD, and Judith Stone (ECW); *Calculus Workbook for Dummies*, 3rd ed., by Mark Ryan (Wiley); *Rock & Roll Women* by Meredith Ochs (Sterling); *Breast Cancer Survival Manual*, 6th ed., by John Link, MD (Holt).

Please describe the kinds of books you want to agent. We have wide-ranging interests and thus an eclectic list. Primarily we want to see books that help the world or entertain, with a special interest in health, business, and pop culture. I would also love to find a page-turning commercial novel with literary appeal by an author with a unique voice. Janet Rosen (janetellenrosen@gmail.com) is concentrating more on our nonfiction portfolio.

What should writers submit for consideration, and how should they send it? Please see our website, shereebee.com, for submission guidelines. Send a query with no attachments to shereebee.com or submitbee.com or directly to Janet Rosen at janetellenrosen@gmail.com.

How do you feel about self-publishing, and what do you see happening with it in the near future? The promise of it seems to be better than the results. It has become a viable option for authors, unlike the vanity self-publishing in days of yore, but authors overall do better when they traverse the normal route of finding an agent and having the agent place their books with appropriate publishers.

Do you think there are too many, too few, or just enough agents? Just enough.

Do you think Amazon will become the country's largest employer within 10 years? Perhaps.

Why do you think some books become super-successful (beyond the obvious reasons)? Publicity, good and bad. Authors who do what it takes to promote their works tend to do better than authors who leave it to the publisher and chance.

Do you think agents are likely to become millionaires? No.

Do you think agents tend toward certain personality types? Interesting question. I do have several good friends who are agents, such as Katharine Sands and Rita Rosenkranz, to name just two. We do have a lot in common, but we are also very different. Overall, I would say we have more in common with each other than most people have in common.

Do you think writers tend to be more or less narcissistic than the population at large? No.

Knowing what you know now, would you become an agent again? It's my passion. And it's rewarding. Emphatically, yes.

Why did you choose to become an agent? I was given the opportunity to start my own business while working for a book producer who suggested it. It was a natural progression in my publishing path and utilized all of my skills.

Do you think many talented writers fail to get published for avoidable reasons? If so, what are some of those reasons? They need to learn the publishing process, conduct themselves like published authors, and thus take all of the same steps a professional writer would take to the best of their ability. That's why I wrote five editions of *The Complete Idiot's Guide to Getting Published*, to help authors approach the process correctly. It's a win-win. When authors succeed, everyone succeeds: agents, publishers, authors, and most notably readers.

SIGNATURE LITERARY AGENCY ❖ signaturelit.com

4200 Wisconsin Avenue NW, #106-233, Washington, DC 20016

Agent's name and contact info: Gary Heidt, gary@signaturelit.com

What would you be doing right now if not responding to this survey? Dandling my wee babe.

What would you be if not an agent (other than a dog, cat, or other mammal)? A street fighter.

Do you think independent (noncorporate) publishing will be stronger, weaker, or the same over the next few years? The same.

Please describe your professional history. I started in 2003 just after moving into an apartment that had been previously occupied by another agent (whom I never met). There must have been a sort of field.

How would you define the "client from hell"? One who is mean.

Do you think Earth was created a few thousand years ago or several billion years ago? I think we each create our own worlds a million times every second (the breath of Brahma).

Please list five books you recently agented. *The Devil's Mercedes* by Rob Klara, *The Insides* by Jeremy Bushnell, *Old Lonesome* by Benjamin Whitmer, *After the Flare* by Deji Olukotun, and *Sacred Geometry of the Earth* by Mark Vidler and Catherine Young.

Describe the kinds of books you want to agent. Books that will stand the test of time.

What should writers submit for consideration, and how should they send it? A page-length query, via email, along with the first five pages, for fiction.

How do you feel about self-publishing, and what do you see happening with it in the near future? I own a lot of self-published books. Gertrude Stein and Walt Whitman self-published. I especially like hand-bound self-published books by original thinkers. But PODs are great too.

Do you think there are too many, too few, or just enough agents? I don't know how I would decide an answer to that question.

Do you think Amazon will become the country's largest employer within 10 years? Depends on whether robots are counted in the employment figures in 10 years.

Why do you think some books become super-successful (beyond the obvious reasons)? Because they are purchased by people who never read books.

Do you think agents are likely to become millionaires? No, unless we have hyperinflation.

Do you think agents tend toward certain personality types? They tend to be intelligent and fairly independent, but other than that they seem to be a diverse crowd.

Do you think writers tend to be more or less narcissistic than the population at large? More, but the very best ones tend to be humble and self-effacing in my experience.

Knowing what you know now, would you become an agent again? Sure.

Why did you choose to become an agent? I like to read.

Do you think many talented writers fail to get published for avoidable reasons? If so, what are some of those reasons? A lot of very talented writers fail to get published, but mainly because the demand for books is low.

SIMENAUER & GREEN LITERARY AGENCY, LLC ❖

sgliteraryagency.com

PO Box 112735, Naples FL 34108

Agents' names and contact info: Jackie Simenauer, jackie@sgliteraryagency.com; Carol Green, carolgreen2@mac.com

What would you be doing right now if not responding to this survey? Carol: Reading.

What would you be if not an agent (other than a dog, cat, or other mammal)? A reporter at the *Washington Post.*

Do you think independent (noncorporate) publishing will be stronger, weaker, or the same over the next few years? Stronger, because it is beginning to carve out niches of quality.

Please describe your professional history. Newspaper reporter for 20 years; lawyer; various management positions in business departments at *Newsday* in Long Island; retired as senior VP and general counsel for the *Denver Post.*

How would you define the "client from hell"? Inflexible, won't take feedback. Emotionally needy and impatient. Mistakes me for "Mother."

Do you think Earth was created a few thousand years ago or several billion years ago? Several billion, and it's still evolving. What a terrifying and wonderful story…

Please list five books you recently agented. Overwatch by Matthew Betley, *Oath of Honor* by Matthew Betley, *Jade's Treasure* by Ana Krista Johnson, *The Insulin-Resistance Diet* by Dr. Cheryle Hart, *I Was a War Child* by Helene Gaillet de Neergaard.

Please describe the kinds of books you want to agent. Thrillers, literary fiction, nonfiction (business, environment, contemplative spirituality, to name just a few of many possible subjects), memoir. Debut authors welcome.

What should writers submit for consideration, and how should they send it? Via email. Fiction: full manuscript with cover letter. Nonfiction: complete proposal and developed "platform" to support marketing (e.g., expertise in the field, presence in the community, strong Web following). *Note: Authors should not send material until they have done everything in their power to make it ready for publication — eliminate sloppiness, clean up grammar and punctuation, fill in "gaps" in the story or logic, cite references in nonfiction, answer the reader's questions before they are asked.*

How do you feel about self-publishing, and what do you see happening with it in the near future? It is an important outlet for writers. We hope mainstream publishers begin to see it as a "training farm" for talent rather than a reason to exclude writers' work.

Do you think there are too many, too few, or just enough agents? Who knows? It will sort itself out!

Do you think Amazon will become the country's largest employer within 10 years? Looks that way, doesn't it?

Why do you think some books become super-successful (beyond the obvious reasons)? The subject matter catches a trend on the upswing at the right moment.

Do you think agents are likely to become millionaires? Hah! Only a few. We love it anyway.

Do you think agents tend toward certain personality types? Probably. Skeptical, yet vulnerable. Demanding, yet a soft touch. Perfectionists. Driven, yet sometimes lazy. Insanely, incurably curious.

Do you think writers tend to be more or less narcissistic than the population at large? In a world filled with narcissists (at least in developed Western societies), writing is right up there with selfies. It just takes more effort.

Knowing what you know now, would you become an agent again? Yes.

Why did you choose to become an agent? I think I mentioned insanely, incurably curious…

Do you think many talented writers fail to get published for avoidable reasons? If so, what are some of those reasons? Inability to absorb feedback and lack of patience.

SPEILBURG LITERARY AGENCY ❖ speilburgliterary.com

Agent's name and contact info: Alice Speilburg, alice@speilburgliterary.com

What would you be doing right now if not responding to this survey? Finishing notes on a requested manuscript.

What would you be if not an agent (other than a dog, cat, or other mammal)? The director of a literary nonprofit.

Do you think independent (noncorporate) publishing will be stronger, weaker, or the same over the next few years? As corporate publishers continue to focus on "bestseller" lists, with fewer midlist and risky acquisitions, small presses will have better material to work with and will become stronger over the next few years.

Please describe your professional history. I worked at John Wiley & Sons before moving to Howard Morhaim Literary and then launching my own agency, Speilburg Literary Agency.

How would you define the "client from hell"? Luckily, I don't have one, but I imagine it would be an author who refuses to make suggested changes to a manuscript, who badgers the agent to send the book to specific editors whom the agent knows will not have an interest in it, who expects the world but won't heed the agent's advice on how to make it happen.

Do you think Earth was created a few thousand years ago or several billion years ago? Several billion years ago.

Please list five books you recently agented. *Barrel-Aged Stout and Selling Out* by Josh Noel, *Jason Molina: Riding with the Ghost* by Erin Osmon, *Sawbones* by Melissa Lenhardt, *Devil and the Bluebird* by Jennifer Mason-Black, *The Fisher King* by Melissa Lenhardt.

Please describe the kinds of books you want to agent. In fiction, I want mystery; fantasy that features women, magic, and folklore; historical novels that reimagine true events or expand on a detail that has been completely lost to history. In nonfiction, I want journalistic narratives that explore a part of our culture (in food, music, literature, etc.); popular-science narratives written by scientists; historical narratives that provide a new perspective on the given topic.

What should writers submit for consideration, and how should they send it? For fiction, please submit a query and the first three chapters. For nonfiction, please submit a query and a proposal. All submissions should be sent to speilburgliterary@gmail.com and should include my name in the subject line.

How do you feel about self-publishing, and what do you see happening with it in the near future? It serves a great purpose, giving writers an outlet for publishing when the market turns them down or if they simply want to publish their memoir for family and friends, but too many writers underestimate the commitment involved and end up doing harm to their potential careers in the long run.

Do you think there are too many, too few, or just enough agents? Publishers probably think there are too many; authors would say there are too few. I think perhaps there are just enough of us.

Do you think Amazon will become the country's largest employer within 10 years? I hope not.

Why do you think some books become super-successful (beyond the obvious reasons)? A blink of luck. A great review here, a chance interview there, a swing in the news cycle that makes the book's topic suddenly relevant. Many great books, with brilliant writing, beautiful storytelling, and esteemed publishers, never make that mark.

Do you think agents are likely to become millionaires? Some of them, but of course it depends on the strength of their client list.

Do you think agents tend toward certain personality types? Agents must be stubborn and determined, but there's also a degree of empathy required (or perhaps acquired through much reading of books) to be a sounding board for so many authors day in and day out.

Do you think writers tend to be more or less narcissistic than the population at large? I tend to think it's a wash. Even the most narcissistic writers can be humbled by a royalty statement.

Knowing what you know now, would you become an agent again? Absolutely.

Why did you choose to become an agent? For the love of books, and admiration and gratitude for those who write them. Being a part of a book from the very beginning is something special.

STEELE-PERKINS LITERARY AGENCY ❖

Agent's name and contact info: Pattie Steele-Perkins, pattiesp@aol.com

What would you be doing right now if not responding to this survey? Reading manuscripts.

Please describe your professional history. Prior to becoming an agent, I was creative director of a major television production company, and before that I was a producer/director. Those positions prepared me to work with creative people.

How would you define the "client from hell"? One who rants and raves online about their editor and publisher.

Please describe the kinds of books you want to agent. Romance novels and women's fiction.

What should writers submit for consideration, and how should they send it? An in-depth synopsis included in an email. No attachments.

Knowing what you know now, would you become an agent again? Absolutely.

Why did you choose to become an agent? I love to read, and I love working with creative people. What better job could a person have than reading the works of the most creative people in the world!!!!!

THE STEPHANIE TADE AGENCY ❖ www.stephanietadeagency.com

7a North Bank Street, Easton, PA 18042

Agents' names and contact info: Stephanie Tade, stade@stadeagency.com; Colleen Martell cmartell@stadeagency.com

What would you be doing right now if not responding to this survey? Stephanie: Answering too many emails to count! Reading something, negotiating something, responding to someone, finding a new client, finding a new writer for a new client, finding a publisher for a new client. Or helping to resettle some refugees.

What would you be if not an agent (other than a dog, cat, or other mammal)? Maybe a shrink, or a meditation teacher.

Do you think independent (noncorporate) publishing will be stronger, weaker, or the same over the next few years? If they are innovators.

Please describe your professional history. Publisher (couple of years), agent (long time), publisher (a few years), agent and agency owner (long time).

How would you define the "client from hell"? Usually someone driven by jealousy, competition, and small-mindedness. I don't mind a lot of work or demands, if someone has a clear message and a passion to get it out there.

Do you think Earth was created a few thousand years ago or several billion years ago? Ha — I'll take the latter. I'm a Buddhist — we tend to align with science rather than beliefs.

Please list five books you recently agented. In Her Own Time by Alisa Vitti; The Autoimmune Solution Cookbook by Amy Myers, MD; How to Be Well by Frank Lipman, MD; How to Stay Human in a F*ed Up World by Timothy Desmond; Standing at the Edge by Roshi Joan Halifax.

Please describe the kinds of books you want to agent. Books that improve, enlighten, uplift, inform.

What should writers submit for consideration, and how should they send it? A digital query. If I say yes, then a proposal.

How do you feel about self-publishing, and what do you see happening with it in the near future? Self-publishing can be a really smart way for people to go and to get educated about what it takes to make a book successful. The problem is overpublishing and confusion.

Do you think there are too many, too few, or just enough agents? I don't really have an opinion on that.

Do you think Amazon will become the country's largest employer within 10 years? Probably.

Why do you think some books become super-successful (beyond the obvious reasons)? They strike the right chord at the right time, with an author's platform that speaks to the right audience for the message.

Do you think agents are likely to become millionaires? *Likely* would be a really strong word…

Do you think agents tend toward certain personality types? Well, I think it's hard to be an agent if you don't know how to express yourself clearly, and repeatedly, and then say it again.

Do you think writers tend to be more or less narcissistic than the population at large? Taking the fifth on that one.

Knowing what you know now, would you become an agent again? Absolutely. I love what I do.

Why did you choose to become an agent? My entire family is made up of writers, artists, singers, and other creatives. Agenting was a way to advocate for creative people, and I believe innovators and creatives will save the world. Not being ironic or sarcastic.

Do you think many talented writers fail to get published for avoidable reasons? If so, what are some of those reasons? Usually not understanding how to build a launching pad.

STONESONG ❖ stonesong.com

270 West 39th Street, New York, NY 10018, 212-929-4600

Agent's name and contact info: Leila Campoli, submissions@stonesong.com

What would you be doing right now if not responding to this survey? Revising a proposal.

What would you be if not an agent (other than a dog, cat, or other mammal)? A jeweler.

Do you think independent (noncorporate) publishing will be stronger, weaker, or the same over the next few years? I hope it will be stronger.

Please describe your professional history. Editor to agent.

How would you define the "client from hell"? A "client from hell" doesn't really want to write a book.

Do you think Earth was created a few thousand years ago or several billion years ago? Several billion.

Please list five books you recently agented. The Million-Dollar One Person Business by Elaine Pofeldt (Lorena Jones Books), *The Science of Selling* by David Hoffeld (Tarcher Perigee), *Next Is Now* by Lior Arussy (Simon & Schuster), *The Person You Mean to Be* by Dolly Chugh (HarperBusiness), *Real Queer America* by Samantha Allen (Little, Brown).

Please describe the kinds of books you want to agent. Serious nonfiction, including business, scientific personal development, science, narrative, current events, and issue-based memoir.

What should writers submit for consideration, and how should they send it? Writers should send me an email and mention my name in the email's subject line. Queries should be about a page and mention a brief description of their book, who they are, and why they're the perfect person to write this book.

How do you feel about self-publishing, and what do you see happening with it in the near future? Self-publishing can be the perfect fit for certain authors. Hopefully self-publishing services will serve authors more and more in the future.

Do you think there are too many, too few, or just enough agents? There's always room for a few more dedicated agents.

Do you think Amazon will become the country's largest employer within 10 years? No.

Why do you think some books become super-successful (beyond the obvious reasons)? Timing.

Do you think agents are likely to become millionaires? No.

Do you think agents tend toward certain personality types? No.

Do you think writers tend to be more or less narcissistic than the population at large? Less.

Knowing what you know now, would you become an agent again? Yes.

Why did you choose to become an agent? I wanted to be able to say yes to authors.

Do you think many talented writers fail to get published for avoidable reasons? If so, what are some of those reasons? Yes. Some writers want to make sure the book idea is perfect before sharing it with anyone else. In my corner of nonfiction, it's always helpful for authors to chat with their colleagues and confidants about what they're working on. Appealing to readers is a tricky business, so the more you can field-test, the better.

Agent's name and contact info: Melissa Edwards, submissions@stonesong.com

Please describe your professional history. I joined Stonesong as a literary agent in August 2016. Previously, I was a literary agent at the Aaron Priest Literary Agency, where I managed the foreign rights for a 40-year backlist. After graduating from Washington University in St. Louis and Vanderbilt Law School, I began my career as a litigation attorney before transitioning into publishing.

Please describe the kinds of books you want to agent. I am looking for warm and timeless middle grade fiction, lively and fun young adult fiction, commercial women's fiction and thrillers, and select pop-culture nonfiction.

Agent's name and contact info: Alison Fargis, Partner, submissions@stonesong.com

Please describe your professional history. I joined Stonesong in 1995, and in 2002 my business partner, Ellen Scordato, and I purchased the company from its founder. My list includes a wide range of bestselling and critically acclaimed titles in subjects ranging from food and wine, lifestyle, pop culture, how-to, and diet to middle grade, young adult, and adult fiction. My roster of authors includes Deb Perelman (*The Smitten Kitchen Cookbook* and *Smitten Kitchen Every Day*), Michael Buckley (*The Sisters Grimm* series, *NERDS* series, *Undertow* trilogy, and the forthcoming *Finn and the Intergalactic Lunchbox* series), Erin Gleeson (*The Forest Feast*, *The Forest Feast for Kids*, *The Forest Feast Gatherings*, and the forthcoming *The Forest Feast Away*), Coco Morante (*The Essential Instant Pot Cookbook*), Stephanie Diaz (*Extraction* trilogy), Alex Myers (*Revolutionary*), April Peveteaux (*Gluten Is My Bitch*, *The Gluten-Free Cheat Sheet*, and *Bake Sales Are My Bitch*), Matt Lewis and Renato Poliafito (*Baked*, *Baked Explorations*, *Baked Elements*, and *Baked Occasions*), and Lukas Volger (*Bowl*) among others.

Please list five books you recently agented. *Finn and the Intergalactic Lunchbox* by Michael Buckley (a three-book middle grade fiction series, Delacorte); *Patterns of India* by Christine Chitnis (lifestyle nonfiction, Clarkson Potter); *Beyond the Point* by Claire Gibson (debut fiction, William Morrow); *Battle for Perfection* by Eric Gorges (narrative nonfiction, Algonquin); *Butcher & Beast* by Angie Mar (cooking nonfiction, Clarkson Potter).

Please describe the kinds of books you want to agent. I am actively looking for lifestyle, narrative nonfiction, pop culture, health/wellness, select middle grade and contemporary young adult fiction, and adult fiction that blurs the line between literary and commercial.

What should writers submit for consideration, and how should they send it? Submit your fiction or nonfiction query addressed to Alison Fargis at submissions@stonesong.com.

Specify the word *Query* in the subject line, and include the first chapter or first 10 pages of your work pasted into the body of your email. Please do not send attachments. Our system is set up so that every email query receives an automatic reply confirming receipt. After that, we will be in touch only if we would like to request more material.

THE STORY MERCHANT ❖ www.storymerchant.com

Agent's name and contact info: Ken Atchity, atchity@storymerchant.com

What would you be doing right now if not responding to this survey? Securing financing for an independent feature film.

What would you be if not an agent (other than a dog, cat, or other mammal)? I'm not an agent — I'm a literary manager and producer. But I would probably be a professor again.

Do you think independent (noncorporate) publishing will be stronger, weaker, or the same over the next few years? Stronger. Its popularity and success only continue to rise with each year.

How would you define the "client from hell"? One who is unwilling to listen to instruction, take criticism, or reasonably separate emotion from business.

Do you think Earth was created a few thousand years ago or several billion years ago? Several billion.

Please list five books you recently agented. I'm the literary manager for *MEG* by Steven Alten, coming in 2018 as a major motion picture; *Head Wounds* by Dennis Palumbo; *Death at the Day Lily Café* by Wendy Sand Eckel; and *Nobody Walks* by Dennis Walsh.

Please describe the kinds of books you want to agent. Open to all genres, so long as the story is high concept and the content is marketable as both a book and film. Currently particularly interested in dramatic Christmas stories.

What should writers submit for consideration, and how should they send it? Please submit a log line, short pitch, and short paragraph about your writing background, all in the body of an email to atchity@storymerchant.com.

How do you feel about self-publishing, and what do you see happening with it in the near future? My imprint, Story Merchant Books, is a facilitator for direct publishing, so I'm an enormous proponent of it. The traditional New York publishers have become nearly impossible to publish with unless you're a household name or celebrity, so direct publishing is a great alternative to get your story out there. Plus, you'll stand to make a lot more money on your sales, so long as you're willing to invest ample time in your marketing!

Do you think there are too many, too few, or just enough agents? Guess I'd have to say just enough — if the material is worthy, there's an agent for it. It's not about quantity; it's about quality.

Do you think Amazon will become the country's largest employer within 10 years? No.

Why do you think some books become super-successful (beyond the obvious reasons)? Marketing, marketing, marketing!

Do you think agents are likely to become millionaires? It all depends on their clients' success.

Do you think agents tend toward certain personality types? Yes. Enthusiastic masochists.

Do you think writers tend to be more or less narcissistic than the population at large? More narcissistic.

Knowing what you know now, would you become an agent again? Probably.

Why did you choose to become an agent? It gives me access to stories I can produce as films.

Do you think many talented writers fail to get published for avoidable reasons? If so, what are some of those reasons? Yes. They are too difficult to work with, too easily dissuaded, don't have strength for rejection, or don't hone their craft relentlessly.

STRACHAN LITERARY AGENCY ❖ strachanlit.com

Agent's name and contact info: Laura Strachan, query@strachanlit.com

What would you be doing right now if not responding to this survey? Reading manuscripts.

What would you be if not an agent (other than a dog, cat, or other mammal)? I don't know. Owning a bookstore or an art gallery. Or a bookstore / art gallery.

Do you think independent (noncorporate) publishing will be stronger, weaker, or the same over the next few years? I predict it will get stronger. Just as we are seeing a resurgence of independent bookstores, we will see more independent publishers who are willing to take risks on books the corporate giants won't.

Please describe your professional history. Long story. English major. Went to law school. Hated practicing law. Did all sorts of things before I hit on the combo of books (which I've always loved) and representation. I've now been an agent for nearly 20 years.

How would you define the "client from hell"? I don't know if there are really "clients from hell." There are clients who don't understand the process and who need to be educated. There are also clients who need constant reassurance and hand-holding, which can be tiresome.

Do you think Earth was created a few thousand years ago or several billion years ago? I'm going with the science, but what do I know? I don't think science and religion are mutually exclusive.

Please list five books you recently agented. *In Pursuit* by David Reichenbaugh (Fore-Word Press, 2019), *Goldens Are Here* by Andrew Furman (Green Writers Press, 2018), *Seven Music Forests* by Jeffrey Greene (University of Virginia Press, 2019), *Café Neandertal* by Beebe Bahrami (Counterpoint, 2017), *Café Oc* by Beebe Bahrami (Shanti Arts, 2016).

Please describe the kinds of books you want to agent. I focus on literary fiction and narrative nonfiction. I like a good story, beautifully told.

What should writers submit for consideration, and how should they send it? Query with a brief description and bio.

How do you feel about self-publishing, and what do you see happening with it in the near future? It makes perfect sense for some authors to self-publish, but they need to understand what that entails.

Do you think there are too many, too few, or just enough agents? Just enough?

Do you think Amazon will become the country's largest employer within 10 years? It certainly is looking that way. It's supposed to be a great place to work, so that's a good thing, but lack of competition creates its own problems.

Why do you think some books become super-successful (beyond the obvious reasons)? Luck. Seriously. And acknowledging that makes it easier to accept.

Do you think agents are likely to become millionaires? Ha.

Do you think agents tend toward certain personality types? I've met all sorts of agents. The media tends to portray agents (of any kind) as gregarious type A personalities. I've met just as many quiet, reflective, serious agents.

Do you think writers tend to be more or less narcissistic than the population at large? Probably more, like any arts genre. Art is the way they express themselves, and so the art is a reflection of the artist.

Knowing what you know now, would you become an agent again? Yes.

Why did you choose to become an agent? Seemed like the best way to combine what I loved with my background.

Do you think many talented writers fail to get published for avoidable reasons? If so, what are some of those reasons? Fiction and nonfiction require two different answers. Talented fiction writers sometimes fail to get published because publishing — and especially fiction publishing — is such a subjective business. So much of it is luck, hitting the right editor on the right day with the right space on his or her list. Nonfiction is a completely different issue. I see many talented authors who simply don't have the platform to convince a publisher that they are a viable investment. I spend a lot of time explaining to authors that they must have that groundwork. "Being willing to go on a book tour" doesn't cut it.

THE STUART AGENCY ❖ www.stuartagency.com

Agent's name and contact info: Rob Kirkpatrick, rob@stuartagency.com

What would you be if not an agent (other than a dog, cat, or other mammal)? An acquisitions editor and/or an author.

Please describe your professional history. In a publishing career of two decades, I have been a senior-level editor at both Big 5 and independent houses and, since 2016, have worked as an agent. I also am a published author. I'm experienced in both ends of book-deal negotiations and am deeply familiar with the journey a book takes from proposal to manuscript to store shelf.

Do you think Earth was created a few thousand years ago or several billion years ago? Several billion. Data > dogma.

Please list five books you recently agented. *The Skeptics' Guide to the Universe* (official book of the podcast) by Dr. Steven Novella and the "Rogues"; *Ninety Percent Mental: An All-Star Player Turned Mental Skills Coach Reveals the Hidden Game of Baseball* by Bob Tewksbury and Scott Miller; *Four-Pack Revolution: How You Can Aim Lower, Cheat on Your Diet, and STILL Lose Weight AND Keep It Off* by Chael Sonnen and Ryan Parsons; *Girl on the Balcony*, memoir of actor Olivia Hussey; *The People's Team: One Hundred Years of Green Bay Packers Football* by Mark Beech of The Players' Tribune.

Please describe the kinds of books you want to agent. Nonfiction, especially narrative nonfiction with a national media platform or tie-in (increasingly important these days). Memoir, sports, pop culture, music, history, current events, etc.

What should writers submit for consideration, and how should they send it? Email: a cover letter in the body of the email describing the project and a thorough book proposal (attached as a Word document, please) with an outline, writing sample, author bio, and details of the author's platform.

Do you think many talented writers fail to get published for avoidable reasons? If so, what are some of those reasons? They need an agent!

TESSLER LITERARY AGENCY ❖ www.tessleragency.com
27 West 20th Street, Suite 1003, New York, NY 10011

Agent's name and contact info: Michelle Tessler, queries through the form at www.tessleragency.com

What would you be doing right now if not responding to this survey? Reading manuscripts.

What would you be if not an agent (other than a dog, cat, or other mammal)? An anthropologist or a world traveler, if I could afford it.

Do you think independent (noncorporate) publishing will be stronger, weaker, or the same over the next few years? Probably the same. It seems small houses close as new small houses emerge.

Please describe your professional history. I worked up the ranks from assistant at William Morris Agency to agent, with a seven-year stint working in the internet industry (beginning in 1992) doing content and business development. I gained experience with marketing while involved in the online world, which helps me as an agent in selling and positioning my clients' books.

How would you define the "client from hell"? Demanding, entitled, and deaf to constructive feedback.

Do you think Earth was created a few thousand years ago or several billion years ago? Several billion, from what I understand.

Please list five books you recently agented. *Salt Houses* by Hala Alyan, *Mama's Last Hug* by Frans de Waal, *Blood & Ivy* by Paul Collins, *Good Talk* by Mira Jacob, *Miss Kopp Won't Quit* by Amy Stewart.

Please describe the kinds of books you want to agent. We are dedicated to writers of high-quality fiction and nonfiction. Our clients include accomplished journalists, scientists, academics, experts in their field, as well as novelists and debut authors with unique voices and stories to tell. We value fresh, original writing that has a compelling point of view.

Our list is diverse and far-reaching. In nonfiction, it includes narrative, popular science, memoir, history, psychology, business, biography, food, and travel. In many cases, we sign authors who are especially adept at writing books that cross many of these categories at once. In fiction, we represent literary, women's, and commercial.

What should writers submit for consideration, and how should they send it? See query requirements and the query form at www.tessleragency.com.

How do you feel about self-publishing, and what do you see happening with it in the near future? It is a good way to build a platform, if other channels are in place, and a way to test-market an idea.

Do you think there are too many, too few, or just enough agents? Too many. Who likes to compete?

Do you think Amazon will become the country's largest employer within 10 years? I hope not.

Why do you think some books become super-successful (beyond the obvious reasons)? They plug into a cultural moment. They have a great title and hook.

Do you think agents are likely to become millionaires? It is my hope and dream.

Do you think agents tend toward certain personality types? We all tend to love talking about ideas.

Do you think writers tend to be more or less narcissistic than the population at large? Less than. I tend to think writers are more observant and sensitive to the world around them than the general population.

Knowing what you know now, would you become an agent again? Yes.

Why did you choose to become an agent? Great combination of many skills. Editing, pitching, negotiating, evaluating, meeting, positioning, marketing, strategizing.

Do you think many talented writers fail to get published for avoidable reasons? If so, what are some of those reasons? Sometimes. I would say write your pitch with the same care and consideration you write your work. Make sure it has a market and potential audience of more than five readers.

THE TOBIAS LITERARY AGENCY ❖ thetobiasagency.com

276 Fifth Avenue, Suite 704, New York, NY 10001

Agent's name and contact info: Lane Heymont, Cofounder and Principal Agent, lane@thetobiasagency.com

What would you be doing right now if not responding to this survey? Reading or editing client material while drinking coffee and possibly stuffing my face with a third cupcake from the two dozen a publisher sent me for the holidays.

What would you be if not an agent (other than a dog, cat, or other mammal)? Those who can, do. Those who can't, teach.

Do you think independent (noncorporate) publishing will be stronger, weaker, or the same over the next few years? Isn't this always the question? Lately, I've seen numerous respected midlist and small presses collapsing into the ether. The Big 5 have made it their business to snap up any publisher successful enough to break out of the small/midlist arena. I see more of the same on the horizon — the weak die and the strong survive.

Please describe your professional history. I started my career as an intern at the Seymour Agency back in 2011 and made my way up to literary agent. I formed the Tobias Literary Agency in August 2016.

How would you define the "client from hell"? Someone who doesn't trust me enough to do my job, refuses to edit or discuss changes to the project (also an editor's nightmare), or only wants to write/shop one book.

Do you think Earth was created a few thousand years ago or several billion years ago? We don't live in a post-fact world, so billions of years ago.

Please list five books you recently agented. *You Get What You Came For* by Rachel Neff, *You Are Not Special* by Dr. Paul M. Sutter, *As Wide as the Sky* by Jessica Pack, *Semper Fi Cowboy* by Heather Long (Simon & Schuster), *Christmas Mystery Series* by Danica Winters (Harlequin, HarperCollins), film rights to *Lune* by Jeff Johnson (Soft Skull).

Please describe the kinds of books you want to agent. Ones that make me laugh, cry, gasp, smile, and think beyond what I already know.

What should writers submit for consideration, and how should they send it? Literary fiction, women's fiction, true crime, mystery/thrillers, nonfiction, fantasy, science fiction, and horror. Send a query and the first five pages (pasted in the body of the email) to query@thetobiasagency.com.

How do you feel about self-publishing, and what do you see happening with it in the near future? Authors who may not be made for traditional publishing are able to find great success in a world untapped — or unutilized — by traditional publishing. For example, paranormal romance is still wildly popular in self-publishing, and sales prove it. However, the Big 5 are almost allergic to it right now. Unless, of course, you have a built-in major readership. Self-publishing is a blessing and a curse. There have been so many fantastic books to come through the ranks, but those ranks are filled with books not ready for the market.

Do you think there are too many, too few, or just enough agents? This isn't for me to answer, but one could say of anything: there's too many bad, too few good, and just enough average.

Do you think Amazon will become the country's largest employer within 10 years? Yes, absolutely. Except maybe for the government — military, etc.

Why do you think some books become super-successful (beyond the obvious reasons)? Besides a wonderful book marketed appropriately? Timing and dumb luck.

Do you think agents are likely to become millionaires? As likely as getting struck by lightning. Sure, it happens, but not often.

Do you think agents tend toward certain personality types? Yes, and no. This job takes a certain amount of nurturing, business/sales acumen, persistence, and creativity.

Do you think writers tend to be more or less narcissistic than the population at large? Creative types, including agents, all tend to be insane. Isn't that the stereotype? And they tend to be alcoholics. Just look at all the greats: Sylvia Plath, Hemingway, Vonnegut, Poe, Woolf.

Knowing what you know now, would you become an agent again? Absolutely. I have the best job in the world, and being able to call an author on her birthday with an offer from a Big 5 publisher is one of the most amazing feelings.

Why did you choose to become an agent? Books, writers, and books.

Do you think many talented writers fail to get published for avoidable reasons? If so, what are some of those reasons? Yes. Don't spam four dozen agents on the same email. Don't write toward trends. The difference between a published and unpublished author is persistence.

Optional shout-outs/comments: "Writing is manual labor of the mind." — John Gregory Dunne

I'd like to thank Nicole Resciniti and Marisa Cleveland, who introduced me to the business; my clients; and the ever-amazing Danica Winters, who was my big first sale.

TONI LOPOPOLO LITERARY MANAGEMENT ❖ lopopololiterary.com

215-353-1151

Agent's name and contact info: Toni Lopopolo, Agent, lopopolobooks@gmail.com

What would you be doing right now if not responding to this survey? Reading Walter Isaacson's *Leonardo Da Vinci*.

What would you be if not an agent (other than a dog, cat, or other mammal)? A reader, that is, having the luxury of reading all the books I've stacked up to read when I have time.

Do you think independent (noncorporate) publishing will be stronger, weaker, or the same over the next few years? Depends on whether those independent publishers know what they're doing, i.e., they've worked in publishing before and have the experience of the market and the business.

Please describe your professional history. I started in book publicity with Bantam Books way before anyone else owned them. Then I became library promotion director at Harcourt Brace; it was fun to travel to all the libraries in the US. I was invited to become paperback marketing manager at Houghton Mifflin in Boston, where we cleaned up with *Even Cowgirls Get the Blues* by Tom Robbins; got them to order the first T-shirts ever for a book. Back in Manhattan, as executive editor, Paperback Books, we cleaned up with *Elvis '54*. Then executive editor at St. Martin's Press. That covered 20 years. I opened my agency in 1991 in Brentwood, Los Angeles. I now teach writers in a program called "Tea with Toni" — something I started the first six months of my agency, because I saw what would-be writers sent me. They needed to know the names of the skills, then master those skills, whether in fiction or in narrative nonfiction, which include memory. Story is king.

How would you define the "client from hell"? Obsessive-compulsive narcissistic personality. I learned early on to interview for the signs, then run like hell.

Do you think Earth was created a few thousand years ago or several billion years ago? The second choice; pretty old.

Please list five books you recently agented. *Watch the Shadows*, Robin Winter, horror novel. Second edition of Shelly Lowenkopf's *The Fiction Writer's Handbook*. About to submit a two-book contract for first-time author Sharon Schlesinger. I service my published authors, teach writers with a lot of talent who need to master the skills needed. I take on editing of manuscripts often, something I enjoy more and more with age. I want to convey knowledge of the conventions that change in writing styles and what readers crave right now: good stories with strong unique voices.

Please describe the kinds of books you want to agent. I look for writers who've mastered the craft of writing their genres. I'm a stickler for "clean" writing. I look for almost any (legal) subject in narrative nonfiction written by a talented writer. Try me.

What should writers submit for consideration, and how should they send it? A terrific query letter via email with something about how and where they've studied their craft; in nonfiction I'd like their credentials for the subject. I need to see the first five pages of the manuscript within the email. I like crime fiction with amazing and different protagonists, women's interests in fiction and narrative nonfiction.

How do you feel about self-publishing, and what do you see happening with it in the near future? Vanity press. No patience. I've been in professional publishing too long to feel positive toward writers who won't put themselves to the test.

Do you think there are too many, too few, or just enough agents? I have no answer.

Do you think Amazon will become the country's largest employer within 10 years? I do a lot of shopping on Amazon. I'm sure a competitor will come forward in that length of time.

Why do you think some books become super-successful (beyond the obvious reasons)? I see many successful novels that go unedited. Ugh. My former boss at St. Martin's, Tom McCormack, wrote a book titled *The Fiction Editor* especially for major publishers' editors. Many miss the mark with head-hopping and 14 *-ly* adverbs per page. Shows many readers care only about story, not the quality or sophistication of the writing.

Do you think agents are likely to become millionaires? I heard tell of one.

Do you think agents tend toward certain personality types? Some agents jibe with the market; that's a gift.

Do you think writers tend to be more or less narcissistic than the population at large? Writers usually are or should be control freaks.

Knowing what you know now, would you become an agent again? Tough question at this late date.

Why did you choose to become an agent? To remain in the business I knew and still love.

Do you think many talented writers fail to get published for avoidable reasons? If so, what are some of those reasons? They're not in harmony with what the editors are looking for or with the changes in the needs and wants of readers.

TRANSATLANTIC LITERARY AGENCY ❖ transatlanticagency.com

Agent's name and contact info: Marilyn Biderman, Senior Literary Agent, marilyn@transatlanticagency.com, 416-488-9214

What would you be doing right now if not responding to this survey? Working through email.

What would you be if not an agent (other than a dog, cat, or other mammal)? A prima ballerina.

Do you think independent (noncorporate) publishing will be stronger, weaker, or the same over the next few years? Stronger.

Please describe your professional history. Before joining Transatlantic Literary Agency, I worked at my own literary agency and consultancy practice for 7 years, where I helped launch the careers of debut and prize-winning authors. I had previously worked at McClelland & Stewart for 12 years, most recently as vice president and director for rights and contracts. At M&S, I handled the international rights for many renowned authors, including Leonard Cohen, Alistair MacLeod, and Madeleine Thien.

I have a BA from the University of Toronto in English literature, graduated from Osgoode Hall Law School, and am a member of the Law Society of Upper Canada. I have guest-lectured at publishing programs at Humber College, Ryerson University, Simon Fraser University, and the University of British Columbia and taught a publishing course at Centennial College. I have also mentored many publishers under the auspices of the Association of Canadian Publishers and the Canada Council and have acted as a juror in literary competitions. I have authored several papers on copyright law, am secretary of the recently formed Professional Association of Canadian Literary Agents, and have served for many years on the organizing committee for the International Visitors Program of Toronto's International Festival of Authors. I also chair the board of Canada's dance magazine, *The Dance Current*, and am especially proud of my work with the St. John Ambulance Therapy Dog program.

How would you define the "client from hell"? I can't mention her name.

Do you think Earth was created a few thousand years ago or several billion years ago? Billions.

Please list five books you recently agented. *The Break* by Katherena Vermette; *Women Who Dig: Farming, Feminism, and the Fight to Feed the World* by Trina Moyles; *The Season of Fury and Wonder* by Sharon Butala; *Into the Current* by Jared Young; *The Long Hello* by Cathie Borrie.

Please describe the kinds of books you want to agent. Literary fiction; sweet-spot fiction, that is, accessible but literary in intent (often found at book clubs); literary crime fiction; and women's commercial and historical fiction. I love memoir with an utterly unique story and brilliant writing; narrative nonfiction on compelling and newsworthy topics that anticipate trends; expert nonfiction with wide appeal from authors with established social-media platforms; and biographies of fascinating lives. I don't handle children's books (except for young adult novels with crossover appeal, very selectively and only by referral), poetry, screenplays, science fiction, paranormal, or fantasy for adult readers.

What should writers submit for consideration, and how should they send it? Please send a brief query by email with a concise description of the manuscript, a small sample of up to 1500 words attached as a plain Word document or PDF, and a short biography. I respond within a week when I am interested in seeing complete manuscripts or additional material. I welcome debut and established authors and diverse voices.

How do you feel about self-publishing, and what do you see happening with it in the near future? Not for me.

Do you think there are too many, too few, or just enough agents? Too many.

Do you think Amazon will become the country's largest employer within 10 years? I'm Canadian, and no, not Canada's largest employer within 10 years.

Why do you think some books become super-successful (beyond the obvious reasons)? Social media, prizes, word of mouth.

Do you think agents are likely to become millionaires? Not a chance for 99 percent of us.

Do you think agents tend toward certain personality types? Yes.

Do you think writers tend to be more or less narcissistic than the population at large? Same.

Knowing what you know now, would you become an agent again? Yes. I love my work.

Why did you choose to become an agent? I combine the business side, being a lawyer and a former VP of rights and contracts, and the editing side, with lots of experience in both.

Do you think many talented writers fail to get published for avoidable reasons? If so, what are some of those reasons? Publishers' interest in a manuscript does not necessarily coincide with literary merit, but what they think will sell.

TRIADAUS LITERARY AGENCY ❖ www.triadaus.com

PO Box 561, Sewickley, PA 15143

Agent's name and contact info: Laura Crockett, Associate Literary Agent, laura@triadaus.com

What would you be doing right now if not responding to this survey? Marathoning season 2 of *The Crown* on Netflix.

What would you be if not an agent (other than a dog, cat, or other mammal)? A librarian.

Do you think independent (noncorporate) publishing will be stronger, weaker, or the same over the next few years? Probably the same.

Please describe your professional history. I received my MA in publishing in 2014 and quickly became an agent with TriadaUS. In the meantime, I've been a bookseller and currently work part-time as a reference librarian at my local public library.

How would you define the "client from hell"? I'm always reachable for my clients, and I prefer open communication, but there's a line between reaching out and incessantly pestering. A client who nags, demands, and tries to tell me how to do my job is not one I can represent properly.

Do you think Earth was created a few thousand years ago or several billion years ago? Several billion years ago.

Please list five books you recently agented. *A Short History of the Girl Next Door* by Jared Reck; *Impossible Saints* by Clarissa Harwood; *Timekeeper*, *Chainbreaker*, and *Firestarter* by Tara Sim (a trilogy); *Saint Rosa of the Sea* by Nina Moreno.

Please describe the kinds of books you want to agent. Voicey, engaging young adult with excellent, authentic worlds (contemporary, fantasy, historical); compelling, interesting, thoughtful women's fiction (contemporary, historical); humorous, millennial-driven women's fiction (contemporary); and profoundly beautiful fantasy, with fleshed-out worlds, intricate plots, and characters with depth.

What should writers submit for consideration, and how should they send it? Writers should send their official query and the first 10 pages pasted into the body of an email (laura@triadaus.com). They will hear from me within two weeks, and if I would like to read more, I will give instructions.

How do you feel about self-publishing, and what do you see happening with it in the near future? Self-publishing is a good avenue for books meant for very niche audiences. I see self-publishing continuing in the future, though it is becoming more difficult for the general public to understand the difference between self-publishing and traditional publishing, and it causes unnecessary frustration with bookstores and libraries not carrying them for consumption.

Do you think there are too many, too few, or just enough agents? There are just enough agents.

Do you think Amazon will become the country's largest employer within 10 years? If not the largest, then one of the largest, though such a monopoly is a frightening thought.

Why do you think some books become super-successful (beyond the obvious reasons)? Something about those books speaks to the audience of readers at large. It could be the topic/premise, it could be the best-written book within that genre's trend, or it could be universal experience. Some are super-successful initially, but no one remembers them in a handful of years; some are quiet and steady and, in my mind, super-successful because they're still printing, they're still being purchased, they're persisting on the shelves. Those are the ones that will last, and a lot of it comes down to voice, universal characterization and identity, and topic.

Do you think agents are likely to become millionaires? Haha! No. We could have a huge docket of bestselling authors, movie deals left and right, foreign rights and subrights exploited, the whole shebang — but no, I don't think agents are likely to become millionaires. We're in the wrong business if that's the goal.

Do you think agents tend toward certain personality types? Absolutely.

Do you think writers tend to be more or less narcissistic than the population at large? Writers are more sensitive than the population at large.

Knowing what you know now, would you become an agent again? Absolutely.

Why did you choose to become an agent? I wanted to become an editor, but after speaking with editors and learning about their everyday tasks, I realized I wanted to work even more closely with authors, and to work with them throughout their career. If I'm to be an author's champion, the best way I can do so is to represent them.

Do you think many talented writers fail to get published for avoidable reasons? If so, what are some of those reasons? A fear of rejection could be holding them back. They can find pleasure in writing, and they can write a story they that themselves would read, but then there's knowing the market and the audience, realizing the business involves a lot of rejection, of really putting yourself out there, of being vulnerable, and it could hold them back. I say shoot for it, try, and try again. There's an agent out there looking for that project.

Agent's name and contact info: Dr. Uwe Stender, uwe@triadaus.com

What would you be doing right now if not responding to this survey? Editing manuscripts or filing 1099 forms.

What would you be if not an agent (other than a dog, cat, or other mammal)? I would be a record producer.

Do you think independent (noncorporate) publishing will be stronger, weaker, or the same over the next few years? It will remain the same.

Please describe your professional history. PhD in German literature, literary agent (since 2004), university lecturer (German, film, writing).

How would you define the "client from hell"? I don't have any. I wouldn't sign them. I have a folder in my email entitled "Nut Jobs" — that is where potential clients from hell reside.

Do you think Earth was created a few thousand years ago or several billion years ago? Several billion years ago.

Please list five books you recently agented. Tiffany Sly Lives Here by Dana L. Davis, Not Perfect by Elizabeth LaBan, Here Comes Trouble by Kate Hattemer, Who's That Girl by Blair Thornburgh, Thieving Weasels by Billy Taylor.

Please describe the kinds of books you want to agent. I want books that make me forget any and everything around me. I want to be abducted into a different world and stay there until I finish reading the book. And then I want to remain obsessed with it.

What should writers submit for consideration, and how should they send it? Just send me a query via email!

How do you feel about self-publishing, and what do you see happening with it in the near future? Self-publishing can be a great tool to get your name out there and to publish books that may otherwise never have sold. I think it will remain the same.

Do you think there are too many, too few, or just enough agents? There are just enough.

Do you think Amazon will become the country's largest employer within 10 years? Aren't they already?

Why do you think some books become super-successful (beyond the obvious reasons)? They hit the zeitgeist at the right moment.

Do you think agents are likely to become millionaires? No.

Do you think agents tend toward certain personality types? No.

Do you think writers tend to be more or less narcissistic than the population at large? The whole population is narcissistic these days, thanks to social media. So they are just more or less the same.

Knowing what you know now, would you become an agent again? One hundred percent — yes!!!

Why did you choose to become an agent? I love the thrill of discovering great new talent and meeting amazingly creative people I otherwise would never have met!

Do you think many talented writers fail to get published for avoidable reasons? If so, what are some of those reasons? They are too stubborn to listen to great advice. That is reason number 1 to reason number 100.

TRIDENT MEDIA GROUP, LLC ❖ www.tridentmediagroup.com

41 Madison Avenue, Floor 36, New York, NY 10010, 212-333-1506

Agent's name: Mark Gottlieb, Literary Agent

What would you be doing right now if not responding to this survey? Watching Ken Burns's documentary on the Civil War or learning to pilot my drone.

What would you be if not an agent (other than a dog, cat, or other mammal)? If you asked me what I would be doing before I even tried my hand at book publishing, I might be a photographer or a chef. Since you asked me after I've been in book publishing, there's really no other way to live.

Do you think independent (noncorporate) publishing will be stronger, weaker, or the same over the next few years? Someday soon I see all publishers having an even bigger presence in the digital sphere for books in terms of placement among online retailers in buying co-op deals, key site placement, and more, exactly the way music and movie companies originated subscription services and digital access. Print won't become a thing of the past but perhaps a nostalgia, much like the way in which music aficionados appreciate vinyl records. Like the LP, the hardcover book is a technology that has been perfected and is ideal for the experience of reading. Regardless, readers will always opt for their preferred format, whether that be print, audio, or ebook.

Please describe your professional history. I attended Emerson College and was president of its Publishing Club, establishing the Wilde Press. After graduating with a degree in writing, literature, and publishing, I began my career with Penguin. My first position at Publishers Marketplace's number-one-ranked literary agency, Trident Media Group, was in foreign rights. I was editorial assistant to Trident's chairman and ran the audio department. I am currently working with my own client list, helping to manage and grow authors' careers with the unique resources available to Trident. I have ranked number one among literary agents on PublishersMarketplace.com in Overall Deals and other categories.

How would you define the "client from hell"? It might be of more use to know what an ideal client would be for me. The ideal client should be patient, since book publishing can be a slow process, but at the same time they should be curious about the book-publishing process, how their role fits into it, and how they can help as a central figure in the success of a book's publication.

Do you think Earth was created a few thousand years ago or several billion years ago? I believe in the big-bang theory and the dinosaurs, if that's what you're getting at.

Please list five books you recently agented. Kate Moretti's *The Blackbird Season*, Christopher Brown's *Tropic of Kansas*, Ruby Karp's *Earth Hates Me*, Deborah A. Wolf's *The Forbidden City*, Samantha Chase's *A Sky Full of Stars*.

Please describe the kinds of books you want to agent. In fiction, I've been focusing most of my efforts in attaining upmarket fiction, which is the crossroads where literary meets commercial fiction. I also look for books that elevate and transcend a given genre, such as literary science fiction, literary fantasy, or literary mystery/crime/thriller. I also like to work with books that carry an important social message. In nonfiction, I tend to look for celebrity memoir or those with massive social-media followings (1M+) or big platforms. Much of the nonfiction I do tends to carry an important social message and in many cases has been born out of fiction, in a sense.

What should writers submit for consideration, and how should they send it? We accept query letters via the contact page on our website, www.tridentmediagroup.com.

How do you feel about self-publishing, and what do you see happening with it in the near future? The self-publishing/indie sphere has become something like what the farm league is to major league baseball, but the odds of success can be lower than if an author were to approach a literary agent to secure a debut in trade publishing. The bar is quite high for self-published authors to attract an agent or publisher. An author usually needs to have sold at least 50,000 copies at a decent price. I see self-publishing continuing on this way for a while, but it may become even more difficult for self-publishing authors if internet neutrality completely falls apart.

Do you think there are too many, too few, or just enough agents? Given what has been happening in our industry with book publishers and smaller boutique literary agencies downsizing, I simply do not see how we can have as many literary agents and editors in the industry as we've had in the past. Of course, that all could change.

Do you think Amazon will become the country's largest employer within 10 years? If you're paying attention, Amazon takes up most of the book market and most every other market. Whether we all work for Amazon or not, we've all come to rely on Amazon.

Why do you think some books become super-successful (beyond the obvious reasons)? The same way some produce is because it's GMO, whereas other plants are organically grown. In the case of the GMO-type book, the publisher puts a lot of publicity/marketing/sales muscle behind it. With the organic book, it sometimes comes completely out of left field as a part of word of mouth.

Do you think agents are likely to become millionaires? Most literary agents are not likely to become millionaires, although I know and have worked with a few.

Do you think agents tend toward certain personality types? Some of the literary agents I know at the top of their game are type A personalities, but then again there are a few of us who are down-to-earth.

Do you think writers tend to be more or less narcissistic than the population at large? Sometimes it takes that type of audacity to achieve a certain level of genius. At the same time I know many authors at the top of their game as *New York Times* bestselling authors who have managed to keep their feet on the ground despite all the success. I've learned to handle most every kind of personality type at this point in my career.

Knowing what you know now, would you become an agent again? Considering it's my family business where I work, I probably wouldn't have much of a choice in the matter, but I'd still do it all over again. It's great to help champion the written word.

Why did you choose to become an agent? I have been working in major trade publishing since 2009, when I started at Penguin Books. I've grown up around books all my life, since both my parents worked in major trade publishing, and my father happens to own and operate the literary agency where I work — Trident Media Group. So I like to tell folks that I've been in publishing from the womb! There was always the expectation that I would study book publishing in college in order to one day go into the family business. That is why I attended Emerson College in Boston, since at the time it was one of only two schools to offer an undergraduate study in book publishing. From there, my company bio charts the rest of my journey.

Do you think many talented writers fail to get published for avoidable reasons? If so, what are some of those reasons? Authors who fail to live by the guiding principles of persistence, patience, and participation might find it difficult to get published.

Persistence: Don't be discouraged by rejection. This being a subjective business, rejection is bound to happen many times over. It does not mean that you're not good — it means you're not quite good enough as of yet. Learn from constructive criticism and grow.

Patience: This is a "hurry up and wait" business, since reading and editing can take time, so it is important to be willing to wait patiently for editors/publishers to consider work once it is submitted by a literary agent. There have been instances, though, where I've sold a project in as little as four days. In other instances, it has taken months. It may seem like a nail-biting experience while rejections start to flow in during the submission process, but it is often worth the wait once an offer finally arrives.

Participation: As I mentioned before, an author has a central role in the book-publishing process. Authors who merely want to write their manuscripts and then check out rarely experience successful publications. Asking one's publisher or literary agent how they can help leading up to publication and in the months thereafter is a great starting point. Being curious about a publisher's marketing/publicity plans and commenting on them is also of key importance.

THE UNTER AGENCY ❖ www.theunteragency.com

23 West 73rd Street, Suite 100, New York, NY 10023, 212-401-4068

Agent's name: Jennifer Unter, jennifer@theunteragency.com

What would you be doing right now if not responding to this survey? Answering emails.

What would you be if not an agent (other than a dog, cat, or other mammal)? An environmental scientist.

Do you think independent (noncorporate) publishing will be stronger, weaker, or the same over the next few years? I would like to say stronger, but I don't think it's going to change much in the next few years unless something drastic happens.

Please describe your professional history. I started out as an editorial assistant at Henry Holt working for a literary fiction editor, then went to the Karpfinger Agency as a junior agent. I went to law school during that time and then worked at an entertainment firm for a few years before going back to being an agent at another agency. I started my own agency in 2008.

How would you define the "client from hell"? Someone who doesn't respect boundaries.

Do you think Earth was created a few thousand years ago or several billion years ago? Billions.

Please list five books you recently agented. *The Parents' Guide to Climate Revolution: 100 Ways to Build a Fossil-Free Future, Raise Empowered Kids, and Still Get a Good Night's Sleep* by Mary DeMocker (New World Library), *Dangerous Alliance* (young adult historical) by Jennieke Cohen (HarperCollins), *Ninja Camp* (picture book) by Sue Fliess (Running Press Kids, Perseus), *Zen and Gone* (young adult mystery) by Emily France (Soho Teen), *The Second Space Race: The True Story of the Women and Men Who Tested to Become America's First Astronauts* by Rebecca Rissman (Scholastic).

Please describe the kinds of books you want to agent. I'm looking for more serious nonfiction (biography, history), which is typically not something I've done in the past.

What should writers submit for consideration, and how should they send it? A query letter via email.

How do you feel about self-publishing, and what do you see happening with it in the near future? It's still tricky to get attention for self-published works, but certainly there have been many writers who benefited from it. Self-publishing will continue to be very popular, and I wouldn't be surprised to see more self-publishing venues pop up.

Do you think there are too many, too few, or just enough agents? There are as many as the market will bear. So, just enough.

Do you think Amazon will become the country's largest employer within 10 years? It's going in that direction.

Why do you think some books become super-successful (beyond the obvious reasons)? Word of mouth and being part of a zeitgeist before knowing what that might be.

Do you think agents are likely to become millionaires? Not always likely, but very possible.

Do you think agents tend toward certain personality types? Not really — there are so many different ones.

Do you think writers tend to be more or less narcissistic than the population at large? No more than in other professions, in fact probably less.

Knowing what you know now, would you become an agent again? Yes.

Why did you choose to become an agent? It speaks to my skills — I love reading to find new talent, nurturing that talent, and negotiating for the best possible outcome for that author.

Do you think many talented writers fail to get published for avoidable reasons? If so, what are some of those reasons? Writers don't realize how important it is to rewrite and to get out and meet people in publishing. If you want it badly enough, it will happen.

VERITAS LITERARY AGENCY ❖ veritasliterary.com

Agent's name and contact info: Michael Carr, michael@veritasliterary.com

What would you be doing right now if not responding to this survey? Answering queries.

What would you be if not an agent (other than a dog, cat, or other mammal)? A writer or a book editor. I love the literary field.

Do you think independent (noncorporate) publishing will be stronger, weaker, or the same over the next few years? I think (hope) we've reached some equilibrium in the industry between Big 5, smaller publishers, and indie writers. At least, it seems that the pace of change is slower.

Please describe your professional history. I have seven years of experience as a literary agent, with a background in writing and editing.

How would you define the "client from hell"? I've been fortunate with my clients; writers are generally lovely people. But a challenging client is one who second-guesses my work, misses deadlines without warning, and fights with editors, cover designers, etc.

Do you think Earth was created a few thousand years ago or several billion years ago? Scientists believe that the earth is approximately 4.54 billion years old. I have no reason to doubt this estimate.

Please list five books you recently agented. The Life She Was Given, The Skyborn Trilogy, Between Earth and Sky, Autumn in Oxford, Soulkeeper.

Please describe the kinds of books you want to agent. I represent science fiction/fantasy, historicals, contemporary thrillers, and science or history nonfiction. Good storytelling is key.

What should writers submit for consideration, and how should they send it? I prefer a straight query with the first five pages included in the body of the email. I tend to skip the outline or synopsis and just get to the pages. I am especially turned off by gimmicky, boastful queries.

How do you feel about self-publishing, and what do you see happening with it in the near future? I'm pro-self-publishing. It's a great option for a lot of writers. One of my most important clients is a hybrid writer, with an indie series and books he writes for a traditional publisher. That's a good model for a prolific writer.

Do you think there are too many, too few, or just enough agents? I haven't given this much thought, to be honest. A lot of people get into it and then leave in a couple of years, indicating that it's harder than they thought.

Do you think Amazon will become the country's largest employer within 10 years? Quite possibly. They keep growing, and they have a lot of natural advantage at this point.

Why do you think some books become super-successful (beyond the obvious reasons)? The super-huge books, books at the level of *Harry Potter* and *The Girl with the Dragon Tattoo*, are just rare events where everything comes together at once. You can't duplicate it.

Do you think agents are likely to become millionaires? Probably not, except through the method of careful saving and funding one's retirement account. There's a lottery aspect to this business, though. All you need is one writer to hit it really big.

Do you think agents tend toward certain personality types? I don't know, to be honest. I would say they lean toward being outgoing, but I've met some shy agents at conferences.

Do you think writers tend to be more or less narcissistic than the population at large? Less narcissistic, more neurotic maybe.

Knowing what you know now, would you become an agent again? Absolutely! I would have started earlier, in fact.

Why did you choose to become an agent? I love books, writers, and the literary field in general.

Do you think many talented writers fail to get published for avoidable reasons? If so, what are some of those reasons? Yes, I do. The number-one reason is that they don't work hard enough. Talent is important, but more important is study, work on the craft, and persistence. A lot of skilled writers never break through, because they don't put in the time.

WALES LITERARY AGENCY ❖ waleslit.com

Agent's name and contact info: Elizabeth Wales, Main Agent, waleslit@waleslit.com

Please describe your professional history. BA, Smith College; graduate work in English and American literature, Columbia University. Past work at Viking Penguin, the Strand, and Oxford University Press. Founded the agency in 1990 with Dan Levant. Member, AAR.

Please list five books you recently agented. *Victory Parade* by Leela Corman (Pantheon); *At Peace* by Samuel Harrington, MD (Grand Central); *Be Brave, Be Kind, Be Thankful* by Heather Lende (Algonquin); *Three Sides Water* by Peter Donahue (Ooligans Press); *In the Province of the Gods* by Kenny Fries (University of Wisconsin Press).

Please describe the kinds of books you want to agent. We represent quality mainstream fiction and narrative nonfiction. In fiction and nonfiction, we look for talented storytellers, both new and established, and we're especially interested in projects that could have a progressive cultural or political impact. Clients are from the entire country; as well, we represent a strong group of Northwest, West Coast, and Alaska writers. We are especially looking for nature and science writing and any compelling new stories and storytellers.

We *don't* represent the following: children's books, how-to, self-help, and almost all genre projects (romance, true crime, horror, action-adventure, science fiction/fantasy, technothrillers).

What should writers submit for consideration, and how should they send it? Writers should send their email queries without attachments to waleslit@waleslit.com. We do not accept queries by phone or regular mail.

WATERSIDE PRODUCTIONS, INC. ❖ www.waterside.com

2055 Oxford Avenue, Cardiff, CA 92007

Agent's name and contact info: Jill Kramer, jkcats210@gmail.com

What would you be doing right now if not responding to this survey? Playing tennis or pickleball.

What would you be if not an agent (other than a dog, cat, or other mammal)? A tennis star or a singer-songwriter.

Do you think independent (noncorporate) publishing will be stronger, weaker, or the same over the next few years? The same.

Please describe your professional history. Former editorial director at major publishing company; currently literary agent and freelance editor/writer/proofreader.

How would you define the "client from hell"? Someone who constantly asks, "Where's my money?," thinks they're going to be able to retire after writing one book, or is angry that they're not going to get a six-figure advance.

Please list five books you recently agented. Indivisible by Jim Hester (political), *Love Is Greater Than Pain* by Marilyn Kapp (mind-body-spirit), *Wrong in All the Right Ways* by Tiffany Brownlee (young adult), *Back to Jesus* by Doreen Virtue (Christian), *I Don't Know How to Grieve* by Rabbi Ben Kamin (spiritual self-help).

Please describe the kinds of books you want to agent. Virtually anything except middle grade and sci-fi/fantasy.

What should writers submit for consideration, and how should they send it? Email: jkcats210@gmail.com. Cover letter and a few chapters.

How do you feel about self-publishing, and what do you see happening with it in the near future? Great avenue for authors without a platform. It will continue to grow.

Do you think Amazon will become the country's largest employer within 10 years? Either Amazon or Google.

Why do you think some books become super-successful (beyond the obvious reasons)? Luck.

Knowing what you know now, would you become an agent again? Yes.

Why did you choose to become an agent? I was on the other side for 18 years and wanted to try my hand on this side.

Do you think many talented writers fail to get published for avoidable reasons? If so, what are some of those reasons? They give up after being rejected a few (or several) times.

Agent's name and contact info: Kristen Moeller, MS, kristen.waterside@gmail.com

What would you be doing right now if not responding to this survey? After finishing work for my clients, I would be hiking with my dogs in the beautiful Colorado mountains. Or reading a book (for fun!).

What would you be if not an agent (other than a dog, cat, or other mammal)? A rock star!

Do you think independent (noncorporate) publishing will be stronger, weaker, or the same over the next few years? Stronger. I love working with independent publishers as both an author and an agent. I find we get a quicker response — and they are more willing to take chances on new authors.

Please describe your professional history. As a formally trained therapist with a master's in counseling and as a life coach, I spent decades helping people move through their fears and create a life they loved. My own life altered when I wrote my first book (*Waiting for Jack*, Morgan James Publishing, 2010, with a foreword by Jack Canfield) — and I fell madly in love with the wonderful world of books.

Enthralled by the "behind the scenes" of publishing, I befriended and became colleagues with bestselling authors, top agents, and savvy editors as I studied the trends. During this time, I shared the stage with well-known thought leaders, hosted a popular internet radio show, and coached new authors in writing their books and getting published. I then joined the Morgan James Publishing team as an acquisitions editor and later became the executive publisher for Persona Publishing, specializing in boutique self-publishing.

In 2012, after losing my dream home and all my worldly possessions to a raging and sudden wildfire that killed 3 people and demolished 21 homes, I began a blog called *Walking through Fire*, which explored our cultural discomfort with grief and became a place to process my own loss. During this time, I was picked up by an independent publisher for my second book, *What Are You Waiting For?* (Viva Editions, 2013). My most recent book, *Phoenix Rising: Stories of Remarkable Women Walking through Fire* (Morgan James Publishing, 2016), tells the heart-wrenching stories of 21 women impacted by Colorado wildfires.

With close to three decades of training in psychology and personal growth, along with my publishing, writing, and editing background, I guide my clients to create a lasting legacy utilizing the power of a book. I am proud to have been featured on NPR, ABC, NBC, and Fox News and in the *New York Times* and the *Huffington Post* — and loved my stint on A&E's *Tiny House Nation*. My husband and I live in the mountains of Colorado with our two Rhodesian ridgebacks and a pit bull rescue.

How would you define the "client from hell"? I tend to take referrals only, so people come to me highly recommended — and they know I will hold them accountable if someone they send me is too high-maintenance. Otherwise, I do try to get to know someone's expectations right off the bat. I like enthusiasm but appreciate when someone has educated themselves about the wonderful world of publishing. I don't mind helping someone learn, but they need to show that they have done their homework. I also don't mind someone checking in to see how things are progressing — but give me enough time to do my job, please!

Do you think Earth was created a few thousand years ago or several billion years ago? Billions (said channeling Dr. Evil from *Austin Powers*).

Please describe the kinds of books you want to agent. I mostly work with women who write real and gritty memoir and literary fiction with strong female leads about walking through the fires of life — exploring depths and darkness while maintaining a strong psychological base.

What should writers submit for consideration, and how should they send it? To start, a mini book proposal via email containing the following: (1) pitch and hook; (2) bio demonstrating why you are an expert or why you should be the one writing this book; (3) short summary; and (4) marketing plan.

How do you feel about self-publishing, and what do you see happening with it in the near future? Self-pub is great, and there is definitely a time and a place for it. I believe that just because someone self-publishes doesn't give license to slack on the quality of the writing. Write with the attention to detail as if you were trying to gain the attention of a major house. We don't need more books — we need more books that matter.

Do you think Amazon will become the country's largest employer within 10 years? It's looking that way. I am not an Amazon basher. I live in a small town, and although we shop locally, we need to supplement from Amazon from time to time. I love browsing for books on Amazon.

Why do you think some books become super-successful (beyond the obvious reasons)? Right voice at the right time driven by passion and blood, sweat, and tears. And they are written by authors who don't give up. Ever.

Do you think agents are likely to become millionaires? Probably not. The game today is smaller numbers — but of course we always look for that uber-breakthrough superstar author too.

Do you think agents tend toward certain personality types? Nope! A wide range of folks who share a love of the written word — and (hopefully) an attention to detail.

Do you think writers tend to be more or less narcissistic than the population at large? I don't believe it's about narcissism. I believe that for most authors it's an art, an expression and a desire to reach into readers' hearts and minds.

Knowing what you know now, would you become an agent again? Yes. It's a career in which I can grow older and wiser.

Why did you choose to become an agent? It was the perfect combination of my love of the world of books and publishing after becoming an author myself, synthesized with my background as a therapist and my years of coaching women in writing their memoirs.

Do you think many talented writers fail to get published for avoidable reasons? If so, what are some of those reasons? They give up. They lose steam. They fail to understand that they have to market their books. They don't develop their writing skills. They don't hire editors.

Optional shout-outs/comments: Thanks for such a great resource! I read your guidebook for years before becoming an agent! And I continue to read it as one of my strategies for keeping up with the trends.

Agent's name and contact info: Johanna Maaghul, johanna@waterside.com, 415-328-5303

What would you be doing right now if not responding to this survey? Reviewing projects for the coming year.

What would you be if not an agent (other than a dog, cat, or other mammal)? Writing software to help agents. I love organized systems, and selling books is all about being organized, knowing what is where, and clearing more space to best get to know the publishers and what they are looking for.

Do you think independent (noncorporate) publishing will be stronger, weaker, or the same over the next few years? It is all getting stronger.

Please describe your professional history. I was a programmer by trade; then, through a series of life-changing events, I became a writer myself. I saw the amount of commitment marketing published work required and decided my energy was best used on the support side as an agent. I have not looked back.

How would you define the "client from hell"? Someone who puts their own success above the feedback of readers and publishers.

Do you think Earth was created a few thousand years ago or several billion years ago? Several billion.

Please list five books you recently agented. *Diet for Divine Connection*, *I Quit Complaining*, *Waking Parent*, several audio titles by Jeff Brown, and an as yet not publicly released exposé on the history of opium.

Please describe the kinds of books you want to agent. Books that make people look at the world differently by authors who spend their waking hours promoting their vision to complement their book.

What should writers submit for consideration, and how should they send it? They should send me a proposal along with a summary of their platform and how they are out and about in the world sharing their gifts in addition to their writing.

How do you feel about self-publishing, and what do you see happening with it in the near future? It's important. If people really are dedicated to getting their work out, they should explore it, and many publishers are becoming more and more open to picking up self-published books.

Do you think there are too many, too few, or just enough agents? I am not sure. I hope just enough.

Do you think Amazon will become the country's largest employer within 10 years? I hope not. I think diversity in the publishing world needs to thrive somehow.

Why do you think some books become super-successful (beyond the obvious reasons)? The author's commitment to continually sharing the message. And not trying to market too many books. Sometimes a lifetime can be spent marketing one powerful book.

Do you think agents are likely to become millionaires? Some do. It's a labor of love. But to make enough money as an agent to become better at it always is my goal.

Do you think agents tend toward certain personality types? It requires a lot of listening and discernment and the ability to say no, with love.

Do you think writers tend to be more or less narcissistic than the population at large? Writers have very busy brains and lots to say, and if they don't get it out and stay connected with their audience (or if they don't have an audience), they can become very self-absorbed.

Knowing what you know now, would you become an agent again? Yes!

Why did you choose to become an agent? Because I love working with authors and helping them get their work into the world.

Do you think many talented writers fail to get published for avoidable reasons? If so, what are some of those reasons? Not necessarily. It really, truly is a lot of work. And more than just writing. It's marketing and putting yourself out there day after day.

WENDY SCHMALZ AGENCY ❖ schmalzagency.com

402 Union Street, #831, Hudson, NY 12534

Agent's name and contact info: Wendy Schmalz, wendy@schmalzagency.com, 518-672-7697

What would you be doing right now if not responding to this survey? Puttering in my woodworking shop.

What would you be if not an agent (other than a dog, cat, or other mammal)? A dog.

Do you think independent (noncorporate) publishing will be stronger, weaker, or the same over the next few years? Stronger.

Please describe your professional history. I founded my agency in 2002 after being a principal agent at Harold Ober Associates for many years.

How would you define the "client from hell"? Passive-aggressiveness seems to be a common malady in authors. It makes for a difficult and unproductive relationship.

Please list five books you recently agented. Caroline: Little House Revisited by Sarah Miller, Everything All at Once by Katrina Leno, Count All Her Bones by April Henry, Echo's Sister by Paul Mosier, Threads by Ami Polonsky.

Please describe the kinds of books you want to agent. Innovative young adult and middle grade novels with strong voices.

What should writers submit for consideration, and how should they send it? They should email a synopsis pasted in a query email. No attachments, and no samples unless requested.

Do you think writers tend to be more or less narcissistic than the population at large? No.

Knowing what you know now, would you become an agent again? Absolutely! It's the only profession I've ever had, and I adore it.

Why did you choose to become an agent? I was reading Tennessee Williams's autobiography and was taken in by his praise for his agent. I was a teenager and had no idea there was such a thing as an agent. Right then and there I decided that's what I wanted to be.

Do you think many talented writers fail to get published for avoidable reasons? If so, what are some of those reasons? Bad social skills.

WILLIAMSON LITERARY ❖ www.esjwilliamson.com

Agent's name: Emily Williamson, emily@chrysaliseditorial.com

What would you be doing right now if not responding to this survey? I would still be opening a dozen raw oysters. For the first time. With a fancy new knife. The ones I successfully opened were delicious, the remaining four were impossible, and I am, as I expected, now bleeding. So if I wasn't answering this survey, I would be licking my salty wounds and cussing. Instead, I am being productive.

What would you be if not an agent (other than a dog, cat, or other mammal)? Jane Goodall. Wait…she's a mammal. A wildlife biologist or animal behaviorist. I would also make a very good doorman (ask my dog).

Do you think independent (noncorporate) publishing will be stronger, weaker, or the same over the next few years? Stronger. With numerous ways for publishers to reach readers (ebooks, print-on-demand, small press distributors, social media, sites like Goodreads, new ways to promote books), there's more opportunity for small publishers to survive. There has always been a huge pool of writers looking to be published, but now these writers also have more opportunities to see their books in print, because independent publishers can take a chance on an unknown author or an unconventional manuscript that just doesn't fit well into corporate publishers' lists.

Please describe your professional history. Prior to becoming an agent, I was an archaeologist for 13 years. I did fieldwork all over the US and the Pacific; I also wrote and edited archaeological field reports and environmental assessments. I decided to make a career change in 2010 and pursue my master's degree in writing at Johns Hopkins University, which I earned in 2012.

In 2011 I began working with my current business partner at Chrysalis Editorial, a small author-services company in Washington, DC. At Chrysalis we provide manuscript critiques, copyediting, publishing advice, and other writing assistance. In 2016 I decided to start my agency. (Chrysalis Editorial is a separate venture, a company owned by my business partner. It and my agency are unrelated, and if a client pays me for editing services through Chrysalis, then I cannot represent them at Williamson Literary. I do not charge fees as an agent. This is clearly stated on my website.)

How would you define the "client from hell"? I had one. I'm not sure what parts of this survey you want to publish, so I won't go into detail and embarrass anyone, but for me a client from hell is one who is verbally abusive in the face of constructive criticism, when things aren't going their way, or when they are not becoming rich and famous fast enough. I also don't want a client who doesn't have a clear vision of why they are doing this, why they write, and what it means to them.

Do you think Earth was created a few thousand years ago or several billion years ago? I used to think about this very thing much more often, when I was older. I'm younger than that now. I can tell you I once found a hadrosaur (duck-billed dinosaur) fossil while on an archaeological survey, and it wasn't even buried, just sitting there like it was dropped yesterday. So several billion years has got to be out of the question, right?

Please list five books you recently agented. *Collision of Wills: Johnny Unitas, Don Shula and the Rise of the Modern NFL* by Jack Gilden (University of Nebraska Press, fall 2018); *Spitfire* (middle grade novel) by Evan Balkan (Amphorae, summer 2018); *Saving Phoebe Murrow* (women's fiction) by Herta Feely (Bonnier Zaffre UK [Twenty7 Books] and Upper Hand Press US, fall 2016); *Making Tracks* (a children's travel/activity book series) by Paige S. Finger and Maria Gorgolas (currently seeking a publisher); *Murder Secret* (mystery/thriller) by C. T. Mitchell (signed last month, manuscript preparation in progress).

Please describe the kinds of books you want to agent. Nonfiction: sports and sports history, science and the environment, world travel, biographies, motivational (i.e., business strategies for aspiring entrepreneurs, work that informs or inspires social change and/or advocates for women and minorities). Commercial fiction: all genres except romance. Clear and fast-paced plot lines, authoritative writing, solid knowledge of the formula for a "page turner," solid author platform. Literary fiction: really stellar, beautiful writing, unusual and unforgettable characters, unique settings. Paint me something. Children's: books that talk up to children, that inspire and build confidence. I like cleverness and humor; I'm not interested in verse unless it is metrically correct and without lazy rhymes; prefer middle grade.

What should writers submit for consideration, and how should they send it? I would like them to submit a query letter in the body of an email and include their proposal or manuscript as an attachment.

How do you feel about self-publishing, and what do you see happening with it in the near future? It's mostly good and somewhat bad for writers. It's good for writers to see their work in print. It's bad in that it has contributed to the creation of a great deal of "noise" out there. All the self-published books flooding the market have made it harder for authors to sell their books successfully, and often they are deceived or disappointed in the process. Many people think they can just throw a book up on Amazon and it will fly off the virtual shelves. Without dedicating yourself to book marketing and self-marketing, it's really hard to get a self-published work noticed at all. It also leads many authors to think that having a self-published book will help their chances of getting an agent or a traditional publishing deal, and that's not the case most of the time. In the near future, I see self-publishing continuing to grow.

Do you think there are too many, too few, or just enough agents? Just enough.

Do you think Amazon will become the country's largest employer within 10 years? They will be the new world order.

Why do you think some books become super-successful (beyond the obvious reasons)? Different genres can have different priorities. However, broadly speaking, big books have clear, clean prose and a human story that hits a cultural nerve at the right time.

Do you think agents are likely to become millionaires? Hint: I play fantasy football. I'm not a millionaire yet, but I'm getting closer by the week!

Do you think agents tend toward certain personality types? Somewhat. I know that I've just gotten a good feeling about some of the authors I have spoken to recently and, in combination with their work, that makes me feel like they'd be someone I'd like to champion. But first and foremost, I think agents look to the quality of the manuscript itself.

Do you think writers tend to be more or less narcissistic than the population at large? About the same, but the danger of becoming narcissistic may be baked into a profession such as writing. If you are dedicated to your craft, you have to be a bit self-absorbed, you have to have a single-minded vision of who you are as a writer and what success looks like to you. You have to sometimes fall in love with your own brilliance on the page.

Knowing what you know now, would you become an agent again? I'm just getting started. Ask me again in 10 years. I suspect the answer will be yes.

Why did you choose to become an agent? It's corny and probably naive, but I really like the idea of helping writers achieve what they've always wanted to achieve. The dream of having your book in print is huge, and I know so many very talented writers who have been working hard for many years, but who haven't yet been able to see their talent realized. I want to find those great writers and be a part of their success. I also find the publishing world fascinating, and I want to prove to myself that I can make this business successful.

Do you think many talented writers fail to get published for avoidable reasons? If so, what are some of those reasons? Yes. For one, I'm continually surprised by how little writers know about how to approach agents and publishers. I didn't know anything when I first started, but there's plenty of opportunity to learn (great books, blogs, guides such as *Jeff Herman's Guide to Book Publishers, Editors & Literary Agents*, writing centers and writer communities, conferences, etc.), and yet so many writers don't know how to present themselves. I've received everything from "Want to be a part of something really lucrative?" to "I'm looking for an agent, give me a call," to weird, handwritten scraps of paper saying, "Seeking Literary Agent!!!!!" I'm not super-cynical; I'll open an attachment. But if a writer can't write a proper query and/or synopsis, can I trust them to pull off a whole novel? A little goes a long way, and if you've got writing chops, it might just come down to unlocking that first door, so why not figure out what the key is for doing that?

Another thing is failing to factor in the importance of an author platform. A lot of writers are resistant to that. I get that. I'm a writer too, and I don't want to spend my days promoting myself. I want to write. But if you're invisible online, you're not helping yourself. Making an effort to be heard above the noise goes a long way. Yes, your writing should speak for itself, and perhaps it's so good it doesn't matter if you're invisible, but this can be a capricious business, and every advantage you give yourself is important.

Optional shout-outs/comments: This has been the most delightful survey I've ever participated in. The one my credit card company requested the other day regarding the usefulness of their bill pay is a close second…not really.

One thing I'd like to say is that I want to build good relationships with authors and help them build good relationships with their publishers. My husband, who has been a poet and professor for 28 years, recently said to me, "When a bunch of writers get together, they don't talk about writing. They bitch about their agents and their publishers." I don't want to be bitched about. I want to find good people with good books and work *for* them, not near them. My most recently published client, Jack Gilden, wrote the following in the acknowledgments of his forthcoming book: "The first person I should thank is my agent, Emily Williamson. Her faith and enthusiasm for my work and her advocacy meant a great deal to me, as did her judgment. She is a first-rate professional who became my friend and confidant as well as my agent." I want to continue to be that for all my clients.

WRITERS HOUSE, LLC ❖ www.writershouse.com

Agent's name and contact info: Stephen Barr, 212-685-2663, sbarr@writershouse.com

What would you be doing right now if not responding to this survey? I can't wait to find out!

What would you be if not an agent (other than a dog, cat, or other mammal)? I hope I never find out!

Do you think independent (noncorporate) publishing will be stronger, weaker, or the same over the next few years? Stronger, almost invariably.

Please describe your professional history. In short, I was always obviously going to be an English major, and then I was (at UCLA). Then I moved to New York 12 seconds after graduating, failed to get about 17 jobs, landed an internship at an awesome, intimate film/literary agency called Hotchkiss & Associates, and then landed a simultaneous internship at an awesome, intimate literary agency called Writers House. I'm so fond of my job that I'll probably do it even after I become a skeleton.

How would you define the "client from hell"? Pitchfork, horns, tail, hooves, carrying a memoir about how hard it is to date.

Do you think Earth was created a few thousand years ago or several billion years ago? Objection: irrelevant!

Please list five books you recently agented. Mourning at White Garden, by Maggie Thrash, author-illustrator of the LA Times Book Prize–nominated Honor Girl; this is her next full-color graphic memoir about the Southern mansion she was raised in and the day her cat disappeared within its walls, which led Maggie to discover a hallway she'd never noticed before, hiding a brother she didn't know she had (Candlewick). Christian Yee's debut The Epic Crush of Genie Lo, launching a series pitched as Buffy the Vampire Slayer in a melee with American-born Chinese, in which a 15-year-old wonders if she's qualified to gain admission to an Ivy League school and then becomes powerful enough to break through the gates of heaven with her fists (Abrams). David Goodner's Kondo and Kezumi Visit Giant Island, the first in a chapter-book series about two island-dwelling best buddies who've never met anyone else, ever, until a map of the surrounding waters washes ashore and turns them into explorers (as well as good neighbors), illustrated by Andrea Tsurumi (Disney-Hyperion). Andrea Tsurumi's debut picture book Accident!, the story of an armadillo kicking off a crescendo of calamities in a Richard Scarry–ish world of infinite, absurd detail (Houghton Mifflin Harcourt). Nate Staniforth's Here Is Real Magic, the memoir of a curiously philosophical magician (who's lectured at Oxford University and the Mayo Clinic) following his evolution from obsessed wunderkind to disillusioned wanderer and telling the story of his rediscovery of astonishment — and the importance of wonder in everyday life — during his trip to the slums of India, where he infiltrated a 3,000-year-old clan of street magicians (Bloomsbury).

Please describe the kinds of books you want to agent. At the moment, I've got a particular hankering for intricate, heart-on-its-sleeve, voice-abundant young adult like *King Dork* or *The Highest Tide* (bonus points for unrequited love stories!); audacious, experimental young adult mysteries or fantasies that handcuff humor and tragedy to the same radiator; middle grade that takes on heavy themes with a light, optimistic, eccentric touch; sweet and/or silly and/or heartbreaking picture books from adventurous author-illustrators; unexpected memoirs with itchy voices; narrative nonfiction that tackles hard-to-tackle issues; and any fiction that rewards readers line by line by letting them get to know at least one character really, really well (recent favorites include *Fourth of July Creek*, *& Sons: A Novel*, *Jeff in Venice*, *The Lazarus Project*, *Diary of a Bad Year*, *Horns*, and *Skippy Dies*). I'm also willing to be a sucker for detective stories that bend reality; ghost stories that blow reality to hell; Secret Book X (I don't know what Secret Book X is, but suffice it to say, I'm open to the occasional curveball).

What should writers submit for consideration, and how should they send it? Far and away the best approach is just to send me an honest, conversational email describing the book, the author, and some hopes and dreams and then let the first 10 or 15 pages do the talking.

How do you feel about self-publishing, and what do you see happening with it in the near future? It's perfect for some, the same way that traditional publishing is perfect for others!

Do you think there are too many, too few, or just enough agents? Apart from being an agent myself, who am I to say?

Do you think Amazon will become the country's largest employer within 10 years? Close, but no cigar (even if they were able to sell cigars).

Why do you think some books become super-successful (beyond the obvious reasons)? As with most successes, it's usually a combination of extraordinary effort and unpredictable fortune.

Do you think agents are likely to become millionaires? Likelihoods are for the birds!

Do you think agents tend toward certain personality types? Perhaps, but with a bundle of exceptions.

Do you think writers tend to be more or less narcissistic than the population at large? Both, depending on the context.

Knowing what you know now, would you become an agent again? I would do it all over again, but with a different haircut.

Why did you choose to become an agent? I became an agent because my favorite thing in the world is talking to people about things that don't exist (or don't exist yet), and writers' brains are full of things that don't exist (or don't exist yet).

Do you think many talented writers fail to get published for avoidable reasons? If so, what are some of those reasons? The only truly identifiable and truly avoidable reason is giving up. ☺

THE ZACK COMPANY, INC. ❖ www.zackcompany.com

Agent's name: Andrew Zack, President

What would you be doing right now if not responding to this survey? Reviewing emails and updating submission records.

What would you be if not an agent (other than a dog, cat, or other mammal)? This is a dangerous question for someone my age. President of the United States (apparently, anyone can do it!)? Scriptwriter? Talent agent?

Do you think independent (noncorporate) publishing will be stronger, weaker, or the same over the next few years? It will continue to grow and to breed many small publishers focused on online sales.

Please describe your professional history. I began working in a bookstore in high school, the same one I'd spent my allowance at for years. Following college, I attended the Radcliffe Publishing Course and then began work in subsidiary rights at Simon & Schuster. From there, I moved to editorial positions at Warner Books, Donald I. Fine, and the Berkley Publishing Group. After Berkley, I did freelance work for several publishers and reviewed books for the Book-of-the-Month Club and Kirkus. I was also a consulting editor for Tom Doherty's Forge Books. From there, I joined the Scovil Chichak Galen Literary Agency, which I left after two and a half years to start my own firm. Since then, I have also launched an author-coaching firm, Author Coach, and a small press, Endpapers Press.

How would you define the "client from hell"? The client from hell has probably published two or three, maybe four, books. These are likely fiction but might be nonfiction. Although not always male, let's just say "he." He has "fired" his previous agent because his career is going nowhere and that is, of course, the agent's fault. He is looking for an agent who can "make things happen." And just to make sure those things happen, he calls a minimum of three or four times a week for updates. He attempts to micromanage me as though I am an employee whom he is paying a six-figure yearly salary (but likely the commissions are far short of even five figures). This client is convinced that his ideas are future bestsellers and can't understand why no one agrees with him. He wants instant feedback from me and never once considers that I may have other clients. Bottom line: clients from hell believe that their needs outweigh everyone else's: their agent's, their editor's, their publicist's, and the needs of all the other clients the agent represents.

Do you think Earth was created a few thousand years ago or several billion years ago? Billions. In fact, if you are a creationist, I am absolutely the wrong agent for you.

Please list five books you recently agented. The best resource for news about the authors and works I represent is the firm's website, www.zackcompany.com.

Please describe the kinds of books you want to agent. Serious narrative nonfiction; history and oral history, particularly military history and intelligence-services history; politics and current affairs by established journalists and political insiders or pundits; science and technology and how they affect society by established journalists, science writers, or experts in their fields; biography, autobiography, or memoir by or about newsworthy individuals, individuals whose lives have made a contribution to the historical record; personal finance and investing; parenting by established experts in their field; health and medicine by doctors or established medical writers; business by nationally recognized business leaders or established business writers, for example, from the *Wall Street Journal*; relationship books by credentialed experts, that is, psychiatrists, psychologists, therapists with prior publishing credits. Commercial fiction (but not "women's fiction"); thrillers in every shape and form — international, serial killer, medical, scientific, computer, psychological, military, legal; mysteries and not-so-hard-boiled crime novels; action novels, but not action-adventure; science fiction and fantasy, preferably hard science fiction or military science fiction (I was a huge Robert Heinlein fan when I was younger) and big, elaborate fantasies (not coming-of-age fantasies) that take you to a new and established world; horror novels that take you on a roller-coaster ride; historical fiction (but not Westerns).

What should writers submit for consideration, and how should they send it? Writers should visit the submissions page on our website and follow the instructions to query us.

How do you feel about self-publishing, and what do you see happening with it in the near future? Self-publishing offers incredible opportunities for authors who know their market and who are willing to put the time and money into properly publishing, marketing, and promoting their work. However, I do think authors need to choose a path. I recommend first trying to get published traditionally and then moving on in a year or so, if you still haven't found an agent or publisher.

Do you think there are too many, too few, or just enough agents? There are too many small agencies, and the business would benefit from the economies of scale created by working together in larger agencies.

Do you think Amazon will become the country's largest employer within 10 years? That's unlikely. As their ability to use automated fulfillment improves, they will need fewer employees. I would not be surprised if the number of employees shrinks over the next 10 years.

Why do you think some books become super-successful (beyond the obvious reasons)? If I knew the answer to this, I'd be living in my villa on Lake Como and enjoying dinners with the Clooneys. And if publishers knew the answer, they would only publish super-successful books, which we all know they do not, so the answer to this question remains a mystery.

Do you think agents are likely to become millionaires? History has given us the answer to this. Very few become millionaires.

Do you think agents tend toward certain personality types? Type A, for the most part.

Do you think writers tend to be more or less narcissistic than the population at large? Less than Donald Trump, more than Punxsutawney Phil.

Knowing what you know now, would you become an agent again? Sure, and I would have flown to wherever John Grisham and Dan Brown and J. K. Rowling lived and offered to represent them before they had an agent. Or maybe I would have just murdered them and written all of their books myself. Knowing the future is tricky. It can tempt you to do things you wouldn't do without knowing what was going to happen.

Why did you choose to become an agent? I had been an editor but was laid off. A number of authors asked me to represent them. I was wary of launching my own firm, but when I had an opportunity to join an agency and work with veteran agents, I took it.

Do you think many talented writers fail to get published for avoidable reasons? If so, what are some of those reasons? No. I don't think it is the writers' fault. Most editors are looking for books they "like." They are less interested in books that will sell and more interested in books that personally appeal to them. Editors too often fail to be blatantly commercial and willing to publish authors who clearly have a market or potential but whom they do not personally want to read.

Optional shout-outs/comments: The agent-author relationship is a business partnership. Agents have their role, and authors have their role. Neither is an employee of the other.

Interestingly enough, I never hear about agents or authors hiring each other, but I hear about them firing one another all the time. Agents, obviously, are businesspeople. Authors need to be businesspeople, too. Authors should do their best to be as informed as possible about the nature of the publishing business. They should talk to their local independent bookseller (and if they really want to learn a few things, they should get a part-time job working in a bookstore). The best client is an educated client. Authors should be able to ask their agents all the questions they want, and if an author's agent disagrees with that, it's time to find another agent. But authors also need to recognize that every minute spent on the phone with them is a minute that could be spent selling their projects. As long as authors understand the job they have and the job agents have in the author-agent relationship, the business partnership will flourish and be profitable.

ZIMMERMANN LITERARY ❖ www.zimmermannliterary.com

Agent's name and contact info: Helen Adams Zimmermann, submit@zimmagency.com

What would you be doing right now if not responding to this survey? Most likely editing a proposal.

Please describe your professional history. I started my publishing career about 25 years ago in the marketing department of Random House. After a dozen years as the director of advertising and promotion for one of their divisions, the Crown Publishing Group, I moved to New York's Hudson Valley, where I worked at an independent bookstore as the author events director. Event-goers would always ask me, "How do I get published?" and I would always say, "You need an agent." Pretty soon one of them convinced me to take their material to an editor and, wham, I was an agent!

How would you define the "client from hell"? One who doesn't take into consideration what I'm telling them.

Please list five books you recently agented. The Champion's Mind by Jim Afremow (Rodale), The Wrecking Crew by Kent Hartman (St. Martin's), Cover Me by Ray Padgett (Sterling), Chosen by a Horse by Susan Richards (Soho, Harcourt), The Normal Bar by Chrisanna Northrup (Crown).

Please describe the kinds of books you want to agent. I am currently concentrating my nonfiction efforts in health and wellness, relationships, pop culture, women's interest, lifestyle, sports, and music. I am also drawn to memoirs that speak to a larger social or historical circumstance or introduce me to a new phenomenon. And I am always looking for a work of fiction that will keep me up at night!

What should writers submit for consideration, and how should they send it? Queries are preferred via email. *Please*, no attachments until I express interest. For nonfiction queries, initial contact should just be a pitch letter. For fiction queries, I prefer a summary, your bio, and the first chapter as text in the email (not as an attachment). If I express interest, I will need to see a full proposal for nonfiction and the remainder of the manuscript for fiction. I receive many submissions and regretfully can't reply to each one, so please understand that if you don't hear from me in two weeks it is most likely because the project isn't right for my agency.

Do you think many talented writers fail to get published for avoidable reasons? If so, what are some of those reasons? Yes, I do. Writing a book is only the very first step to getting published. You need to study the industry, do your agent research carefully, and be willing to go the *long* haul. A detailed video to help new authors is available on my other website, www.projectpublish.com — I've been told it's a valuable resource.

Part 5
INDEPENDENT EDITORS

INTRODUCTION
EDITORS VS. SCAMMERS

Jeff Herman

What Is an Independent Book Editor?

Someone who is qualified to make your proposal and/or manuscript better than you could do by yourself.

Why Might You Want to Retain an Editor?

Because even "perfect" writers are imperfect and can greatly benefit from an objective and qualified edit. Selling your work to agents and publishers is extremely competitive, so you want your editorial product to be as strong as possible. Typos, grammatical errors, and missed opportunities to say it better can mean the difference between "yes" and "no." The high-end editors and consultants listed here offer years of specialized experience along the lines of what one would expect from any other high-end consultant, whether legal, medical, or financial. Their services are not about copyediting and proofreading. Most editors of this ilk not only ensure that the text is as strong as it should be for the given market but also guide writers on navigating the publishing arena. Even if you already have a publishing deal, the reality is that in-house editors are not necessarily going to do a pristine editing job, and what gets published is a reflection on you, not them. Self-publishers should be especially vigilant about having their work professionally vetted and edited prior to publication.

What Kind of Editor Should You Retain?

Someone who has a genuine history of editing the kind of work you are writing. It's best if you actually read some of the works they have edited and communicate with some of the people who have used their services.

Where Can You Find Qualified Editors?

This section lists dozens of the most experienced and qualified independent editors in America. Most of them have many years of traditional in-house publishing experience, and they may have even edited one or more of your favorite books. The editors in this section are members of small, informal organizations that enable freelance editors to network, teach, and support each other in mutually beneficial ways. For instance, an editor who specializes in romance novels can refer science fiction writers to an appropriate editor, and vice versa. The editors prefer to keep their groups no larger than the number of people that can comfortably fit in a Manhattan living room, which is why new groups keep forming.

Most affiliated members reside in and around New York City, which is only natural since almost all of them have worked for New York publishers. However, there surely are many excellent editors throughout the country who don't belong to one of these organizations and haven't worked for a New York publisher. They can be found through Google, Editcetera (www.editcetera.com), or the Editorial Freelancers Association (www.the-efa.org) and by networking with fellow writers. No editor should be dismissed simply because they aren't listed in this section. I was only able to list the editors I have personal confidence in, and membership in one of these groups gives me that confidence. I welcome your suggestions for additional editors to include in future editions (jeff@jeffherman.com).

What Does It Cost to Hire an Editor?

Frankly, I'm not sure. It obviously depends on what type or level of editing you need, who you use, and when you use them. More experienced editors, and those with some "big hits" on their résumés, will presumably charge more than others. Even stated rates might be negotiable. For instance, someone who is unbooked at the time you approach them will probably be more price-flexible than someone who's carrying a waiting list. The best thing to do is ask experienced people and maybe shop around.

What about Scams?

Unfortunately, scams are legion in all areas of enterprise. You need to be careful and discerning without becoming cynical or paranoid. Here are some tips.

- Only retain the actual person who will be working with you, not a company that will randomly assign someone to you.
- Avoid anyone who makes outlandish promises before they have even seen your work. Actually, don't give anyone money before they see your work and give you a proposal for what they will do and what it will cost.
- It's always smart to get everything in writing. This doesn't mean retaining a lawyer to negotiate your arrangement with the editor. The editor probably has a standard

template stating what they will do, when they will do it, a payment structure, and a termination procedure. If the editor doesn't already have a template, you should ask him or her to put all this information in writing for both of you to sign off on. Just remember that these kinds of "adult" procedures are meant to protect both of you.
- Check references, and surf the internet for complaints.

An independent editor isn't a literary agent or a publisher. If they are offering to represent and/or publish you for money (you pay them), it's likely a scam. If someone is promising to fulfill your most cherished publishing dreams for a fee, it's probably too good to be true. It no longer surprises me that intelligent people are sometimes suckered. The hunger to be published is generally governed by our emotions, and what our brains have to say about such things can often be rather boring.

AN EDITOR OF ONE'S OWN

Members of Words into Print

(For information about Words into Print, see page 460.)

Are book doctors really worth it? What do they do that agents and in-house editors might not? With all the help a writer can get on the journey from manuscript to published book, why hire an editor of one's own?

Before the Age of the Independent Editor, literary agents and publishing staff were the first publishing insiders to read a proposal or manuscript. Today, however, the focus on business interests is so demanding and the volume of submissions so great — agents alone take in hundreds of query letters a month — that a writer's work has to be white-hot before receiving serious consideration. In light of these developments, a writer may turn to an independent editor as the first expert reader in the world of publishing's gatekeepers.

What Do Independent Editors Do, and How Much Do They Charge?

Services. Not every writer and project will call for the services of an independent editor. However, if you are looking for the kind of personalized and extensive professional guidance beyond that gained from workshops, fellow writers, online sources, magazines, and books, hiring an editor may well be worth the investment. An editor of your own can provide a professional assessment of whether or not your project is ready to submit, and to whom you should submit it; expert assistance to make your manuscript or book proposal as good as it should be; help with preparing a convincing submissions package; and an advocate's voice and influence to guide you in your efforts toward publication.

Another key role an independent editor plays is to protect writers from querying their prospects before their material is irresistible. Premature submissions cause writers needless disappointment and frustration. Your editor can zero in on the thematic core, central idea, or story line that needs to be conveyed in a way that is most likely to attract an agent and a publisher. In short, an editor of your own can identify the most appealing, salable aspects of you and your work.

Rates. "Good editing is expensive," our venerable colleague Jerry Gross, editor of the book *Editors on Editing*, prudently notes. What kind of editing is good editing, and how expensive is it? The internet and other sources quote a wide range of rates from a variety of editors. The numbers are not necessarily accurate or reliable. We've seen hourly rates ranging from about $50 to well above $200. Several factors account for this spread: the type of editing, the editor's level of experience, and the publishing venue. For example, rates for copyediting are lower than those for substantive editing. Moreover, standards in book publishing are particularly rigorous because books are long, expensive to produce, made to last, and vulnerable to the long-term impact of reviewer criticism.

Process. Book editors are specialists. Every book project arrives on the desk of an independent editor at a certain level of readiness, and the first task is to determine what the project needs. A deep book edit is typically a painstaking, time-consuming process that may move at the pace of only three or four manuscript pages per hour — or, when less intensive, eight to twelve pages per hour. Occasionally a manuscript received by an independent is fully developed, needs only a light copyedit, and may well be ready to submit as is. In other cases, the editorial process may require one or more rounds of revisions. If you are hiring an editor to critique your work, you should be aware that reading the material takes considerably more time than writing the critique. Sometimes a flat fee, rather than an hourly rate, may be appropriate to the project. Sometimes an editor will offer a brief initial consultation at no charge. A reputable independent book editor will be able to recommend a course of action that may or may not include one or more types of editorial services, and give you a reliable estimate of the time and fees involved.

But Won't the In-House Editor Fix Your Book?

Sometimes. Maybe. To an extent. Independents and in-house editors are, in many ways, different creatures. For starters, in-house editors spend much of the day preparing for and going to meetings. Marketing meetings. Sales meetings. Editorial meetings. Production meetings. The mandate for most of these in-house editors is to acquire new book projects and to shepherd those that are already in the pipeline. With so many extended activities cutting into the business hours, the time for actually working on a manuscript can be short.

Many in-house editors have incoming manuscripts screened by an already overworked assistant. (The days of staff readers are long gone.) The only quiet time the editor has for reading might be evenings and weekends. We have known editors to take a week off from work just to edit a book and be accessible to their authors. These days, too, the acquiring editor may not do any substantive work on a book project under contract, leaving that task to a junior editor. There is also a distinct possibility the acquiring editor may leave the job before that book is published, and this can occur with the next editor, too, and the next, threatening the continuity of the project. All of which doesn't mean that there aren't a lot of hardworking people at the publishing house; it means that editors have more to do than ever before and must devote at least as much time to crunching numbers as to focusing on the writer and the book.

Independent editors, on the other hand, spend most of their business days working exclusively with authors and their texts. They typically handle only a few manuscripts at a time and are free from marketing and production obligations. An independent editor's primary interest is in helping you get your book polished and published. An editor of your own will see your project through — and often your next book, too.

What Do Agents Say about Independent Editors?

"As the book market gets tougher for selling both fiction and nonfiction it is imperative that all submissions be polished, edited, almost ready for the printer. Like many other agents, I do as much as possible to provide editorial input for the author, but there are time constraints. So independent editors provide a very valuable service these days in getting the manuscript or proposal in the best shape possible to increase the chances of impressing an editor and getting a sale with the best possible terms." — **Bill Contardi**

"Agents work diligently for our clients, but there are situations in which outside help is necessary. Perhaps a manuscript has been worked on so intensively that objectivity is lacking, or perhaps the particular skill required to do a job properly is not one of an agent's strong suits. Maybe more time is required than an agent can offer. Fortunately, agents and authors are able to tap into the talent and experience of an outside editor. The outside editors I've worked with offer invaluable support during the editing process itself and for the duration of a project. Their involvement can make the difference between an author getting a publishing contract or having to put a project aside, or the difference between a less- or more-desirable contract." — **Victoria Gould Pryor**

"The right editor or book doctor can make all the difference in whether a manuscript gets sold. A debut novelist, for example, may have a manuscript that is almost there, but not quite. With the input of a good editor, the novel can reach its full potential and be an attractive prospect to a potential publisher. Similarly, someone writing a memoir may have had a fascinating life but may not really have the God-given writing talent that will turn that life into a compelling and readable book. An editor can take that person's rough-hewn words and thoughts and turn them into a memoir that really sings on the printed page." — **Eric Myers**

"Occasionally a novel will land on my desk that I feel has talent or a good concept behind it but for whatever reason (the writing, the pacing) needs an inordinate amount of work. Instead of just rejecting it flat out I may then refer the author to a freelance editor, someone who has the time and expertise to help the author further shape and perfect their work."
— **Nina Collins**

"I have had several occasions to use the help of freelance editors and think they provide incalculable good service to the profession. In these competitive times, a manuscript has to be as polished and clean as possible to garner a good sale to a publisher. If it needs work, it simply provides an editor with a reason to turn it down. My job is to not give them any excuses. I do not have either the time or the ability to do the editorial work that may be required to make the manuscript salable. Paying a freelance professional to help shape a book into its most commercially viable form ultimately more than pays for itself."
— **Deborah Schneider**

So How Can You Find the Right Editor?

You've searched online. You've looked in directories such as this one. You've asked around. A personal recommendation from a published writer-friend who has used an independent editor for his or her work may or may not do the trick. Every author has different needs, every author-editor dynamic a different chemistry.

Although sometimes an author and editor "click" very quickly, many editors offer free consultations, and it's fine to contact more than one editor at this stage. A gratis consult may involve an editor's short take, by phone or in writing, on sample material the editor asked you to send. But how to distinguish among the many independent editors?

Some editorial groups are huge, and they are open to all who designate themselves as editors; it might take some additional research to identify the members who are most reputable and best suited to your work. The smaller groups consist of editors who have been nominated, vetted, and elected, which ensures the high quality of the individual professionals. They meet with regularity, share referrals, and discuss industry developments. Your consultation, references offered, and the terms of any subsequent agreement can tell the rest.

Another way to find the right editor is to prepare your manuscript to its best advantage — structurally, stylistically, and mechanically. Asking the opinion of one or more impartial readers — that is, not limiting your initial reviewers to friends and relatives — is a great strategy as well. If you have the benefit of a disinterested reader, you may be able to make some significant changes before sending an excerpt to an independent editor. One more element to consider: editors often will take your own personality and initial written inquiry into account as carefully as they do your writing. Seasoned independents do not take on every project that appears on their desk; they can pick and choose — and, working solo, they must.

Tales from the Trenches

We hope we've given you a sense of what an editor of your own can do for you and where we fit into the publishing picture. But next to firsthand experience, perhaps nothing communicates quite as sharply as an anecdote. Here are a few of ours from past and present members:

"An in-house editor called me with an unusual problem. He had signed up an acclaimed author for a new book project. She had written a number of stories — nonfiction narratives about her life in an exotic land. The problem was this: some of the stories had already been published in book form in England, and that collection had its own integrity in terms of theme and chronology; now she had written another set of stories, plus a diary of her travels. How could the published stories and the new ones be made into one book?

"I decided to disregard the structure of the published book altogether. As I reexamined each story according to theme, emotional quality, geographical location, and people involved, I kept looking for ways in which they might relate to each other. Eventually, I sensed a new and logical way in which to arrange them. I touched not one word of the author's prose. I did the same thing I always try to do when editing — imagine myself inside the skin of the writer. A prominent trade book review had this to say about the result: 'One story flows into the next....'" — **Alice Rosengard**

"A writer had hired me to help with his first book after his agent had sold it to a publisher because he wanted to expedite the revisions and final approval of his manuscript. As a result of our work together, the book came out sooner than anticipated; it also won an award and the author was interviewed on a major TV news program. The same author hired me a year later for his second book, purchased by a larger publisher, and this book, too, entailed some significant developmental editing. At that point we learned the in-house editor had left the publisher and a new one had come aboard. This editor not only objected strongly to one whole section of the book; she also gave the author a choice: revise the section in one week or put the project on hold for at least six more months.

"From halfway across the world, the writer called me on a Friday to explain his publishing crisis, which was also coinciding with a personal crisis, and asked if we could collaborate closely on the fifty pages in question over the weekend. I agreed and canceled my weekend plans, and we camped out at each end of the telephone and emailboxes almost nonstop for three days. He resubmitted the book on Tuesday, the book received all requisite signatures in-house, and a month later it went into production. This hands-on and sometimes unpredictable kind of collaboration with writers helps illustrate the special nature of independent editing." — **Katharine Turok**

"A writer with a truly astonishing story to tell received only rejections when he sent his query letter to agents. He had an informal proposal and assumed that his extraordinary experiences on the Amazon River would be enough to get him a book deal for his memoir. I could see right away that the query letter was confusing and didn't present him or his story in a powerful-enough light.

"I culled the most effective parts of his story and reworked the book proposal so that his enthusiasm and vivid tales dominated. We hammered out a succinct and compelling query letter. I offered the names of several agents I thought might be interested, and this time it worked. He signed with an agent who sold his manuscript to a major publisher."
— **Linda Carbone**

"My work on a book about a near-extinct bird species was greatly enhanced when the author gave me a tour of a California estuary. Guided by his passion and on-site expertise, I was able to spot exquisite birds, hear bird-watching lingo, and see his high-end scope in action. Now I understood the thrill of what he was writing about and was better able to help him communicate it.

"One of my most challenging assignments was to add action scenes to a memoir by an Olympic fencing champion. Here was a subject I knew nothing about. I tried to bone up in advance through reading, but my author had a better idea. Working his way across my living room floor, he sparred with an invisible opponent, demonstrating what he wished to describe in his book. I wrote down what I saw.

"As an independent editor, I have the time and freedom to work 'outside the book,' to literally enter the worlds my authors are writing about." — **Ruth Greenstein**

WHEN TO CALL THE (BOOK) DOCTOR

Sandi Gelles-Cole

Suppose you are an author with an inkling that you might require editorial assistance. Of course, in the world of legendary editor Maxwell Perkins and novelist William Faulkner — or, for that matter, the world of Carole Baron and Judith Krantz, or many other contemporary editors and the authors they have worked with — it's understood that every author needs an editor, just as every actor needs a director. Traditionally, the editor was provided by the publisher. But this is no longer the case. Editors who work for publishing houses have had their job descriptions changed in recent years. Their mission now is generally to acquire books and help package and market them — not to edit them.

Maybe you've been getting the message that your book needs editorial work. The message may be coming from that nagging voice inside you, from your dearest friend and critic, from every agent you have submitted the material to, or even, if you are lucky, from a publisher who has committed to the book provided you improve it. No matter the source, if that message is reaching you persistently, then it is probably time to call the book doctor.

It's fine to seek editorial help after writing a complete first draft of your book. However, it is easier and more productive to begin working with an editorial consultant much earlier. For example, consider nonfiction. The author in any field, whether writing a memoir, a biography, or a book about business, health, science, or psychology, would do well to begin working with an editor as soon as the book idea begins to take shape. The editor will help you develop your idea into a full-fledged book concept and then help you put together the book proposal.

Suppose you are an astronomer who has discovered a new galaxy. Maybe the entire world knows your name, and you have been on talk shows and radio call-in shows. You may have already made it to the late-night talk circuit, and Jimmy Fallon and Stephen Colbert may already be making fun of you. When you decide to write your book, it may take many forms. It might be a dramatic narrative relating how you found the galaxy. It might be a groundbreaking exploration of what finding the galaxy means to scientists and to our future. It might even be a "tell-all" book exposing the seamy side of scientific competition. An outside editor can help you choose among these and other options, expanding your thinking from the outset.

On the other hand, it may be that your nonfiction idea is quite fully developed, but you have come to realize that the book's organization is making it less broadly appealing than it could be. An editor can help you find the largest concept in the material and a form of presentation that will highlight the facets of the idea that are new or uniquely yours. Even familiar material can be made more appealing through shrewd editorial intervention. For example, there are zillions of self-help guides, but the bestsellers in the category have some unique concept, structure, or organization that puts them over the top.

If your material is not reader-friendly, is disorganized, or fails to fulfill its potential, consult an editor before you submit your book to agents. If you do, the agents will ultimately have the opportunity to consider the best possible material you can turn out, avoiding frustration and loss of time on all sides.

For the fiction writer, there are different considerations. Perhaps you have written and tucked away a thousand pages. When you think you finally have something worth showing to other people, this is a really good time to call an independent editor. For a fee, the editor can read and evaluate your work, providing a detailed editorial letter that will honestly appraise the book's chances of getting published and explain how you can make it the best book it can be.

Some would-be novelists have a great idea (a "high concept" in industry parlance) or special and unique knowledge suited to a fictional recounting, but don't know where to begin to tell a story. An independent editor can help develop a story around your concept, help you build characters and subplot, and either write the book for you or review the book as it leaves your computer. An experienced editor knows what works for your market and can help to ensure you have created the optimal story to wrap around your idea.

Perhaps you've been getting really nice rejection letters from agents rather than form letters. These suggest that your work is promising, though currently inadequate. Consider digesting what all the agents have to say and then finding an outside editor to help you deliver. An independent editor may be called when you find that you need help in applying various literary techniques, such as flashback; flash-forward; prologue; use of various narrative voices; the third-person-limited point of view; or any other elements of the craft of writing that you have not mastered on your own.

For example, the complicated plots necessary for mysteries, thrillers, psychological suspense, romantic suspense, science fiction, and so on can be daunting to work out. A seasoned, objective editor may be able to "see" the ending of your book even when you can't.

A fictionalized memoir can also benefit from an objective eye. An editor can weed out those parts of the book that are not interesting to readers (even though you may consider them the high points of your life story). And an editor can help you organize the events, reordering and modifying them if that makes for a better story.

Still in doubt as to whether it's time for you to call the book doctor? Visit the website of the editors' group I belong to, the Book Editors Alliance (www.bookeditorsalliance.com; and see page 453). Examine the lists of genre specialties for each member, and find an editor with expertise in your field of writing. Send a query describing your project, and the editor will be happy to advise you as to whether you might benefit from professional help.

Sandi Gelles-Cole, a member of the Book Editors Alliance, founded Gelles-Cole Literary Enterprises in 1983, after eleven years as an acquisitions editor for major New York publishers. Authors she has worked with include Danielle Steel, Alan Dershowitz, Victoria Gotti, Christiane Northrup, Rita (Mrs. Patrick) Ewing, and Chris Gilson, whose first novel, *Crazy for Cornelia*, was sold in an overnight preemptive sale as a major hardcover and became a *Los Angeles Times* bestseller. She can be reached at sandigc@gmail.com.

TRUST AND PERFECT FIT

Michael Wilde

Trust, as any editor can tell you, is the most important basis of our relationships; without it, nothing worthwhile can be accomplished. What we do depends on this basic ingredient. While the résumé is key, nothing beats first contact — that voice to voice, when early threads of enthusiasm begin to spin between author and prospective editor, opening the vital channel of communication. The flow of ideas required for shaping and developing a work in progress demands an open line, and trust undergirds this channel.

How then to determine the best possible fit when choosing an editor, after those initial contacts? Presumably she or he has gone over the query letter, read the synopsis, and responded in some way. Is there an element of caring, of excitement? Is there a spark? A spark can be anything from a perceptive idea — an insight, maybe — to overall comfort with the sense that your work will be in safe hands. Developing a manuscript may involve deep changes; it can mean restructuring a plot, changing scenes or portions of narrative, rearranging and combining chapters, adding where there isn't, subtracting where there is. Arc, flow, style, and voice all may be affected. Ultimately, and ideally, the editor leaves no fingerprints. At the end, what you hold in your hands is your book in your voice; getting there, though, takes willingness and time to see why something might need to be changed. Trust becomes all-important. How can you know that the editor has your back?

One thing to look for, in addition to an editor's resonance with your work's subject and themes, are the heads-ups she or he gives you in advance of some big change. Tight deadlines may limit turnaround, in which case preapproval is necessary. A good editor will let you know ahead of time the nature and remedy of specific problems, or how together you might address any issue. I had just such a case, a whistleblower's memoir, with a drop-dead due date and very little time for review. The assignment involved reducing the manuscript by a third — a daunting responsibility, since we're talking about someone's life. The solution was anything but simple. In one way, an editor needs to turn her- or himself into the world's most clueless reader, in order that everything will be properly explained and set up; meaning, where not explicit, is seldom intuited. A Byzantine story, with three separate threads, may leave us scratching our heads halfway through, and it was here I questioned what anyone reading up to this point might fairly ask of the author: Why is she doing this, at such great risk to life and limb, including harm to her family? Why would she take such a chance? The answer — or solution to the riddle of the book, including its considerable reduction — involved braiding the three narratives into one trajectory, whereby an "open" resolution was achieved (despite her status as forever classified, the tale is ongoing) and her fateful decision made clear at the end. A tangential story line was removed for focus, overall tightening heightened suspense, and the book wound up a page-turner. None of this could have happened without the author's faith throughout, where first there had to be trust; good and timely communication provided both.

In another instance, the task involved similar reduction but with a twist: part memoir, part cultural history about a storied nightclub — one with a soul — by an author who is neither a cultural historian nor particularly well known but who is nonetheless vital in shaping that history and without whom the history would have been different. In this case, the club was a central character that developed and evolved, its nightly doings essential, with the narrator present in real time. The storytelling required a telescoping technique: to look back and be in the moment at once, to both capture the zeitgeist and reflect on it. From an editor's view, those are treacherous sands, with hidden pitfalls when deleting and reshaping. (Narrative is just that: remove or change it, and a crucial piece may vanish.) Collapsing time — that is, alternating period-present with the point of view of now — presents added difficulty: for example, the narrator remembering in the moment. Which moment, then? Without careful attention and consulting with the author, this can lead to a paradox that may befuddle readers, a risk when things move around. With input from the literary agent, further changes were made, and the work underwent multiple revisions that required new rounds of editing, in coordination with the drafting of new sections. This went on. Some books are like that. The way forward was to work in tandem with the author on his schedule, as he was writing; the book needed to come out soon, and our window of opportunity was closing. At such times, any form of resistance is your enemy, and the author-editor bond, precious. No moment was wasted, every good idea was used, and the result, by all accounts, was a success.

Miscommunication is a devil. Sometimes you'll agree or otherwise signal approval to your editor about something imperfectly understood, which can lead to a collapse of trust. In any and all such cases, use the telephone or, even better, meet. A good editor should always be available and ready to address any issue. A book is no place for simmering resentments, a manuscript in development no place for surprises. If something was done without your consent that isn't to your liking, call the editor and work it out. You have final say. It is rare, in my experience, that something along these lines is not the result of a misperception or mistaken impression — signals that were crossed rather than a lapse in judgment. Allowing for such a possibility goes a long way in mending a broken relationship.

As independents, we want nothing more than to fulfill the promise of your work and to help make it shine; to be the perfect fit; and successfully, with enthusiasm, to earn your trust.

Michael Wilde provides first-time and experienced authors with all manner of editorial services and help with writing. He has more than 25 years' experience working with major publishers in a wide range of subjects that include literary and mainstream fiction (various genres); children's books (especially young adult and middle grade); behavioral, social, and political science; history, biography, and memoir; and music and popular culture. Projects include bestselling and award-winning titles by authors as diverse as Steven Pinker, Glenn Cooper, and Lemony Snicket. Michael can also assist in finding an agent when appropriate. For more information, see www.publishersmarketplace.com/members/mewilde. Contact Michael at 518-672-7172 or michaelwildeeditorial@earthlink.net.

THE LISTINGS

BOOK DEVELOPMENT GROUP ❖ www.bookdevelopmentgroup.com

Book Development Group (BDG) is an alliance of independent New York City publishing professionals. All the BDG editors have at least 25 years of experience, and they work with first-time and seasoned writers in both fiction and nonfiction. The editors work independently of one another with services that range from developing a strong book concept to completely editing a manuscript and — for authors who wish to self-publish — producing a printed book.

The editors of Book Development Group can help you with:

- idea and concept development
- manuscript evaluation
- in-depth manuscript editing
- query letters and book proposals for agents
- project management for self-publishing books and ebooks
- coaching throughout the writing process
- assistance and advice for related publishing services

Whether you are a writer of fiction or nonfiction, BDG editors can help you transform your manuscript into a polished and professional book.

Janet Spencer King, janet@bookdevelopmentgroup.com

Specialties: Fiction — most genres in commercial/mainstream fiction including, among others, thrillers, mysteries, and women's literature. Nonfiction — health/fitness/nutrition, relationships, medical, self-help/popular psychology, business, spirituality, travel, women's interest, and others.

Janet Spencer King has been an editor and writer for more than 30 years and was at one time a literary agent, placing both fiction and nonfiction with key publishing houses. King has been the author or coauthor of four books published by major houses. She started her career in magazine publishing, eventually becoming editor in chief of three national magazines. Today she works one-on-one with writers, providing them with editing and professional guidance throughout the entire book-writing process; additionally, she manages production of self-published books.

Diane O'Connell, diane@bookdevelopmentgroup.com

Specialties: Fiction — commercial/mainstream, thriller/mystery/suspense, fantasy/science fiction, women's, young adult. Nonfiction — business, biography/memoir, health/fitness/nutrition, narrative, self-help/popular psychology, spirituality/New Age, true crime.

Diane O'Connell has over 25 years' publishing experience as a Random House editor and author of six books, including the award-winning *The Novel-Maker's Handbook: The No-Nonsense Guide to Crafting a Marketable Story*. She specializes in working with first-time authors and has helped numerous authors get deals with major publishers, including some that have become bestsellers. She edits manuscripts, coaches writers, writes and edits book proposals, and is available to work in person with authors. She welcomes authors at any stage of the book-writing process.

Olga Vezeris, olga@bookdevelopmentgroup.com

Specialties: Fiction — commercial/mainstream, general, thriller/mystery/suspense, historical novels and sagas. Nonfiction — narrative, self-help/popular psychology, health/fitness/nutrition, art/architecture, business, food/entertaining, illustrated and gift books on all subjects, lifestyle/decorating, travel, true crime.

Olga Vezeris has extensive experience in the publishing industry, having held senior editorial and subsidiary rights positions at companies including Simon & Schuster, Hachette Book Group, Workman, and HarperCollins, where she has acquired, edited, or licensed many commercial fiction and nonfiction titles and illustrated books. Currently she works with authors, editing proposals and manuscripts and guiding them in all aspects of traditional and ebook publishing.

THE BOOK EDITORS ALLIANCE ❖ www.bookeditorsalliance.com

The Book Editors Alliance (formerly the Consulting Editors Alliance) is a group of highly skilled independent editors, each with a minimum of fifteen years' New York publishing experience. BEA members have edited hundreds of acclaimed titles in virtually every category of fiction and nonfiction, including many national bestsellers. They can help you get your book ready to publish and advise you on every aspect of publishing, from the editorial process to ebooks.

To learn more, visit the BEA website at www.bookeditorsalliance.com.

Members of BEA include the following:

Marlene Adelstein, marlene@fixyourbook.com

Marlene is a freelance developmental editor. She specializes in commercial and literary novels: thriller, mystery, historical and women's fiction, first novels; memoir; and screenplays.

Arnold Dolin, abdolin@sprynet.com

In five decades as editor/publisher, Arnold Dolin has worked on literary fiction and serious nonfiction — politics, business, memoir, popular psychology.

Sandi Gelles-Cole, sandigc@gmail.com

Sandi edits both fiction and nonfiction and enjoys working with authors early in their book's life to build concepts into plot lines and to structure works of nonfiction and memoirs.

David Groff, davidagroff@gmail.com

A poet and writer, David focuses on editing narrative — literary and popular fiction, memoir, history, science, sexuality, and politics.

Hilary Hinzmann, hinzmann@earthlink.net

Hilary coaches writers on developing their work and serves as ghostwriter/collaborator or editor/book doctor on varied nonfiction projects.

Judith Kern, kernjt@aol.com

Judith is an editor, ghostwriter, and collaborator in areas including food, health, memoir, spirituality, self-improvement, mystery, and women's fiction.

Carla Jablonski, carla@carlajablonski.com

Carla is a writer, editor, and ghostwriter specializing in middle grade and young adult fiction, as well as adult science fiction/fantasy and historical fiction.

Carole Lalli, clalli3@gmail.com

Carole is a writer and editor specializing in food, lifestyle, and design, with extensive experience in illustrated books.

Danelle McCafferty, writerseditor@gmail.com

Danelle offers all stages of editorial development for thrillers, mysteries, historicals, women's fiction (all genres), first-time "debut" novels, and nonfiction memoirs.

Nancy Nicholas, nacnich@cs.com

Nancy is an editor and writer who works on many kinds of books, from literary fiction to cookbooks.

Toni Sciarra Poynter, tonionemail@yahoo.com

Toni is a nonfiction book editor, book doctor, writer, and collaborator. Specialties: psychology/science, social trends, lifestyle/wellness, work/family, self-help.

Nan Gatewood Satter, nangatewoodsatter@gmail.com

Nan edits fiction — debut, literary, women's, thrillers; narrative nonfiction, particularly memoir; and books dealing with contemporary social issues.

Karl Weber, karlweberliterary@yahoo.com

Karl is a writer and editor who specializes in such serious nonfiction topics as business, politics, and social issues.

THE INDEPENDENT EDITORS GROUP ❖ www.bookdocs.com or www.independenteditorsgroup.com

The IEG is an alliance of professional freelance editors in New York City, all of whom have held senior editorial positions in major publishing houses. We meet monthly with current industry leaders from the top publishers and literary agencies, which allows us to give our clients the best and most up-to-date guidance as they develop and seek to prepare their projects for the marketplace. A changing industry has made our role more important than ever, as agents tell us that their submissions need to be pitch-perfect to have a chance of selling. The good news is that publishers are always looking for new work, and the rise of self-publishing has broadened opportunities for fresh voices and ideas to emerge. We encourage you to visit our website, www.independenteditorsgroup.com, for our full bios. There we speak in our individual voices about ourselves and our work, and it's the best way to find out who might be a good match for you.

How we can help you:

- You need a professional's evaluation — aside from your family, friends, or writers' group
- You want your manuscript critiqued before undertaking a final revision
- You want your manuscript professionally edited/polished before submission to an agent
- You are looking for a fresh approach after one rejection letter too many
- You are self-publishing and seeking editorial services or project oversight
- You want strategic advice in creating/developing a salable book

Sally Arteseros, sarteseros@cs.com

Having worked as an editor and then senior editor at Doubleday for more than 25 years, Sally edits all kinds of fiction: literary, commercial, women's, historical, and contemporary, as well as short stories. And in nonfiction: biography, history, science, psychology, anthropology, business, religion, inspiration, essays, academic books.

Harriet Bell, harrietbell@verizon.net, www.bellbookandhandle.com

Specializes in nonfiction categories such as memoir, lifestyle, cookbooks, self-help, illustrated books, business, health and fitness, diet, and fashion. Writes proposals and website copy, ghostwrites books, edits manuscripts, and packages books. See her website for more information.

Toni Burbank, burbank.toni5@gmail.com

Former vice president and executive editor at Bantam Dell / Random House, with particular interest/expertise in psychology, neuroscience, health, women's issues, spirituality, and self-help. She has edited more than 10 *New York Times* bestsellers; authors include Daniel Goleman, Christiane Northrup, MD, Daniel Siegel, MD, Tara Brach, Jack Kornfield, Brian

Wansink, and Bessel van der Kolk, MD. Offers developmental and line editing, manuscript evaluation, and proposal writing. Nonfiction only.

Susan Dalsimer, susan.dalsimer@gmail.com

Former East Coast vice president of Warner Bros. and vice president and publisher of Miramax Books, specializing in editing literary and commercial fiction, young adult fiction, and mysteries. In nonfiction, areas include memoir, spirituality, biography, psychology, theater, film, and television. Authors have included David Levien, John Pierson, Iris Krasnow, Fredric Dannen, and Padma Lakshmi.

Paul De Angelis, 860-672-6882, pdabooks@optonline.net www.pauldeangelisbooks.com

Manuscript evaluations, rewriting or ghostwriting, and editing. Thirty-five years' book-publishing experience in significant positions at St. Martin's Press, E.P. Dutton, and Kodansha America. Special expertise in history, current affairs, music, biography, literature, and translations. Authors have included the Delany sisters, Mike Royko, and Jorge Luis Borges.

Michael Denneny, 212-362-3241, mldenneny@aol.com

Thirty years' editorial experience at the University of Chicago Press, Macmillan, Crown, and St. Martin's Press. Edits commercial, literary, and mystery fiction; in nonfiction, works with biography, history, current affairs, memoir, psychology, and almost any narrative nonfiction. Also works with writers on book-proposal packages.

Paul Dinas, dinas.paul@gmail.com, www.pauldinasbookeditor.com

As an editor for more than 30 years in trade book publishing, Paul has enjoyed being part of the creative process, helping to develop and shape manuscripts from inception through final publication. His experience embraces nearly every genre of book-length work, both fiction and nonfiction. He works with many experienced authors but finds great satisfaction in helping develop and shape the works of first-time writers. Many have gone on to find publishers or to have great success in the vibrant self-publishing arena. See his website for more details about his career and services.

Aliza Fogelson, aliza@alizafogelson.com, www.alizafogelson.com

Editor and writer specializing in developing and improving books at all stages of the process, from initial concept to proposal to complete manuscript. Special expertise in creating critically acclaimed and bestselling lifestyle books, including cooking, decorating, personal style, and advice/how-to/reference; personal and celebrity memoir; literary and commercial fiction; nonfiction narrative/general interest; and cowriting. Significant editorial experience at Clarkson Potter/Penguin Random House, ReganBooks/HarperCollins, and Rizzoli. See her website for more information.

Emily Heckman, emilyheckman@aol.com

Editor of adult nonfiction and fiction, writer of nonfiction. Areas of interest in nonfiction include health, psychology, business, memoir, and spirituality. Areas of interest in fiction include women's, suspense, thriller, and horror. Coauthor/ghostwriter of health, wellness, diet, and memoir. Training includes senior editorial positions at major publishing houses (Simon & Schuster, Random House, etc.).

Susan Leon, Scribe914@gmail.com

Susan edits literary and commercial fiction and serious nonfiction, and offers manuscript evaluations, project development, and heavy rewrites. Ghostwriter of two *New York Times* bestsellers; editor of award-winning titles across categories. Fiction interests: historical novels and smart, relationship-driven stories in all settings. Nonfiction interests: American/European history (special expertise), personal memoir, biography, the Holocaust, World War II, travel, women/family and the life cycle, film and television history. Susan especially enjoys working with new and emerging writers.

Richard Marek, rwmarek@earthlink.net

Former president and publisher of E.P. Dutton. Specializes in editing and ghostwriting, both fiction and nonfiction. Edited Robert Ludlum's first nine books, James Baldwin's last five, and Thomas Harris's *The Silence of the Lambs*. Ghostwrote 14 books, including Trisha Meili's *I Am the Central Park Jogger* and James Patterson's *Hide and Seek*.

Sydny Miner, sydny.miner@gmail.com

Sydny has extensive experience as an editor at major publishing houses (Crown Publishing Group, Simon & Schuster), working primarily in nonfiction, with a special emphasis on cookbooks, food and nutrition, health and wellness, diet, fitness, exercise, psychology, and self-help. She has worked closely with high-profile authors (including two First

Ladies) and edited numerous bestselling and award-winning titles, taking projects from concept to outline to finished book. She sees herself as a midwife, helping authors put their unique voice and vision on the page, deconstructing their expertise and making it accessible to the layperson.

Beth Rashbaum, bethrashbaum@gmail.com

A veteran of over 35 years in publishing, Beth was an editor most recently at Bantam Dell/Random House. She edits all kinds of nonfiction — including memoir, biography, investigative journalism, Judaica, health and wellness, yoga, psychology, and popular science. She also edits and writes proposals, has ghostwritten one *New York Times* bestseller, and was coauthor, with Olga Silverstein, of *The Courage to Raise Good Men*. Authors she has worked with include Gretchen Rubin, Gloria Steinem, Leonard Mlodinow, Stephen Hawking, Mildred Kalish, Daniel Coyle, Luke Barr, Alexander Masters, and Candace Pert.

Betty Kelly Sargent, bettysargent@me.com

Founder and CEO of BookWorks.com — The Self-Publishers Association, and former editor in chief of William Morrow. Specializing in collaborations and developmental editing for both literary and commercial fiction as well as general nonfiction, including memoir, health, humor, psychology, and spirituality. Coauthor of seven published books and recent consultant for those who want to self-publish and take advantage of social media for book promotion. She is currently editing all of Danielle Steel's work.

James O'Shea Wade, jwade@bookdocs.com

With 30 years' experience as editor in chief and executive editor for major publishers, including Crown/Random House, Macmillan, Dell, and Rawson-Wade, James edits and ghostwrites in all nonfiction areas and specializes in business, science, history, biography, and militaria. Also edits all types of fiction, prepares book proposals, and evaluates manuscripts.

MARVELOUS EDITIONS ❖ www.marvelouseditions.com, www.facebook.com/MarvelousEditors

Marvelous Editions is the partnership of respected independent editors Marlene Adelstein and Alice Peck. They each have over two decades of expertise in developmental and line editing as well as ghostwriting, proposal drafting, and screenplay editing. They provide comprehensive guidance for writers from the first inspiration to the published work — be it through a mainstream publisher, independent press, self-publishing venture, periodical, or website. When appropriate, they also offer referrals to reliable and talented designers, copyeditors, proofreaders, publicists, and agents. Marlene and Alice usually work independently but have joined forces when appropriate, editing authors including Kristen Wolf, Nicole Bokat, and Kim Powers.

Marlene Adelstein, marlene@fixyourbook.com, www.fixyourbook.com

Provides thorough, constructive critiques, developmental and line editing, advice on a book's commercial potential, and agent referrals when appropriate. Over 20 years' experience in publishing and feature-film development. Specializes in commercial and literary fiction: mystery, thriller, women's, romance, historical; young adult; memoir; screenplays. Recent authors include Karan Bajaj, Michael Barsa, Peter Golden, Violet Ramis Stiel, Beth Hoffman, Douglas Carlton Abrams, Kim Powers, Antoinette May, and Anne Serling.

Alice Peck, alicepeck@alicepeck.com, www.alicepeckeditorial.com

Edits, evaluates, and cowrites memoir, narrative nonfiction, psychology, spirituality/religion, and fiction; writes and edits proposals; ghostwrites. Acquired books and developed them into scripts for film and television before shifting her focus to editing in 1998. Recent authors include Chris Grosso, Dr. Miles Neale, Lama Surya Das, Bassam Tarazi, Kelly Boys, Jeri Parker, Dr. Jeffrey B. Rubin, Mark Schimmoeller, Joanie Schirm, and Bonnie Myotai Treace.

WORDS INTO PRINT ❖ www.wordsintoprint.org

Words into Print is one of New York's top networks of independent book editors, writers, and publishing consultants. Founded in 1998, WiP is a professional alliance whose members provide editorial services to publishers, literary agents, and book packagers, as well as to individual writers. Members of WiP have extensive industry experience, averaging 20 years as executives and editors with leading trade book publishers. As active independent professionals, members meet individually and as a group with agents and other publishing colleagues; participate in conventions, conferences, panels, and workshops; and maintain affiliations with organizations that include PEN, AWP, the Authors Guild, the Women's Media Group, Lambda Literary Foundation, the CLMP, the Modern Language Association, and the Academy of American Poets.

The consultants at Words into Print are committed to helping established and new writers develop, revise, and polish their work. They also guide clients through the publishing process by helping them find the most promising route to publication. WiP's editors and writers provide:

- detailed analyses and critiques of proposals and manuscripts
- editing, cowriting, and ghostwriting
- expert advice, ideas, and techniques for making a writer's project the best it can be
- assistance in developing query letters and synopses for literary agents and publishers
- referrals to literary agents, publishers, book packagers, and other publishing services
- guidance in developing publicity and marketing strategies
- project management — from conception through production
- inside information writers need to make their way successfully through the publishing world

Words into Print's editors are nominated, vetted, and elected to membership. Members conform to group guidelines, so potential clients can be confident of the highest caliber of skills and conduct. Each member has his or her own contracts, fee structures, and business arrangements. The range of rates is in keeping with market rates for independent editors with longtime experience at major publishing houses. Estimates and individualized agreements will be provided, as appropriate, on a project-by-project basis. Brief profiles appear below. For more information, please visit www.wordsintoprint.org.

Jeff Alexander, alexandereditorial@gmail.com

Twenty years of editing experience in magazines and book publishing, editing nonfiction with a focus on science, history, politics, sociology, technology, and current events. Has edited books for Vintage/Anchor, Pantheon, Knopf, and the Penguin Press. Has worked with Robert Reich, Jaron Lanier, David Grann, Alice Dreger, Charles C. Mann, Michael Dobbs, and Simon Critchley. Offers a full range of editorial services for manuscripts and proposals, including ghostwriting.

Becky Cabaza, rtcbooks@gmail.com

Becky Cabaza has more than 20 years of full-time publishing experience as an acquisitions editor and editorial director and an additional 11 years as a freelance editor, ghostwriter/collaborator, and consultant to numerous authors. Freelance services include writing and restructuring from idea/proposal phase through finished manuscript, as well as thorough project evaluation and editing at any level. Specialties: self-help, practical nonfiction, health and wellness, parenting/family, book proposals, ghostwriting, collaboration.

Jane Fleming Fransson, jffeditor@gmail.com

More than 15 years of experience editing narrative nonfiction and fiction (both adult and young adult). Former editor at Penguin Press. Has worked with Frank Bruni, Novella Carpenter, Pamela Druckerman, Deanna Fei, Camilla Gibb, Paul Greenberg, Emma Larkin, Marina Lewycka, Christine Montross, Craig Mullaney, Ann Napolitano, Georgia Pellegrini, Jim Sheeler, Sadia Shepard, Jane S. Smith, and Dana Thomas. Offers manuscript critiques, proposal editing and writing, developmental and line editing of manuscripts, ghostwriting, project management, and general publishing consulting.

Ruth Greenstein, rg@greenlinepublishing.com

Editing independent voices since 1989. Literary fiction, biography/memoir, social issues, arts and culture, nature and popular science, travel, religion/spirituality, poetry, photography, media companions. Founding member of WiP, publisher of Turtle Point Press, formerly with Harcourt and Ecco. Has worked with Anita Shreve, Erica Jong, John Ashbery, Gary Paulsen, Alice Walker, Sallie Bingham, and Dennis Lehane. Offers a wide range of editorial and consulting services, plus synopsis writing, submissions guidance, career strategy, and Web presence development.

Emily Loose, emilylooselit@gmail.com

Twenty-five years' experience editing nonfiction for Random House, Penguin, Simon & Schuster, and Cambridge University Press. Seventeen *New York Times* bestsellers. Has worked with Lawrence Wright, Ross Douthat, Arianna Huffington, Charles Fishman, Gillian Tett, Peter Sims, and Nicholas Wade. Offers proposal development, detailed critiques, developmental and line editing, and consultation about agents, building a promotional platform, marketing, and self-publishing. Specializes in narrative nonfiction, business, politics, history, science, social science, women's interest, memoir, biography, psychology.

Julie Miesionczek, julie@writewithjulie.com

Ten years' experience with literary to commercial fiction, including historical, thriller, women's fiction, and select narrative nonfiction and memoir. Worked at Doubleday Broadway, the Crown Publishing Group, Pamela Dorman Books/Viking, and Viking Books at

Penguin Random House. Has worked with Jojo Moyes, Luanne Rice, Jasper Fforde, Paolo Giordano, Anne M. Fletcher, and Beth Hoffman. Offers detailed critique, developmental editing, and line editing services as well as submissions/publishing guidance.

Anne Cole Norman, acole157@gmail.com

Specializing in nonfiction projects including memoir, self-help, how-to, health, relationships, lifestyle, parenting, and personal finance. Offers developmental and detailed editing, rewriting/book doctoring, manuscript evaluation, proposal writing, and ghostwriting. Fifteen years' experience as an acquiring editor at Hyperion, Doubleday, and HarperCollins. Can assist in finding an agent when appropriate.

ACKNOWLEDGMENTS

I wish to express my deep gratitude and appreciation for my publisher, New World Library, and the two individuals I have the most interaction with, Georgia Hughes and Kristen Cashman. Surely there are several others who labor and contribute behind the scenes, whose names and voices I don't know, but please know that I appreciate you.

Georgia is my current editor and also one of my first editors, from a different time and place, where she supported my morale and efforts more than she probably knows. Kristen's deep dives into this book's interminable conundrums, and her capacity for challenging my occasional complacency and spells of pure laziness, have earned her multiple gold stars and my respect.

I must not forget the various four-legged entities that snore, snort, and howl as I toil. And the other ones, who aggressively edit my prose with sharp-nailed toes and with zero respect for my simian ego. Sometimes the muse arrives as a gentle breeze through an open window, whereas other times it drools on everything.

Finally, I thank my wife, who for many years has helped shape and invigorate this project in countless ways.

GLOSSARY

A

abstract A brief sequential profile of chapters in a nonfiction book proposal (also called a synopsis); a point-by-point summary of an article or essay. In academic and technical journals, abstracts often appear with (and may serve to preface) the articles themselves.

adaptation A rewrite or reworking of a piece for another medium, such as the adaptation of a novel for the screen. (*See also* **screenplay**.)

advance Money paid (usually in installments) to an author by a publisher prior to publication. The advance is paid against royalties: if an author is given a $5,000 advance, for instance, the author will collect royalties only after the royalty moneys due exceed $5,000. A good contract protects the advance if it should exceed the royalties ultimately due from sales.

advance orders Orders received before a book's official publication date, and sometimes before actual completion of the book's production and manufacture.

agent The person who acts on behalf of the author to handle the sale of the author's literary properties. Good literary agents are as valuable to publishers as they are to writers; they select and present manuscripts appropriate for particular houses or of interest to particular acquisitions editors. Agents are paid on a percentage basis from the moneys due their author clients.

American Booksellers Association (ABA) The major trade organization for retail booksellers, chain and independent. The annual ABA convention and trade show offers a chance for publishers and distributors to display their wares to the industry at large and provides an incomparable networking forum for booksellers, editors, agents, publicists, and authors.

American Society of Journalists and Authors (ASJA) A membership organization for professional writers. ASJA provides a forum for information exchange among writers and others in the publishing community, as well as networking opportunities. (*See also* **Dial-a-Writer**.)

anthology A collection of stories, poems, essays, and/or selections from larger works (and so forth), usually carrying a unifying theme or concept; these selections may be written by different authors or by a single author. Anthologies are compiled as opposed to written; their editors (as opposed to authors) are responsible for securing the needed reprint rights for the material used, as well as supplying (or providing authors for) pertinent introductory or supplementary material and/or commentary.

attitude A contemporary colloquialism used to describe a characteristic temperament common among individuals who consider themselves superior. Attitude is rarely an esteemed attribute, whether in publishing or elsewhere.

auction Manuscripts a literary agent believes to be hot properties (such as possible bestsellers with strong subsidiary rights potential) will be offered for confidential bidding from multiple publishing houses. Likewise, the reprint, film, and other rights to a successful book may be auctioned off by the original publisher's subsidiary rights department or by the author's agent.

audiobooks Works produced for distribution on audio media, typically MP3, other downloadable electronic formats, or audio compact disc (CD). Audiobooks are usually spoken-word adaptations of works originally created and produced in print; these works sometimes feature the author's own voice; many are given dramatic readings by one or more actors, at times embellished with sound effects.

authorized biography A history of a person's life written with the authorization, cooperation, and, at times, participation of the subject or the subject's heirs.

author's copies/author's discount Author's copies are the free copies of their books that the authors receive from the publisher; the exact number is stipulated in the contract, but it is usually at least 10 hardcovers. The author may purchase additional copies of the book (usually at 40 percent discount from the retail price) and resell them at readings, lectures, and other public engagements. In cases where large quantities of books are bought, author discounts can go as high as 70 percent.

author tour A series of travel and promotional appearances by an author on behalf of the author's book.

autobiography A history of a person's life written by that same person, or, as is typical, composed conjointly with a collaborative writer ("as told to" or "with"; *see also* **coauthor; collaboration**) or ghostwriter. Autobiographies by definition entail the authorization, cooperation, participation, and ultimate approval of the subject.

B

backlist The backlist comprises books published prior to the current season and still in print. Traditionally, at some publishing houses, such backlist titles represent the publisher's cash flow mainstays. Some backlist books continue to sell briskly; some remain bestsellers over several successive seasons; others sell slowly but surely through the years. Although many backlist titles may be difficult to find in bookstores that stock primarily current lists, they can be ordered either through a local bookseller or internet retailer or directly from the publisher.

backmatter Elements of a book that follow the text proper. Backmatter may include the appendix, notes, glossary, bibliography and other references, lists of resources, index, author biography, offerings of the author's and/or publisher's additional books and other related merchandise, and colophon.

bestseller Based on sales or orders by bookstores, wholesalers, and distributors, bestsellers are those titles that move the largest quantities. Lists of bestselling books can be local (as in metropolitan newspapers), regional (typically in geographically keyed trade or consumer periodicals), or national (as in *USA Today, Publishers Weekly*, or the *New York Times*), as well as international. Fiction and nonfiction are usually listed separately, as are hardcover and paperback classifications. Depending on the list's purview, additional industry-sector designations are used (such as how-to/self-improvement, religion and spirituality, business and finance); in addition, bestseller lists can be keyed to particular genre or specialty fields (such as bestseller lists for mysteries, science fiction, or romance novels, and for historical works, biography, or popular science titles) — and virtually any other marketing category at the discretion of whoever issues the bestseller list (for instance, African American interests, lesbian and gay topics, youth market).

bibliography A list of books, articles, and other sources that have been used in the writing of the text in which the bibliography appears. Complex works may break the bibliography down into discrete subject areas or source categories, such as General History, Military History, War in the Twentieth Century, or Unionism and Pacifism.

binding The materials that hold a book together (including the cover). Bindings are generally denoted as hardcover (featuring heavy cardboard covered with durable cloth and/or paper, and occasionally other materials) or paperback (using a pliable, resilient grade of paper, sometimes infused or laminated with other substances such as plastic). In the days when cloth was used lavishly, hardcover volumes were conventionally known as clothbound; and in the very old days, hardcover bindings sometimes featured tooled leather, silk, precious stones, and gold and silver leaf ornamentation.

biography A history of a person's life. (*See also* **authorized biography; autobiography; unauthorized biography**.)

blues (or bluelines) Printer's proofs. The term refers back to a time when photographic proofs of the printing plates for a book had a telltale blue hue. Although the technology has changed — today proofs are typically delivered electronically as PDF files —

the archaic name endures. Publishers review bluelines as a last chance to inspect the type and layout of the book's pages before it goes on press.

blurb   A piece of written copy or extracted quotation used for publicity and promotional purposes, as on a flyer, in a catalog, or in an advertisement. (*See also* **cover blurbs**.)

book club   A book club is a book-marketing operation that ships selected titles to subscribing members on a regular basis, sometimes at greatly reduced prices. Sales of a work to book clubs are negotiated through the publisher's subsidiary rights department (in the case of a bestseller or other work that has gained acclaim, these rights can be auctioned off). Terms vary, but the split of royalties between author and publisher is often 50 percent/50 percent. Book club sales are seen as blessed events by author, agent, and publisher alike.

book contract   A legally binding document between author and publisher that sets the terms for the advance, royalties, subsidiary rights, advertising, promotion, and publicity — plus a host of other contingencies and responsibilities. Writers should therefore be thoroughly familiar with the concepts and terminology of the standard book-publishing contract.

book distribution   The method of getting books from the publisher's warehouse into the reader's hands. Distribution is traditionally through bookstores but can include such means as telemarketing and mail-order sales, and of course online via websites, as well as sales through a variety of special-interest outlets such as health-food or New Age venues, sports and fitness emporiums, or sex shops. Publishers use their own sales forces as well as independent salespeople, wholesalers, and distributors. Many large and some small publishers distribute for other publishers, which can be a good source of income. A publisher's distribution network is extremely important, because it not only makes possible the vast sales of a bestseller but also affects the visibility of the publisher's entire list of books.

book jacket   *See* **dust jacket**.

book producer (or **book packager**)   An individual or company that can assume many of the roles in the publishing process. A book packager or producer may conceive the idea for a book (most often nonfiction) or series, bring together the professionals (including the writer) needed to produce the book(s), sell the individual manuscript or series project to a publisher, take the project through to manufactured product — or perform any selection of those functions, as commissioned by the publisher or other client (such as a corporation producing a corporate history as a premium or giveaway for employees and customers). The book producer may negotiate separate contracts with the publisher and with the writers, editors, and illustrators who contribute to the book.

book review   A critical appraisal of a book (often reflecting a reviewer's personal opinion or recommendation) that evaluates such aspects as organization and writing style, possible market appeal, and cultural, political, or literary significance. Before the public reads book reviews in the local and national print media, important reviews have been published in such respected book-trade journals as *Publishers Weekly, Kirkus Reviews, Library Journal,* and *Booklist.* A gushing review from one of these journals will encourage booksellers to order the book; copies of these raves will be used for promotion and publicity purposes by the publisher and will encourage other book reviewers nationwide to review the book.

Books in Print   Listings published by R.R. Bowker, of books currently in print; these were once yearly printed volumes (along with periodic supplements such as *Forthcoming Books in Print*). Now they exist more online than in print; they provide ordering information, including titles, authors, ISBNs, prices, whether the book is available in hardcover or paperback, and publisher names. Intended for use by the book trade, *Books in Print* (www.booksinprint.com) is also of great value to writers who are researching and market-researching their projects. Listings are provided alphabetically by author, title, and subject area. Most libraries subscribe to their service or have access to some form of the metadata.

bound galleys   Copies of uncorrected typesetter's page proofs or printouts of electronically produced mechanicals that are bound together as advance copies of the book (*compare* **galleys**). Bound galleys are sent to trade journals (*see also* **book review**) as well as to a limited number of reviewers who work under long lead times.

bulk sales   The sale, at a set discount, of many copies of a single title (the greater the number of books, the larger the discount).

byline   The name of the author of a given piece, indicating credit for having written a book or article. Ghostwriters, by definition, do not receive bylines.

C

casing   Alternate term for binding; *see* **binding**.

category fiction   Also known as genre fiction. Category fiction falls into an established (or newly originated) marketing category (which can then be subdivided for more precise target marketing). Fiction categories include action-adventure (with such further designations as military, paramilitary, law enforcement, romantic, and martial arts); crime novels (with points of view that range from deadpan cool to visionary, including humorous capers as well as gritty urban sagas); mysteries or detective fiction (hard-boiled, soft-boiled, procedurals, cozies); romances (including historical as well as contemporary); horror (supernatural, psychological, or technological); thrillers (tales of espionage, crisis, and the chase); Westerns; science fiction; and fantasy. (*See also* **fantasy**; **horror**; **romance fiction**; **science fiction**; **suspense fiction**; **thriller**.)

children's books   Books for children. As defined by the book-publishing industry, children are generally readers ages 17 and younger; many houses adhere to a fine but firm editorial distinction between titles intended for younger readers (under 12) and young adults (generally ages 12 to 17). Children's books (also called juveniles) are produced according to a number of categories (often typified by age ranges), each with particular requisites regarding such elements as readability ratings, length, and inclusion of graphic elements. Picture books are often for very young readers, with such designations as toddlers (who do not themselves read) and preschoolers (who may have some reading ability). Other classifications include easy storybooks (for younger schoolchildren), middle grade books (for elementary to junior high school students), and young adult (sometimes abbreviated YA, for readers through age 17).

coauthor   One who shares authorship of a work. Coauthors all have bylines. Coauthors share royalties based on their contributions to the book. (*Compare* **ghostwriter**.)

collaboration   Writers can collaborate with professionals in any number of fields. Often a writer will collaborate in order to produce books outside the writer's own areas of formally credentialed expertise (for example, a writer with an interest in exercise and nutrition may collaborate with a sports doctor on a health book). Though the writer may be billed as a coauthor (*see also* **coauthor**), the writer does not necessarily receive a byline (in which case the writer is a ghostwriter). Royalties are shared, based on respective contributions to the book (including expertise or promotional abilities as well as the actual writing).

colophon   Strictly speaking, a colophon is a publisher's logo; in bookmaking, the term may also refer to a listing of the materials used, as well as credits for the design, composition, and production of the book. Such colophons are sometimes included in the backmatter or as part of the copyright page.

commercial fiction   Fiction written to appeal to as broad-based a readership as possible.

concept   A general statement of the idea behind a book.

cool   A modern colloquial expression that indicates satisfaction or approval, or may signify the maintenance of calm within a whirlwind. A fat contract for a new author is definitely cool.

cooperative advertising (co-op)   An agreement between a publisher and a bookstore. The publisher's book is featured in an ad for the bookstore (sometimes in conjunction with an author appearance or other special book promotion); the publisher contributes to the cost of the ad, which is billed at a lower (retail advertising) rate.

copublishing   Joint publishing of a book, usually by a publisher and another corporate entity such as a foundation, a museum, or a smaller publisher. An author can copublish with the publisher by sharing the costs and decision making and, ultimately, the profits.

copyeditor   An editor, responsible for the final polishing of a manuscript, who reads primarily in terms of appropriate word usage and grammatical expression, with an eye toward clarity and coherence of the material as presented, factual errors and inconsistencies, spelling, and punctuation. (*See also* **editor**.)

copyright   The legal proprietary right to reproduce, have reproduced, publish, and sell copies of literary, musical, and other artistic works. The rights to literary properties reside in the author from the time the work is produced — regardless of whether a formal copyright registration is obtained. However, for legal recourse in the event of plagiarism or other infringement, the work must be registered with the US Copyright Office, and all copies of the work must bear the copyright notice. (*See also* **work-for-hire**.)

cover blurbs   Favorable quotes from other writers, celebrities, or experts in a book's subject area, which appear on the dust jacket and are used to enhance the book's point-of-purchase appeal to the potential book-buying public.

crash   Coarse gauze fabric used in bookbinding to strengthen the spine and joints of a book.

curriculum vitae (CV)   Latin expression meaning "course of life" — in other words, the résumé.

D

deadline   In book publishing, this not-so-subtle synonym is used for the author's due date for delivery of the completed manuscript to the publisher. The deadline can be as much as a full year before the official publication date, unless the book is being produced quickly to coincide with or follow up on a particular event.

delivery   Submission of the completed manuscript to the editor or publisher.

Dial-a-Writer   A project-referral service of the American Society of Journalists and Authors, in which members, accomplished writers in most specialty fields and subjects, list their services.

direct marketing   Advertising that involves a "direct response" (which is an equivalent term) from a consumer — for instance, an order form or coupon in a book-review section or in the back of a book or mailing (direct-mail advertising) to a group presumed to hold a special interest in a particular book.

display titles   Books that are produced to be eye-catching to the casual shopper in a bookstore setting. Often rich with flamboyant cover art, these publications are intended to pique bookbuyer excitement about the store's stock in general. Many display titles are stacked on their own freestanding racks; sometimes broad tables are laden with these items. A book shelved with its front cover showing on racks along with diverse other titles is technically a display title. Promotional or premium titles are likely to be display items, as are mass-market paperbacks and hardbacks with enormous bestseller potential. (Check your local bookstore and find a copy of this *Guide to Book Publishers, Editors, and Literary Agents* — if not already racked in "display" manner, please adjust the bookshelf so that the front cover is displayed poster-like to catch the browser's eye — that's what we do routinely.)

distributor   An agent or business that buys or warehouses books from a publisher to resell, at a higher cost, to wholesalers, retailers, or individuals. Distribution houses are often excellent marketing enterprises, with their own roster of sales representatives, publicity and promotion personnel, and house catalogs. Skillful use of distribution networks can give a small publisher considerable national visibility.

dramatic rights   Legal permission to adapt a work for the stage. These rights initially belong to the author but can be sold or assigned to another party by the author.

dust jacket (or **dustcover** or **book jacket**)   The wrapper that covers the binding of hardcover books, designed especially for the book by either the publisher's art department or a freelance artist. Dust jackets were originally conceived to protect the book during shipping, but now their function is primarily promotional — to entice the browser to actually reach out and pick up the volume (and maybe even open it up for a taste before buying) by means of attractive graphics and sizzling promotional copy.

dust-jacket copy   Descriptions of books printed on the dust-jacket flaps. Dust-jacket copy may be written by the book's editor but is often either recast or written by in-house copywriters or freelance specialists. Editors send advance copies (*see also* **bound galleys**) to other writers, experts, and celebrities to solicit quotable praise that will also appear on the jacket. (*See also* **cover blurbs**.)

E

ebook   Refers to any book that exists in digital form, regardless of whether or not it also exists in a traditional physical form.

editor   Editorial responsibilities and titles vary from house to house (often being less strictly defined in smaller houses). In general, the duties of the editor in chief or executive editor are primarily administrative: managing personnel, scheduling, budgeting, and defining the editorial personality of the firm or imprint. Senior editors and acquisitions editors acquire manuscripts (and authors), conceive project ideas and find writers to carry them out, and may oversee the writing and rewriting of manuscripts. Managing editors have editorial and production responsibilities, coordinating and scheduling the book through the various phases of production. Associate and assistant editors edit; they are involved in much of the rewriting and reshaping of the manuscript and may also have acquisitions duties. Copyeditors read the manuscript and style its punctuation, grammar, spelling, headings and subheadings, and so forth. Editorial assistants, laden with extensive clerical duties and general office work, perform some editorial duties as well — often as springboards to senior editorial positions.

Editorial Freelancers Association (EFA)   This organization of independent professionals offers a referral service, through both its annotated membership directory and its job phone line, as a means for authors and publishers to connect with writers, collaborators, researchers, and a wide range of editorial experts covering virtually all general and specialist fields.

el-hi   Books for elementary and/or high schools.

endnotes   Explanatory notes and/or source citations that appear either at the end of individual chapters or at the end of a book's text; used primarily in scholarly or academically oriented works.

epilogue   The final segment of a book, which comes "after the end." In both fiction and nonfiction, an epilogue offers commentary or further information but does not bear directly on the book's central design.

F

fantasy   Fantasy is fiction that features elements of magic, wizardry, supernatural feats, and entities that suspend conventions of realism in the literary arts. Fantasy can resemble prose versions of epics and rhymes or it may be informed by mythic cycles or folkloric material derived from cultures worldwide. Fantasy fiction may be guided primarily by the author's own distinctive imagery and personalized archetypes. Fantasies that involve heroic-erotic roundelays of the death dance are often referred to as the sword-and-sorcery subgenre.

film rights   Like dramatic rights, these belong to the author, who may sell or option them to someone in the film industry — a producer or director, for example (or sometimes a specialist broker of such properties) — who will then try to gather the other professionals and secure the financial backing needed to convert the book into a film. (*See also* **screenplay**.)

footbands   *See* **headbands**.

footnotes   Explanatory notes and/or source citations that appear at the bottom of a page. Footnotes are rare in general-interest books, the preferred style being either to work such information into the text or to list informational sources in the bibliography.

foreign agents   Persons who work with their US counterparts to acquire rights for books from the United States for publication abroad. They can also represent US publishers directly.

foreign market   Any foreign entity — a publisher, broadcast medium, etc. — in a position to buy rights. Authors share royalties with whoever negotiates the deal, or they keep 100 percent if they do their own negotiating.

foreign rights   Translation or reprint rights that can be sold abroad. Foreign rights belong to the author but can be sold either country by country or en masse as world rights. Often the US publisher will own world rights, and the author will be entitled to anywhere from 50 percent to 85 percent of these revenues.

foreword   An introductory piece written by the author or by an expert in the given field. A foreword by a celebrity or well-respected authority is a strong selling point for a prospective author or, after publication, for the book itself. (*See also* **introduction**.)

Frankfurt Book Fair   The largest international publishing exhibition — with 500 years of tradition behind it. The fair takes place every October in Frankfurt, Germany. Thousands of publishers, agents, and writers from all over the world negotiate, network, and buy and sell rights.

Freedom of Information Act   A federal law that ensures the protection of the public's right to access public records — except in cases violating the right to privacy, national security, or certain other instances. A related law, the Government in the Sunshine Act, stipulates that certain government agencies announce and open their meetings to the public.

freight passthrough   The bookseller's freight cost (the cost of getting the book from the publisher to the bookseller). It is added to the basic invoice price charged the bookseller by the publisher.

frontlist   New titles published in a given season by a publisher. Frontlist titles customarily receive priority exposure in the front of the sales catalog — as opposed to backlist titles (usually found at the back of the catalog), which are previously published titles still in print.

frontmatter   The frontmatter of a book includes the elements that precede the text of the work, such as the title page, copyright page, dedication, epigraph, table of contents, foreword, preface, acknowledgments, and introduction.

fulfillment house   A firm commissioned to fulfill orders for a publisher — services may include warehousing, shipping, receiving returns, and mail-order and direct-marketing functions. Although more common for magazine publishers, fulfillment houses also serve book publishers.

G

galleys   Typeset proofs (or copies of proofs) on sheets of paper, or printouts of the electronically produced setup of the book's interior — the author's last chance to check for typos and make (usually minimal) revisions or additions to the copy. (*See also* **bound galleys**.)

genre fiction *See* **category fiction**.

ghostwriter (or **ghost**)   A writer without a byline, often without the remuneration and recognition that credited authors receive. Ghostwriters often get flat fees for their work, but even without royalties, experienced ghosts can receive quite respectable sums.

glossary   An alphabetical listing of special terms as they are used in a particular subject area, often with more in-depth explanations than would customarily be provided by dictionary definitions.

H

hardcover   Books bound in a format that uses thick, sturdy, relatively stiff binding boards and a cover composed (usually) of a cloth spine and finished binding paper. Hardcover books are conventionally wrapped in a dust jacket. (*See also* **binding**; **dust jacket**.)

headbands   Thin strips of cloth (often colored or patterned) that adorn the top of a book's spine where the signatures are held together. The headbands conceal the glue or other binding materials and are said to offer some protection against accumulation of dust (when properly attached). Such bands placed at the bottom of the spine are known as footbands.

hook   The distinctive concept or theme of a work that sets it apart as being fresh, new, or different from others in its field. A hook can be an author's special point of view, often encapsulated in a catchy or provocative phrase intended to attract or pique the interest of a reader, editor, or agent. One specialized function of a hook is to articulate what might otherwise be seen as dry, albeit significant, subject matter (academic or scientific topics; number-crunching drudgery such as home bookkeeping) into an exciting, commercially attractive package.

horror   The horror classification denotes works that traffic in the bizarre, awful, and scary in order to entertain as well as explicate the darkness at the heart of the reader's soul. Horror subgenres may be typified according to the appearance of werecreatures, vampires, human-induced monsters, or naturally occurring life-forms and spirit entities — or absence thereof. Horror fiction traditionally makes imaginative literary use of paranormal phenomena, occult elements, and psychological motifs. (*See also* **category fiction**; **suspense fiction**.)

how-to books   An immensely popular category of books ranging from purely instructional (arts and crafts, for example) to motivational (popular psychology, inspirational, self-awareness, self-improvement) to get-rich-quick (such as in real estate or personal investment).

I

imprint   A separate line of product within a publishing house. Imprints run the gamut of complexity, from those composed of one or two series to those offering full-fledged and diversified lists. Imprints also enjoy different gradations of autonomy from the parent company. An imprint may have its own editorial department (perhaps consisting of only one editor), or the house's acquisitions editors may assign particular titles for release on appropriate specialized imprints. An imprint may publish a certain kind of book (juvenile or paperback or travel books) or have its own personality (such as a literary or contemporary tone). An individual imprint's categories often overlap with other imprints or with the publisher's core list, but some imprints maintain a small-house feel within an otherwise enormous conglomerate. The imprint can offer the distinct advantages of a personalized editorial approach while availing itself of the larger company's production, publicity, marketing, sales, and advertising resources.

index   An alphabetical directory at the end of a book that references names and subjects discussed in the book and the pages where such mentions can be found.

instant book   A book produced quickly to appear in bookstores as soon as possible after (for instance) a newsworthy event to which it is relevant.

international copyright   Rights secured for countries that are members of the International Copyright Convention (*see* **International Copyright Convention**) and that respect the authority of the international copyright symbol, ©.

International Copyright Convention   Countries that are signatories to the various international copyright treaties. Some treaties are contingent upon certain conditions being met at the time of publication, so an author should, before publication, inquire into a particular country's laws.

introduction   Preliminary remarks pertaining to a piece. Like a foreword, an introduction can be written by the author or an appropriate authority on the subject. If a book has both a foreword and an introduction, the foreword will be written by someone other than the author; the introduction will be more closely tied to the text and will be written by the book's author. (*See also* **foreword**.)

ISBN (International Standard Book Number)   A 13-digit number that is linked to and identifies the title and publisher of a book. It is used for ordering and cataloging books and appears on the dust jackets of hardcovers, the back covers of paperbacks, and all copyright pages.

ISSN (International Standard Serial Number)   An 8-digit cataloging and ordering number that identifies all US and foreign periodicals.

J

juveniles See **children's books**.

K

kill fee A fee paid by a magazine when it cancels a commissioned article. The fee is only a certain percentage of the agreed-on payment for the assignment (no more than 50 percent). Not all publishers pay kill fees; a writer should make sure to formalize such an arrangement in advance. Kill fees are sometimes involved in work-for-hire projects in book publishing.

L

lead The crucial first few sentences, phrases, or words of anything — be it a query letter, book proposal, novel, news release, advertisement, or sales tip sheet. A successful lead immediately hooks the reader, consumer, editor, or agent.

lead title A frontlist book featured by the publisher during a given season — one the publisher believes should do extremely well commercially. Lead titles are usually those given the publisher's maximum promotional push.

letterhead Business stationery and envelopes imprinted with the company's (or, in some cases, the writer's) name, address, and logo — a convenience as well as an impressive asset for a freelance writer.

letterpress A form of printing in which set type is inked, then impressed directly onto the printing surface. Now used primarily for limited-run books-as-fine-art projects. (*See also* **offset**.)

libel Defamation of an individual or individuals in a published work, with malice aforethought. In litigation, the falsity of the libelous statements or representations, as well as the intention of malice, has to be proved for there to be libel; in addition, financial damages to the parties so libeled must be incurred as a result of the material in question for there to be an assessment of the amount of damages to be awarded to a claimant. This is contrasted to slander, which is defamation through the spoken word.

Library of Congress (LOC) The largest library in the world, located in Washington, DC. As part of its many services, the LOC will supply a writer with up-to-date sources and bibliographies in all fields, from arts and humanities to science and technology. For details, write to the Library of Congress, Central Services Division, Washington, DC 20540.

Library of Congress Catalog Card Number An identifying number issued by the Library of Congress to books it has accepted for its collection. The publication of those books, which are submitted by the publisher, is announced by the Library of Congress to libraries, which use Library of Congress numbers for their own ordering and cataloging purposes.

Literary Market Place (LMP)   An annual directory of the publishing industry that contains a comprehensive list of publishers, alphabetically and by category, with their addresses, phone numbers, some personnel, and the types of books they publish. Also included are various publishing-allied listings, such as literary agencies, writers' conferences and competitions, and editorial and distribution services. *LMP* is published by Information Today and is available in most public libraries.

literature   Written works of fiction and nonfiction in which compositional excellence and advancement in the art of writing are higher priorities than are considerations of profit or commercial appeal.

logo   A company or product identifier — for example, a representation of a company's initials or a drawing that is the exclusive property of that company. In publishing usage, a virtual equivalent to the trademark.

M

mainstream fiction   Nongenre fiction, excluding literary or avant-garde fiction, that appeals to a general readership.

marketing plan   The entire strategy for selling a book: its publicity, promotion, sales, and advertising.

mass-market paperback   Less expensive smaller-format paperbacks that are sold from racks (in such venues as supermarkets, variety stores, drugstores, and specialty shops) as well as in bookstores. Also referred to as rack (or rack-sized) editions.

mechanicals (or **pasteups**)   Typeset copy and art mounted on boards to be photocopied and printed.

middle grade   Just like the name implies, books for fourth to eighth graders.

midlist books   Generally mainstream fiction and nonfiction books that traditionally formed the bulk of a publisher's list (nowadays often by default rather than intent). Midlist books are expected to be commercially viable but not explosive bestsellers — nor are they viewed as distinguished, critically respected books that can be scheduled for small print runs and aimed at select readerships. Agents may view such projects as a poor return for the effort, since they generally garner a low-end advance; editors and publishers (especially the sales force) may decry midlist works as being hard to market; prospective readers often find midlist books hard to buy in bookstores (they have short shelf lives). Hint for writers: Don't present your work as a midlist item.

multimedia   Presentations of sound and light, words in magnetically graven image —

and any known combination thereof as well as nuances yet to come. Technological innovation is the hallmark of the electronic-publishing arena, and new formats will expand the creative and market potential. Multimedia books are publishing events; their advent suggests alternative avenues for authors as well as adaptational tie-ins with the world of print. Meanwhile, please stay tuned for virtual reality, artificial intelligence, and electronic end-user distribution of product.

multiple contract   A book contract that includes a provisional agreement for a future book or books. (*See also* **option clause/right of first refusal**.)

mystery stories (or **mysteries**)   *See* **suspense fiction**.

N

net receipts   The amount of money a publisher actually receives for sales of a book: the retail price minus the bookseller's discount and/or other discount. The number of returned copies is factored in, bringing down even further the net amount received per book. Royalties are sometimes figured on these lower amounts rather than on the retail price of the book.

New Age   An eclectic category that encompasses health, medicine, philosophy, religion, and the occult — presented from an alternative or multicultural perspective. Although the term has achieved currency relatively recently, some publishers have been producing serious books in these categories for decades.

novella   A work of fiction falling in length between a short story and a novel.

O

offset (or **offset lithography**)   A printing process that involves the transfer of wet ink from a (usually photosensitized) printing plate onto an intermediate surface (such as a rubber-coated cylinder) and then onto the paper. For commercial purposes, this method has replaced letterpress, whereby books were printed via direct impression of inked type on paper.

option clause/right of first refusal   In a book contract, a clause that stipulates that the publisher will have the exclusive right to consider and make an offer for the author's next book. However, the publisher is under no obligation to publish the book, and in most variations of the clause the author may, under certain circumstances, opt for publication elsewhere. (*See also* **multiple contract**.)

outline   Used for both a book proposal and the actual writing and structuring of a book, an outline is a hierarchical listing of topics that provides the writer (and the proposal reader) with an overview of the ideas in a book in the order in which they are to be presented.

out-of-print books   Books no longer available from the publisher; rights usually revert to the author.

P

package   The package is the actual book; the physical product.

packager   See **book producer**.

page proof   The final typeset copy of the book, in page-layout form, before printing. Proofs are read and reviewed by the author and the publisher's proofreader for errors.

paperback   Books bound with a flexible, stress-resistant, paper covering material. (*See also* **binding**.)

paperback originals   Books published, generally, in paperback editions only; sometimes the term refers to those books published simultaneously in hardcover and paperback. These books are often mass-market genre fiction (romances, Westerns, Gothics, mysteries, horror, and so forth) as well as contemporary literary fiction, cookbooks, humor, career books, self-improvement, and how-to books — the categories continue to expand.

pasteups   See **mechanicals**.

permissions   The right to quote or reprint published material, obtained by the author from the copyright holder.

picture book   A copiously illustrated book, often with very simple, limited text, intended for preschoolers and other very young children.

plagiarism   The false presentation of someone else's writing as one's own. In the case of copyrighted work, plagiarism is illegal.

platform   Refers to the author's professional connections and popularity, measured by internet and media presence, and the extent to which such can be leveraged to sell books.

preface   An element of a book's frontmatter. In the preface, the author may discuss the purpose behind the format of the book, the type of research upon which it is based, its genesis, or an underlying philosophy.

premium   Books sold at a reduced price as part of a special promotion. Premiums can thus be sold to a bookseller, who in turn sells them to the bookbuyer (as with a line of modestly priced art books). Alternatively, such books may be produced as part of a broader marketing package. For instance, an organization may acquire a number of books (such as its own corporate history or the biography of its founder) for use in personnel training and as giveaways to clients; or a nutrition/recipe book may be displayed along with a company's diet foods in nonbookstore outlets. (*See also* **special sales**.)

press agent   See **publicist**.

press kit   A promotional package that includes a press release, tip sheet, author biography and photograph, reviews, and other pertinent information. The press kit can be put together by the publisher's publicity department or an independent publicist and sent with a review copy of the book to potential reviewers and to media professionals responsible for booking author appearances.

price   There are several prices pertaining to a single book: the invoice price is the amount the publisher charges the bookseller; the retail, cover, or list price is what the consumer pays.

printer's error (**PE**)   A typographical error made by the printer or typesetting facility, not by the publisher's staff. PEs are corrected at the printer's expense.

printing plate   A surface that bears a reproduction of the set type and artwork of a book, from which the pages are printed.

producer   *See* **book producer**.

proposal   A detailed presentation of the book's concept, used to gain the interest and services of an agent and to sell the project to a publisher.

publication date (or **pub date**)   A book's official date of publication, customarily set by the publisher to fall six weeks after completed bound books are delivered to the warehouse. The publication date is used to focus the promotional activities on behalf of the title — so that books will have had time to be ordered, shipped, and available in the stores to coincide with the appearance of advertising and publicity.

public domain   Material that is uncopyrighted, whose copyright has expired, or that is uncopyrightable. The last category includes government publications, jokes, titles — and, it should be remembered, ideas.

publicist (or **press agent**)   The publicity professional who handles the press releases for new books and arranges the author's publicity tours and other promotional venues (such as interviews, speaking engagements, and book signings).

publisher's catalog   A seasonal sales catalog that lists and describes a publisher's new books; it is sent and/or emailed to all potential buyers, including individuals who request one. Catalogs range from the basic to the glitzy and often include information on the author, on print quantity, and on the amount of money slated to be spent on publicity and promotion. Now also available online.

publisher's discount   The percentage by which a publisher discounts the retail price of a book to a bookseller, often based in part on the number of copies purchased.

Publishers' Trade List Annual   A collection of current and backlist catalogs arranged alphabetically by publisher, available in many libraries.

Publishers Weekly (*PW*)   The publishing industry's chief trade journal. *PW* carries announcements of upcoming books, respected book reviews, interviews with authors and publishing-industry professionals, special reports on various book categories, and trade news (such as mergers, rights sales, and personnel changes).

Q

quality   In publishing parlance, the word *quality* in reference to a book category (such as quality fiction) or format (quality paperback) is a term of art — individual works or lines so described are presented as outstanding products.

query letter   A brief written presentation to an agent or editor designed to pitch both the writer and the book idea.

R

remainders   Unsold book stock. Remainders can include titles that have not sold as well as anticipated, in addition to unsold copies of later printings of bestsellers. These volumes are often remaindered — that is, remaining stock is purchased from the publisher by specialty distributors at a huge discount and resold to the public. Both online and physical bookstores have high-discounted sections where these books can be bought for pennies on the dollar.

reprint   A subsequent edition of material that is already in print, especially publication in a different format — the paperback reprint of a hardcover, for example.

résumé   A summary of an individual's career experience and education. When a résumé is sent to prospective agents or publishers, it should contain the author's vital publishing credits, specialty credentials, and pertinent personal experience. Also referred to as the curriculum vitae or, more simply, vita.

returns   Unsold books returned to a publisher by a bookstore, for which the store may receive full or partial credit (depending on the publisher's policy, the age of the book, and so on).

reversion-of-rights clause   In the book contract, a clause that states that if the book goes out of print or the publisher fails to reprint the book within a stipulated length of time, all rights revert to the author.

review copy   A free copy of a (usually) new book sent to electronic and print media that review books for their audiences.

romance fiction (or **romance novels**)   Modern or period love stories, always with happy endings, which range from the tepid to the torrid. Except for certain erotic specialty lines, romances do not feature graphic sex. Often mistakenly pigeonholed by those who do not read them, romances and romance writers have been influential in the movement away from passive and coddled female fictional characters to the strong, active modern woman in a tale that reflects areas of topical social concern.

royalty   The percentage of the retail cost of a book that is paid to the author for each copy sold after the author's advance has been recouped. Some publishers structure royalties as a percentage payment against net receipts.

S

sales conference   A meeting of a publisher's editorial and sales departments and senior promotion and publicity staff members. A sales conference covers the upcoming season's new books, and marketing strategies are discussed. Sometimes sales conferences are the basis upon which proposed titles are bought or not.

sales representative (sales rep)   A member of the publisher's sales force or an independent contractor who, armed with a book catalog and order forms, visits bookstores in a certain territory to sell books to retailers.

SASE (self-addressed stamped envelope)   It is customary for an author to enclose SASEs with query letters, proposals, and manuscript submissions sent via snail mail. Many editors and agents do not reply if a writer has neglected to enclose an SASE with correspondence or submitted materials.

satisfactory clause   In book contracts, a publisher will reserve the right to refuse publication of a manuscript that is not deemed satisfactory. Because the author may be forced to pay back the publisher's advance if the complete work is found to be unsatisfactory, the specific criteria for publisher satisfaction should be set forth in the contract to protect the author.

science fiction   Science fiction includes the hardcore, imaginatively embellished technological/scientific novel as well as fiction that is even slightly futuristic (often with an after-the-holocaust milieu — nuclear, environmental, extraterrestrial, genocidal). An element much valued by editors who acquire for the literary expression of this cross-media genre is the ability of the author to introduce elements that transcend and extend conventional insight.

science fiction/fantasy   A category-fiction designation that actually collapses two genres into one (for bookseller-marketing reference, of course — though it drives some devotees of these separate fields of writing nuts). In addition, many editors and publishers specialize in both these genres and thus categorize their interests with catchphrases such as *sci-fi/fantasy*.

screenplay   A film script — either original or based on material published previously in another form, such as a television docudrama based on a nonfiction book or a movie thriller based on a suspense novel. (*Compare* **teleplay**.)

self-publishing   A publishing project wherein an author pays for the costs of manufacturing and selling his or her own book and retains all money from the book's sale. This is a risky venture but one that can be immensely profitable (especially when combined with an author's speaking engagements or imaginative marketing techniques); in addition, if successful, self-publication can lead to distribution or publication by a commercial publisher. (*Compare* **subsidy publishing**.)

self-syndication   Management by writers or journalists of functions that are otherwise performed by syndicates specializing in such services. In self-syndication, it is the writer who manages copyrights, negotiates fees, and handles sales, billing, and other tasks involved in circulating journalistic pieces through newspapers, magazines, or other periodicals that pick up the author's column or run a series of articles.

serialization The reprinting of a book or part of a book in a newspaper or magazine. Serialization before (or perhaps simultaneously with) the publication of the book is called *first serial*. The first reprint after publication (either as a book or by another periodical) is called *second serial*.

serial rights Reprint rights sold to periodicals. First serial rights include the right to publish the material before anyone else (generally before the book is released, or coinciding with the book's official publication) — either for the United States, a specific country, or a wider territory. Second serial rights cover material already published, in either a book or another periodical.

series Books published as a group either because of their related subject matter (such as a series on modern artists or on World War II aircraft) and/or single authorship (a set of works by a famous romance writer, a group of books about science and society, or a series of titles geared to a particular diet-and-fitness program). Special series lines can offer a ready-made niche for an industrious author or compiler/editor who is up-to-date on a publisher's program and has a brace of pertinent qualifications and/or contacts. In contemporary fiction, some genre works are published in series form (such as family sagas, detective series, fantasy cycles).

shelf life The amount of time an unsold book remains on the bookstore shelf before the store manager pulls it to make room for newer incoming stock with greater (or at least untested) sales potential.

short story A short work that is more pointed and more economically detailed as to character, situation, and plot than a full novel. Published collections of short stories — whether by one or several authors — often revolve around a single theme, express related outlooks, or comprise variations within a common genre.

signature A group of book pages that have been printed together on one large sheet of paper that is then folded and cut in preparation for being bound, along with the book's other signatures, into the final volume.

simultaneous publication The issuing at the same time of more than one edition of a work, such as in hardcover and trade paperback. Simultaneous releases can be expanded to include (though rarely) deluxe gift editions of a book as well as mass-market paper versions. Audio versions of books are most often timed to coincide with the release of the first print edition.

simultaneous (or **multiple**) **submissions** The submission of the same material to more than one publisher at the same time. Although simultaneous submission is a common practice, publishers should always be made aware that it is being done. Multiple submissions by an author to several agents is, on the other hand, a practice that is sometimes not regarded with great favor by agents.

slush pile The morass of unsolicited manuscripts at a publishing house or literary agency, which may fester indefinitely awaiting (perhaps perfunctory) review. Some publishers or agencies do not maintain slush piles per se — unsolicited manuscripts are slated for instant or eventual return without review (if an SASE or email address is included) or may otherwise be literally or figuratively pitched to the wind. Querying a targeted publisher or agent before submitting a manuscript is an excellent way of avoiding, or at least minimizing the possibility of, such an ignoble fate.

software Programs that run on a computer. Word-processing software includes programs that enable writers to compose, edit, store, and print material. Professional-quality software packages incorporate such amenities as databases that can feed the results of research electronically into the final manuscript, alphabetization and indexing functions, and capabilities for constructing tables and charts and adding graphics to the body of the manuscript. Software should be appropriate to both the demands of the work at hand and the requirements of the publisher (which may contract for a manuscript suitable for electronic editing, design, composition, and typesetting).

special sales Sales of a book to appropriate retailers other than bookstores (for example, wine guides to liquor stores). This classification also includes books sold as premiums (for example, to a convention group or a corporation) or for other promotional purposes. Depending on volume, per-unit costs can be very low, and the book can be custom designed. (*See also* **premium**.)

spine That portion of the book's casing (or binding) that backs the bound page signatures and is visible when the volume is aligned on a bookshelf among other volumes.

stamping In book publishing, the stamp is the impression of ornamental type and images (such as a logo or monogram) on the book's binding. The stamping process involves using a die with a raised or intaglioed surface to apply ink stamping or metallic-leaf stamping.

submission guidelines An agent or publisher's guidelines for approaching them about publication of a work. Usually can be found on the agency or publisher website.

subsidiary rights The reprint, serial, movie and television, and audiotape and videotape rights deriving from a book. The division of profits between publisher and author from the sales of these rights is determined through negotiation. In more elaborately commercial projects, further details such as syndication of related articles and licensing of characters may ultimately be involved.

subsidy publishing A mode of publication wherein the author pays a publishing company to produce his or her work, which may thus appear superficially to have been published conventionally. Subsidy publishing (a.k.a. vanity publishing) is generally more expensive than self-publishing, because a successful subsidy house makes a profit on all its contracted functions, charging fees well beyond the publisher's basic costs for production and services.

suspense fiction   Fiction within a number of genre categories that emphasize suspense as well as the usual (and sometimes unusual) literary techniques to keep the reader engaged. Suspense fiction encompasses novels of crime and detection (regularly referred to as mysteries). These include English-style cozies, American-style hard-boiled detective stories, dispassionate law-enforcement procedurals, crime stories, action-adventure, espionage novels, technothrillers, tales of psychological suspense, and horror. A celebrated aspect of suspense fiction's popular appeal — one that surely accounts for much of this broad category's sustained market vigor — is the interactive element: the reader may choose to challenge the tale itself by attempting to outwit the author and solve a crime before the detective does, figure out how best to defeat an all-powerful foe before the hero does, or parse out the elements of a conspiracy before the writer reveals the whole story.

syndicated column   Material published simultaneously in a number of newspapers or magazines. The author shares the income from syndication with the syndicate that negotiates the sale. (*See also* **self-syndication**.)

syndication rights   *See* **self-syndication**; **subsidiary rights**.

synopsis   A summary in paragraph form, rather than in outline format. The synopsis is an important part of a book proposal. For fiction, the synopsis portrays the high points of story line and plot, succinctly and dramatically. In a nonfiction book proposal, the synopsis describes the thrust and content of the successive chapters (and/or parts) of the manuscript.

T

table of contents   A listing of a book's chapters and other sections (such as the front matter, appendix, index, and bibliography) or of a magazine's articles and columns, in the order in which they appear; in published versions, the table of contents indicates the first page of each section.

tabloid   A smaller-than-standard-size newspaper (daily, weekly, or monthly). Traditionally, certain tabloids are distinguished by sensationalism of approach and content rather than by straightforward reportage of newsworthy events. In common parlance, *tabloid* is used to describe works in various media (including books) that cater to immoderate tastes (for example, tabloid exposé, tabloid television, the tabloidization of popular culture).

teleplay   A screenplay geared toward television production. Similar in overall concept to screenplays for the cinema, teleplays are nonetheless inherently concerned with such TV-loaded provisions as the physical dimensions of the smaller screen and formal elements of pacing and structure keyed to stipulated program length and the placement of commercial advertising. Attention to these myriad television-specific demands is fundamental to the viability of a project.

terms   The financial conditions agreed to in a book contract.

theme   A general term for the underlying concept of a book. (*See also* **hook**.)

thriller   A thriller is a novel of suspense with a plot structure that reinforces the elements of gamesmanship and the chase, with a sense of the hunt being paramount. Thrillers can be spy novels, tales of geopolitical crisis, legal thrillers, medical thrillers, techno-thrillers, domestic thrillers. The common thread is a growing sense of threat and the excitement of pursuit.

tip sheet   An information sheet on a single book that presents general publication information (publication date, editor, ISBN, etc.), a brief synopsis of the book, information on relevant other books (sometimes competing titles), and other pertinent marketing data such as author profile and advance blurbs. The tip sheet is given to the sales and publicity departments; a version of the tip sheet is also included in press kits.

title page   The page at the front of a book that lists the title, subtitle, author (and other contributors, such as translator or illustrator), as well as the publishing house and sometimes its logo.

trade books   Books distributed through the book trade — meaning bookstores and major book clubs — as opposed to, for example, mass-market paperbacks, which are often sold at magazine racks, newsstands, and supermarkets as well.

trade discount   The discount from the cover or list price that a publisher gives the bookseller. It is usually proportional to the number of books ordered (the larger the order, the greater the discount) and typically varies between 40 percent and 50 percent.

trade list   A catalog of all of a publisher's books in print, with ISBNs and order information. The trade list sometimes includes descriptions of the current season's new books.

trade (or **quality**) **paperbacks**   Reprints or original titles published in paperback format, larger in dimension than mass-market paperbacks, and distributed through regular retail book channels. Trade paperbacks tend to be in the neighborhood of twice the price of an equivalent mass-market paperback version and about half to two-thirds the price of hardcover editions.

trade publishers   Publishers of books for a general readership — that is, nonprofessional, nonacademic books that are distributed primarily through bookstores.

translation rights   Rights sold either to a foreign agent or directly to a foreign publisher, either by the author's agent or by the original publisher.

treatment In screenwriting, a full narrative description of the story, including sample dialogue.

U

unauthorized biography A history of a person's life written without the consent or collaboration of the subject or the subject's survivors.

university press A publishing house affiliated with a sponsoring university. The university press is usually nonprofit and subsidized by the respective university. Generally, university presses publish noncommercial scholarly nonfiction books written by academics, and their lists may include literary fiction, criticism, and poetry. Some university presses also specialize in titles of regional interest, and many acquire projects intended for commercial book-trade distribution.

unsolicited manuscript A manuscript sent to an editor or agent without being requested by the editor or agent.

V

vanity press A publisher that publishes books only at an author's expense — and will generally agree to publish virtually anything that is submitted and paid for. (*See also* **subsidy publishing**.)

vita Latin word for "life." A shortened equivalent term for *curriculum vitae*. (*See also* **résumé**.)

W

word count The number of words in a given document. When noted on a manuscript, the word count is usually rounded off to the nearest 100 words.

work-for-hire Writing done for an employer, or writing commissioned by a publisher or book packager who retains ownership of, and all rights pertaining to, the written material.

Y

young adult books Books for readers generally between the ages of 12 and 17. Young adult fiction often deals with issues of concern to contemporary teens.

young readers (or **younger readers**) Publishing terminology for the range of publications that address the earliest readers. Sometimes a particular house's young-readers program typifies books for those who do not yet read, which means these books have to hook the caregivers and parents who actually buy them. In certain quirky turns of everyday publishing parlance, *young readers* can mean anyone from embryos through young adults (and *young* means you when you want it to). This part may be confusing (as is often the case with publishing usage): sometimes *younger adult* means only that the readership is allegedly hip, including those who would eschew kids' books as being inherently lame and those who are excruciatingly tapped into the current cultural pulse, regardless of cerebral or life-span quotient.

Z

zombie (or **zombi**)   In idiomatic usage, a zombie is a person whose conduct approximates that of an automaton. Harking back to the term's origins as a figure of speech for the resurrected dead or a reanimated cadaver, such folks are not customarily expected to exhibit an especially snazzy personality or be aware of too many things going on around them; hence some people in book-publishing circles may be characterized as zombies.

INDEX

Advice for Writers

AAR (Association of Authors' Representatives), 8
advances, 38, 61, 131
agents, 5–19
    AAR, 8
    assessing, 13–14
    becoming an agent, 12
    client relations, 6–7, 17–19, 61–64, 66–67
    clients found by, 16–17
    commissions earned by, 5, 7, 9, 62–63
    contracts with, 62–65
    vs. editors, 12
    email and snail mail to, 10–11, 23–24
    false, 7
    fee-based services by, 8–9, 63, 66
    fees for reading your book, 7, 66, 171–72
    finding an agent, 9–12
    future of, 15
    multiple submissions to, 11
    need for, 5–6, 28
    unresponsiveness of, 48–49
    pitching to, 9–12, 23
    query letters to, 10, 20–25
    rejections from, 9, 17, 19, 67–68
    representation by, 13, 62–63
    sales process of, 15–16
    services provided by, 8–9
    success in selling projects, 15
    sweetheart deals by, 13
    switching agents, 18
    and unsold work, 14–15
    when you can't get an agent, 28–31
Amazon, 42–46
Association of Authors' Representatives (AAR), 8
attention getting, 57

biography, author's, 22–23
book proposals, 32–37
business of writing. *See* writing, business of

cease-and-desist orders, 69–70
cold-calling, 28–29
contracts, 62–65, 69
copyright, 69
creativity, 73

depression after publication, 59–60

ebooks, 41–43
editors
    vs. agents, 12
    agents' views of, 442–43
    anecdotes by, 444–45
    author's relationship with, 449–51
    benefits/services of, 29–30, 437, 440, 446–48
    cold-calls to, 28–29
    defined, 437
    fees of, 438, 441
    finding/choosing, 437–38, 443–44, 449–51
    independent vs. in-house, 441–42
    need for, 437
    unresponsiveness of, 48–49
    pitching to, 29–30
    process of editing, 441
    vs. scammers, 438–39
    sweetheart deals by, 13

Facebook, 41

human potential, 72

ignored authors, 48–49

Kindle ereaders, 43

libel, 69
literary agents. *See* agents

marketing, 40–41

"over the transom." *See* unagented/unsolicited submissions

pitching, 9–12, 23, 29–30. *See also* query letters
planning and overplanning, 3–4
platform of author, 41, 46, 70–71
production process for manuscripts, 39–40
promotion, 40

493

publishers
    advances from, 38, 61, 131
    vs. Amazon, 43–44
    conglomerates (Big 5), 77–79, 132
    contracts with, 69
    future of, 47
    independent presses, 131–33
    in-house functions of, 5
    manuscript in production, 39–40
    need for writers, 5
    promotion of books by, 40
    royalties paid by, 39
    what they do, 30–31

query letters, 10, 20–25. *See also* pitching

rejections, 9, 17, 19, 27–28, 48, 67–68
royalties, 39

scientific explanations, 72–73
self-publishing, 44–47, 70
slander, 69
slush piles, 26–31
solicited books, 6
spiritual writing, 50–54
success, factors affecting, 15

unagented/unsolicited submissions, 5, 11, 21, 25, 27–28
unknown writers, 55–58

visibility of authors, 56–58

the writer's journey, 50–54
writing, business of, 61–71
author-agency relationship, 6–7, 17–19, 61–64, 66–67
cease-and-desist orders, 69–70
contracts with agents, 62–65
contracts with publishers, 69
copyright, 69
fees to agents, 7–9, 63, 66, 171–72
libel and slander, 69
for money, 61
platform, 41, 46, 70–71

rejections, 67–68
self-publishing disadvantages, 70

zero, meaning of, 72–73

Publishers and Imprints

ABC-CLIO, 134
Abingdon Press, 134
Abrams, 135
Abrams Books for Young Readers, 135
Ace/Roc Books, 112
Akashic Books, 135
Aladdin, 126
Alfred A. Knopf Books for Young Readers, 110
Algonquin Books, 167–68
All Points Books, 93
Amacom Books, 136
Amistad, 87
Andrews McMeel Publishing, 136
Arte Público Press, 136–37
Arthur A. Levine Books, 161
Artisan, 167
Atheneum Books for Young Readers, 126
Atlantic Monthly Press, 145
Atria Publishing Group, 120–21
Avery, 111–12
Avon, 87

Baen Books, 137
Baker Books (imprint), 137
Baker Publishing Group, 137–38
Ballantine Books, 108
Balzer + Bray, 94
Basic Books, 84–85
Beach Lane Books, 126
Beacon Press, 138
BenBella Books, 138
Berkley, 112
Berrett-Koehler Publishers, 139
Bethany House, 137
Beyond Words Publishing, 139
Bloomsbury Publishing, 139–40
Blue Rider Press, 113
Broadside Books, 88

Celadon Books, 93
Central Recovery Press, 140
Chelsea Green Publishing, 140
Chicago Review Press, 141
Chronicle Books, 141
Clarion, 148
Clarkson Potter, 103
Cleis Press, 141–42
Coffee House Press, 142
Convergent Books, 103
The Countryman Press, 142
Crown Archetype, 103
Crown Children's, 110
Crown Forum, 103
Crown Publishing Group, 102–5
Currency, 103
Custom House, 91

Da Capo Press, 85
Dafina, 149
Daw, 113
Delacorte, 110
Del Rey, 108–9
DeVorss & Company, 142
Dey Street Books, 91
Dial Books for Young Readers, 117
Doubleday, 106–7
Dutton, 113
Dutton Children's Books, 117

Ecco Books, 88
Eerdmans Publishing Co., 143
Emily Bestler Books, 121
Enliven Books, 121
Entrepreneur Press, 143
Europa Editions, 143
The Experiment Publishing Company, 144

Fair Winds Press, 157
Fantagraphics Books, 144
Farrar, Straus and Giroux, 95
Farrar, Straus and Giroux Books for Young Readers, 100
Feiwel and Friends, 101
First Second Books, 101
Flatiron Books, 95
Forever Yours, 82

Gallery Books, 122–23
Globe Pequot, 160
G. P. Putnam's Sons, 114–15
G. P. Putnam's Sons Books for Young Readers, 118
Grand Central, 80–81
Grand Central Life & Style, 82
Graydon House, 92
Graywolf Press, 144
Greenwillow Books, 94
Grosset & Dunlap, 117
Grove Atlantic, 145–46
Grove Press, 145

Hachette Book Group, 80–84
Hachette Books, 81
Hachette Nashville, 82–83
Hanover Square Press, 92–93
Harlequin, 91–92
Harlequin TEEN, 92
Harmony Books, 104
Harper, 88
Harper Business, 88
HarperCollins Children's Books, 94
HarperCollins Christian Publishing, 92
HarperCollins Leadership, 89
HarperCollins Publishers, 87–94
Harper Design, 89
HarperOne, 89
Harper Perennial, 89
HarperTeen, 94
Harper Voyager, 90
Harper Wave, 90
Harvard Common Press, 157
Harvest House, 146
Hay House, 146
Hazelden Publishing, 146–47
Health Communications, Inc., 147
Henry Holt and Company, 96–97
Henry Holt Books for Young Readers, 101
Hogarth, 104
Houghton Mifflin Harcourt, 147–48
Houghton Mifflin Harcourt Children's, 148

Howard Books, 122
Human Kinetics Publishers, Inc., 148

Inner Traditions/Bear & Company, 149

Jimmy Patterson, 84

Katherine Tegen Books, 94
Kensington (imprint), 149–50
Kensington Publishing, 149–50
Knopf Doubleday Publishing Group, 106–7

Little, Brown and Company, 83
Little, Brown Children's, 84
Little Simon, 127
Liveright, 150
Llewellyn Worldwide, 150
Loveswept, 109

Macmillan Children's, 100–101
Macmillan Publishers, 95–101
Manic D Press, 150
Margaret K. McElderry Books, 127
McGraw-Hill Professional, 151
Metropolitan Books, 97
Milkweed Editions, 151
Minotaur, 98–99
Mira Books, 92
Mulholland Books, 83
The Mysterious Press, 146

National Geographic Books, 151
Nation Books, 85
Naval Institute Press, 152
New Directions, 152
New Harbinger Publications, 152
New Horizon Press, 153
The New Press, 153
New World Library, 153
North Star Way, 123
No Starch Press, 154

One World, 109
Orbit, 82
The Overlook Press, 155

Pam Krauss Books, 112
Park Row Books, 92
Paula Wiseman Books, 127
Paulist Press, 155
Peachtree Publishers, 155
Pegasus Books, 155
Pelican Publishing Company, 156
Penguin, 111–19
Penguin Books (imprint), 116
The Penguin Press (imprint), 114
Penguin Random House, 102–19
Penguin Young Readers Group, 116–19
The Permanent Press, 156
The Perseus Books Group, 84–86
Philomel Books, 118
Picador, 93–94
Portfolio, 114
Praeger, 134
Prometheus Books, 156–57
Public Affairs, 85–86

Quarto Publishing Group, 157
Quirk Books, 158

Random House, 102–5
Random House (imprint), 107–8
Random House Books for Young Readers, 111
Random House Children's Books, 110–11
Razorbill, 118
Red Wheel, 158
Regnery Publishing, Inc., 159
Revell, 138
Riverhead Books, 115
Roaring Brook Press, 101
Rodale Books, 105
Rowman & Littlefield, 159–60
Running Press, 86

Saga Press, 127
Salaam Reads, 126
Sasquatch Books, 160
Schocken Books, 107
Scholastic Inc., 160–61
Schwartz and Wade, 111
Scribner, 123–24
Seal Press, 86

INDEX

495

Sentinel, 115
Seven Stories Press, 161
Shambhala Publications, 161
Simon Pulse, 128
Simon & Schuster, 120–25
Simon & Schuster (imprint), 124–25
Simon & Schuster Books for Young Readers, 128
Simon & Schuster Children's Publishing, 126–28
Skyhorse Publishing, 162
Smithsonian Books, 162
Soho Press, 162
Sounds True, Inc., 163
Sourcebooks, 163–64
Spiegel & Grau, 109
Square One Publishers, Inc., 164
St. Martin's Press, 97–98
Storey Publishing, 168

Tarcher Perigee, 115–16
Ten Speed Press, 104–5
Thames & Hudson, 164
37 Ink, 121
Thomas Dunne Books, 98
Thomas Nelson, 92
Three Rivers Press, 105
Threshold Editions, 123
Tin House Books, 164–65
Tor/Forge, 100
Touchstone Books, 125
Turner Publishing Company, 165
Twelve, 82
Tyndale House Publishers, Inc., 165

Ulysses Press, 165–66

Verso Books, 166
Viking Books, 116–17
Viking Children's Books, 119

Waterbrook Multnomah Publishing Group, 106
Weinstein Books, 86
Wiley, 166

William Morrow, 90
Workman Publishing Company, 167–68
W. W. Norton & Company, Inc., 154

Zondervan, 92
Zondervan Children's, 92

Agents and Agencies

Altshuler, Miriam, 213–14
Anderson-Wheeler, Claire, 360–61
Andrea Brown Literary Agency, Inc., 173–75
Andrea Hurst & Associates, LLC, 175–76
Annie Bomke Literary Agency, 176–79
Atchity, Ken, 395–96
The August Agency LLC, 179–84

Baldi, Malaga, 317–19
Barbara, Stephen, 260–61
Barbour, Bruce R., 308–9
Barr, Stephen, 427–29
Becker, Laney Katz, 331–32
Beren, Peter, 346–49
Betsy Amster Literary Enterprises, 184–87
Biderman, Marilyn, 405–6
Bieker, Lauren, 229–30
Bilmes, Joshua, 264–66
BJ Robbins Literary Agency, 187
Blue Ridge Literary Agency, LLC, 188–89
Bomke, Annie, 176–79
Bradford Literary Agency, 189–94
Brady, Mackenzie, 345–46
Brewer, Amy, 339–40
Brown, Andrea, 173–75
Bykofsky, Sheree, 383–85

Campoli, Leila, 392–93
Carnicelli Literary Management, 194–96
Carothers, Patty, 340–42

Carr, Michael, 415–16
Chilton, Jamie Weiss, 173–75
Claggett, Hilary, 371–73
Clark, June, 230
Cloughley, Amy, 294–95
Collins, Nina, 443
Contardi, Bill, 442
Corvisiero Literary Agency, 196–207
Creative Media Agency, 207–9
Crockett, Laura, 407–8
CSG Literary Partners/MDM Management, 209–10
Cummings, Mary, 184–87
Curtis, Richard, 363–64
Curwen, Ginger, 292–93
Cusick, John, 233–35

Dana Newman Literary, LLC, 210–13
De Chiara, Jennifer, 275
DeFiore and Company Literary Management, Inc., 213–15
Denise Shannon Literary Agency, Inc., 215–16
Devlin, Anne G., 333–34
Diana Finch Literary Agency, 216–19
Dilanyan, Rema, 349
Diver, Lucienne, 295–96
Domínguez, Adriana, 242–43
Dontzin, Ginger Harris, 311–13
Doug Grad Literary Agency, Inc., 219–22
Dowdle, Dawn, 188–89
Dunham Literary, Inc., 222–26
Dunton, David, 255–57

Ebeling & Associates, 226–27
Edwards, Melissa, 394
Ekstrom, Rachel, 264
Ekus, Lisa, 305–6
The Evan Marshall Agency, 228

Fargis, Alison, 394–95
Finch, Diana, 216–19

FinePrint Literary Management, 229–33
Fleissig, Liza, 311–13
Folio Literary Management / Folio Jr., 233–41
Fraser, Stephen, 277–78
Fraser-Bub Literary, LLC, 241–42
Frederick, Dawn, 352–53
Fredericks, Jeanne, 267–72
Freeman, Cricket, 179–84
Full Circle Literary, 242–43
Fuse Literary, 243–51

Ghahremani, Lilly, 243
Global Lion Intellectual Property Management, Inc., 251–53
Goetz, Adria, 324–26
Gomez, Leticia, 373–78
Goodman, Irene, 262–64
Gore, Clelia, 328–31
Gottlieb, Mark, 410–13
Grad, Doug, 219–22
Graham, Stacey, 356–57
Grazian, Natalie, 326–28
Green, Carol, 387–88

Hagan, Lisa, 306–8
Hales, Katelyn, 365–67
Hane, Erik, 357–58
Hansen, Stephanie, 337–38
Harris, Erin, 235–38
Harris, Steven, 209–10
Hart, Cate, 202–4
Hart, Jim, 251–53
Hartline Literary Agency, 253–55
Harvey Klinger, Inc., 255–58
Haskin, Jennifer, 197–200
Hawkins, Anne, 288–90
Heather Jackson Literary Agency, 258–60
Hedrick, Catherine, 352
Heidt, Gary, 385–86
Herman, Jeff, 272–74
Heymont, Lane, 401–2
Hill, Julie, 293–94
Hoffmann, Markus, 362–63
Hurst, Andrea, 175–76

Inkwell Management, 260–61
Irene Goodman Literary Agency, 262–64

JABberwocky Literary Agency, Inc., 264–66
Jackson, Heather, 258–60
Janklow & Nesbit Associates, 266–67
Jeanne Fredericks Literary Agency, Inc., 267–72
The Jeff Herman Agency, LLC, 272–74
The Jennifer De Chiara Literary Agency, 275–86
Jennifer Lyons Literary Agency, 286–87
Jill Cohen Associates, LLC, 287–88
John Hawkins & Associates, Inc., 288–92
Johnson, Kaitlyn, 200–202
Julia Lord Literary Management, 292–93
Julie A. Hill and Associates, LLC, 293–94

Karinch, Maryann, 370–71
Kean, Taylor Martindale, 243
Kilkelly, Lori, 367–68
Kimberley Cameron & Associates, 294–95
Kirkpatrick, Rob, 398–99
Kleinman, Jeff, 238–40
Knapp, Peter, 346
The Knight Agency, 295–96
Konner, Linda, 304–5
Kramer, Jill, 417–18
Kriss, Miriam, 264
Kronenberg, Annie, 290–92

The LA Literary Agency, 296–300
Lamba, Cari, 278–79
Lampack, Andrew, 349
Lampack, Peter, 349
Lasher, Maureen, 296–300
Laughran, Jennifer, 173–75
Laurell, David, 279–81

Levine | Greenberg | Rostan Literary Agency, 300–303
Linda Konner Literary Agency, 304–5
The Lisa Ekus Group, 305–6
Lisa Hagan Literary, 306–8
Literary Management Group, LLC, 308–9
Literary Services, Inc., 309–11
Liza Royce Agency, LLC, 311–13
Lopopolo, Toni, 403–4
Lord, Julia, 292–93
Lowenstein Associates, 313–15
Lynn Seligman, Literary Agent, 315–17

Maaghul, Johanna, 420–22
Mackwood, Robert, 382–83
Malaga Baldi Literary Agency, 317–19
Marini, Victoria, 264
Marsal Lyon Literary Agency, LLC, 319–21
Marshall, Evan, 228
Martin Literary & Media Management, 321–31
Massie & McQuilkin Literary Agents, 331–32
Mattson, Jennifer, 173–75
Max Gartenberg Literary Agency, 333–34
McCollum, Kim, 352
McLean, Laurie, 243–45
McNicholl, Damian, 281–82
Mendel Media Group, LLC, 334–37
Metamorphosis Literary Agency, 337–42
Miller, Peter, 251–53
Moeller, Kristen, 418–20
Myers, Eric, 442
Myers Literary Management, 342–44

New Leaf Literary & Media, Inc., 344–46
Newman, Dana, 210–13

Ortiz, Kathleen, 345
Ourvan, Jeff, 286–87

Parry, Emma, 266–67
Perel, Kim, 264
Perkins, Laura, 173–75
The Peter Beren Agency, 346–49
Peter Lampack Agency, Inc., 349
Poelle, Barbara, 264
Posner, Marcy, 240–41
Price, Kortney, 204–7
Pryor, Victoria Gould, 442
P.S. Literary Agency, 349–50
The Purcell Agency, LLC, 350–52

Rahn, Liz, 359
Red Sofa Literary, 352–59
Regal Hoffmann & Associates, LLC, 360–63
Rennert, Laura, 173–75
Richard Curtis Associates, Inc., 363–64
Richter, Michelle, 245–47
Rita Rosenkranz Literary Agency, 365
Robbins, BJ, 187
Robin Straus Agency, Inc., 365–67
Rodeen Literary Management, 367–68
Rodgers, Lisa, 266
Rofé, Jennifer, 173–75
The Rohm Literary Agency, 368–69
Rosen, Janet, 383–85
Rosenkranz, Rita, 365
Ross, Grace, 361–62
Ross, Whitney, 264
Rubie, Peter, 230–33
The Rudy Agency, 369–73
Rushall, Kathleen, 173–75
Russell, Curtis, 349–50
Rutter, Amanda, 355–56

Savvy Literary Services, 373–78
The Schisgal Agency, LLC, 378–80
Schmalz, Wendy, 422–23
Schneider, Deborah, 443

Schneider, Eddie, 266
Schwartz, Tina P., 350–52
Second City Publishing Services, LLC, 380–82
Seligman, Lynn, 315–17
Selvaggio, Victoria, 282–84
Seventh Avenue Literary Agency, 382–83
Sheree Bykofsky Associates, Inc., 383–85
Signature Literary Agency, 385–86
Simenauer & Green Literary Agency, LLC, 387–88
Skinner, Tricia, 247–48
Skurnick, Victoria, 302–3
Smith, Bridget, 224–26
Soloway, Jennifer March, 173–75
Somberg, Andrea, 257–58
Sonnack, Kelly, 173–75
Speilburg Literary Agency, 388–90
Steele-Perkins Literary Agency, 390
Stender, Uwe, 409–10
Stephanie Tade Agency, 391–92
Stonesong, 392–95
The Story Merchant, 395–96
Strachan Literary Agency, 396–98
Straus, Robin, 365–67
The Stuart Agency, 398–99
Svetcov, Danielle, 300–302

Tade, Stephanie, 391–92
Temperly, Jaida, 346
Tessler Literary Agency, 399–400
The Tobias Literary Agency, 401–2
Toni Lopopolo Literary Management, 403–4
Townsend, Suzie, 345
Tran, Jennifer Chen, 191–94
Transatlantic Literary Agency, 405–6
TriadaUS Literary Agency, 407–10
Trident Media Group, LLC, 410–13

The Unter Agency, 413–14

Veritas Literary Agency, 415–16
Volpe, Joanna, 345
Von Borstel, Stefanie Sanchez, 242

Wales Literary Agency, 416–17
Warnock, Gordon, 248–50
Waterside Productions, Inc., 417–22
Watters, Carly, 350
Webber, Carlisle K., 250–51
Weiss, Alexandra, 276–77
Wells, Roseanne, 284–86
Wendy Schmalz Agency, 422–23
Wheeler, Paige, 207–9
Williamson Literary, 423–26
Willig, John, 309–11
Wiseman, Caryn, 173–75
Wood, Laura, 229
Writers House, LLC, 427–29

The Zack Company, Inc., 429–32
Zats, Laura, 354–55
Zigmund, Cynthia, 380–82
Zimmermann Literary, 432–33

Independent Editors

Adelstein, Marlene, 454, 460
Alexander, Jeff, 461
Arteseros, Sally, 456

Bell, Harriet, 456
Book Development Group, 452–53
The Book Editors Alliance, 453–55
Burbank, Toni, 456–57

Cabaza, Becky, 461–62
Carbone, Linda, 445
Dalsimer, Susan, 457
De Angelis, Paul, 457
Denneny, Michael, 457
Dinas, Paul, 457
Dolin, Arnold, 454

Fogelson, Aliza, 458
Fransson, Jane Fleming, 462

Gelles-Cole, Sandi, 446–48, 454
Greenstein, Ruth, 445, 462
Groff, David, 454

Heckman, Emily, 458
Hinzmann, Hilary, 454

The Independent Editors Group, 455–59

Jablonski, Carla, 454

Kern, Judith, 454
King, Janet Spencer, 452–53

Lalli, Carole, 455
Leon, Susan, 458
Loose, Emily, 462

Marek, Richard, 458
Marvelous Editions, 459–60
McCafferty, Danelle, 455
Miesionczek, Julie, 462–63
Miner, Sydny, 458–59

Nicholas, Nancy, 455
Norman, Anne Cole, 463

O'Connell, Diane, 453

Peck, Alice, 460
Poynter, Toni Sciarra, 455

Rashbaum, Beth, 459
Rosengard, Alice, 444

Sargent, Betty Kelly, 459
Satter, Nan Gatewood, 455

Turok, Katharine, 444–45

Vezeris, Olga, 453

Wade, James O'Shea, 459
Weber, Karl, 455

Wilde, Michael, 449–51
Words into Print, 440–45, 460–63

Publishers, Imprints, and Agents by Subject

addiction. *See also* health care / medicine
    Central Recovery Press, 140
    Hazelden Publishing, 146–47
adult fiction. *See also* historical fiction; horror; magical realism; mystery; paranormal/supernatural; science fiction / fantasy; suspense/thriller/crime; urban fantasy/fiction; women's fiction
    Abrams, 135
    Algonquin Books, 167–68
    Altshuler, Miriam, 213–15
    Atlantic Monthly Press, 145
    Atria Publishing Group, 120–21
    Baldi, Malaga, 317–19
    Barbara, Stephen, 260–61
    Becker, Laney Katz, 331–32
    Biderman, Marilyn, 405–6
    Bieker, Lauren, 229–30
    Bilmes, Joshua, 264–66
    BJ Robbins Literary Agency, 187
    Bloomsbury Publishing, 139–40
    Blue Rider Press, 113
    Bradford Literary Agency, 189–94
    Brady, Mackenzie, 345–46
    Carnicelli Literary Management, 194–96
    Carothers, Patty, 340–42
    Celadon Books, 99
    Cloughley, Amy, 294–95
    Coffee House Press, 142
    Corvisiero Literary Agency, 196–207
    Creative Media Agency, 207–9

Crown Publishing Group, 102–5
Custom House, 91
De Chiara, Jennifer, 275
DeFiore and Company Literary Management, Inc., 213–15
Del Rey, 108–9
Denise Shannon Literary Agency, Inc., 215–16
Diana Finch Literary Agency, 216–19
Dontzin, Ginger Harris, 311–13
Doubleday, 106–7
Dunham Literary, Inc., 222–26
Dutton, 113
Ecco Books, 88
Emily Bestler Books, 121
Europa Editions, 143
The Evan Marshall Agency, 228
Fargis, Alison, 394–95
Farrar, Straus and Giroux, 95
Finch, Diana, 216–19
FinePrint Literary Management, 229–33
Flatiron Books, 96
Fleissig, Liza, 311–13
Folio Literary Management / Folio Jr., 233–41
Fraser-Bub Literary, LLC, 241–42
Fuse Literary, 243–51
Gallery Books, 122–23
Gomez, Leticia, 373–78
Gottlieb, Mark, 410–13
G. P. Putnam's Sons, 114–15
Grand Central, 80–81
Graywolf Press, 144
Green, Carol, 387–88
Grove Atlantic, 145–46
Grove Press, 145
Hachette Nashville, 82–83

adult fiction (continued)
Hales, Katelyn, 365–67
Hane, Erik, 357–58
Hanover Square Press, 92–93
Harper, 88
Harper Perennial, 89
Harris, Erin, 235–38
Hart, Jim, 253–55
Hartline Literary Agency, 253–55
Hawkins, Anne, 288–90
Heather Jackson Literary Agency, 258–60
Henry Holt and Company, 96–97
Hoffmann, Markus, 362–63
Hogarth, 104
Houghton Mifflin Harcourt, 147–48
Inkwell Management, 260–61
JABberwocky Literary Agency, Inc., 264–66
Jackson, Heather, 258–60
Janklow & Nesbit Associates, 266–67
The Jennifer De Chiara Literary Agency, 275–86
John Hawkins & Associates, Inc., 288–92
Johnson, Kaitlyn, 200–202
Julia Lord Literary Management, 292–93
Kensington (imprint), 149–50
Kimberley Cameron & Associates, 294–95
Kleinman, Jeff, 238–40
Knapp, Peter, 346
Knopf Doubleday Publishing Group, 106–7
The LA Literary Agency, 296–300
Lamba, Cari, 278–79
Lasher, Maureen, 296–300
Levine | Greenberg | Rostan Literary Agency, 300–303

Little, Brown and Company, 83
Liveright, 150
Liza Royce Agency, LLC, 311–13
Lord, Julia, 292–93
Lowenstein Associates, 313–15
Lynn Seligman, Literary Agent, 315–17
Malaga Baldi Literary Agency, 317–19
Manic D Press, 150
Marsal Lyon Literary Agency, LLC, 319–21
Marshall, Evan, 228
Massie & McQuilkin Literary Agents, 331–32
McLean, Laurie, 243–45
McNicholl, Damian, 281–82
Mendel Media Group, LLC, 334–37
Milkweed Editions, 151
Moeller, Kristen, 418–20
Mulholland Books, 83
Naval Institute Press, 152
New Directions, 152
New Leaf Literary & Media, Inc., 344–46
One World, 109
The Overlook Press, 155
Park Row Books, 92
Parry, Emma, 266–67
Pelican Publishing Company, 156
The Penguin Press (imprint), 114
The Permanent Press, 156
Picador, 99–100
P. S. Literary Agency, 349–50
Quirk Books, 158
Random House (imprint), 107–8
Red Sofa Literary, 352–59
Regal Hoffmann & Associates, LLC, 360–63
Richter, Michelle, 245–47

Riverhead Books, 115
Robbins, BJ, 187
Robin Straus Agency, Inc., 365–67
The Rohm Literary Agency, 368–69
Ross, Grace, 361–62
Rubie, Peter, 230–33
Russell, Curtis, 349–50
Savvy Literary Services, 373–78
The Schisgal Agency, LLC, 378–80
Scribner, 123–24
Second City Publishing Services, LLC, 380–82
Seligman, Lynn, 315–17
Selvaggio, Victoria, 282–84
Seven Stories Press, 161
Shannon, Denise, 215–16
Simenauer & Green Literary Agency, LLC, 387–88
Simon & Schuster (imprint), 124–25
Skurnick, Victoria, 302–3
Skyhorse Publishing, 162
Smith, Bridget, 224–26
Soho Press, 162
Sourcebooks, 163–64
Spiegel & Grau, 109
Square One Publishers, Inc., 164
St. Martin's Press, 97–98
Stonesong, 392–95
Strachan Literary Agency, 396–98
Straus, Robin, 365–67
Svetcov, Danielle, 300–302
Temperly, Jaida, 346
Tessler Literary Agency, 399–400
Thomas Dunne Books, 98
Tin House Books, 164–65
Tor/Forge, 100
Touchstone Books, 125
Townsend, Suzie, 345
Tran, Jennifer Chen, 191–94

Transatlantic Literary Agency, 405–6
Trident Media Group, LLC, 410–13
Turner Publishing Company, 165
Viking Books, 116–17
Volpe, Joanna, 345
Wales Literary Agency, 416–17
Warnock, Gordon, 248–50
Waterside Productions, Inc., 417–22
Wells, Roseanne, 284–86
Wheeler, Paige, 207–9
William Morrow, 90
Williamson Literary, 423–26
W. W. Norton & Company, Inc., 154
The Zack Company, Inc., 429–32
Zigmund, Cynthia, 380–82
Zimmermann Literary, 432–33

adult nonfiction
   Algonquin Books, 167–68
   Altshuler, Miriam, 213–15
   Atlantic Monthly Press, 145
   Atria Publishing Group, 120–21
   The August Agency LLC, 179–84
   Baldi, Malaga, 317–19
   Barbara, Stephen, 260–61
   Becker, Laney Katz, 331–32
   Beren, Peter, 346–49
   Biderman, Marilyn, 405–6
   Bilmes, Joshua, 264–66
   BJ Robbins Literary Agency, 187
   Bloomsbury Publishing, 139–40
   Blue Rider Press, 113
   Bradford Literary Agency, 189–94
   Bykofsky, Sheree, 383–85
   Campoli, Leila, 392–93
   Carnicelli Literary Management, 194–96
   Celadon Books, 99
   Chronicle Books, 141
   Cloughley, Amy, 294–95
   Coffee House Press, 142
   Corvisiero Literary Agency, 196–207
   Creative Media Agency, 207–9
   Custom House, 91
   Dana Newman Literary, LLC 210–13
   De Chiara, Jennifer, 275
   DeFiore and Company Literary Management, Inc., 213–15
   Denise Shannon Literary Agency, Inc., 215–16
   Devlin, Anne G., 333–34
   Dontzin, Ginger Harris, 311–13
   Doubleday, 106–7
   Dunham Literary, Inc., 222–26
   Dunton, David, 255–57
   Dutton, 113
   Ebeling & Associates, 226–27
   Ecco Books, 88
   Emily Bestler Books, 121
   Europa Editions, 143
   Farrar, Straus and Giroux, 95
   FinePrint Literary Management, 229–33
   Fleissig, Liza, 311–13
   Folio Literary Management / Folio Jr., 233–41
   Fraser-Bub Literary, LLC, 241–42
   Freeman, Cricket, 179–84
   Full Circle Literary, 242–43
   Fuse Literary, 243–51
   Gallery Books, 122–23
   Gomez, Leticia, 373–78
   Goodman, Irene, 262–64
   Gottlieb, Mark, 410–13
   G. P. Putnam's Sons, 114–15
   Graham, Stacey, 356–57
   Grand Central, 80–81
   Graywolf Press, 144
   Green, Carol, 387–88
   Grove Atlantic, 145–46
   Grove Press, 145
   Hachette Books (imprint), 81
   Hales, Katelyn, 365–67
   Hane, Erik, 357–58
   Hanover Square Press, 92–93
   Harper, 88
   Harper Perennial, 89
   Harris, Erin, 235–38
   Hart, Cate, 202–4
   Hart, Jim, 253–55
   Hartline Literary Agency, 253–55
   Harvey Klinger, Inc., 255–58
   Hawkins, Anne, 288–90
   Heather Jackson Literary Agency, 258–60
   Henry Holt and Company, 96–97
   Herman, Jeff, 272–74
   Hoffmann, Markus, 362–63
   Houghton Mifflin Harcourt, 147–48
   Inkwell Management, 260–61
   Irene Goodman Literary Agency, 262–64
   JABberwocky Literary Agency, Inc., 264–66
   Jackson, Heather, 258–60
   Janklow & Nesbit Associates, 266–67
   The Jeff Herman Agency, LLC, 272–74
   The Jennifer De Chiara Literary Agency, 275–86
   John Hawkins & Associates, Inc., 288–92
   Julia Lord Literary Management, 292–93
   Kensington (imprint), 149–50

adult nonfiction (*continued*)
Kimberley Cameron & Associates, 294–95
Kirkpatrick, Rob, 398–99
Knopf Doubleday Publishing Group, 106–7
Konner, Linda, 304–5
The LA Literary Agency, 296–300
Lasher, Maureen, 296–300
Levine | Greenberg | Rostan Literary Agency, 300–303
Linda Konner Literary Agency, 304–5
Literary Services, Inc., 309–11
Little, Brown and Company, 83
Liveright, 150
Liza Royce Agency, LLC, 311–13
Lopopolo, Toni, 403–4
Lord, Julia, 292–93
Lowenstein Associates, 313–15
Lynn Seligman, Literary Agent, 315–17
Mackwood, Robert, 382–83
Malaga Baldi Literary Agency, 317–19
Manic D Press, 150
Marsal Lyon Literary Agency, LLC, 319–21
Martin Literary & Media Management, 321–31
Massie & McQuilkin Literary Agents, 331–32
Max Gartenberg Literary Agency, 333–34
Mendel Media Group, LLC, 334–37
Milkweed Editions, 151
Myers Literary Management, 342–44
National Geographic Books, 151
New Leaf Literary & Media,
Inc., 344–46
Newman, Dana, 210–13
One World, 109
The Overlook Press, 155
Parry, Emma, 266–67
The Penguin Press (imprint), 114
The Permanent Press, 156
The Peter Beren Agency, 346–49
P. S. Literary Agency, 349–50
Random House (imprint), 107–8
Red Sofa Literary, 352–59
Regal Hoffmann & Associates, LLC, 360–63
Richter, Michelle, 245–47
Riverhead Books, 115
Robbins, BJ, 187
Robin Straus Agency, Inc., 365–67
The Rohm Literary Agency, 368–69
Rosen, Janet, 383–85
Ross, Grace, 361–62
Rowman & Littlefield, 159–60
Rubie, Peter, 230–33
Russell, Curtis, 349–50
Savvy Literary Services, 373–78
The Schisgal Agency, LLC, 378–80
Second City Publishing Services, LLC, 380–82
Seligman, Lynn, 315–17
Selvaggio, Victoria, 282–84
Seven Stories Press, 161
Seventh Avenue Literary Agency, 382–83
Shannon, Denise, 215–16
Sheree Bykofsky Associates, Inc., 383–85
Simenauer & Green Literary Agency, LLC, 387–88
Simon & Schuster (imprint), 124–25
Skurnick, Victoria, 302–3
Smithsonian Books, 162
Sourcebooks, 163–64
Spiegel & Grau, 109
Square One Publishers, Inc., 164
St. Martin's Press, 97–98
Stonesong, 392–95
Strachan Literary Agency, 396–98
Straus, Robin, 365–67
The Stuart Agency, 398–99
Tessler Literary Agency, 399–400
Thomas Nelson, 93
Tin House Books, 164–65
Toni Lopopolo Literary Management, 403–4
Tor/Forge, 100
Tran, Jennifer Chen, 191–94
Transatlantic Literary Agency, 405–6
Trident Media Group, LLC, 410–13
Turner Publishing Company, 165
Ulysses Press, 165–66
Verso Books, 166
Volpe, Joanna, 345
Von Borstel, Stefanie Sanchez, 242
Wales Literary Agency, 416–17
Warnock, Gordon, 248–50
Wells, Roseanne, 284–86
Wheeler, Paige, 207–9
William Morrow, 90
Williamson Literary, 423–26
Willig, John, 309–11
Wood, Laura, 229
Workman Publishing Company, 167–68
The Zack Company, Inc., 429–32
Zigmund, Cynthia, 380–82
adventure
Aladdin, 126

Cloughley, Amy, 294–95
Corvisiero Literary Agency, 196–207
Julia Lord Literary Management, 292–93
Kimberley Cameron & Associates, 294–95
Lord, Julia, 292–93
Price, Kortney, 204–7
St. Martin's Press, 97–98

advice
Da Capo Press, 85
Gomez, Leticia, 373–78
Grand Central, 80–81
Hachette Nashville, 82–83
Houghton Mifflin Harcourt, 147–48
Running Press, 86
Savvy Literary Services, 373–78
Seal Press, 86
Skyhorse Publishing, 162
Tarcher Perigee, 115–16
William Morrow, 90

African and African American
Amistad, 87
Atria Publishing Group, 120–21
Beacon Press, 138
Dafina, 149
Dial Books for Young Readers, 117
Rowman & Littlefield, 159–60
37 Ink, 121
W. W. Norton & Company, Inc., 154

aging/gerontology
Folio Literary Management / Folio Jr., 233–41
The Jennifer De Chiara Literary Agency, 275–86
Kleinman, Jeff, 238–40
Konner, Linda, 304–5
Laurell, David, 279–81
Linda Konner Literary Agency, 304–5

Amish
Abingdon Press, 134
Blue Ridge Literary Agency, LLC, 188–89
Dowdle, Dawn, 188–89
Kensington (imprint), 149–50

animals
The Countryman Press, 142
Devlin, Anne G., 333–34
Folio Literary Management / Folio Jr., 233–41
Globe Pequot, 160
Kensington (imprint), 149–50
Kleinman, Jeff, 238–40
Max Gartenberg Literary Agency, 333–34
New World Library, 153
Simon & Schuster (imprint), 124–25
Skyhorse Publishing, 162
St. Martin's Press, 97–98
Storey Publishing, 168

anthropology/ethnology
Rowman & Littlefield, 159–60

archaeology
Rowman & Littlefield, 159–60

art/architecture
Abrams, 135
Beren, Peter, 346–49
Corvisiero Literary Agency, 196–207
Crown Publishing Group, 102–5
Folio Literary Management / Folio Jr., 233–41
Fredericks, Jeanne, 267–72
Harper Design, 89
Jeanne Fredericks Literary Agency, Inc., 267–72
Kleinman, Jeff, 238–40
Pelican Publishing Company, 156

The Penguin Press (imprint), 114
The Peter Beren Agency, 346–49
Price, Kortney, 204–7
Rowman & Littlefield, 159–60
Ten Speed Press, 104–5
Thames & Hudson, 164
Viking Books, 116–17

beauty/fashion
Artisan, 167
Bieker, Lauren, 229–30
Bradford Literary Agency, 189–94
Clark, June, 230
Cohen, Jill, 287–88
FinePrint Literary Management, 229–33
Fraser-Bub Literary, LLC, 241–42
Harper Design, 89
Jill Cohen Associates, LLC, 287–88
Thames & Hudson, 164
Tran, Jennifer Chen, 191–94

biography/memoir
Algonquin Books, 167–68
Anderson-Wheeler, Claire, 360–61
Annie Bomke Literary Agency, 176–79
Atria Publishing Group, 120–21
The August Agency LLC, 179–84
Becker, Laney Katz, 331–32
Biderman, Marilyn, 405–6
Bloomsbury Publishing, 139–40
Bomke, Annie, 176–79
Bradford Literary Agency, 189–94
Brady, Mackenzie, 345–46
Campoli, Leila, 392–93
Carnicelli Literary Management, 194–96

INDEX

503

biography/memoir (*continued*)
　　Cloughley, Amy, 294–95
　　Coffee House Press, 142
　　Crown Publishing Group, 102–5
　　CSG Literary Partners / MDM Management, 209–10
　　Dana Newman Literary, LLC, 210–13
　　De Chiara, Jennifer, 275
　　DeFiore and Company Literary Management, Inc., 213–15
　　Denise Shannon Literary Agency, Inc., 215–16
　　Devlin, Anne G., 333–34
　　Dey Street Books, 91
　　Doubleday, 106–7
　　Dunton, David, 255–57
　　Dutton, 113
　　Ecco Books, 88
　　FinePrint Literary Management, 229–33
　　Folio Literary Management / Folio Jr., 233–41
　　Frederick, Dawn, 352–53
　　Freeman, Cricket, 179–84
　　Gallery Books, 122–23
　　Gomez, Leticia, 373–78
　　Gottlieb, Mark, 410–13
　　Grand Central, 80–81
　　Green, Carol, 387–88
　　Hachette Books (imprint), 81
　　Hales, Katelyn, 365–67
　　Harper, 88
　　Harper Business, 88
　　Harris, Erin, 235–38
　　Harris, Steven, 209–10
　　Hart, Jim, 253–55
　　Hartline Literary Agency, 253–55
　　Harvey Klinger, Inc., 255–58
　　Henry Holt and Company, 96–97
　　Houghton Mifflin Harcourt, 147–48
　　The Jennifer De Chiara Literary Agency, 275–86
　　Julia Lord Literary Management, 292–93
　　Kimberley Cameron & Associates, 294–95
　　Kirkpatrick, Rob, 398–99
　　Kleinman, Jeff, 238–40
　　Laurell, David, 279–81
　　Levine | Greenberg | Rostan Literary Agency, 300–303
　　Little, Brown and Company, 83
　　Liveright, 150
　　Lord, Julia, 292–93
　　Lynn Seligman, Literary Agent, 315–17
　　Martin Literary & Media Management, 321–31
　　Massie & McQuilkin Literary Agents, 331–32
　　Max Gartenberg Literary Agency, 333–34
　　McNicholl, Damian, 281–82
　　Mendel Media Group, LLC, 334–37
　　Moeller, Kristen, 418–20
　　Myers Literary Management, 342–44
　　New Leaf Literary & Media, Inc., 344–46
　　Newman, Dana, 210–13
　　The Penguin Press (imprint), 114
　　P. S. Literary Agency, 349–50
　　Random House (imprint), 107–8
　　Red Sofa Literary, 352–59
　　Regal Hoffmann & Associates, LLC, 360–63
　　Regnery Publishing, Inc., 159
　　Robin Straus Agency, Inc., 365–67
　　The Rohm Literary Agency, 368–69
　　Rubie, Peter, 230–33
　　Russell, Curtis, 349–50
　　Savvy Literary Services, 373–78
　　Scribner, 123–24
　　Seligman, Lynn, 315–17
　　Shannon, Denise, 215–16
　　Simenauer & Green Literary Agency, LLC, 387–88
　　Simon & Schuster (imprint), 124–25
　　Soho Press, 162
　　Spiegel & Grau, 109
　　St. Martin's Press, 97–98
　　Stonesong, 392–95
　　The Stuart Agency, 398–99
　　Svetcov, Danielle, 300–302
　　Tessler Literary Agency, 399–400
　　Tran, Jennifer Chen, 191–94
　　Transatlantic Literary Agency, 405–6
　　Trident Media Group, LLC, 410–13
　　Twelve, 82
　　The Unter Agency, 413–14
　　Viking Books, 116–17
　　Waterside Productions, Inc., 417–22
　　Wells, Roseanne, 284–86
　　William Morrow, 90
　　Williamson Literary, 423–26
　　W. W. Norton & Company, Inc., 154
　　The Zack Company, Inc., 429–32
　　Zimmermann Literary, 432–33
biology/bioethics. *See* science / natural history
botany/plant sciences. *See* science / natural history
business/management
　　Annie Bomke Literary Agency, 176–79
　　Basic Books, 84–85
　　Berrett-Koehler Publishers,

139
Bomke, Annie, 176–79
Bradford Literary Agency, 189–94
Bykofsky, Sheree, 383–85
Campoli, Leila, 392–93
Carnicelli Literary Management, 194–96
Clark, June, 230
Creative Media Agency, 207–9
Crown Publishing Group, 102–5
CSG Literary Partners/MDM Management, 209–10
Currency, 103
Da Capo Press, 85
Dana Newman Literary, LLC, 210–13
Denise Shannon Literary Agency, Inc., 215–16
Devlin, Anne G., 333–34
Diana Finch Literary Agency, 216–19
Ebeling & Associates, 226–27
Entrepreneur Press, 143
Finch, Diana, 216–19
FinePrint Literary Management, 229–33
Gomez, Leticia, 373–78
Grand Central, 80–81
Green, Carol, 387–88
Hachette Books (imprint), 81
Harper Business, 88
HarperCollins Leadership, 89
HarperOne, 89
Harris, Steven, 209–10
Hill, Julie, 293–94
Houghton Mifflin Harcourt, 147–48
Julie A. Hill and Associates, LLC, 293–94
Literary Services, Inc., 309–11

Lowenstein Associates, 313–15
Marsal Lyon Literary Agency, LLC, 319–21
Max Gartenberg Literary Agency, 333–34
McGraw-Hill Professional, 151
Newman, Dana, 210–13
Portfolio, 114
Praeger, 134
P.S. Literary Agency, 349–50
Public Affairs, 85–86
Random House (imprint), 107–8
Red Wheel, 158
Riverhead Books, 115
The Rohm Literary Agency, 368–69
Rowman & Littlefield, 159–60
Rubie, Peter, 230–33
Russell, Curtis, 349–50
Savvy Literary Services, 373–78
Scribner, 123–24
Second City Publishing Services, LLC, 380–82
Shannon, Denise, 215–16
Sheree Bykofsky Associates, Inc., 383–85
Simenauer & Green Literary Agency, LLC, 387–88
Simon & Schuster (imprint), 124–25
Sourcebooks, 163–64
St. Martin's Press, 97–98
Stonesong, 392–95
Tarcher Perigee, 115–16
Ten Speed Press, 104–5
Tessler Literary Agency, 399–400
Tran, Jennifer Chen, 191–94
Twelve, 82
Viking Books, 116–17
Wheeler, Paige, 207–9
Wiley, 166

Williamson Literary, 423–26
Willig, John, 309–11
Wood, Laura, 229
W. W. Norton & Company, Inc., 154
The Zack Company, Inc., 429–32
Zigmund, Cynthia, 380–82

celebrities
Atria Publishing Group, 120–21
Crown Archetype, 103
De Chiara, Jennifer, 275
Devlin, Anne G., 333–34
Gallery Books, 122–23
Gottlieb, Mark, 410–13
Howard Books, 122
The Jennifer De Chiara Literary Agency, 275–86
Laurell, David, 279–81
Martin Literary & Media Management, 321–31
Max Gartenberg Literary Agency, 333–34
Simon & Schuster (imprint), 124–25
Spiegel & Grau, 109
Three Rivers Press, 105
Trident Media Group, LLC, 410–13
William Morrow, 90
chemistry. *See* science/natural history
childbirth. *See* parenting
children through young adult. *See also* picture books
Abrams, 135
Abrams Books for Young Readers, 135
Aladdin, 126
Alfred A. Knopf Books for Young Readers, 110
Algonquin Books, 167–68
Altshuler, Miriam, 213–15
Anderson-Wheeler, Claire, 360–61

children through young adult (*continued*)
Andrea Brown Literary Agency, Inc., 173–75
Arthur A. Levine Books, 161
Atheneum Books for Young Readers, 126
Balzer + Bray, 94
Barbara, Stephen, 260–61
Barr, Stephen, 427–29
Beach Lane Books, 126
Beren, Peter, 346–49
Betsy Amster Literary Enterprises, 184–87
Bieker, Lauren, 229–30
Bloomsbury Publishing, 139–40
Bradford Literary Agency, 189–94
Brady, Mackenzie, 345–46
Brewer, Amy, 339–40
Brown, Andrea, 173–75
Chicago Review Press, 141
Chilton, Jamie Weiss, 173–75
Chronicle Books, 141
Clarion, 148
Corvisiero Literary Agency, 196–207
Crockett, Laura, 407–10
Crown Children's, 110
CSG Literary Partners/MDM Management, 209–10
Cummings, Mary, 184–87
Cusick, John, 233–35
De Chiara, Jennifer, 275
DeFiore and Company Literary Management, Inc., 213–15
Delacorte, 110
Dial Books for Young Readers, 117
Dunham Literary, Inc., 222–26
Dunton, David, 255–57
Dutton Children's Books, 117
Edwards, Melissa, 394

Eerdmans Publishing Co., 143
The Evan Marshall Agency, 228
Fargis, Alison, 394–95
Farrar, Straus and Giroux Books for Young Readers, 100
Feiwel and Friends, 101
FinePrint Literary Management, 229–33
First Second Books, 101
Folio Literary Management/Folio Jr., 233–41
Fraser-Bub Literary, LLC, 241–42
Full Circle Literary, 242–43
Fuse Literary, 243–51
Goetz, Adria, 324–26
Gomez, Leticia, 373–78
Gore, Clelia, 328–31
G. P. Putnam's Sons Books for Young Readers, 118
Graham, Stacey, 356–57
Greenwillow Books, 94
Grosset & Dunlap, 117
Hansen, Stephanie, 337–38
HarperCollins Children's Books (imprint), 94
HarperTeen, 94
Harris, Erin, 235–38
Harris, Steven, 209–10
Hart, Cate, 202–4
Hart, Jim, 253–55
Hartline Literary Agency, 253–55
Harvest House, 146
Harvey Klinger, Inc., 255–58
Haskin, Jennifer, 197–200
Henry Holt Books for Young Readers, 101
Houghton Mifflin Harcourt, 147–48
Houghton Mifflin Harcourt Children's, 148
Inkwell Management,

260–61
The Jennifer De Chiara Literary Agency, 275–86
Jennifer Lyons Literary Agency, 286–87
Jimmy Patterson, 84
John Hawkins & Associates, Inc., 288–92
Katherine Tegen Books, 94
Kean, Taylor Martindale, 243
Kilkelly, Lori, 367–68
Knapp, Peter, 346
Kronenberg, Annie, 290–92
Lamba, Cari, 278–79
Laughran, Jennifer, 173–75
Little, Brown Children's, 84
Little Simon, 127
Lowenstein Associates, 313–15
Lynn Seligman, Literary Agent, 315–17
Margaret K. McElderry Books, 127
Marshall, Evan, 228
Martin Literary & Media Management, 321–31
Mattson, Jennifer, 173–75
McLean, Laurie, 243–45
Metamorphosis Literary Agency, 337–42
Milkweed Editions, 151
Myers Literary Management, 342–44
New Leaf Literary & Media, Inc., 344–46
Ortiz, Kathleen, 345
Ourvan, Jeff, 286–87
Paula Wiseman Books, 127
Peachtree Publishers, 155
Pelican Publishing Company, 156
Perkins, Laura, 173–75
The Peter Beren Agency, 346–49
Philomel Books, 118
Posner, Marcy, 240–41
Price, Kortney, 204–7

P.S. Literary Agency, 349–50
The Purcell Agency, LLC, 350–52
Quirk Books, 158
Random House Books for Young Readers, 111
Razorbill, 118
Red Sofa Literary, 352–59
Regal Hoffmann & Associates, LLC, 360–63
Rennert, Laura, 173–75
Revell, 138
Richter, Michelle, 245–47
Roaring Brook Press, 101
Rodale Books, 105
Rodeen Literary Management, 367–68
Rofé, Jennifer, 173–75
The Rohm Literary Agency, 368–69
Rowman & Littlefield, 159–60
Rubie, Peter, 230–33
Rushall, Kathleen, 173–75
Russell, Curtis, 349–50
Rutter, Amanda, 355–56
Saga Press, 127
Salaam Reads, 126
Savvy Literary Services, 373–78
Schmalz, Wendy, 422–23
Scholastic Inc., 160–61
Schwartz, Tina P., 350–52
Schwartz and Wade, 111
Seligman, Lynn, 315–17
Selvaggio, Victoria, 282–84
Simon Pulse, 128
Simon & Schuster Books for Young Readers, 128
Skinner, Tricia, 247–48
Skyhorse Publishing, 162
Smith, Bridget, 224–26
Soho Press, 162
Soloway, Jennifer March, 173–75
Somberg, Andrea, 257–58
Sonnack, Kelly, 173–75

Sourcebooks, 163–64
St. Martin's Press, 97–98
Stonesong, 392–95
Temperly, Jaida, 346
Tor/Forge, 100
Townsend, Suzie, 345
Tran, Jennifer Chen, 191–94
TriadaUS Literary Agency, 407–10
Tyndale House Publishers, Inc., 165
Viking Children's Books, 119
Volpe, Joanna, 345
Von Borstel, Stefanie Sanchez, 242
Warnock, Gordon, 248–50
Webber, Carlisle K., 250–51
Weiss, Alexandra, 276–77
Wells, Roseanne, 284–86
Wendy Schmalz Agency, 422–23
Williamson Literary, 423–26
Wiseman, Caryn, 173–75
Workman Publishing Company, 167–68
Writers House, LLC, 427–29
Zats, Laura, 354–55
Zondervan Children's, 93
Christian/faith. *See also* inspiration
 Abingdon Press, 134
 Baker Books (imprint), 137
 Eerdmans Publishing Co., 143
 Goetz, Adria, 324–26
 Hachette Nashville, 82–83
 HarperCollins Christian Publishing, 93
 Hart, Jim, 253–55
 Hartline Literary Agency, 253–55
 Harvest House, 146
 Howard Books, 122
 The Jennifer De Chiara Literary Agency, 275–86
 Laurell, David, 279–81
 Martin Literary & Media Management, 321–31
 Paulist Press, 155
 Revell, 138
 Thomas Nelson, 93
 Tyndale House Publishers, Inc., 165
 Waterbrook Multnomah Publishing Group, 106
 Zondervan, 93
 Zondervan Children's, 93
classics
 Penguin Books (imprint), 116
comic books / graphic novels
 Abrams, 135
 Abrams Books for Young Readers, 135
 Bradford Literary Agency, 189–94
 Fantagraphics Books, 144
 First Second Books, 101
 Fuse Literary, 243–51
 Henry Holt and Company, 96–97
 Levine | Greenberg | Rostan Literary Agency, 300–303
 Little, Brown and Company, 83
 Metropolitan Books, 97
 Svetcov, Danielle, 300–302
 Tran, Jennifer Chen, 191–94
 Warnock, Gordon, 248–50
communications
 Rowman & Littlefield, 159–60
computers/technology
 Basic Books, 84–85
 Dana Newman Literary, LLC, 210–13
 FinePrint Literary Management, 229–33
 McGraw-Hill Professional, 151
 Newman, Dana, 210–13
 No Starch Press, 154
 Portfolio, 114
 Riverhead Books, 115

computers/technology (*continued*)
- Rowman & Littlefield, 159–60
- Rubie, Peter, 230–33
- Simon & Schuster (imprint), 124–25
- Smithsonian Books, 162
- Wiley, 166
- The Zack Company, Inc., 429–32

cooking/food/wine
- Abrams, 135
- Andrews McMeel Publishing, 136
- Artisan, 167
- Atria Publishing Group, 120–21
- Ballantine Books, 108
- Basic Books, 84–85
- Bloomsbury Publishing, 139–40
- Bradford Literary Agency, 189–94
- Chelsea Green Publishing, 140
- Chicago Review Press, 141
- Clark, June, 230
- Clarkson Potter, 103
- CSG Literary Partners / MDM Management, 209–10
- Da Capo Press, 85
- Devlin, Anne G., 333–34
- Ecco Books, 88
- Ekus, Lisa, 305–6
- FinePrint Literary Management, 229–33
- Flatiron Books, 96
- Folio Literary Management / Folio Jr., 233–41
- Fraser-Bub Literary, LLC, 241–42
- Fredericks, Jeanne, 267–72
- Full Circle Literary, 242–43
- Ghahremani, Lilly, 243
- Gomez, Leticia, 373–78
- Grand Central, 80–81
- Grand Central Life & Style, 82
- Harper Design, 89
- Harris, Steven, 209–10
- Harvard Common Press, 157
- Houghton Mifflin Harcourt, 147–48
- Jeanne Fredericks Literary Agency, Inc., 267–72
- The Jennifer De Chiara Literary Agency, 275–86
- Kleinman, Jeff, 238–40
- Konner, Linda, 304–5
- Levine | Greenberg | Rostan Literary Agency, 300–303
- Linda Konner Literary Agency, 304–5
- The Lisa Ekus Group, 305–6
- Literary Services, Inc., 309–11
- Little, Brown and Company, 83
- Max Gartenberg Literary Agency, 333–34
- New Leaf Literary & Media, Inc., 344–46
- Pam Krauss Books, 112
- Pelican Publishing Company, 156
- Penguin Books (imprint), 116
- Quirk Books, 158
- Riverhead Books, 115
- Rodale Books, 105
- Rowman & Littlefield, 159–60
- Rubie, Peter, 230–33
- Running Press, 86
- Sasquatch Books, 160
- Savvy Literary Services, 373–78
- Scribner, 123–24
- Simon & Schuster (imprint), 124–25
- Skyhorse Publishing, 162
- Square One Publishers, Inc., 164
- St. Martin's Press, 97–98
- Svetcov, Danielle, 300–302
- Ten Speed Press, 104–5
- Tessler Literary Agency, 399–400
- Touchstone Books, 125
- Tran, Jennifer Chen, 191–94
- Volpe, Joanna, 345
- Wells, Roseanne, 284–86
- William Morrow, 90
- Willig, John, 309–11
- Workman Publishing Company, 167–68

crafts/hobbies
- Abrams, 135
- Chicago Review Press, 141
- Harper Design, 89
- Quirk Books, 158
- Running Press, 86
- Shambhala Publications, 161
- Skyhorse Publishing, 162
- Storey Publishing, 168
- Ten Speed Press, 104–5
- Workman Publishing Company, 167–68

crime fiction. *See* suspense/thriller/crime

criminology
- Rowman & Littlefield, 159–60

cultural history/studies
- Abrams, 135
- Beacon Press, 138
- Dutton, 113
- Ecco Books, 88
- Farrar, Straus and Giroux, 95
- Grove Atlantic, 145–46
- HarperOne, 89
- Henry Holt and Company, 96–97
- Little, Brown and Company, 83
- The Overlook Press, 155
- Pegasus Books, 155
- Penguin Books (imprint), 116

The Penguin Press
(imprint), 114
Riverhead Books, 115
Scribner, 123–24
Simon & Schuster (imprint), 124–25
Skyhorse Publishing, 162
Smithsonian Books, 162
Viking Books, 116–17
W. W. Norton & Company, Inc., 154
current events. *See* politics/public policy/current events

dance. *See* performing arts
decorating. *See* interior design
diet/nutrition. *See also* health/wellness/diet/fitness
Annie Bomke Literary Agency, 176–79
Atria Publishing Group, 120–21
Ballantine Books, 108
Bomke, Annie, 176–79
Ekus, Lisa, 305–6
Fair Winds Press, 157
Fraser-Bub Literary, LLC, 241–42
Gallery Books, 122–23
Gomez, Leticia, 373–78
Grand Central Life & Style, 82
Hachette Books (imprint), 81
Harmony Books, 104
HarperOne, 89
Konner, Linda, 304–5
Linda Konner Literary Agency, 304–5
The Lisa Ekus Group, 305–6
Rodale Books, 105
Savvy Literary Services, 373–78
Skyhorse Publishing, 162
Ten Speed Press, 104–5
Touchstone Books, 125
drama. *See* entertainment/theater

dystopian fiction
Bieker, Lauren, 229–30
Corvisiero Literary Agency, 196–207
FinePrint Literary Management, 229–33
Grazian, Natalie, 326–28
Harlequin TEEN, 92
Haskin, Jennifer, 197–200
Martin Literary & Media Management, 321–31

economics/finance
Ballantine Books, 108
Basic Books, 84–85
Beacon Press, 138
Dutton, 113
Full Circle Literary, 242–43
Fuse Literary, 243–51
Ghahremani, Lilly, 243
Grand Central Life & Style, 82
Jennifer Lyons Literary Agency, 286–87
McGraw-Hill Professional, 151
Nation Books, 85
Ourvan, Jeff, 286–87
Portfolio, 114
Public Affairs, 85–86
Richter, Michelle, 245–47
Simon & Schuster (imprint), 124–25
Tarcher Perigee, 115–16
Viking Books, 116–17
Wiley, 166
The Zack Company, Inc., 429–32

education
Arthur A. Levine Books, 161
Beacon Press, 138
Chicago Review Press, 141
Devlin, Anne G., 333–34
Max Gartenberg Literary Agency, 333–34
Praeger, 134
Rowman & Littlefield, 159–60
Scholastic Inc., 160–61
Ten Speed Press, 104–5

entertainment/theater
Clark, June, 230
Da Capo Press, 85
FinePrint Literary Management, 229–33
Gallery Books, 122–23
Hart, Jim, 253–55
Hartline Literary Agency, 253–55
The Jennifer De Chiara Literary Agency, 275–86
Laurell, David, 279–81
Lynn Seligman, Literary Agent, 315–17
Random House (imprint), 107–8
Rowman & Littlefield, 159–60
Seligman, Lynn, 315–17
Simon & Schuster (imprint), 124–25

entomology. *See* science/natural history
environment/green living/ecology
Beacon Press, 138
Chelsea Green Publishing, 140
Devlin, Anne G., 333–34
Diana Finch Literary Agency, 216–19
Enliven Books, 121
Finch, Diana, 216–19
Folio Literary Management/Folio Jr., 233–41
Fredericks, Jeanne, 267–72
Green, Carol, 387–88
Jeanne Fredericks Literary Agency, Inc., 267–72
Kleinman, Jeff, 238–40
Max Gartenberg Literary Agency, 333–34
Riverhead Books, 115

509

environment / green living / ecology (*continued*)
    Rowman & Littlefield, 159–60
    Shambhala Publications, 161
    Simenauer & Green Literary Agency, LLC, 387–88
    Storey Publishing, 168
    Williamson Literary, 423–26

erotica. *See also* sexuality
    Avon, 87
    Gomez, Leticia, 373–78
    Kensington (imprint), 149–50
    Savvy Literary Services, 373–78
    Sourcebooks, 163–64

ethnology
    Rowman & Littlefield, 159–60

faith. *See* Christian/faith
family. *See* parenting
fantasy. *See* science fiction/fantasy; urban fantasy
fashion. *See* beauty/fashion
feminism. *See also* women's interest/studies
    Becker, Laney Katz, 331–32
    Chicago Review Press, 141
    Folio Literary Management / Folio Jr., 233–41
    HarperOne, 89
    Harris, Erin, 235–38
    Massie & McQuilkin Literary Agents, 331–32
    Red Sofa Literary, 352–59
    Zats, Laura, 354–55

fiction. *See* adult fiction; historical fiction; horror; magical realism; mystery; paranormal/supernatural; science fiction/fantasy; suspense/thriller/crime; urban fantasy/fiction; women's fiction

film/media
    Abrams, 135
    Basic Books, 84–85
    Beacon Press, 138
    Bloomsbury Publishing, 139–40
    Chicago Review Press, 141
    Da Capo Press, 85
    Del Rey, 108–9
    Dey Street Books, 91
    Globe Pequot, 160
    Hachette Books (imprint), 81
    Harper Design, 89
    Simon & Schuster (imprint), 124–25
    Skyhorse Publishing, 162

finance. *See* economics/finance
fine arts. *See* art/architecture; music
fitness. *See* health/wellness/diet/fitness
food. *See* cooking/food/wine

gardening/nature
    Abrams, 135
    Chelsea Green Publishing, 140
    Chicago Review Press, 141
    Folio Literary Management / Folio Jr., 233–41
    Fredericks, Jeanne, 267–72
    Hawkins, Anne, 288–90
    Jeanne Fredericks Literary Agency, Inc., 267–72
    John Hawkins & Associates, Inc., 288–92
    Kleinman, Jeff, 238–40
    Rodale Books, 105
    Simon & Schuster (imprint), 124–25
    Skyhorse Publishing, 162
    St. Martin's Press, 97–98
    Storey Publishing, 168

gender studies/issues. *See also* men's interest/fiction; women's interest/studies
    Little, Brown and Company, 83
    Scribner, 123–24
    Seal Press, 86
    Simon & Schuster (imprint), 124–25
    Viking Books, 116–17
    W. W. Norton & Company, Inc., 154

geography
    National Geographic Books, 151
    Rowman & Littlefield, 159–60

gift books
    Abrams, 135
    Andrews McMeel Publishing, 136
    Brady, Mackenzie, 345–46
    The Jennifer De Chiara Literary Agency, 275–86
    New Leaf Literary & Media, Inc., 344–46
    Sourcebooks, 163–64
    Wells, Roseanne, 284–86
    Workman Publishing Company, 167–68

government. *See* politics / public policy / current events
graphic novels. *See* comic books / graphic novels

health care / medicine. *See also* lifestyle
    Beacon Press, 138
    Bradford Literary Agency, 189–94
    Central Recovery Press, 140
    Chelsea Green Publishing, 140
    Doubleday, 106–7
    Fuse Literary, 243–51
    Hazelden Publishing, 146–47
    Lynn Seligman, Literary Agent, 315–17
    New Harbinger

Publications, 152
Richter, Michelle, 245–47
Seligman, Lynn, 315–17
St. Martin's Press, 97–98
Tran, Jennifer Chen, 191–94
The Zack Company, Inc., 429–32
health/wellness/diet/fitness. *See also* lifestyle
   Amacom Books, 136
   Andrews McMeel Publishing, 136
   Annie Bomke Literary Agency, 176–79
   Atria Publishing Group, 120–21
   Avery, 111–12
   Ballantine Books, 108
   Bomke, Annie, 176–79
   Bykofsky, Sheree, 383–85
   Carnicelli Literary Management, 194–96
   Central Recovery Press, 140
   CSG Literary Partners / MDM Management, 209–10
   Da Capo Press, 85
   Dana Newman Literary, LLC, 210–13
   De Chiara, Jennifer, 275
   Denise Shannon Literary Agency, Inc., 215–16
   Devlin, Anne G., 333–34
   Diana Finch Literary Agency, 216–19
   Ekus, Lisa, 305–6
   Enliven Books, 121
   The Experiment Publishing Company, 144
   Fair Winds Press, 157
   Fargis, Alison, 394–95
   Finch, Diana, 216–19
   FinePrint Literary Management, 229–33
   Flatiron Books, 96
   Folio Literary Management / Folio Jr., 233–41
   Fraser-Bub Literary, LLC, 241–42
   Fredericks, Jeanne, 267–72
   Gallery Books, 122–23
   Gomez, Leticia, 373–78
   Grand Central Life & Style, 82
   Hachette Books (imprint), 81
   Harmony Books, 104
   HarperOne, 89
   Harper Wave, 90
   Harris, Steven, 209–10
   Health Communications, Inc., 147
   Houghton Mifflin Harcourt, 147–48
   Human Kinetics Publishers, Inc., 148
   Jeanne Fredericks Literary Agency, Inc., 267–72
   The Jennifer De Chiara Literary Agency, 275–86
   Kensington (imprint), 149–50
   Kleinman, Jeff, 238–40
   Konner, Linda, 304–5
   Linda Konner Literary Agency, 304–5
   The Lisa Ekus Group, 305–6
   Literary Services, Inc., 309–11
   Little, Brown and Company, 83
   Llewellyn Worldwide, 150
   Lowenstein Associates, 313–15
   Lynn Seligman, Literary Agent, 315–17
   Marsal Lyon Literary Agency, LLC, 319–21
   Max Gartenberg Literary Agency, 333–34
   Mendel Media Group, LLC, 334–37
   New Harbinger Publications, 152
   Newman, Dana, 210–13
   New World Library, 153
   Peachtree Publishers, 155
   Praeger, 134
   P. S. Literary Agency, 349–50
   Red Wheel, 158
   Rodale Books, 105
   Rowman & Littlefield, 159–60
   Rubie, Peter, 230–33
   Running Press, 86
   Russell, Curtis, 349–50
   Savvy Literary Services, 373–78
   Scribner, 123–24
   Seal Press, 86
   Seligman, Lynn, 315–17
   Shambhala Publications, 161
   Shannon, Denise, 215–16
   Sheree Bykofsky Associates, Inc., 383–85
   Skyhorse Publishing, 162
   Sounds True, Inc., 163
   Square One Publishers, Inc., 164
   Stonesong, 392–95
   Tarcher Perigee, 115–16
   Ten Speed Press, 104–5
   Touchstone Books, 125
   Viking Books, 116–17
   William Morrow, 90
   Willig, John, 309–11
   Workman Publishing Company, 167–68
   W. W. Norton & Company, Inc., 154
   Zimmermann Literary, 432–33
historical fiction
   Altshuler, Miriam, 213–15
   Annie Bomke Literary Agency, 176–79
   Atria Publishing Group, 120–21
   The August Agency LLC, 179–84

historical fiction (*continued*)
Becker, Laney Katz, 331–32
Betsy Amster Literary Enterprises, 184–87
Biderman, Marilyn, 405–6
Blue Ridge Literary Agency, LLC, 188–89
Bomke, Annie, 176–79
Carr, Michael, 415–16
Cloughley, Amy, 294–95
Corvisiero Literary Agency, 196–207
Crockett, Laura, 407–10
Cummings, Mary, 184–87
De Chiara, Jennifer, 275
DeFiore and Company Literary Management, Inc., 213–15
Devlin, Anne G., 333–34
Dowdle, Dawn, 188–89
Dunham Literary, Inc., 222–26
Folio Literary Management / Folio Jr., 233–41
Fraser-Bub Literary, LLC, 241–42
Freeman, Cricket, 179–84
Full Circle Literary, 242–43
Gallery Books, 122–23
Gomez, Leticia, 373–78
G. P. Putnam's Sons, 114–15
Graydon House, 92
Grazian, Natalie, 326–28
Hart, Cate, 202–4
The Jennifer De Chiara Literary Agency, 275–86
Julia Lord Literary Management, 292–93
Kean, Taylor Martindale, 243
Kimberley Cameron & Associates, 294–95
Kleinman, Jeff, 238–40
The LA Literary Agency, 296–300
Lasher, Maureen, 296–300
Literary Services, Inc., 309–11

Liveright, 150
Lord, Julia, 292–93
Lynn Seligman, Literary Agent, 315–17
Marsal Lyon Literary Agency, LLC, 319–21
Martin Literary & Media Management, 321–31
Massie & McQuilkin Literary Agents, 331–32
Max Gartenberg Literary Agency, 333–34
Mendel Media Group, LLC, 334–37
Myers Literary Management, 342–44
Pegasus Books, 155
Posner, Marcy, 240–41
Richter, Michelle, 245–47
Savvy Literary Services, 373–78
Seligman, Lynn, 315–17
Skinner, Tricia, 247–48
Smith, Bridget, 224–26
Sourcebooks, 163–64
Speilburg Literary Agency, 388–90
St. Martin's Press, 97–98
Tor/Forge, 100
Transatlantic Literary Agency, 405–6
TriadaUS Literary Agency, 407–10
Veritas Literary Agency, 415–16
Willig, John, 309–11
The Zack Company, Inc., 429–32

history
Abrams, 135
Basic Books, 84–85
Beacon Press, 138
Bradford Literary Agency, 189–94
Brady, Mackenzie, 345–46
Carnicelli Literary Management, 194–96

Carr, Michael, 415–16
Chicago Review Press, 141
CSG Literary Partners / MDM Management, 209–10
Da Capo Press, 85
Dana Newman Literary, LLC, 210–13
Devlin, Anne G., 333–34
Diana Finch Literary Agency, 216–19
Dutton, 113
Ecco Books, 88
Farrar, Straus and Giroux, 95
Finch, Diana, 216–19
FinePrint Literary Management, 229–33
Folio Literary Management / Folio Jr., 233–41
Globe Pequot, 160
G. P. Putnam's Sons, 114–15
Grove Atlantic, 145–46
Hachette Books (imprint), 81
Hane, Erik, 357–58
Hanover Square Press, 92–93
Harper Business, 88
Harris, Steven, 209–10
Hawkins, Anne, 288–90
Henry Holt and Company, 96–97
Houghton Mifflin Harcourt, 147–48
The Jennifer De Chiara Literary Agency, 275–86
Jennifer Lyons Literary Agency, 286–87
John Hawkins & Associates, Inc., 288–92
Julia Lord Literary Management, 292–93
Kensington (imprint), 149–50
Kirkpatrick, Rob, 398–99
Levine | Greenberg | Rostan Literary Agency, 300–303

Literary Services, Inc., 309–11
Little, Brown and Company, 83
Liveright, 150
Lord, Julia, 292–93
Lynn Seligman, Literary Agent, 315–17
Marsal Lyon Literary Agency, LLC, 319–21
Max Gartenberg Literary Agency, 333–34
Mendel Media Group, LLC, 334–37
New Leaf Literary & Media, Inc., 344–46
Newman, Dana, 210–13
Ourvan, Jeff, 286–87
The Overlook Press, 155
Pegasus Books, 155
Portfolio, 114
Posner, Marcy, 240–41
Praeger, 134
P. S. Literary Agency, 349–50
Random House (imprint), 107–8
Red Sofa Literary, 352–59
Rowman & Littlefield, 159–60
Rubie, Peter, 230–33
Russell, Curtis, 349–50
Scribner, 123–24
Seligman, Lynn, 315–17
Simon & Schuster (imprint), 124–25
Skurnick, Victoria, 302–3
Skyhorse Publishing, 162
Smithsonian Books, 162
Sourcebooks, 163–64
St. Martin's Press, 97–98
The Stuart Agency, 398–99
Tessler Literary Agency, 399–400
Thomas Dunne Books, 98
Tran, Jennifer Chen, 191–94
The Unter Agency, 413–14
Veritas Literary Agency, 415–16

Viking Books, 116–17
Wells, Roseanne, 284–86
William Morrow, 90
Willig, John, 309–11
Wood, Laura, 229
The Zack Company, Inc., 429–32
hobbies. *See* crafts/hobbies
horror. *See also* suspense/thriller/crime
   Annie Bomke Literary Agency, 176–79
   Bomke, Annie, 176–79
   De Chiara, Jennifer, 275
   Doubleday, 106–7
   Fuse Literary, 243–51
   Gallery Books, 122–23
   Harlequin TEEN, 92
   Harper Voyager, 90
   The Jennifer De Chiara Literary Agency, 275–86
   John Hawkins & Associates, Inc., 288–92
   Knapp, Peter, 346
   Kronenberg, Annie, 290–92
   McLean, Laurie, 243–45
   New Leaf Literary & Media, Inc., 344–46
   Webber, Carlisle K., 250–51
   The Zack Company, Inc., 429–32
horticulture. *See* gardening/nature
how-to
   Abrams, 135
   Bradford Literary Agency, 189–94
   Clark, June, 230
   Devlin, Anne G., 333–34
   Entrepreneur Press, 143
   Fair Winds Press, 157
   FinePrint Literary Management, 229–33
   Folio Literary Management / Folio Jr., 233–41
   Gomez, Leticia, 373–78

Hachette Nashville, 82–83
Kleinman, Jeff, 238–40
Max Gartenberg Literary Agency, 333–34
North Star Way, 123
Running Press, 86
Savvy Literary Services, 373–78
Skyhorse Publishing, 162
Square One Publishers, Inc., 164
Ten Speed Press, 104–5
Touchstone Books, 125
Tran, Jennifer Chen, 191–94
Workman Publishing Company, 167–68
humor/satire
   Aladdin, 126
   Andrews McMeel Publishing, 136
   Atheneum Books for Young Readers, 126
   Atria Publishing Group, 120–21
   Corvisiero Literary Agency, 196–207
   Crockett, Laura, 407–10
   CSG Literary Partners / MDM Management, 209–10
   Flatiron Books, 96
   Gomez, Leticia, 373–78
   G. P. Putnam's Sons, 114–15
   Grand Central, 80–81
   Grazian, Natalie, 326–28
   Hachette Books (imprint), 81
   HarperOne, 89
   Harper Perennial, 89
   Harris, Steven, 209–10
   The Jennifer De Chiara Literary Agency, 275–86
   Julia Lord Literary Management, 292–93
   Levine | Greenberg | Rostan Literary Agency, 300–303
   Little, Brown and Company, 83

humor/satire (*continued*)
    Lord, Julia, 292–93
    Martin Literary & Media Management, 321–31
    The Penguin Press (imprint), 114
    Price, Kortney, 204–7
    P. S. Literary Agency, 349–50
    Running Press, 86
    Russell, Curtis, 349–50
    Savvy Literary Services, 373–78
    Simon & Schuster (imprint), 124–25
    Skyhorse Publishing, 162
    Sourcebooks, 163–64
    Svetcov, Danielle, 300–302
    Tarcher Perigee, 115–16
    Ten Speed Press, 104–5
    Three Rivers Press, 105
    Touchstone Books, 125
    TriadaUS Literary Agency, 407–10
    Wells, Roseanne, 284–86
    William Morrow, 90
    Workman Publishing Company, 167–68

industrial and labor relations. *See* business/management
inspiration. *See also* Christian/faith
    Atria Publishing Group, 120–21
    Bethany House, 137
    Convergent Books, 103
    CSG Literary Partners / MDM Management, 209–10
    Enliven Books, 121
    Gallery Books, 122–23
    Hachette Nashville, 82–83
    Harris, Steven, 209–10
    Hart, Jim, 253–55
    Hartline Literary Agency, 253–55
    Harvest House, 146

    Howard Books, 122
    The Jennifer De Chiara Literary Agency, 275–86
    Laurell, David, 279–81
    Paulist Press, 155
    Revell, 138
    Rodale Books, 105
    Sounds True, Inc., 163
    Sourcebooks, 163–64
    Tarcher Perigee, 115–16
    Thomas Nelson, 93
interior design
    Abrams, 135
    Cohen, Jill, 287–88
    Harper Design, 89
    Jill Cohen Associates, LLC, 287–88
international relations. *See* politics / public policy / current events

journalism
    Bradford Literary Agency, 189–94
    Brady, Mackenzie, 345–46
    Denise Shannon Literary Agency, Inc., 215–16
    Diana Finch Literary Agency, 216–19
    Dutton, 113
    Finch, Diana, 216–19
    G. P. Putnam's Sons, 114–15
    Levine | Greenberg | Rostan Literary Agency, 300–303
    New Leaf Literary & Media, Inc., 344–46
    Public Affairs, 85–86
    The Rohm Literary Agency, 368–69
    Shannon, Denise, 215–16
    Simon & Schuster (imprint), 124–25
    Speilburg Literary Agency, 388–90
    St. Martin's Press, 97–98
    Svetcov, Danielle, 300–302
    Touchstone Books, 125
    Tran, Jennifer Chen, 191–94

landscaping. *See also* gardening/nature
    Chelsea Green Publishing, 140
    Chicago Review Press, 141
law
    Basic Books, 84–85
    Beacon Press, 138
leadership. *See* business/management
LGBTQ issues
    Atria Publishing Group, 120–21
    Beacon Press, 138
    Brewer, Amy, 339–40
    Cleis Press, 141–42
    Kensington (imprint), 149–50
    Metamorphosis Literary Agency, 337–42
lifestyle. *See also* health/wellness/diet/fitness
    Abrams, 135
    Andrews McMeel Publishing, 136
    Avery, 111–12
    Bradford Literary Agency, 189–94
    Brady, Mackenzie, 345–46
    Clarkson Potter, 103
    Cleis Press, 141–42
    The Countryman Press, 142
    CSG Literary Partners / MDM Management, 209–10
    Dey Street Books, 91
    Diana Finch Literary Agency, 216–19
    The Experiment Publishing Company, 144
    Fargis, Alison, 394–95
    Finch, Diana, 216–19
    Fredericks, Jeanne, 267–72
    Full Circle Literary, 242–43
    Gallery Books, 122–23
    Ghahremani, Lilly, 243
    Globe Pequot, 160

Gomez, Leticia, 373–78
Grand Central, 80–81
Hachette Books (imprint), 81
Hachette Nashville, 82–83
Harper Design, 89
HarperOne, 89
Harper Wave, 90
Harris, Steven, 209–10
Houghton Mifflin Harcourt, 147–48
Jeanne Fredericks Literary Agency, Inc., 267–72
Kensington (imprint), 149–50
Little, Brown and Company, 83
New Leaf Literary & Media, Inc., 344–46
Quirk Books, 158
Rodale Books, 105
Running Press, 86
Sasquatch Books, 160
Savvy Literary Services, 373–78
Simon & Schuster (imprint), 124–25
Skyhorse Publishing, 162
Square One Publishers, Inc., 164
Stonesong, 392–95
Tarcher Perigee, 115–16
Ten Speed Press, 104–5
Touchstone Books, 125
Tran, Jennifer Chen, 191–94
William Morrow, 90
Zimmermann Literary, 432–33

magical realism
　Annie Bomke Literary Agency, 176–79
　Betsy Amster Literary Enterprises, 184–87
　Bomke, Annie, 176–79
　Corvisiero Literary Agency, 196–207
　Cummings, Mary, 184–87
　Full Circle Literary, 242–43
　G. P. Putnam's Sons, 114–15
　Kean, Taylor Martindale, 243
management. *See* business/management
marketing. *See* business/management
marriage/family. *See also* parenting
　Revell, 138
mathematics/statistics
　Diana Finch Literary Agency, 216–19
　Finch, Diana, 216–19
　No Starch Press, 154
media. *See* film/media
medicine. *See* health care/medicine
memoir. *See* biography/memoir
men's interest/fiction
　New Horizon Press, 153
　St. Martin's Press, 97–98
　Touchstone Books, 125
middle grade. *See* children through young adult
military
　Ballantine Books, 108
　Da Capo Press, 85
　Dutton, 113
　FinePrint Literary Management, 229–33
　Folio Literary Management/Folio Jr., 233–41
　Globe Pequot, 160
　Houghton Mifflin Harcourt, 147–48
　Julia Lord Literary Management, 292–93
　Kensington (imprint), 149–50
　Kleinman, Jeff, 238–40
　Lord, Julia, 292–93
　Naval Institute Press, 152
　Praeger, 134
　Rowman & Littlefield, 159–60
　Rubie, Peter, 230–33
　Simon & Schuster (imprint), 124–25
　St. Martin's Press, 97–98
　Tor/Forge, 100
　William Morrow, 90
　W. W. Norton & Company, Inc., 154
　The Zack Company, Inc., 429–32
mind-body-spirit
　Beyond Words Publishing, 139
　Bradford Literary Agency, 189–94
　CSG Literary Partners/MDM Management, 209–10
　DeVorss & Company, 142
　Harper Wave, 90
　Harris, Steven, 209–10
　Hay House, 146
　Inner Traditions/Bear & Company, 149
　Llewellyn Worldwide, 150
　Red Wheel, 158
　Rodale Books, 105
　St. Martin's Press, 97–98
　Tran, Jennifer Chen, 191–94
motivation
　Convergent Books, 103
　Enliven Books, 121
　Hachette Nashville, 82–83
　The Jennifer De Chiara Literary Agency, 275–86
　Laurell, David, 279–81
　North Star Way, 123
　Rodale Books, 105
　Sourcebooks, 163–64
　Williamson Literary, 423–26
music
　Bradford Literary Agency, 189–94
　Chicago Review Press, 141
　Da Capo Press, 85
　Devlin, Anne G., 333–34

INDEX

515

music (*continued*)
  Dutton, 113
  FinePrint Literary Management, 229–33
  Harper Design, 89
  Hart, Jim, 253–55
  Hartline Literary Agency, 253–55
  Kirkpatrick, Rob, 398–99
  Max Gartenberg Literary Agency, 333–34
  Rubie, Peter, 230–33
  Simon & Schuster (imprint), 124–25
  Sounds True, Inc., 163
  St. Martin's Press, 97–98
  The Stuart Agency, 398–99
  Tran, Jennifer Chen, 191–94
  Zimmermann Literary, 432–33
mystery. *See also* suspense/thriller/crime
  Abingdon Press, 134
  Annie Bomke Literary Agency, 176–79
  Atria Publishing Group, 120–21
  Berkley, 112
  Blue Ridge Literary Agency, LLC, 188–89
  Bomke, Annie, 176–79
  Cloughley, Amy, 294–95
  Corvisiero Literary Agency, 196–207
  Creative Media Agency, 207–9
  Curwen, Ginger, 292–93
  De Chiara, Jennifer, 275
  Doubleday, 106–7
  Dowdle, Dawn, 188–89
  Dutton, 113
  Ecco Books, 88
  Emily Bestler Books, 121
  FinePrint Literary Management, 229–33
  Fraser-Bub Literary, LLC, 241–42
  Fuse Literary, 243–51
  Gomez, Leticia, 373–78
  Gottlieb, Mark, 410–13
  G. P. Putnam's Sons, 114–15
  Grand Central, 80–81
  Harper, 88
  Harper Perennial, 89
  Henry Holt and Company, 96–97
  Houghton Mifflin Harcourt, 147–48
  The Jennifer De Chiara Literary Agency, 275–86
  Jennifer Lyons Literary Agency, 286–87
  Julia Lord Literary Management, 292–93
  Kensington (imprint), 149–50
  Kimberley Cameron & Associates, 294–95
  The LA Literary Agency, 296–300
  Lamba, Cari, 278–79
  Lasher, Maureen, 296–300
  Little, Brown and Company, 83
  Lord, Julia, 292–93
  Lowenstein Associates, 313–15
  Marsal Lyon Literary Agency, LLC, 319–21
  McLean, Laurie, 243–45
  Mulholland Books, 83
  New Leaf Literary & Media, Inc., 344–46
  Ourvan, Jeff, 286–87
  Pegasus Books, 155
  Picador, 99–100
  Price, Kortney, 204–7
  P. S. Literary Agency, 349–50
  Richter, Michelle, 245–47
  Russell, Curtis, 349–50
  Savvy Literary Services, 373–78
  The Schisgal Agency, LLC, 378–80
  Second City Publishing Services, LLC, 380–82
  Skyhorse Publishing, 162
  Sourcebooks, 163–64
  Speilburg Literary Agency, 388–90
  St. Martin's Press, 97–98
  Tor/Forge, 100
  Townsend, Suzie, 345
  Trident Media Group, LLC, 410–13
  Viking Books, 116–17
  Webber, Carlisle K., 250–51
  Wheeler, Paige, 207–9
  William Morrow, 90
  Wood, Laura, 229
  The Zack Company, Inc., 429–32
  Zigmund, Cynthia, 380–82

narrative
  Algonquin Books, 167–68
  Altshuler, Miriam, 213–15
  Annie Bomke Literary Agency, 176–79
  Atria Publishing Group, 120–21
  The August Agency LLC, 179–84
  Baldi, Malaga, 317–19
  Ballantine Books, 108
  Becker, Laney Katz, 331–32
  BenBella Books, 138
  Biderman, Marilyn, 405–6
  Bloomsbury Publishing, 139–40
  Bomke, Annie, 176–79
  Bradford Literary Agency, 189–94
  Campoli, Leila, 392–93
  Cloughley, Amy, 294–95
  Creative Media Agency, 207–9
  Dana Newman Literary, LLC, 210–13
  DeFiore and Company Literary Management, Inc., 213–15

Denise Shannon Literary Agency, Inc., 215–16
Devlin, Anne G., 333–34
Dey Street Books, 91
Diana Finch Literary Agency, 216–19
Doubleday, 106–7
Dunton, David, 255–57
Dutton, 113
Fargis, Alison, 394–95
Finch, Diana, 216–19
FinePrint Literary Management, 229–33
Folio Literary Management / Folio Jr., 233–41
Freeman, Cricket, 179–84
Gallery Books, 122–23
Global Lion Intellectual Property Management, Inc., 251–53
G. P. Putnam's Sons, 114–15
Grand Central, 80–81
Grazian, Natalie, 326–28
Hachette Books (imprint), 81
Hales, Katelyn, 365–67
Hanover Square Press, 92–93
Harper Business, 88
Harris, Erin, 235–38
Harvey Klinger, Inc., 255–58
Heather Jackson Literary Agency, 258–60
Henry Holt and Company, 96–97
Houghton Mifflin Harcourt, 147–48
Jackson, Heather, 258–60
The Jennifer De Chiara Literary Agency, 275–86
Jennifer Lyons Literary Agency, 286–87
Julia Lord Literary Management, 292–93
Kimberley Cameron & Associates, 294–95

Kirkpatrick, Rob, 398–99
Kleinman, Jeff, 238–40
Knopf Doubleday Publishing Group, 106–7
The LA Literary Agency, 296–300
Lasher, Maureen, 296–300
Little, Brown and Company, 83
Liveright, 150
Lopopolo, Toni, 403–4
Lord, Julia, 292–93
Lowenstein Associates, 313–15
Malaga Baldi Literary Agency, 317–19
Marsal Lyon Literary Agency, LLC, 319–21
Martin Literary & Media Management, 321–31
Massie & McQuilkin Literary Agents, 331–32
Max Gartenberg Literary Agency, 333–34
McNicholl, Damian, 281–82
Mendel Media Group, LLC, 334–37
Miller, Peter, 251–53
Nation Books, 85
Newman, Dana, 210–13
Ourvan, Jeff, 286–87
Portfolio, 114
Posner, Marcy, 240–41
Public Affairs, 85–86
Random House (imprint), 107–8
Red Sofa Literary, 352–59
Regnery Publishing, Inc., 159
Riverhead Books, 115
Robin Straus Agency, Inc., 365–67
Rodale Books, 105
The Rohm Literary Agency, 368–69
Rubie, Peter, 230–33
Seal Press, 86
Shannon, Denise, 215–16

Simon & Schuster (imprint), 124–25
Soho Press, 162
Speilburg Literary Agency, 388–90
Spiegel & Grau, 109
St. Martin's Press, 97–98
Stonesong, 392–95
Strachan Literary Agency, 396–98
The Stuart Agency, 398–99
Tarcher Perigee, 115–16
Tessler Literary Agency, 399–400
Three Rivers Press, 105
Toni Lopopolo Literary Management, 403–4
Touchstone Books, 125
Tran, Jennifer Chen, 191–94
Transatlantic Literary Agency, 405–6
Twelve, 82
Viking Books, 116–17
Wales Literary Agency, 416–17
Wells, Roseanne, 284–86
Wheeler, Paige, 207–9
W. W. Norton & Company, Inc., 154
The Zack Company, Inc., 429–32
Zats, Laura, 354–55
nature. *See* environment / green living / ecology; gardening / nature; science / natural history
New Age. *See also* mind-body-spirit
    Inner Traditions / Bear & Company, 149
    Llewellyn Worldwide, 150
    Red Wheel, 158
nonfiction, adult. *See* adult nonfiction; *specific subject areas*
nutrition. *See* diet / nutrition; health / wellness / diet / fitness

paranormal/supernatural
- Ace/Roc Books, 112
- Avon, 87
- Corvisiero Literary Agency, 196–207
- Gomez, Leticia, 373–78
- Harlequin TEEN, 92
- Harper Voyager, 90
- Kensington (imprint), 149–50
- Price, Kortney, 204–7
- Saga Press, 127
- Savvy Literary Services, 373–78
- St. Martin's Press, 97–98

parenting
- Atria Publishing Group, 120–21
- Ballantine Books, 108
- Bradford Literary Agency, 189–94
- Chicago Review Press, 141
- Clark, June, 230
- Da Capo Press, 85
- Dana Newman Literary, LLC, 210–13
- Devlin, Anne G., 333–34
- Fair Winds Press, 157
- FinePrint Literary Management, 229–33
- Folio Literary Management/Folio Jr., 233–41
- Fredericks, Jeanne, 267–72
- Full Circle Literary, 242–43
- Ghahremani, Lilly, 243
- Globe Pequot, 160
- Gomez, Leticia, 373–78
- Grand Central Life & Style, 82
- Hachette Books (imprint), 81
- Harper, 88
- Hart, Jim, 253–55
- Hartline Literary Agency, 253–55
- Harvard Common Press, 157
- Jeanne Fredericks Literary Agency, Inc., 267–72
- Kensington (imprint), 149–50
- Kleinman, Jeff, 238–40
- Little, Brown and Company, 83
- Marsal Lyon Literary Agency, LLC, 319–21
- Max Gartenberg Literary Agency, 333–34
- New Harbinger Publications, 152
- New Horizon Press, 153
- Newman, Dana, 210–13
- Peachtree Publishers, 155
- Rodale Books, 105
- Rubie, Peter, 230–33
- Running Press, 86
- Savvy Literary Services, 373–78
- Seal Press, 86
- Skyhorse Publishing, 162
- Sourcebooks, 163–64
- Tarcher Perigee, 115–16
- Touchstone Books, 125
- Tran, Jennifer Chen, 191–94
- Viking Books, 116–17
- Workman Publishing Company, 167–68
- The Zack Company, Inc., 429–32

performing arts. *See also* entertainment/theater; music
- Human Kinetics Publishers, Inc., 148
- St. Martin's Press, 97–98

pets. *See* animals

philosophy
- DeVorss & Company, 142
- HarperOne, 89
- Hawkins, Anne, 288–90
- John Hawkins & Associates, Inc., 288–92
- Julia Lord Literary Management, 292–93
- Llewellyn Worldwide, 150
- Lord, Julia, 292–93
- New World Library, 153
- Pegasus Books, 155
- Penguin Books (imprint), 116
- Portfolio, 114
- Prometheus Books, 156–57
- Shambhala Publications, 161
- Simon & Schuster (imprint), 124–25
- W. W. Norton & Company, Inc., 154

photography
- Abrams, 135
- Beren, Peter, 346–49
- The Peter Beren Agency, 346–49
- Thames & Hudson, 164

picture books. *See also* children through young adult
- Aladdin, 126
- Atheneum Books for Young Readers, 126
- Beach Lane Books, 126
- Betsy Amster Literary Enterprises, 184–87
- Clarion, 148
- Crown Children's, 110
- Cummings, Mary, 184–87
- De Chiara, Jennifer, 275
- Dontzin, Ginger Harris, 311–13
- Fleissig, Liza, 311–13
- Goetz, Adria, 324–26
- Gore, Clelia, 328–31
- G. P. Putnam's Sons Books for Young Readers, 118
- Houghton Mifflin Harcourt Children's, 148
- Janklow & Nesbit Associates, 266–67
- The Jennifer De Chiara Literary Agency, 275–86
- Kilkelly, Lori, 367–68
- Lamba, Cari, 278–79
- Little, Brown Children's, 84
- Liza Royce Agency, LLC, 311–13

Martin Literary & Media Management, 321–31
New Leaf Literary & Media, Inc., 344–46
Parry, Emma, 266–67
Paula Wiseman Books, 127
Peachtree Publishers, 155
Philomel Books, 118
P. S. Literary Agency, 349–50
Rodeen Literary Management, 367–68
Russell, Curtis, 349–50
Selvaggio, Victoria, 282–84
Simon & Schuster Books for Young Readers, 128
Volpe, Joanna, 345
Weiss, Alexandra, 276–77
Wells, Roseanne, 284–86
plant sciences. *See* science/natural history
poetry
    Betsy Amster Literary Enterprises, 184–87
    Coffee House Press, 142
    Cummings, Mary, 184–87
    Milkweed Editions, 151
    New Directions, 152
    Tin House Books, 164–65
politics/public policy/current events
    Abrams, 135
    All Points Books, 98
    Atria Publishing Group, 120–21
    Ballantine Books, 108
    Basic Books, 84–85
    Bloomsbury Publishing, 139–40
    Bradford Literary Agency, 189–94
    Broadside Books, 88
    Campoli, Leila, 392–93
    Carnicelli Literary Management, 194–96
    Chicago Review Press, 141
    Crown Archetype, 103
    Crown Forum, 103
    Crown Publishing Group, 102–5
    CSG Literary Partners/MDM Management, 209–10
    Da Capo Press, 85
    Dana Newman Literary, LLC, 210–13
    De Chiara, Jennifer, 275
    Denise Shannon Literary Agency, Inc., 215–16
    Devlin, Anne G., 333–34
    Dey Street Books, 91
    Diana Finch Literary Agency, 216–19
    Doubleday, 106–7
    Dutton, 113
    Ecco Books, 88
    Farrar, Straus and Giroux, 95
    Finch, Diana, 216–19
    Flatiron Books, 96
    Folio Literary Management/Folio Jr., 233–41
    Gallery Books, 122–23
    Globe Pequot, 160
    Gomez, Leticia, 373–78
    G. P. Putnam's Sons, 114–15
    Grove Atlantic, 145–46
    Hachette Books (imprint), 81
    Hales, Katelyn, 365–67
    Hane, Erik, 357–58
    Harper, 88
    HarperOne, 89
    Harris, Steven, 209–10
    Henry Holt and Company, 96–97
    Houghton Mifflin Harcourt, 147–48
    The Jennifer De Chiara Literary Agency, 275–86
    Jennifer Lyons Literary Agency, 286–87
    Kirkpatrick, Rob, 398–99
    Kleinman, Jeff, 238–40
    Knopf Doubleday Publishing Group, 106–7
    Laurell, David, 279–81
    Levine | Greenberg | Rostan Literary Agency, 300–303
    Literary Services, Inc., 309–11
    Little, Brown and Company, 83
    Liveright, 150
    Marsal Lyon Literary Agency, LLC, 319–21
    Max Gartenberg Literary Agency, 333–34
    Metropolitan Books, 97
    Nation Books, 85
    Newman, Dana, 210–13
    The New Press, 153
    Ourvan, Jeff, 286–87
    Penguin Books (imprint), 116
    The Penguin Press (imprint), 114
    Picador, 99–100
    Praeger, 134
    P. S. Literary Agency, 349–50
    Public Affairs, 85–86
    Random House (imprint), 107–8
    Red Sofa Literary, 352–59
    Regnery Publishing, Inc., 159
    Riverhead Books, 115
    Robin Straus Agency, Inc., 365–67
    Rowman & Littlefield, 159–60
    Russell, Curtis, 349–50
    Savvy Literary Services, 373–78
    Scribner, 123–24
    Second City Publishing Services, LLC, 380–82
    Sentinel, 115
    Seven Stories Press, 161
    Shannon, Denise, 215–16
    Simon & Schuster (imprint), 124–25
    Skurnick, Victoria, 302–3

politics / public policy / current
events (*continued*)
   Skyhorse Publishing, 162
   St. Martin's Press, 97–98
   Stonesong, 392–95
   The Stuart Agency, 398–99
   Thomas Dunne Books, 98
   Threshold Editions, 123
   Tran, Jennifer Chen, 191–94
   Twelve, 82
   Viking Books, 116–17
   William Morrow, 90
   Willig, John, 309–11
   W. W. Norton & Company, Inc., 154
   The Zack Company, Inc., 429–32
   Zigmund, Cynthia, 380–82
pop culture
   Abrams, 135
   Andrews McMeel Publishing, 136
   Atria Publishing Group, 120–21
   Beren, Peter, 346–49
   Bradford Literary Agency, 189–94
   Bykofsky, Sheree, 383–85
   Carnicelli Literary Management, 194–96
   Chicago Review Press, 141
   Clarkson Potter, 103
   Creative Media Agency, 207–9
   CSG Literary Partners / MDM Management, 209–10
   Da Capo Press, 85
   Dana Newman Literary, LLC, 210–13
   De Chiara, Jennifer, 275
   Del Rey, 108–9
   Dey Street Books, 91
   Dunton, David, 255–57
   Dutton, 113
   Edwards, Melissa, 394
   Fargis, Alison, 394–95
   FinePrint Literary Management, 229–33
   Flatiron Books, 96
   Fuse Literary, 243–51
   Gallery Books, 122–23
   Globe Pequot, 160
   Gomez, Leticia, 373–78
   G. P. Putnam's Sons, 114–15
   Grand Central, 80–81
   Hachette Books (imprint), 81
   Hales, Katelyn, 365–67
   Harmony Books, 104
   Harper, 88
   Harper Design, 89
   Harris, Steven, 209–10
   Harvey Klinger, Inc., 255–58
   Howard Books, 122
   The Jennifer De Chiara Literary Agency, 275–86
   Kensington (imprint), 149–50
   Kirkpatrick, Rob, 398–99
   Laurell, David, 279–81
   Little, Brown and Company, 83
   Martin Literary & Media Management, 321–31
   New Leaf Literary & Media, Inc., 344–46
   Newman, Dana, 210–13
   The Peter Beren Agency, 346–49
   P. S. Literary Agency, 349–50
   Random House (imprint), 107–8
   Richter, Michelle, 245–47
   Robin Straus Agency, Inc., 365–67
   Rowman & Littlefield, 159–60
   Rubie, Peter, 230–33
   Running Press, 86
   Russell, Curtis, 349–50
   Savvy Literary Services, 373–78
   Sheree Bykofsky Associates, Inc., 383–85
   Simon & Schuster (imprint), 124–25
   Sourcebooks, 163–64
   St. Martin's Press, 97–98
   Stonesong, 392–95
   The Stuart Agency, 398–99
   Ten Speed Press, 104–5
   Thomas Dunne Books, 98
   Touchstone Books, 125
   Tran, Jennifer Chen, 191–94
   Viking Books, 116–17
   Volpe, Joanna, 345
   Warnock, Gordon, 248–50
   Wells, Roseanne, 284–86
   Wheeler, Paige, 207–9
   Zimmermann Literary, 432–33
popular science
   Abrams, 135
   Beren, Peter, 346–49
   Chicago Review Press, 141
   Curtis, Richard, 363–64
   Diana Finch Literary Agency, 216–19
   Doubleday, 106–7
   Dutton, 113
   Farrar, Straus and Giroux, 95
   Finch, Diana, 216–19
   FinePrint Literary Management, 229–33
   Hachette Books (imprint), 81
   Henry Holt and Company, 96–97
   Houghton Mifflin Harcourt, 147–48
   The Jennifer De Chiara Literary Agency, 275–86
   New Leaf Literary & Media, Inc., 344–46
   Pegasus Books, 155
   Penguin Books (imprint), 116
   The Penguin Press (imprint), 114
   The Peter Beren Agency, 346–49

Prometheus Books, 156–57
P. S. Literary Agency, 349–50
Richard Curtis Associates, Inc., 363–64
Riverhead Books, 115
Rubie, Peter, 230–33
Russell, Curtis, 349–50
Scribner, 123–24
Simon & Schuster (imprint), 124–25
Speilburg Literary Agency, 388–90
St. Martin's Press, 97–98
Tessler Literary Agency, 399–400
Volpe, Joanna, 345
Wells, Roseanne, 284–86
W. W. Norton & Company, Inc., 154

psychology/psychiatry
Algonquin Books, 167–68
Annie Bomke Literary Agency, 176–79
Atria Publishing Group, 120–21
Avery, 111–12
Basic Books, 84–85
Bomke, Annie, 176–79
Bradford Literary Agency, 189–94
Carnicelli Literary Management, 194–96
Dana Newman Literary, LLC, 210–13
Dutton, 113
Ebeling & Associates, 226–27
Folio Literary Management / Folio Jr., 233–41
Fraser-Bub Literary, LLC, 241–42
Harmony Books, 104
Houghton Mifflin Harcourt, 147–48
Kensington (imprint), 149–50
Literary Services, Inc., 309–11

Little, Brown and Company, 83
Lowenstein Associates, 313–15
Lynn Seligman, Literary Agent, 315–17
Marsal Lyon Literary Agency, LLC, 319–21
New Harbinger Publications, 152
Newman, Dana, 210–13
Penguin Books (imprint), 116
Posner, Marcy, 240–41
Praeger, 134
Prometheus Books, 156–57
P. S. Literary Agency, 349–50
Public Affairs, 85–86
Rowman & Littlefield, 159–60
Russell, Curtis, 349–50
Scribner, 123–24
Seal Press, 86
Seligman, Lynn, 315–17
Simon & Schuster (imprint), 124–25
Tarcher Perigee, 115–16
Tessler Literary Agency, 399–400
Touchstone Books, 125
Tran, Jennifer Chen, 191–94
Viking Books, 116–17
Willig, John, 309–11
public policy. *See* politics / public policy / current events

race issues
Hane, Erik, 357–58
Red Sofa Literary, 352–59
Scribner, 123–24
Simon & Schuster (imprint), 124–25
reference
ABC-CLIO, 134
Baker Books (imprint), 137
Clark, June, 230
CSG Literary Partners / MDM Management, 209–10

Entrepreneur Press, 143
FinePrint Literary Management, 229–33
Fredericks, Jeanne, 267–72
Globe Pequot, 160
Harris, Steven, 209–10
Jeanne Fredericks Literary Agency, Inc., 267–72
Julia Lord Literary Management, 292–93
Literary Services, Inc., 309–11
Lord, Julia, 292–93
Penguin Books (imprint), 116
Running Press, 86
Skyhorse Publishing, 162
Ten Speed Press, 104–5
William Morrow, 90
Willig, John, 309–11
relationships
Atria Publishing Group, 120–21
Bradford Literary Agency, 189–94
Cleis Press, 141–42
Fraser-Bub Literary, LLC, 241–42
Gomez, Leticia, 373–78
Graydon House, 92
Harmony Books, 104
Harper, 88
Kensington (imprint), 149–50
Marsal Lyon Literary Agency, LLC, 319–21
Mendel Media Group, LLC, 334–37
Penguin Books (imprint), 116
Red Wheel, 158
Running Press, 86
Savvy Literary Services, 373–78
Skyhorse Publishing, 162
Sourcebooks, 163–64
Thomas Nelson, 93

relationships (*continued*)
    Tran, Jennifer Chen, 191–94
    The Zack Company, Inc., 429–32
    Zimmermann Literary, 432–33
religion/theology. *See also* Christian/faith
    Beacon Press, 138
    Bethany House, 137
    Eerdmans Publishing Co., 143
    Gomez, Leticia, 373–78
    HarperOne, 89
    Howard Books, 122
    Inner Traditions / Bear & Company, 149
    The Jennifer De Chiara Literary Agency, 275–86
    Praeger, 134
    Red Wheel, 158
    Rowman & Littlefield, 159–60
    Savvy Literary Services, 373–78
    Simon & Schuster (imprint), 124–25
    Wells, Roseanne, 284–86
romance
    Abingdon Press, 134
    Atria Publishing Group, 120–21
    Berkley, 112
    Bethany House, 137
    Blue Ridge Literary Agency, LLC, 188–89
    Brewer, Amy, 339–40
    Corvisiero Literary Agency, 196–207
    Creative Media Agency, 207–9
    Curtis, Richard, 363–64
    Dafina, 149
    Dowdle, Dawn, 188–89
    Forever Yours, 82
    Fraser-Bub Literary, LLC, 241–42
    Fuse Literary, 243–51
    Gallery Books, 122–23
    Gomez, Leticia, 373–78
    Graham, Stacey, 356–57
    Grand Central, 80–81
    Graydon House, 92
    Hansen, Stephanie, 337–38
    Harlequin, 91–92
    Harlequin TEEN, 92
    Hart, Cate, 202–4
    Hart, Jim, 253–55
    Hartline Literary Agency, 253–55
    Jennifer Lyons Literary Agency, 286–87
    Kensington (imprint), 149–50
    Loveswept, 109
    Lynn Seligman, Literary Agent, 315–17
    Marsal Lyon Literary Agency, LLC, 319–21
    McLean, Laurie, 243–45
    Metamorphosis Literary Agency, 337–42
    New Leaf Literary & Media, Inc., 344–46
    Ourvan, Jeff, 286–87
    P.S. Literary Agency, 349–50
    Red Sofa Literary, 352–59
    Richard Curtis Associates, Inc., 363–64
    Richter, Michelle, 245–47
    Russell, Curtis, 349–50
    Savvy Literary Services, 373–78
    Seligman, Lynn, 315–17
    Skinner, Tricia, 247–48
    Skyhorse Publishing, 162
    Sourcebooks, 163–64
    Steele-Perkins Literary Agency, 390
    St. Martin's Press, 97–98
    Townsend, Suzie, 345
    Wheeler, Paige, 207–9
    Zats, Laura, 354–55
satire. *See* humor/satire
science fiction / fantasy. *See also* urban fantasy/fiction
    Ace/Roc Books, 112
    Aladdin, 126
    Baen Books, 137
    Bieker, Lauren, 229–30
    Brewer, Amy, 339–40
    Carr, Michael, 415–16
    Corvisiero Literary Agency, 196–207
    Crockett, Laura, 407–10
    Crown Publishing Group, 102–5
    Daw, 113
    Del Rey, 108–9
    Dunham Literary, Inc., 222–26
    FinePrint Literary Management, 229–33
    Folio Literary Management / Folio Jr., 233–41
    Full Circle Literary, 242–43
    Fuse Literary, 243–51
    Gallery Books, 122–23
    Gomez, Leticia, 373–78
    Gottlieb, Mark, 410–13
    Grazian, Natalie, 326–28
    Hales, Katelyn, 365–67
    Hansen, Stephanie, 337–38
    Harper, 88
    Harper Voyager, 90
    Harris, Erin, 235–38
    Hart, Cate, 202–4
    Hart, Jim, 253–55
    Hartline Literary Agency, 253–55
    Haskin, Jennifer, 197–200
    The Jennifer De Chiara Literary Agency, 275–86
    Jennifer Lyons Literary Agency, 286–87
    John Hawkins & Associates, Inc., 288–92
    Kean, Taylor Martindale, 243
    Kensington (imprint), 149–50

Kronenberg, Annie, 290–92
Little, Brown Children's, 84
Martin Literary & Media Management, 321–31
McLean, Laurie, 243–45
Metamorphosis Literary Agency, 337–42
New Leaf Literary & Media, Inc., 344–46
Orbit, 82
Ourvan, Jeff, 286–87
Price, Kortney, 204–7
Red Sofa Literary, 352–59
Robin Straus Agency, Inc., 365–67
Rubie, Peter, 230–33
Rutter, Amanda, 355–56
Saga Press, 127
Savvy Literary Services, 373–78
Skinner, Tricia, 247–48
Smith, Bridget, 224–26
Speilburg Literary Agency, 388–90
St. Martin's Press, 97–98
Tor/Forge, 100
Townsend, Suzie, 345
TriadaUS Literary Agency, 407–10
Trident Media Group, LLC, 410–13
Veritas Literary Agency, 415–16
Wells, Roseanne, 284–86
Wood, Laura, 229
The Zack Company, Inc., 429–32
Zats, Laura, 354–55
science/natural history. *See also* popular science
 Abrams, 135
 Avery, 111–12
 Basic Books, 84–85
 Beacon Press, 138
 Brady, Mackenzie, 345–46
 Campoli, Leila, 392–93
 Carnicelli Literary Management, 194–96
 Carr, Michael, 415–16
 Chelsea Green Publishing, 140
 The Countryman Press, 142
 Crown Publishing Group, 102–5
 CSG Literary Partners/MDM Management, 209–10
 Da Capo Press, 85
 Dana Newman Literary, LLC, 210–13
 Dutton, 113
 Ecco Books, 88
 FinePrint Literary Management, 229–33
 Fredericks, Jeanne, 267–72
 Fuse Literary, 243–51
 G. P. Putnam's Sons, 114–15
 Grove Atlantic, 145–46
 Hane, Erik, 357–58
 HarperOne, 89
 Harris, Steven, 209–10
 Hawkins, Anne, 288–90
 Jeanne Fredericks Literary Agency, Inc., 267–72
 The Jennifer De Chiara Literary Agency, 275–86
 Jennifer Lyons Literary Agency, 286–87
 John Hawkins & Associates, Inc., 288–92
 Julia Lord Literary Management, 292–93
 Levine | Greenberg | Rostan Literary Agency, 300–303
 Literary Services, Inc., 309–11
 Little, Brown and Company, 83
 Lord, Julia, 292–93
 Lowenstein Associates, 313–15
 Lynn Seligman, Literary Agent, 315–17
 Marsal Lyon Literary Agency, LLC, 319–21
 New Leaf Literary & Media, Inc., 344–46
 Newman, Dana, 210–13
 No Starch Press, 154
 Ourvan, Jeff, 286–87
 Public Affairs, 85–86
 Random House (imprint), 107–8
 Red Sofa Literary, 352–59
 Richter, Michelle, 245–47
 Rodale Books, 105
 Scribner, 123–24
 Second City Publishing Services, LLC, 380–82
 Seligman, Lynn, 315–17
 Simon & Schuster (imprint), 124–25
 Smithsonian Books, 162
 Stonesong, 392–95
 Svetcov, Danielle, 300–302
 Thomas Dunne Books, 98
 Touchstone Books, 125
 Veritas Literary Agency, 415–16
 Viking Books, 116–17
 Wales Literary Agency, 416–17
 Weiss, Alexandra, 276–77
 Williamson Literary, 423–26
 Willig, John, 309–11
 Wood, Laura, 229
 The Zack Company, Inc., 429–32
 Zigmund, Cynthia, 380–82
screenplays
 Barbara, Stephen, 260–61
 Inkwell Management, 260–61
self-help
 Annie Bomke Literary Agency, 176–79
 Atria Publishing Group, 120–21
 Avery, 111–12
 Baker Books (imprint), 137

self-help (continued)
   Ballantine Books, 108
   BenBella Books, 138
   Beren, Peter, 346–49
   Bomke, Annie, 176–79
   Carnicelli Literary Management, 194–96
   Clark, June, 230
   Creative Media Agency, 207–9
   CSG Literary Partners / MDM Management, 209–10
   Dana Newman Literary, LLC, 210–13
   DeFiore and Company Literary Management, Inc., 213–15
   Devlin, Anne G., 333–34
   Dutton, 113
   Ebeling & Associates, 226–27
   Entrepreneur Press, 143
   Fair Winds Press, 157
   FinePrint Literary Management, 229–33
   Fraser-Bub Literary, LLC, 241–42
   Gallery Books, 122–23
   Grand Central, 80–81
   Hachette Books (imprint), 81
   Hachette Nashville, 82–83
   Hagan, Lisa, 306–8
   Harmony Books, 104
   HarperOne, 89
   Harris, Steven, 209–10
   Hart, Jim, 253–55
   Hartline Literary Agency, 253–55
   Harvest House, 146
   Hay House, 146
   Health Communications, Inc., 147
   Henry Holt and Company, 96–97
   Kensington (imprint), 149–50
   Konner, Linda, 304–5
   Linda Konner Literary Agency, 304–5
   Lisa Hagan Literary, 306–8
   Little, Brown and Company, 83
   Marsal Lyon Literary Agency, LLC, 319–21
   Max Gartenberg Literary Agency, 333–34
   McGraw-Hill Professional, 151
   New Harbinger Publications, 152
   Newman, Dana, 210–13
   New World Library, 153
   North Star Way, 123
   The Peter Beren Agency, 346–49
   Revell, 138
   Rubie, Peter, 230–33
   Running Press, 86
   Seal Press, 86
   Skyhorse Publishing, 162
   Sourcebooks, 163–64
   Spiegel & Grau, 109
   Square One Publishers, Inc., 164
   Tarcher Perigee, 115–16
   Ten Speed Press, 104–5
   Thomas Nelson, 93
   Touchstone Books, 125
   Wheeler, Paige, 207–9
   Workman Publishing Company, 167–68
sexuality. *See also* erotica
   Cleis Press, 141–42
   Fair Winds Press, 157
   Rowman & Littlefield, 159–60
social justice / issues
   Algonquin Books, 167–68
   Beacon Press, 138
   Bloomsbury Publishing, 139–40
   Crown Publishing Group, 102–5
   De Chiara, Jennifer, 275
   Denise Shannon Literary Agency, Inc., 215–16
   Diana Finch Literary Agency, 216–19
   Dutton, 113
   Finch, Diana, 216–19
   Folio Literary Management / Folio Jr., 233–41
   Hane, Erik, 357–58
   Harper, 88
   Harris, Erin, 235–38
   Hart, Jim, 253–55
   Hartline Literary Agency, 253–55
   Henry Holt and Company, 96–97
   Houghton Mifflin Harcourt, 147–48
   The Jennifer De Chiara Literary Agency, 275–86
   Little, Brown and Company, 83
   Lowenstein Associates, 313–15
   Metropolitan Books, 97
   Nation Books, 85
   New Horizon Press, 153
   Penguin Books (imprint), 116
   Random House (imprint), 107–8
   Red Sofa Literary, 352–59
   Regal Hoffmann & Associates, LLC, 360–63
   Riverhead Books, 115
   Ross, Grace, 361–62
   Scribner, 123–24
   Shannon, Denise, 215–16
   Skyhorse Publishing, 162
   St. Martin's Press, 97–98
   Viking Books, 116–17
   Williamson Literary, 423–26
   W. W. Norton & Company, Inc., 154
sociology / social sciences
   Basic Books, 84–85

Fuse Literary, 243–51
Henry Holt and Company, 96–97
Public Affairs, 85–86
Richter, Michelle, 245–47
Rowman & Littlefield, 159–60
spirituality. *See also* mind-body-spirit
   Atria Publishing Group, 120–21
   DeVorss & Company, 142
   Ebeling & Associates, 226–27
   Enliven Books, 121
   FinePrint Literary Management, 229–33
   Global Lion Intellectual Property Management, Inc., 251–53
   Gomez, Leticia, 373–78
   Green, Carol, 387–88
   HarperOne, 89
   Miller, Peter, 251–53
   New Harbinger Publications, 152
   New World Library, 153
   Rubie, Peter, 230–33
   Savvy Literary Services, 373–78
   Simenauer & Green Literary Agency, LLC, 387–88
   Sounds True, Inc., 163
sports
   Algonquin Books, 167–68
   Ballantine Books, 108
   Brady, Mackenzie, 345–46
   Carnicelli Literary Management, 194–96
   Chicago Review Press, 141
   Crown Publishing Group, 102–5
   CSG Literary Partners / MDM Management, 209–10
   Da Capo Press, 85
   Dana Newman Literary, LLC, 210–13

Devlin, Anne G., 333–34
Dey Street Books, 91
Diana Finch Literary Agency, 216–19
Finch, Diana, 216–19
Fredericks, Jeanne, 267–72
Gomez, Leticia, 373–78
G. P. Putnam's Sons, 114–15
Hachette Books (imprint), 81
Hane, Erik, 357–58
Harris, Steven, 209–10
Henry Holt and Company, 96–97
Houghton Mifflin Harcourt, 147–48
Human Kinetics Publishers, Inc., 148
Jeanne Fredericks Literary Agency, Inc., 267–72
The Jennifer De Chiara Literary Agency, 275–86
Jennifer Lyons Literary Agency, 286–87
Kirkpatrick, Rob, 398–99
Laurell, David, 279–81
Little, Brown and Company, 83
Max Gartenberg Literary Agency, 333–34
New Leaf Literary & Media, Inc., 344–46
Newman, Dana, 210–13
Ourvan, Jeff, 286–87
The Penguin Press (imprint), 114
P.S. Literary Agency, 349–50
Random House (imprint), 107–8
Red Sofa Literary, 352–59
Rodale Books, 105
Rowman & Littlefield, 159–60
Russell, Curtis, 349–50
Savvy Literary Services, 373–78
Scribner, 123–24

Simon & Schuster (imprint), 124–25
Skyhorse Publishing, 162
St. Martin's Press, 97–98
The Stuart Agency, 398–99
Thomas Dunne Books, 98
William Morrow, 90
Williamson Literary, 423–26
Zimmermann Literary, 432–33
spy stories. *See* suspense/thriller/crime
statistics. *See* mathematics/statistics
supernatural. *See* paranormal/supernatural
suspense/thriller/crime. *See also* horror
   Abingdon Press, 134
   Andrea Hurst & Associates, LLC, 175–76
   Annie Bomke Literary Agency, 176–79
   Atria Publishing Group, 120–21
   The August Agency LLC, 179–84
   Becker, Laney Katz, 331–32
   BenBella Books, 138
   Berkley, 112
   Bethany House, 137
   Biderman, Marilyn, 405–6
   Bloomsbury Publishing, 139–40
   Blue Ridge Literary Agency, LLC, 188–89
   Bomke, Annie, 176–79
   Carnicelli Literary Management, 194–96
   Carr, Michael, 415–16
   Cloughley, Amy, 294–95
   Corvisiero Literary Agency, 196–207
   Creative Media Agency, 207–9
   Crown Publishing Group, 102–5

suspense/thriller/crime (*continued*)
- Curtis, Richard, 363–64
- Curwen, Ginger, 292–93
- De Chiara, Jennifer, 275
- Devlin, Anne G., 333–34
- Doubleday, 106–7
- Dowdle, Dawn, 188–89
- Dutton, 113
- Ecco Books, 88
- Edwards, Melissa, 394
- Emily Bestler Books, 121
- Europa Editions, 143
- FinePrint Literary Management, 229–33
- Folio Literary Management / Folio Jr., 233–41
- Fraser-Bub Literary, LLC, 241–42
- Freeman, Cricket, 179–84
- Fuse Literary, 243–51
- Gallery Books, 122–23
- Gomez, Leticia, 373–78
- Gottlieb, Mark, 410–13
- G. P. Putnam's Sons, 114–15
- Grand Central, 80–81
- Green, Carol, 387–88
- Hanover Square Press, 92–93
- Hansen, Stephanie, 337–38
- Harlequin, 91–92
- Harper, 88
- Harper Perennial, 89
- Hart, Jim, 253–55
- Hartline Literary Agency, 253–55
- Hawkins, Anne, 288–90
- Henry Holt and Company, 96–97
- Houghton Mifflin Harcourt, 147–48
- Hurst, Andrea, 175–76
- The Jennifer De Chiara Literary Agency, 275–86
- Jennifer Lyons Literary Agency, 286–87
- John Hawkins & Associates, Inc., 288–92
- Julia Lord Literary Management, 292–93
- Kensington (imprint), 149–50
- Kimberley Cameron & Associates, 294–95
- Kleinman, Jeff, 238–40
- Knapp, Peter, 346
- The LA Literary Agency, 296–300
- Lasher, Maureen, 296–300
- Levine | Greenberg | Rostan Literary Agency, 300–303
- Little, Brown and Company, 83
- Lord, Julia, 292–93
- Marsal Lyon Literary Agency, LLC, 319–21
- Martin Literary & Media Management, 321–31
- Massie & McQuilkin Literary Agents, 331–32
- Max Gartenberg Literary Agency, 333–34
- McLean, Laurie, 243–45
- Mendel Media Group, LLC, 334–37
- Metamorphosis Literary Agency, 337–42
- Minotaur, 98–99
- Mira Books, 92
- Mulholland Books, 83
- Myers Literary Management, 342–44
- The Mysterious Press, 146
- New Leaf Literary & Media, Inc., 344–46
- Ourvan, Jeff, 286–87
- Pegasus Books, 155
- Picador, 99–100
- Posner, Marcy, 240–41
- Price, Kortney, 204–7
- P.S. Literary Agency, 349–50
- Random House (imprint), 107–8
- Richard Curtis Associates, Inc., 363–64
- Richter, Michelle, 245–47
- Rowman & Littlefield, 159–60
- Rubie, Peter, 230–33
- Russell, Curtis, 349–50
- Savvy Literary Services, 373–78
- The Schisgal Agency, LLC, 378–80
- Scribner, 123–24
- Selvaggio, Victoria, 282–84
- Simenauer & Green Literary Agency, LLC, 387–88
- Simon & Schuster (imprint), 124–25
- Skurnick, Victoria, 302–3
- Skyhorse Publishing, 162
- Soho Press, 162
- Sourcebooks, 163–64
- St. Martin's Press, 97–98
- Stonesong, 392–95
- Tor/Forge, 100
- Touchstone Books, 125
- Townsend, Suzie, 345
- Transatlantic Literary Agency, 405–6
- Trident Media Group, LLC, 410–13
- Veritas Literary Agency, 415–16
- Webber, Carlisle K., 250–51
- Wheeler, Paige, 207–9
- William Morrow, 90
- The Zack Company, Inc., 429–32

technology. *See* computers/technology
theater. *See* entertainment/theater
theology. *See* Christian/faith; religion/theology
thriller. *See* suspense/thriller/crime
travel/recreation
- Abrams, 135
- Atria Publishing Group, 120–21

Bradford Literary Agency, 189–94
Chicago Review Press, 141
Cloughley, Amy, 294–95
The Countryman Press, 142
Globe Pequot, 160
G. P. Putnam's Sons, 114–15
Human Kinetics Publishers, Inc., 148
The Jennifer De Chiara Literary Agency, 275–86
Kimberley Cameron & Associates, 294–95
New Leaf Literary & Media, Inc., 344–46
No Starch Press, 154
Pelican Publishing Company, 156
Riverhead Books, 115
Sasquatch Books, 160
St. Martin's Press, 97–98
Tessler Literary Agency, 399–400
Thames & Hudson, 164
Tran, Jennifer Chen, 191–94
Volpe, Joanna, 345
Wells, Roseanne, 284–86
Williamson Literary, 423–26

urban fantasy/fiction
Akashic Books, 135
Avon, 87
Gallery Books, 122–23
New Leaf Literary & Media, Inc., 344–46
Saga Press, 127
Townsend, Suzie, 345

wellness. See health/wellness/diet/fitness

Westerns
Fuse Literary, 243–51
McLean, Laurie, 243–45
Tor/Forge, 100

wine. See cooking/food/wine

women's fiction
Andrea Hurst & Associates, LLC, 175–76
Annie Bomke Literary Agency, 176–79
Atria Publishing Group, 120–21
Avon, 87
Berkley, 112
Biderman, Marilyn, 405–6
Bieker, Lauren, 229–30
Bomke, Annie, 176–79
Bradford Literary Agency, 189–94
Cloughley, Amy, 294–95
Creative Media Agency, 207–9
Crockett, Laura, 407–10
Dana Newman Literary, LLC, 210–13
Edwards, Melissa, 394
Emily Bestler Books, 121
FinePrint Literary Management, 229–33
Folio Literary Management / Folio Jr., 233–41
Fraser-Bub Literary, LLC, 241–42
Fuse Literary, 243–51
Gallery Books, 122–23
Gomez, Leticia, 373–78
G. P. Putnam's Sons, 114–15
Grand Central, 80–81
Graydon House, 92
Hart, Jim, 253–55
Hartline Literary Agency, 253–55
Hurst, Andrea, 175–76
Kimberley Cameron & Associates, 294–95
Loveswept, 109
Lynn Seligman, Literary Agent, 315–17
Marsal Lyon Literary Agency, LLC, 319–21
McLean, Laurie, 243–45
Mendel Media Group, LLC, 334–37
Newman, Dana, 210–13
Posner, Marcy, 240–41
Richter, Michelle, 245–47
The Rohm Literary Agency, 368–69
Savvy Literary Services, 373–78
Seligman, Lynn, 315–17
Sourcebooks, 163–64
Steele-Perkins Literary Agency, 390
St. Martin's Press, 97–98
Stonesong, 392–95
Tessler Literary Agency, 399–400
Tor/Forge, 100
Touchstone Books, 125
Tran, Jennifer Chen, 191–94
Transatlantic Literary Agency, 405–6
TriadaUS Literary Agency, 407–10
Warnock, Gordon, 248–50
Webber, Carlisle K., 250–51
Wheeler, Paige, 207–9
William Morrow, 90

women's interest/studies
Beacon Press, 138
Chicago Review Press, 141
Creative Media Agency, 207–9
Dana Newman Literary, LLC, 210–13
Devlin, Anne G., 333–34
Fredericks, Jeanne, 267–72
HarperOne, 89
Houghton Mifflin Harcourt, 147–48
Jeanne Fredericks Literary Agency, Inc., 267–72
Kensington (imprint), 149–50
Little, Brown and Company, 83
Lowenstein Associates, 313–15
Max Gartenberg Literary Agency, 333–34

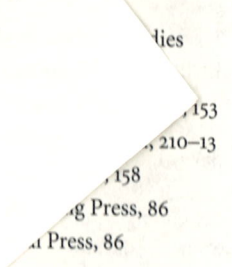

Skyhorse Publishing, 162
Sourcebooks, 163–64
St. Martin's Press, 97–98
Thomas Nelson, 93
Viking Books, 116–17
Wheeler, Paige, 207–9
Workman Publishing
   Company, 167–68

W.W. Norton & Company,
   Inc., 154
Zimmermann Literary,
   432–33

young adult. *See* children through young adult

ABOUT THE AUTHOR

Jeff Herman opened his literary agency in the mid-1980s while in his mid-20s. He has made nearly 1,000 book deals, including many bestsellers. His own books include *Jeff Herman's Guide to Publishers, Editors & Literary Agents* (more than 500,000 copies sold) and *Write the Perfect Book Proposal* (coauthored with Deborah Herman). He has presented hundreds of workshops about writing and publishing and has been interviewed for dozens of publications and programs.

In 1981, shortly after graduating from Syracuse University, Herman was riding the subway on a hot summer day when he spotted an ad stating: "I found my job in *The New York Times*." He promptly bought a copy and answered some Help Wanted ads. A few days later he was summoned for an interview with the publicity director at an independent publishing house and was hired on the spot as her assistant for $200 a week. Showering, shaving, wearing a suit, saying little, and promising to show up were the clinchers.

The publicity department comprised Herman and his boss, who took her summer vacation his first week on the job. He was left "in charge," though he knew nothing about publicity, publishing, or how an office functioned. But he was a quick study and soon helped make *When Bad Things Happen to Good People* a massive bestseller.

In time, Herman followed the money into corporate marketing, where he worked on various product-promotion campaigns for Nabisco, AT&T, and many other large and small brands. But books were his passion and calling.

Today, Jeff Herman is an exceptionally successful veteran literary agent, entrepreneur, and author. His areas of editorial expertise include popular business, spirituality, and most other areas of nonfiction. "If I feel I can sell it, I'll represent it," says Herman.

The Jeff Herman Agency, LLC
PO Box 1522 • 29 Park Street • Stockbridge, MA 01262
413-298-0077 • jeff@jeffherman.com • www.jeffherman.com

LIBRARY is dedicated to publishing books and other media that inspire and challenge us to improve the quality of our lives and the world.

We are a socially and environmentally aware company. We recognize that we have an ethical responsibility to our customers, our staff members, and our planet.

We serve our customers by creating the finest publications possible on personal growth, creativity, spirituality, wellness, and other areas of emerging importance. We serve New World Library employees with generous benefits, significant profit sharing, and constant encouragement to pursue their most expansive dreams.

As a member of the Green Press Initiative, we print an increasing number of books with soy-based ink on 100 percent postconsumer-waste recycled paper. Also, we power our offices with solar energy and contribute to nonprofit organizations working to make the world a better place for us all.

Our products are available in bookstores everywhere.

www.newworldlibrary.com

At NewWorldLibrary.com you can download our catalog,
subscribe to our e-newsletter, read our blog,
and link to authors' websites, videos, and podcasts.

Find us on Facebook, follow us on Twitter, and watch us on YouTube.

Send your questions and comments our way!
You make it possible for us to do what we love to do.

Phone: 415-884-2100 or 800-972-6657
Catalog requests: Ext. 10 | Orders: Ext. 10 | Fax: 415-884-2199
escort@newworldlibrary.com

NEW WORLD LIBRARY
publishing books that change lives   14 Pamaron Way, Novato, CA 94949